ARCHAIC GREECE:
NEW APPROACHES AND NEW EVIDENCE

ARCHAIC GREECE: NEW APPROACHES AND NEW EVIDENCE

Edited
by
Nick Fisher
and
Hans van Wees

Contributors:
Deborah Boedeker, Paul Cartledge, Andrew Dalby,
Philip de Souza, Lin Foxhall, Stephen Hodkinson,
Ian Morris, Daniel Ogden, Robin Osborne, Anton Powell,
Kurt A. Raaflaub, Alexandra Villing,
Hans van Wees, James Whitley

Duckworth
with
The Classical Press of Wales

First published in 1998 by
Gerald Duckworth & Co. Ltd.
The Old Piano Factory
48 Hoxton Square, London N1 6PB
Tel: 0171 729 5986
Fax: 0171 729 0015
with The Classical Press of Wales

Published in the United States of America
by the David Brown Book Co.
PO Box 511, Oakville, CT 06779
Tel: (860) 945–9329
Fax: (860) 945–9468

Originated and prepared for press by
The Classical Press of Wales
15 Rosehill Terrace, Swansea SA1 6JN
Tel: 01792 458397
Fax: 01792 419056

ISBN 0 7156 2809 7

A catalogue record for this book is available from the British Library

Typeset by Ernest Buckley, Clunton, Shropshire
Printed and bound in Great Britain by Antony Rowe Ltd.,
Chippenham, Wiltshire

CONTENTS

PREFACE

This book derives from a conference held in Aberdare Hall, Cardiff, 19–21 September, 1995. We are grateful to the *University of Wales Institute of Classics and Ancient History* for including both the original conference and the present volume in its programmes, and to all those who contributed to the Cardiff conference as speakers, chairs, and participants, and made it such a lively and enjoyable occasion. In particular, we should like to thank the British Academy for its contribution towards the expenses of our overseas speakers; the Warden of Aberdare Hall (now, very sadly, no longer with us) and her staff for providing excellent facilities and constant, friendly service; the *School of History and Archaeology* of the University of Wales Cardiff, for general support; and Karen Pierce and Louis Rawlings for ensuring that everything ran smoothly and an appropriately convivial atmosphere was created.

The publication of this volume was much helped by all our contributors' prompt submission of revised papers and proofs, by the unfailing advice and assistance, academic and technical, of Anton Powell, as Director of the Institute and manager of the Classical Press of Wales, and finally by Ernest Buckley's rapid and expert production of copy.

Note that in the application of conventions we have aimed for consistency within each chapter, but have allowed authors their own preferred spellings of Greek names (thus both Alkaios and Alcaeus appear) and transliterations of Greek words (with or without indicating long vowels), as well as their choice of American or English spelling, and dates rendered as BC or BCE.

ABBREVIATIONS

AA	*Archäologischer Anzeiger*	FGH	F. Jacoby, *Die Fragmente der griechischen Historiker*
AAA	*Athens Annals of Archaeology*		
Acta Arch	*Acta Archaeologica*	Fornara	C.W. Fornara, *Archaic Times to the end of the Peloponnesian War*, 2nd edn
AD	*Archaiologikon Deltion*		
AE	*Archaiologiki Ephemeris*		
AEMTh	*To Archaiologiko Ergo sti Makedonia kai Thraki*	I.C(ret.)	*Inscriptiones Creticae*
AION	*Annali di Archeologia e Storia Antica, Instituto Orientali di Napoli*	IG	*Inscriptiones Graecae*
		IM	*Istanbuler Mitteilungen*
		LIMC	*Lexicon Iconographicum Mythologiae Classicae*
AJA	*American Journal of Archaeology*	L-P	E. Lobel and D.L.Page, *Poetarum Lesbiorum Fragmenta*
AM	*Athenische Mitteilungen*		
Anat St	*Anatolian Studies*	ML	R. Meiggs and D.M. Lewis, *A Selection of Greek Historical Inscriptions*
AntJ	*Antiquaries Journal*		
AntK	*Antike Kunst*		
AR	*Archaeological Reports*		
ASAA	*Annuario della Scuola Archeologica di Atene*	ÖJh	*Österreichische Jahreshefte*
		Op Ath	*Opuscula Atheniensa*
BCH	*Bulletin de correspondance hellénique*	PMG (Page)	D.L. Page, *Poetae Melici Graeci*
BdA	*Bollettino d'Arte*		
BSA	*Annual of the British School at Athens*	Praktika	*Praktika tis en Athinais Archaiologikis Etaireias*
ClR	*Clara Rhodos*	PZ	*Prähistorische Zeitschrift*
DAI	*Deutsches Archäologisches Institut*	RA	*Revue archéologique*
		SEG	*Supplementum Epigraphicum Graecum*
D-K	H. Diels and W. Kranz, *Die Fragmente der Vorsokratiker*, 10th edn	SIG	W. Dittenberger, *Sylloge Inscriptionum Graecarum*, 3rd edn
Ergon	*Ergon tis en Athinais Archaiologikis Etaireias*	TGF N²	A. Nauck, *Tragicorum Graecorum Fragmenta*, 2nd edn
F(r.)	fragment		
FGE	D.L. Page, *Further Greek Epigrams*		

INTRODUCTION

Nick Fisher and *Hans van Wees*

The writing of the history of archaic Greece has been transformed between the 1970s and the end of the millenium. Two key stages in this process may in due course come to be distinguished. In 1980, Anthony Snodgrass's *Archaic Greece* and Oswyn Murray's *Early Greece* sought to demonstrate, in their different ways, the fundamental importance of placing the archaeological evidence at the centre of interpretation, and adopting a more sceptical approach to the later literary evidence.[1] Since then, there has been a steady and judicious introduction of the principles of post-processual archaeology into the Greek Iron Age, which has placed a solid emphasis on the study of the symbolic meaning of systems of material culture, and on the diversity of developments in different regions.[2] This, and other new approaches, such as those borrowed from anthropology, have fundamentally altered our views on such issues as the rise of the *polis*, the relations between *poleis* and *ethne*, the development of sanctuaries and territorial consolidation, the introduction and growth of literacy and written law, the interaction of oral and literary systems, and the processes by which the written evidence has suffered major distortions through the centuries of oral transmission and through the varied contemporary agendas of those engaged in writing it down.[3]

By the mid-1990s, the time seemed ripe for incorporation of the mass of new archaeological material – now produced by survey as much as by excavation – into new, more complex, pictures of development, for reflection on the wider implications of the more critical approach to the literary evidence, and for a move away from the narrative political history which had come to seem largely unattainable. One major manifestation of these concerns is *Greece in the Making* (1996), Robin Osborne's bold attempt at a broad history of the period from the end of the Bronze Age to the Persian Wars. Worthy of honourable mention will also be the records of two conferences on Archaic Greece held in September 1995: the Durham conference on *The Development of the Polis in Archaic Greece*,[4] and the Cardiff conference whose product is this volume. Both attracted many leading scholars in the

UK and from wider afield, four of whom contributed papers to both volumes.

The papers gathered here are divided into three groups. The first consists of four chapters which deal predominantly with material evidence and share a concern with the extent to which different parts of Greece developed in different directions. The next four chapters reassess the significance of major works of poetry as evidence for the archaic period, and the remaining six papers, which range across archaeological, iconographical, epigraphical, and literary evidence, address a series of related issues concerning social status, power, and state-formation. This division is slightly arbitrary: most of the contributors cover such broad historical questions, and give such prominence to explicit confrontation and integration of the various kinds of evidence, that their papers might almost as easily have been assigned to one of the other sections.

In Part I, Ian Morris' long introductory article offers a *catalogue raisonnée* of material culture, organised thematically (under the categories of burials, sanctuaries and settlements), regionally (divided between Central Greece, Northern Greece, Western Greece, and Crete), and historically (three key stages are distinguished). His presentation of this vast mass of material will serve as an invaluable data-bank for historians less *au fait* with the material scattered through excavation reports and journals; but it offers much more. As is his wont, Morris launches a set of provocative hypotheses of regionally diverse cultural and ideological patterns. He explores ways in which broad-brush interpretations of the surviving archaic poetry can suggest, or set limits to, a range of possible explanations of patterns of material culture, and interprets both kinds of evidence as a reflection of conflict between an egalitarian or proto-democratic 'middling' tradition and an 'elitist' counterpart, dominating the history of archaic Greece from *c.* 750–500 BC. This theory will provoke fierce debate, here already taken up to an extent in Paul Cartledge's concluding chapter.

Two complementary, though methodologically diverse, chapters address the question of whether archaic Sparta was as unique a *polis* as the later literary evidence would have us believe. Stephen Hodkinson takes the hard quantitative approach favoured by such as Snodgrass and Morris, and on the basis of a detailed scrutiny of Lakonian pottery, bronzework, and lead figurines, demonstrates that talk of a peculiarly Spartan 'artistic decline' after the mid-sixth century, and of the imposition of a culture of austerity at this time, is unwarranted. He concludes with a call for more systematic analysis of all the finds from Spartan sanctuaries, and for a change of focus from *production* to the Spartans' *use* of wealth, a theme echoed in this volume in Lin Foxhall's application of the theory of *consumption* to explain the extent of exchange in early Greece.

Anton Powell turns to the iconography of Lakonian figured pottery, and in a subtle study of predominant themes on Spartan pots (favourite mythological characters, unusual religious imagery, and a range of sympotic, komastic, and sexual representations) brings to light features characteristic of Spartan culture. Yet he also finds evidence for a relaxed and pleasure-loving atmosphere in Sparta even after the middle of the sixth century, confirming Hodkinson's thesis of a Spartan society not fundamentally different from other Greek communities. Powell suggests that the 'Lykourgan reform' may have been a late archaic reaction to an aristocratic regime seen as excessively soft-living, a reaction which encouraged a more austere life style and gave a new twist to such Spartan practices as public nudity, homosexual relations, and whipping. A general retreat from 'luxury' is, according to Morris, signalled by Central Greek archaeological evidence from 500 BC onwards, and in a later chapter Hans van Wees argues that a similar trend is discernible in Athenian iconography of the mid-fifth century.

Finally in this section, and moving across the Aegean, Alexandra Villing focuses on the contribution of iconography to issues of regional diversity in cult and culture. Her detailed study of the distinctive representation in East Greece of a spinning Athena, and the goddess's strong presence also there in warlike poses, leads to cautious, but stimulating, conclusions: it may be possible to discern some Anatolian influence on the material culture and ideology of these cities (perhaps involving a slightly higher valuation of women's work than elsewhere), and it is necessary to cast serious doubt on the image of the east Greeks as 'softies' which comes to us from later, mainland Greek, literary sources.

Part II focuses on the literary sources for archaic Greece, the sadly few major poems to have survived complete, and the fragmentary remains, constantly expanding as new papyri are published. The first category is represented here by two essays on Homer and one on Hesiod, which explore in different ways the contexts and complexities of these texts. Kurt Raaflaub's assault on the mass of problems associated with the phrase 'a historical Homeric society' aligns itself firmly with those who believe that the poems presuppose, and work with, a coherently presented social order which was in many ways close to that of the poet's or poets' own time. He argues, moreover, that the *effective* span of the oral tradition is likely not to have exceeded three generations and that consciously 'archaizing' elements in the poems are drawn from living memory of the world as it was before the dramatic changes of the mid-eighth century. While favouring a date in the late eighth century for the composition of the epics, Raaflaub considers possible the early seventh-century date favoured by many others recently.[5]

This later dating of the epics, making 'Homer' a poet inhabiting much the same world as Archilochos or Tyrtaeus, is the starting point of Andrew Dalby's investigation into the different types of songs and singers (more or less professional), that are revealed in the Homeric poems. The traditional view, that epic came first, and that all the songs mentioned in the Homeric poems were modelled, in metrical form, tone, or ethos, on hexameter epic, is properly challenged. Dalby shows that there is reason to suppose that the full range of songs – hymnic, lyric, iambic, paraenetic and so on – is known to the epic poets. The writing of archaic history has often relied heavily on comparisons and contrasts between the world of Homer and the worlds revealed by other poets and by the archaeological record, and Raaflaub's and Dalby's reassessments of the nature and date of the epic tradition, and of its relation to other poetic genres, therefore have dramatic implications for the study of early Greece.

As for Hesiod, Daniel Ogden's subtle analysis of the Pandora myth finds another significant strand of associations and beliefs – to do with the *teras*-baby, a deformed child, bringer of plague or famine if it is not expelled from the community – which further enriches this famous myth, which, as has been shown by the studies of scholars such as Vernant and Faraone,[6] is fundamental to so much of Greek thinking about gender difference and marriage, sacrifice and agriculture, and the relations between gods, humans and animals. Throughout, and also in his trenchant Appendix, Ogden applies his characteristic combination of close attention to linguistic meaning and structural analysis of *mentalités*[7] to reveal how densely-packed, long-lasting, and essentially Greek is the thinking that produced such stories, for all that elements in the Prometheus and Pandora stories may find parallels in Near Eastern myths.

Among recent additions to remains of Greek poetry found on papyrus, few have attracted as much attention as the forty-seven fragments of Simonides' elegies first published in 1992. Among these by far the the most extensive and interesting are more than fifty lines from a lengthy narrative elegy on the Greeks' victory over the Persians at Plataea in 479, probably composed for recitation at a victory celebration very soon afterwards, and thus falling precisely on the disputable boundary between the archaic and the classical periods.[8] Deborah Boedeker's paper, besides contributing to the debate of the poem's plan and occasion, explores sensitively the ways in which poetic honours can express these Greek achievements by a striking analogy between the contemporary Greeks, celebrated by the poet Simonides, and such men as Achilles, the 'heroes' of Homer's Greek war against Troy, and an emphasis on the ways in which both sets of 'heroes' were connected to, and supported by, the gods. She suggests poems of this kind helped to create the climate which enabled the glorious dead of the Persian Wars to be themselves 'immortalized' in cult.

Many of the chapters in Part III draw out various ways in which careful attention to the totality of the primary evidence and scepticism towards our later accounts enables new questions to be pursued, and traditional views undermined. The predominant themes are state-formation and the activities of smaller groups, including the extent of state-involvement and private enterprise in exchange, settlement, and warfare, and the gradual, regionally diverse, establishment of social control inside the community over the lives of individuals.

Robin Osborne provocatively seeks to demonstrate that early Greek 'colonization' is not an expression – let alone a cause – of state-formation. Indeed, he wishes to remove altogether from our accounts of early Greece the term 'colonization' (which was always recognised to be problematic). His argument, based alike on the Homeric and Hesiodic pictures of widespread individual movement and individual settlement, and on the archaeological picture of overseas settlement (e.g. in Southern Italy and Sicily), is that there was much trade and other traffic across the Aegean, and that Greek settlements, from Pithecusae in the middle of the eighth century onwards, were normally founded by privately organised groups, often drawing manpower from several Greek communities. The alternative vision of a decision taken by a single mother-city, reinforced by a Delphic oracle, to send out, perhaps by conscription, a proportion of the citizen body led by a single founder – a model which appears from Herodotus onwards and has traditionally been accepted by scholars – should be seen as a 'charter' put about to legitimise relations between the settlement and one or more cities back in the heartland of Greece.

The decline of private raiding parties and the development of formal 'navies', that is, state-managed stores of dedicated warships with

supporting harbour installations, is a clear index of growing governmental centralization. In tracing this development, Philip de Souza
shows that, unfortunately, archaeological evidence is at present of
limited use and that one therefore has to operate – sceptically – with
the traditions that began with the fifth-century historiography of
Herodotus, Thucydides, and more shadowy precursors of the 'Eusebian
thalassocracy list'. Much in detail remains uncertain, but de Souza
argues plausibly that much of what is attributed to 'naval states' before
Polycrates of Samos is fantasy and the product of facile schematization.
Systematic and widespead development of mostly small navies got
under way, largely in response to non-Greek states such as Carthage
and Phoenicia/Persia, only in the latter part of the sixth century.

Lin Foxhall adds strikingly to the thesis of considerable overseas
movement of goods and people in our period, here concentrating on
the multiplicity of contacts between Greeks and non-Greeks to the
East. Like Osborne, she starts from the totality of the material record.
Her chapter suggests that the application of 'consumption theory',
with its emphasis on the rapid development of desires for luxuries,
varieties, and fashionable products, as much as the need for agricultural or metallurgical products and materials, can help explain both
the archaeological record and the expressions of longings and
enjoyments found in the poets.

Turning to relations of power within the city-states, James Whitley's
treatment of literacy in archaic Crete, currently itself such an enigma
archaeologically,[9] reinforces another central theme of the book: the
importance of attending to archaeologically revealed regional variations in the nature and pace of developments. He emphasizes the stark
contrast in the early uses of writing and monumental display between
Attica and Crete; his elegant explanation (reinforced by a telling analogy from *Animal Farm*) of the functions of the inscribing of so many
laws and regulations in the oligarchic and apparently reclusive Cretan
poleis, and of these cities' apparently specialist, elite, 'public scribes',
like Spensithios of the Dataleis, reminds us that inscriptions can be
monuments to be viewed and admired, but not necessarily to be read,
and can serve as tools of repression as well as of liberation.

Connecting the internal development of the state and the changing
life styles of the archaic upper classes, Hans van Wees focuses on the
under-studied question of when, and why, Greek men, especially
among the elite, abandoned the habit of appearing under arms in
civilian life. His detailed analysis of the iconographical record suggests
that the carrying of swords and spears was abandoned in favour of

wearing ever more cumbersome and luxurious clothes, and posing with staffs. It is argued that this increasingly 'elegant' and 'civilised' style of self-presentation – culminating in the late sixth century, and perhaps, as Thucydides claimed, first adopted in Athens – was integral to a more general development towards the competitive display of leisure and wealth in *gymnasia* and *symposia*, and away from the display of physical prowess, as demonstrated above all in the violent settlement of disputes. The extent to which this process was encouraged by state-regulation or by social pressure, from peers or from below, remains obscure, above all because of the gaps in our evidence for early law and the unreliability of the traditions about the 'lawgivers', but its result would have been to enable Greek communities to exercise a greater degree of central control over the use of force.

Finally, Paul Cartledge's overview of the political theory and practice that led to the explicit creation of complex structures of male citizen democracy in Athens and elsewhere, links back to the themes of Morris' initial paper. Cartledge considers the issue of whether reforms such as those of Cleisthenes of Athens presuppose any form of coherent democratic or egalitarian theory, or whether in contrast successful practice supported by relatively vague sloganising later produced some theory, in support, or, more substantially, in opposition to democratic practice. He also questions the relative roles of leading individuals with new ideas and of collective, politicised ideologies, and suggests that there were at the end of the archaic age remarkable advances in collective preparedness to attempt new solutions to political and social problems,[10] but that the convictions and rhetoric of certain elite individuals, against the apparent traditions and interests of their class, played a major part in making change acceptable.

The Cardiff conference was originally called *Archaic Greece: The Evidence and Its Limitations*. As the papers published here show beyond a doubt, this was an unduly negative title: for every limitation exposed in the sources, a new direction for research has opened up. Not only does new evidence, material and literary, continue to accumulate, but there is, it appears, no end to the new approaches to be explored.

Notes

[1] At the Cardiff conference, both Anthony Snodgrass and Oswyn Murray gave papers; these are appearing elsewhere (as is the paper given by Sitta von Reden).

[2] See Snodgrass 1987; Morris (ed.) 1994, and below; Davies in Mitchell and

Rhodes 1997.

[3] See Morris 1987; Whitley 1991a, b; Morgan 1990; Marinatos and Hägg (eds.) 1993; Alcock and Osborne (eds.) 1994; de Polignac 1995a; Thomas 1989, 1991; Hölkeskamp 1992 a, b.

[4] Published as Mitchell and Rhodes 1997.

[5] See Van Wees 1994; West 1995; Crielaard (ed.) 1995; Andersen and Dickie (eds.) 1995.

[6] Vernant 1980, 1989; Faraone 1992.

[7] Shown extensively in his innovative book *The Crooked Kings of Ancient Greece* (1997), which shows how many repeated patterns of myth-making, and how few pieces of reliable 'information', are to be found in the stories about early tyrants, lawgivers and poets.

[8] On which see Cartledge, pp. 386–7 below.

[9] See Morris, pp. 61–8 below.

[10] See Ober 1996.

ARCHAEOLOGY AND
ARCHAIC GREEK HISTORY

Ian Morris

What role for archaeology in the writing of archaic Greek history? How we answer this question depends in large part on how we define its terms, and the kind of definitions favored by historians and archaeologists have changed significantly in the last twenty years. Nothing illustrates this better than the brief methodological statements in two of the best-known English-language studies of early Greece. In his magisterial account of *Geometric Greece*, Nicolas Coldstream suggested that the methods appropriate to the study of the Greek Dark Age (by which he meant the period *c.* 1100–900 BC) were totally different from those needed for analysis of the archaic period (700–500). He observed that Vincent Desborough's book *The Greek Dark Ages* (1972), published in the same series as *Geometric Greece*, was 'based almost wholly on the material remains recovered from excavation, which offer the only evidence at first hand', while Lilian Jeffery's *Archaic Greece* (1976), the third book in the same series, 'draws upon a rich variety of literary sources, supplemented by contemporary inscriptions; in reconstructing the history of those times, archaeology performs only an ancillary function' (Coldstream 1977, 17).

Coldstream's judgments rested on two assumptions. The first was that archaeology was the history of art, subdivided into 'the local pottery style, the local burial customs, the jewelry, bronzes, ivories, and seals' (Coldstream 1977, 19). The second was that archaic history meant political narrative: 'Although no systematic records were kept before the fifth century, the main course of events in archaic Greece has been saved from oblivion in the central narrative and long digressions of Herodotus, and in the more disjointed memories recorded by other ancient historians' (1977, 17). No proper history in this sense can be written for the years before 700, so they should be studied by the methods of archaeology (as he defined them). Some kind of narrative can be reconstructed from written sources for the post-700 period, so archaeology, as Coldstream puts it, 'performs only an ancillary function' for the archaic historian.

But just a few years later, Anthony Snodgrass offered very different definitions of the key terms in his survey of *Archaic Greece*. He suggested that classicists had started to define 'the field of archaeology [as] the entire material culture – so far as it is recoverable – of an ancient society' (1980, 12). He concluded that:

> by enlarging their horizons in this way, ancient history and classical archaeology have also become much closer. Once historians extend their interests from political and military events to social and economic processes, it is obvious that archaeological evidence can offer them far more; once classical archaeologists turn from the outstanding works of art to the totality of material products, then history (thus widely interpreted) will provide them with a more serviceable framework, not least because Greek art is notoriously deficient in historical reference. As a result of this *rapprochement*, it will be difficult for a future researcher to embark on an historical subject in the field of archaic Greece without becoming involved in archaeological questions, and vice versa. (Snodgrass 1980, 13)

Given such radically different assumptions, expressed by leading scholars in widely read books, we might expect that classical scholars would have rushed to debate in print the merits and possibilities of each vision of the field. But as is often the case in academia, this did not happen. Rather, a revolution in thought has taken place in the quietest of ways. Little by little, one step at a time, archaeologists and historians have been slipping away from the entrenched positions of the 1960s and '70s. There is no obvious way to quantify such a shift, but my impression is that by the end of the 1980s Snodgrass's way of defining the issues had won general acceptance in English-language scholarship, showing how the systematic study of archaeology could illuminate archaic history. Yet despite what seems to be near-consensus on the theoretical level, the number of actual published studies treating archaeology (broadly defined) as a basic source for archaic cultural history remains small.

I see two major reasons for this. The first is structural. Ever since scholarship on ancient Greece was institutionalized in universities in the late nineteenth century, ancient history and classical archaeology have normally been pursued together within Classics departments, but with archaeology taking a subordinate role. Its practitioners established a niche for themselves by monopolizing the study of artifacts, at the cost of renouncing claims to impinge on the dominant text-based fields. Students of classical archaeology and ancient history sit in the same classes, but the goals, methods, and forms of discourse which they are encouraged to internalize scarcely overlap.[1]

I have written at length about this great divide elsewhere (Morris 1992; 1994a), and will not repeat my arguments here. In this paper I concentrate on a second problem. Until the late 1970s, historians and archaeologists generally approached the Early Iron Age (c. 1100–700 BC) in much the same way that they continue to approach the archaic period twenty years later. It seems that nearly everyone agreed that artifacts and texts ought to be combined, but hardly anyone actually did so. In one camp were the historians, who worked from Homer and Hesiod, and argued back from later sources. They usually envisaged a complex and warlike early Greek 'heroic age' obsessed with honor and status. In the other camp were archaeologists, who worked from pottery and metalwork, usually seeing a simple, isolated, backward, and poor Dark Age, preoccupied with just surviving (Morris 1997a).

This academic division of labor broke down by 1980. The main reason, I believe, was the publication of three monumental surveys of the material record (Snodgrass 1971; Desborough 1972; Coldstream 1977). Reading these books was not the same thing as reading the primary sources (the excavation reports), but they suddenly made it much easier for the Homerist who believed that she or he ought to draw on archaeology to go out and do so. The 1970s syntheses were comprehensive, authoritative, and accessible. The footnotes to the proceedings of the four great international conferences on the Early Iron Age held between 1979 and 1988[2] illustrate the impact of the syntheses. Snodgrass, Desborough, and Coldstream feature as prominently in the papers of philologists, historians, and linguists as in those of archaeologists.

But there are no equivalent syntheses of archaic archaeology,[3] and the growing theoretical sophistication among ancient historians about the possible uses of archaeology is often held back by empirical ignorance about what actually survives from archaic times. There are excellent surveys, easily available, of the best examples of sculpture, architecture, and vase painting. But the historian who wants to know about the kinds of material culture which have become central to historical writing on the Early Iron Age – say, about seventh-century houses in the Cyclades or sixth-century burials in Thessaly – has to go to the original site reports, scattered across a century of journal issues in half a dozen languages; and most historians are unwilling to do this. I cannot provide a thorough survey of the evidence in a single chapter, but I can offer at least a quick sketch and indicate some of the main areas of debate.

Material culture and historical writing

My goal, then, is highly empirical: I want to provide a picture of archaic archaeology. But my decisions about which parts of the record deserve description inevitably depend on prior non-empirical assumptions. In this section, I set out what I see as the four main presuppositions guiding my choices.

The first is that archaic Greeks, like humans everywhere, used material culture to say things about themselves. The recent fascination with material culture among modern historians and the 'post-processual' movement in prehistoric archaeology rest on the recognition that material culture is part of a symbolic field which real people manipulate in pursuit of their goals.[4] Archaeology is thus an example of what Clifford Geertz (1973, 15) calls a second-order interpretation – that is, it is our interpretations of ancient interpretations (an idea emphasized by Christopher Tilley in his edited volume *Interpretative Archaeology* (1993)). It may be possible to read through this human manipulation of material culture to obtain objective information about trade patterns, levels of wealth, etc. But we first have to recognize that everything in the archaeological record which survives from archaic Greece comes to us mediated through a series of filters. The first of these – certainly the most interesting, and arguably the most important – consists of the individual decisions made by breathing, thinking people in the past, which led to some objects entering the archaeological record, and others disappearing forever. Contrary to the assumptions behind Christopher Hawkes's still-influential model of a 'ladder of inference', economic analyses are not more secure than inferences about ideas or institutions, because economic arguments are in fact third-order interpretations – i.e., our readings of ancient readings of symbolic processes, followed by our imaginative attempts at reading away the ancient interpretations to gain access to a body of un-interpreted data.

The significance of these ancient decisions about what to do with material objects is obvious when we are talking about objects which have come from contexts of deposition like offerings to the dead or the gods. It would be ridiculous to assume that the objects we excavate in cemeteries and sanctuaries represent a cross-section of the goods people would have encountered in their everyday lives. What we learn about when we dig these things up is primarily what kinds of things people thought it was appropriate to bury with their relatives or offer to the immortals. We can certainly try to use them as evidence for something else, such as the overall level of wealth in society or changes in technology. But such arguments always depend on a further level of interpretation, predicated on our understanding of why these particular things, and not other things, were being used. All archaeological analysis must begin with an effort to enter into the non-verbal symbolic languages of people in the past – the 'system of objects', as Baudrillard (1968) called it – which generated the patterns of deposition which originally formed the archaeological record.

Archaeologists usually recognize this in principle, but often forget it when they get down to the serious job of analyzing artifacts. And when archaeologists are confronted with the remains of houses or garbage pits, rather than of temples or graves, even the principle that material culture always comes to us mediated through past symbolic activity is sometimes forgotten. There is a temptation to see the physical remains of these kinds of activity as a transparent window onto the realities of the past, in contrast to slippery sources like literature or rituals, which are full of distortion.[5] Nothing could be further from the truth. Few things are more important to most people than what they throw away and where they do it, as was made clear in a famous study of colonial New England (Deetz 1977) which showed how changes in refuse disposal formed part of a much larger shift in the ways people understood the world. Equally, every element of the house can be the scene of complex signification. Many anthropologists and historians have explored how the experience of domestic space contributes to people's sense of the proper structure of the world.[6]

Ian Hodder has summed up the situation by suggesting that 'in archaeology *all* inference is via material culture. If material culture, all of it, has a symbolic dimension such that the relationship between people and things is affected, then *all* of archaeology, economic and social, is implicated' (Hodder 1991, 3). Archaeology thus draws close to the central ideas of the self-styled 'new cultural history' (Chartier 1988; Hunt 1989) in insisting that we cannot reduce cultural practices to underlying economic and social realities which have analytical priority. Our understanding of the world is always discursively constituted, through the manipulation of words and things, and through competing interpretations of what such manipulations mean. Archaeology has to be about the contextual analysis of meanings. However, as Hodder concedes, '...in the construction of the cultural world, all dimensions (the height and color of pottery for example) already have meaning associations. An individual in the past is situated within this historical frame, and interprets the cultural order from within its perspective. The archaeologist seeks also to get "inside" the historical context, but the jump is often a considerable one' (Hodder 1987, 7).

Prehistorians normally make the jump by using general theoretical propositions or analogical arguments as springboards (see Hodder 1992), but here the Hellenist has a distinct advantage. The Greeks themselves show how aware they were of material culture as something they could use creatively, in the same way as language, and which required interpretation. For Homer, a large part of Odysseus' skill was that he could apply his *noēsis* (intelligence) more successfully than anyone else to the material *sēmata* (signs) which he confronted, identifying meanings in them which eluded others, and taking advantage of this knowledge to further his own ends (Nagy 1990b, 202–22). The hero had to be adept at reading all manner of non-verbal signals, from smiles to architecture (Lateiner 1995). In the fifth century, Aeschylus could take it for granted that his audience would be attuned to the ambiguities of the carpet scene in the *Agamemnon* (Crane 1993); and in the fourth, any good orator knew that a passing reference to hairstyle, choice of cloak, or taste in tableware spoke volumes about the wicked intentions of his rivals (Ober 1989). Just as cultural historians of fourth-century Athens have moved away from reading the orations as direct evidence for everyday life toward seeing them as speakers' competing efforts to fashion images of themselves as idealized Athenian men,[7] so we should see the archaeological record primarily as the residue of non-verbal languages in which these (and other) debates were also going on (Morris 1992, 1–30).

My second assumption is that we will make most sense of our evidence by combining archaeological/non-verbal communication acts with textual/verbal ones. We can use the literary record to constrain somewhat the almost endless interpretive possibilities which the artifacts present. When we look at the archaeological data in the light of what Sappho, Archilochus, Pindar, and others were saying about wealth, restraint, the East, and the past, we get a clearer sense of how material culture was used in competing efforts at self-fashioning; and, conversely, the detail and geographical spread of the non-verbal remains allow us to understand better the panhellenizing simplifications of archaic poetic genres.[8]

Third, I take it for granted that we can read this non-verbal language best if we follow a method pioneered by Anthony Snodgrass in his work on the Early Iron Age. We need to collect *all* the evidence to find out what belongs to a general pattern and what is unique, and the temporal and spatial scales on which processes operated. Snodgrass explained that his method

> is to examine the whole period in chronological sequence, scrutinizing the evidence as it comes, assembling the facts and endeavouring to face them. This sounds banal enough, but in this instance it involves abandoning the normal priorities of the historian, the literary scholar or the classical archaeologist... This method also entails an almost obsessional insistence on chronology. Much of the material that is available is trivial in itself and ambiguous as to the conclusions that can be drawn from it; yet this same material has some security as a basis for a broader understanding of the period. (Snodgrass 1971, vii–viii)

This method is the greatest legacy of the structural interests of historians and archaeologists in the 1960s and '70s. Words and things, they argued, could only be understood in terms of their relations to other words and things, that is, from their position in an overall system. Examining an individual find or site in isolation, or solely in relationship to earlier or later finds or sites, began to seem pointless; we could only know what something meant by looking at it synchronically, in the most complete context possible. Pushed to extremes, this reduces archaeology to an abstract formalism, but it remains a basic starting point.[9]

This is not always (indeed, not often) how archaeologists approach archaic data. For example, Robin Osborne (1988; cf. 1989) has argued that the contrasts between the funerary scene on the name vase of the Dipylon Master, probably painted about 750 BC, and the blinding scene on the name vase of the Polyphemus Painter, *c.* 675 BC, reveal a profound shift in Athenian mentalities. Almost all of the funerary scenes by the Dipylon Master and his circle come from one small cemetery on the north-west edge of Athens, while buriers using the dozens of other known cemeteries in Attica apparently felt no need for such scenes. Seventh-century painted grave pots like that of the Polyphemus Painter, found in the West Cemetery at Eleusis, are even less common. Fewer than 2% of seventh-century child burials in Attica were made in decorated pots. This does not undermine the interest of these paintings, but it does affect their historical significance.[10] Whose mentalities were changing? Do the two pots relate to comparable groups within Attic society? Why did so few people want (or perhaps have access to) such images? These questions can only be approached through systematic analysis of the whole range of evidence. Snodgrass has pointedly summed up the problem: 'make no mistake, the real

7

opponents of [Whitley's] new approach [to early Greek art...are] the new art historians who regard the concept of "total material culture" as an impediment to their own mystic communion with the viewers and users of the pottery.'[11]

My final assumption is that we should be looking at *contexts of behavior*, not at decontextualized artifacts, whether singly or in quantity. So, I divide the evidence into categories of graves, sanctuaries, and settlements, not the more conventional pottery, metalwork, and sculpture. This focus also grows out of the structural approach: since the ancient users of objects expected them to signify meaning by virtue of their position within the overall cultural system, looking at them as isolated works of art will get us nowhere.

The point has been made repeatedly by archaeologists of the post-processual school pioneered by Ian Hodder. A gold cup that has been put in a grave may mean something radically different from one that has been given to a god, or displayed in a dining room. The best example of this is the so-called 'Orphic' graves of the late fourth and third century BC: their grave goods are much like those which we find in other rich burials of these years, yet the buriers assumed that the deceased was heading for a next life radically different from that expected within mainstream versions of Greek religion. Gold cups did not have the same meanings for different buriers (Morris 1992, 17–18, 104).

Some associations may carry over from one context to another, and in that sense we can talk about an irreducible core of meanings attributed to gold cups by a particular group at a particular moment; but many important meanings were entirely context-dependent. To pour libations to the gods from gold cups as the Athenian fleet sailed for Sicily in 415 BC was apparently a fine and patriotic thing (Thucydides 6.32), but to say that a man took pride in owning gold cups was to imply that he was vulgar, lacking in the qualities of the true citizen (Demosthenes 22.75). To say that your enemy went round positively bragging about his cups was even worse – it evoked the image of a rich man who harbored anti-social *hubris* (Demosthenes 21.133, 158). When Pseudo-Andocides (4.29) wanted to convince a jury that Alcibiades was beyond the pale of civilized society, he took advantage of these associations by alleging that Alcibiades had deliberately tried to create an impression that gold vessels belonging to an Athenian embassy were his own, not only pretending that cups made him a better man, but even lying about owning them.

To bury a gold cup with a dead relative may have been even more hubristic. In the three thousand or so fifth- and fourth-century graves which have been excavated and published from Athens, there is not a single case of this happening (Morris 1992, 108–27). The literary sources do not give us 'the' meaning of the gold cup, which we can then mechanically apply to such finds. But they do give us a sense of the semantic range of artifacts, of how the possibilities available to the people who used them varied from context to context, and of the limits of plausible interpretation.

These three anaytical categories – the burial, the sanctuary, and the house – are not the only ones I could have chosen,[12] but they do have three great merits. Two of these merits are obvious: first, the vast majority of our surviving evidence comes from one or another of these contexts; and second, these contexts transcend the limitations of the written record in that they come from the whole Greek world and potentially represent the activities of ordinary men and women, slave as well as free. Of course, they also have limitations. Most activities do not leave residues for us to dig up. We can recognize funerals, for example, but not weddings. And even in the case of the funeral, the burial may be the only phase to produce a deposit, although mourning may have mattered more than burying, and marrying may have been a more significant ritual than either (Morris 1992, 104–8). We do not have the whole story. But then, of course, neither do we have the whole story when we use literary sources. If we had to have all the evidence before we could say anything, history-writing of any kind would be impossible. In archaeology as in text-based history, we work by interrogating the evidence in its context, looking for patterns and trying to make sense of them. Studying house remains requires different methods from studying epic, and archaeological data constrain interpretation less than textual ones; but the principles of analysis are much the same.

The third merit of my chosen categories, that they would have made abundant sense to ancient Greeks, calls for more discussion.

THE BURIAL. As is well known, Herodotus was obsessed with the disposal of the dead, and treated it as a key to national character. It was in the context of discussing funeral customs that he made explicit his (Pindaric) view that *nomos* was king of all (3.38). A century later, Athenian orators presented their audiences with similar views of the importance of the grave. For Aeschines, a man's ancestral tombs and shrines were the best proof that he was a citizen (2.23); he could even say that graves and shrines *were* a man's homeland (2.152). And, he alleged, if the Athenians let Demosthenes keep a gold crown he had been awarded, the very tombs of their fathers would groan aloud

(3.239). None of these claims was exactly true, but Aeschines would hardly have wasted time on them had he not been confident that tombs were highly charged symbols of community, which would evoke useful emotions in his listeners.

THE SANCTUARY. Herodotus is again a valuable witness. His Athenians used the ways Greeks worshipped their gods, along with the Greek language itself, as the twin pillars defining *to Hellēnikon*, 'Greekness,' in the face of the Persian threat (8.144). For Aristotle, sacrificing properly was a major component of a man's standing in the community (*Rhetoric* 1361a); and for Xenophon, the ability to make good sacrifices was central to living a good life (*Oeconomicus* 11.9). Plato believed that shared sacrifices built a sense of community (*Laws* 771d), and Theophrastus regularly used the image of inappropriate behavior at sacrifices to mock undesirable types of men (*Characters* 9.2; 19.4; 20.12; 21.7, 11; 22.4). Correct sacrifice was fundamentally important, and variations from expectations were loaded with significance.

THE HOUSE. This too was a basic metaphor for the social order, and particularly gender relations (D. Cohen 1991, 72–97; Nevett 1994; 1995). To enter another citizen's house without an invitation was *hubris*, a penetration of his personal space with extremely strong sexual overtones (e.g., Lysias 1.4, 25, 36; Demosthenes 18.132). It is not likely that women were secluded in the secure rear parts of houses, but the *idea* that space was gendered was very important to Athenians. Cohen and Nevett argue that the courtyard house, with its controllable entry point and restricted lines of vision, maximized opportunities for Greek men to create an image of gendered space, which then became a powerful metaphor for the structure of the community. The house also played a major part in thinking about class. Demosthenes (23.207–8; cf. 3.25–6; 13.20) claimed to be scandalized that whereas in the good old days public temples were grand and private homes simple, by 352 BC 'some men have built private dwellings more magnificent than many public buildings'. As with the grave and the sanctuary, the house was overflowing with meanings, a place to assert notions of the proper constitution of the group, or to challenge conventions.

Regional patterns

These, then, are my guiding assumptions. I now turn to the archaic finds.[13] The most striking feature of the record is regional diversity, and I break the Aegean world down into four broad spatial groups (*Fig.* 1). These regions are not homogeneous. No two archaeological sites are ever exactly alike, and grouping them into geographical units

Fig. 1. The four regions: A Central Greece, B Northern Greece,
C Western Greece, D Crete.

(or 'cultures,' as they are generally called among prehistorians) is
always an interpretive act (see Hodder 1987). Other scholars, looking
at other elements within the overall assemblage, might come up with
very different spatial units. Nor are the boundaries between the regions which I identify always clear-cut. For example, while Boeotia
belongs fairly clearly in the central Greek area, just a few miles to the
west, in Phthiotis, Locris, and perhaps Phocis, we see a mixture of
central and western elements. Similarly, some Thessalian sites have
much in common with those in my central area, while others seem to
look more toward Macedonia.

But for all the definitional problems, I suggest that this geographical
organization of the data clarifies much more than it obscures. These
four broad zones of material culture seem to be very old. Snodgrass
(1971, 228–68) sees similar regional patterns of pottery decoration,

11

metal use, and building taking shape as early as the eleventh century. They may well have been the outcome of different responses to the breakup of palatial civilization; or were perhaps already present in the late Mycenaean world. What he called the 'advanced' regions of Protogeometric Greece (Snodgrass 1971, 374–6) correspond roughly to my central Greek area, around the shores of the Aegean Sea. This was the homeland of the most famous archaic and classical *poleis*. I begin my survey with these city-states, partly because they have attracted far more attention from historians than other parts of Greece, and partly because this is the best-explored region. I empha-size the variations within central Greece as much as the factors which unite it, but argue that this area as a whole went through a profound social and cultural revolution in the eighth century, which created a unique archaic civic society.

The eighth-century revolution was less pronounced in other parts of Greece. I group Thrace, Macedonia, Epirus, and Thessaly together as a northern zone. As noted above, Thessaly is in many regards transi-tional, and as we move further north, pottery, metalwork, burials, houses, and religion all show stronger links to the Balkans than to the Aegean. The establishment of central Greek colonies along the coasts had a dramatic impact on their immediate hinterlands in the seventh century, but it was only in the later sixth century that the Balkan orientation of northern Greek material culture changed significantly.

Western Greece is also a loose grouping. From early in the Iron Age, the whole area from Ithaca to Laconia had shared a common ceramic tradition, which paid little attention to the Protogeometric and Geo-metric styles popular in the Aegean. After 700 Corinthian pottery reached the West in quantity, but the Dark Age tradition had a strong legacy. The second element was the widespread use of *pithos* burial for adults, which was unusual (though not unknown) elsewhere in the Aegean. Third is the structure of the material: we have few traces of burial and settlement, but extensive cult remains, often going back to the tenth century.[14]

Crete, being an island, is the easiest region to define. In some ways it had much in common with the Aegean world, and the scale of changes in the eighth century is undeniable, but its distinctive features (par-ticularly openness to the east and continuities from the Minoan past) are even more striking. The most peculiar feature of Cretan archaeol-ogy is the virtually complete disappearance of evidence at the end of the seventh or beginning of the sixth century. This 'period of silence', as some call it, lasted through the fifth century. It probably has enormous historical significance, but has received little sustained analysis.

I begin my review of the evidence from each region with a short discussion of absolute chronology. I opened this chapter by discussing definitions of 'archaeology' and 'history', and before plunging into the data, I also need to comment on what I mean by 'archaic'.[15] Historians normally set the beginning of an archaic period around 700 BC, and end it *c.* 480. But Snodgrass made an unanswerable case in *Archaic Greece* that we can only make sense of the seventh and sixth centuries if we foreground what he called the 'structural revolution' of the late eighth century (1980, 15–84). I suggest in the conclusion to this chapter that archaeology's greatest contribution to archaic history lies in the study of such structural changes.

Central Greece (*Fig.* 2)
Under this heading I group together most of the *poleis* around the shores of the Aegean. I emphasize the variations within this central Greek region on p. 30 below, but nonetheless see underlying similarities across the area. To a considerable extent the colonies established by Greeks all around the Mediterranean in archaic times reproduced central Greek culture, and Malkin (1994a) has made a good case that the act of founding colonies was itself a crucial step in the creation of such a culture. However, constraints of space mean that I can only touch briefly on the colonial *poleis* of Italy and Sicily here, although I say more about the northern Aegean colonies and their interactions with the native populations.[16]

There was until recently general agreement on the absolute dates of central Greek pottery, but this has now been challenged. Francis and Vickers (1985a) and James et al. (1991) would downdate the end of Late Geometric pottery styles from *c.* 700 to the 670s. This is hardly a radical revision, but Francis and Vickers (1981; 1983) also lowered the origins of Red Figure painting at Athens from around 530 to roughly 450 BC. This would mean that what I am calling the third archaic transformation in fact took place some way into the fifth century. There are acute problems with some local pottery sequences, to which I return in my conclusions, but I remain confident that the broad outlines of the conventional relative and absolute chronologies for the eighth and seventh centuries are solid (Morris 1993b; 1996b), and Shear (1993) has convincingly restated the case for the traditional late archaic and early classical dating. I use absolute dates throughout this review to avoid cluttering it with technical jargon and to make cross-referencing

13

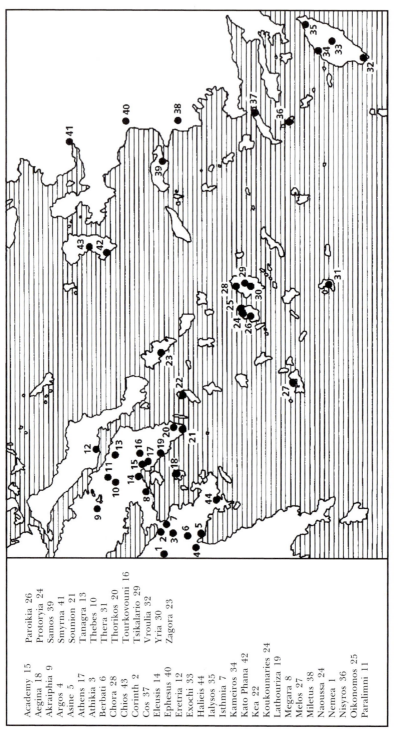

Academy 15	Paroikia 26
Aegina 18	Protoryia 24
Akraiphia 9	Samos 39
Argos 4	Smyrna 41
Asine 5	Sounion 21
Athens 17	Tanagra 13
Athikia 3	Thebes 10
Berbati 6	Thera 31
Chora 28	Thorikos 20
Chios 43	Tourkovouni 16
Corinth 2	Tsikalario 29
Cos 37	Vroulia 32
Eleusis 14	Yria 30
Ephesus 40	Zagora 23
Eretria 12	
Exochi 33	
Halieis 44	
Ialysos 35	
Isthmia 7	
Kameiros 34	
Kato Phana 42	
Kea 22	
Koukounaries 24	
Lathouriza 19	
Megara 8	
Melos 27	
Miletus 38	
Naoussa 24	
Nemea 1	
Nisyros 36	
Oikonomos 25	
Paralimni 11	

Fig. 2. Sites in central Greece.

14

between regions easier, but as Cook (1969) has insisted, by its very nature, archaeological dating always leaves a margin of error of at least ±25 years. All the dates I give are to some extent merely accepted conventions.

I subdivide Snodgrass's structural revolution into two phases. The first falls between 750 and 725, and the second between 725 and 700. As I commented in the last paragraph, we should not put too much confidence in such precise absolute dates, but the relative chronology of the two phases is clear enough. We can raise or lower the beginning and end of these transformations by 25 years or more, but the important points – that there was a period of dizzyingly rapid change, and that we need to divide it into two phases – are beyond dispute. I also see a third major transformation around 550–500. I summarize the evidence under my three headings of burials, sanctuaries, and settlements, and then discuss its implications.

Phase 1, c. 750–725 BC

BURIALS. Before 750, very few burials are known; after 750, there are many. Throughout the Iron Age, each part of central Greece had its own burial customs. Thus in the early eighth century, Athenians cremated adults and put their ashes in fine clay vessels, while Argives inhumed them in a contracted position in stone cist graves. But within each area, customs were rather homogeneous, and graves were generally poor and simple. This changed after 750. In some regions, new rites appeared (adult inhumation in shaft and pit graves at Athens, and for a few men, cremation in a bronze urn; multiple use of cists and increasing use of giant *pithoi* at Argos), and everywhere variability increased dramatically. In Attica, virtually every village had its own twist on the normative practices, and even within cemeteries it was rare for two graves to be very similar. Some graves were now very rich, like the famous warrior burial (French gr. 45) at Argos, or had monumental markers, like the Dipylon graves at Athens.[17] The explosion in the quantity and variety of evidence is most pronounced in Attica, Corinthia, the Argolid, Megara, Euboea, and the Dodecanese; in the Cyclades burials remain rare until 700, and in Ionia and Boeotia, until 550.[18]

SANCTUARIES. Before 750, few sites have clear evidence for sacrifice. Whatever Dark Age Greeks did when they worshipped the gods did not produce substantial deposits. At Isthmia, Asine, Yria on Naxos, and Ephesus, we can perhaps trace cult activity across most of the Dark Age (and at Yria and Ephesus perhaps small cult buildings in the early eighth century), and several more sites have evidence of sacrifices beginning around 900.[19] Alexandros Mazarakis-Ainian argues that worship was dominated by chiefs within their own dwellings (1985; 1988), which might explain why it has been so difficult to detect. But whether he is right or not, Dark Age cult had little impact on the physical world. That changed after 750. Stone altars appeared at many sites, and clear evidence for repeated animal sacrifice. Large deposits of ash could form, and whereas before 750 only a handful of sherds can be associated with cult, after 750 regular votive offerings of pottery began. Most sites now had discrete cult spots, often marked off by *peribolos* walls, and usually with a temple. Many of these were small (although by the standards of the villages they were in, they were very imposing structures), but others, like the first *hekatompedon* at Eretria, were impressive.[20]

SETTLEMENTS. Before 750, most houses were single-room, curvilinear structures, apsidal or oval. Sometimes they were built from mud and reeds woven around a structure of posts, and sometimes from mudbricks, with or without a low stone foundation. Beaten earth or clay floors and simple open hearths were normal, and pitched thatched roofs. Most activities – eating, sleeping, cooking, storage, stalling animals – must have gone on in this undivided main room or in the open air. The best examples come from Asine (Wells 1983).

After 750, these simple structures were replaced by rectilinear houses. At first, these were usually also one-room structures, or modest *megaron* houses with a small front porch, like the earliest houses at Zagora (see *Fig.* 11, below). The best examples come from colonial sites on Sicily, such as Naxos, Syracuse, and Megara Hyblaea. Some oval houses were renovated as rectangular ones by just adding corners, as at Pithekoussai on Ischia, or the seventh-century House A at Miletus (*Figs.* 3, 4). At Eretria, we see a clear progression during the eighth century from small one-room oval huts, to larger mudbrick houses, and finally to rectangular stone *megara* (*Fig.* 5). At Smyrna, on the other hand, the excavator identified a more complex sequence, seeing a multi-room rectilinear structure in the ninth century, only for apsidal houses to return around 750, before multi-room rectilinear houses again took over in the seventh century.[21]

Dark Age settlements are rare, small, and often short-lived, but the evidence of excavation and particularly intensive surface survey suggests that the size of settlements increased rapidly after 750 and that there was a rapid infilling of the landscape by new villages.[22]

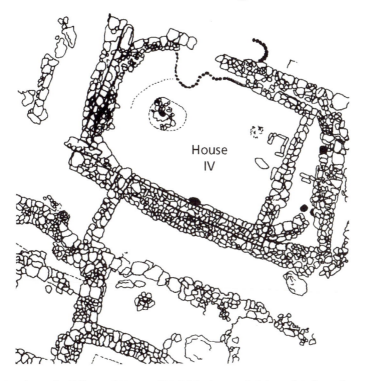

Fig. 3. The rebuilding of House IV, Pithekoussai (Mazzola) (based on plan in *Archaeological Reports* 1970/71, 65).

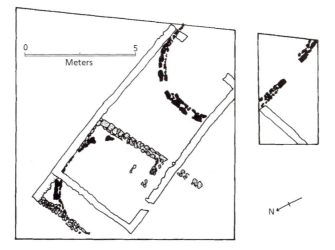

Fig. 4. The rebuilding of Südschnitt House A, Miletus (based on plans in *Istanbuler Mitteilungen* 23/24 (1973/74) 71–3).

17

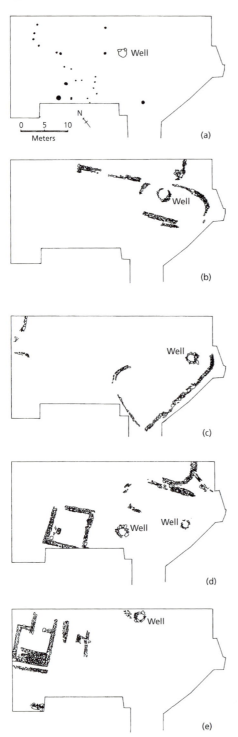

Fig. 5. Building sequence in the Roussou plot, Eretria.
a) Phase 1, probably early eighth century
b) Phase 2, probably mid-eighth century
c) Phase 3, probably late eighth century
d) Phase 4, probably around 700 BC
e) Phase 5, probably early seventh century

Figures a–e are all based on the composite plan in *Antike Kunst* 24 (1981) 85. I have separated the walls into phases on the basis of the elevations published for their lower courses. This is not the ideal method, particularly since the excavated area slopes gently from west to east. Some of the structures will of course have remained in use across several phases, and the doubled walls of some houses suggest re-buildings on almost the same alignment. But until the full publication appears, this is the only way to make sense of the sequence. I am most grateful to Drs Alexandros Mazarakis-Ainian and Petros Themelis for suggesting the idea to me in discussions at Eretria in 1984.

Phase 2, c. 725–600 BC

BURIALS. Around 700, rich graves, especially warrior graves, disappeared. At Argos and particularly at Eretria, where a series of male cremations in bronze urns has been found, the richest warrior burials date close to 700, perhaps continuing a decade or so into the seventh century, but they had no successors.[23] Mortuary variability declined, and most seventh-century cemeteries are characterized by monotonously normative customs – at Argos, inhumation in cylindrical *pithoi*; at Corinth and Megara, inhumation in simple stone sarcophagi; on Thera, small primary cremations in rock-cut pits.

The age structure changed dramatically in most cemeteries. Before 725 there are few known child graves; after 725, they make up roughly half our sample, which is what we would expect in an ancient agrarian society. Sometimes children were buried with adults, and sometimes they had their own graveyards. Archaeologists often react to child cemeteries by assuming that they must be evidence for plagues, famines, or other crises, but this was just a normal archaic practice. Intramural burial ended virtually everywhere for adults before 700, and even child graves among houses were rare by the sixth century. By 675 or 650, most sites in mainland central Greece and the Cyclades had large, homogeneous cemeteries along the roads away from town, without lavish monuments. Grave goods were very poor; anything more than two or three pots is exciting in archaic funerary archaeology, and metal almost disappears from the record.

Despite their importance, seventh-century cemeteries are badly known, probably because few archaeologists want to excavate them in a systematic way, and fewer still want to publish such material. The Hospital and Gymnasium cemeteries at Argos and the West Cemetery at Eretria seem to be good examples of this pattern; the North Cemetery at Corinth is unique in the care the excavators took to publish every deposit.[24]

Attica is the major exception. Here, although the graves are very homogeneous and grave goods are limited largely to pottery, almost all adult cremations were marked by monuments (mounds, mudbrick tombs, or, in the sixth century, sculpture), and Houby-Nielsen (1992) argues that even the pottery associated with the graves was designed to evoke images of wealthy feasting.[25]

SANCTUARIES. There was an explosion of temple-building around 700. By 650, every little village had its own temple, and big sites had monumental stone structures with clay roof tiles, architectural terracottas, and pedimental sculptures. Some builders used huge blocks of stone, perhaps as a deliberate statement of the effort felt to be needed to honor the gods. Votive dedications also intensified. Even modest shrines now often had a few metal offerings. Kato Phana on Chios, for example, yielded gold, scarabs, two bronze cauldron attachments, and a miniature silver tripod. Literally tons of pottery accumulated at these sites during the seventh century, only to be swept into vast garbage pits. At Koukounaries on Paros, my initial on-site counts suggested that the quantity of pots dedicated to Athena increased something like one thousand-fold between 750 and 650.[26]

At major temples – of which there were surprisingly many – the level of seventh-century activity was truly breathtaking. At Ephesus, for example, a peripteral apsidal temple was rebuilt in the early seventh century as a bigger rectangular stone temple with a new altar, and rebuilt again in the early sixth century; and another sequence of temples culminated around 550 in a massive stone structure for which king Croesus of Lydia provided columns (Herodotus 1.26). The whole area is strewn with rich offerings, including gold, ivory, electrum, Phoenician imports, and the earliest known Greek coins, probably deposited between 650 and 625. At Samos, the first *hekatompedon* for Hera was probably built around 725; in the seventh century the sanctuary filled up with other buildings, and by 600 a monumental paved Sacred Way linked it with the main town. Two more temples were built in the sixth century, and Herodotus (3.60) says that the final version (109 x 55 m) was the biggest Greek temple he had ever seen. The dedications included magnificent jewelry, a zoo of exotic animals, and at some point in the late seventh century a whole ship.[27] Seventh-century archaeology is primarily the archaeology of sanctuaries.

Once again, Attica is the exception: here there are remarkably few seventh-century temples. The Sacred House at the Academy and 'tholos' at Lathouriza had extremely odd architectural plans, and the sanctuary on Tourkovouni was a very simple structure. Even the richest sanctuary, at Sounion, was poorer than a minor Chian shrine like Kato Phana. It seems that monumental religious architecture only appeared in Attica around 600 BC, with a large stone altar on the acropolis, and the Old Temple of Athena perhaps in the 590s.[28]

SETTLEMENTS. There was an overall chopping-up of space. The removal of cemeteries and demarcation of sanctuaries meant that domestic space was more sharply defined, a trend which was reinforced by the spread of defensive perimeter walls for villages and cities around 700, and much more complex rectilinear houses. Drerup (1967, 11–12) and Krause (1977) see continuity from the earliest rectilinear houses to the fourth-century *pastas*-house as defined at Olynthus by Robinson and Graham (1938), via a common archaic house shape of two rooms opening off a corridor along the front of the house (e.g., Aegina houses 2 and 3, shown in *Fig.* 6). Development was uneven: these simple houses on Aegina continued in use until about 500, while corridor-style House I at Corinth was modified substantially in the sixth century. At Koukounaries and Smyrna, much more complex houses were already the norm by the middle of the seventh century (*Fig.* 7).[29]

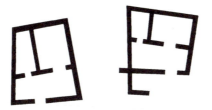

Fig. 6. Archaic houses 2 and 3, Aegina (based on drawings in *Archäologischer Anzeiger* 1925, 5–6).

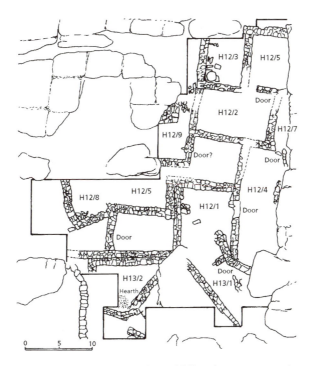

Fig. 7. Seventh-century houses on the Middle Plateau at Koukounaries on Paros (based on plan in *Praktika* 1988, 198).

21

At Zagora, developments were even faster. Already by 700 we can identify genuine courtyard houses of just the kind which Nevett (1995) sees as important to classical concepts of space, inward-turned and accessible only via a narrow door on to a street. Houses were being built more sturdily, especially in the Cyclades, where all-stone construction was common. At Zagora, one wall was preserved intact when it fell: the house was a little over 2 m high, with a small triangular window near the top. The same design is attested in all-stone House 1 at fourth-century Ammotopos in Epirus. These stone houses normally had flat roofs, with wooden beams supporting thin slabs of stone, sealed by clay (*Fig.* 8). Hearths were sometimes carefully built, with stone slabs around them, and drains became common. A bathtub built into a fortification wall at Miletus is probably as early as the seventh or even the end of the eighth century.[30]

At most sites, the transition from one-room or *megaron* houses to courtyard houses took longer, and, not surprisingly, we can document old and new designs in use alongside each other. At Miletus, one rectilinear house was built early enough to have been destroyed by fire *c.* 750, and stretches of late eighth-century walls found in the early excavations also seem to belong to rectilinear houses. But oval huts were still being built in the seventh century, and the first indisputable courtyard house here dates after 650, when an early seventh-century multi-room rectilinear house was replanned (*Fig.* 9).[31] On Sicily, the simple rectangular houses of the first settlers at Naxos gave way to

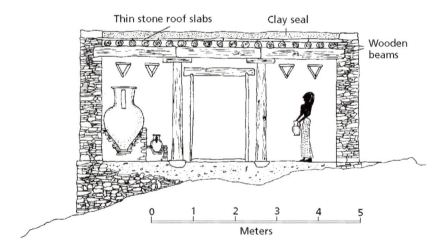

Fig. 8. House construction at Zagora on Andros (based on drawing by J.J. Coulton in Cambitoglou 1981, fig. 8).

courtyard houses in the seventh century, perhaps even by 700, but at Megara Hyblaea, founded in 728, the conversion of one-room or *megaron* houses into courtyard houses was a very gradual process, proceeding unevenly across the whole seventh century. It was not until after 650 that the area around the *agora* began to look like late eighth-century Zagora, as the original plots of 100–120 m² were filled by courtyard houses.[32] By 600, the courtyard house was normal everywhere.

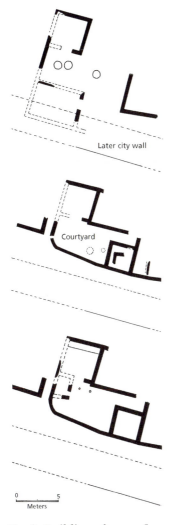

Fig. 9. Building phases of seventh-century courtyard house on Kalabaktepe, Miletus (based on plans in *Istanbuler Mitteilungen* 40 (1990) 44–7).

Formal agoras probably began to be laid out in this period too. Homer (*Od.* 8.6–7) said that the *agora* at Phaeacia had 'polished stone' seats, and on Ithaca, Odysseus had his own seat (*Od.* 2.14). The clearest central Greek archaeological evidence comes from colonial Megara Hyblaea, which included an open central space in its original plan of 728 BC. Older cities, already built up, may only have made provisions for formal agoras quite late in the sixth century (Snodgrass 1980, 154–8).

Finally, Attica was again an exception. A group of rectilinear rooms dating around 700 has been found at Thorikos, but the most substantial group of early houses, from Lathouriza, combines rectilinear and curvilinear styles in a very unusual way (*Fig.* 10), and a recently reported excavation at Eleusis exposed an early archaic apsidal house. Some of these houses retained old-fashioned pitched thatch roofs. By the early sixth century, though, a group of houses and shops in Athens were typical of the rest of central Greece.[33]

Fig. 10. Seventh-century houses at Lathouriza (based on plans in Mazarakis-Ainian 1994, 1995).

Discussion of phases 1 and 2

These changes created the spatial structures which characterized Greek civilization for the next half-millennium. But after a dizzying, even revolutionary, period between 750 and 700, the rate of change slowed down, and in most parts of central Greece the seventh and early sixth century saw the gradual unfolding of patterns initiated at the end of the eighth. How we interpret the archaeology of the seventh century depends largely on what we make of the events between 750 and 700; and that, in turn, hinges on what vision we have of the Dark Age order which crumbled in these years. The dominant model is that proposed by Snodgrass in the 1970s, of a Dark Age of small, poor, and isolated egalitarian groups, perhaps mobile and partly pastoral. As summed up by Chester Starr, this view holds that 'during the Dark Ages...men struggled to survive and to hold together the tissue of society' (1977, 47). A population explosion in the eighth century, linked to more intensive agriculture, ended this, and led to new wealth, political centralization, increasing hierarchy, and massive cultural changes (Snodgrass 1977; 1980, 15–84; 1987, 170–210; 1993).

I have argued that this model is too positivist, assuming that the data passively mirror prior demographic, economic, and political forces. It seems to me that the homogeneity of Dark Age burials, cult observances, and housing was not a simple reflection of an egalitarian society.

Rather, I argue, our evidence is heavily skewed toward elite groups, who used material culture as one way to construct an image of themselves as an internally equal class ruling over excluded lower groups (Morris 1987; forthcoming). I interpret the changes I described above as follows:

BURIALS. Detailed analysis of burials, particularly the well published Athenian Kerameikos cemetery, remains fundamental to our understanding of central Greece. Between 1000 and 725 BC, only about one in ten of the excavated graves in most central Greek cemeteries belongs to a child or infant. In *Burial and Ancient Society*, I argued that this cannot directly reflect the demographic structure of the living populations, but must be a side-effect of ritual distinctions, with most children being buried in ways which have low archaeological visibility.[34] I went on to suggest that a similar phenomenon partly accounts for the tiny numbers of Dark Age adult burials: as well as an age boundary, death-rituals created a class boundary between a high-status group with formal cemeteries, and a low-status group excluded from these rites. Whitley (1991b) and Houby-Nielsen (1992, 1995), authors of the most detailed re-analyses of the Kerameikos evidence since *Burial and Ancient Society*, both accept some version of the exclusion hypothesis which I advanced there.[35]

I suggested that rather than reflecting the rise of the first aristocracies, as in Snodgrass's model, the eighth-century changes were part of the collapse of the old Dark Age hierarchy and the creation of something like the citizen communities we know from later literature. The years between 750 and 700 were a period of chaotic transition, when new ideas about how to order the world were being worked out, in part through the manipulation of material culture in ritual settings. Instead of a funerary community rigidly divided into elite and non-elite, everyone now claimed access to the same kinds of funerals. Some of the rich responded by differentiating themselves in new ways, using lavish grave goods and markers, or complicating the treatment of the dead (Phase 1), but after a generation or so, a more egalitarian ethos won out. Lavish spending was no longer appropriate in burial: families could not get away with representing those they buried as special warriors or great men (or as the dependents of such men). The citizens relocated their cemeteries outside the city and established a new, civic space of the dead (Phase 2). In most *poleis*, there was no significant challenge to this vision of the cemetery until late in the sixth century.

SANCTUARIES. The new forms of worship created at the end of the eighth century, like the new funerals, offered an arena where competing visions of how mortals should relate to the gods – and thus conflicting views of the nature of humanity itself and the good society – were made explicit. François de Polignac (1995a) argues that the new sanctuaries defined the spatial limits of the citizen state as well as its relationships with the gods. And if Mazarakis-Ainian is right about the form of Dark Age worship, the shift from rituals within a chief's house, which physically restricted involvement to a select group, to open-air sacrifices, also implies a widening membership of the religious corporation paralleling the widening of the 'burying family', to borrow Houby-Nielsen's (1995) useful term.

Snodgrass has called the chronological coincidence between the abandonment of rich grave goods and the appearance of rich votives around 700 'a big social change with the redirection of attention towards the communal sanctuary and away from the individual grave' (1980, 54). This is a compelling argument, but the literary sources suggest that it may only be half the story. Archaic Greek poetry breaks down into two cultural traditions, which I have labeled the 'middling' and the 'elitist'.[36] The former – generally expressed in elegiac and iambic meters by poets like Archilochus, Solon, Phocylides, Xenophanes, and to some extent Theognis, but drawing on ideas going back to Hesiod's hexameters – insisted that the best man was middling (*metrios* or *mesos*), with controlled appetites, neither rich nor poor, tending his farm, standing his place in the hoplite ranks, and fathering sturdy children. Gender distinctions were sharp (most notoriously in Hesiod's myth of Pandora and in Semonides F7 West). The good community was a group of such men, and there could be no source of human authority higher than this group. The *metrios* was pious, but the gods were utterly removed from mankind, and no one in the *polis* could claim privileged access to them.

The elitist poets, mostly working in lyric meters, took an entirely opposed view. The community of middling men was just a rabble of peasants, while the good society was a group of like-minded aristocrats who transcended the boundaries of the individual *polis*. Such creatures lived in a world of luxury, using the same kinds of vessels, clothes, and houses as the gods, heroes, and Lydians, and they claimed to draw authority from their links with these privileged groups. Their special knowledge, beauty, and athletic skills set them above everyone else.

The two traditions explicitly confronted one another. The words that Archilochus put into the mouth of Charon the carpenter – 'I don't care for Gyges the Golden's things, and I've never envied him. I'm not jealous of the works of gods either, and I don't lust after a magnificent tyranny. These are beyond my gaze' (F19 West) – are a virtual checklist of elitist culture, at least in the eyes of its critics. They saw elitists as hankering after tyrannical rule like oriental despots such as Gyges of Lydia, impiously setting themselves up as rivals to the very gods. In the end, the differences between the two traditions came down to a single point: the elitists would legitimate their claims to be a special elite by appeals to sources of authority outside the *polis*; and the middling poets absolutely rejected this. The former blurred distinctions between male and female, present and past, mortal and divine, Greek and Lydian, to create a single distinction, between aristocrat and commoner; the latter did precisely the opposite. Each was doubtless guilty of disgusting and polluting behavior in the eyes of the other.

We are dealing with competing constructions of identity, involving radically opposed notions of class, gender, ethnicity, and cosmology. To someone steeped in middling values, the rejection of rich grave goods and monuments around 700 probably did seem like a victory, as Snodgrass suggests. Grave goods brought honor only to an individual family, but a gift to the gods, far removed from the petty struggles of mortals, won favor for the whole *polis*. But to those men and women who felt that they virtually lived, loved, and dined among the gods, matters probably looked very different. Giving a golden cup to Aphrodite was precisely the kind of action which Sappho represented as involving a personal epiphany; and when votives were not only expensive but also evoked the worlds of the East and the heroes, like the bronze tripods which accumulated in large numbers in seventh-century sanctuaries, all sources of external power flowed together in the act of dedication.

The cemetery had been the scene of cultural conflict in the late eighth century; in the early seventh, the action shifted to the sanctuary. Breathtaking wealth was diverted in this direction both by individual nobles, and by *poleis* acting as communities.[37]

SETTLEMENTS. Changes in eighth- and seventh-century settlements have received much less attention than those in burials and sanctuaries. The conflict of values in archaic poetry was as much about gender as class, and in the reorganization of domestic space around 700, I suggest, we see evidence for profound changes in gender ideology.

The symbolic association of the outer/public/light areas of a house with masculinity and the inner/private/dark areas with femininity, which was so fundamental to classical Athenian thought about gender, appears as early as Hesiod.[38] This linkage only became possible with the emergence of multi-room houses, and particularly with the courtyard

27

house, which we first see on Zagora around 700. Before 750, almost all houses were flimsy, one-roomed, and open, with very few physical separators to break up the flow of activity. It is certainly possible for people to develop complex spatial symbolism without solid physical boundaries (the contemporary Brazilian Mehinaku are a famous case in point; Gregor 1977, 48–62), but societies with rigid and hierarchical gender and age structures tend to construct them in part through subdividing domestic space (Lawrence and Low 1990; Kent 1990).

At Zagora, the best published site, older single-room houses or *megara* built between 775 and 725 were broken up into multi-room structures with functionally specific spaces after 725 (Cambitoglou et al. 1971; 1988). For example, in the third quarter of the eighth century, unit H24/25/32 formed a *megaron* house with a simple porch in front (*Fig.* 11). The sherds from the floor show that cooking, storage, eating, and drinking all went on in the one main room. By 700, though, the people who lived here had broken this one room into three smaller rooms (H24, H25, H32). Judging from the finds in them, all three were used solely for storage. The south wall of the old porch was extended 8 m, and two new rooms, H40 and H41, were

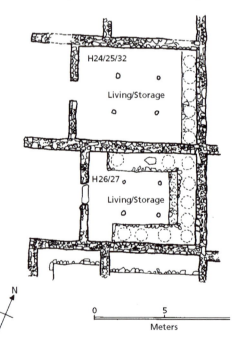

Fig. 11. Units H24/25/32 and H26/27 at Zagora, phase 1, *c.* 750–725 (based on drawing by J.J. Coulton in Cambitoglou 1981, fig. 9).

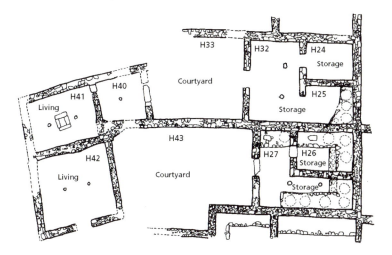

Fig. 12. Units H24/25/32/33/40/41 and H26/27/42/43 at Zagora, phase 2, *c.* 725–700 (based on drawing by J.J. Coulton in Cambitoglou 1981, fig. 9).

built at its end (*Fig.* 12). H40, which had an unusually wide door, was probably an ante-room to H41, with a monumental stone hearth and dense concentrations of sherds from fine cups. The new version of the house was reached from the courtyard now formed by the space between H32 and H40. Turning right, the visitor entered through the wide doorway into the public area of the house for feasting; turning left, into an area of storage at the back of the house. The house immediately to the south went through a very similar transformation at just the same time.

Interpreting these finds, and the replacement of single-roomed by courtyard houses all over central Greece during the seventh century, is no easy matter. Attributing gender to excavated space is almost impossible (Conkey and Gero 1991), but I am not trying to suggest that men or women were restricted to any particular part of the house.[39] No doubt women often went into Zagora H40 and H41, and men into H24, H25, and H32. But what I want to suggest is that the kind of *ideas* about gendered space which we see in Hesiod and classical Athenian literature began to take shape in the late eighth century as part of the formation of the middling ideology.[40] Historians often point out that Homeric notions of gender seem less rigid than those in Hesiod and later authors.[41] The evidence of housing suggests that gender ideologies were changing rapidly in the late eighth and seventh centuries, as part of a general shift toward 'middling' values.

29

Regional variation in eighth- and seventh-century central Greece.
So far, I have discussed central Greece in terms of a single general
pattern, but no two *poleis* were exactly the same. The model which
I have set out so far works best for places like Corinth, Argos, Eretria,
Megara, and the Aegean islands, though even within this group there
is some variation. For instance, on Thera we have substantial cemeteries of multiple burials from about 775 on, replaced by individual
burials after 700, though on Naxos and Paros major cemeteries only
begin around 700. On Rhodes, seventh-century burials were definitely
poorer than those of the eighth century, but still richer than those on
the mainland. The cities of Ionia, including Samos and Chios, are very
similar in terms of settlements and sanctuaries, but have produced
very few graves at all before 550. Boeotia is rather similar, though we
know little as yet about housing there.[42]

Some *poleis* moved further than others toward a 'middling' material
culture. I would suggest that Corinth, Argos, and the other cities
which I listed above embraced the new ways most enthusiastically; the
Ionians and the Boeotians perhaps rather less so; while in Athens, the
middle way was rejected altogether in the years around 700. In the
middle of the eighth century, the Athenians had been at the forefront
of developments, but by 700 they had become exceptions to every
generalization. Seventh-century Athenian cemeteries of adult cremations under mounds contain very few graves, and I have argued
(Morris 1987; 1993a, 32–7; 1995) that the Athenians returned to
a divided ritual world like that of the Dark Age, in a conscious effort
by the aristocracy to turn the clock back. They built no great temples
until 600, and their votives were very poor. De Polignac (1995a, 81–8)
suggests that Athens also ignored the bipolar religious spatial structure
which was typical of archaic *poleis*. The early seventh-century houses
on Velatouri hill at Thorikos seem to be going in the same direction as
other central Greeks, but the larger area of housing at Lathouriza is
most peculiar by the standards of contemporary housing in Corinth or
the Cyclades. Seventh-century Attica must have looked very old-
fashioned to visitors from anywhere else in central Greece.

This variability is important. The world was being turned upside
down, and not everyone liked it. We hear stories in Aristotle's *Politics*
and other late sources about outbreaks of violence, redistribution of
land, and struggles over the formalization of law. In some places,
a new civic ideology was very successful; in others, moderately so. In
Athens, it was halted, then reversed, around 700. Solon's reforms in
594 destroyed the economic basis for this reactionary society, and in

the second half of the sixth century Athens fell back in line with the rest of central Greece.

Phase 3, c. 550–500 BC

In most central Greek *poleis* the upheavals between about 750 and 675 set the pattern for some hundred and fifty years. This is again a point that Snodgrass has made, identifying renewed structural changes in the late sixth century (1980, 201–18). As with the earlier changes, I begin with a brief description of my three categories of evidence.

BURIALS. Outside Attica, there are very few rich graves or striking monuments between 700 and 550.[43] But in the mid and late sixth century, we see a small movement back toward display. At Corinth, for instance, North Cemetery gr. 206 (*c.* 550) held an iron spearhead, and gr. 262 (shortly before 500) some bronze armor. Around 525, gr. 250 contained two gold, two silver, and three bronze ornaments, as well as an iron pin, a necklace of glass beads, and ten pots; and shortly before 500, gr. 257 had a silver ring. The only monument post-dating 750 BC is a small tombstone over gr. 240, around 550 BC. A little way outside the city, a marble sphinx was found at Aetopetra, perhaps set up as early as 575; and the famous 'Tenean Apollo' *kouros* of *c.* 550 found near Athikia was probably also a grave marker. These graves are not impressive for such a rich city, but they are more lavish than anything from the previous hundred years. On Samos, there are also some post-550 burials with interesting grave goods, but Boehlau (1898, 22) explicitly noted the contrast between the poverty of the cemetery and the famous wealth of the Polycratean *polis*.[44]

The same trend toward slightly richer grave goods and occasional use of funerary sculpture after 550 can be seen elsewhere. In the cemeteries of Naxos, for example, only one statue can be dated between 600 and 550, but at least five between 550 and 500. On Thera, one statue of about 600 BC may have come from a grave, but three more found *in situ* date to the second half of the century. A few Theran tombs have faïence ornaments, gilt bronze vessels, and even gold and silver trinkets in the late sixth century. On Paros, an unusual chamber tomb containing 50 cremations was marked by a tall stele around 700 BC, and another stele of the same date was found in the early 1960s; but then no more markers are known until two late sixth-century *kouroi* from Naoussa and Protoryia.[45]

For most of the archaic period, Attica was a marked exception to the central Greek pattern. Nearly all known adult burials can be associated with a monument. In the seventh century this usually meant a mound, but by 600 it could also be a mudbrick tomb, often decorated with painted plaques, or a stone sculpture. The monuments got bigger and bigger in the early sixth century, culminating in the huge Mound G and South Mound in the Kerameikos, dating between 560 and 520 BC. Houby-Nielsen (1995, 142, 166–9) also draws attention to the use of Lydian vessel types in these two mounds, and their remarkable Lydian-style wooden biers decorated with ivory panels. She sees this as a flirtation with eastern luxury and a partial redefinition of gender roles. There was also a minor revival of the late eighth-century heroizing vogue for cremations in bronze urns in the mid and late sixth century. Attic buriers after 550 paralleled the increase in spending which we see in the rest of central Greece, but having started off from a much higher level in the early sixth century, its late sixth-century monuments were particularly spectacular.[46]

But around 500, there was an abrupt collapse in funerary display all over central Greece. The situation at Athens has been much discussed: grave monuments almost completely disappeared around 500, only to return after 425 in very different forms. No rich grave goods have been reported from this seventy-five year period. What is less commonly recognized, however, is that this fifth-century austerity affected the *whole* Greek world. Defining the scale of this transformation radically changes the nature of the problem to be explained: Atheno-centric explanations, focusing on the goals of this or that lawgiver or the contingencies of Athenian public building programs, cannot account for the pattern as a whole (Morris 1992, 108–55; 1997d).[47]

SANCTUARIES. At most sites the number and wealth of excavated votives decline steadily across the sixth century, reaching quite low levels in the fifth (Snodgrass 1989/90). The main exceptions are small shrines of non-Olympian deities. However, inscribed inventories from the Parthenon, Erechtheion, and Asklepieion in Athens, and several other sanctuaries, along with descriptions of elaborate athletic victory monuments in the literary sources, show that magnificent objects were dedicated in the fifth and particularly the fourth century. As Snodgrass observes, contrary to what the archaeological record by itself reveals, the grandest offerings of the sixth and fifth centuries were probably much more expensive than those of the eighth and seventh centuries. These spectacular dedications have all but disappeared. It may be that by the time looting sanctuaries became a real problem, in the fourth century, archaic bronzes were too old to be worth much, and are thus over-represented relative to classical offerings. But on the other hand, Diodorus (16.56.6) explicitly mentions gold and silver treasures given by Croesus of Lydia in the sixth century among the 10,000 talents worth of booty which the Phocians stole from Delphi around 350. There is no obvious reason why temple-robbing would have affected either very rich (gold and silver) or very poor (pottery) classical dedications more severely than those of archaic times; yet at all levels, seventh-century offerings dominate the record. This may be good enough grounds to assume that we should take the decline in excavated offerings after 600 (and particularly after 500) as reflecting a real decline in the number of dedications originally made, but the problem needs more study.[48]

The sixth century also saw something of a boom in temple-building, the formalization of the Doric and Ionic orders, and revolutionary advances in technology (Snodgrass 1980, 149–51). Many of the finest mainland Greek temples date to the years around 500, and Snodgrass (1986) has suggested that *poleis* were consciously competing against one another in the grandeur of their temples. Although the data have never been systematically collected, there also seems to be an increase in the building of small shrines around 500.

SETTLEMENTS. By 600 BC, the shift to courtyard houses was almost complete.[49] Changes in domestic space in the late sixth century were less striking than those in cemeteries or sanctuaries, but were still significant. In Athens, there is some evidence for a fundamental re-thinking of public space, involving increasingly rigid divisions between communal and private areas, which Lévêque and Vidal-Naquet (1995 (1964)) associate with Cleisthenes' reforms. Hoepfner and Schwand-ner (1986) have argued that there were also major changes in housing around 500. They suggest that new cities were now being planned on a 'Hippodamian' system, using equal sized lots and uniform courtyard plans. The evidence, however, remains unclear (Schuller et al. 1989). At Miletus, digging behind the Bouleuterion revealed a late sixth-century grid plan, which Müller-Wiener (1986, 102) calls 'Hippo-damian'; but at Halieis a grid plan goes back earlier into the sixth century, while most of Hoepfner and Schwandner's examples belong later in the fifth or even in the fourth century. The evidence is sugges-tive, but there is not yet enough of it to pin down new styles of planning as a specifically late sixth-century phenomenon.[50]

Our knowledge of eighth- and seventh-century houses comes mainly from the well preserved villages of the Cyclades, but most of these were abandoned before 600, with people probably moving to larger towns like Paroikia on Paros or Chora on Naxos. These towns have been almost continuously occupied ever since, and have yielded little archaic evidence. The only substantial excavated areas of sixth-century central Greek housing are in colonial sites (notably Megara Hyblaea, Selinus, Acragas, and Elea).[51] Courtyard houses laid out in regular-sized plots along straight roads were normal in these cities. As noted above, many of the houses of Megara Hyblaea filled up their original lots of 100–120 m² with multi-room courtyard structures by 600; thereafter they changed little before the city's destruction in 476.

Our evidence from the older towns of the Aegean is scrappy, but it seems that the people who lived here did not have such freedom to reshape their domestic space. At Corinth, houses II and III and the final phase of house I date to the sixth century (*Fig.* 13), and the 'Traders' Complex', built in the late seventh century, probably remained in use until about 575. The sixth-century houses are similar to those of the fifth century, though smaller and plainer. At Athens, only the barest traces of sixth-century houses have been preserved around

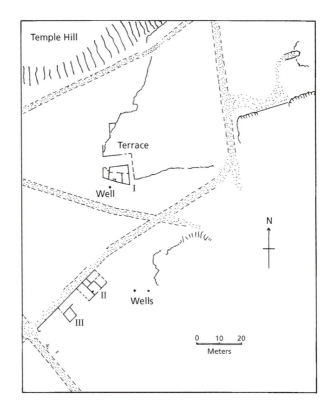

Fig. 13. Archaic Houses I, II, and III, Corinth (based on plans in *Hesperia* 40 (1971)–43 (1974).

the Agora. At Thorikos, the classical settlement began to take shape around 525. At Argos, the excavators repeatedly commented that Hellenistic activity had destroyed the archaic and classical houses. A small building of around 550 with massive stone foundations but measuring just 3 x 3 m has been found, but no complete house plans.[52]

On current evidence, it seems that most archaic houses – like those of the fifth century – were more or less the same size. Shear (1994) suggests that Buildings F, C, and D in the Athenian Agora should be identified as a sixth-century Pisistratid palace, but despite the traditions of tyrannies at Corinth, Samos, and numerous other central Greek *poleis*, no palace has been definitely identified. There are many possible explanations for this lacuna, but it may well be that even sixth-century tyrants lived in relatively modest structures.

Discussion of phase 3

The changes of the late sixth century are less dramatic than those of the late eighth, but are nonetheless important. I argued above that the period 750–700 saw a decisive shift toward the middling ideology in central Greece; in 550–500, I suggest, there was a second shift, going still further in this direction. Aristocrats briefly contested this, adorning their family tombs with statues, but their reaction was not very successful. By the end of the century, there was no major context in which the rich could make permanent material displays of their own specialness. By 500, the most important form of spending on the gods may have been state-funded temple-building.[53] Jameson (1998) shows that at Athens there was no abrupt break in religious practices around 500, only a gradual communal and eventually democratic expansion and takeover of older forms of worship. The patterns in settlement space probably also indicate a steady transformation: between 550 and 450 there was a general move toward more regular and uniform housing, but this was more an acceleration of trends underway across the whole archaic period than an abrupt break with the past.

The disappearance of the last contexts for the material display of special status coincided with an important change in literary culture. The elitist ideology crumbled, and new poetic forms like the epinician ode, mediating between the interests of the aristocratic household and the community of citizens, took its place.[54] The middling ideology reigned supreme in the early and mid-fifth century, and opposition was driven underground or to the margins of mainstream society. It is no coincidence that this was the very period in which the first male citizen democracies seized power, in which the visual imagery of aggressive male sexuality is most pronounced in Athenian art (Keuls 1985), and in which elitist appeals to the East were most problematic (although, as Miller (1997) shows, never entirely forgotten). The use of material culture in the years between 500 and 425 suggests to me that this was an age of consensus around the core values of the middling ideology. But by the end of the fifth century, this quarter-millennium-old trend toward increasing male citizen power was being reversed (Morris 1992, 145–55; 1997d).

Northern Greece (*Fig.* 14)

Under this heading I include Thessaly, Epirus, Macedonia, and Thrace. Thessalian archaic chronology is closely tied to the Corinthian and Attic series, but further north there are fewer connections. Corinthian pottery appears on a number of Epirote sites from 700 on, and after 600 penetrates the Thracian interior, but in Macedonia the problems are severe. A little central Greek pottery appears along the coast as early as 900, and many archaeologists see Euboean colonies in Chalcidice at that time. There is plenty of Geometric and archaic Greek pottery in Chalcidice, but further north there are fewer finds. At Vardaroftsa, for example, Greek pottery shows up in the sixth century, but only becomes dominant in the fourth. Most of the time we must deal with a very conservative 'Early Iron Age' pottery style, probably used from the eleventh century into the sixth, which can only rarely be divided into phases.[55]

Thessaly

BURIALS. There were certainly changes in the eighth century, but they were not as pronounced as in central Greece. Multiple burial, particularly in small *tholos* tombs, had continued across the Dark Age. Most of these tombs were modest and were used only briefly, but a few lasted for several generations, accumulating many burials and rich offerings, particularly iron weapons. The *tholos* tombs were probably often marked by grave mounds, but only one very large Dark Age mound – 27 m in diameter and 5 m high – is so far known, from Ayioi Theodoroi. Alongside the multiple burials, a tradition of single burial in cists also flourished across the Dark Age. This does not seem to be a regional distinction: cists and *tholoi* are known from the same sites, so we must assume that the two grave types were used for different categories of people, however these were defined.[56]

Some archaic cemeteries developed along similar lines to those in central Greece. At Nea Ionia, for instance, the large, rich cist graves of

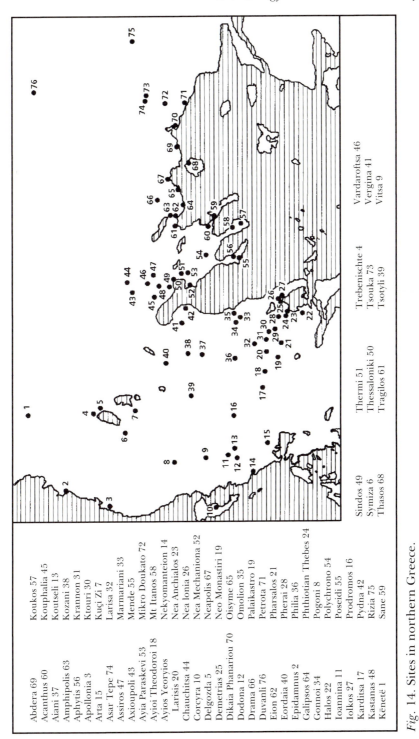

Fig. 14. Sites in northern Greece.

Abdera 69
Acanthus 60
Aiani 37
Amphipolis 63
Aphytis 56
Apollonia 3
Arta 15
Asar Tepe 74
Assiros 47
Axioupoli 43
Ayia Paraskevi 53
Ayioi Theodoroi 18
Ayios Yeoryios
Larisis 20
Chauchitsa 44
Corcyra 10
Delgozda 5
Demetrias 25
Dikaia Phanariou 70
Dodona 12
Drama 66
Duvanli 76
Eion 62
Eordaia 40
Epidamnus 2
Galipsos 64
Gonnoi 34
Halos 22
Ioannina 11
Iolkos 27
Karditsa 17
Kastanas 48
Kenetë 1

Koukos 57
Kouphalia 45
Koutseli 13
Kozani 38
Krannon 31
Ktouri 30
Kuçi Zi 7
Larisa 32
Marmariani 33
Mende 55
Mikro Doukato 72
Mt Itanos 58
Nekyomanteion 14
Nea Anchialos 23
Nea Ionia 26
Nea Mechaniona 52
Neapolis 67
Neo Monastiri 19
Oisyme 65
Omolion 35
Palaikastro 19
Petrota 71
Pharsalos 21
Pherai 28
Philia 36
Phthiotian Thebes 24
Pogoni 8
Polychrono 54
Poseidi 55
Prodromos 16
Pydna 42
Rizia 75
Sane 59

Sindos 49
Symiza 6
Thasos 68

Thermi 51
Thessaloniki 50
Tragilos 61

Trebenischte 4
Tsouka 73
Tsotyli 39

Vardaroftsa 46
Vergina 41
Vitsa 9

Geometric times gave way around 700 to poor and simple sarcophagi, smaller cists, and child pot burials. At the end of the sixth century, new, simple, and homogeneous cemeteries began at Prodromos (including tile graves, which are very common in fifth-century central Greece) and Demetrias. But Dark Age traditions survived alongside these cemeteries. A sixth-century *tholos* tomb found at Iolkos in 1915 contained four hundred pots, plus iron swords, daggers, and arrowheads, bronze fibulas, shield bosses, and helmets, bronze and gold rings, and gold nails. For many years this remarkable warrior burial was unique, but since 1975 a series of similar tombs has come to light at Ayios Yeoryios Larisis, a suburb of Krannon. Most of the thirty-one tombs on the Zapheirouli farm date 650–600, though a few poorer sarcophagi and a tile grave (gr. 15) probably belong around 500. The seventh-century burials were in rough stone-built chamber tombs with multiple cremations in urns. Tomb 2, for example, probably held eight or more urns, along with an undetermined number of iron knives, daggers, spearheads, arrowheads, and swords, and assorted bronze ornaments. Tomb 9 held three cremations in bronze urns.[57]

The eighteen tombs containing 157 burials on the Nanouli farm, four kilometers to the north, were even more interesting. These were better preserved, and were found under a very big, low mound covering the entire field. Most date to the period 550–525. Tomb 8, the biggest, contained twenty-seven burials with fifty-seven iron weapons. Tomb 2 yielded seventeen clay urns and three bronze urns, along with iron swords, spearheads, knives, wheel rims from funerary wagons or chariots, and bronze fibulas; tomb 1 had similar grave goods, but also a gold crown (an extremely unusual find before the late fourth century).[58]

The excavator initially suggested that the burials were a *polyandrion*, a mass tomb for the war dead. That remains possible, but the parallel between these finds and the older discovery at Iolkos, plus the likelihood that the Ayios Yeoryios warrior tombs formed a large cemetery spanning the whole seventh and sixth centuries, make it more likely that this was a minority funerary rite which allowed some families to represent their dead men as heroic warriors. The grave goods have strong parallels going back into the Thessalian Dark Age, particularly in the ninth- to eighth-century warrior cremations at Halos.[59]

None of the other Thessalian cemeteries are quite as striking as Ayios Yeoryios, but at Pharsalos and Krannon very large mounds were heaped up over burials at the end of the sixth century. The excavated mound at Pharsalos covered a spectacular *tholos* tomb, which had been built on top of a Mycenaean chamber tomb. Nearby there was another

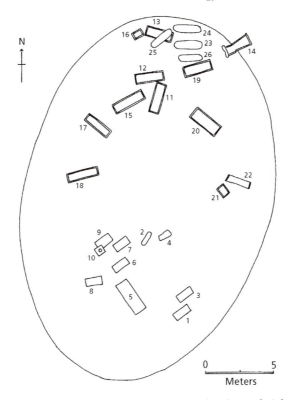

Fig. 15. Burial mound at Krannon (based on plan in *Archaiologikon Deltion* 44:2 (1989) 215).

late sixth-century *tholos* tomb. At Krannon, some sixteen tumuli are known. The main excavated example was oval, 25 x 15 m, and covered twenty-six graves (*Fig.* 15). Grave goods were not rich at either site, although Krannon gr. 20 did contain an iron sword, and gr. 5 eight alabaster vessels. These mounds remained in use through the first quarter of the fifth century.[60]

SANCTUARIES. As in central Greece, there is little evidence for worship of the gods in Dark Age Thessaly, although some of the bronzes found in archaic sanctuaries date back to the tenth century. There is a sharp increase in evidence in the late eighth century. At Pherai, Philia, Gonnoi, and Phthiotian Thebes, excavations have recovered vast numbers of bronzes dedicated between 750 and 600; and still more were looted and sold at Athens between 1917 and 1921.[61] This boom in dedications resembles central Greece, but whereas in the Aegean area the sanctuaries with spectacular bronzes flourished alongside many smaller shrines with much pottery but little metal, the early archaic

Thessalian record is so far restricted to a few great sanctuaries. But here we confront a serious methodological problem. Most of these sites are known only from the whirlwind campaigns conducted by Antonios Arvanitopoullos before the First World War, targeting the acropoleis of what he hoped would be major cities. He published short accounts in *Praktika*, but few excavators have been interested in collecting more Iron Age evidence, or even in publishing Arvanitopoullos's finds. Serious salvage archaeology began in the 1970s, but most of this work, driven by urban expansion, has uncovered cemeteries. At the moment, the absence of poor seventh-century shrines distinguishes the Thessalian religious record from the central Greek, but further work may change that.

Thessaly also differs from central Greece in having no good evidence for eighth-century temples. At Pherai, Arvanitopoullos found no temple earlier than the sixth century, but did find late seventh-century architectural terracottas; and at Phthiotian Thebes while no temple was earlier than 550, he found an early seventh-century Doric capital, and hypothesized that there had been a wooden temple here around 700. The apsidal temple at Gonnoi probably belongs in the late seventh century, as do architectural terracottas from a wooden temple at Omolion. But again, the quality of this early fieldwork may be limiting our knowledge. Recent work at Ephesus (n. 27 above) and Tegea (n. 95 below) has found traces of eighth-century temples missed in the original digs, and further work in Thessaly may change the picture radically. At the moment, though, temple-building seems to be very much a sixth-century phenomenon.[62]

SETTLEMENTS. There is little evidence. An archaic *megaron* house is reported from Larisa, and Arvanitopoullos mentioned archaic houses at several sites, but rarely gave details. At Iolkos he found large stone houses, and claimed to have located the palace of the Scopad dynasty on the acropolis of Krannon. If his observations were sound, it may be that some houses in sixth-century Thessaly were more ostentatious than those in central Greece.[63]

Epirus [64]

BURIALS. Inhumation in cist graves grouped under large tumuli was common in Late Bronze and Early Iron Age Epirus, and continued into the fourth century in southern Illyria. But by the ninth century it seems to have disappeared in Epirus, and the burials at Vitsa were in cists under individual stone cairns. This tradition continued until the fourth century. Warrior burials were common across much of this period, and also continued into the fourth century at Vitsa (gr. 166) and Ioannina (gr. 76). A few graves even included Illyrian bronze helmets (e.g., Ioannina grs. 43 and 52, the latter with the bones of a child in the helmet; and a grave from Koutseli, dating *c.* 525–500). However, even the limited evidence currently available hints at diachronic changes within the archaic period: at Vitsa, only seven graves can be dated to the seventh century, and these are also rather poor compared to those of the eighth and later sixth century.[65]

Corinthian colonists settled Corcyra in the late eighth century, perhaps displacing earlier Euboean occupants, and spread to Ambracia (modern Arta) on the mainland by 625. The colonists did not retain the normal Corinthian rite of inhumation in sarcophagi. On Corcyra, cremation in *pithoi* was preferred, and at Ambracia, sixth-century funerary *pithoi* are again reported (though it is not clear whether they contained cremations). Further north on the Illyrian coast, the Corcyrean colony of Epidamnus also has urn cremations. The different terms used by the excavators perhaps all refer to the same type of burial, which might mean that, like colonists in Sicily, those in northwest Greece forged a new identity in part through developing a new shared burial rite.[66]

On Corcyra, where we have most evidence, a large extramural cemetery of simple and homogeneous graves was established in the earliest days of the colony. As well as about one hundred poor burials, a few seventh-century monuments have been published. The best known is a round stone structure 4.7 m in diameter topped by a sculpted lion, for Menekrates of Oiantheia in Ozolian Locris, who died on Corcyra in the late seventh century (*Fig.* 16). The inscription on the monument (ML 4 = Fornara 14) tells us that the Corcyrean *demos* joined forces with Menekrates' brother to build

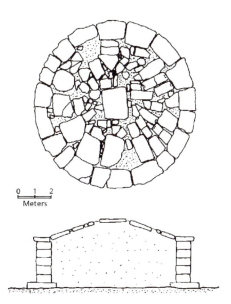

Fig. 16. The funerary monument of Menekrates on Corcyra.

the tomb in honor of their former *proxenos*. This is clearly a public monument. But just a few meters away, a rectangular stone monument of the same date, measuring 6.1 x 5.5 m, formed the center of a small cemetery which remained in use into Hellenistic times, and a third monument has been found, dated only as 'archaic'. In the absence of other inscriptions, there is no way of knowing whether this was a cluster of state-sponsored tombs or, as is perhaps more likely, whether some Corcyrean families were also honoring their own dead with elaborate structures. A major monument from Ambracia, however, is even more communal than the tomb in honor of Menekrates: it seems to be a *polyandrion* or cenotaph dating around 600 BC, with a long inscription recording a military adventure into the Epirote interior.[67]

There is a little evidence for an increase in spending in the later sixth century. On Corcyra, gr. 1968/α (*c.* 550–525) may have had a stele, and a late archaic gold ring inscribed *Menandros* probably came from a destroyed grave. At Peritheia, in the north part of the island, a huge oval mound (42 x 27.5 m, preserved height 4.9 m) may date to late archaic times. Ambracia gr. 60, containing two bronze vessels, may also date to the late sixth century.[68]

SANCTUARIES. There is little evidence outside Dodona, but a rich array of bronzes begins here in the late eighth century. There is a little pottery of the same period, but ceramic finds only become common in the sixth century. The earliest known temple was only built around 400 BC. There is strong evidence for Corinthian interest at Dodona, which may help explain the similarities between Dodona and some other west and central Greek sanctuaries. The sanctuary of Zeus at Dodona and its oracle were already known to Homer (*Iliad* 16.233–5; *Odyssey* 14.327–30 = 19.296–9), and was a major center at least by 550 (Herodotus 1.46). Herodotus (5.92) also says that Periander consulted the Nekyomanteion, an oracle of the dead, some time around the end of the seventh century, and the earliest terracottas there may go back to this date; potsherds and a series of small marble heads certainly appear in the sixth. Epirote religious activity from the period before the central Greek expansion, and at inland archaic sites, remains obscure. An altar and remains of sacrifices of the seventh through fifth centuries has been found at Kënetë in southern Illyria.[69]

On Corcyra, there is as yet no good evidence for cult activities in the earliest days of the colony, but a late seventh-century altar has been found in the main town. The famous 'Gorgon temple' dates to the early sixth century, and remains of sixth-century pedimental sculptures have turned up in two more excavations. There is a great increase in evidence around 500, including another temple at Kardaki. Very rich bronzes were dedicated at a series of temples beginning shortly before 600 in the former royal park called Mon Repos. Generally the Corcyrean evidence is like that from central Greece, though, as at most colonial sites, it seems to begin rather later. Possibly the colonial cities were not rich enough for major architectural projects until the sixth century. At Ambracia, the earliest temples date around 500 BC, though one of them had votives going back to the early sixth century.[70]

SETTLEMENTS. At Vitsa, primitive-looking huts run from the eighth century through the fourth, although only a short stretch of wall survives from archaic times. The Vitsa houses may be slightly misleading, since the site is perched 1000 m above sea level, and has often been interpreted as a summer pasture for transhumant pastoralists. However, as Halstead (1987) and Hodkinson (1988) point out, modern Epirote transhumance may be a function of factors which were not relevant in archaic times, and we should not rush to assume that a site was only occupied seasonally unless there is direct physical evidence for this. The houses in north Epirote settlements like Symiza seem to be more substantial.[71] At Ambracia and on Corcyra, traces of archaic courtyard houses have been found, going back to the late seventh century, and a sixth-century house on Corcyra had drains and paved floors.[72]

Macedonia

BURIALS. Vergina is the major site. Here more than three hundred Early Iron Age mounds are known, covering cist graves and *pithoi*, often equipped with iron weapons and/or bronze ornaments. Andronikos (1969) argued that since there are no Corinthian pots in the graves, the cemetery must have gone out of use soon after 700, but, as Snodgrass points out (1971, 139 n. 30), hardly any Macedonian sites have Corinthian imports, and the mounds probably remained in use in the seventh century. Relatively few Macedonian burials can be dated firmly to the seventh century, but the stylistic development of the bronzes from Chauchitsa, Vergina, and sites further north makes it likely that many 'Early Iron Age' mounds date after 700. One of the few sites with clear continuity across the seventh century is Kuç i Zi in the far northwest. Mound I, of the late eighth and early seventh century, contained rich cremations, but mound II, beginning around 650 and continuing into the early sixth century, produced relatively few weapons and only a little gold.[73] The evidence remains unclear, largely because of the chronological problems. The numbers and richness of graves may have declined after 700, but the changes seem less dramatic than in the Aegean.

In the course of the seventh century, central Greeks settled densely along the Aegean shore, particularly in Chalcidice. Seventh-century urn cremations have been found at Tragilos and Acanthus, and infant pot burials at Mende, but these show no sign of native Macedonian influence.[74]

There were big changes in the middle of the sixth century. Greek imports became much more common in Macedonian graves, and the burial styles and grave goods of Chalcidice, linked more to the Aegean than the Balkans in the seventh century, suddenly start to show strong similarities with those of inland Macedonia. This episode is best known from the truly magnificent late archaic cemeteries of Trebenischte in the far northwest, and Vergina and Sindos in central Macedonia.

At Trebenischte, sixteen large pit graves dating 550–500, marked with small mounds, contained hundreds of gold and silver ornaments and vessels, along with iron weapons and bronze armor. Graves 1 and 5 even contained gold leaf death masks, very like those from the shaft graves of Mycenae, more than a millennium earlier. They may be evidence for an early stage of the Macedonian aristocracy's identification with the Homeric heroes (if we can assume that sixth-century Greeks were aware of Bronze Age death-masks). The contemporary grave goods from the larger cemetery at Sindos were similar, including more gold death masks (grs. 20, 56, 62, 67, 115) and outstanding gold filigree jewelry. The two recently-found late archaic graves at Vergina, proving continuity between the Early Iron Age and Hellenistic mound cemeteries, had no death masks, but produced jewelry very like Trebenischte and Sindos, even down to the use of tiny iron toy chariots and spits.[75]

The wealth of these graves is extraordinary. As just one example from the dozens available, Sindos gr. 20, the burial of an adult woman around 510 BC, contained – in addition to its gold death mask – a gold leaf band, six fragments from other gold leaf bands, a conical gold ornament, a filigree gold necklace, two filigree gold earrings, an electrum necklace, two silver pins with gold heads, a silver bracelet with a gold snakehead on each end, two plain silver pins, a silver double pin, two silver fibulas, two silver bracelets, a bronze cauldron, a bronze bowl on a tripod, a bronze oinochoe, a miniature iron tripod, a miniature iron table-and-chair set, an ivory ring, four glass beads, a faïence bead, a bone rosette, and two pots. And although the three sites mentioned in the last paragraph are the richest so far known, virtually every corner of Macedonia has produced late sixth-century burials which would, in any other period, be considered outstanding.[76] I pile up examples in n. 76 to make the point clear: there was a staggering reorientation of wealth toward the cemetery after 550, forming an elite style shared all the way from the wilds of Upper Macedonia to the shores of the Aegean.

Palavestra (1994) has stressed the links that Trebenischte, and other spectacular central Balkan cemeteries such as Novi Pazar and Atenica, seem to have with west and central European 'princely' tombs around 500. He argues that the main Balkan sites lay on caravan routes to the Adriatic, and that long-distance trade briefly encouraged the emergence of a warrior ideology connecting areas as far apart as Gaul and Illyria. He makes no reference to the extension of these types of burial all the way to the shores of the Aegean, but the data he collects do demonstrate the extent to which even late in the sixth century northern Greece remained a cultural buffer zone. The chronological coincidence between the central Balkan horizon of princely burials and the temporary upswing in grave goods and monuments in central Greece after 550 is intriguing. Possibly we should see fashions flowing from south to north, as part of Alexander I's well known attempt to Hellenize his monarchy around 500.[77] However, Sindos and the other Macedonian cemeteries have much more in common with the Illyrian burials than they do with Corinth or Athens, and we should probably accept Palavestra's suggestion that the Balkans (including Macedonia) formed the southeastern tip of a central European pattern in the late sixth century.

SANCTUARIES. As elsewhere in northern Greece, there is little evidence for the worship of the gods outside the central Greek colonies along the coasts.[78] At Aphytis, evidence for worship goes back to the late eighth century; on Mt Itamos a peak cult was active in the seventh century; and at Sane, a cult of Artemis had definitely begun by 650. Cult activity at Koukos probably goes back to the ninth century. Here a building at least 14 m long was built over the ruins of an earlier apsidal structure, with its porch partially covering a pit of ash, which may be the remains of an early ash altar. But the most interesting site is Poseidi near Mende. Apsidal building Στ', in what became the archaic and classical sanctuary of Poseidon, probably dates to the eleventh century. It is hard to say what evidence we would need to find to prove that this was the earliest known Greek temple, but the area was certainly in use for sacrifices by the eighth century, and the lowest levels in sacrificial pit δ included early sherds. In the fourth century an altar (inscribed as being dedicated to Poseidon) was set up on the same alignment as Στ'.[79] Like the central Greek colonies on the coast of Epirus, there are few early temples. At Poseidi, the ancient building Στ' probably stayed in use until the early sixth century, and was only replaced by apsidal building Γ after a flood. The people of Chalcidice apparently did not share in the great temple-building craze of central Greece, but otherwise worship followed much the same pattern as in the Aegean world.

SETTLEMENTS. Eighth- and seventh-century Macedonian settlements were very different from those in the central Greek colonies in the north. There was an ancient local tradition of building in wattle-and-daub or mudbrick without stone foundations, leading to the formation of *tell* sites. These sites were anything but static; at Assiros, for example, the village of multi-room rectilinear houses with narrow streets which had flourished across most of the Early Iron Age was completely replanned around 800, and a pair of apsidal houses was set up on the top of the mound with a cobbled alley between them. The site was abandoned by 750. At Thessaloniki, by contrast, an apsidal house formed part of a larger complex with rectilinear rooms in the eleventh and tenth centuries, then went out of use by the ninth. At Kastanas, mudbrick houses were replaced by wattle-and-daub and post structures *c.* 1000 BC, only for mudbricks to return in the eighth century, as part of another substantial replanning. A '*Großhaus*' with a central courtyard then filled the small excavated part of the site (*Fig.* 17), being replaced by simpler houses in the sixth century.[80]

Fig. 17. The Kastanas 'Großhaus' (based on plans in Hänsel 1989).

In Chalcidice, houses followed central Greek patterns. There were apsidal buildings at Koukos in the tenth and ninth century, but at Sane, with the exception of a tiny (3.8 x 2.6 m) seventh-century oval hut, all the houses were rectilinear. House B, probably built around 700, was small (6 x 4 m) and rectangular, like some of the contemporary houses on Sicily (see above); while House A was at least 10 m long, and probably had two rooms. By the sixth century, we see definite courtyard houses at Tragilos. At Mende, House Δ, built around 600, had at least four rectilinear rooms, with storage bins and *pithoi* in room δ, and hearths in room α. This was probably a courtyard house.[81]

There is some evidence that Macedonian houses were starting to look more like those of central Greece in the sixth century. At Vardaroftsa, the first stone foundations and *pithoi* set into house floors appear around this time, in connection with Corinthian pottery, and at Thessaloniki Ano Toumba, there seems to have been a major replanning in the early or mid-sixth century. On the top of the mound, after five centuries of great continuity in house plans, the older buildings were abandoned; on the north-west side of the mound, under modern Ortansias Street, sixth-century builders began to use stone foundations and set *pithoi* into the ground, as at Vardaroftsa, and to use Greek pottery; and to the southeast, under Kalavryton Street, a layer of red soil 1 m thick covers the older houses, and new buildings were put up on strong stone foundations, again associated with *pithoi*.[82]

Thrace [83]

BURIALS. At Roussa, Balkan-style burial in megalithic dolmens probably continued into the ninth century, but this rite is otherwise unknown south of the Rhodope range. In the eighth and seventh century, cremations in cists, pit graves, and urns, often accompanied by weapons and covered by small stone cairns (rather like those in Epirus) are typical of this site and the large pre-colonization cemeteries on Thasos. Further west, we find tumulus burials, forming a transitional zone between Thrace and Macedonia, where such burials were more common. At the Kastas site at Amphipolis there was a truly enormous Early Iron Age mound, said to be 165 m in diameter and 21 m high. Sixty-three graves, some of them with weapons, have been excavated. The earliest examples probably date to the seventh century. At Drama, three large mounds covering warrior burials, some with gold jewelry, are firmly dated to the seventh century.[84]

Central Greek colonization began on Thasos around 650. Parian migrants apparently chased the Thracians off the island, and before the end of the seventh century had set up colonies of their own on the mainland. Graves dating back to 625 have been found at Galipsos and Oisyme, two of these Thasian foundations. The publications are brief, but at Oisyme the graves are typical of the northern colonies, with cremations under small mounds and a late archaic stele. At Galipsos, the late archaic burials were rather rich, paralleling developments in Chalcidice. On Thasos itself, the early Greek graves are poorly known, but it seems that a large extra-mural cemetery was immediately established. Sixth-century relief tombstones have been found, and poor burials in *pithoi* and pits which would be perfectly normal in a central Greek cemetery.[85]

The most interesting site is Abdera. Here large cemeteries were immediately established around 650. In one, 88% of the graves belong to children, while a second was mainly for adults. The adult cemeteries featured large and small mounds. In area Π, two large mounds date back to the seventh century, covering urn cremations accompanied only by pottery. There seems to have been a second period of mound-building in the late sixth century, accompanied by more diverse and sometimes richer graves. The mounds continued into the early fifth century. The Abderans' fondness for mounds has no precursors in their mother-city of Clazomenae, where no burials of any kind are documented until large, homogeneous cemeteries appear in the sixth century, but neither was it exactly an adoption of local customs. Large mounds were common north of the Rhodope range, but were unusual in Iron Age coastal Thrace. Clazomenian sarcophagi appear at the end of the sixth century. Some of these contained silver and gold jewelry, and were marked by stelai.[86]

By 600, Thracian burial customs were showing central Greek influences. A group of sixth- and fifth-century graves under small mounds at Dikaia Phanariou seem to be like those at Oisyme, and the thirteen cist graves and four *pithoi* at Mikro Doukato, probably of the first half of the sixth century, combine Greek and Balkan styles of grave goods. The latest graves in the Kastas mound at Amphipolis, around 500 BC, would not look out of place in Chalcidice. However, with the exception of Duvanli, the Thracians did not take part in the great expansion of grave goods and shared symbolic system which stretched from central Illyria to Chalcidice after 550.[87]

SANCTUARIES. As elsewhere in northern Greece, there are few traces of pre-colonization religious activity (see n. 78 above), but the central Greek settlers immediately set about reproducing the religious forms of their mother cities. On Thasos, the earliest votives in the sanctuaries of Athena and Artemis go back to the first half of the seventh century, and in the second half of the century Artemis was receiving gold, bronze, and ivory. By 600, both sites had massive terraces. No structural remains survive from the Artemision, but Athena had a stone temple in the early sixth century, replaced with a more monumental one around 500. Heracles was worshipped at a rock-cut altar in the seventh century, and his sanctuary contained a building, the 'polygonal *oikos*' (possibly a dining room rather than a temple), by *c.* 550 BC. Cult activity also began in the cave of Aliki around 650. The cities of the Thasian *peraia* gave equally prompt attention to the gods: at Neapolis (Kavala), dedications began before 650, including bronze tripods, and at Oisyme a temple had been built by 600.[88]

SETTLEMENTS. Pre-colonization settlements were varied. On Thasos, stone foundations of simple huts have been found, and at Petrota, a round stone hut. At the settlement sites of Tsouka, Rizia, and Asar Tepe in the Rhodope mountains, however, very few structural remains were detected. It may be that these Thracians were highly mobile, like the inhabitants of Vitsa in Epirus, living only in simple shelters at their summer pastures.[89] The best evidence for the central Greek colonists' houses comes from Abdera. The earliest layers have only been explored in one area, where a seventh-century apsidal house was replaced around 600 by two *megaron* houses, and a larger house was built at the end of the sixth century. At Thasos, little survives of the seventh-century settlement, but by the late sixth century courtyard houses have been found all over the city, laid out on a regular grid pattern.[90]

Discussion of northern Greece

'Northern Greece', as I have defined it here, was a large and varied area, but I draw two general conclusions about it. First, the eighth century did not see such dramatic transformations as in the Aegean. This is particularly true of burials. Second, until the sixth century at the earliest, the area looks distinctly more Balkan than Aegean; and the 'Hellenizing' of the north was accompanied by major social changes. Neither generalization applies as strongly to Thessaly as to the areas further north, but even as far south as Iolkos, Balkan material and patterns of behavior are prominent in the seventh and sixth centuries.

The most striking continuity from Early Iron Age into archaic times is in warrior burials and other kinds of rich graves, and in many places in the use of large grave mounds. The shift of wealth from grave goods to votives which has received such attention in central Greek archaeology is simply not relevant to most of the North. Warrior burials are perhaps less prominent in Thessaly after 700 than they had been before, but nonetheless Iolkos and Ayios Yeoryios Larisis have produced spectacular examples even in the late sixth century. In Macedonia, although the chronological problems are acute, the Iron Age warrior burial tradition may have been in decline by 650 or 600; if so, it reappeared in a new guise after 550. In Thrace, warrior graves only decline in the late sixth century; and in Epirus, they are less common at Vitsa in the seventh century than in the eighth, but then revive in the sixth through fourth centuries.

The worship of the gods is as archaeologically elusive in archaic northern Greece as it is in Dark Age central Greece, though Thessaly follows the Aegean pattern more closely, with rich bronzes at a few sites from 750 on, and temple-building in the sixth century. Further north, Aegean-style religious practices are almost entirely restricted to the central Greek colonies until the fifth century, with the striking exception of Dodona in Epirus.

The settlement evidence is more varied. In the mountains of Epirus and Thrace, we may be dealing with transhumant pastoral groups, building flimsy structures in their summer pastures and only slightly more substantial winter homes in the lowland. In Macedonia, however, we see continuous occupation of *tell* sites like Kastanas, Vardaroftsa, Chauchitsa, and Thessaloniki from the Bronze Age into Hellenistic times. These were substantial villages, whose inhabitants used domestic space in more complex ways than those of central Greek towns, at least until the eighth century. In the sixth century, more substantial houses appear at several sites, often giving more prominence to storage.

The societies of northern Greece were clearly very varied. Thrace and Epirus give every impression of being lightly settled by fairly simple, mobile groups into the sixth century. Even in the fifth century, Herodotus (2.167; 5.3–8; 9.119) and Thucydides (2.29, 67, 95–101) saw the Thracians as backward barbarians, and Thucydides' brief comments on the Chaonians and other groups in Epirus (1.136; 2.68, 80–1) convey a similar impression of warlike and disorganized tribes. According to Plutarch (*Pyrrhus* 1), it was only under king Tharyps, around 400 BC (cf. Thucydides 2.80), that Greek customs came to Epirus in a serious way. Thucydides seems to have thought that the Macedonians were rather better than the Thracians (2.95–101), but still an uncivilized bunch. The massive tumuli and elaborate warrior burials of archaic Macedonia led Hammond (1972, 370) to identify a warrior aristocracy, probably with powerful kings whose authority depended on their ability to lead their nobles in successful battles. It seems to me that this is the kind of image the buriers at Vergina, Duvanli, Trebenischte, and other presumably royal cemeteries wanted to project; and the occurrence of warrior graves at smaller sites like Chauchitsa, Eordaia, Thermi, and Drama suggests to me that there was a widely spread upper class who shared this point of view and imposed it on the villagers of sites like Kastanas and Thessaloniki. But we should not simply assume that this was an ancient 'tribal' or 'Balkan' custom; the burial rites associated with being a warrior, and very probably the ideologies associated with this status, went through enormous changes in the sixth century.

Thessaly was famous for its powerful warrior aristocracy in the late sixth century (Helly 1995). In 511 Thessalian cavalry descended on Attica to sweep away an invading Spartan force (Herodotus 5.63; Aristotle, *Ath. Pol.* 19.5), and until the 480s they may have controlled Phocis (Larsen 1968, 18–19). Their burials celebrated this military prowess, and, if Arvanitopoullos is to be believed, Krannon and other sites boasted palatial architecture. Classical writers never doubted that Thessalians were Greeks, but their social structures, with masses of dependent serfs whom Aristotle (*Politics* 1269a37–9) represented as always being on the verge of revolt,[91] set them apart from the world of the city-states. The decline of warrior burials and the eventual abandonment of tumuli by 470 may have been part of a rapprochement with Greek culture, and we even hear of attempts to do away with serfdom in the late fifth century (Xenophon, *Hellenica* 2.3.36). But in Plato's day, the nobles were still notorious for their violent and impetuous ways (*Crito* 53e).

For the far north, the arrival of central Greek colonists in the late eighth and seventh centuries eventually triggered major, and perhaps traumatic, changes. Corinthians may have been visiting Epirus by 900, and Euboeans settling in Chalcidice by the same date, but the archaic colonizers probably came in greater numbers, and were more aggressive. We hear of a series of wars between Greeks and natives in Thrace and Epirus (Hammond 1967, 487–507; Isaac 1986, 291–2). According to Thucydides (2.92), the first powerful king of the Odrysians in Thrace was Teres, who would have taken the throne in the later sixth century, and it may be that the struggles with the predatory central Greek colonies stimulated secondary state-formation in Thrace.

By the middle of the sixth century, the central Greek presence was having a serious impact. In Macedonia, while the new upper-class burial style probably owed more to Balkan than to Aegean influences, we also see the gradual replacement of 'Early Iron Age' pottery by Greek forms and the adoption of Greek-style architecture in villages. In Thrace, the distinctive burial styles of the earlier Iron Age lost popularity in the later sixth century in favor of more typically Greek fashions. But lumping all these changes together under the single rubric of 'Hellenization' would be a gross oversimplification. By 550 northern Greece was being drawn into a wider economic and political network centered on the Aegean city-states, and the local populations had to find ways to come to terms with that. These local responses need more study.

There is rather less evidence for the Epirotes, Macedonians, and Thracians having a major impact on the central Greeks who took their lands. As in Sicily, most colonists abandoned the burial customs of their mother-cities on reaching the north. But in no case did they simply adopt local norms: usually they created a brand new set of rites, like the *pithos* cremations of Corcyra. The closest thing to Greeks 'going native' is the mounds of Abdera, although these burials have as much in common with Macedonian and Thessalian as with Thracian practices. The colonists always directed considerable sums of money into their sanctuaries, continuing Aegean forms of worship, and lived in Aegean-style courtyard houses (at Abdera we can even follow the progression from apsidal to *megaron* to courtyard houses). Colonial central Greek culture seems predatory and chauvinistic.

Western Greece (*Fig.* 18)
Dark Age pottery styles in the West are hard to date, having few contacts with Aegean Protogeometric and Geometric. But after 750 a variety of local Late Geometric styles developed (Coldstream 1968, 223–32; Morgan 1990). It is not easy to know how far Sub-Geometric versions of these survived into archaic times, but by 700 Corinthian pottery was being widely used for grave goods and offerings to the gods, even in quite remote locations. On the whole, the western and central Greek archaic deposits can be tied together well, and there are fewer chronological problems than in northern Greece.

Burials. There is no sharp boundary between the western and central regions. Phthiotis, Locris, and perhaps Phocis form a transitional area. Cemeteries at Atalandi and Tragana had been like those in Attica and Euboea since 900, and in the late eighth they show a similar explosion in numbers and wealth. A group of twenty-two graves dating

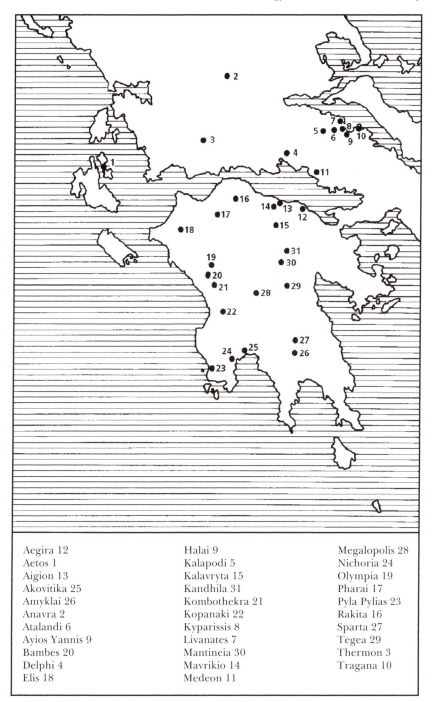

Fig. 18. Sites in western Greece.

Aegira 12	Halai 9	Megalopolis 28
Aetos 1	Kalapodi 5	Nichoria 24
Aigion 13	Kalavryta 15	Olympia 19
Akovitika 25	Kandhila 31	Pharai 17
Amyklai 26	Kombothekra 21	Pyla Pylias 23
Anavra 2	Kopanaki 22	Rakita 16
Atalandi 6	Kyparissis 8	Sparta 27
Ayios Yannis 9	Livanates 7	Tegea 29
Bambes 20	Mantineia 30	Thermon 3
Delphi 4	Mavrikio 14	Tragana 10
Elis 18	Medeon 11	

53

750–700 at Anavra produced just one pot but 116 bronzes. Tragana gr. Π9, dating around 750, a woman aged about eighteen years, held two necklaces (one of glass beads, one of bronze), a further forty-nine bronze ornaments, and two bronze bowls, one of them inscribed *Muzawi* in Neo-Hittite (*Fig.* 19). And like many cemeteries in Athens, Tragana had a layer of child burials in pots dating around 700 overlying the adult graves. Further west, Medeon in Phocis went through similar but slightly less pronounced changes; in Achaea, the increase in numbers and wealth is barely perceptible; and by the time we reach Arcadia, Laconia, Messenia, Elis, and Aetolia, there are no observable changes at all.[92]

No rich archaic graves have been reported from Phthiotis and eastern Locris, which probably means that these regions shared in seventh-century central Greek developments. At Medeon, only one poor grave dates to the seventh century, paralleling another common central Greek pattern of declining numbers of graves after 700. At the end of the sixth century, extensive new cemeteries are known from Ayios Yannis Theologos, Halai, and Livanates, again following Aegean trends. At Delphi, extra-mural cemeteries began in the seventh century, but there were some rich graves, such as a well-shaped pit containing more than thirty skulls and pots, bronzes, iron, and ivories spanning the archaic period.[93]

Further west, archaic graves are rare. Only thirty-five have been published from Achaea, Aetolia, Arcadia, Elis, Laconia, and Messenia combined, but five of these were warrior burials. Warrior burials were not new in West Greece, going back as far as the well known eleventh- or tenth-century bronze sword in Elis gr. 1963/4, but the bulk of the Dark Age examples come from Tragana and Atalandi and should probably be seen as the westernmost fringe of the central Greek pattern. Some of the western archaic warrior burials are also much more impressive than those of the earlier periods, with an Illyrian bronze helmet, bronze greaves, three iron spearheads, and an iron

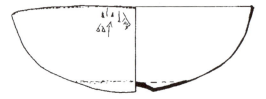

Fig. 19. Bronze bowl from Tragana, inscribed 'Muzawi' in Neo-Hittite (based on drawing in *Archaiologikon Deltion* 36:1 (1981) 42).

sword at Kalavryta, thirty iron spearheads, three iron swords, and iron arrowheads from (several) destroyed graves at Kandhila, and another Illyrian bronze helmet at Olympia.[94] Trends in the west seem diametrically opposed to those in the Aegean; rather than disappearing after 700, warrior burials became more prominent.

SANCTUARIES. The worship of the gods is highly visible in Dark Age western Greece. Each region seems to have at least one major shrine by the tenth century, often with more bronzes than pottery (a situation which perhaps also applies at Dodona). Some of these, such as Kalapodi, Aetos on Ithaca, Olympia, and possibly Thermon, may have been the sites of continuous worship since the Bronze Age.[95] Morgan (1990) argues that the main shrines, such as Olympia, were periodic gathering places for the chiefs of widely scattered pastoral groups, and that in offering expensive bronzes to the gods, the chiefs could assert their own importance. Olympia probably also drew central Greek visitors, judging from the numbers of Argive bronzes dedicated there in the tenth and ninth centuries.

On the whole, Dark Age cult seems to have gone on in the open air. This changed in the late eighth century: like central Greece, the west saw a revolution in religious practices, with a massive increase in votive offerings (particularly bronzes) and a wave of temple construction. Even old sites like Kalapodi and Olympia saw a dramatic increase in bronze offerings around 700. Old shrines like Tegea had temples built at them, and new shrines sprang up everywhere. Jost (1985, 549) counts eleven sanctuaries operating in Arcadia by 700; and even such a remote site as Rakita in Achaea not only received rich votives but also had an apsidal peripteral *hekatompedon* before 700.[96] Olympia and Delphi became truly panhellenic in the seventh century, and even drew dedications from Italy.[97] As in central Greece, the sixth century perhaps saw a decline in offerings, but new levels of state spending on temples and treasuries.[98] However, Hodkinson's detailed quantification of Spartan dedications (1997; and in this volume) shows the difficulties of trying to impose a single model on all sites: while votives at the Menelaion and Artemis Orthia definitely declined, the Acropolis and possibly the Amyklaion saw an increase.

SETTLEMENTS. The evidence is very poor. Large apsidal houses of the tenth through mid-eighth century have been excavated at Nichoria in Messenia, but this site was abandoned around 750. At Aigion in Achaea, an apsidal house probably dates to the seventh century; and sixth-century farmsteads excavated at Bambes in Elis (*Fig.* 20), Kopanaki in Messenia, and on Ithaca, all seem to be rectilinear courtyard

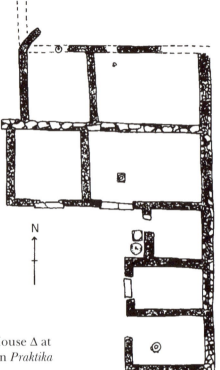

N
↑

Fig. 20. Sixth-century House Δ at Bambes (based on plan in *Praktika* 1956, 195).

houses. The Kopanaki example, built around 550, had eleven rooms forming a Π-shape around a central courtyard. One house on Ithaca was at least 12 m across, and a second had a functionally specific kitchen. At Kyparissi in Locris, a major stone stoa, 21.8 m long, was set up around 540 BC. Meager as the evidence is, it suggests that western Greek settlements developed along more or less the same lines as those in central Greece.[99]

Discussion of western Greece

Western and central Greece had been very different in the Dark Age, but to some extent their material cultures converged in archaic times. Insofar as we can talk about western houses, their development followed roughly the same pattern as in the Aegean and its colonies. But these houses were only grouped into very small settlements. Sparta's notorious lack of urban development (Thucydides 1.10) seems to be typical of the region, which remained much more rural than the Aegean.

Western sanctuaries have much in common with those of central

Greece, its colonies in the north, and Thessaly; so much so that Olympia and Delphi are often treated as paradigms of 'the' Greek sanctuary. The seventh-century boom in votive dedications and temple-building affected all these areas. But again we must be sensitive to differences in context. Some of the western sites had a tradition of substantial offerings going back to the tenth century. This must have made the religious significance of the new practices of the eighth and seventh centuries rather different in this area from in the Aegean, not so much a break with past practices as their rapid expansion. Again paralleling Aegean developments, the increase in metal offerings to the gods after 700 coincided with a decline in the quantities of grave goods used, from 3.3 metal objects per grave in Late Geometric to 1.2 in Archaic, though pottery grave goods increased from 1.2 to 3.2. But the one striking difference between western and central Greece is that warrior burials, some of them quite rich, flourished in the west in the seventh century, just at the time they disappeared in the Aegean; and burial mounds also appeared at Kandhila and perhaps Megalopolis.[100]

This is an important difference between the two areas. In a famous passage, Thucydides (1.5–6) singled out the Locrians, Acarnanians, and Aetolians for their habit of carrying weapons, which, to his mind, signified backwardness (see also Van Wees, this volume). Lest any doubts remain, he reported that 'it is said' that the Aetolians not only spoke an almost incomprehensible language but also lived on raw meat (3.94). Possibly it suited Thucydides' purposes to paint an extreme picture of the West; or possibly we should draw a contrast between the wild areas he describes and more civilized cities like Sparta, home to Alcman and Tyrtaeus, or Mantineia, whence Demonax was invited to Cyrene around 550 to draw up a lawcode (Herodotus 4.161). But archaic warrior burials are known from Arcadia and Achaea as well as the backwoods of Aetolia. This emphasis on a man's status as a warrior in archaic funerals suggests to me that at least some westerners did see themselves as belonging to a more violent world than that of the Aegean *poleis*, though no doubt, like the inhabitants of mountains and forests of the Mediterranean in other ages (Braudel 1972, 38–41), they may have felt that it was not so much backward as more virile. But the presence of archaic warrior burials was not simply a 'survival' from simpler times, as Thucydides understood the carrying of arms to be. The fact that such burials first became prominent in the seventh century suggests that new ideas of manhood were forming in western Greece at this time.

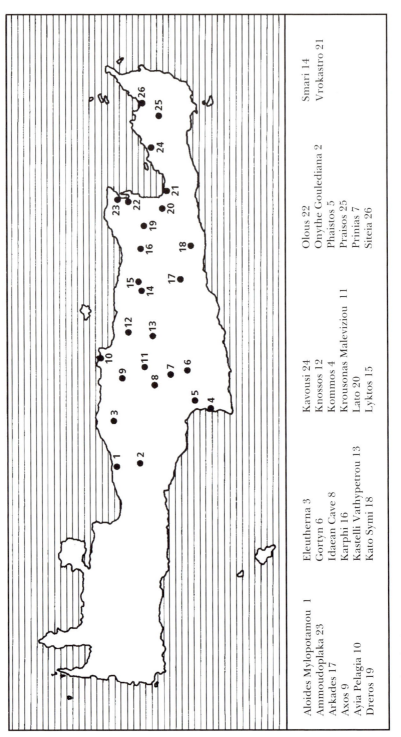

Fig. 21. Sites in Crete.

Aloïdes Mylopotamou 1
Ammoudoplaka 23
Arkades 17
Axos 9
Ayia Pelagia 10
Dreros 19

Eleutherna 3
Gortyn 6
Idaean Cave 8
Karphi 16
Kastelli Vathypetrou 13
Kato Symi 18

Kavousi 24
Knossos 12
Kommos 4
Krousonas Maleviziou 11
Lato 20
Lyktos 15

Olous 22
Onythe Goulediana 2
Phaistos 5
Praisos 25
Prinias 7
Siteia 26

Smari 14
Vrokastro 21

Crete (*Fig.* 21)[101]

There has been general agreement about archaic Cretan ceramic chronology, although, as we shall see, there may be some serious problems.

BURIAL. Compared with the rest of Greece, there was strong continuity from the Bronze Age. Multiple burial in chamber tombs and small *tholoi* remained normal until the end of the seventh century, although at most sites few new multiple tombs were dug after 700. The major change in rites during the Iron Age had been a switch from inhumation to cremation in clay urns, which allowed more burials to be packed into each tomb. This shift was complete in central Crete well before the end of the tenth century, but at some east Cretan sites it took rather longer.

There was much regional variation in the seventh century. Large cemeteries of chamber tombs stuffed with urns were the norm for adults at Knossos, but buriers at Arkades preferred to place their urns individually under upturned *pithoi* in small stone settings. Some families at Eleutherna cremated the dead in trenches, and others just on the surface of the ground. A third practice at this site involved burying the bones along with the pyre under a small mound, while still other buriers washed off the bones and placed them in urns. Yet another rite at Eleutherna involved 'bone enclosures', paralleled at Prinias and Vrokastro, while some buriers at Praisos used shaft graves, and others continued an old tradition of cave burial.[102]

Multiple burial makes it difficult to assess the scale of changes in the eighth century. In tombs in use for ten generations or more – which are by no means unusual – it is hard to know which objects belong with which urn, and preliminary reports, often the only published sources of information, rarely specify how many burials were made in each phase. Fortetsa, one of the cemeteries of Knossos, was, until the publication of the North Cemetery (Catling and Coldstream 1996), the best published site (Brock 1957). Here the number of burials made each year went up from 0.4 in Early and Middle Geometric times (conventionally assigned the implausibly precise dates of 810–745 BC) to 1.3 in Late Geometric and Orientalizing times (745–630). But there is little evidence for a shift in the age balance. Brock rarely mentioned infant or child graves. This may just be an example of the usual lack of interest in demography, but more recent work suggests that we should take it seriously, and that a 'Dark Age' demographic structure, skewed toward adults, continued into the seventh century. At Kavousi Vronda, the preliminary reports list fifty-two adults and just ten children (with another ten unclear cases). Some of the infants had been cremated and their bones, which were mixed with those of adults, were only recovered by water-sieving. Since this technique is not commonly practised, children may be under-represented in the bones collected on other sites. But the only other detailed published skeletal study, of tomb EPH/75 at Knossos, detected just one baby, one child, and nine adults (with a further five cases undetermined).[103]

Snodgrass's recent report on the iron objects from the large North Cemetery at Knossos (1996) shows little change in the rate of deposition in the eighth century, with 148 artifacts dating to Protogeometric (i.e., about 1.5 objects per annum), 78 to Early and Middle Geometric (about 1.0 per annum), and 51 to Late Geometric (1.7 per annum).

There were some unusual late eighth-century burials, most notably Eleutherna ΛΛ/90–91 pyre B, which included a beheaded human sacrifice. But overall, continuity overshadowed change. Late eighth-century tombs included weapons and imports from the Near East, but so had those of the tenth and ninth centuries, sometimes on a grander scale (see TABLE 1 for Fortetsa, and Stampolidis 1993, 42–4, on Eleutherna). As Burkert puts it, the Cretans 'have been "orientalizing" all the time' (1992, 16). Similarly, archaic Cretan towns had large extramural cemeteries, just like those in central Greece, but had had them right across the Dark Age.

The average wealth of grave goods declined at Fortetsa after 700

TABLE 1. Grave goods at Fortetsa (data from Brock 1957).

	Number of burials	Mean number of objects per burial:			
		Pots	Gold	Bronze	Iron
Late Protogeometric/ Protogeometric B (*c.* 870–810 BC)	54	6.4	0.4	0.7	0.6
Early and Middle Geometric (810–745 BC)	21	5.3	0	0.1	0.6
Late Geometric (745–710 BC)	46	4.2	0.1	0.3	0.6
Orientalizing (710–630 BC)	102	2.9	0.1	0.1	0.1

(TABLE 1), chiefly because a large class of cremations accompanied only by a single aryballos appeared (Brock 1957, 3). But warrior burials continued throughout the seventh century, and some magnificent gold jewelry was buried with the dead (particularly the dromos deposit in the Khaniale Teke *tholos* at Knossos, around 675 BC). The seventh-century cemetery at Arkades was similar, with many cremations accompanied only by an aryballos or small jug, while a few tombs contained weapons and jewelry. Cremations in bronze urns, intimately linked to the notion of the hero in central Greece, and largely restricted to the late eighth century, made their first appearance in Crete in the seventh century, with numerous examples from Arkades (often with the urn resting on an iron tripod), two from Lyktos, and two more from Fortetsa tomb II. Horse burials, another 'heroic' trait, also appear only after 700, with two complete skeletons in Prinias tomb BU, another two in Knossos North Cemetery tomb 79, and a skull in tomb 168.[104]

Even more striking is the first appearance of stone funerary monuments. The earliest, a small Π-shaped structure over Eleutherna pyre A1/K1, may date around 700, but by 650, pyre 4A was marked by an elaborate construction of ashlar masonry, enclosed by a *peribolos* wall, and probably crowned by small limestone figures of warriors. Nearby, fragments of five limestone sculptures turned up, including the body of a seventh-century Daedalic *kore* and pieces of an early sixth-century *kouros* which would originally have stood 2 m tall. Similar seventh- and early sixth-century tomb architecture has been found at Prinias.[105]

But between 625 and 575 BC, virtually all the known cemeteries on Crete end, and we enter what Stampolidis (1990, 400) describes as 'the so-called "period of silence" in Crete, that is the 6th and the 5th centuries'. The lacuna is astonishing: at Knossos, one of the most intensely explored archaeological regions in the world (see Hood and Smyth 1981), every one of the dozens of tombs in use in the seventh century was apparently abandoned, and no sixth- and fifth-century cemetery is known. There are only a handful of exceptions from the whole of Crete. At Arkades, a sarcophagus contained an adult skeleton, two sixth-century pots, and an iron knife; at Kastello Vathypetrou, a group of *pithos* graves dates around 500 BC; and at Praisos, a handful of graves in the 'Hellenic' cemetery seem to belong to the sixth century. Graves only become common again in the fourth century.[106]

SANCTUARIES. Continuities from the Dark Age (and even the Bronze Age) into archaic times are still more striking in Cretan religion, in sacred iconography as well as the continuity of cult places. The peaktop sanctuary of Kato Symi saw unbroken activity on the same spot from the Middle Bronze Age until Roman times, and the subterranean Idaean Cave from Neolithic until Roman.[107]

These religious continuities spanning two or three millennia are quite astonishing, but they should not be allowed to mask equally important developments through time. At Kato Symi, the huge Late Bronze Age processional way, podium, and sacred enclosure continued in use through most of the Dark Age, gradually decaying, until replaced in Geometric times by an altar and series of massive terraces. In the archaic period, Building G, with a pavement and hearth, was set up over the Minoan remains. The nature of offerings changed too, with a sharp increase in dedications of bronzes around 700. Angeliki Lebessi, the excavator, describes the seventh century as the zenith of the sanctuary. The Idaean Cave also saw an explosion of bronze dedications in the seventh century; the most recent excavations, in the early 1980s, uncovered many thousands of bronzes (including 1,153 recovered from sieving the older spoil tips), most of them miniature votive bronze shields, chiefly of the seventh century.[108]

Through the Dark Age, as in the Late Bronze Age, most Cretan cult had taken place either in caves or in the open air, often on mountain tops. There were exceptions, such as Kommos, which had a ninth-century temple, although this was radically redesigned in the late eighth century; and perhaps Smari, where a temple may date back before 800. Some cult spots, like Arkades, Ayia Pelagia, and the sanctuary of Demeter at Knossos, on current evidence got along perfectly well in the seventh and sixth centuries with no temples at all. But other sites, notably Dreros, Gortyn, and Prinias, did share the central Greek fondness for temple-building at the end of the eighth and in the seventh century. The Cretan temples were, however, architecturally different from those on the mainland, normally having an interior sacrificial pit or hearth, benches around the walls, and a squarish plan.[109]

In the early sixth century, our evidence for most of these shrines dries up. This is just as surprising (although not as complete) as the abandonment of the cemeteries. At Kato Symi, Building F dates to the end of the sixth century, but offerings dwindled to the point that Lebessi even speaks of a break in the use of the shrine. Of the bronze reliefs which have been published in detail, sixty-one date to the seventh century, just thirteen to the sixth, and two to the fifth. At Kommos, after a massive deposit of imported pottery around 600 BC in Building Q, there are hardly any votives from the sixth and fifth centuries. At Gortyn, only a few vases belong to the sixth century.

Again, the list of negative instances could easily be extended. Few sites have good evidence for sixth-century activity. Praisos is the most interesting, with not only votives but also a new temple with architectural terracottas. At Axos the rich bronzes break off around 600, although terracottas continued across the sixth century. At Knossos, a small shrine for the hero Glaukos probably dates to the sixth century, and at Arkades, an inscribed bronze headband and bronze cuirass attest to sixth-century offerings. At Ayia Pelagia, a pit contained two bronze cauldrons, one of them inscribed as a dedication to Apollo in script of 550–525 BC, and an altar was associated with mid-sixth-century Attic pottery.[110]

SETTLEMENTS. Again, there were strong continuities from the Bronze Age across the Dark Age, despite a massive disruption of settlement patterns in the twelfth century. Cretan houses were always rectilinear, built entirely of stone, and protected by a flat roof. Many of them had only one room, or one room and a small porch, but from the 'Great House' of eleventh-century Karphi onward, there was always a significant minority with two, three, or four rooms, occasionally with evidence for functional specialization. The same architectural forms survived into the seventh century; indeed, at Vrokastro, Kavousi Kastro, and Phaistos there is clear stratigraphical evidence that some houses stayed in constant use for three, four, or five centuries, with minimal architectural changes.[111]

Substantial areas of eighth-century housing have been exposed at locations varying from small mountain sites like Vrokastro to major towns like Phaistos, but very often the houses go out of use in the early seventh century. At Prinias the houses near the temples remained occupied throughout the seventh century, and some even have a little early sixth-century material; but (unlike contemporary sanctuaries and cemeteries) seventh-century houses are less common than their Late Geometric predecessors. There was a major urban reorganization at Dreros around 700, with the establishment of the earliest known formal *agora* in Greece, with a stepped area which probably served as public seating.[112]

The most interesting group of houses comes from a late seventh-century village at Onythe Goulediana. *Fig.* 22 shows what is probably the remains of four houses, with rooms Γ–Δ making a *megaron*, I and K being one-roomed houses (each of these rooms was well supplied with storage *pithoi*), and a larger cluster of rooms at the south end of the row. This cluster was entered through porch Θ into courtyard Z, which then gave admittance to corridor E and from it rooms H, A,

63

and B. The houses are architecturally very distinctive, with their large rooms (room K measures 11 x 6 m) and liberal use of wooden columns on stone bases. These houses have a certain amount in common with those on the mainland (particularly with the contemporary site of Vroulia on Rhodes; see n. 49 above), but much about them is also distinctively Cretan. Eighth- to seventh-century Building II at Krousonas Maleviziou, with a porch, large hearth, internal corridor, and central column base, sounds very similar to these examples, as does another archaic house on the same site, with a paved courtyard open on one side, rectangular rooms, and column bases.[113]

The Onythe houses were occupied into the early sixth century, and the courtyard house at Krousonas also dates to the sixth century. But as with the cemeteries and sanctuaries, settlement evidence dating after 575 is extremely rare. Ayia Pelagia House II, a courtyard structure with a drain and a pitched tiled roof, is firmly dated by Attic pottery to the sixth and fifth centuries, and a probable farmstead of late archaic and classical times has been found at Aloides Mylopotamou. But the extensively explored settlements at Phaistos, Kavousi, and Vrokastro have produced little or nothing. Even at Knossos, only a few wells and a handful of sherds can be dated to the sixth century.[114]

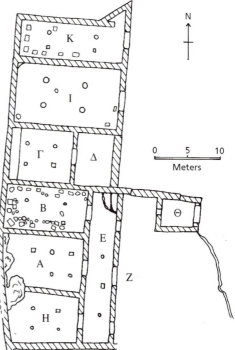

Fig. 22. Seventh-century houses at Onythe Goulediana (based on plan in *Praktika* 1958, 227).

Discussion of Crete

Whitley (1991b, 186–9) emphasizes that Dark Age Knossos was a very different place from the Dark Age towns of central Greece, and this was also true in the archaic period. Cretan sanctuaries probably had more in common with those in central Greece than did houses or cemeteries, with a clear increase in votive activity and temple-building around 700. But even here the differences are strong. Changes in Cretan practices took place within a context of significant dedications spanning the whole Dark Age. As in western Greece, the late eighth-century changes were more a revision and expansion than a revolution. And throughout the seventh century, the Cretans remained firmly attached to open-air peak and cave sanctuaries, which certainly have parallels on the mainland, but were never so important there. Cretan temples also had a distinctly local, even Minoan, flavor.

The archaic courtyard houses at Onythe and Krousonas have links to the mainland, but again uniquely Cretan features and continuities from the Early Iron Age or even Bronze Age were strong. The rapid evolution of central Greek house forms in the eighth and seventh centuries has no parallel on Crete.

Many of the same comments apply to the cemeteries. The eighth-century Aegean funerary revolution is only dimly echoed at Fortetsa, and warrior burials and deposits of gold continued through the seventh century. Monumental grave markers, which disappeared in seventh-century central Greece outside Attica, flourished at Prinias and Eleutherna.

Seventh-century Crete was very different from other parts of the Greek world. Its burials were more open to outside (particularly eastern) elements than those of the Aegean, but nevertheless remained firmly rooted in very ancient traditions, as did its sanctuaries, and even more so its settlements. The range of forms of funerary display at Knossos, Arkades, and Eleutherna, and the variety of house types and sizes at Onythe, Arkades, and Krousonas suggest societies in which an aristocracy had a clear sense of itself as distinct from the lower orders, and perhaps also much more complex hierarchies than we see in central Greece. The written evidence reveals archaic and classical Cretans thinking about their societies in such ways. The Gortyn Code of *c.* 450–400 BC (*IC* 4.72; Willetts 1967) is filled with obscure status terms, some of which (e.g., *woikeus, dolos*) refer to servile dependents, yet ones whose position was less rigidly fixed than that of the Athenian *douloi* (Aristotle, *Politics* 1272a1, likened the Cretan *perioikoi* to the Spartan helots). The famous 'Song of Hybrias' (Athenaeus 695f–96a) expresses a militaristic, aristocratic ethos which seems consistent with the tone of the seventh-century cemeteries.

The archaic Cretan status system was very different from the citizen-states of central Greece. The central Greek hierarchies were largely created in the struggles of the eighth century, but all the archaeological evidence suggests that eighth-century changes were much weaker in Crete. Given the strong signs of material continuity, it might be tempting to see archaic Cretan social structure as a legacy from the Bronze Age. Aristotle (*Politics* 1271b31), after all, claimed that the Cretan *perioikoi* were still living under the laws of king Minos in the fourth century. But this is only one element in the social order of archaic Crete. I have argued elsewhere against theories which interpret the Gortyn Code as evidence for the survival of a very primitive kinship system (Morris 1990), and the astonishing gaps in the sixth- and fifth-century record surely point to very serious social transformations.

The obvious interpretation of the near-total absence of funerary, religious, and domestic evidence after 600 is that Crete suffered a massive depopulation. But I find it hard to believe that such an event, leaving Crete virtually empty through the fifth century, could have no echo in our literary sources. Further, one class of evidence – inscriptions – does continue across the 'period of silence' (*Fig.* 23; cf. Whitley, this volume). Our question has to be not where all the people went, but why the only way they made a serious physical impact on the world for two centuries was through the inscribed word.

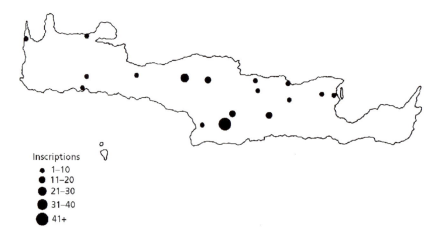

Inscriptions
- 1–10
- 11–20
- 21–30
- 31–40
- 41+

Fig. 23. Cretan inscriptions from the 'period of silence', *c.* 625-400 BC (based on Bile 1988).

But to some extent, even this reframed question may be misleading. It is often suggested that Crete was isolated from the rest of the Mediterranean in the sixth and fifth centuries (see Perlman 1992, 201–4). The written record provides us with indisputable evidence for contacts, notably a Greek embassy to seek Cretan aid in 480 (Herodotus 7.169–70; perhaps significantly, the Cretans refused to help), a treaty between Argos, Tylissos, and Knossos around 450 BC (ML 42 = Fornara 89), and a brief Athenian military adventure in 429 (Thucydides 2.85). But overall we hear little about Cretan involvement in Greek affairs in Herodotus and Thucydides, and in the fourth century Plato (*Laws* 886b-e) represented Crete as not sharing in current social and cultural developments at Athens. When Aristotle did discuss Crete (*Politics* 1271b32–40, 1272b17–18), he emphasized its geographical isolation.

The silence of the archaeological record may partly be an illusion caused by the Cretans turning away from the outside world around 600 BC. In the absence of imported Corinthian and Attic pottery, sixth- and fifth-century deposits might be very difficult to identify. But if this were to explain the whole of the problem, we would have to argue that much of the 'Orientalizing' pottery conventionally dated to the seventh century was in fact produced in the sixth and even the fifth century. Alternatively, we might suggest that buriers virtually abandoned grave goods after 600, but went on putting the dead in the same kinds of plain *pithoi* in old chamber tombs. Given the confusion of these multiple burials, excavators might have dated large numbers of 'Orientalizing' burial *pithoi* in tombs like Fortetsa P to the seventh century, instead of realizing that they should really be spread out across the sixth and even the fifth century. But this would not work for individual burials like those at Arkades, and we would also have to assume that imported pottery disappeared from settlements, and that plain pottery of basically the same types as were used in the early seventh century continued into classical times. When mixed with residual sherds from earlier layers, as inevitably happens on long-lived sites, the sixth- and fifth-century levels of settlements would in effect 'disappear' against the Late Geometric and Orientalizing background. The absence of votive evidence could be explained as an extreme version of the decline in such activity which we see everywhere in Greece in the sixth century.

But the need to multiply hypotheses like this, and to invoke the coincidence of different factors for each category of evidence, suggests this is at best only a partial explanation of the pattern. Further, there is little in the stratified settlement deposits from the Unexplored Mansion at Knossos to support such a theory.

For archaic archaeologists and historians, the 'period of silence' should be a major research topic. If we take the evidence at face value, then Crete suffered a rapid population decline, which would have had a traumatic impact on landholding, inheritance, marriage, and the distribution of power. On the other hand, if the silence is more a product of fluctuations in archaeological visibility than of demographic factors, then the sixth and fifth centuries were an extraordinary episode in which the Cretans turned their backs on the outside world every bit as thoroughly as did Tokugawa Japan between 1639 and 1854. Either way, the early sixth century was decisively important in Cretan history, and no explanation of Cretan society in terms of vaguely defined 'continuities' from the Bronze Age will make sense unless it faces this issue.

Conclusions and debates
Archaeological time
I close by returning to my opening question: what role for archaeology in the writing of archaic Greek history? My conclusion is that it allows us to write a kind of structural history, reaching back across the entire archaic period and extending to every corner of the Greek world. The literary record cannot provide the materials for such a history, but without a structural framework, our text-based histories are seriously misleading.

This conclusion, of course, depends more on the assumptions about material culture which I outlined at the beginning of this chapter than on the mass of data I have provided. The finds themselves determine the content of my archaeological interpretation of archaic Greek history, but not the kind of history I think we can write. I argued that we must begin from the standpoint that material culture was a non-verbal language which archaic Greeks used to construct images of how they wanted the world to be, and that the archaeological record is an imperfect residue left behind by these activities. We can perhaps read away the games people played to reach an authentic understanding of non-discursive realities, effectively reducing material culture to a passive reflection of economics, politics, or other forces; but before we can begin to do so, we must recognize that our data always come to us already implicated in competing attempts to fashion images of the world. We must begin our analyses by trying to understand the cultural systems (or mentalities, or ideologies, or whatever we choose to call them) which lie behind the finds. As a result, I concentrated in this review on seeing the archaeological data as evidence for a long-term history of ideologies, spanning a quarter of a millennium.

Fernand Braudel (1972 (1949), 21) suggested that the best way to understand the history of the Mediterranean 'is to dissect history into various planes, or, to put it another way, to divide historical time into geographical time, social time, and individual time'.[115] Braudel criticized his predecessors for concentrating obsessively on the doings of kings and diplomats, measured in individual time, what he elsewhere called '*l'histoire événementielle*'. To understand the Mediterranean world, he argued, we must situate the experiences of individual time within the imperceptibly slow history of geological, climatic, and environmental change, measured in millennia, and the history of institutions, economic systems, and ideologies, measured in centuries or generations.

The *Annales* school inspired by Braudel's work was, to some extent, repudiated in the 1980s in favor of new forms of cultural history (e.g., Furet 1983; Hunt 1984), but no one would suggest for a moment that the study of the Mediterranean should return to pre-Braudelian models. However, when classical archaeologists have tried to wring 'history' from artifacts, they have generally assumed that such an activity means turning the material record into something like the textual record, contributing to a narrative political history in 'individual time'. Snodgrass (1987, 36–66) has shown the inadequacy of this kind of writing: there is no way to use these data to generate a story of year-by-year happenings.[116] Even when our dating and stratigraphical resolution are as good as they can get, a quarter-century (in antiquity, effectively the span of an adult lifetime) will be our basic chronological unit. This is a viable timeframe for social time, 'the history of groups and groupings...with slow but perceptible rhythms' (Braudel 1972, 20–1), but not for the history of events. The great contribution of archaeology to the archaic historian, I contend, is that it allows us – for the first time – to think in social time.

Those who want to think in individual time must continue to make do with the textual sources. However, even for them, archaeological history written in social time is indispensable. The texts encourage chronological foreshortening and geographical tunnel vision. The only place for which an archaic political narrative can conceivably be written is sixth-century Athens, and even there the source problems are formidable. The foreshortening effect is a tendency to assume that everything important about archaic Greece can be explained in terms of the handful of processes and events, mainly in the sixth century, mentioned in the surviving sources. Even those who are confident in their powers to divine from Aristotle and Plutarch the situation in pre-Solonian Athens only dare to venture two or three decades back into the seventh century. After all, what else can be done? Before Cylon all is darkness, and there is no way to relate conjectures to firm evidence. Yet as Snodgrass (1980) insisted, and as the steadily accumulating evidence underlines, there is really no way to understand archaic Greece without plunging into the revolutionary ferment of the eighth-century Aegean. Further, there is no way to interpret the eighth-century transformation without exploring the Dark Age, and no way to make sense of Athens without putting it into a broader geographical context.

A second strategy is to combine a sixth-century Athenian narrative with seventh-century stories about the tyrants of Corinth, Argos, and other cities, and fragments of poets, particularly Homer and Hesiod, to make a composite picture of archaic 'Greece'. This tunnel-vision blurs all geographical and synchronic distinctions to create its single diachronic sequence; it also does violence to the generic distinctions between the sources, requiring a naïve confidence in the factuality of the early poets' personas (Morris 1996a, 25–8).

We will only understand individual time if we ground it in social time, and vice versa. Archaeology contributes most to archaic history when woven together with the textual evidence. When discussing the meanings of the finds from each region in this chapter, I regularly turn to the literary sources, where we can find first-hand observations on the world of events which illuminate social time just as much as the longer-term history which I have tried to generate from the excavated finds illuminates the experience of the individuals who produced our texts.

Archaeology is also our most important source for Braudel's 'geographical time', the famous *longue durée* of the *Annales* historians. A history of climate, geology, and ecology at this level would necessarily dwarf the archaic period within a span of millennia, producing a very different kind of history from that which I have offered here. It is sorely needed, but at the moment the data are inadequate. The finds of surface surveys are particularly important. The chronological imprecision of these data, usually involving time-bands closer to a quarter of a millennium – the whole archaic period – than a quarter of a century, probably makes them too coarse-grained for a history on social time. But that is much less of a problem on the grander scale of geographical history, and, as Alcock (1993; 1994) in particular has shown for Hellenistic and Roman Greece, an archaeological history written in geographical time will nevertheless transform our understanding of the social scale.

The history of archaic ideologies

I filled most of this chapter with an account of developments from 750 to 500 in three categories of deposits – burials, sacrifices, housing – in the belief that these are the most useful contexts to look at to write a long-term history of ideologies. I identified four broad regional material culture groups (*Fig.* 1), which go back at least as far as the eleventh century. I argued that the eighth century saw a dramatic social and cultural revolution in central Greece. New rituals were invented, constructing visions of the community and its relationships to excluded groups (whether living, dead, or immortal) which differed radically from those which had prevailed during the Dark Age. The core ideas of these new ideologies, I suggested, can be summed up as a 'middling' ideology, of the good society as a group of restrained, honorable men, farming their fields, fighting in the phalanx, beating their slaves, and impregnating their wives. The new rituals brought these men together, denying wealth or any other distinctions within their ranks. The middling ideology was a coherent system of class, gender, ethnicity, and cosmology. The middle had its opponents, who may have been largely responsible for filling the sanctuaries of the seventh century with magnificent offerings. But from 700 onward, these men and women were an embattled minority. Archaic central Greek *poleis* were unusually egalitarian within the male citizen community, but combined that sense of equality with a rigid gender hierarchy, increasing use of non-citizen (and ideally non-Greek) chattel slaves, and a predatory cultural chauvinism.

Snodgrass's greatest contribution to archaic history was to focus attention on what he called the 'structural revolution' of the eighth century. But in the early 1990s, some archaeologists began to deny that there was such a transformation. Sarah Morris, for instance, says that 'in my view, the Greek community-by-consensus evolved slowly, gradually, and continuously since the Late Bronze Age...without the "explosion" or "renaissance" attached to the eighth century' (1992b, xvii–xviii). In a similar vein, Lin Foxhall says that 'I am not at all sure that [a site like Nichoria] is very different in fundamental organizational terms from what I would call a *polis* in the eighth, seventh, or even sixth century, though it may sometimes differ in scale. The image of coherent, well-organized political entities coming into view only in the eighth century seems to me largely a product of the preceding "darkness". If this darkness is illuminated, where does that leave us?' (1995, 249).

Examples could be multiplied. But none of the gradualists have responded to Snodgrass's arguments with a detailed examination of evidence, explaining why what he saw as a fundamental structural revolution was in fact no such thing. The way I presented the evidence in this chapter will have made it clear that, although I disagree with Snodgrass on its interpretation, I see no empirical reason to deny the reality of massive changes in eighth-century central Greece. A full-length gradualist analysis of the by now very large body of evidence might persuade me that, like everyone who has worked in detail with this material in the last fifty years, I am mistaken in identifying a profound rupture around 750–700, though I cannot imagine how anyone could explain away the upheavals in funerals, sacrifice, building styles, artwork, the overall quantity and distribution of finds, etc. The data seem to me to be utterly resistant to the claims of the gradualists, who argue more from assertion than from appeal to evidence or challenges to the methods of earlier interpreters. The eighth century saw ferment, experiment, and change in central Greece on a scale that has few parallels in Mediterranean history. Everything was open to challenge: the world was turned upside down.

This was much less true outside central Greece, and if the gradualists restricted their arguments to these areas, they would have a stronger case. Of the three contexts of deposition which I reviewed in this chapter, sacrifice is the only one in which Aegean developments are strongly paralleled on Crete and in western Greece, although in both these areas, the eighth century saw the expansion of older practices rather than radical innovation, as in central Greece. It may well be that in the charged atmosphere of the late eighth century, central Greeks borrowed heavily in the religious realm from Cretans and westerners, as well as from Levantines. To some extent, we may speak of a common religious revolution in the eighth century. But once we travel north of Thessaly, the newly created 'Greek' way of worship had no perceptible impact, except where central Greek colonists brought it with them.

The rapid development of house types in the eighth century was more restricted to central Greece, where apsidal and oval one-roomed houses had been so common in the Dark Age, and perhaps also to western Greece. But so far we have no good evidence for Aegean-style towns packed with courtyard houses in the West. On Crete, stone rectilinear houses, some with as many as four rooms, had been normal across the Dark Age. The eighth century saw no very abrupt change, although in the seventh there are indications of a partial move toward the courtyard house. In the north, only very simple houses are known from Aegean Thrace and Epirus, perhaps because only exposed mountain-top sites have been excavated, but in Macedonia a tradition of multi-room rectilinear mudbrick houses went back to the Bronze Age. Apsidal houses, like those at Thessaloniki and Assiros, were unusual, and some of the rectilinear houses, like the Kastanas '*Großhaus*', were very substantial. Here too the eighth century seems to have made little difference.

The regional differences are most pronounced in burials. The homogeneous, poor cemeteries typical of seventh-century central Greece have few parallels elsewhere. The Iron Age tradition of warrior burial under mounds may have been in decline in seventh-century Macedonia and Epirus, although that is far from certain; but in Thessaly, western Greece, and Crete, the seventh century was the golden age of rich and martial graves.

The Aegean world went its own way after the eighth century. The structural revolution was not only a break with the past but also a break with the rest of the Mediterranean, including near neighbors in the north, the west, and on Crete. I have suggested, as did Snodgrass (1980), that the later seventh and earlier sixth century saw a gradual playing out of movements started around 700. Large, plain, and poor cemeteries became more and more normal in central Greece, spreading across the islands to Ionia, and eastward to Boeotia. Aegean-style worship of the gods, involving a large temple as well as an altar and votives, was established in the colonial sites by 600, and spread across Thessaly. The new courtyard houses gradually squeezed out old-fashioned curvilinear and even one-roomed rectangular types, though this took most of the century, perhaps because of the expense of building a house in the new style.

The pace of change increased after 550. After a short period in which the plain archaic style of cemetery was contested by high spending, there was an absolute collapse of monumental burial (Aegina seems to be the only exception in the fifth century). Even Athens, which had followed a unique path across the archaic period, now fell into line. Courtyard houses generally became more sturdy and probably more rigorously organized, and there may have been big changes in the use of public space. The architectural orders of the houses of the gods were formalized, and there was probably a decline in the kind of votives favored by archaic 'elitists'. At this point, central Greek material culture began to penetrate the west and north on a much larger scale than before. We hear of wars in the north, central Greek military adventurers making their fortunes there, and secondary state formation.

By 500, a genuinely panhellenic material culture was taking shape on the mainland, involving poor inhumation cemeteries (most often in pit or tile graves in the fifth century, though *pithoi* remained popular in the West), courtyard houses on regular and even Hippodamian plans, substantial Doric temples, and generally low levels of votive offerings, and a common repertoire of pottery shapes and imported Attic Black Glaze vases. But none of this applied to Crete. Whatever the Cretans were doing in the sixth and fifth centuries left few archaeological traces, and it is not until some way into the fourth that the island can be said to have rejoined the panhellenic trajectory.

I have argued (Morris 1996a; forthcoming) that the changes of the late sixth century represent a further general shift toward middling values. They coincided with the beginning of a seventy-five-year eclipse of elitist literary traditions, the hardening of gender boundaries, the extreme ethnic chauvinism brought to perfection by the Persian wars, a rapid expansion of slave labor, and the most dynamic form of class leveling within the male citizen community, Greek-style democracy. All these were forces set in motion by 700 BC, and all began to be reversed by 400, beginning a long process of the unraveling of the *polis* (Morris 1992, 130–55; 1997d).

From cultural history to social history

This is an archaeological history of ideologies, played out on a social time scale. It is, I believe, an important contribution to understanding archaic Greece, but I suspect that most historians, even if they accept my main conclusions, will feel that it is at best incomplete. A history of ideologies begs the question of what caused these great shifts in mentality in the later eighth and later sixth centuries.

To put the issue this way is to assume that ideologies are epiphenomenal, dependent on deeper social and economic forces. Not everyone sees a need to reduce cultural history to something else; in Lynn Hunt's words, 'economic and social relations are not prior to or determining of cultural ones; they are themselves fields of cultural practice and cultural production – which cannot be explained deductively by reference to an extracultural dimension of experience' (1989, 7). The approach to material culture which I set out in my introduction involves accepting at least part of the new cultural historians' case. If, as I suggested, all excavated materials come to us already implicated in competing efforts at self-fashioning, it may be impossible simply to cut through the discursively constituted realm of culture to reach objective economic and social structures.

But I do not want to push the claims of cultural history so far,[117] and I conclude this chapter by suggesting that we can in fact see how the ideological changes of the eighth and sixth centuries were connected to broader and perhaps deeper forces. One of the best ways to do this is to put the evidence into a broader geographical context. The archaeological records of Italy or Iran were the products of cultural negotiations just as complex as those in Greece, but they were the products of *different* negotiations, and cross-cultural comparison may show what were shared problems, and what were culturally specific responses.

In the eighth and seventh century, the whole Mediterranean basin experienced substantial population growth. From Anatolia to Iberia, cemeteries became more complex, and in the Aegean and Italy rich warrior burials appeared. In many places there is evidence for new fortifications, and perhaps more intense warfare. There is much evidence for connections between regions, largely through the activities of Phoenicians and Greeks, and possibly evidence for agricultural advances and the centralization of power in aristocratic or royal hands. In the old kingdoms of Egypt and Assyria, local priests, officials, and chiefs were the first to take advantage of the new possibilities, and the middle of the eighth century saw political fragmentation, but by 700 the centralized palaces had revived in both cases. From Babylonia to Greece, the surviving written evidence grows by leaps and bounds from 725 on.[118]

These processes operated on a truly Braudelian scale, which is perhaps why they have so far received little attention. But they have serious consequences for efforts to understand the small world of the Aegean. As across most of the Mediterranean, in central Greece we have evidence for population growth, fortification, more intense warfare, monumental building, and state formation. Yet these processes led to different results. Instead of struggles between local officials and palaces, as in Egypt and Assyria, or the emergence of powerful princes and nobles, as in Italy and eventually in Spain, we get broad male citizen communities, led by aristocrats, but ones who generally felt themselves to be answerable to the ordinary folk of their *polis*.

Explaining what happened in eighth-century central Greece will require both a general account of the sudden increase in the pace of life across the whole Mediterranean and a series of particularized accounts of what made each region unique. We might compare the problems of the archaic period with the famous 'Brenner debate' about Europe in the fourteenth through sixteenth centuries AD. The whole area from Muscovy to Ireland experienced severe population decline after the onset of the Black Death in 1348, but generally recovered before 1600. West of the Elbe, feudalism collapsed; to the east, a particularly repressive 'second feudalism' was created in the sixteenth century. Rejecting the demographic determinism popular in the 1970s, Brenner argued that pre-existing class structures were decisive in determining how de- and re-population affected societies. In the West, despite the efforts of the aristocracy and church, peasant communities generally turned the labor shortage of the late fourteenth century to their advantage to escape bondage; while in the East, the decline in the workforce left the poor even more vulnerable to exploitation than before.

Brenner's thesis is contested (Aston and Philpin 1985), but right or wrong, it provides a very helpful model for thinking about the eighth-century Mediterranean. For reasons which lie buried in the Dark Age, the big men of eighth-century Greece generally did not succeed in harnessing the new forces to their own ends. Rather than rising to the rank of 'princes', as probably happened in Etruria and Campania, such men were marginalized, to be stigmatized in the seventh century as *tyrannoi*, totally anti-social creatures who negated the very principle of community. The details of how this happened are lost forever, though from the stories about genuine archaic tyrants we may be able to piece together something of the competing discourses of power and authority (as McGlew (1993) tries to do, with mixed success). The Dark Age ruling-class ideology of the elite as a very homogeneous group may have made it harder for any individual to rise above the rest of his peers than in more fragmented elites like those in Villanovan Italy. The struggle to preserve the Dark Age order of an internally egalitarian elite against the challenge of tyrants succeeded, but only, I suggest, at the cost of the collapse of its boundaries, and the generalization of the concept to include the whole male community (Morris, forthcoming, ch. 8). Attica was the great exception within central Greece. Here, after being at the forefront of the shift to a broader conception of the community around 750, a closed aristocracy of *Eupatridai* succeeded in reasserting an older vision in the seventh century, only to be overthrown by the threat of civil war in 594 (Morris 1987, 205–10).

This is not the only possible interpretation of the structural revolution. Starr (1977; 1986) and Snodgrass (1977; 1980; 1993) saw in it not the defeat of a West-Mediterranean-style elite, but the original emergence of an aristocracy after four centuries of simpler societies, in a process of rapid state-formation. Snodgrass's argument rests on treating the increase in numbers of graves and settlements after 750 as a fairly direct reflection of an increase in population, but, as Camp (1979) pointed out, if this is the case, then we should also assume that the fall in numbers after 700 reflects a serious depopulation. Excavators from Eretria to Epirus have suggested that their particular part of Greece suffered a seventh-century demographic decline. If they are right, then demography must be seen as the driving force in archaic history. Regardless of how we interpret the eighth-century revolution, it was overshadowed by the consequences of the massive population slump in the seventh century and recovery in the later sixth.

Demography has been central to interpretations of the early archaic period for many years, as the background to colonization and the Solonian crisis, but Camp's thesis has not generated much discussion. Snodgrass (1983) replied with cogent criticisms of his treatment of the number of wells in the Athenian Agora, and I have tried to show that in the case of Eretria and Chalcis, the most extreme examples of apparent depopulation, we are dealing with a problem in identifying diagnostic wares in settlement contexts (Morris 1987, 158–67). But the issue is far from closed. I cannot bring myself to believe that a demographic collapse on this scale could have had so little impact on the literary tradition, particularly if it was combined with an equally dramatic sixth-century depopulation of Crete. The most economical explanation is that both phenomena are technical, archaeological problems of chronology. But the fact remains that in many parts of Greece cemeteries seem to shrink and settlements become hard to identify after 700. *Ad hoc* explanations are possible for each case, but as Camp pointed out, this is a systematic pattern, which needs to be investigated as a whole.

If Camp's interpretation is correct, the rapid changes of the later sixth century might be the result of the revival of population, but again there are other ways of seeing the issue. In recent years, some economic historians have drawn on survey data and ethnoarchaeology to suggest that there was something of an agricultural revolution in classical Greece. Historians normally assume that most classical Greeks lived in nucleated villages. Their landholdings would often be fragmented by partible inheritance into very small, scattered plots, which would mean that farm animals would have to be stalled or kept in distant pastures. The land would be under-fertilized, since most of the manure produced by the animals would be wasted. Consequently, the land would require frequent, perhaps even biennial, fallow. This regime would produce low yields, but would also reduce the farmers' vulnerability to localized variations in rainfall.

But several recent surface surveys have detected a shift toward dispersed settlement in classical times. It seems that many classical Greeks lived in isolated farmsteads. Combining this with evidence from Euboea and Greek colonial sites in the Crimea and Italy for consolidated landholdings ranging from four to twenty-five hectares, some historians are now proposing a so-called New Model of classical agriculture. Farmers living in the center of a single block of land would save on travel time to and from their fields, and could keep their animals on the arable, dropping manure where it would do most good. Instead of biennial fallow, cereal/pulse rotation would provide animal fodder. This regime would improve crop yields, although the concentration of holdings would also increase climatic risk.[119]

Several of the survey reports date the shift in residence patterns to late archaic or early classical times, and I have suggested (1994b, 361–6) that this process might provide an economic explanation for the great cultural changes of the years around 500. Rather than hovering on the brink of subsistence crisis, which would regularly make them dependent on patronage from richer neighbors, farmers started trying to concentrate their holdings, and moved out of the villages to live on them. The new regime would have meant higher yields and greater overall prosperity, but also higher labor inputs and more risks. Some historians claim that such a pattern suggests a maximizing strategy aimed more toward production for markets than toward traditional peasant subsistence.

The new economy would not have appealed to everyone. In some areas, it may be that only the rich could afford to take these risks; elsewhere a broader group of middling farmers may have established themselves in the countryside, with their new-found economic independence underwriting the cultural transformations of the years around 500.

Every part of the arguments behind the 'New Model' is open to challenge,[120] and trying to connect this thesis to the late sixth-century changes described above only creates further problems. Survey data operate best on a geographical time scale, with a margin of error centuries wide. Correlating them with a social time scale is no easy matter. Hanson (1995, 50–5) claims that this new agricultural regime lay behind the changes of the eighth century, while Jameson et al. (1994, 383–94) see it as a fourth-century phenomenon. Excavations on farmsteads will eventually narrow the margin of error to match the tolerances of social time, but many years will pass before enough sites have been explored to inspire confidence in general patterns.

I conclude on a deliberately polemical note: there will be no proper cultural, social, and economic histories of archaic Greece until archaeologists become historians, and historians become archaeologists. The textual data suffer from such narrow chronological and geographical limits that in order to explain anything significant about the archaic period, historians ultimately either have to turn to archaeology or to make up the past on the basis of comparative materials, evolutionary assumptions, or guesswork. Yet when historians have turned to archaeology, they have not always done so in a very productive way. The study of archaic material culture is above all a form of cultural history. We can only use archaeology as a source for a more traditional social and economic history if we first understand the non-verbal languages through which objects made sense to archaic Greeks. To do that, we need to approach the evidence comprehensively, paying fanatical attention to chronological and geographical distinctions, and always reading it against the surviving literary record. As the subtitle to this volume implies, new evidence and new approaches must go together.

Acknowledgements

I would like to thank the participants in the 'Archaic Greece' conference for their comments on the original version of this paper, and Jan Paul Crielaard, Steve Hodkinson, Lisa Nevett, Kurt Raaflaub, Anthony Snodgrass, and Hans van Wees for reading an earlier draft. They have saved me from countless errors of fact and fancy and have made many valuable suggestions, but are not, of course, responsible for what I have done with their advice.

Notes

In presenting the evidence from archaic Greece, I need to refer to a large number of preliminary archaeological reports. The simplest way to do this is to modify the bibliographical system used in the other papers in this volume, and to refer to reports by the abbreviated title of the journal in which they appear (see p. *viii* for abbreviations).

[1] Morris 1994a, Shanks 1996, cf. Whitley 1997.

[2] *ASAA* 59–61 (1981–3), Hägg 1983, Deger-Jalkotzy 1983, Musti et al. 1991.

[3] Robin Osborne's excellent recent book *Greece in the Making* (1996) reviews the archaeological evidence from some regions, but is not intended as an archaic version of the Dark Age syntheses.

[4] e.g., Brewer and Porter 1993, Lubar and Kingery 1994, Auslander 1996. For postprocessual archaeology, Hodder 1992. Much of the inspiration for these studies can be traced to Bourdieu 1984 and sometimes to Baudrillard 1981.

[5] e.g., Blanton 1994, 13–16; Rathje 1992.

[6] Most recently Richards and Parker Pearson 1994, Carsten and Hugh-Jones 1995.

79

[7] Particularly Foucault 1985; Ober 1989; Johnstone 1994, forthcoming; D. Cohen 1995. I set out my views on these developments more fully in Morris 1994b, 355–60.

[8] Morris 1996a, 1997b, cf. Shanks 1995.

[9] See Leach 1976; Gellner 1985, 128–57; Tilley 1990, 65–6. I expand on this argument in Morris 1992, 17–21.

[10] Morris 1993a, 28–32; Whitley 1994b; cf. D'Onofrio 1995, 76–81.

[11] Snodgrass 1994a, 198, with reference to Whitley 1991b.

[12] Nor are they entirely discrete. In particular, cult in honor of the occupants of tombs (both the recent dead and the dead of the Bronze Age) blurs the categories of the sanctuary and the burial. This was an extremely important activity which has rightly attracted considerable attention in recent years, but pressure of space does not allow me to treat it here. I set out my own views in Morris 1988; but see also Snodgrass 1982a, 1988; Whitley 1988, 1994b, 1995; Antonaccio 1995a.

[13] The eighth-century finds made up to the 1970s are admirably summarized in Snodgrass 1971 and Coldstream 1977. There are also reviews of settlements in Drerup 1969 and Fagerström 1988 (with Mazarakis-Ainian's review in *Op Ath* 20 (1992) 183–6), and sanctuaries in Mazarakis-Ainian 1985, Hägg et al. 1988, Hägg and Marinatos 1994. I present the more recent finds and those of the archaic period in detail in Morris, forthcoming, chs. 5–7. In the notes that follow, I normally provide references only for excavations which I specifically mention in the text.

[14] Pottery: Coulson 1986, *BSA* 80 (1985) 29–84, 83 (1988) 21–4, 86 (1991) 43–64. *Pithoi*: *AD* 34:1 (1979) 56–61. Sanctuaries, Morgan 1990, 1991; and p. 55 below.

[15] My fourth key word, 'Greek', is (and was) just as contested as the other three (see Cartledge 1993). I use it rather loosely, to include all those who made serious claims to be regarded as Greeks in classical times, including Macedonians, Epirots, and Thracians, even though, as I suggest in the text, their archaic material culture often has more in common with the Balkans than with the Aegean world. This is once again a controversial issue in the 1990s (see e.g. Danforth 1995).

[16] For introductions to the tremendous wealth of Greek archaeological data from Italy and Sicily, see *ASAA* 59–61 (1981–3), Graham 1982, Descoeudres 1990, Ridgway 1992, D'Agostino and Ridgway 1994. I treat the western evidence in more detail in Morris, forthcoming, chs. 5–7.

[17] Argos: *BCH* 81 (1957) 322–84; cf. *AD* 26:2 (1971) 81–2, 28:2 (1973) 97–9. Dipylon: *AM* 18 (1893) 73–191, Villard 1954.

[18] Attica: see Morris 1987, 1997b; Whitley 1991b. Corinthia: Dickey 1995. Argolid: Hägg 1974, Foley 1988. Megara: *Praktika* 1934, 54–6; *AAA* 2 (1969) 339–43; *AD* 25:2 (1970) 101–2, 106; 30:2 (1975) 46–8; 33:2 (1978) 42; 34:2 (1979) 49–51, 54; 36:2 (1981) 33, 33–34, 39; 37:2 (1982) 36–7; 38:2 (1983) 33–8; 40:2 (1985) 44, 45; 42:2 (1987) 36–7, 43, 48; 43:2 (1988) 64; 44:2 (1989) 42, 44, 49; 45:2 (1990) 62; 46:2 (1991) 51. Euboea: *AntK* 39 (1987) 1–30. Dodecanese: Ialysos: *ASAA* 6/7 (1923/24) 83–341; *ClR* 3 (1929) *passim*; 8 (1936) 7–207; *AD* 23:1 (1968) 77–98; Kameiros: *ClR* 4 (1931) *passim*; 6/7 (1933) 7–219; *AD*

35:3 (1980) 547; Exochi: *Acta Arch* 28 (1957) 1–192. Nisyros: *ClR* 6/7 (1932) 469–552; Vroulia: Kinch 1914; Cos: *ASAA* 56 (1978) 9–427; *AD* 35:3 (1980) 552–3; 39:2 (1984) 331; 42:3 (1987) 625; Kantzia 1988. Cyclades: Paros: Zapheiropoulou 1994; *AD* 16:2 (1960) 245; 18:3 (1963) 273–4; 38:3 (1983) 347–58; 39:2 (1984) 295; 41:2 (1986) 213; 43:3 (1988) 490–1; *Praktika* 1978, 197–8; 1983, 284–5; Naxos, main town: Lambrinoudakis 1988; *AD* 14 (1935), Paratema 50; 17:2 (1961/62) 271–2, 274–5; 18:3 (1963) 275; 31:3 (1976) 343–4; 34:2 (1979) 366; 42:3 (1987) 493; 43:3 (1988) 494; *Praktika* 1937, 115–22; 1960, 259–62; 1961, 195–200; 1963, 154–5; 1965, 172–3; 1970, 152; 1971, 174–5; 1972, 143–5; 1978, 215; 1980, 259–62; 1982, 253–5; 1983, 299–308; 1984, 301–4, 313–39; 1985, 145–52, 162–7; Naxos, Tsikalario: *AD* 18:3 (1963) 279–81; 20:4 (1965) 515–22; 21:3 (1966) 391–6. Ionia: Akurgal 1983, 58; *IM* 31 (1981) 149–66; 38 (1988) 253–62; 41 (1991) 163–82. Boeotia: Symeon-oglou 1985 reviews the evidence from Thebes; for Akraiphia, Andreiomenou 1980; 1991; *AD* 29:3 (1973/74) 425–7; 31:2 (1976) 119; 32:2 (1977) 95–7; 36:2 (1981) 187–8; 37:2 (1982) 164; 38:2 (1983) 129; 40:2 (1985) 149–52; *AAA* 7 (1974) 325–8; 10 (1977) 273–86; *Praktika* 1989, 125–45; 1990, 113–41; 1991, 131–45; Tanagra: Andreiomenou 1985; *AD* 31:2 (1976) 120–1; 32:2 (1977) 97; 34:2 (1979) 160–3; Paralimni: *AD* 21:2 (1966) 198–201; 22:2 (1967) 243; 26:2 (1971) 215–17; 27:3 (1972) 316; 28:2 (1973) 265–6; *AAA* 4 (1971) 325–8.

[19] Isthmia: *Hesperia* 61 (1992) 18–22. Asine: Wells 1983, 29, 34, 160, 279–82, with Mazarakis-Ainian 1988, 116 n. 35. Yria, *AA* 1987, 569–621; *AE* 1992, 201–16. Ephesus: *ÖJh* 38 (1988) 1–23, Beiblatt 1–38. I follow Mallwitz (*AA* 1981, 624–33) on a low dating for the first Heraion at Samos. See p. 45 below for Poseidi and Koukos in Chalcidice.

[20] Eretria: Auberson 1968; *AntK* 39 (1987) 10–14, with references to earlier work; 34 (1991) 127–31; 36 (1993) 122–4. For the dating of the *hekatompedon* c. 750, see *Praktika* 1981, 144–6.

[21] Zagora: Cambitoglou et al. 1988. Sicilian Naxos: *ASAA* 59 (1981) 297. Syracuse: *ASAA* 60 (1982) 119–34. Megara Hyblaea: Vallet and Villard 1976. Pithekoussai: *AR* 1970/71, 63–7; *Expedition* 14 (1971) 34–9. The Pithekoussai houses are often interpreted as a specialized metalworking district. Until the finds are fully published, this is hard to assess, but evidence of metalworking has been found in most early Greek houses. Miletus: *IM* 23/24 (1973/74) 68–85; 29 (1979) 115–23. Eretria: *AntK* 30 (1987) 4. Smyrna: Akurgal 1983. There may be some stratigraphic problems at Smyrna. Akurgal (1983, 23) comments that the ninth-century phase was dated by pottery found 30 cm below the first phase of room 41, but there is also evidence for ninth-century experiments with rectilinear houses at Thorikos (*Thorikos* 3 (1965) 25–34), and the Smyrnaeans may have used the half-cellar design popular in the Cyclades in the eighth and seventh century, with the floor dug out beneath the level of the foundations to give more head room.

[22] Dark Age settlements: Whitley 1991a, Morris 1991. Sites known from excavations in Attica, Corinthia, and the Argolid: Morris 1987, 156–8. Survey data: Renfrew and Wagstaff 1982 (Melos); *JFA* 12 (1985) 123–61 (Boeotia); Munn and Zimmerman Munn 1989 (eastern Attica); *Hesperia* 59 (1990) 579–659 (Nemea); *OpAth* 18 (1990) 207–38 (Berbati); Cherry et al. 1991 (Kea);

Jameson et al. 1994 (southern Argolid).

[23] Argos: see Whitley 1991b, 189–91. Eretria: Bérard 1970.

[24] Argos extramural cemeteries: *AD* 16:2 (1960) 93; 19:2 (1964) 123–6; 21:2 (1966) 126, 128–9; 22:2 (1967) 174; 46:2 (1991) 93–5; *RA* 1977, 326–30. Child burials continued within the settlement space: to Hägg 1974, 30–5, add now *AD* 26:2 (1971) 81; 27:2 (1972) 200, 202–3; 28:2 (1973) 113, 121, 132; 29:3 (1973/74) 219; 38:2 (1983) 80; *BCH* 96 (1972) 168; 113 (1989) 721; 116 (1992) 683. A couple of seventh-century intramural graves did have interesting grave goods: see *BCH* 79 (1955) 312; 91 (1967) 825. On seventh-century Argos generally, see Foley 1988. Eretria: *Praktika* 1891, 35–6; 1897, 21–2; 1898, 95–8; 1899, 36–7; 1900, 55–6; *AE* 1903, 1–43; *BSA* 47 (1952) 1–48; 52 (1957) 1–29; *AD* 23:2 (1968) 230, 231; 27:3 (1972) 355–7; 29:3 (1973/74) 467; 31:2 (1976) 135; 36:1 (1981) 58–81; 38:2 (1983) 148–9; *AAA* 7 (1974) 238–41; 9 (1976) 202. Corinth: Palmer 1964.

[25] Attica: Morris 1987, 1997c; Houby-Nielsen 1992, 1995, 1996.

[26] Kato Phana: *AD* 1 (1915) 64–93; 2 (1916) 190–212; *AntJ* 39 (1959) 170–89; *BSA* 35 (1934/35) 138–64; 56 (1961) 105–6. Koukounaries: Schilardi 1988; *Praktika* 1986, 182–7; 1987, 227–36; 1988, 202–7; 1989, 257–61. The sherd counts are my own, taken on site; I thank Dr Demetrius Schilardi for giving me the invaluable experience of excavating this temple between 1984 and 1989.

[27] Ephesus: Hogarth 1908; Bammer 1984; *AnatSt* 35 (1985) 103–8; 40 (1990) 137–60; *ÖJh* 56 (1985) 39–58; 58 (1988) 1–23, Beiblatt 1–31; 61 (1991/92) 18–54; 62 (1993) 120–67; *RA* 1991, 63–83; *AJA* 99 (1995) 239; Williams 1991/93. Samos: Kyrieleis 1994, with references; on the date of the first temple, see n. 19 above.

[28] Sacred House: *Praktika* 1958, 6–8; 1960, 322; 1961, 8–10; 1962, 5–8. Lathouriza: Mazarakis-Ainian 1994. Tourkovouni: Lauter 1985a. Sounion: *AE* 1917, 168–213. Athens: Plommer 1960.

[29] Aegina: *Praktika* 1894, 17–18; *EA* 1895, 238–42; *AA* 1925, 5–9. Corinth: *Hesperia* 40 (1971) 5–9, 26–34; 41 (1972) 145–8; 42 (1973) 12. Koukounaries: *Praktika* 1982, 235, 248–50; 1983, 282–6; 1984, 276–85; 1986, 172–6; 1987, 220–6; 1988, 197–200. Smyrna: Akurgal 1983; *BSA* 53/54 (1958/59) 55, 58, 66, 75–87, 91–4.

[30] House construction and Zagora: Cambitoglou et al. 1971, 1988; Cambitoglou 1972, 1981. Ammotopos: *AE* 1986, 108–14. Drains: e.g., Koukounaries (*Praktika* 1985, 121–6; 1986, 179; 1987, 228–31) and Miletus (*IM* 16 (1966) 21–2). Bathtub: Von Gerkan 1925, 29–30; cf. Akurgal 1983, 36, for a separate bathroom in a seventh-century house at Smyrna.

[31] Early rectilinear house: *IM* 9/10 (1959/60) 38–40, 57–8, with comments of Snodgrass 1971, 430; Coldstream 1977, 270 n. 53. Late eighth-century houses: Von Gerkan 1925, 8–9. Seventh-century oval houses: *IM* 16 (1966) 21–2. Courtyard house: *IM* 40 (1990) 44–8; 41 (1991) 127–33; 42 (1992) 100–4.

[32] Naxos: *BdA* 57 (1972) 211–19; *ASAA* 59 (1981) 299–301; *Kokalos* 30/31 (1984/85) 809–38. Megara Hyblaea: Vallet and Villard 1976; Fusaro 1982, 15–26; cf. De Angelis 1994. Di Vita (1990) suggests that most colonies went through a two-stage process, with major changes in plan once the community

was properly established, two or three generations after its foundation.

[33] Thorikos: *Thorikos* 3 (1965) 9–19. Lathouriza: *AA* 1936 177–8; Lauter 1985b; Mazarakis-Ainian 1994, 1995. Eleusis: *AD* 46:2 (1991) 38–9. Athens: *Hesperia* 23 (1954) 36; 25 (1956) 48. *Ergon* 1996, 27–38, with houses at Skala Oropos, appeared too late for me to discuss it in the text.

[34] Morris 1987. Sallares 1991, 122–9, defends the view that the cemeteries do reflect a living age structure (so too Coldstream 1995, 401); I have replied in Morris 1992, 79–81.

[35] The most detailed critiques of *Burial and Ancient Society* have come from Papadopoulos (1993, with response in Morris 1993c), Sallares (n. 34 above), and Humphreys (1990). I respond to Humphreys and discuss the archaeo-logical finds made since the mid-1980s in Morris 1997c.

[36] Morris 1996a, forthcoming, ch. 3; cf. Kurke 1992.

[37] Kyrieleis 1979 argues that most Near Eastern votives were actually dedi-cated by oriental visitors to Greek sanctuaries, and Strøm 1992 suggests that officials from each temple were responsible for obtaining orientalia. No theory can be proven (De Polignac 1992, 122–3, gives good reasons not to think that all Near Eastern objects were deposited by non-Greeks), but neither of these models seems to me to account either for the mass of imports or the large numbers of orientalizing imitations of Near Eastern goods. See Snodgrass 1980, 131, on the scale of *polis*-dedications.

[38] *Works and Days* 519–25; on classical Athens, see Keuls 1985, 95–7; D. Cohen 1991, 75.

[39] Walker 1983 did make an argument of this kind, but D. Cohen 1991, 133–70, and Nevett 1994 present abundant evidence to undermine any simple reading of domestic space.

[40] Fusaro 1982, 13–15, drew a rather similar conclusion. In a forthcoming paper, Whitley suggests that Athenian graves may also reveal a shift toward more rigidly opposed gender categories around 700.

[41] e.g., Arthur 1973, 1982, 1983; Van Wees 1995, 154–63; Zeitlin 1996, 19–86.

[42] See references in nn. 18, 24, above. Thera: Dragendorff 1903; *AM* 28 (1903) 1–288; 73 (1958) 117–39; *Praktika* 1961, 201–6; 1963, 156–7; 1965, 183–6; 1966, 135–8; 1968, 128–32; 1969, 193–6; 1970, 205–7; 1971, 226–30; 1973, 121–6; 1974, 194–200; 1975, 230–4; 1976, 330–3; 1977, 400–2; 1978, 229–31; 1981, 329–30; 1982, 267–71; *AD* 17:2 (1961/62) 268–71; 19:4 (1964) 409; 43:3 (1988) 504–10. Samos: Boehlau 1898; *AAA* 2 (1969) 202–5; *AD* 24:3 (1969) 388–90; 25:3 (1970) 417–18; 30:3 (1975) 318, 321; 32:3 (1977) 301–3; 33:3 (1978) 333–4; 37:3 (1982) 351–2; 43:3 (1988) 486–90. Chios: *AD* 1 (1915) 67–71; *Praktika* 1952, 520–30; *Chiaka Chronika* 15 (1983) 93–104; *BCH* 109 (1985) 831. *AD* 44:3 (1989) 397 mentions a Protogeometric grave on Chios.

[43] Among the most interesting mid-seventh-century grave goods is a clay house model painted with the words 'I belong to Archidikas... Andrias made me', holding 98 miniature pots, a silver *aryballos*, silver rings, and other small ornaments, from the Sellada cemetery on Thera (*Praktika* 1982, 268–71). See also nn. 24, 42, above, for Argos and Samos respectively.

[44] North Cemetery: Palmer 1964. Aetopetra: *AAA* 6 (1973) 181–8; *AD* 29:2

(1973/74) 200. Tenean Apollo: Wiseman 1978, 90. Samos: Boehlau 1898; *AD* 24:3 (1969) 376–90; *AAA* 2 (1969) 202–5. The richest grave, T6, in fact dates to the late seventh century.

[45] Naxos: *Praktika* 1951, 222; 1971, 172; 1972, 144–5; 1976, 301; 1980, 259. Thera statues: *AM* 73 (1958) 117–39; *Praktika* 1965, 183; 1968, 131. Thera grave goods: Dragendorff 1903, grs. 42, 69; *Praktika* 1961, 201; 1969, 195. Paros sculptures: *AD* 16:2 (1960) 245; 23:3 (1968) 383; *Praktika* 1985, 104–8. Paros grave goods: Zapheiropoulou 1994; *AD* 16:2 (1960) 245; 18:3 (1963) 273–4.

[46] Monuments: Richter 1961; Jeffery 1962; D'Onofrio 1982, 1988; Morris 1987, 128–37, 151–5. Mound G: Kübler 1976, 5–21. South Mound: Knigge 1976. Bronze urns: Acharnai: *AD* 42:2 (1987) 67; Anavyssos: *AAA* 7 (1974) 224; Liopesi: *AD* 25:2 (1970) 126–7.

[47] Aegina is the only central Greek exception to the fifth-century pattern of restraint. Here a two-century-old tradition of single burial in sarcophagi ended around 550, when quite elaborate chamber tombs, usually containing two or three burials, came into use, and remained popular throughout the fifth century: Welter 1938, 51–7; *AA* 1928, 612; 1930, 128–9; 1931, 275; 1938, 496–524; *AD* 19:2 (1964) 74–9; 21:2 (1966) 100–3; 22:2 (1967) 147; 25:2 (1970) 130–2; 27:2 (1972) 182; 28:2 (1973) 50–1; 32:2 (1977) 43; 33:2 (1978) 53; 34:2 (1979) 68–70; 35:2 (1980) 92–5; 36:2 (1981) 65–9; 38:2 (1983) 63; 40:2 (1985) 52; 42:2 (1987) 68; 44:2 (1989) 84–7; 45:2 (1990) 81.

[48] Inventories: Aleshire 1989; Harris 1995. Looting: see Thucydides 1.143, 4.97; Diodorus 16.30.

[49] There are a few odd sites, such as Oikonomos on Paros (*Praktika* 1975, 205–9; Schilardi 1983, 180–2) and Vroulia on Rhodes (Kinch 1914; Morris 1992, 193–9).

[50] Miletus: *IM* 22 (1972) 51–60. Halieis: *Hesperia* 47 (1978) 333–55; 50 (1981) 327–42.

[51] Vallet and Villard 1976; *ASAA* 59 (1981) 63–79; 60 (1982) 173–88; Bencivenga Trillmich 1990.

[52] Corinth: *Hesperia* 40 (1971) 3–10, 26–34; 41 (1972) 145–9; 42 (1973) 12; 43 (1974) 14–24. An earlier excavation (*Praktika* 1892, 125–32) uncovered a courtyard house of the sixth or fifth century. Athens: see n. 33, above. Thorikos: *Thorikos* 2 (1964) 52; 3 (1965) 9–19; 7 (1970/71) 39. Argos: de-stroyed deposits, e.g., *BCH* 94 (1970) 766; 95 (1971) 748–9; 96 (1972) 178–80; 99 (1975) 801–2. Small building: *BCH* 81 (1957) 673–7. Assorted house walls and floors: *BCH* 83 (1959) 755; 92 (1968) 1020–1; 93 (1969) 976; 94 (1970) 766. There is also an unusually shaped early seventh-century monumental building: *BCH* 96 (1972) 171–7.

[53] There are exceptions to this trend, such as the Alcmaeonids' use of their wealth between 514 and 510 to finish the new temple of Apollo at Delphi much more lavishly than the contract had demanded, but the way Herodotus (5.62) reports the story suggests that he thought this was highly unusual. According to Plutarch (*Themistocles* 22), when Themistocles built a shrine of Artemis Aristoboule with his own money and near his own house in the 470s, he gave serious offense to the Athenian people. The classical inventories

record many rich gifts given by entire communities to the gods (Harris 1995, 238–40, 250–2), but there is no good evidence for whether this went on on a larger scale in the fifth century than before.

[54] Kurke 1991; Morris 1996a; forthcoming, ch. 3.

[55] Greek pottery *c.* 900: *ÖJh* 62 (1993), Beiblatt 1–12. Chalcidice: Snodgrass 1994b; Papadopoulos 1996. Vardaroftsa: *BSA* 27 (1925/26) 30, 59–61. Macedonian Early Iron Age pottery: Andronikos 1969. Snodgrass (1971, 132–3, 160–3, 253–5), Hammond (1972, 219–36, 384–99), and Kilian (1975, 65–74) propose lower dates than Andronikos.

[56] Long-lived *tholoi*: Kapakli, *AE* 1914, 141 (70+ burials, perhaps from Protogeometric into the sixth century); Nea Anchialos, *AD* 42:2 (1987) 255 (used 900–750, but only 3 cremations reported); Ayioi Theodoroi, *AD* 45:2 (1990) 204–5 (in use 200 years, many burials, large mound); perhaps Marmariani Tomb VI, *BSA* 31 (1930/31) 9–10. Cists and *tholoi* at same site: e.g., Dark Age Pherai, *Praktika* 1925/26, 37; Béquignon 1937, 51–5; *AD* 44:2 (1989) 223; archaic Iolkos, *Praktika* 1909, 160; 1915, 158–9; and for the cists of nearby Nea Ionia, see n. 57, below.

[57] Nea Ionia: *AD* 18:2 (1963) 140–1; 36:3 (1981) 252; 37:2 (1982) 225–6; 38:2 (1983) 196; 39:2 (1984) 140–2; 42:2 (1987) 254. Prodromos: *AD* 39:2 (1984) 148; 40:2 (1985) 156. Demetrias: *AD* 40:2 (1985) 189–91; 42:2 (1987) 247. Iolkos: *Praktika* 1915, 158–9. Ayios Yeoryios Zapheirouli farm: *AD* 30:2 (1975) 194–6; 31:2 (1976) 181–2; 39:2 (1984) 150–1; 42:2 (1987) 274–6.

[58] *AD* 31:2 (1976) 182–3; 38:2 (1983) 208–11. General account of both cemeteries in *AAA* 11 (1978) 156–82. Large mound: *AD* 31:2 (1976) 182.

[59] *Polyandrion*: *AD* 31:2 (1976) 183. Halos: *BSA* 18 (1911/12) 1–29.

[60] Pharsalos: *Praktika* 1951, 157–63; 1952, 185–98, 201–3; 1953, 120–32; 1954, 153–5; *AD* 20:3 (1965) 319. Krannon: *AD* 16:2 (1960) 179–81; 25:3 (1970) 279–82; 27:3 (1972) 416; 44:2 (1989) 231–3. The latest report suggests that graves were still being dug into the Krannon mound at the end of the fifth century. A tomb at Neo Monastiri, in use from archaic through Hellenistic times, contained an archaic *kore* head (*AD* 19:3 (1964) 263).

[61] Pherai: *Praktika* 1915, 166; 1922/24, 195–6; Béquignon 1937, 43–7, 57–72. Philia: *AE* 1925/26, 187–9; *AD* 17:2 (1961/62) 179; 18:2 (1963) 135–9; 19:3 (1964) 247; 20:3 (1965) 312; 22:3 (1967) 295–6; 43:2 (1988) 257; Kilian 1983. Gonnoi: *Praktika* 1910, 252–8. Thebes: *Praktika* 1907, 167–9; 1908, 178–80; 1925/26, 39–41, 115–16. Looting: *Praktika* 1925/26, 40–1. The rich bronzes at Proerni apparently only begin in the sixth century (*AD* 21:3 (1966) 249–52). Many of the bronzes finally received publication in Kilian 1975.

[62] Pherai: *Praktika* 1922/24, 107. Thebes: *Praktika* 1925/26, 39–41. Gonnoi: *Praktika* 1910, 252–8; Helly 1978, 72–4. Omolion: *Praktika* 1910, 189. Other sixth-century temples: Pherai: Béquignon 1937, 43–7; Prodromos: *AD* 39:2 (1984) 148; 42:2 (1987) 269; Demetrias: *Praktika* 1915, 159; Ktouri: *BCH* 56 (1932) 139–47; Koropaios: *Praktika* 1906, 124–5; Krannon: *Praktika* 1915, 173–4; possibly Palaiokastro: *Praktika* 1915, 157; Pharsalos: *Praktika* 1907, 151–3; 1915, 195–6.

[63] Larisa: *AD* 34:2 (1979) 221. Iolkos: *Praktika* 1910, 171. Krannon: *Praktika* 1915, 173–4; 1922/24, 35. Arvanitopoullos also reported palaces at Amphanai

(*Praktika* 1909, 168) and Gonnoi (*Praktika* 1910, 249). Other houses: *Praktika* 1909, 162–70; 1910, 226; *BCH* 56 (1932) 147–8.

[64] General accounts in Hammond 1967; 1982; *ASAA* 60 (1982) 77–100.

[65] Hammond (1967, 199–204, 227–30, 289–363, 401–6) surveys the early mounds, but see also Snodgrass 1971, 257–61, and the newly found tumuli at Pogoni, in *AD* 35:2 (1980) 303–7; 36:3 (1981) 271–3; 37:3 (1982) 259; 38:3 (1983) 229–30; 43:2 (1988) 302–4. Vitsa: Vokotopoulou 1986. Ioannina: *AD* 31:3 (1976) 206–9; 32:2 (1977) 149–52; 33:2 (1978) 181–2; 34:2 (1979) 240; 35:3 (1980) 301–2; 36:3 (1981) 271; 38:3 (1983) 229. Koutseli: *AD* 23:3 (1968) 292. There are some large mounds from archaic Epirus: at Shuec, a sixth- to fifth-century mound covered sixty-six pit and cist graves, many with weapons (*AR* 1991/92, 85).

[66] Colonization: see Hammond 1967, 425–6; 1982, 266–73; Graham 1982, 130–3. For Corcyra, *ASAA* 60 (1982) 57–76. Corcyra graves: *AD* 17:2 (1961/62) 204–5; 20:3 (1965) 397–9; 23:3 (1968) 313–15; 25:3 (1970) 322–5; 27:3 (1972) 479–80, 481; 35:3 (1980) 351–5; 38:3 (1983) 258–61; 41:2 (1986) 125; 43:2 (1988) 336–8. Ambracia: *AD* 42:2 (1987) 318. Epidamnus: *AR* 1983/84, 108; and, in detail, *Iliria* 13 (1983) 137–80. Sicilian burial: Shepherd 1995.

[67] Tomb of Menekrates: *AD* 24:3 (1969) 260–2; 26:3 (1971) 346–7; 35:3 (1980) 349. Rectangular monument: *AD* 35:3 (1980) 351. Third monument: *AD* 41:2 (1986) 125. There are also fragments of three stelai (*AD* 25:3 (1970) 325) and a cremation in a bronze urn (*AD* 41:2 (1986) 125), all late seventh-century. Ambracian monument: *AD* 41:1 (1986) 425–46; 41:2 (1986) 103–5; 43:1 (1988) 109–13.

[68] Corcyra gr. α: *AD* 23:3 (1968) 314; gold ring: *AD* 43:2 (1988) 338. Peritheia: *AD* 38:3 (1983) 251–2; 39:2 (1984) 211; 40:2 (1985) 225–6; 41:2 (1986) 121–2. Ambracia gr. 60: *Praktika* 1957, 85–8.

[69] Bronzes: Carapanos 1878; Dakaris 1971; *Praktika* 1929, 111–22; 1930, 65–8; 1931, 86–8; 1932, 47–52; 1952, 283–92; 1953, 162–3; 1954, 188–93; 1955, 170; 1956, 154–7; 1967, 38; 1985, 44; *AD* 16:1 (1960) 14–15. Pottery: *Praktika* 1965, 54; 1967, 46–7; 1985, 42. Nekyomanteion: *Ergon* 1960, 102–11; *AD* 18:3 (1963) 153–4; *AntK* Beiheft 1 (1963) 35–42. Kënetë: *AR* 1991/92, 78.

[70] Corcyrean temples: Rodenwaldt et al. 1939–40. Altar: *AD* 32:2 (1977) 181. Pedimental sculptures: *Praktika* 1911, 164–204; *AAA* 7 (1974) 183–6; 13 (1980) 284–96; *AD* 29:4 (1973/74) 634–5, 642–4. Late sixth- and fifth-century boom: *Praktika* 1939, 85–7; *AD* 17:2 (1961/62) 204–6; 20:3 (1965) 399; 22:3 (1967) 367–9; 24:3 (1969) 264–7; 29:4 (1973/74) 630–2; 32:2 (1977) 182; 39:2 (1984) 206–9; *BCH* 115 (1991) 183–211. Mon Repos: *AA* 1912, 248; 1914, 48; *AM* 29 (1914) 270–1; *AJA* 32 (1936) 4–8, 55–6; *AD* 1 (1915) 81; 18:3 (1963) 161–80; 19:4 (1964) 317–28; 20:3 (1965) 381–91; 21:3 (1966) 317–21; 22:3 (1967) 360–6; 23:3 (1968) 303–13. Ambracia: *AD* 24:3 (1967) 246–7; 30:3 (1975) 210–11; 31:3 (1976) 193; 32:2 (1977) 145–6; 33:2 (1978) 179.

[71] Vitsa: *AD* 27:3 (1972) 445; *ASAA* 60 (1982) 86–7. Symiza: *AR* 1983/84, 114–15.

[72] Ambracia: *AD* 25:3 (1970) 303–5; 26:3 (1971) 331–2; 30:3 (1975) 209, 218; 31:3 (1976) 193–4; 39:2 (1984) 178–80. Corcyra: *AD* 18:3 (1963) 182; 20:3 (1965) 394; 22:3 (1967) 366–7; 29:4 (1973/74) 639; 32:2 (1977) 181, 186–

9; 33:2 (1978) 218, 219–21; 35:3 (1980) 350; 38:3 (1983) 256–8; 41:2 (1986) 125–7; 42:2 (1987) 339–40; 43:2 (1988) 338–42. House with drains: *AD* 29:4 (1973/74) 627–8.

[73] Vergina: Andronikos 1969; *AD* 17:1 (1961/62) 218–88; 18:3 (1963) 217–32; 25:3 (1970) 395–6; 26:3 (1971) 411–12; *PZ* 64 (1989) 86–149. Chauchitsa: *BSA* 24 (1919–21) 1–33; 26 (1923–25) 1–29. Bronzes: Bouzek 1973; *AAA* 21 (1988) 91–101 (Axioupoli); *AD* 43:3 (1988) 401 (Aiani). Kuç i Zi: *Iliria* 6 (1976) 165–233; 7/8 (1977/78) 127–55. Summaries in Hammond 1982, 263; Wilkes 1992, 47.

[74] Colonization: Graham 1982, 113–18; Isaac 1986, 4–13. Tragilos: *AD* 40:2 (1985) 270–1. Acanthus: *AD* 42:3 (1987) 366; 44:3 (1989) 328–9; *AEMTh* 1 (1987) 295–304; Mende, *AEMTh* 3 (1989) 414–16; 4 (1990) 411–23.

[75] Generally, see Bouzek and Andrejovà 1988. Trebenischte: Filow 1927; *ÖJh* 27 (1931) 1–42; *RA* 1934, 26–38; *AA* 1933, 459–82; Konova 1995. Sindos: Vokotopoulou et al. 1985. Vergina: *Praktika* 1987, 126–48; 1988, 99–107; *AEMTh* 1 (1987) 81–91; 2 (1988) 1–4. Macedonian identification with the heroes: A. Cohen 1995.

[76] e.g., in Chalcidice: 435 graves from Ayia Paraskevi: *AD* 36:3 (1981) 300; 37:3 (1982) 282–3; 38:3 (1983) 269–70; 39:2 (1984) 216–17; 40:2 (1985) 235; 41:2 (1986) 138–9; hundreds more from Tragilos: *AD* 26:3 (1971) 418; 33:3 (1978) 297–9; 40:2 (1985) 270–1; Aphytis: *AD* 34:1 (1979) 70–84; probably hundreds of this period among the more than 5000 graves excavated at Acanthus, noted in *AD* each year since 1971. See particularly *AD* 26:3 (1971) 393–5; 42:3 (1987) 366; 43:3 (1988) 364–5; 44:3 (1989) 328. Nea Syllata: *AD* 17:2 (1961/62) 207; *AAA* 14 (1981) 246–50. Polygyros: *AD* 43:3 (1988) 361. In Macedonia proper, as well as graves discussed above, there are a *kouros, kore,* and stone lion at Aiani (*AD* 42:3 (1987) 423; 43:3 (1988) 398–401; *AEMTh* 2 (1988) 19–25), plus warrior burials, rich bronzes, and toy wagons like those from Sindos (*AEMTh* 3 (1990) 46–50). See also Eion: *AD* 34:2 (1979) 275–6; Eordaia: *Praktika* 1934, 87–9; Kouphalia: *AD* 40:2 (1985) 235; Kozani: *AE* 1948/49, 85–111, gr. 5; Nea Michaniona: *AD* 35:3 (1980) 368; Vokotopoulou 1990; Pydna gr. 91: *AEMTh* 3 (1989) 156; Sianisti: *Praktika* 1934, 75–6; Thermi: *AD* 43:3 (1988) 359; *AEMTh* 2 (1988) 283–6; Thessaloniki: *BCH* 45 (1921) 541; Tsotyli: *Praktika* 1933, 68–9. The list could probably be extended.

[77] Badian 1982, 33–7; Borza 1990, 110–15.

[78] Gergova 1993 summarizes the evidence for Macedonian and Thracian cult.

[79] Aphytis: *AAA* 4 (1971) 356–67. Mt Itamos: *AEMTh* 4 (1990) 425–38. Sane: Vokotopoulou 1993, 181–6. Koukos: *AEMTh* 1 (1987) 284–5; 2 (1988) 358–9; 3 (1989) 425–7; 4 (1990) 439–47; 6 (1992) 496–502; in English: *Mediterranean Archaeology* 5/6 (1992/93) 184–5. Poseidi: *AEMTh* 3 (1989) 416–17; 4 (1990) 401–3; 5 (1991) 303–18; 6 (1992) 443–50; 7 (1993) 401–12.

[80] Assiros: *BSA* 75 (1980) 229–67; 82 (1987) 313–29; 83 (1988) 375–87; 84 (1989) 447–63. Thessaloniki: *AEMTh* 5 (1991) 212–17. Kastanas: Hänsel 1989.

[81] Koukos: see n. 79 above. Sane: Vokotopoulou 1993, 186–8. Tragilos: *AD* 27:3 (1972) 531–2; 28:3 (1973) 454. Mende: *AD* 41:2 (1986) 147–9; 42:3 (1987) 368–9; 43:3 (1988) 361; 44:3 (1989) 327; *AEMTh* 1 (1987) 281–2; 2 (1988) 331–5; 3 (1989) 409–14; 5 (1991) 303–15; 6 (1992) 443–50.

[82] Vardaroftsa: *BSA* 27 (1925/26) 11, 42–5. Thessaloniki: *AEMTh* 1 (1987) 235–45; 2 (1988) 243–55; 3 (1989) 201–13; 4 (1990) 289–313; 5 (1991) 209–12.

[83] Here I concentrate on Aegean Thrace, south of the Rhodope mountains. See general discussions in Triandaphyllos 1990a, b; Koukouli-Chrysanthaki 1993.

[84] Roussa: *AAA* 6 (1973) 241–55; *AD* 35:3 (1980) 432. Thasos: Koukouli-Chrysanthaki 1984. Amphipolis: *Praktika* 1965, 49–50; 1971, 57–9; 1972, 70; 1973, 50–3; 1974, 63–4; 1975, 69–71; 1976, 94–8; 1977, 42–4; 1978, 58; 1979, 79; 1981, 25; 1982, 50–1; *AD* 32:3 (1977) 254. Drama: *AD* 34:2 (1979) 333–4.

[85] Galipsos: *AD* 16:2 (1960) 218; 20:4 (1965) 451 n. 20; 27:3 (1972) 527; 29:4 (1973/74) 785–6. Oisyme: *AD* 20:4 (1965) 447–51; 24:3 (1969) 349–51; 30:3 (1975) 286. Thasos: *BCH* 78 (1954) 225–51; *AD* 27:3 (1972) 520; 32:3 (1977) 246; 34:3 (1979) 330. General comments in Isaac 1986, 18–21, 35–48, 75–88.

[86] Scarlatidou 1986 provides a general discussion of the cemeteries. In detail, see *Praktika* 1954, 170–1; 1966, 65–6; 1982, 6–12; 1983, 10–12; 1984, 6–11; 1987, 183–5; *AD* 19:4 (1964) 377; 20:4 (1965) 460–1; 23:3 (1968) 361; 25:3 (1970) 404; 39:2 (1984) 283; *BCH* 94 (1970) 327–60; *AEMTh* 1 (1987) 421–38. Clazomenae: *Praktika* 1921, 63–74; 1922/23, 34.

[87] Dikaia Phanariou: *AD* 27:3 (1972) 535–6; 28:3 (1973) 469–73. Mikro Doukato: *AD* 29:4 (1973/74) 802–3; *ASAA* 61 (1983) 179–207. Amphipolis: see n. 84, above. Duvanli: Filow 1934. Delgozda: Bitrakova-Grozdanova 1993.

[88] Athena: *JHS* 29 (1909) 206–10; *BCH* 84 (1960) 864–6; 85 (1961) 930. Artemis: *BCH* 82 (1958) 808–14; 83 (1959) 775–81; 84 (1960) 656–62; 85 (1961) 919–30. Heracles: Bergquist 1973, 39–45. Aliki: *AD* 18:3 (1963) 257–8. Neapolis: *AD* 16:2 (1960) 219–20; 17:2 (1961/62) 235–8; 18:3 (1963) 257; 19:4 (1964) 370–1. Oisyme: *AD* 42:3 (1987) 444; 43:3 (1988) 427; *AEMTh* 1 (1987), 363–87.

[89] Thasos: Koukouli-Chrysanthaki 1984. Petrota: *Praktika* 1972, 86–90; *AD* 33:3 (1978) 307. Tsouka: *BSA* 88 (1993) 135–71. Rizia: *Praktika* 1984, 95–106; *AEMTh* 1 (1987) 487–97. Asar Tepe: *Praktika* 1971, 90.

[90] Abdera: *Praktika* 1991, 195–201. Thasos: *BCH* 52 (1928) 494–6; 53 (1929) 512; 55 (1931) 502–4; 57 (1933) 285–96; 78 (1954) 191–6; 86 (1962) 935–42; 87 (1963) 846; 92 (1968) 1092; Grandjean 1988; *AD* 31:3 (1976) 290; 32:3 (1977) 239, 241, 242; 33:3 (1978) 286; 34:3 (1979) 322, 326, 329; 35:3 (1980) 419; 36:3 (1981) 333; 37:3 (1982) 307–14; 39:2 (1984) 279.

[91] Ducat (1994) argues that the central Greek literary sources persistently misrepresent the Thessalian *penestai*; but see also Cartledge's review (1996d).

[92] Atalanti: *AD* 40:2 (1985) 165–7; 42:2 (1987) 226–8. Tragana: *AD* 36:1 (1981) 1–57; 42:2 (1987) 235–8. Anavra: *AD* 32:2 (1977) 104–5. Medeon: Vatin 1969. Achaea: see Morgan 1991, and add *AD* 45:2 (1990) 136, 137. Geometric graves from Laconia: *BSA* 56 (1961) 158; *AD* 28:2 (1973) 175. Messenia: *AD* 16:2 (1960) 108; 17:2 (1961/62) 95–6; 22:2 (1967) 207; McDonald et al. 1983, 260–5. Aetolia: *AD* 17:2 (1961/62) 184–5 (with Coldstream 1968, 223); 22:3 (1967) 323; 27:3 (1972) 439; 34:2 (1979) 208. I know of no eighth-century graves from Arcadia.

[93] Ayios Yannis: *AD* 42:2 (1987) 228–31. Halai, *Hesperia* 11 (1942) 366–83;

AD 44:2 (1989) 178–83. Livanates: *AD* 37:2 (1982) 181–7. Delphi well grave: *AD* 22:2 (1967) 291; other graves: Perdrizet 1908, 133, 153–4; *BCH* 61 (1937) 45–52; 64/65 (1940/41) 270–2; 68/69 (1944/45) 51–6; 89 (1965) 898.

[94] Elis grave: *Praktika* 1963, 137–40; *AD* 19:2 (1964) 180–2. Tragana grs. Π10, Π11, Π14, T4, T5, K1, 1986/1, 1987/5, 1987/6, and Atalandi grs. 1985/1 and 2: see n. 92 above. Other examples: *AR* 1960/61, 14; *BSA* 56 (1961) 115–17; *AD* 22:3 (1967) 323; 26:2 (1971) 186–7; 29:3 (1973/74) 378; 30:2 (1975) 120; 34:2 (1979) 208; *AE* 1972, 201–5; McDonald et al. 1983. Archaic: Kalavryta: *AD* 17:2 (1961/62) 130–2 (with Morgan 1991, 141); Kandhila: *AD* 26:2 (1971) 122–3; Olympia: *BCH* 78 (1954) 269. The other archaic warrior graves are at Mavrikio (Kourou 1980) and Pyla Pylias (*AD* 20:2 (1965) 208).

[95] e.g., in Laconia: Artemis Orthia (Dawkins 1929) and Amyklai (*AM* 52 (1927) 1–85); on the border with Messenia: Akovotika (*AAA* 2 (1969) 352–7); in Arcadia: Tegea (Voyatzis 1990; *OpAth* 20 (1994) 89–141; *AR* 1993/94, 18; 1994/95, 14); in Messenia: possibly Mila (*AD* 27:2 (1972) 262); in Elis: Olympia (Morgan 1990, 26–105; Kyrieleis 1992) and Kombothekra (*AM* 96 (1981) 25–71); on Ithaca: Polis cave (*BSA* 35 (1934/35) 45–73) and Aetos (*Praktika* 1989, 295; 1990, 271–8; 1992, 200–10; *Ergon* 1995, 63–7); in Phocis: Kalapodi (Felsch 1983; Felsch et al. 1996; *AAA* 8 (1975) 1–24; *AA* 1980, 38–123; 1987, 1–99); in Achaea: Aegira (*ÖJh* 50 (1972/75) 9–31; 51 (1976/77) 30–4; 53 (1981/ 82) 8–15; 54 (1983) 35–40; *AAA* 6 (1973) 193–200; 7 (1974) 157–62; 9 (1976) 16–65; 11 (1978) 147–56). At Thermon, Megaron B is now firmly dated to the Early Iron Age (*Ergon* 1994, 48), perhaps developing from an earlier cult of the dead, though it remains unclear how late Megaron A continued in use (see *AE* 1990, 191–200; *Praktika* 1992, 88–120; 1993, 73–102; *Ergon* 1994, 43–9; 1995, 36–42).

[96] Rakita: *Praktika* 1982, 187–8; *AD* 34:2 (1979) 153; 39:2 (1984) 103; 42:2 (1987) 170; 44:2 (1989) 133–4.

[97] Herrmann 1983; Kilian-Dirlmeier 1985, 215–54; panhellenic status: Rolley 1983; Morgan 1994.

[98] Snodgrass 1989/90; for Sparta, Hooker 1980, 47–70.

[99] Nichoria: McDonald et al. 1983, with *OpAth* 17 (1988) 33–50; 19 (1992) 75–84. Aigion: *AD* 40:2 (1985) 120–3. Bambes: *Praktika* 1956, 187–92; 1958, 194–8. Kopanaki: *AD* 36:2 (1981) 151–2; 37:2 (1982) 136–7. Ithaca: *Praktika* 1986, 234–40. Kyparissi: *AD* 33:2 (1978) 139–40; 34:2 (1979) 187.

[100] Kandhila: *AD* 26:2 (1971) 122–3; Megalopolis: *Praktika* 1907, 124–5. A late eighth-century grave at Pharai in Achaea had also been marked by a mound of stones (*Praktika* 1956, 197).

[101] Pendlebury (1939, 327–44) has a very good review of the older finds, though he glosses over the contrast between the seventh and the sixth century. Di Vita et al. 1984 describe Italian excavations.

[102] Arkades: *ASAA* 10/12 (1927/29) 78–400. Eleutherna: Stampolidis 1990; 1993; 1995. Vrokastro: Hall 1914, 154–71. Prinias: Di Vita et al. 1984, 238– 56. Praisos: *BSA* 8 (1901/2) 235–6; 80 (1985) 129–37; *Praktika* 1952, 639–42; 1953, 292–4; 1954, 363–4.

[103] Kavousi Vronda: *Hesperia* 57 (1988) 283–96; 60 (1991) 152–67; 64 (1995)

70–89. Water sieving described in a lecture by Leslie Day at Stanford University, March 1996. EPH/75: *BSA* 76 (1981) 162–5.

[104] Warrior burials: Ammoudoplaka (*AD* 21:3 (1966) 407); Kavousi Vronda gr. 26, possibly grs. 16, 28 (see n. 103, above); Knossos North Cemetery tombs 25, 56, 60, 75, 106, 107, 123, 219, 292, 294, 306 (Snodgrass 1996); and perhaps Hogarth's tombs (*BSA* 31 (1930/31) 98–102; 58 (1963) 42–3); Praisos tomb C1 (*BSA* 8 (1901/2) 248–51; though Coldstream 1977, 277, calls it 'shortly before 700 BC'); Siteia (*AD* 16:2 (1960) 261–2); Vrokastro bone enclosures I, VI (see n. 102, above). Rich grave goods: Fortetsa tombs I, II, P; North Cemetery tomb 112 (*AR* 1978/79, 50); Khaniale Teke (*BSA* 62 (1967) 57–75). Bronze urns: Arkades (*ASAA* 10/12 (1927/29) 78–400); Fortetsa tomb II (Brock 1957); Lyktos (*AD* 41:2 (1986) 224. Horses: Rizza 1973; *AR* 1978/79, 50–1.

[105] Eleutherna: see n. 102, above; Prinias: Lebessi 1974; 1976. At Arkades, a Doric capital and dado were found in chamber tomb B (*ASAA* 10/12 (1927/29) 184–7).

[106] Arkades: *AD* 30:3 (1975) 341–2. Kastello Vathypetrou: *AD* 25:3 (1970) 468. Praisos: *BSA* 12 (1905/6) 63–70.

[107] Iconography: Coldstream 1984. Kato Symi: *Praktika* 1972, 193–203; 1973, 188–99; 1974, 222–7; 1975, 322–9; 1976, 400–7; 1977, 403–18; 1981, 380–96; 1983, 348–66; 1984, 440–63; 1985, 263–85; 1989, 296–303; 1990, 300–8; 1992, 211–30; *AAA* 6 (1973) 104–14; Kanta 1991. Idaean Cave: Kunze 1931; Boardman 1960; *BSA* 39 (1938/39) 52–64; 40 (1939/40) 82; *BCH* 68/69 (1944/45) 45–8; *AJA* 54 (1950) 295–9; *Praktika* 1956, 224–5; 1983, 415–500; 1984, 507–99.

[108] Kato Symi: *Praktika* 1972, 200; Lebessi 1985. Idaean Cave spoil tips: *Praktika* 1983, 434–47. General discussion of earlier finds: Canciani 1978.

[109] Bronze Age cult: Gesell 1985; Rutkowski 1986. Kommos: *Hesperia* 46 (1977) 145–9; 49 (1980) 229–45; 50 (1981) 230–50; 51 (1982) 186–90. Smari: *AAA* 13 (1980) 20–60, although see now *AD* 44:3 (1989) 441–7. Arkades: *AD* 20:4 (1965) 554; 25:3 (1970) 455–60; 26:3 (1971) 499–500; 28:3 (1973) 569. Ayia Pelagia: *AAA* 5 (1972) 230–44; *AD* 33:3 (1978) 353–5. Knossos: Coldstream 1973. Dreros: *BCH* 60 (1936) 214–85; Beyer 1976. Gortyn: Scrinari and Rizza 1968; *BCH* 106 (1982) 447–64. Prinias: *ASAA* 1 (1914) 18–111; Beyer 1976; Rizza 1991.

[110] Kato Symi: *Praktika* 1972, 201; 1973, 198; 1974, 223–9; 1977, 403; 1985, 277; Lebessi 1985. Kommos: *Hesperia* 62 (1993) 339–82. Gortyn: *ASAA* 33/34 (1955/56) 45–57. Praisos: *AJA* n.s. 5 (1901) 385–92; *BSA* 8 (1901/2) 254–9, 271–81; 11 (1904/5) 243–57. Axos: *ASAA* 13/14 (1930/31) 411–98; 45/46 (1967/68) 211–302. Knossos: *BSA* 73 (1978) 1–30. Arkades: *AD* 20:4 (1965) 554. Ayia Pelagia: see n. 109, above. Cf. the large deposit of pottery at Olous: *AD* 16:2 (1960) 259–60; and possible temple: *BCH* 61 (1937) 474; 62 (1938) 386–7; Drerup 1969, 21–2.

[111] Generally: Renard 1967; Drerup 1969, 36–44. Disruptions: *Hesperia* 62 (1993) 229–30; 65 (1996) 408–15; *BSA* 89 (1994) 235–68. Karphi: *BSA* 38 (1937/38) 57–145. Continuity at Vrokastro: *Hesperia* 52 (1983) 384; Phaistos: *ASAA* n.s. 35/36 (1974/76) 173, 197–9, 200, 201, 204, 212, 242, 300; Kavousi

Kastro: *Hesperia* 64 (1995) 101–7.

[112] Vrokastro: Hall 1914; *Hesperia* 52 (1983) 367–87. Phaistos: *ASAA* 35/36 (1957/58) 265–74. Prinias: Rizza 1991. See also Lato: *BCH* 25 (1901) 282–97; 27 (1903) 206–234; 53 (1929) 382–429; although more recent work, in *BCH* 93 (1969) 792–822 and 95 (1971) 603–11, has shown that the public buildings are Hellenistic, not archaic. Dreros: *BCH* 61 (1937) 10–15.

[113] Onythe Goulediana: *Praktika* 1954, 377–82; 1955, 298–305; 1956, 226–8. Krousonas Maleviziou: *AD* 38:3 (1983) 355–6; 42:3 (1987) 530–1. The 'casa grande' at Arkades has similarities (*ASAA* 10/12 (1927/29) 51–7, 446–7).

[114] Ayia Pelagia: *AD* 28:3 (1973) 560–2; 29:4 (1973/74) 899–900. Aloides Mylopotamou: *AD* 28:3 (1973) 583. Knossos: *BSA* 68 (1973) 33–63; Coldstream 1992; Callaghan 1992.

[115] After many years of neglect, Mediterranean archaeologists are now very aware of Braudel's work (e.g., Bintliff 1991; Knapp 1992).

[116] Shanks (1996, 33–5, 49–52) discusses some of the reasons for this obsessive concern to locate individual time in classical archaeology.

[117] I set out my thoughts on this in more detail in Morris 1993a; 1994b; forthcoming, ch. 1.

[118] General reviews in Champion et al. 1984, 238–67; Kitchen 1986; Grayson 1991; Sherratt and Sherratt 1993; Fernández Castro 1995, 159–235; Bats and Ruby, forthcoming.

[119] Burford (1993, 59–61) has a balanced discussion of the issues. Alcock et al. (1994, 163–4) integrate the survey data and ethnoarchaeology most fully.

[120] See Isager and Skydsgaard 1992, 108–14; Burford 1993, 76.

2

LAKONIAN ARTISTIC PRODUCTION AND THE PROBLEM OF SPARTAN AUSTERITY

Stephen Hodkinson

The idea that the citizens of classical Sparta lived a lifestyle character-ised by a high degree of austerity looms large in ancient literary accounts. This notion appears in its most extreme form in Plutarch's *Life of Lykourgos* (8–10, esp. 9.3), written in the early Roman imperial period. Plutarch claims that the (legendary) lawgiver neutralised the role of wealth in Spartan society through a range of measures, includ-ing one especially relevant to the subject of this paper: the banishment from the territory of Lakonia of superfluous crafts which did not produce functional items necessary for the practicalities of life. Although his depiction is an extreme development of the image of austerity, the essence of Plutarch's ideas is foreshadowed in earlier, non-Spartan writings from the classical period itself, including some authors whom Plutarch explicitly cites.[1] The combination of this legacy with the generic impression of Sparta as a militaristic society has conveyed to the modern era the predominant image of a society marked by an austere lifestyle and a disdain for material goods and the possession of private wealth.

   In recent years aspects of this literary image have been subjected to severe questioning by a number of scholars.[2] My concern in this paper, however, is not to continue that particular interrogation, but rather to express my doubts about the evidential value of the other main prop for the idea of classical Spartan austerity: namely, the modern ar-chaeological and art-historical notion of the 'decline' of Lakonian artistic production towards the end of the archaic period. I began with the literary image, however, because until very recently modern inter-pretations of the history of Lakonian artistic production have typically been constructed under its influence. A survey of these interpretations will both illustrate this point and introduce my concern about the ways in which changes in Lakonian artistic production have been used as a basis for tracing the development of Spartan austerity.[3]

During the nineteenth century the visible remains at the site and the increasing collection of chance finds (which necessitated the opening of a new local museum in 1872) led some commentators to question the literary image of Spartan austerity; but the framework for modern debate was set by the excavations at Sparta conducted by the British School between 1906 and 1910.[4] The wealth of artefacts which the excavators found at early levels at the sanctuary of Artemis Orthia seemed to furnish decisive proof, to borrow the words of Paul Cartledge (1979, 155), 'that the "austere" Sparta of the myth had had no counterpart in reality before the mid-sixth century at the earliest'.

In their assessment of the late archaic and classical levels, however, the excavators were faced with a different picture, for these later strata were much less rich in finds and the artefacts generally poorer in quality. Now, this disparity was at least partly due to the physical conditions of the site. In the early sixth century the Spartans had covered the sanctuary with a layer of sand which had had the effect of sealing in the earlier deposits, whereas material deposited after this date had had no such protection and was probably seriously denuded by such factors as flooding from the nearby River Eurotas, erosion and plunder of the better artefacts. The excavators acknowledged these factors, but explicitly discounted them in order to reconcile their findings with the literary evidence for Spartan austerity. According to their chief spokesman, Guy Dickins (1908, 67), 'it is impossible to determine how much has been lost [from the classical strata] owing to erosion and spoliation, but by the beginning of the fifth century *we know from history* that...there was no room for artistic production in a state where money was of purely local value, where intercourse with foreigners was restricted, and commerce confined to a subject class' (my emphasis). In a subsequent article Dickins ascribed the origin of austerity, involving what he deemed to be the 'more or less complete abandonment of artistic development' to 'the Settlement of 550 BC... the carefully considered policy of Sparta's greatest statesman, Chilon the Ephor' (1912, 19 and 17).

In the two decades immediately following the excavations, although some scholars preferred a slightly different date for the transformation, the basic theory of a sharp cultural break caused by a decisive political change of direction on the part of the Spartan state continued to hold sway. In the late 1920s leading Greek historians such as Wade-Gery and Ehrenberg enshrined the view that the archaeological record provided 'conclusive evidence at this period of a great change in Spartan life' in their contributions to the 'canonical' publications of the *Cambridge Ancient History* and the *Real-Encyclopädie der classischen Altertumswissenschaft*.[5] After a time, however, this simple political explanation began to founder on a growing perception of the gradual nature of the decline of Lakonian art, and scholars began to look instead for more slow-acting, economic causes. Blakeway (1935) suggested that the critical factor was Sparta's retention of her outdated iron currency which discouraged foreign traders at a time when new silver coinages were being minted by other Greek states, with a consequent adverse effect upon local arts and crafts. Other scholars looked to the Persian conquest of Asia Minor around 550 which supposedly ruptured Sparta's eastern trade and impoverished her commercial partners, thus undermining both her exports and her import of luxuries.[6]

More recently, however, these economic theories have themselves gone out of fashion and there has been a general return to political (or socio-political) explanations. The trend was started by Holladay (1977, 111–14), who pointed out obvious flaws in the theories based on economic causes: for example, that there were other states which issued no coinage without suffering economic or artistic decline, and that there is no reason to think that the Spartan or Lakonian economy was dependent on trade with the East or that the Persian conquest did in fact rupture trade between Greece and Asia. Instead, Holladay ascribed the gradual development of austerity to Sparta's (re)-imposition of the strict public upbringing in the sixth century. Two years later Paul Cartledge (1979, 156) explained artistic decline in terms of a more long-term phenomenon, the 'complex and gradual transformation of the Spartan social system' towards a more military society. The resulting 'reduction of non-military wants to the barest minimum', he argued, led to the decay of Spartiate patronage of the arts, and consequently to the decline of craftsmanship. Similarly, Massimo Nafissi has attempted to explain the earlier *rise* of Lakonian artistic production in the late seventh and early sixth centuries in terms of socio-political developments connected with the growing influence of the mass of Spartan citizens. In his view, the development of Lakonian art reflected 'the demand for status symbols on the part of the new *damos* of hoplites' which attracted a growing number of merchants to Lakonia. As a consequence, 'the established workshops and the foreign potters who came to Laconia benefited from the new economic circumstances, which favoured equally the expansion of the domestic market and the increase of outlets elsewhere in the Mediterranean'.[7]

These new socio-political interpretations are clearly of a different order of sophistication from the earlier ideas of Dickins. But recent years have also seen a somewhat unfortunate revival of the older kind of political explanations, especially in the writings of some of the most distinguished contemporary art historians. Claude Rolley has suggested that the supposed end of bronze vessel production and of figured pottery exports around 530–525 BC might be ascribed to a prohibition of trading middlemen, especially those from Samos, from landing in Lakonia, due to the rupture of relations between Sparta and Samos during the expedition against the tyrant Polykrates.[8] We shall see cause later to question whether pottery exports, and even bronze vessel production, did in fact cease at this time. But, quite apart from these matters of detail, the basic assumptions underlying the hypothesis are unsound. There is little reason to suppose that Lakonian bronze production or pottery exports in general would have been curtailed by a particular dispute with Samos: Samians were surely not the only carriers of Lakonian products which travelled, as we know, across the length and breadth of the Mediterranean;[9] and why should a particular dispute with Samos have led to the exclusion of all other traders?[10] Conrad Stibbe (1985, 16–18) has argued that, far from introducing an austere 'barrack life', the ephor Chilon was partly responsible for the *flourishing* of sixth-century Lakonian art. In his view, Chilon's policies were a response to political pressure for tyranny on the part of prospering Lakonian craftsmen and 'would have had the same stimulating effect on the impetus of small industry which the tyrants had elsewhere'. However, not only does Stibbe fail to indicate precisely how Chilon's policies are supposed to have stimulated craft activity; the general presuppositions behind his argument are also historically improbable. It is highly unlikely that Lakonian craftsmen, many of them non-citizens, could exert significant political pressure on the Spartiate elite; and the claimed connection between tyranny and craft or commercial interests is a now long-outdated notion which runs counter to the conclusions of recent studies of Greek tyranny.[11] In sum, whilst acknowledging the invaluable contributions of art historians to the study of Lakonian art, I would argue that such attempts to explain trends in artistic production with reference to the political *histoire événementielle* of archaic Sparta are essentially a retrograde step.

The more sophisticated recent attempts to associate changes in artistic production with longer-term socio-political developments clearly do not suffer from the inadequacies just suggested; but I should, nevertheless, like to question whether artistic developments ultimately link in any more satisfactorily with these socio-political explanations than they do with the *histoire événementielle*. I suggested earlier that interpretations of the history of Lakonian artistic production have typically been constructed under the influence of the literary evidence. This was explicitly acknowledged by Dickins, and it remains implicit even in more recent interpretations. The consequence has been to distort the history of Lakonian production into an oversimplified picture of a general 'decline' in the late sixth and fifth centuries (which some scholars then balance with the notion of an equally general 'rise' in the late seventh and early sixth centuries). I would suggest that, had we possessed only the material evidence, this oversimplified picture of rise and decline would not have arisen, given the uneven and diverse chronological trajectories displayed by different media and types of artefact; nor would these trajectories ever have been regarded as indicators of a society finally lapsing into a self-imposed austerity. In what follows, I shall look first at the patterns of Lakonian artistic production, concentrating on the question of the 'decline' of Lakonian art, as a basis for considering what conclusions may and may not legitimately be drawn from those patterns. Since limits of space prevent me from discussing the entire range of Lakonian production, I shall of necessity restrict my attention to those artefacts which have featured most prominently in modern debate: the pottery, bronzework and lead figurines.[12]

I start with the pottery. Although the most recent study of early Lakonian pottery (Margreiter 1988) lays greater stress than previous studies upon continuities in development from the earliest periods to the apogee of figured pottery in the sixth century, even on this reading the early sixth century is clearly the beginning of a new phase in the production and export of Lakonian ceramics. The survival pattern indicated by Massimo Nafissi's analysis of a sizeable *corpus* of datable finds (*Fig.* 1) suggests that the volume of pottery production rose sharply during the early sixth century, reaching a peak in the second quarter. This peak was not maintained, however, and levels seem to fall throughout the rest of the century, before tailing off still further in the fifth century. This would appear, at first blush, to be a classic example of the rise and decline of Lakonian art in the sixth century, one pregnant with implications for the growth of local austerity. The picture, however, is not so straightforward.

First, it should be noted that the decline in production is rather drawn out: in the first quarter of the fifth century numbers of datable pots remain higher than in the later seventh century; not until the

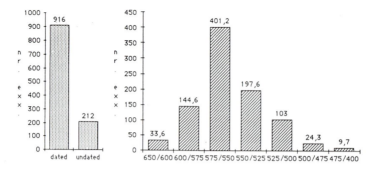

Fig. 1. Chronological distribution of Lakonian pottery production (reproduced from Nafissi 1989, 79, Graph 1b).

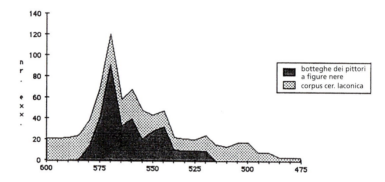

Fig. 2. Changes in production of black-figure and other Lakonian pottery (reproduced from Nafissi 1991, 252, fig.13b). Black-figure production represented by darker-shaded area.

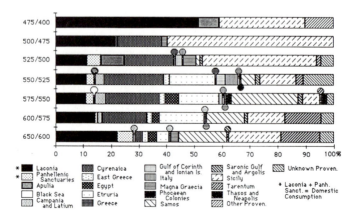

Fig. 3. Geographical distribution of Lakonian pottery finds (reproduced from Nafissi 1989, 83, Graph 5b).

98

second quarter of the fifth century do they fall clearly below. (This point is somewhat obscured by the unequal timespans in Nafissi's histogram reproduced in *Fig.* 1, in which a 50-year timespan is employed for the period 650–600, but only a 25-year span for the period 500–475.) Secondly, as is evident from *Fig.* 2, the fluctuations in production revealed in Nafissi's statistics, and in particular the later sixth-century fall, are largely due to the rise and subsequent decline of one particular kind of ceramics: the high-quality, black-figured pottery (PLATE 1) which has been the subject of considerably more study than other Lakonian work. It is important to note the scale of black-figure production. Recent research (Stibbe 1972; Pompili 1986) has shown that even in its heyday the success of Lakonian black figure was dependent upon the impetus and reputation of a very small number of major painters. Black figure was the product of a mere two workshops, one of which was absorbed by the other *c.* 555–550 BC when its head, the Naukratis Painter, ceased production.[13] The quantity and quality of work produced by the new, unified workshop itself subsequently went into decline from the 530s, after the career of the last major painter, the Hunt Painter, came to an end; the final demise of black figure followed sometime towards the end of the century, perhaps during the 510s (Stibbe 1972). The small-scale nature of black-figure production and its dependence upon the leadership of so few painters makes it an insecure base for generalisations about wide-ranging changes in Spartan society. In any case, the proportion of Lakonian black figure consumed locally was small. *Fig.* 3 shows that it was largely

PLATE 1. Interior of Lakonian black-figure kylix (Wine Cup), from Sikyon, by the Rider Painter (British Museum, B3).

an export product, whose distribution in different regions of the Mediterranean varied considerably over time, suggesting that its overseas outlets were by no means stable or secure.[14] On these grounds too, it is hard to see how the history of its rise and fall tells us much about attitudes to property and wealth among the Spartiate elite. Finally, even though it is true that the cessation of significant overseas export of black figure occurred around the time of Sparta's conflict with Polykrates of Samos *c.* 525, this was clearly not true of non-figured pottery whose export continued long afterwards. Hence it is hard to see the hand of state intervention behind the fate of black figure, whose significance for our understanding of the development of Spartan society once again appears overrated.

Scholarly concentration on black figure has indeed tended to overshadow the fact that it was only a relatively small part of a much wider spectrum of Lakonian black-glazed fine ware, some bearing non-figured decoration, some entirely black-glazed (PLATE 2). This non-figured work covered virtually the entire range of standard ceramic shapes. It is severely under-represented in the *corpus* of Lakonian pottery on which Nafissi's statistics (*Figs.* 1–3) are based – a direct reflection of the paucity of systematic studies of non-figured work, a gap which is only now in the process of being filled by recent, more systematic research.[15] Even Nafissi's statistics, however, show that these other types of black-glazed pottery originated well before the emergence of black figure and long outlived its demise. The modern neglect of non-figured pottery in comparison with black figure does not

PLATE 2. Sixth-century Lakonian black-glazed aryballos in the shape of a fig. Provenance unknown (Manchester Museum, 1991.89).

accurately reflect their true relation in antiquity. Even during the heyday of black figure, the leading potter-painters and their work-shops were also engaged in the manufacture of other black-glazed ware.[16] Indeed, the largest group of sixth-century Lakonian cups, the stemmed cups, are found contemporaneously in various guises, some entirely black-glazed, others decorated either in black figure or simply with secondary ornaments.[17] Hence, the decline of black-figure paint-ing in the final third of the century did not signify the decline of potting; and it has been suggested that the remaining black-figure workshop simply shifted more of its efforts towards its existing pro-duction of non-figured pottery (Nafissi 1989, 70). Like black figure, many items of this non-figured ware were exported abroad, a phe-nomenon which continued into the early fifth century; and at a number of southern and western Peloponnesian sites the ware can be seen to have exercised a continuing influence through import or imitation in both the archaic and classical periods.[18] A greater propor-tion – mostly not yet adequately published – derives, however, from excavations or finds at Sparta itself and was clearly manufactured for home consumption.[19] Owing to its current inadequate state of publica-tion, a systematic statistical analysis of the chronological distribution of this non-figured, black-glazed ware is not at present feasible; but some well-founded observations have emerged from the recent studies by Stibbe. In general terms, the bulk of the pottery dates to the sixth century, and its volume seems to have lessened in classical times. But this was not a universal story of decline betokening an unmistakeable onset of austerity. Several shapes in fact possessed a considerable longevity, continuing (and developing) down to the early or mid-fifth century, and some even down into the fourth century, a period which has been given little attention in comparison with earlier centuries.[20]

One often gets the impression from the total silence of many general works on Sparta that Lakonian ceramic production in the late fifth and fourth centuries somehow disappeared into a late classical 'black hole'.[21] This was clearly not the case. It was not the view of the Artemis Orthia excavators, who wrote of 'an unbroken continuity' of Lakonian pottery 'for at least six centuries before the various Hellenistic wares took its place' (Droop 1929, 52); and the excavators' view is clearly supported by the recent evidence for continuities in several black-glazed shapes noted above. The impression should now be further dispelled by Ian McPhee's recent publication (1986) of fifth- and early-fourth century Lakonian red-figure pottery from the Spartan acropo-lis, a previously neglected ware which received little more than passing

PLATE 3. Sherd of classical Lakonian red-figure pottery, from the Spartan acropolis (McPhee Catalogue no. 3; photo courtesy of the author).

mention by the excavators (PLATE 3). The emergence of this new type of ware indicates that the work of classical Lakonian potter-painters was not restricted to continuing older techniques, but was open to new developments and outside influences. Lakonian red figure was largely an imitation of Attic red figure and, as McPhee points out, its development parallels that of other similar, contemporary local fabrics elsewhere in mainland Greece. Since Lakonian red figure was not an export ware but for local use, it can clearly inform us more directly about Spartiate pottery usage than its more famous black-figured predecessor; and its similarity to wares in other parts of Greece indicates that this aspect of Spartan material culture was far from unusual.

I turn now to the bronzework. It is of course necessary to distinguish between different types of bronze artefacts which each served different purposes and frequently a different clientele. The most famous, but also the most controversial, type of Lakonian bronzework is the vessels. Finds of vessel ornaments and attachments at Spartan sanctuaries suggest a flourishing production of bronze vessels already in the seventh century.[22] This production developed during the early and mid-sixth century, with increasing production for export evidenced by the discovery outside Lakonia of several large vessels (hydrias, kraters and tripods) or their attachments (PLATE 4),[23] before coming to an end at some point during the second half of the century. The experts disagree about the precise extent of Lakonian manufacture. In particular, there is longstanding dispute concerning the attribution of the famous Vix krater – a large, richly ornamented vessel found in the tomb of a Celtic princess in Northern Burgundy and most frequently dated

102

PLATE 4. Lakonian hydria
(lower part modern),
provenance uncertain, said
to have been found near
Mainz, 610–590 (Ashmolean
Museum, Oxford 1890.590).

between 530 and 520 – whose possible Lakonian origin was originally suggested by its excavator (Joffroy 1954; 1962). This hypothesis has been developed and defended by a number of scholars, but has also been vigorously challenged by several scholars who have advocated a Corinthian origin for the krater and by others (including, most notably, Claude Rolley) who have advanced the case for South Italian manufacture.[24] The question of attribution is significant because the Vix krater would appear to share a common origin with a number of other vessels normally dated between 540 and 520: two kraters from Trebenischte near Lake Ochrid in former Yugoslavia, and a number of hydrias from Paestum and Sala Consilina in Southern Italy.[25] The question also has a bearing on the chronology of Lakonian bronze vessel production, since Rolley's exclusion of a Lakonian origin for the Vix krater and associated vessels leads him to the date of *c.* 530 for its final termination. On this dating, he argues, the production of bronze vessels ceased abruptly at the very height of its development – only a decade, in fact, after the introduction of a new type of hydria with palmette handles which betokens the influence of Eastern models (1982, 75–8). Hence his hypothesis that its termination should be ascribed to a sudden official exclusion of foreign traders. Acceptance of a Lakonian origin for the Vix krater would clearly cast doubt upon this notion of an abrupt termination, although there are proponents of the Lakonian case who argue that the krater and its associates should be dated much earlier, around 570–560, on the basis of comparisons with Lakonian relief and fictile kraters.[26] But, even if we were to accept, for the sake of argument, that this group of vessels was either not Lakonian or, if Lakonian, not datable to the period *c.* 540–520, it is still uncertain whether the bronze vessels do end as suddenly as Rolley suggests. The recent monograph of Herfort-Koch has identified a number of Lakonian vessel ornaments from Delphi, Dodona and Olympia which she dates within the decade 530–520, and which perhaps suggest a more gradual end to vessel production.[27]

Thus far, the picture emerging is that the chronologies of Lakonian material culture do not display the neat synchronisms which have sometimes been claimed. The claimed synchronism between the end of the bronze vessels and the conflict with Samos remains at best uncertain. The termination of both the export and production of the bronze vessels differs greatly from the chronology of exported pottery as a whole which continues, as already noted, into the fifth century. Other types of Lakonian bronze artefacts also had their own divergent

PLATE 5. Bronze mirror with nude female stand, from woods of Vasiliki on Mt Taygetos, 550–540 BC (Sparta Museum 3302; photo *DAI*).

PLATE 6. Bronze statuette of the god Apollo, from Kosmas in Lakonia, 500–490 (Athens, National Museum 16365; photo *DAI*).

chronologies. One notable innovation of Lakonian bronzeworkers was the production of mirrors with stands consisting of a nude female figure (PLATE 5).[28] Most have been found outside Lakonia, although three come from Sparta or its neighbourhood. Their production began early in the sixth century and seems to have continued into the early years of the fifth.[29] The production of free-standing bronze statuettes (PLATE 6) was yet different again. This was the type of bronze most closely linked to local consumption, being used by Lakedaimonians as votive offerings not only within the region but also at sanctuaries elsewhere in Greece (Rolley 1982, 76). In the eighth century there had been a considerable production of horse statuettes; but these had ended at the start of the seventh century (Zimmermann 1989, 171–5). For the next hundred years Lakonian bronze statuettes in general became somewhat rare and it is not until around 560 that their manufacture again became numerically significant.[30] TABLE 1 provides evidence for trends in the production of free-standing statuettes between *c.* 650 and *c.* 350, as indicated by datable finds.[31] After rising to a peak in the second half of the sixth century, their number subsequently declined significantly. Nevertheless, production between *c.* 500 and *c.* 450 still exceeded that of the first half of the sixth century. It then continued at a decreasing level into the later fifth century, and perhaps even into the fourth century.[32]

TABLE 1

Datable Finds of Lakonian Bronze Statuettes
(Finds from Sparta itself in parentheses)

c. 650–600	*c. 600–550*	*c. 550–500*	*c. 500–450*	*c. 450–400*	*c. 400–350*
5(3)	11(4)	52(24)	19(11)	6(6)	1(1)

My final class of artefacts is the lead figurines (PLATE 7), a votive offering found at almost every shrine in or near Sparta, often in great numbers, especially at the sanctuary of Artemis Orthia. The lead figurines have played a curious dual role in modern scholarship. Although they are sometimes used as evidence for the emerging self-consciousness of the hoplite *damos* in the late seventh and sixth centuries, they have also traditionally been cited as proof of the Spartans' disdain for more precious metals which, it is argued, led them to use

PLATE 7. Lead figurines from the sanctuary of Artemis Orthia, Lead V, 500–425 BC (Courtesy of the British School at Athens Archives).

a base metal in place of richer votives.[33] TABLE 2 documents their increasing use at the sanctuary of Artemis Orthia from the later seventh century, rising to a dramatic peak in the second half of the sixth century, followed by a decline in numbers during the fifth century and later. What is remarkable about the pattern revealed in TABLE 2 is its similarity to the chronology of the finds of bronze statuettes.[34] Spartiates were not abandoning bronze dedications for cheaper lead; dedications of bronze statuettes and of lead figurines rise and fall in parallel. It is notable that use of the leads declines in the fifth and fourth centuries, precisely at the time when Spartan austerity and militarism were supposedly at their height. Indeed, the lead figurines depicting warriors seem to share the same trend as the leads as a whole (Wace 1929). Appearing in the Lead 0 period, they diversified into 15 separate varieties in Lead I, rising to 26 varieties by Lead III–IV (when they occurred in great numbers); but they then declined to only 10 varieties in Lead V (though they remained quite popular) and a mere 3 varieties in Lead VI.

TABLE 2

Chronology of Lead Figurines from Artemis Orthia[35]

Period		*Number*	*No. per annum*
Lead 0	(? –650)	23	–
Lead I	(650–620)	5719	191
Lead II	(620–580)	9548	239
Lead III–IV	(580–500)	68822	860
Lead V	(500–425)	10617	152
Lead VI	(425–250)	4773	27

This brief and partial survey of the main forms of Lakonian art suggests, in sum, that the existing evidence for the history of Lakonian artistic production offers little assistance to those who would use it to exemplify the development of Spartiate society. The increasing numbers of lead figurines may betoken a newly self-confident Spartiate *damos*; but it is hard to see the *damos* behind the overall growth of artistic production in the sixth century. Among the bronzework, production of the more export-oriented vessels and mirrors increased at an earlier date than the locally-oriented statuettes. Among Lakonian pottery, the earlier of the two black-figure workshops, that of the Boreads Painter, seems to have been located in perioikic territory rather than at Sparta itself and worked for an almost exclusively external clientele.[36]

Similarly, although it cannot be denied that there was less native Lakonian artistic production by the late classical period than in the sixth century, this phenomenon does not constitute proof of the growth of Spartiate austerity. Unqualified talk of a general 'decline of Lakonian art' gives a misleading impression. There is little correlation between the decline of different media and art-forms, some of which end suddenly but at different dates, whilst others fall away gradually over an extended period. Each art-form follows its own chronological path and each surely demands a separate explanation. Nor is it plausible to view these different trajectories as evidence of a progressive societal transformation towards an increasingly barrack-like culture. The decline of those products which were produced primarily for external outlets cannot be satisfactorily explained in terms of a decay of patronage from a minority clientele inside Lakonia. Moreover, in general, it is the more export-oriented products which tail away first, and those more geared to local investment which continue longer.

A look at developments elsewhere adds a further important point. The trajectories of Lakonian production in the late archaic and classical periods were far from unusual. Lakonia was not the only region whose black-figure pottery declined in the sixth century, as we know from the earlier demise of Corinthian black-figure. Study of the Corinthian case suggests that it resulted from a combination of declining quality of production and competition from Attic potter-painters (Salmon 1984, 101–16), and comparable factors have been adduced in the case of Lakonian black figure.[37] We have also already noted that the development of Lakonian red figure either side of 400 BC parallels similar local developments in other regions of mainland Greece. In the case of the bronze statuettes, the fifth century saw a general decline of production throughout much of Greece, a change at least partly connected with a major shift in dedication patterns involving an overall decrease both in numbers of offerings and in the votive use of bronze statuettes. In this period Lakonia was one of the few smaller centres of bronze statuette production which remained active.[38] These parallels between trends in artistic production in Lakonia and elsewhere make it hard to sustain the thesis that the history of Lakonian art attests the growth of a uniquely austere society. Indeed, in the fifth and fourth centuries Lakonian art was increasingly influenced by the production of other regions. Attic influence, for example, is evident from the mid-fifth century onwards in a number of black-glazed pottery shapes and in the emergence of Lakonian red figure; and several bronze statuettes are local imitations of foreign work.[39] These influences were, as Richard Catling (1996, 88) has aptly remarked, part of a long-term process of artistic convergence, marked by increasing contact with the outside world, in which by the end of the classical period Lakonia became 'a producer of provincial versions of types widespread in much of the Greek world', sharing in a 'trend towards uniformity...common to nearly all regions which had possessed their own distinctive ceramic styles in the archaic period'. Although, in purely artistic terms, this development might be decried as indicative of the decline of an authentically Lakonian art, it fits rather badly with the notion of a uniquely austere society closed off from the outside world.

There are also fundamental considerations concerning the character of craft production which prohibit using its history as an indicator of socio-political developments. We have already noted the small-scale nature of the operations and limited number of craftsmen responsible for the bulk of Lakonian pottery. Similarly, it seems that Lakonian bronzework was the product of a number of small workshops in various parts of Spartan territory.[40] Some scholars have suggested that certain Lakonian art-forms may have been the product of just a single workshop or even a single master craftsman.[41] The small-scale nature of most craft production rendered it extremely susceptible to changeable contingent factors such as the life-chances of individual master craftsmen, organisational problems within individual workshops, personal misfortune or the vagaries of consumer taste.[42] It is no surprise, therefore, that the history of Lakonian art is littered with instances of artefacts – such as the Geometric horse figurines, the seventh-century marble perirrhanteria (Carter 1988), the archaic relief pithoi and the red-figure pottery – which flourished for limited periods before vanishing. There may be no need to search for deep-rooted societal causes for most of these disappearances. Moreover, the fact that several of these products came to an end during the seventh and early sixth centuries, which (to judge from the poems of Alkman and from finds at Spartan sanctuaries) were a period of prosperity and cultural openness, shows that the demise of particular art-forms, even those intended primarily for local consumption, does not carry any necessary implications for a growth in domestic austerity.

The tenor of this paper has thus far been largely negative. I have restricted myself to arguing within the terms of the existing academic debate, in order to expose the limitations of the approaches and the evidence which have been deployed by past and by current scholarship. I will end, however, by suggesting how the evidence of Lakonian material culture might be viewed in a different and more fruitful way to illuminate the questions of Spartiate austerity and use of wealth. I should like, in the spirit of this volume, to advocate a new approach, utilising a somewhat different body of evidence which, if not exactly new, has lain neglected for almost the whole of this century and is in need of a fresh and more systematic treatment than it has received hitherto.

The fundamental problem with the existing archaeological debate about Spartan austerity is that, from the time of Dickins' original article, what should logically have been a discussion about Spartiate *expenditure* and *investment* – as revealed by the dedications discovered at Artemis Orthia and other Spartan sanctuaries – was distorted instead into a debate about artistic *production*, and about the supposed rise and fall of Lakonian art. The socio-economic character of the Spartiate polis was treated as a given (as revealed by the literary sources), and the art-historical interest took over. This concentration on production has rendered the entire debate vulnerable to the fundamental objection made by Cook (1962) that 'there need not be any relationship between Laconian art and Spartan austerity' because the vast bulk of artistic production lay in the hands of non-Spartiates. Even if it is true that full-time craftsmen were not excluded from citizenship in the early archaic period and that citizens may not have been formally prohibited from engagement in craft activity before the fifth century,[43] no one would seriously doubt that after the early sixth century the Spartiates were essentially a body of full-time warriors whose economic support came from their landholdings and whose lives were devoted principally to civic and military concerns. Scholars are agreed that much Lakonian pottery and bronze production took place within perioikic territory distant from Sparta itself;[44] and, although the perioikoi were not just a population of craftsmen and traders (Shipley 1992), they must have been responsible for the bulk of artistic production. It has also been suggested that some Lakonian art was produced by itinerant potters operating abroad; and some of the leading craftsmen in Lakonia itself were apparently foreigners, such as the Boreads Painter who seems to have come from Ionia around 580 BC.[45]

Since the involvement of Spartan citizens in artistic production was minimal, there are only two indirect ways in which the history of Lakonian art might conceivably shed light on the supposed growth of Spartiate austerity: if changes in Spartan society led the *polis* to impose permanent restrictions on artistic production or commercial dealings by the entire non-Spartiate population throughout the whole of Lakonia (and Messenia); or, if a decline in Spartiate expenditure on material goods undermined the market for Lakonian production. But our discussion has shown that neither proposition is likely. First, there is no evidence that the polis ever restricted the productive activities of the perioikoi, and we have seen that the notion of commercial restrictions rests upon the improbable supposition that the state imposed a blanket *xenelasia* upon all foreign traders. In fact, *xenelasiai* are not attested at Sparta until the late fifth and early fourth centuries, when they are portrayed by contemporary sources as occasional and temporary expulsions of foreigners rather than a longstanding exclusion.[46] Equally, the second proposition falters, since many prominent Lakonian products, including most of those which ceased production at a relatively early date, were mainly for a foreign clientele. But, in any case, this second hypothesis merely illustrates the fallacy of approaching these issues solely from the perspective of production. The proposition that changes in Spartan society led to the demise of artistic production due to a decline in Spartiate expenditure merely demonstrates that, if we want to shed direct light on the question of Spartiate austerity and use of wealth through the archaeological record, we should focus primarily not on Lakonian artistic *production*, but on the surviving evidence for Spartiate *expenditure* on material goods.

Ideally, we would examine the material evidence for expenditures in several spheres of Spartiate life; but the extremely patchy coverage of current archaeological research renders this unfeasible. There are few excavated burial sites from Sparta or its environs and no complete Spartiate house from our period has yet been discovered. On the other hand, the wealth of excavated evidence which has long existed from the major Spartan sanctuaries could be used to inform us about the Spartiates' expenditure of wealth on religious offerings and provide a direct insight into one sphere in which we might test the material record for signs of the development of austerity.[47] Unfortunately, the potential of this evidence has to date been largely neglected. This is not to deny that the most perceptive recent studies have been alert to the dimension of expenditure and investment at Spartan sanctuaries. Paul Cartledge (1979, 156) has suggested, for example, that in the new austere Sparta 'there was no longer any room for expensive private dedications'. To test such claims, however, we need a systematic chronological analysis of all the excavated finds. At present we are some way from this goal, since few of the older reports published all the finds and many artefacts which do appear are given merely the briefest of mentions.[48] The inadequacies of the current state of the published evidence are graphically illustrated in TABLE 3 which attempts to express the chronological distribution of the published bronze finds from the four main Spartan sanctuaries. Note, in particular, the frequent vagueness concerning numbers of finds and the large quantity of bronzes undated or only loosely dated in existing reports. I would suggest, however, that even the flawed and incomplete statistics currently available may suggest hypotheses which might serve as a focus for future, more comprehensive study.[49] The current state of affairs can, moreover, be turned to advantage in that it highlights the need for the construction of a systematic database of finds from earlier excavations, utilising developments in expertise and technology unavailable to the original excavators. The conjunction of a new theoretical approach focusing on religious expenditure and investment with a new post-excavation methodology focusing on the complete assem-

---

TABLE 3

Chronological Distribution of Published Bronzes from Spartan Sanctuaries, c. 650–c. 350

	Orthia	Acropolis	Menelaion	Amyklai	Total
c. 650–*c.* 600	40+	3	22+	5+	70+
c. 600–*c.* 550	22	7/8	21+	4+	54+
c. 550–*c.* 500	6	15–18	6+	8/9	35+
c. 500–*c.* 450	2	10–14	1+	1/2	14+
c. 450–*c.* 400	1	5–7	Ind	0/1	7+
c. 400–*c.* 350	–	1	–	–	1
Early Archaic	1	–	–	–	1
Archaic	13	–	Ind	5	18+
Late Archaic	–	–	–	3	3
Lak. III–V and later	–	–	11+	–	11+
DNG	3	77+	3+	115+	198+

Key: DNG = Date Not Given
The signs '+' and 'Ind' signify the existence of an indefinite number of artefacts whose limit is not specified in the excavation reports.

---

blage of finds would create the potential for important new perspectives on Spartan society and its use of wealth which could stand independently of the literary evidence which has dominated the study of Lakonian material culture for far too long.[50]

Acknowledgements

The research for this article was performed during my tenure of a Nuffield Foundation Social Science Research Fellowship and an award under the Research Leave Scheme of the British Academy Humanities Research Board. I am also grateful to Massimo Nafissi, Conrad Stibbe, the Allard Pierson Museum and the Università degli Studi di Perugia for their kind permission to reproduce Figures 1–3. Since the article represents an attempt by a non-specialist to re-direct study of the Lakonian material record towards a more realistic historical perspective, I should like to express my thanks to several scholars (Paul Cartledge, Richard Catling, Robin Osborne, John Salmon, Christopher Simon, Anthony Snodgrass and Nigel Spencer) for their assistance in the navigation of unfamiliar terrain. I regret that the important recent *Habilitationsschrift* by Reinhard Förtsch (1994) came to my attention too late to incorporate into this essay.

Notes

[1] Plutarch's sources for the Spartans' austere lifestyle include Ephoros, Theopompos and Theophrastos (cf. Plut. *Lys.* 17.2; *Lyk.* 10.2). Among significant comments by other classical writers, note Hdt. 2.167: Spartan disdain for craftsmen; Thuc. 1.6: the life of rich Spartans was assimilated to that of the many; Xen. *Lak. Pol.* 7.3–5: physical condition and hard work were more important than expenditure. On the general development of images of Spartan wealth, Hodkinson 1994.

[2] Against the notion of public, equal landholdings, Hodkinson 1986. Against the idea of a prohibition of foreign currency: Michell 1964, 298–303; MacDowell 1986, 119; Noethlichs 1987, 129–70.

[3] My survey draws in part on the discussion of Fitzhardinge 1980, 10–14; cf., also, Förtsch (forthcoming).

[4] For nineteenth century commentators, Fitzhardinge 1980, 9–11. For the artefacts available before the British excavations, Tod and Wace 1906, esp. iii. The initial excavations at a number of sites in Sparta and environs were reported in *BSA* 12 (1905/6)–16 (1909/10). The excavations at the sanctuary of Artemis Orthia were later published separately in a final report (Dawkins 1929). Subsequent years of work at Sparta in the 1920s, including a season's cleaning at Artemis Orthia (not mentioned in the final publication) were reported in *BSA* 26 (1923/4)–30 (1928/9).

[5] Wade-Gery 1925, 562, dating the change to the late seventh century; Ehrenberg 1929. Cf. the similar view expressed in Ehrenberg 1925, 10.

[6] Stubbs 1950; Huxley 1962, 73–4.

[7] Nafissi 1989, 75; cf. 1991, 253.

[8] Rolley 1977, 136–7; cf. 132; 1982, 75–8.

[9] On carriers of Lakonian products from cities other than Samos, Nafissi 1989, 74. Study of the distribution of Corinthian pottery has suggested, in particular, a divorce between carriers of cargoes in the Aegean and in the Western Mediterranean: Salmon 1984, 115.

[10] The improbability of this eventuality is implicitly demonstrated by Nafissi 1989, 73–4. As he points out, the rupture in Spartan–Samian relations in fact came well before the conflict with Polykrates, around the middle of the sixth century amidst the mutual accusations surrounding the diversion to Samos of the bronze krater sent by the Spartans to King Kroisos of Lydia and the linen corselet sent by the Egyptian king Amasis to Sparta (Hdt. 1.70, 3.48). But, although this dispute may have led to a decline in pottery exports to Samos, there was no detectable effect on Lakonian pottery production or exports in general; as *Fig.* 2 (below) shows, the late 550s and early 540s were a period of modest recovery after earlier falls in production.

[11] The connection was advanced earlier this century by Ure 1922 and Nilsson 1936, but has now been almost universally abandoned by historians (e.g. Andrewes 1956, 80, 154; Murray 1993, 140–1, 331). Note that the older interpretation of Chilon as the destroyer of Lakonian art still lingers on in some quarters (e.g. Christou 1964a). All notions about the work of Chilon also suffer from the difficulty that, although he was from an early date regarded by Spartans as a sage (Hdt. 1.59, 7.235) and probably hero (Wace 1937), details of his substantive political influence – which were evidently unknown to Herodotus – appear only in much later sources (*Rylands Papyrus* 18; Diog. Laert. 1.68).

[12] For a systematic survey of developments over the entire range of Lakonian artistic production, see now Förtsch 1994.

[13] Cook (1959) has shown that the entire production of Attic pottery will at any one time in the fifth century have involved no more than *c.* 500 men, including unskilled labour. He estimates that the maximum number at the height of Corinthian production may have been half that. The numbers involved in sixth-century Lakonian production, which was minuscule compared with both Attic and Corinthian, will have been rather small.

[14] Nafissi 1989, 72; 1991, 246–53. Cf. the comments of Salmon (1984, 115–16) on the rapidity of changes of both consumer taste and commercial initiative within the sphere of export pottery.

[15] Cf. esp. Stibbe 1978, 1984a, 1989, 1994; Pelagatti 1989; Pelagatti and Stibbe 1988, 1990. Cf., most recently, the publication of black-glazed fine ware sherds from the recently-completed Laconia Survey (Catling 1996). When he compiled his *corpus*, Nafissi had available to him only Stibbe's published studies of black-glazed kantharoi, stamnoi and certain types of kraters (mainly stirrup-kraters, volute-kraters and krateriskoi) augmented by a few other finds from published excavations: Nafissi 1989, 143 n. 254.

[16] Stibbe 1994, 16, 73–4, 78.

[17] This statement is true of both types of stemmed cup, the canonical and the 'Doric' cup: Stibbe 1994, 75.

[18] Cf. the notable amounts of non-figured ware at Tocra in Cyrenaica and in Sicily: Boardman and Hayes 1966, 81–95, 117–17; 1973, 39–41; Pelagatti and Stibbe 1990, 123–247. On its influence in the Peloponnese, see the brief discussion and references in Catling 1996, 34.

[19] Cf. Stibbe 1994, 16. There is much material awaiting systematic publication in the storerooms of the Sparta Museum – for example, from the British excavations earlier this century (cf. Catling 1996, 34) and from the rich votive pit associated with the heroon of Agamemnon at Amyklai, which contained *inter alia* about 2,000 kylix feet. The 'home' sample is also usually more continuous and representative than those at foreign sites, where the pattern of finds may often be irregular. At Selinos, for example, the finds include 10 fine kraters but hardly any other Lakonian pottery; at Taras, in contrast, there are numerous drinking cups and aryballoi but no kraters: Stibbe 1989, 20.

[20] All-black stirrup kraters (Groups 2 and 3), large kraters, krateriskoi, black-glazed cups with flat base (Group D), and cups with low base-moulding (Group E) continued into the fifth century: Stibbe 1989, 42–3, 45, 49–50; 1994, 66, 69. Cylindrical mugs (Group E), their 'successors', the one-handled mugs (Groups F and G), and possibly the black-glazed small bowls without handles (Groups C and E), continued into the fourth century: Stibbe 1994, 42, 46, 93; Catling 1996, esp. 39, 48. Miniature vases of various kinds continued from the seventh until at least the third century: Catling 1996, 84–5.

[21] Cf. the silences in Fitzhardinge 1980, ch. 3 and Hooker 1980, ch. 2.

[22] Note, in particular, the surviving female protomes, handles and ornaments of animals and mythical creatures published in Wace 1908/9; Lamb 1926/7; Buschor and von Massow 1927; Droop 1929; Herfort-Koch 1986.

[23] See esp. Politis 1936; Johannowsky 1974; Fitzhardinge 1980, 108–16; Rolley 1982, 31–47; Herfort-Koch 1986, 13–19; Stibbe 1989, 59–65. Note also the literary evidence for the bronze krater which the Spartans sent as a gift for King Kroisos of Lydia (Hdt. 1.70).

[24] The thesis of Lakonian manufacture was originally developed by Rumpf 1957 and Gehrig 1971 and has been defended more recently by Cartledge 1985, 1988; Stibbe 1989, 59–67. The Corinthian hypothesis advanced esp. by Gjødesen 1963, but for a time thought to have been refuted by Jucker 1966, 107–12, has recently been revived by Croissant 1988, 150–66. Advocates of a South Italian origin include Vallet and Villard 1955; Rolley 1958, 1982, 52–71; Herfort-Koch 1986, 70–4.

[25] Popovic 1956; Diehl 1964a, nos. B26, 28–30; cf. Griffith 1988, 19 n. 7.

[26] Stibbe 1989, 60–7, with 141 n. 223. Gjødesen 1963, 338 had earlier proposed a similar date in terms of Corinthian manufacture.

[27] Herfort-Koch 1986, nos. K104, K137–9, K147–50. Rolley does not comment upon Herfort-Koch's dating of these ornaments in his brief review of her monograph (1989, 352–3), though elsewhere (*RA* 1993, 391) he notes that his dates are generally often higher than hers: the dating of Greek bronzes is inevitably an inexact science. It might be argued, in defence of Rolley's case for a sudden official prohibition of foreign traders, that it is significant that these last vessels were restricted to sites in mainland Greece accessible without overseas transport. But this would be to forget that even in its heyday much

Lakonian vessel production never found its way outside the Greek mainland; and, if it is conceded that some bronze vessel production survived the effects of state intervention, this then raises the question why Lakonian bronze vessel production then ceased entirely after 520.

[28] See esp. Karagiorga 1965. The mirrors are listed in the general study of 'Caryatid' mirrors by Keene Congdon 1981, 46; but cf. the severe criticisms of her work by Rolley 1986a, 378–84.

[29] The last extant example, from Sparta itself (Sparta Museum no. 594), is given an early fifth-century date by Fitzhardinge 1980, 100; Congdon 1981, no. 28; Steinhauer (n.d.), 28 fig. 6; Pipili 1987, no. 216j; although Herfort-Koch 1986, K68, dates it to 520–500.

[30] Herrmann 1964; Rolley 1982, 39 and 76 n. 201.

[31] The statistics in TABLE 1 represent the results of my own trawl through art-historical studies and excavation reports. Owing to the scattered character of modern publications and scholarly uncertainties or disagreements concerning many matters of dating and identifications, the statistics are to be taken as indicative rather than definitive; but the overall chronological pattern is unlikely to be inaccurate.

[32] On the continuation of the statuettes into the late fifth century, Rolley 1977, 129 n. 17; 1986b, 113. On possible fourth-century work, cf. the helmeted nude hoplite (Sparta Museum no. 970), which Rolley (1986b), Catalogue no. 24, dates not earlier than the second half of the fifth century, and Steinhauer (n.d.), 36 fig.10a–b, assigns to the early fourth century.

[33] For the first approach, Nafissi 1989, 75; 1991, 253. For the second approach, Wace 1929, 250.

[34] Although the numbers of surviving bronze statuettes are rather small, one must remember that they were considerably more susceptible than the leads to post-depositional factors (corrosion, plunder, melting-down by temple officials) which have considerably reduced their numbers.

[35] TABLE 2 is based upon the figures in Wace 1929, 251–2, but with a revised chronology. The excavators based their classification of the leads upon their chronology for Lakonian I–VI pottery. The chronology used here is a compromise between that of the excavators, the revision proposed by Boardman 1963 and the recent reconsideration by Cavanagh and Laxton 1984.

[36] Pompili 1986; Nafissi 1989, 82, Graph 4b.

[37] e.g. Cook 1962, 156; Holladay 1977, 116; Rolley 1977, 128; Pompili 1986; Nafissi 1989, 77.

[38] On these changes, Lamb 1969, 144–5 and 150–1; Rolley 1986b, 169; Snodgrass 1989/90.

[39] Attic-influenced pottery: Stibbe 1989, 45 – large kraters; 59 – handles of column kraters; 1994, 43 and 46–7 – one-handled mugs; 93 – small handleless bowls. Cf. also the numerous points of influence noted in Catling 1996, 88. Imitative bronze statuettes: Rolley 1977, 129 with nn. 16–17.

[40] Leon 1968; Rolley 1982, 76.

[41] This suggestion has been made, for example, regarding Lakonian I pottery and the terracotta relief vessels (cf. Fitzhardinge 1980, 26 and 54). The longevity of the latter is disputed, with some scholars (Christou 1964b;

Andersen 1977, 62; Stibbe 1989, 142 n. 248) suggesting a chronological range between *c*. 625 and *c*. 550, others (Lauter-Bufe 1974, 89; Fitzhardinge 1980, 54) a range of no more than thirty years.

[42] A case in point is the demise of one of the black-figure workshops around 555–550 following the disappearance of its leader, the Naukratis Painter. The departure of its remaining craftsmen to join the workshop of the Hunt Painter has been interpreted as an enforced relocation closer to the coast of Lakonia, due to the expulsion of foreign merchants from Sparta itself (Nafissi 1989, 76). This hypothesis is unnecessary, since the departure of the workshop's personnel may be satisfactorily explained by a weakness in its internal division of labour (Pompili 1986). It seems that the Naukratis Painter appropriated to himself the principal decoration of the workshop's painted ware, thus leaving his assistants unable to continue such projects in his absence.

[43] Cartledge 1976; 1979, 183–4. Cf. the potter's kiln excavated in the region of the Spartan village of Mesoa, in association with remains of a house wall and a tumulus mound containing a burial group of four cist graves marked by a terracotta relief amphora of *c*. 600 or perhaps slightly later (Christou 1964a). Note, however, the *caveat* entered by Steinhauer (1972, 244 n. 15), that 'the Spartan graves published by Christou as archaic are, we fear, very much more recent'.

[44] See Stibbe 1972, 11–12; Nafissi 1989, 76; and the refs. in nn. 36 and 40.

[45] Stibbe 1972, 12 n. 2; 1984b; Pompili 1986, 66.

[46] The impermanence of the phenomenon is indicated by the fact that it is typically described as *xenelasiai*, in the plural: Thuc. 1.144, 2.39; Aristoph. *Birds* 1012–13; Xen. *Lak. Pol.* 14.4; Plato *Protagoras* 342C; *Laws* 950B, 953E.

[47] Besides the early British excavations at Artemis Orthia, the Acropolis and the Menelaion cited in n. 5, cf. the more recent Menelaion excavations reported in *JHS, Arch. Reports* 23 (1977) 24–42 and in *Lakonikai Spoudai* 2 (1975) 258–69; 3 (1977) 408–16; 8 (1986) 205–16; and the older Greek and German work at the Amyklaion reported in *Archaiologikê Ephemeris* (1892) 1–26; Buschor and von Massow (1927).

[48] Several chapters of the final publication of the original Artemis Orthia excavations (Dawkins 1929) either give a complete inventory or specify exact numbers of finds. But not all the chapters follow this practice (e.g. chs. 2 and 7 on the pottery and the bronzes) and the finds from the early work at the Acropolis, Menelaion and other sites are much less well published. Publication of the finds from Tsountas' 1890 excavations at the Amyklaion was similarly incomplete: Calligas 1992, 31–3 and 41.

[49] The implications of these statistics are discussed in Hodkinson 1998.

[50] There are already some propitious signs for the future. Calligas (1992, 41) has promised a more extensive publication of material, especially the bronzes, from the Amyklaion. The final publication of the recent Menelaion excavations should provide a more complete coverage of the rich new finds from that site. Finally, the proposed foundation of a Sparta Study Centre by the British School augurs well for the possibilities of a systematic new study and publication of material from the older excavations.

3

SIXTH-CENTURY LAKONIAN VASE-PAINTING
Continuities and discontinuities with the 'Lykourgan' ethos

Anton Powell

In the Greek literary record, there is little which throws immediate light on the general nature of Spartan culture in the mid-sixth century. A few highly pejorative remarks in Herodotos and Thucydides, describing a time before the coming of εὐνομία ('good order'), *may* reflect the period.[1] In this paper it is argued that scenes of human activity painted on Lakonian vases give a more revealing, as well as a more sympathetic, view of the age; that they suggest a society which was not austere but which had characteristics which were to shape the severe Lykourgan* regime.

Many of the vases identified by scholars as Lakonian black-figure were found in the area of Sparta. The other great find area, more important numerically than Lakonia, is Samos: in Stibbe's survey of Lakonian black-figure vases the ratio of Samian to Lakonian provenance is some 114:45.[2] Political links between Samos and Sparta in the sixth century are made clear by Herodotos.[3] I follow the consensus of modern scholarship in dating the Lakonian black-figure vases to the sixth century and, for the most part, to the second and third quarters thereof.[4] This consensual chronology rests in turn on the dating of

---

*Uses of the term 'Lykourgan' in this paper do not imply the historicity of Lykourgos; they refer to the famous austere culture within the Spartan citizen body.

Certain works are cited by author's name only:

Amyx = Amyx, D.A. (1988) *Corinthian Vase-Painting of the Archaic Period*

Pipili = Pipili, M. (1987) *Laconian Iconography of the Sixth Century BC.*

Stibbe = Stibbe, C.M. (1972) *Lakonische Vasenmaler des 6. Jhs. v. Chr.*

Where possible I have referred to vases by the numbers assigned by Pipili, for the sake of accessibility. In other cases, as indicated, I have used the numbering of Stibbe.

Corinthian and Attic vases, the imprecision of which dating is widely
known. I shall not, therefore, try to date any particular Lakonian vase
to a particular decade. However, the approximate general chronology
of the Lakonian vases has confirmation of another kind. One such vase
depicts, perhaps in an African setting, an authoritative figure named
on the vase as Arkesilas; whether this is, as usually thought, Arkesilas II of
Cyrene, or even Arkesilas I, a date in or near the first half of the sixth
century is appropriate. [5]

That the number of surviving decorated Lakonian vases of the sixth
century is low, 360+9 as catalogued by Stibbe, reminds us of the need
to be very careful with arguments from silence.[6] (The number of
surviving decorated vases from archaic Corinth is several times as
great.[7]) The small number of producers – Stibbe assigns names to
fourteen – also invites caution when we enquire whether themes which
may appear to predominate in their output represent general taste
within a Spartan clientele. Whether the vases were made under the
direct supervision of Spartiates, or of *perioikoi*, or of others in Lakonia,
two preliminary considerations, taken together, suggest that we may
expect the vases to reflect Spartiate culture. Many are found at Sparta
itself; the paintings show males of a very wealthy class and so, if
modelled to any extent on local manhood, are more likely to reflect
Spartiates than *perioikoi*. Other possible points of contact, between the
vase-paintings and what we know from elsewhere about the Spartiates,
form a main theme of this paper.

In the shapes of Lakonian vases much independence has been observed.[8] There is agreement, however, that – in Pipili's words (84) –
'the Laconian vases with figured decoration…were indebted mainly to
Corinth for both their style and iconography'. [9] Corinthian influence is
particularly evident in early Lakonian vases, those of the Naukratis
and Boreads Painters (Pipili, ibid.). The Rider Painter, in Stibbe's
judgment, was hardly affected by Attic work,[10] and only with the Hunt
Painter, he observes, does Attic influence first become apparent.[11] As
to the choice of subjects for illustration, there are also interesting
differences between Lakonian and Corinthian vases. The comparison
between Lakonian and Corinthian work is central to the argument of
this paper. Allowances must be made for the fact that vases with
particular functions and shapes are differently represented as a proportion within the two sets of material; thus kylikes form a larger part
of the Lakonian remains than of the Corinthian. Since vase-type
affected the choice of painted image, a thorough exploration of possibly

significant differences between Lakonian and Corinthian iconography would involve a detailed and wide-ranging taxonomy within both sets, which would be beyond the scope of the present study. In this respect some allowance has been made here, but still the author runs the risks of the pioneer. Apparent differences in the two sets of iconography have been explored helpfully by Pipili; one may now try to add to her findings.

It may be helpful to summarise at this point, even though that is partly to anticipate what follows. Scenes connected with the Trojan War were less favoured by Lakonian than by Corinthian vase-painters.[12] Spartans of the sixth century seem, unlike the consumers of Corinthian vases, to have been at least as fond of stories with Boiotian and Thessalian connections.[13] The myth of Herakles, common in Corinthian vase-painting, appears on a higher proportion of Lakonian vases.[14] Athletics may have been less favoured by Lakonian artists than by archaic artists elsewhere,[15] though one athletic activity forms an exception, as we shall see.[16] Athletic scenes surviving on Corinthian vases occur particularly on aryballoi.[17] Among Lakonian figured vases aryballoi number only six in Stibbe's catalogue.[18] However, a well-represented form of Lakonian vase is the kylix, and the kylix was thought an appropriate setting for the two scenes of athletics which survive (below, n. 25). On other points of difference from Corinthian art: Lakonian artists had a distinctive liking for enthroned figures, as Pipili observed;[19] in addition it now appears that musical instruments are shown more frequently, as a proportion, in the scenes of komos, and that scenes of symposion occur on a far higher proportion of Lakonian than of Corinthian vases. Most intriguing perhaps, and, on our present state of knowledge, all but peculiar to Lakonia are certain flying, winged but largely anthropomorphic, figures, to be considered below.[20] Lakonian pictures, then, were not a mere provincial echo of Corinth. We can hope for Lakonian vase-painting to offer some reflections of Spartan society in particular. That Lakonian painters often deviated from Corinthian may add to the significance even of those spheres in which Corinthian norms *were* followed.

First, let us consider features of the archaic vase-painting which can be seen as substantially *coinciding*, on the face of it, with the ideals of Lykourgan Sparta as they appear from literary testimony of the classical period and later. The vase-painters' reluctance to write is a clear case. There is far less writing on Lakonian than on Corinthian vases; for the Lakonian, Stibbe records seven cases, for the Corinthian, Amyx counts some 156.[21] Such is the scarcity of surviving written records from classical Sparta that the question whether the Spartiates were illiterate has been addressed, rightly, by modern scholarship, albeit to be answered in the negative.[22] The mistrust of writing can readily be aligned with Lykourgan ideals.[23] The absence of almost all forms of athletic scene from the vases also coincides interestingly with the Lykourgan ethos. We think of how the numbers of victorious Spartan athletes in the Olympic games, for long spectacularly predominant, appear to have fallen away in the sixth century (see Appendix) and to have remained low through the late archaic and classical periods. Post-classical anecdote has Spartans expressing contempt for mere athletic, that is non-military, feats.[24] This, however, might reflect the rationalisation of failure rather than abstention on principle; compare the comment of Aristotle that the Spartans in his day were losers in athletic as well as military contests (*Pol.* 1338b). In earlier classical literature there is an apparent exception: boxing. The Xenophontic *Lak. Pol.* (4.6) tells of Spartans boxing each other from rivalry; there is also at least one reference in Plato (*Laws* 633b; cf. *Protag.* 342bc) to boxing in Sparta. On the archaic vases, too, there is an exception – the same one; two vases show boxing.[25] Depiction of boxing among surviving Corinthian vases is confined to a single, dubious, instance.[26]

Two prominent elements of the Lykourgan system noted by non-Spartan contemporaries, religiosity and the use of music, have been discussed at length in recent studies.[27] Religion served classical Sparta by underpinning the obedience required of Spartiates. The kings were of divine descent through Herakles; Apollo had approved the setting-up of the Lykourgan system; oracular guidance validated numerous decisions of state. Religious themes feature largely in our vase-paintings, though we should note the skew towards religious find-spots, especially on Samos. Vases may have been chosen for offering at the shrine of Hera because of religious elements in their composition. Aspects of religion in Lakonian art will be treated below.

On music, it was in the late archaic period that Pratinas of Phleious described the Spartans as like cicadas, ready for a chorus (*ap.* Athen. 633a). We are familiar with the use of music as Spartan troops marched into battle in Thucydides' day (and later?), and of chanting and dancing at the militaristic festival of the Gymnopaidiai.[28] In the *Laws*, while suggesting that his Spartan interlocutor is saturated (διακορής) with the songs of Tyrtaios, the philosopher lays down that in his ideal city (in many ways an imaginary super-Sparta, as I argue elsewhere)[29] all the principles of that long work are to be uttered in song (664b). Plato writes of the need for the 'whole city never to cease working on the whole city with songs of enchantment from itself to itself' (665c). Music is a prominent feature of our vases. Many vases portray komos – thirty-one, as listed by Pipili (118 f.). The komasts were not dancing abstractly; lyres and pipes are shown accompanying them, on nine of those thirty-one.[30] (Among komos scenes on Corinthian vases, the proportion showing instruments is much lower – about one in twenty.)[31] On the famous 'Mitra Vase' two female pipe-players regale a symposion (*Fig.* 1). But we shall see that in these two interrelated things, religion and music, although there is a community of strong interest, as between the ethos of the vases and that of austere Sparta, there is also a marked difference of application.

The distinctively Lakonian winged youths accompany human figures (and in one case probably that of a divinity). To be clear about a distinction: we are not now concerned with winged, bearded, running figures: the so-called *Knielauf* figures, which are familiar also from

Fig. 1. The 'Mitra Vase'; Lakonian cup attributed to Arkesilas Painter, found on Samos. Pipili no. 196; Samos K1203, K1541, K2402 and Berlin 478X, 460X. (Drawing after Pipili.)

Fig. 2.
The 'Symposion-of-
Five Vase'; Lakonian
cup attributed to
Naukratis Painter.
Pipili no. 194; Louvre
E667.

Corinthian art. The *Knielauf* figures occur in isolation, of interest in
their own right. In contrast the winged youths are shown as small and
contingent, accompanying larger figures 'in complete scenes which
would have made sense without them' (Pipili, 64). The youths have
wings on their shoulders, and in some cases at or near their feet;
otherwise they are anthropomorphic, but are shown in some cases
flying and more-or-less horizontal. They have masculine chests but
lack beards. We can see four of these winged youths on the Mitra Vase,
at a symposion.[32] They appear also on the Symposion-of-Five vase,
where they alternate with other, bird-like, airborne figures identified
as sirens (*Fig.* 2). How to interpret the winged youths? They are not
the quirk of an individual artist: they are shown by three or four of the
five main painters.[33] A theory which has won little support is that these
figures represent the souls of the departed in a feast of the dead, a
Totenmahl.[34] Against such a theory may be the generally cheerful context. 'Context' in two senses. The vases on which such scenes are
shown tend to be cups, associated with happy, earthly occasions. And
the details of the Mitra Vase suggest a setting anything but sombre. In
addition to the female flute-players, there is a youth presented with a
cock, the symbol of homo-erotic courtship. Elsewhere on the vase we
may see his lover, with long hair, beard, and wreath, catching the cock,
with the aid of a tethered decoy. Behind a pomegranate tree lurks
a cock of implausible size. There is a scene of komos, in a different
register of the vase. Pipili (54) notes that '...most of the symposia with
winged daemons are shown together with komos scenes...'.

Fig. 3. Lakonian cup
by Rider Painter.
Pipili no. 214; British
Museum B1.

A winged youth is typically shown in close connection with an individual, sometimes presenting him or her with a garland. Similar
winged creatures attend a very large female, presumably a goddess, on
a vase of the Naukratis Painter (Pipili no. 101). Also there are three
vases on which a winged youth accompanies a young man, who sits
serene on horseback; these are the 'Lakonian rider' vases (*Fig.* 3 and
Pipili nos. 213–15;), after which the Rider Painter is named.[35] All three
show water-birds; Pipili notes that Orthia had her shrine in an area
close to the River Eurotas, exposed to flooding and indeed called
Marshes (Λίμναι).[36] As a control on the significance of winged youths,
we look for the sort of human figure they do *not* attend. They do not
accompany any komast, so far as I am aware, even though – as we have
seen – they can be shown on the same vase as a komast, in a different
register. In the Symposion-of-Five, the 'sirens' and the winged youths
join forces with a single human who brings, to the only symposiast
without a supernatural attendant, wine in one hand and a garland in
the other. It appears, then, that the winged youth is a mark of high
status. But the analogy with the human servant, and the frequency of
these winged figures – the four on the Mitra Vase attend three or four
different individuals – suggest that the status in question need not be
quite the most august. On the Mitra Vase, the flying youth who attends
the mitra-wearing woman points to her lips, the lips with which she is
playing her double pipe. Her musical skill, we are being told, is what
makes her eminent. The other female pipe-player on the vase is
herself attended by a winged figure, in this case one proffering

125

a wreath. Was the supernatural association devalued, if it could be assigned to females in a sympotic setting, who were quite likely foreign and hired? Or, rather than degrading the supernatural aura, does the Mitra Vase perhaps fit with our evidence for the high importance of music in Spartan life?

Few may wish to adopt the suggestion, put up to be refuted by Stibbe, that the mature (bearded) participants in the Symposion-of-Five vase are five ephors. However, an objection raised by Stibbe (70) should be set aside. Stibbe rejected the identification with ephors on the grounds that the winged figures showed the scene not to be one from real life. This may involve an important misunderstanding of Spartan culture. Both Plato and Aristotle found it noteworthy that Spartans (of the classical period) used, as a term of praise for people, θεῖος (or rather, in Lakonian, σεῖος): 'godlike', 'superhuman'. In the *Meno* (99d) we read (Sokrates speaking): 'The Spartans, whenever they celebrate a good man, say that he is θεῖος ἀνήρ'. Similarly Aristotle writes: '…just as the Spartans habitually call him; whenever they very much admire someone, they say he is σεῖος ἀνήρ' (*NE* 1145a, cf. Plat. *Laws* 626c).

A theme of Pipili's study is that many of the scenes of Lakonian vase-painting refer to cult (e.g. 83); for example, the Mitra Vase may show part of a temple (71),[37] the water-birds on the rider vases may refer to Orthia, the riders themselves may echo the procession of riders at the Hyakinthia (76). The finding of figured vases at Orthia's shrine undeniably makes a connection with cult. But cult itself serves secular needs, not least the compulsion to display wealth. The painters' reluctance to show flying youths with komasts, those oft-portrayed performers of cult, suggests that the flying youth says of the figure it accompanies not simply 'he/she is with divinity'; rather the exalted nature of the accompanied figures – goddess, symposiasts, riders, and inspired female musicians – implies 'divinity is with them'. At one symposion, as we have seen, the flying youths are made co-ordinate with a human cup-bearer. Compare the way that in classical Sparta divinity could be subordinated to the secular needs of the authorities.[38]

Herakles, the most popular mythical figure in Lakonian art of the sixth century, is shown on some seventeen vases (Pipili 1–13, 83). Herakles is popular also in archaic Corinthian vase-painting, but not to this extent, proportionally; Amyx (628–32) catalogues slightly more than forty occurrences of Herakles on Corinthian vases. It may be tempting to see the extraordinary concentration on Herakles in sixth-century Lakonia as reflecting Spartan isolationism, a kind of *xenelasia* of myth, with only that myth allowed which did most to validate the Spartan polity. Such an approach might not be wholly wrong. But, as has already been observed, various non-Homeric myths set in central and northern Greece are treated in sixth-century Lakonian art at least as often as Homeric and Trojan material.[39] As a proportion of the surviving material, references to these myths of central and northern Greece on the Lakonian vases seem to exceed by far those in Corinthian vase-painting (Amyx 644 f.). Pipili plausibly suggests (83) a revulsion not against all non-Spartan mythical themes but against the cycle which had at its centre a Mycenaean, by implication Argive, overlordship of Greece, at a period when Sparta was pushing to dominate the Peloponnese and Argos was the great obstacle. Sensitivity on this subject would help to explain the conspicuous sixth-century adventure as Sparta claimed to retrieve from Tegea the bones of Agamemnon's son.[40]

It would be wrong to describe the emphasis on Herakles only in modern secularizing terms, as purely an assertion of how long-established were Sparta and her Heraklid kings in Greek story – though we can be sure that Spartans in the classical period were interested in claims about the great age of their state.[41] The role of Herakles in archaic Lakonian art coheres with other features of that art which we have already touched on. Herakles, like the Dioskouroi (shown several times, in the bronze of Athena Khalkioikos and by Bathykles at Amyklai)[42] and Helen (shown, probably, twice on a single archaic stone sculpture and certainly on the Amyklai throne),[43] combined strong Spartan connections with a hybrid existence on the religious plane: divine ancestry, earthly life and death, promotion to divine existence thereafter. The altar-tomb of Hyakinthos, human companion of Apollo, had sculptural decoration which portrayed other deities and humans introduced to them (Paus. III.19.3–5). The sculptor showed the translation to heaven of Hyakinthos, of his sister Polyboia, and of Herakles. The 'daughters of Thestios' mentioned in this connection by Pausanias included Leda, and perhaps Althaia (said to have had children by both Ares and Dionysos) and Klytia (lover of Helios).[44] On our vases the winged figures, 'sirens' as well as flying youths, give a supernatural dimension to several earthly scenes. Spartan thoughts about the interpenetration of divine and human spheres are also reflected in the liberal application of the term σεῖος. In addition we read of the supposed descent of the earthly Spartan kings from Herakles, which had perhaps its clearest celebration in the Spartan royal funerals of the classical period, more suitable for heroes than men, according to the Xenophontic *Lak. Pol.* (15.9).[45] It could be claimed that Sparta's kings had an aura which made even enemies on the battlefield unwilling, out of fear and reverence, to attack them.[46] Lykourgos was worshipped as a god. In the *Laws* (634de), Plato commends classical Sparta for its doctrine that everything about the Spartan constitution was divinely arranged. From vase-painting of the early and mid-sixth century, through sculpture later in that century, to literary evidence on the classical period and beyond, the theme of divine relations with humanity in Lakonia is continuous and prominent even in our far-from-copious material. The interaction of divine and human was, of course, an interest of very many Greeks in early and classical times. We are reminded of the judgement of a distinguished student of Greek religion: that (to paraphrase) Spartan belief was Hellenic, only more so.[47]

We move now to certain contrasting features of Lakonian art: those which, at least at first sight, may seem to be at odds with the austere Lykourgan system. The Lakonian vases do not show a consistent interest in warfare. Of the five vase-painters who (on Stibbe's analysis), with their associates, account for the great majority of our material, three – the Arkesilas Painter, the Boreads Painter and the Rider Painter – have left no surviving image of a foot-soldier. There are none of the rows of marching hoplites common on aryballoi from Corinth. Occasionally two or three warriors with hoplite equipment are shown fighting in alignment, in a way which might be artistic shorthand for a phalanx (Stibbe nos. 36, 206b, 214). The Lakonian vases which do show warriors are assigned to – or associated with – the Naukratis Painter (six)[48] and the Hunt Painter (eight).[49] This sparing treatment of military subjects is, of course, the opposite of what we might have expected if we believed Thucydides (and later writers) on the extreme antiquity of the Spartan constitution.[50]

Other non-austere features are linked by the themes of fun and self-indulgence, in particular among the wealthy. Pipili notes (71 f.) that nineteen Lakonian vases of the sixth century show symposia. This may actually exceed the total of surviving Corinthian portrayals of this subject;[51] in any case it far exceeds the Corinthian material as a proportion. There are signs of extravagance in furniture and fabric. On the Mitra Vase, for example, a symposion is attended by two female pipe players, expensively dressed; one has a headdress which is usually identified as a Lydian mitra. Alkman famously described the wearing of the mitra by young women of Sparta: μίτρα Λυδία, νεανίδων... ἄγαλμα.[52]

It is now widely accepted that the most characteristic gathering of the austere Sparta, the *syssition*, was both a pointed rejection, and an adaptation, of the aristocratic symposion.[53] The symposion had been, to coin a term, lykourgised. For the principle, compare the Lykourgan institution of the *hippeis*, an elite group, named after an aristocratic symbol, but seemingly not owning horses (Appendix, below). The Lykourgan physical training for war may itself be a mutation of aristocratic training for athletics. Lakonian vases, with their numerous convivial scenes, suggest how ingrained in pre-Lykourgan Sparta was the idea of symposion. Images of symposion were, of course, particularly appropriate on cups, and cups seem to be the most common Lakonian vase-types to survive. But this last fact in itself suggests something about the ethos of the Lakonia which produced the cups; in proportion Corinth seems to have produced fewer (cf. Amyx, 462–4). The distinctive local feature of these symposia, the flying youths, confirms that in this sphere it was not merely foreign images which influenced Lakonian vase-painters. Intimations given by Alkman of luxurious parties (and of social division) are borne out by the vases; for wealthy Spartans, the symposion was probably a prominent part of their own lives, in the years before austerity.[54]

Lakonian vase-painters, like Corinthian, expected their clients to have a taste for scenes of drunken revelry, of komos; komos-vases form a similar proportion of the surviving material from each territory (cf. Seeberg 1971, 71). Seeberg pointed to a possibly mythic element in the revelling scenes (73) – the commonness of drinking-horns. He suggested that the horn also had rustic or barbarian associations; it was perhaps meant to hint at a link with the Thracian Dionysos. Seeberg raised the question how far komos as portrayed ever happened (74 f., 79 f.). He called attention to the fatness of many dancers, and observed that in Corinthian painting false bulk is often shown as derived from folds of clothing (72). We should add the buttock-caps worn by dancers in Corinthian scenes (73) – and also by participants in the highly sexual revelry of a Lakonian vase to be discussed shortly. Perhaps the purpose of the caps was, as with the folds of clothing, to give a bulbousness required by the genre. Buttock-caps and clothes-as-padding may help with the question how far these komos scenes were understood as mythical. If the aim had been simply to show jolly fatties dancing in another world, another time, the simplest thing for the artist, and the most satisfying thing for the consumer, would surely have been to show genuine fatness. To depict carefully, if only in a minority of cases, the mechanisms of false fatness surely implies that we have here a known, no doubt contemporary, human activity with dress for a special occasion. The scenes of komos probably represent in a stereotyped and exaggerated way some historical festival.[55]

Drunken revels, and the complaisant portrayal of fatness, seem unLykourgan in several ways. The sombre Spartan character Megillos in Plato's *Laws* (637a–b) emerges from his silence to contrast the general intoxication he had witnessed at 'our colony Taras' with the sobriety of Sparta, where there were no symposia and (as Kritias also attests)[56] there was no day set aside for heavy communal drinking. Megillos states that any Spartan, if he met someone engaging in drunken *komos* (κωμάζοντί τινι μετὰ μέθης), would immediately inflict the severest punishment; not even the celebration of Dionysia would be accepted as an excuse. On fatness, contrast the dietary restrictions upon classical Spartiates ([Xen.] *Lak. Pol.* 5.3; Ar. *Pol.*1294b) and the late, unreliable reports of Spartans punished for being fat.[57] Sobriety and leanness had clear importance for a community which pursued military excellence. We think of the moralising vignette in Plato's *Republic* (556d) in which a lean pauper sees a bloated oligarch on the battlefield and concludes that the oligarch is an ineffective soldier. Drunkenness at a festival, suggested on our vases, had more serious military implications than excess in individuals or at a symposion. The timing of a festival was predictable; a drunken festival, by incapacitating an entire community, would have presented enemies with a fine *kairos*.[58]

The images of komos on Lakonian vases suggest not just that the Spartans practised communal drinking but that they did not mind outsiders knowing about it.[59] Spartans of the classical period were noted for their sensitivity about the image of themselves projected abroad.[60] Yet on the komos vases we get an impression that was very different from the messages which classical and post-classical Sparta wished to project. At the Gymnopaidiai, in the presence of foreigners,[61] Spartans displayed physical endurance amid intense summer heat;[62] the cult of Orthia involved boys' endurance of flogging.[63] These vases seem to come from a Sparta not yet intensely interested in advertising that it was militarily unapproachable. However, different though the festivals were, their prominence in our source material – literary and iconographic respectively – is something which later Sparta has in common with the Lakonia of the sixth century.

Another kind of physical pleasure, again with no obvious military application, is depicted on a fragmentary cup recovered at Sparta, at the shrine of Orthia (*Fig.* 4 = Pipili no. 179).[64] In the judgment of

Fig. 4. Lakonian cup found at shrine of Orthia; now in Sparta Museum. Pipili no. 179. (Drawing from Lane 1933/4.)

Stibbe (221 f.), this vase is from the workshop of the Naukratis Painter, and was made *c.* 580–575. From the treatment of sexual matters on the vase it may be possible now to produce some tempting ideas about the origins of Lykourgan practices. We must try to keep in mind that, in the relevant sexual aspects, this vase is to date unique within the Lakonian material; inferences drawn from it must be tentative. A collection of revellers includes one man who is sexually penetrating a person on all fours; another figure, either a satyr or a man in satyr costume, implicitly has sex in mind while chasing someone else. Apart from the satyr-figure, the figures seem to fall into two categories. Two bearded men wear cloaks; neither of them is dancing, one of them is the penetrator. The second group of figures, which includes the two who are sexually approached, comprises four people who seem to be beardless and naked, apart from buttock-caps.[65] The two members of this group who are not sexually approached appear to be dancing. Now, is the penetrated person female or male? The question is of some importance. Lane thought that it was a woman (1933/4, 160); so did Stibbe (222). Seeberg made a case for agnosticism (1966, 66). Lane's drawing has a clear if slight swelling in the area of the breast. However, such swelling is not visible on his or Pipili's photograph, nor was I able to detect any in examining the vase-fragments (albeit through their glass case) at the Sparta Museum. Both of the virtually-naked and thus apparently related dancers to the right of the copulating pair have prominent bellies, more suggestive of a male komast than of a fe-male.[66] The penetrated person seems at least as likely to be male as female. Spartans in the classical period were mocked, even by the friendly Aristophanes, for their degree of male homosexuality.[67] More sober sources confirm that pederasty, and sexual pairing between men, were prominent, if problematic, institutions of classical Sparta (see below).

To clarify the politics of the sexual act shown on this vase, it may help to consider now the scene at the left of the vase-fragments. The satyr-figure, with prodigious penis,[68] is aligned with the two standing adult men by his possession of a beard. He strides after a near-naked, beardless person who has a buttock-cap. Of this latter figure Seeberg wrote: 'fear...may be drastically indicated by a shower of dots under his (her) buttocks...' (1966, 66). In fact the marks are rather more substantial and elongated than dots; see *Fig.* 4 above and the photograph in Stibbe (pl. 26.7). (Comparable at first sight is the Lakonian vase (Pipili no. 92) where a Promethean figure, whose chest is being assaulted by a bird, has below his buttocks many elongated marks and directly beneath them a pile. However, the marks here proceed from the chest wound and represent blood.) Do we have here an early case of Spartan interest in the visible effects of that key emotion, physical fear? Were there χέσαντες, as we might call them, forerunners of the τρέσαντες ('Tremblers') of classical times who were themselves named after a florid manifestation of fear? The significance of all this for our komos vase is that the scene to the left is not of free bonding but of imminent rape.

Was the ancient viewer of the vase to imagine that the fleeing person would have fled any form of copulation in this festival context, or was it the monstrous appearance of the pursuer which alone caused fear? We return to the actual copulators. The penetrator holds over the back of his mate what may seem to be a distended arm; even though he leans back, his penis partly withdrawn, the arm, or whatever, still reaches half-way along the back of the partner. The vase-painter is capable of distorting an arm, as on the reveller immediately to the right of the coupling pair. But no arm on the vase-fragment appears so exaggerated as this projection from the penetrator. The other arm of the penetrator is of normal proportions. Why should the arm be stretched along the back? It is clear, both in the photographs of Lane and Pipili and also in autopsy, that the arm, or whatever, is in the air just above – separated from and not gripping – the back of the partner. Indeed, the middle of the back of a naked person would not be an obvious place to grip. Also, on other figures of the vase there is some clear, if crude, attempt to represent hands as distinct from arms: in contrast, on the projection above the partner's back there is no such representation *at the end*. Rather the projection tapers smoothly at its end, whereas some *half way along* the projection there is – even more clearly in autopsy than in the photographs – a swelling consistent with a hand. I suggest that what is held above the back is not an arm but a stick. In the hand of the reveller immediately to the right can be seen a stick, or some other long, straight object held aloft; this is clear in Lane's photograph and clearer in autopsy.[69] Among the other features of the scene are dark parallel stripes on the flank of the passive figure. No such stripes appear elsewhere on the fragments of this vase. On other Lakonian vases similar marks denote the prominent ribs of men or animals;[70] the marks here may very well be merely a representation of ribs, perhaps with a comment on the animal posture adopted by the person. If, on the other hand, these were stripes from whipping administered when the recipient was upright, we might better understand why the tip of the projection from the active partner ends above dead-centre of the marks. The interpretation of the marks cannot be pressed. However, that the projection is a stick seems likelier than not, especially when we remember in particular that the near-naked figure to the left is also involved in a scene of unwanted sexual attention, and in general that stories of Lakonia involve rape, attempted rape, and abduction to a marked degree.[71]

On Corinthian komos vases, which are very numerous,[72] actual copulation between human figures is rare. Amyx (658) knows of only two cases, but one of these is relevant here. On the Corinthian kylix shown below (*Fig.* 5 = Oxford 1968.1835) the wearer of a buttock cap

Fig. 5. Corinthian kylix. Oxford 1968.1835. (Photo courtesy of Ashmolean Museum.)

is penetrated from the rear by a man, while (as in our vase) another man looks on. The penetrated person is male. In contrast with our vase there is no indication of reluctance or of violence. (For a Corinthian scene of possibly impending rape, of a robed female by an ithyphallic man wielding a 'club-like object', Seeberg 1966, 58 f.)

On our Lakonian vase, then, one dedicated at the shrine of Orthia, there is a scene of sex forced upon young people, quite likely adolescent males, and probably involving whipping; the context is probably a festival, as the buttock-caps indicate. In classical times and later, Orthia's festival was famous for the whipping of boys for different purposes. The Xenophontic *Lak. Pol.* suggests that the whipping was represented as training for battle; the boys were aiming to grab cheeses from the shrine of Orthia, encouraged no doubt by the salutary hunger of the Lykourgan educational regime.[73] Is this a case of religious forms adjusted, as political culture changed? In a lykourgising spirit, was the element of casual sex removed and the whipping of the young – an exciting spectacle, no doubt – retained, redirected towards militarist ends?

From archaic times we have both a familiar scene of sympotic homoeroticism (on the Mitra Vase) and quite probably, here, the whipping and penetration of a youth. From classical times the literary record contains much evidence that homosexual relationships flourished at Sparta, and could be seen as giving a degree of support to the Lykourgan ethic.[74] But in classical Sparta the explicit attitude towards homosexuality may have involved condemnation of hedonism. The Xenophontic *Lak. Pol.* emphatically denies what was evidently a widespread belief in Greece: that at Sparta men were allowed to seek the company of boys from desire for their bodies. Rather, the author claims, Lykourgos brought it about that sexual intercourse between such parties was reckoned as shameful as incest. Elsewhere in the same work we read that the Spartan citizen gave to his peers authority over his own children, and even the right to hit them; in explanation it is stated '...they trust each other not to order the boys to do anything dishonourable' (6.2). As Spartan men thus became 'fathers of the children' (πατέρες...τῶν παίδων), it might well have been rational to deploy the incest taboo against pederastic abuse. But we are told also that Lykourgos approved of good men who desired to improve, and keep company with, boys whose characters they admired (2.12–14). There is little doubt that, in the love of men for boys, sublimation became the ideal, under the austere Spartan culture.[75] Was this partly why at the Gymnopaidiai, the festival of naked boys, unmarried men –

who might be thought to include dedicated pederasts – were excluded from the spectacle (Plut. *Lyk.* 15.2)? Megillos in the *Laws* (636e) says that the Spartan lawgiver ordered the shunning of pleasures (τὸ τὰς ἡδονὰς φεύγειν διακελεύεσθαι); compare the *Lak. Pol.* (2.9) on the importance of pain in classical Sparta.[76] If sexual relationships between men and boys had been lykourgised to reduce pleasure, that would provide an appropriate context for the austere flogging of youths to develop out of a more frankly erotic and self-indulgent form of whipping.

The assumption that sexual intercourse in public was a feature of pre-Lykourgan festivals, would also supply a possible origin for the (by general Greek standards) extraordinary uses of public nudity at Sparta for purposes of the Lykourgan state. Plutarch in the *Lykourgos* writes of Spartan girls' undressing and competing in the view of young men as an incentive to marriage (15.1), and of a ritual wherein bachelors were made naked in public as a disincentive to male infertility (15.1 f.). That Plutarch is to be taken seriously with these reports is confirmed by Plato's commendation in the (lakonising) *Laws* of mutual display of near-nudity by young men and women, as a preliminary to marriage (771e–772a; cf. 925a).

The Lakonian vases seem to present a picture of a society which combined forms of self-indulgence, which austere classical Sparta would not admit (or at least admit to), with practices that would eventually be recast in the service of austerity. Is there any sign on the vases that the movement to austerity had already begun? Given that Sparta had long excelled at athletics, the scarcity of athletic scenes may seem a pointer to the rise of militaristic thinking. Perhaps athleticism was on the way out because militarism was on the way in? But if so why do the vase-painters pay such scant attention to the phalanx? Given that the ideal of the effective hoplite was at the heart of the Lykourgan system, the Lakonian vases suggest that Lykourgan ideals were as yet far from dominant. If, on the other hand, there was in the era of these vases a *non*-Lykourgan reason for athletics to be in disfavour among the patrons of the vase-painters, what might that have been?

As compared with the images of classical Sparta derived from litera-ture, as compared even with the images on vases from archaic Corinth, the general tone of Lakonian vase-imagery is suggestive of soft living: little soldiering or athleticism; much symposion and komos. The lavish use, by the vase-painters, of supernatural symbols may point to an associated complacency. The divine attended so many grandees: the young man luxuriating on his horse, the older man (and the younger) at his symposion. While one outsider (the female musician) may be felicitated for an achievement, the general impression is of a wealthy class congratulating itself on its moments of supreme luxury. Now, we have learned to be cautious, if not dismissive, about ('broad-brush') claims that any society or substantial class has 'gone soft'. Yet about Sparta most, if not all, scholars would accept the logically rather similar claim that with the Lykourgan reforms, however dated, a society 'went hard'. If, in the sixth century, the rich of Sparta were indeed unusually averse to physical discomfort, that might account for the distinct pattern of images on the Lakonian vases. To explain the success of the revolution into austerity we might wish to posit *some* form of incompetence on the part of the aristocracy, even if that consisted only of giving a false impression of softness, one which might prove inflammatory if compounded, for example, by a military defeat. In the classical period the concept of decline into softness was applied to Sparta; Thucydides records that the Spartan victory at Mantineia in 418 refuted the charge of other Greeks, derived from events on Sphakteria in 425, that the Spartans had fallen into μαλακία (V.75.3).

Let us recall some elementary generalities. Revolutions, energetic if not dangerous things, need inflammatory ideals; the history of recent centuries suggests that those ideals may in general draw heavily on a negative image, or caricature, of the Old Regime, whether that be the callousness of Marie-Antoinette, the conditions in Tsarist factories, the corruption of Batista's Cuba, or even the Means-Test in Britain before the Welfare State. Post-revolutionary governments have commonly preserved, enhanced, and repeated to the point of tedium such negative images, while of course suppressing more attractive aspects of the past. In the *demokratia* of classical Athens memories of the sixth-century tyranny were overwhelmingly negative. What of Sparta? There is in the Greek historians no image of a pleasurably relaxed, pre-Lykourgan Sparta in the sixth century, such as we get from the vases. The closed nature of Sparta's oligarchic structures, and the anxious conformism of the Lykourgan citizens, made it far easier than at Athens to impose a 'party line'. Yet in the classical period Sparta knew the value of the negative image as an incentive, as defining the ideal;[77] that was the point of displaying, in their misery or absurdity, the Tremblers, the drunken helots, the men who refused to marry. By the classical period at least, it had seemingly become Spartiate ideology that Sparta had passed through lamentable times, long before. Surviving comment on these times, which were seen as characterised by acute political disorder, is emphatic but vague. Herodotos describes the

Spartans then as the most lawless (κακονομώτατοι) of almost all the Greeks (I.65.2); for Thucydides Sparta 'had the longest period of internal conflict (στασιάσασα) [of any state] that we know of' (I.18.1). These negative superlatives, in context, act as a foil, bringing into relief Sparta's achievement of εὐνομία (mentioned here by both writers) while implicitly warning against complacency. The combination of pride, uncomplacency and negative image-making would be appropriate in material deriving from austere Sparta. The Spartans seemingly refused to issue – at least to outsiders – an image of the old regime which was locatable in the century before the Persian Wars. Yet Thucydides describes the fear of revolution at Sparta after the Arkhidamian War, a fear so intense as to cause the precautionary disfranchisement of a large number of well-connected citizens who were tainted with military softness (V.34.2). The Spartans who made this abrasive move were obviously not persuaded that revolution was remote and impracticable. Did they still remember a Spartan society in which soft men had dominated? It seems that helots still knew Alkman as late as *c.* 370, not from recitations of their own but presumably from hearing Spartans. The latter, then, may well have known of the relaxed carnality – even, perhaps, loquacity in men – which the poems implicitly attribute to Alkman's (Spartan) environment, unless the poet's *oeuvre* had been subject to drastic selection.[78]

One cannot reconstruct the culture of pre-Lykourgan Sparta simply by reading back, and inverting, the austere culture of the classical period. There is too much apparent continuity in such matters as religiosity, the prominence of music, of homosexuality. Indeed, in political history generally if by 'revolution' we mean the complete inversion or effacing of a political culture, we may conclude that we know of no revolution. In the case of early 20th-century Russia, if we knew only that there had been a change of regime, and that after it Lenin lived in a palace and was transported in a Rolls Royce, we should be wrong to proceed by inversion to conclude that his predecessors had avoided luxuries. But the Kremlin and the Rolls were not central parts of explicit public ideology under the new regime. Extreme collectivism was; from that fact by inversion one could successfully infer that there had earlier been offensive extremes in the distribution of wealth. Likewise from the prominence of republican ideals in the United States and France one could successfully infer an earlier period of painful monarchy in the history of each. Even in public ideology there may of course be continuities between an old regime and its revolutionary successor; we think, for example, of the appeal to nationalism made by Stalin's regime during World War II. But the ideology, more than the actual practice, of a new regime may in general be a helpful basis for the historian to infer, by inversion, how the old regime was popularly perceived after, and shortly before, its fall. With classical Sparta, if we try to identify the overarching public ideals, then we may find something interestingly close to the inverse of the picture suggested by our vases. Those ideals were: the cultivation of hoplite expertise and discipline; homogeneity rather than exclusiveness among citizens; austerity rather than luxury; self-sacrifice rather than self-indulgence. Incidentally, if the coercive power of the Lykourgan ideal did depend on Spartan memories, however inaccurate, of an undesirable regime in the sixth century, it may be easier to explain why from the early fourth century there are reports of a falling away from austerity. It was not just that empire brought too many physical temptations and too much sense of security. After all, empire vanished; insecurity was restored by the Theban invasion and maintained by Macedon. But vigorous austerity was never successfully reinstated, even though a revered local model was available. Was that partly because bad memories from the sixth century had become too remote to commend so arduous a life?

Appendix
Notes on Spartan athleticism and attitudes to the horse

Records of Spartan victors at Olympia are mostly late and unreliable. But they have the attraction of dealing with Spartan events which were widely famed in Greece, and which were perhaps less exposed than usual to Spartiate myth-making of the classical period. Though in few cases can the details of a particular victory be depended upon, in the mass the information on victors may present a pattern congruent with our other information on pre-classical Sparta. De Ste. Croix, in his seminal treatment of Spartiate names in the records of Olympic victors, noted the falling off of Spartan athletic victories, and their replacement by victories for Spartan owners in the chariot-races (1972, 354 f.). A Spartan is recorded as winning an Olympic foot-race, 'about 552'. This is the terminal date, for the era of Spartan athletic success, to which de Ste. Croix calls attention. He noted correctly that mere accident of survival is not likely to have caused a shift from a record of Spartan athletic victories which formed a high proportion of the total (pre–550) to one comprising a small-to-vanishing proportion (for most of the fifth and fourth centuries). Rather, the apparent coincidence with another shift, from success in athletics to success in chariot racing, suggests a change of system. (It is only a slight qualification of de Ste. Croix's general argument to note that, from the early sixth century, there is an overall decline in the proportion of Olympic victors from states in or near the Peloponnese; overseas victors, especially from Magna Graecia and Sicily, become more common than previously.) De Ste. Croix stresses the 'astonishingly large number of Spartans who won chariot races between *c.* 548 and *c.* 368 – there are thirteen or fourteen, winning seventeen or eighteen victories between them... No other Greek state, as far as we know, provided anything like so many chariot victors (cf. Paus. VI.2.1).' To which one should add that in the earlier period Sparta has a similar predominance in the surviving athletic records of the Olympics. (For details see especially Moretti 1957). Here perhaps is an instance of continuity through change at Sparta comparable with those discussed above.

However, for the change in the pattern of Olympic results our evidence is less tidy than might be inferred from de Ste. Croix's account, with its picture of athletic victories down to about 552, and chariot victories from *c.* 548. For the decline of Spartan athletics we should perhaps look at a significant date rather earlier than 552. Spartan victories are recorded with remarkable regularity over the entire period 720–592, usually for runners, less often for wrestlers and pentathletes; for most Olympiads over that period one or two Spartan victors are named. (The main source is Eusebius, *Chron.* I, followed by Pausanias. The bias of our information towards sprinters reflects the practice, followed by Eusebius, of using the stadion-winners as chronological indicators. On the question of Eusebius' own source for the victors, for long assumed to be the chronographer Sextus Iulius Africanus, see now Mosshammer 1979, 138 ff.) For Sparta, it is after 592 that the sequence falters. The last victory of the Spartan Hetoimokles, a wrestler, may be put, according to Poralla (1913, no. 285) in 588, but precision is impossible (cf. Paus. III.13.9). In the stadion of 580 Epitelidas the Spartan is recorded as victor (Diod. Sic. V.9.2; D.H. IV.1; Eusebius). Thereafter comes a stray Spartan victory in 552 (Eusebius) for one Ladromos ('People's-Race', a name that might even reflect a clash of ideologies applying to athletics in the time of an athletically-minded father). After Ladromos, for more than seventy years no Spartan runner is recorded as having won. The date *c.* 548, for the first of Sparta's recorded chariot victories, relates to Euagoras (Herod. VI.103; Paus. VI.10.8), whom Herodotos records as having won three times at Olympia before the similar feat of the Athenian Kimon. (The latter's *floruit* is put around 530, because of his links, recorded by Herodotos, with Peisistratos and his sons.) However, while Euagoras' victories should very probably be put before the late 530s, to assign his first victory to a particular decade – let alone to a particular Olympiad – seems unjustified. After Euagoras the next Spartan chariot-victor whose epoch is approximately known is Damaratos (Herod. VI.70), king at the turn of the century.

The athletic record may in part reflect Sparta's political relations with Olympia. We hear that Sparta was involved, alongside Elis, in a war which led to the deposing of Pisatans who had dominated Olympia. These hostilities may belong to the early sixth century (Cartledge 1979, 138, suggests 572); a period of actual fighting implies an additional, prior, period of bad relations between Sparta and Olympia. We *may* see the faltering after 592 in Sparta's athleticism as a sign that the wealthy, from whose ranks leisured and well-fed athletes were likeliest to emerge, were coming under political pressure; perhaps movement towards austerity was beginning. Alternatively, if for some forty years after 592 Spartan athletes failed to win anything like the proportion of Olympic victories which had long seemed their due, that in itself might well have produced adverse comment among the citizens concerning the wider competence of their own privileged class. Athletic capacity was seen, later at least, as closely linked with military power. Aristotle wrote that in his own time the Spartans were 'defeated by others in athletic contests as well as military ones' (*Pol.* 1338b). Thucydides attributes to Alkibiades an argument that successful outlay on Olympic chariot racing was taken by Greeks as a measure of a state's military might (VI.16.2). If, against a background of striking athletic failure, unusual military failure should occur, the two kinds of bad impression would reinforce each other.

The horse was, notoriously, the chief symbol of aristocratic luxury in archaic and classical Greece: the *locus classicus* is Aristophanes' *Clouds* (ll. 60–70), where a socially-ambitious mother, inspired by the thought of an adult grandee in his chariot, gives a ἱππο- name to her son. (On the horse in aristocratic culture see the references collected at Davies 1971, xxv–xxvi esp. n. 7.) The horse had commonly symbolised wealth on vases since the Geometric period. The prominence of the horse on certain Lakonian vases is easiest to interpret, like the scenes of symposion, as symbolic in this way. Also, a horseman, unlike a hoplite, was well equipped to flee a battlefield. The horse, therefore, was likely to be a symbol exposed to attack in the Lykourgan revolution. Our study so far might make us suspect, however, that the horse – rather than being discarded completely – would be lykourgised, like those other charismatic institutions the symposion, the festival, physical training and pederasty, and would be reused, harnessed, as it were, to the values of austere Sparta. Sure enough, it is clear that personal names involving ἱππο-, or πωλο- (foal), were common in classical Sparta, notably (as Hodkinson has reminded us; 1989, 99) in the period 432–362.

If it was not politic, under the Lykourgan ethos of the Similars, to celebrate publicly the possession of riches, how did ἱππο- names have legitimate cachet? How was horse-culture lykourgised? An elite institution for 300 men, named 'the cavalry' (οἱ ἱππεῖς) existed in classical Sparta (Herod. VIII.124; Thuc. V.72.4; cf. [Xen.] *L.P.* 4.3). We hear from a late source that its members owned no horses (Strabo 481). This is indirectly supported by Thucydides' statement (IV.55.2) that the Spartans, early in the Peloponnesian War, created a cavalry force (of 400) 'contrary to their custom' (παρὰ τὸ εἰωθός). If, as is likely, it was the elite institution of the ἱππεῖς which the author of the *Lak. Pol.* had in mind when he referred to the selection of 300 young men by the ἱππαγρέται, the method of recruiting the ἱππεῖς was pointedly un-aristocratic. The ἱππαγρέται published their reasons for selecting some and rejecting others: this seems eminently Lykourgan, to be compared with Sparta's use of public humiliation against cowards and bachelors. The recorded role of the ἱππεῖς was to act as bodyguard of men whom the state cherished: most importantly the kings. This required supreme military competence as a coherent unit, rather than as heroes who risked lives – their own and indirectly their comrades' – in conspicuous isolation for personal glory; service as bodyguards also involved subordination to the authorities. Military coherence and personal subordination were characteristic Lykourgan values.

What of chariot racing? King Agesilaos' attempt to teach Spartans that success in this field was proof not of manly virtue but of wealth, by use of his sister Kyniska (Xen. *Ages*.9.6), has understandably encouraged scholars to see chariot-racing as something of an excrescence, arising from the problematic survival (and development) under the Lykourgan system of inequalities of private wealth. However, a military and political virtue of successful chariot-racing has already been noted: the Spartan community might expect to benefit if Greeks generally could be persuaded that the Spartans had wealth to spare for expensive pursuits. Such wealth (as Alkibiades reportedly implied) might support war. In a forthcoming study Hodkinson calls attention to the remarkable number of prominent memorials to equestrian victories dedicated by Spartans at Olympia; these might reflect a policy of advertising Sparta's corporate wealth and power. Rich Spartans, we know, were expected to aid their fellow citizens by sharing their property, as by contributing extra food to the messes, and lending their slaves, or their dogs ([Xen.] *L. P.* 5.3, 6.3–5; Arist. *Pol.* 1263a; Athen. 140c–141e; Fisher 1989, 31 f.). [Xenophon] and Aristotle also make clear that horses might be borrowed at Sparta by those with some personal need. The chariot-horse was perhaps seen as performing a similar service, this time for the repute (and thereby the security) of the whole citizen body, again as Alkibiades is reported as claiming in the case of Athens. The objection of Agesilaos has yet to be explained. Isokrates (VI.55) comments adversely (and with conscious paradox?) on Spartans' toleration of voracity in their racehorses. The various forms of sharing required of wealthy Spartans had the effect, surely intentional, of defusing political tensions by reducing the dissimilarities in resources. Was this very capacity of horses to eat excess wealth something which Spartans usually valued under the Lykourgan regime? More speculatively, was Agesilaos' objection in the days of Sparta's empire caused by the new level of private wealth, in the sense that race-horses could at last be comfortably afforded? Rather than eating away their owners' excess, was a multiplying horde of horses merely advertising it?

Notes

[1] See below, pp. 136 f.

[2] Rolley 1977, 135, suggests a ratio of 110:79. I am unable to understand the figure of 79.

[3] III.46 f., 54 ff., 148; Cartledge 1982.

[4] Stibbe, esp. 9, 48–51, 90, 109, 124 f., 153 f., 178, 181 f., 184–6, 188, 190–3; followed by Pipili, see esp. Introduction; Rolley 1977, 128.

[5] Stibbe no. 194. An African setting may be suggested by the presence of a monkey in the scene. For the (approximate) chronology of the rulers Arkesilas I–III, Hdt. IV.159–67, 200–5. Arkesilas III, grandson of Arkesilas II, is synchronised with Cambyses (IV.165).

[6] For Lakonian vases published after Stibbe's survey, Rolley 1977, 134 f.; Stibbe 1976, 7–16; Schaus 1978.

[7] Amyx's main catalogue, for the Early Corinthian through to the Late Corinthian ware, lists over 2,400 vases, covering – according to his tentative calculation – a period from 620/15 to 'after 550'. He knows of many other Corinthian vases within that period; see his Appendix II and (e.g.) p. 252. A single sub-group of Corinthian figured vases, those showing komos, numbers some 401 (below, n. 31).

[8] e.g. Lane 1933/4, 149.

[9] Cf. Lane 1933/4, 149, Stibbe, 47, 122.

[10] 1972, 152.

[11] 1972, 6, 122 f. Stibbe's estimate of dates for the five main painters is as follows:

Naukratis Painter: *c.* 580 – *c.* 565–550 (pp. 49 f.)

Boreads Painter: *c.* 575 – *c.* 565 (p. 90)

Arkesilas Painter: *c.* 565 – *c.* 555 (p. 109)

Hunt Painter: *c.* 565–560 – 530s (pp. 124 f.)

Rider Painter: pre-565 – *c.* 540 (or later?) (pp. 153 f.)

[12] Pipili, 83–4.

[13] See below, p. 127.

[14] (Below, p. 126.) This is unlikely to be an accident of survival. Images of Herakles were predominant on the Amyklai Throne of Apollo, a late archaic structure for which Pausanias gives us something much closer to a thorough catalogue of artistic scenes. At Amyklai there were several scenes closely linked with the Trojan War and the Homeric poems, and a similar if slightly lesser number linked with Thessaly and Boiotia. But by far the most prominent individual in Pausanias' record of Amyklai is Herakles, with appearances in no fewer than thirteen scenes: Paus. III.18.10–13, 15 f.; 19.5. (This is to include one scene from the altar-tomb of Hyakinthos.)

[15] Pipili, 24. On athletic scenes in early sixth-century Corinthian art, Roller 1981b, 110, 115 ff.

[16] See p. 122. Mythical games were shown on the public art of the Amyklai Throne; Paus. III.18.16.

[17] Amyx, 647–50.

[18] Stibbe nos. 6, 106–7, 290, 323, 357.

[19] Pipili, 60.

[20] Pipili, 64. Cf. Stibbe 1974.

[21] Stibbe counts the instances of writing by the five main Lakonian painters as follows: Naukratis Painter 0; Boreads Painter 1; Arkesilas Painter 1; Rider Painter 0; Hunt Painter 5: (1972, 52, 93, 110, 126, 155). It may be relevant that in other respects the Hunt Painter is singled out by Stibbe (122) for the extent of Attic influence in his work. For writing on Corinthian ware, Amyx, 547–612; he counts 130 Corinthian vases with painted inscriptions and some 26 with inscriptions incised.

[22] Cartledge 1978, 25–37, cf. Boring 1979.

[23] A low value was put on the abundance of words, as contrasted with deeds (Powell 1988, 235). The reading of books conduced to privacy rather than to collectivity, to idiosyncrasy rather than to homogeneity. It was a channel for foreign influences – a route by which even in his absence the *xenos* might corrupt. In the story involving Gorgo's *mot*, the Milesian brings in support of his *logoi* a special instrument of temptation, an engraved document – a map in the form of a bronze *pinax*. Forms of the word *logos* are used four times in this context – V.49 f.; Herodotos claims this is a story told by the Spartans.

[24] e.g. Plut. *Mor.* 224f, 233e, 236e. Tyrtaios is recorded as having made remarks depreciating athletic prowess, some time before the falling-away of Spartan success in inter-state athletic contests: F 12 West.

[25] Pipili, 24 and nos. 75–6. The problematic subject of boxing at Sparta will

be dealt with by Stephen Hodkinson in a forthcoming work. See also Crowther 1990.

[26] Amyx, 650.

[27] Hodkinson 1983, 273–6; Parker 1989, 142–72 (religion); Michell 1952, 182–90; Powell 1994, 302 f. (music).

[28] Thuc.V.70, Plut. *Lyk.* 22.5; Xen. *Hell.* VI.4.16; Plat. *Laws* 633bc. Bölte 1929, 124–30.

[29] Powell 1994.

[30] Pipili nos. 205a–e (lyre); 206a, d, 210b, d (pipes). For an illustration, see this volume p. 99.

[31] Seeberg (1971) catalogues 401 Corinthian komos-vases. Only 17 (?18) of these show pipe(s), 2 show a lyre. With both the Corinthian and the Lakonian vases, the proportion showing instruments would no doubt have been considerably higher if all the known vases had been preserved intact.

[32] One winged youth presents a garland. For 'thousands' of lead wreaths found among the dedications at the shrine of Orthia, Pipili, 42. Other dedications there involve pomegranates, again as prominent on the Mitra Vase: Pipili ibid.

[33] Naukratis Painter, Pipili nos. 194–5; Arkesilas Painter, Pipili no. 196; Rider Painter, Pipili no. 198 (very fragmentary); ?Hunt Painter, Pipili no. 197. Further on the Lakonian winged youths, Stibbe 1974; Isler-Kerenyi 1984.

[34] Weicker 1902, 14 ff.; cf. for bibliography and review of the debate Dentzer 1982, 90–5; Pipili, 72.

[35] See Stibbe 1974.

[36] 1987, 76, citing Strabo VIII.5.1.

[37] cf. Diehl 1964b, 561 f.

[38] This was a delicate process, sometimes no doubt performed unconsciously, though indelicately exploited and consciously built up to form a political system by Plato in the *Laws*. On the question of Spartan self-awareness here, Parker 1989, 160; Powell 1994, 290–1.

[39] Pipili, 21–6, on her nos. 65–78. While in several cases there are problems with identifying a particular myth (most importantly in showing that the boarhunt of nos. 69–73 is indeed the Kalydonian and not merely generic), Pipili's argument for Spartan interest in stories linked with Boiotia and Thessaly is strongly supported by Pausanias' record that four such were depicted on the Amyklai Throne (III.18.12, 15 f.).

[40] Hdt. I.67 f. Malkin (1994b) has collected probable instances of the positive use of myth by Sparta, to support state ventures of the sixth and fifth centuries.

[41] Thucydides' claim (I.18.1) that the Spartan constitution went back 'slightly more than 400 years approximately' must depend on Spartan informants. Cf., on reported Spartan interest in the origins of communities, [Plat.] *Hipp. Maj.* 285d.

[42] Paus. III.17.3; 18.11, 14.

[43] Pipili, 30–1; Paus. III.18.15.

[44] Also shown on the altar-tomb were Semele (mother of Dionysos, by Zeus) and her sister Ino (who became the sea-goddess Leukothea).

[45] cf. Hdt. VI.58 and esp. Xen. *Hell.* III.3.1. Cartledge 1987, ch. 16.

[46] Plut. *Agis* 21.2.

[47] Parker 1989, 161 f.: '...their [the Spartans'] eccentricity is merely to believe with unusual seriousness what other Greeks believed too.'

[48] Stibbe nos. 26, 30, 36, 93–4, 107.

[49] Stibbe nos. 206b, 213–14, 218–19, 221, 230, 239.

[50] Thuc. I.18.1 and (e.g.) Plut. *Lyk.* 1.

[51] Payne (1931, 118) listed 12 banqueting scenes, comparing 4 others (and observing that such scenes do not occur on Protocorinthian vases); cf. Amyx 1988, 647. Bakır (1974) adds two (his K37, K40).

[52] F 1.67–9 (Campbell, Page).

[53] Bowie 1990, 225 n. 16; Murray 1993, 177; Hodkinson 1997.

[54] Nafissi 1991, ch. 4; Nafissi observes (220) that the surviving work of the Arkesilas Painter shows a particular bias towards the representation of banquets. The totals, for the main painters, are: Naukratis Painter 5, Arkesilas Painter 4, Hunt Painter 4, Rider Painter 3.

[55] Compare modern Christmas-card scenes of fat, grotesque, revelling Santas and Santas on sleighs, with their real-life analogues in padded Santas and children's sledging. Also, Payne 1931, 118.

[56] D-K 88 no. 6. Compare the picture in Plutarch's *Lykourgos* (28) of tableaux mounted to impress young Spartiates with the idea that drunkenness was servile and ridiculous; helots, made drunk for the purpose, provided the lesson.

[57] Athen. 550d–e, Aelian *VH* 14 7.

[58] Xenophon's tale of the conspiracy of Kinadon implies that the Spartans in the early fourth century saw themselves as permanently surrounded in their own land by bitter enemies, in the persons of their own non-citizen population (*Hell.* III.3 4–11, esp. 5–6). Spartiates and helots alike were acutely aware of the principle of military opportunity, in the classical period; Powell 1980.

[59] This is, of course, to assume that the Spartiates generally and not just the Lakonian vase-painters, whatever their status, knew something of the export of numerous Lakonian vases.

[60] Spartans withheld knowledge of military significance, as Thucydides reported Perikles as suggesting, concerning the *xenelasia* (II.39.1); Thucydides in his own person wrote of the general secretiveness of the Spartan polity (V.68.2).

[61] Xen. *Mem.* I.2.61, cf. Plut. *Kim.* 10.6.

[62] Plat. *Laws* 633bc; Wade-Gery 1949, 79–81.

[63] [Xen.] *Lak. Pol.* 2.9; Plut. *Lyk.* 18.2; [Plut.] *Mor.* 239d; cf. Plat. *Laws* 633b.

[64] The photograph in Lane 1933/4, his plate 40a, is at some points clearer than that at Pipili , 66, though see n. 65, below.

[65] Three of the four certainly have buttock-caps. Lane's drawing represents the penetrated figure as lacking one, probably rightly. The buttock-cap on the reveller at far right is best seen in the photograph of Pipili, 66. On anklets worn by revellers here, Seeberg 1966, 66. In autopsy they are clearly visible on the two revellers to the right.

[66] Seeberg 1966, 66 n. 1. That the passive copulator, and the dancers, are shown with dark flesh is not decisive; Pipili, 22 n. 195, observes that some of the Lakonian vase-painters render female flesh in black.

[67] Harvey 1994, 41–2.

[68] Amyx, 658 reports 'oversized or misshapen penises' on Corinthian komos vases, 'in some cases evidently part of the costume'. Several lead figurines from the shrine of Orthia, now in the Sparta museum, show male dancers with prominent penises and buttocks.

[69] Pipili's photograph does not make it apparent.

[70] e.g. Pipili nos. 1, 15, 58, 72, 103, 133, 149, 215 (animals); 89, 92 (human).

[71] For example, on the Amyklai Throne were scenes involving sexual attempts on Taygete, Alkyone, the Leukippids, Kephalos, Io, Athena and Helen (Paus. III.18.10–13, 15). Plutarch's famously obscure reference to historical Spartan marriage by ἁρπαγή (rape or abduction) is at *Lyk.* 15.4 f. The present writer hopes to deal more fully elsewhere with the subject of heterosexual activity among the Spartans.

[72] Seeberg (1971) catalogues 401 such.

[73] [Xen.] *Lak. Pol.* 2.9; cf. Plut. *Lyk.* 18.1 f. for whipping at a much later period with, no doubt, a different rationale.

[74] In the *Hellenica* Xenophon has two sympathetic stories involving same-sex pairing of Spartiate males, both stories suggesting that an enduring emotional bond conduced to a key Lykourgan virtue, willingness to die for the community in battle (IV.8.38 f.; V.4.25–33). Indeed, his story about Arkhidamos and Kleonymos implies that such relationships might intensify pressure to accept the Lykourgan code in its entirety.

[75] For further references, and discussion, see Cartledge 1981, 19–22. Cartledge suggests that any Spartan rule requiring continence in homosexual affairs was probably widely flouted.

[76] Cf. Ar. *Pol.* 1338b on ταῖς φιλοπονίαις of the Spartans.

[77] David 1989, 7 f.

[78] For helot knowledge of Alkman, Plut. *Lyk.* 28.10. For Alkman and hedonism see F 4a (Campbell, Loeb ed.) on marital sex; 19, 96, cf. 17, 134 (Campbell, Page) on food; 92 (Campbell, Page) on wine. On loquacity in men, see the fragment Πολλαλέγωhν ὄνυμ᾽ ἀνδρί, γυναικὶ δὲ Πασιχάρηα – quoted and glossed at Ael. Arist. *Or.* 45.32 (=107, Campbell, Page). Custom may succeed in hiding inconvenient elements even of a text regarded as sacred, and publicly accessible in its entirety; compare the obscurity in modern times of Christ's words to the Syrophoenician woman, as reported in Mark 7.27.

4

ATHENA AS ERGANE AND PROMACHOS
The iconography of Athena in archaic east Greece

Alexandra Villing

'The history of the eastern Greeks still remains to be written', J.M. Cook stated in 1962, [1] and this assessment continues to hold true today for much of archaic east Greece. Our knowledge of the history and culture of many Greek cities and settlements on the western coast of Asia Minor and its islands is still rather limited. However, archaeological research in recent years has helped to sharpen our views, in particular regarding the interaction between the Greeks and their Anatolian cultural environment.

The emerging picture is one of the archaic east Greek cities – joined in a cultural *koinē* – and their eastern neighbours living together in what could be called in some respects a 'cultural symbiosis', based largely on exchange between the elites, and visible especially in the large number of Oriental imports and the adaptation of eastern motifs in the arts.[2] Eastern links are also apparent in the complex field of religion. The worship of Syro-Phrygian Kybele was widespread in archaic east Greece,[3] and major Greek deities are also known to reveal foreign traits, for example Samian Hera and Artemis at Ephesos (Fleischer 1973). Associated in particular with these two goddesses is a specific 'Anatolian' type of cult statue, characteristic for the east Greek area and based at least partly on native Anatolian iconography. It is in this context that the present chapter attempts to review what we know about another Greek goddess, Athena, in one of the oldest and most famous cities of western Asia Minor, Troy.

Homer (*Il.* 6.269–311) describes at length a ceremony in which Hekabe offers a robe to Athena in her local temple at Troy, which is commonly taken to indicate that a cult of Athena existed at Ilion at the time of the creation of the *Iliad*. What is the image of Athena that a visitor to Ilion might have encountered in the eighth or seventh century? Coins of Ilion show the local cult statue of Athena in a pose and dress similar to the 'Anatolian' type of cult statue, carrying a spear and a distaff, attributes which refer to her functions as patroness of crafts and warlike protectress. Unfortunately, these coins, and virtually all our other evidence for Athena at Ilion, date from the Hellenistic and later periods, raising the question of whether the statue displayed on them, or even the cult of Athena as a whole, is of ancient Anatolian origin or is a Hellenistic 'archaizing' creation. This is a problem which has long been recognized – as for other east Greek cults and cult statues – but which has not so far been approached systematically. We shall re-examine the Hellenistic and later data, and attempt to place the iconography of Athena Ilias – the combination of the patroness of spinning and the warlike protectress – in the context of the archaic iconography of east Greek Athena.

The cult of Athena at Ilion

Very little is known about Troy/Ilion in historical times.[4] There is scant archaeological evidence for the archaic and classical settlement (Troy VIII and IX), although pottery finds suggest that the site was occupied from the eighth century onwards, or even from around 1000 BC.[5] Architectural remains most notably include a sanctuary – possibly of Kybele – at the southern foot of the hill, which was in use from 700 through to the Roman period, making it the first known religious complex to have been built at Troy after the Bronze Age. The recent discovery of an archaic building incorporating Aiolic columns at this site (Rose 1995) disproves ancient claims that Ilion before the time of Lysimachus (or even before the Romans) was virtually uninhabited.[6]

However, archaeological evidence for the cult of Athena from this period is lacking. There appear to be no early traces of cult on the site of the Hellenistic temple of Athena, although it is possible, of course, that they went unnoticed by Schliemann and Dörpfeld, or that the site of the sanctuary was moved in the Hellenistic period.[7] The extant temple, according to ancient sources, was built under Lysimachus, after 301[8] (although planned already under Alexander the Great; see Diodorus 18.4.5; Strabo 13.1.26), as part of a larger building programme. The existence of a cult predating the temple is implied by a third-century mention of 'traditional ancestral sacrifices'[9] and the allegedly ancient custom – first referred to in the third quarter of the fourth century – of sending maidens from south-Italian Locri to serve in the sanctuary of Athena Ilias.[10] However, the first inscriptions mentioning a festival called Ilieia or (Greater and Lesser) Panathenaia, celebrated by a league of cities worshipping Athena Ilias, only date from around 300.[11] We can reasonably assume that the festival was instituted – or at least modified and embellished – around the time the temple was built, especially as the idea of calling it Panathenaia is almost certainly neither of ancient nor local origin. In all likelihood it was borrowed from Athens, as may have been the provision of sacrificial cows by members of the league, suggesting an attempt on the part of Ilion to emulate Athens at the height of its glory as the head of the Delian League. In this, Ilion follows a fashion that can also be traced in a number of other east Greek *poleis* in the early Hellenistic period, for example Priene and Pergamon.[12]

Most archaeological and epigraphical records of Athena's cult at Ilion thus do not predate the Hellenistic period; our only pre-Hellenistic sources for Athena's cult at Ilion are literary. Herodotus (7.43) mentions that Xerxes on his march to Abydos in 480 sacrificed a thousand oxen to Athena Ilias; Xenophon (*Hell.* 1.4) describes how the Spartan Mindaros looked down at a battle while he was sacrificing to Athena at Ilion; and Arrian (*An.* 1.11.7; 6.9.3), Strabo (13.1.26), Diodorus (18.1) and Plutarch (*Alex.* 15.4) record that Alexander sacrificed to Athena Ilias at Ilion, exchanging his own panoply for one kept in the temple. Are these incidents simply literary embellishments or inventions? Herodotus' account of Xerxes' sacrifice does not specifically mention a temple or sacred precinct of Athena, nor can we exclude the possibility that the story is a Greek re-interpretation of what was in fact a sacrifice to a Persian god on a hill-top near Ilion. However, the accounts of Alexander's visit are so numerous and varied – including the specific references to an existing sanctuary[13] – that it would be difficult to consider them all literary elaborations. Moreover, the sources indicate that at least from the fifth century onwards the Greeks knew of the early history of Ilion as Homeric Troy, and we can assume that the local Aiolian population of Troy would have striven to live up to their great heritage by continuing, or even instigating, a local Athena cult. As Aiolians possibly from Lesbos – an island with many important cults of Athena – they would probably have been familiar with the worship of Athena as a city goddess (Hertel 1991, 134).

Homer, the Palladion and the iconography of Athena Ilias

Evidence for the cult statue of Athena at Ilion is not much clearer than that for the cult itself. What comes to mind first in this context is the Trojan Palladion, which appears in archaic and later art as the cult statue at which Kassandra took refuge or which was stolen by Diomedes and/or Odysseus, and which by the classical period had acquired the standardized iconography of a small, archaizing, armed figure. The myths that record the theft of the Palladion from Troy during the Trojan war date back to at least the sixth century, and from about the same time onwards, several cities, among them Athens and Argos, claimed possession of the Trojan statue. Artistic renderings of the Palladion may thus reflect local statues believed to be the stolen Palladion, or – more likely – conventions for depicting an epitomized 'old statue of Athena'. In any case they are unlikely to have been based on any actual statue at Ilion.[14]

Closer to Ilion, the *Iliad* (6.269–311) describes how Hekabe places a robe on Athena's knees (ἐπὶ γούνασι) when asking for her support as the protectress of Ilion. The episode is often believed to have been inspired by an actual cult statue which stood at Ilion at the time of the creation of the poem, and both ancient and modern scholars[15] have taken it to indicate that the ancient cult statue of Athena at Troy was seated. The description may be based on an actual cult image at Ilion, but it is just as possible that Homer simply described a generic cult statue, or that the 'placing on the knees' is merely a figure of speech. The passage therefore need not be taken as evidence for the appearance of a Trojan cult statue.[16] As Strabo points out, moreover, it conflicts with the fact that 'the wooden image of Athena now to be seen [at Ilion] stands upright',[17] from which he (or presumably his second-century source Demetrios) concludes that Ilion could not have been the site of ancient Troy. This standing Athena can probably be identified on Hellenistic coins of Ilion, the most reliable source for the iconography of Athena at Ilion.

It is commonly assumed that the minting of coins at Ilion began under Lysimachus around 300 BC. The earliest coins are civic bronze issues with the head of Athena on the obverse and the full figure of Athena on the reverse (*Figs.* 1, 2), while from the second century onwards, silver coins were minted in connection with the league worshipping Athena Ilias.[18] The coins represent Athena with a fairly consistent iconography, dressed in an Attic peplos, standing or walking, carrying a spear over her shoulder and a distaff in her hand. Knotted bands are dangling from the spear or distaff, similar to the ones found on Artemis of Ephesos and other statues of the so-called 'Anatolian type'. This type is characterized by a rigid frontal stance, extended lower arms often with attached beaded bands, a tight dress (*ependytes*) around the legs, and a high *polos* with attached veil-like mantle.[19] In common with this type Athena also wears a *polos* and veil, a feature possibly derived ultimately from Hittite prototypes (Fleischer 1973, 122, 209–10). Several factors strongly suggest that the figure was

Figs. 1a, b. Bronze coins of Ilion, around 300 or early third century (Ashmolean Museum, Oxford).

Fig. 2: Hemidrachm of Ilion, last quarter third century (Ashmolean Museum, Oxford).

intended to represent the cult statue of Athena Ilias: the figure is sometimes shown on a base, on second-century issues the depiction is inscribed with 'ΑΘΗΝΑΣ ΙΛΙΑΔΟΣ', and Roman Imperial coins show the same figure inside a temple.[20] It moreover corresponds to Apollodorus' description – dating from the first century AD and probably based on the statue at Troy – of the Palladion of Troy as 'three cubits in height, its feet joined together; in its right hand it held a spear aloft, and in the other a distaff and spindle'.[21]

But to which period does the image belong? Is it an ancient *xoanon* or an archaizing statue made for the temple built by Lysimachus? [22] Similar questions have been asked with respect to most of the other cult statues of the so-called 'Anatolian type'. There is virtually no iconographic evidence before the Hellenistic period for any of these statues, and an archaic origin can only be hypothesized. Even the prime example of the type, Artemis Ephesia, has been considered a Hellenistic creation (Simon 1985, 163). However, it is difficult to imagine that the 'Anatolian type' of cult statue as such was a Hellenistic

151

invention, and the late appearance of the type in art could be explained by Hellenistic antiquarian interest (Förtsch 1995). For Artemis Ephesia, an early origin appears in fact quite probable, since her cult can be traced back archaeologically into the early archaic period (Bammer and Muss 1995).

The 'Athena Ilias' type has a close iconographical parallel that might push back its dating at least slightly. A fourth-century tetradrachm of Assos, another city in the Troad, features an Athena which deviates from the Ilion coin type only in the stiff, stationary pose of Athena, and in the fact that the object in her left hand cannot be identified with certainty as a distaff (*Fig.* 3).[23] Athena's cult at Assos probably dates back to the archaic period[24] and the coin might depict an ancient local cult statue (which might have provided a model for a later statue at Ilion; Lacroix 1949, 122–3). Alternatively, as we know that Assos belonged to the confederation celebrating the festival of Athena Ilias in later times, the coin might represent the statue at Ilion. The coin is difficult to date, but in all likelihood predates Lysimachus, indicating that the type of 'Athena Ilias' was known in the area before the third century.[25] There is, moreover, an archaic representation of Athena from Assos, a terracotta figurine dating from around 500 (*Fig.* 4).[26] It shows the goddess standing in a stiff pose not dissimilar to the representation on the coin, with both lower arms extended forward (the hands and possible attributes are lost), with a *gorgoneion* on her chest and a high head-dress with attached veil or mantle. The head-dress[27] might go back to Hittite origins, as male gods (and Ishtar-Shaushga in her male incarnation) wear similar head-dresses on Hittite reliefs, while a mantle-veil was commonly worn over the *polos* of female deities.[28] One could easily imagine that in Greek art the distinction

Fig. 3a, b. Tetradrachm of Assos, mid to second half fourth century (Paris, Cabinet des Médailles; after cast in the British Museum).

between the two types of divine head-dresses was blurred. Thus, from an early period onwards, we find that Athena at Assos took a peculiar iconographical shape which included local Anatolian elements.

Returning to the iconography of the coin representations, there are two further unusual features which might have a bearing on the dating of the type. The first is the way the spear is carried across the shoulder, a pose rare in archaic art, particularly for Athena.[29] In sculpture in the round, the motif was probably rarely used before Polykleitos' Doryphoros, suggesting that the creation of the Athena Ilias type would fit better into the period after the mid-fifth century. The second feature is the unique combination of the distaff and spear, a highly effective means of conveying the two main areas of protection commonly associated with Athena, war and (female) crafts, in one single image. This double function of Athena appears already in Homer,[30] who describes Athena both as a goddess of war and as one adept at fashioning clothes and teaching woolwork. As the Homeric poems are commonly believed to have originated in an Aiolian/Ionian setting,[31] we might therefore suspect that the Athena Ilias type and the poems belong to a common context – east Greece in the archaic period. The iconographical combination of the two spheres of activity could then be interpreted as a synoptic effort, characteristic of archaic narrative, applied to a cult statue.[32] Alternatively, one could suspect a Hellenistic desire to create an all-encompassing image of the goddess, in line with the syncretistic tendencies of the period. Such a creation, based on Homeric ideas, would have appeared particularly appropriate for a statue of

Fig. 4. Terracotta figurine from Assos (Athens, National Museum, Coll. Misthos; after Langlotz 1975, pl. 25.4).

Athena on the site of Homeric Troy.[33] On the other hand, if the cult-image were a Hellenistic creation, it would be surprising that the far more common iconographic type of the 'Palladion' was not used, as this would have evoked the image of 'Trojan Athena' far better.

It therefore remains for us to examine further the possibility that the iconography of the combined spear and distaff was developed in the archaic period rather than later. This will involve tracing the 'history' of these attributes in the context of Athena's iconography, especially in east Greece, as well as her role as a goddess of crafts and war in the region.

Athena Ergane – an Ionian concept?

The cult of Athena Ergane as the patron deity of skilful craftsmanship and art (from ἔργα as the product of τέχνη, artful craft) is well attested in Greece. In myth, the goddess is credited with the invention and teaching of various crafts, ranging from the art of building a ship, to bridling a horse, to women's weaving, all closely linked to her character of practical intelligence (μῆτις). Under the epithet Ergane, Athena was worshipped in much of Greece.[34] Pictorial representations referring to these functions are, however, rare, especially those depicting the goddess holding the tools for spinning, distaff and spindle. It is therefore of considerable importance that the few known mentions or actual examples of this type in archaic and classical Greek art appear to centre on western Asia Minor (Graf 1985, 214).

The earliest known secure evidence for spinning Athena anywhere in the Greek world are fifth-century Sicilian terracotta figurines from Scornavacche (*Fig. 5*)[35] and Kamarina[36] which show Athena seated and holding tools for spinning. Representations of a spinning owl on loomweights found in various places in south Italy (Demargne 1984, 962 no. 44, pl. 708) are a further indication of the presence of a concept relating Athena to spinning. As both Scornavacche and Kamarina had close links with Gela, which in turn was said to be a foundation by Crete and Rhodian Lindos, an east Greek origin of the type has been suspected. At Lindos itself, two terracotta statuettes of seated, spinning females have been found and identified as Athena (*Fig. 6*), but there is insufficient evidence to support such an identification.[37]

Athena is unequivocally connected with spinning, however, at Ionian Erythrai.[38] Athena Polias/Poliouchos was the main deity here, with a sanctuary on the acropolis from the late eighth century onwards.[39] Her cult statue is described by Pausanias (7.5.9) as 'a wooden image of great size seated on a throne and holding a distaff [ἠλακάτη]

Fig. 5. Terracotta figurine from Scornavacche, fifth century (Syracuse, National Museum; after Di Vita 1952–4, 144 fig. 2).

Figs. 6a, b. Terracotta figurines from Lindos, fifth century (after Blinkenberg 1931, pl. 102).

in each hand, and also having a *polos* on its head'.[40] It is commonly assumed that Pausanias mistook a spindle for a second distaff – a mistake easily made, as the spindle and distaff can look rather similar; but it can also be argued that the word ἠλακάτη in its strict sense only refers to a spinning 'staff', i.e. either a distaff (staff with clump of wool) or spindle (staff with whorl; Bianchi 1953, 212). If Pausanias was not mistaken in his attribution of the statue to Endoios, then the cult statue at Erythrai dates back to the second half of the sixth century, and was made by a sculptor whose name is intimately linked both with Greek Asia Minor and Athens, an example of the close contact which existed in the late archaic period between the art of Athens and Ionia.[41] At Athens, Pausanias (1.26.5) credits Endoios with being the sculptor of a seated Athena statue dedicated by Kallias on the Acropolis. This statue is commonly identified with a late archaic marble statue of the goddess which might also have been equipped with spindle and distaff (*Fig.* 7; Ridgway 1992, 138–9), based on iconographic parallels with representations of a seated spinning woman on terracotta plaques from the Acropolis (*JHS* 17 (1897), 309, pl. 7,1).

An early classical bronze figurine of seated Athena has been suggested as another possible spinning Athena, but this identification is also uncertain (*Fig.* 8; Charbonneaux 1958, pl. 7,1). The figurine

Fig. 7. Athens, Acropolis Museum 625 (after H. Payne and G.M. Young, *Archaic Marble Sculpture from the Acropolis II*, London 1936, pl. 116).

Fig. 8. Bronze statuette of Athena, first quarter fifth century (Paris, Br 4196; photo *La Licorne*, courtesy of *Musée du Louvre*).

shows the goddess with her right hand – once holding an attribute – in front of her chest and her left arm extended forward. Charbonneaux believed the figure to be Attic, but its incongruous style, unusual aegis type and virtually unparalleled rendering of the helmet crest make this appear unlikely,[42] and one might rather suspect an east Greek craftsman, perhaps working in Italy. A spindle and a distaff can be safely identified as attributes on a seventh-century incised stele from Prinias on Crete (*Fig.* 9), where they are held by a woman standing on a small pedestal (possibly a statue base). The woman might be Athena, as we know the goddess was worshipped on the acropolis of Prinias.[43] On the Greek mainland, representations of a spinning Athena are virtually non-existent.[44] Even if we take into account the possible late archaic spinning Athena from the Acropolis, the lack of representations of spinning Athena at Athens is surprising, given that Athena Ergane enjoyed worship from an early period onwards, and that female crafts were certainly amongst her responsibilities; moreover, the iconography of spinning was well known in archaic and classical Attic vase-painting for mortal women.

The only secure representations of Athena with spinning tools are thus the fifth-century Sicilian terracotta figurines, the coins of Ilion, and – if we trust Pausanias – the cult statue at Erythrai. Given such a small sample, the preponderance of east Greek evidence may not weigh very heavily in favour of an east Greek origin of the type, were it not for a remarkable feature shared by the evidence from Ilion and Erythrai. In both cities, the representation of Athena with distaff is not just a votive offering, but a cult statue, the incarnation of Athena as Polias, protectress of the whole city. In spite of this important position, she is alluding to a task – spinning – which at first glance appears to be of little direct relevance to the well-being of the city and which moreover is usually confined to women – hardly the most prominent social group in the Greek polis. Spinning is not normally a divine activity, and no other spinning cult statues are known to me in Greece, nor, in fact, are there any securely identifiable representations of other Olympian goddesses occupied in such a way.[45] One possible exception is an archaic ivory figurine of a spinning woman from the sanctuary of Artemis at Ephesos, but it is not clear whether Artemis or some other goddess, priestess or votary is represented (*Fig.* 10; Akurgal 1987, 32–3, pl. 69). According to Lucian (*Syr.D.* 32), the cult statue of the Dea

Fig. 9. Engraved stele from Prinias, seventh century (Heraklion Museum 234).

Fig. 10. Ivory figurine from Ephesos, late seventh century.

Fig. 11. Neo-Hittite grave relief from Marash, eighth/seventh century (Adana Museum 175b).

Syria of Hierapolis – Syrian Atargatis – held a spindle (ἄτρακτος),[46] but this is quite probably a Hellenistic statue reflecting syncretistic tendencies, and it does not represent an Olympian goddess. What is remarkable, though, is that these two possible examples of spinning goddesses are again located in Asia Minor, and this – together with the evidence for spinning Athena – raises the question of whether the inspiration for the motif might have come from the Near East, and whether this might explain the high value attached to it by the eastern Greeks.

A Syrian or Hittite 'spinning goddess' has been proposed as a possible model (Suhr 1969), but, as pointed out by Bianchi (1953, 205–20) and Graf (1985, 213), there is virtually no evidence for the existence of such a goddess. The female spinners on two Neo-Hittite grave stelai of Marash (*Fig.* 11) and on a Neo-Elamite relief from Susa, all dating from the eighth or seventh century, are probably mortals and not deities,[47] and if Near Eastern goddesses are described as spinning in literary sources, this is probably thought of merely as an appropriate female occupation. An indication that spinning had a certain cosmological significance in the ancient Near East may, however, be deduced from a Hittite text found at Boghazköi, which describes a spindle in the hands of one of the three Hittite goddesses who determine the fate of the king during the building of a new palace.[48] This idea could have been transferred into the Greek realm, where we know that from Homeric times onwards the spindle was used by the Moirai, the 'Fates', who are 'spinning men's destiny' (Bianchi 1953). Their action gains cosmological significance perhaps already in the work of east Greek philosophers such as Parmenides, but definitely by the time of Plato's *Republic*, in the myth of Er (617c). The picture evoked here of cosmic order is that of ἀνάγκη ('Necessity'), on whose knees rests the spindle which governs the movement, in concentric spheres or 'whorls', of the heavenly bodies, and who is assisted by her daughters, the Moirai.[49]

Could the spinning Athena thus primarily be a manifestation of an early Ionian philosophical concept of a goddess determining the fate of men and the movement of the world? This seems unlikely, as the average ancient viewer would rarely have made such a connection, and probably rather assumed a reference to the more mundane daily work of spinning wool. Spinning and weaving were common among the Greeks – some east Greek cities in particular were renowned for the quality of their wool – but were common also among their eastern neighbours. Phrygian textiles, for example, were famous all around the Mediterranean.[50] In this context, one should expect spinning to be part of human iconography, both in Near Eastern and Greek art. The idea of a spinning goddess therefore could have developed anywhere, but perhaps the presence of an established iconography of the spinning female in Near Eastern art meant that in east Greece the conditions were ideal for a Greek iconographical rendering of divine patronage for this activity. Of course, such a borrowing of an iconographical motif could only have taken place if it conformed to Greek ideas, and this is where the importance of woolworking, the – possibly – higher social position of women (Cook 1975, 800–1), and perhaps the wider cosmological implications may have come into play. A merging of Greek and eastern concepts and iconography seems to be reflected particularly in the seated spinning Athena as found at Erythrai, since the seated pose itself in Greek and east Greek art in particular developed under eastern (Assyrian and Egyptian) influence.[51] Moreover, it conformed best to the Greek ideal of the woman as comparatively passive, concerned with handicrafts and the sphere of the house in general, in contrast to the strong and active, standing man (Jung 1982, 117–23). As the divine incarnation of the seated, spinning mistress of the *oikos* described in the *Odyssey*, the seated, spinning Athena would have symbolized the wealth and status of local aristocratic households (cf. Wickert-Micknat 1982, 39–41).

Warlike Athena in east Greece

We might be tempted to infer from the picture of a seated, spinning Athena a generally peaceful, inactive character of east Greek Athena, but this would be a misconception nourished by the equally misconceived notion of the soft and weak nature of the east Greeks. The assumption is probably justified that within the archaic Greek aristocracy – not just in east Greece – imported Oriental goods, eastern contacts and a luxurious life-style were highly valued, but the equating of 'Eastern luxury', and everyone who was associated with it, with weakness and decadence probably resulted from a change of attitudes after the Persian wars and with the rise of Athenian democracy.[52] This mainly classical Athenian image of the unwarlike Ionians continues to tint our view of the art and culture of archaic east Greece, but it is easily dispelled if we consider the fact that east Greek cities boast some of the earliest Greek fortifications, that the earliest extant war-poet, Kallinos, was east Greek, and that the east Greeks were popular mercenaries (Murray 1993, 231–2). To this we can now add that some of the earliest representations of an armed Athena actually come from east Greece.

Our main source for the iconography of warlike Athena in east

Greece is Chian vase-painting, which is particularly notable considering that Chios was located just opposite Erythrai, with which it had close links.[53] Among the finds from the only excavated sanctuary of Athena on the island, at Emporio – in use from the Late Geometric to the Hellenistic periods[54] – was a Chian plate dated to the first quarter of the sixth century with a representation of an armed Athena striding forward, carrying a shield and a spear in a diagonal position (*Fig.* 12).[55] It seems likely that the plate was made specifically as a votive offering to the goddess, especially as it shows Athena on her own without a mythical context. There has even been speculation that it represents the local cult statue, but this cannot be considered certain.[56] Nonetheless, the plate reflects the contemporary Chian/Emporian concept of Athena, suggesting that the goddess was regarded as warlike already in the early sixth century, a time when at Athens, for example, Athena only just began to carry arms on vases.[57] The picture of an armed Athena is repeated again on a fragment of archaic Chian pottery from Naukratis (*Fig.* 13),[58] while two more fragments feature helmeted heads, presumably of Athena (*Figs.* 14, 15).[59] All three fragments date from the second quarter of the sixth century and confirm that from an early stage, Athena was represented as a warlike goddess in Chian art. Even though they do not allow extrapolation concerning a 'Chian' character of the goddess, they nevertheless suggest that on Chios the warlike attitude was a prominent character trait of archaic Athena. Of course, it needs to be taken into account that different media belong to different contexts and have different iconographic traditions, and that a warlike Athena in vase-painting does not necessarily carry the same weight with respect to the way Athena was perceived in a local cult as a

Fig. 12. Athena on a Chian plate from Emporio, first quarter sixth century.

Fig. 13. Chian fragment from Naukratis, second quarter sixth century (London, BM 1888.6-1.493; photo courtesy of *British Museum*).

Fig. 14. Chian fragment from Naukratis, second quarter sixth century (British School at Athens).

Fig. 15. Athena on a Chian fragment from Naukratis, second quarter sixth century (Cambridge, Fitzwilliam Museum 94-6, N.88.G.20).

cult statue or even a votive figurine. When we look at late archaic Athens, for example, we find that Athena appears warlike throughout in vase-painting, while terracotta figurines from the Acropolis show her as a more 'peaceful', seated figure. Both nevertheless represent aspects of Athena's Athenian character as we know it from other sources, and constitute valid evidence for reconstructing the way the deity was perceived by the local population.

Representations of armed Athena are also known in later periods from a number of other east Greek regions. One of these is a bronze statuette of unknown provenance, but attributable to an east Greek, south Ionian (Milesian/Samian) workshop. It represents Athena striding forward, with both arms lowered but slightly extended forward; both hands and the attributes they once held are lost (*Fig*. 16). Herdejürgen (1969) has suggested that the statuette should be restored as carrying spear and shield, similar to the late archaic Athenian bronze statuettes of the 'Promachos'-type. She argues that this would make the statuette one of the earliest known sculptural representations of this type, which might

Fig. 16. Bronze statuette of Athena, around 540/530 (Basle, Antikenmuseum und Sammlung Ludwig BS 509; photo C. Niggli, courtesy of *Antikenmuseum*).

even indicate that its origins could be in east Greece. However, the 'Promachos' type occurs already much earlier in different media, for example, on Athenian Panathenaic prize-amphorae. More importantly, we cannot be sure that the figure actually carried a shield and spear, and even though the reconstruction appears likely, the statuette cannot strictly be counted among the 'Promachoi'. That term implies an active fighting attitude, with a spear in the raised right hand, and the Ionian statuette has her right hand lowered. We do not know whether the spear was held in a horizontal (attacking) or diagonal/vertical position; if it was diagonal, possibly leaning against her shoulder, the figure would repeat the pose of the Athena on the earlier Chian plate. The origins of the fighting Athena are thus unlikely to be found in east Greece, but armed Athena was certainly a common phenomenon in the area.

This is further confirmed by a number of armed terracotta figurines from Rhodes, especially Lindos (*Fig.* 17).[60] Winged Athena – a type that appears to be largely confined to late archaic east Greece and areas under east Greek influence – also generally appears armed (Demargne 1984, 1019), for example on Klazomenian sarcophagi dating from the decades around 500 (ibid., 964 no. 62, pl. 710). It has been argued by Cook that winged women appear on Klazomenian sarcophagi in many different situations, often duplicated, and should

Fig. 17a, b. Terracotta figurines of Athena from Lindos, fifth and fourth century (after Blinkenberg 1931, pls. 109, 133).

162

therefore rather be understood as supernatural beings without a specific divine identity (1981, 121–2). This interpretation is a possibility, but it is equally likely that the armed winged beings represent Athena as a warlike guardian of the hoplite both in life and in death, especially as a winged Athena can be clearly identified in other media, for example, an east Greek or Cypriot scarab of around 500 (*Fig.* 18),[61] and a late archaic Attic vase created under east Greek influence (*Fig.* 19).[62] Further possible winged and armed Athenas appear on the friezes of the Artemision of Ephesos and the Siphnian treasury.[63] The concentration of winged, armed Athenas in east Greece suggests that

Fig. 18. Onyx scarab from Amathus, around 500 (London, BM 437; photo courtesy of *British Museum*).

Fig. 19. Attic black-figured amphora, late sixth century (Paris, F 380; photo *La Licorne* courtesy of *Musée du Louvre*).

the type was developed locally, quite possibly under influence from Eastern winged deities such as Ishtar-Shaushga and Anat (with Cyprus being a possible point of contact), but a general divine/demonic connotation of wings may have also played a role.

East Greek Athena between Greece and Anatolia

In this chapter we have investigated the iconography of east Greek Athena in the context of the east Greeks' relations with their eastern neighbours, using Athena at Troy – Greek Ilion – as a starting point for addressing the broader question of Anatolian influences on the development of the prime Greek *polis* goddess. Evidence for the cult statue of Athena at Ilion is essentially limited to early Hellenistic coins of Ilion, which represent an Athena type in many ways conforming to patterns characteristic of Anatolian cult statues. Although these Anatolian features are not attested at Ilion or in most other places before the Hellenistic period, we can reasonably assume that they originated in the archaic period; for Athena, this is confirmed by the evidence for an unusual, Anatolian-influenced iconography at Assos, a city close to Ilion. We cannot be certain that the Ilion image, with its unique combination of warlike spear and craft-related spindle, was an ancient east Greek *xoanon* rather than a Hellenistic creation drawing on earlier iconographic and poetic concepts. However, as our examination of the iconography of Athena in archaic east Greece has revealed that the dichotomy in the goddess's character certainly existed in archaic east Greece, the odds may be in favour of an earlier date.

The consideration of the broader question of the iconography of archaic east Greek Athena in an Anatolian context has shown that the iconography of the spinning Athena quite probably originated in archaic east Greece under the influence of the art and ideology of the Greeks' eastern neighbours, with whom the Greeks had in common the economic importance of woolworking, and who are known to have represented women from local ruling families as seated and spinning in funerary art. Similarly, in a Greek context, the representation of Athena with spinning implements can be seen as a reference to the wealth and status of the local Greek aristocracy. But this same goddess was also intimately associated with the attributes of war, which, contrary to the common (classical Athenian) perception of the 'soft' east Greeks, was a constant feature of life in the east Greek cities, a feature that left its mark also on art and poetry. It should not surprise us to find that the account of the Trojan war largely took shape in this environment, and that Athena – as in other areas of Greece – was represented with implements of war in east Greek art from the early sixth century onwards.

Both economic wealth and the defence of the people were thus central concerns of east Greek Athena, with the craft-oriented and the warlike aspects of the iconographic image of Athena present already in the archaic period. While warlike Athena is found throughout the archaic Greek world – possibly also ultimately of eastern origins, though earlier – it appears to have been east Greece which was the origin of the spinning Athena and her association with wool-working as one of the basic aspects of city-life. It is not inconceivable that the presence of this character trait in the Homeric epics is directly linked to its prominence in east Greece, which resulted, at least partly, from the interactions of the Greeks with their Anatolian cultural environment.

Acknowledgements

I would like to thank the editors for their patience and helpful suggestions, and the conference participants for their comments. I am also grateful to John Boardman, Nigel Spencer, Astrid Möller, Susanne Ebbinghaus and Brian Rose for constructive criticism and advice, and to Sophie Descamps, Ute Wartenberg, Dyfri Williams, Henry Kim, Vera Slehoferova, Richard Tomlinson and Lesley Beaumont for help with obtaining photographs and permission to publish them.

Notes

[1] Cook 1962, 15.

[2] Cf. Kurke 1992; Georges 1994, 1–46; De Vries 1975; Cook 1975.

[3] Cf. e.g. Spencer 1995, 296–9; Rose 1993, 98–104; also Hanfmann 1983, 90–6, 128–36.

[4] The most recent comprehensive work on Greek Ilion, the unpublished Habilitation thesis by D. Hertel, *Eine Stadt als Zeugnis ihrer Geschichte: Troja/ Ilion in griechischer und hellenistisch-römischer Zeit* (University of Cologne 1993), has not been accessible to me.

[5] Cf. Rose 1992, 43–5; Hertel 1991.

[6] e.g. Strabo 13.1.26; cf. Rose 1993, 98–104; Leaf 1923, 141–50.

[7] On the excavations by Schliemann and Dörpfeld, cf. Goethert and Schleif 1962, 1–3; Dörpfeld 1902, 208–11. The identification of the temple as that of Athena Ilias appears relatively secure on the basis of its position and the finds of inscriptions.

[8] Cf. Rose 1992, 45–6. Goethert and Schleif (1962) dated the temple into the Augustan period, and more recently, Schmidt-Dounas (1991) suggested a second-century date.

[9] An inscription dating to shortly after 280 (Frisch 1975, 84–91 no. 32, lines 20, 28–9) mentions traditional ancestral sacrifices (νομιζομένην καὶ πάτ[ριον θυ]σίαν) which can perhaps be recognized in representations of a cow (sometimes in the process of being stabbed by a man) suspended from a pole or tree on Roman coins of Ilion. The iconography is unique and has been thought to represent a rite of early Greek, pre-Hellenic or Anatolian origins (Lacroix 1949, 110 n. 5; Brückner 1902, 563–6). Cf. also Miller 1994, 271–2, pl. 84f, for Hellenistic antefixes from Ilion representing a female head (Athena?) with a horned helmet as a possible reference to this rite.

[10] This seems to suggest that a sanctuary of Athena existed at Troy at least

from the mid-fourth century onwards; however, it is not clear whether the destination of the maidens was Athena Ilias at Troy, or rather Athena Ilias at Physkos, a city in Locris. On the Locrian maidens, see most recently Bonnechere 1994, 150–63.

[11] Hesychius 2.1.556a s.v. *Ilieia*; Frisch 1975, 59–62 no. 24, 123–6 no. 51. On the history of the league: Frisch 1975, xi–xv; Boffo 1985, 114–23.

[12] Cf. Rose 1992, 44. For Pergamon, cf. Schalles 1985, 5–7, 13–22.

[13] Strabo (13.1.26) mentions that Athena's sanctuary at the time of Alexander's visit was 'small and cheap' (μικρὸν καὶ εὐτελές).

[14] On Palladia in Greek art, see Demargne 1984, 965–9, 1019–20.

[15] Strabo 13.1.41; cf. e.g. Ziehen 1949, 174.

[16] Cf. Jung 1982, 47–9 and Burkert 1991b, 88. Note, however, that the passage has been taken by some to be a later Athenian interpolation (Lorimer 1950, 442–9).

[17] ...τῆς Ἀθηνᾶς τὸ ξόανον νῦν μὲν ἑστηκὸς ὁρᾶται, Ὅμηρος δὲ καθήμενον ἐμφαίνει.

[18] Bellinger 1961; Lacroix 1949, 103–12, pl. 7.

[19] Cf. Fleischer 1973, 107–11. The bands also appear on other representations of Athena in an east Greek context, such as on coins of Pergamon (Lacroix 1949, 124–5, pl. 9.5–6).

[20] On the identification of statues on coins in general, cf. Lacroix 1949, 10–28.

[21] Ἦν δὲ τῷ μεγέθει τρίπηχυ, τοῖς δὲ ποσὶ συμβεβηκός, καὶ τῇ μὲν δεξιᾷ δόρυ διηρμένον ἔχον, τῇ δὲ ἑτέρᾳ ἠλακάτην καὶ ἄτρακτον (Apollodorus 3.12.3; tr. J. Frazer). Cf. Lacroix 1949, 103–12. Apollodorus reports that the legs of the statue were joined, as on some of the early coins, while we see her walking especially on the later coins, but this may merely be an element of variation added by the die-cutter in order to bring to life the otherwise stiff statue, in keeping with the tastes of the time. On the repetition of the type in the coinage of other cities, cf. Lacroix 1949, 111–12, pl. 7.

[22] Proponents of these opposing views: e.g. Graf 1985, 213–14; Bellinger 1961, 15.

[23] Demargne 1984, 966 no. 77, pl. 712. On the history of Assos, cf. Strabo 13.1.59. Cf. also Serdaroglu 1990; Leaf 1923, 289–303.

[24] Cf. Merkelbach 1976, 30–5 no. 14; 51–9 no. 26.

[25] The tetradrachm has been assigned by some scholars to the late fifth or first half of the fourth century, but, judging from the style of the obverse, a date around or soon after the mid-fourth century seems more likely. One could imagine the coin to have been minted, for example, in the third quarter of the fourth century, or around the time of Alexander, when it would have fitted well into the framework of an awakening of antiquarian interest in the fourth century, possibly in connection with the 'Ionian Renaissance'; cf. Isager 1994.

[26] Demargne 1984, 962 no. 46, pl. 708; Langlotz 1975, 100–1 pl. 25.4–5.

[27] For parallels of the pointed headdress in east Greek coroplast art, cf. Langlotz 1975, 101, pl. 25.6; Blinkenberg 1931, 542 no. 2246b, pl. 103; Akurgal 1987, 36, pl. 14.a–b.

[28] Cf. Akurgal 1987, 36, and Akurgal 1949, 1–12. Ishtar-Shaushga appears on the thirteenth century reliefs at Yazilikaya, cf. Bittel 1975, 141–2 no. 38,

pls. 23–4. A representation on a Hittite relief at Fraktin of a goddess in profile wearing a high pointed head-dress (Trémouille 1994, pls. I, II) may in fact represent a large circular head-dress in profile view.

[29] Among the earliest examples of the motif are a metope of the Sicyonian treasury, dated to around 560, and a bilingual vase by the Andokides Painter of around 520 which shows Ajax and Achilles playing dice (Boston, MFA 01.8037). Athena is carrying a spear across her shoulder on an early classical red-figured lekythos (London market: *Christie's Sales Catalogue 20th Feb. 1979*, 20 no. 99, pl. 6.99) and on a somewhat later red-figured pyxis lid (Copenhagen, National Museum 731: Demargne 1984, 992 no. 411, pl. 750). The motif becomes popular in Hellenistic glyptic art; cf. Thomas 1982, 60–2.

[30] See e.g. *Od.* 20.72; *Il.* 14.178–9.

[31] Cf. Gauer 1996; Forssman 1991, 269–74.

[32] Cf. Snodgrass 1987, 135–46; Raeck 1984. On the kind of attributes held by archaic cult statues in general: Romano 1980, 399–404.

[33] This contradicts, of course, the well-attested crucial role allocated to the removal of the Palladion in making possible the fall of Troy (Dionysius of Halikarnassos 1.69), and the claim by a number of other Greek cities to possess the stolen Palladion.

[34] Cf. Demargne 1984, 961–4, 1019. On Athena's connection with spinning and weaving, cf. Graf 1985, 211. On her cult as Ergane, cf. Di Vita 1952–4, 149–54; Ridgway 1992, 137–40. On spinning in general, cf. Forbes 1956, 151–74. Dedications of spinning and weaving equipment, such as spindles and loomweights, are common in sanctuaries of Athena, but also of other gods; cf. Simon 1986, 263–70.

[35] Di Vita 1952–4; Stucchi 1956.

[36] Κώκαλος 18/19 [1972/3], 184, pl. 34.2.

[37] Blinkenberg 1931, 535–6 no. 2217, pl. 102, cf. Graf 1985, 210, 214. Alternatively, Di Vita (1952–4) and Stucchi (1956) propose a derivation of the type from an Athenian statue.

[38] On Erythrai, see Graf 1985, 147–375.

[39] Engelmann and Merkelbach 1973, 347–64 nos. 207, 208, 210; also Simon 1986, 131–5.

[40] ἄγαλμα ξύλου μεγέθει μέγα καθήμενόν τε ἐπὶ θρόνου καὶ ἠλακάτην ἐν ἑκατέρᾳ τῶν χειρῶν ἔχει καὶ ἐπὶ τῆς κεφαλῆς πόλον.

[41] On Endoios and his works, cf. most recently Viviers 1992, 55–102, esp. 56–62.

[42] For a detailed discussion of the helmet and aegis types, see the present author's doctoral thesis on the iconography of Athena in classical Greece, soon to be completed at Oxford.

[43] Lebessi 1976, 21–2 no. A1, 86–90, 173–4, pl. 2–3. The piece belongs to a series of similar stelai with representations of women, warriors and seated figures, the original use of which is unclear.

[44] For a Roman relief from Philippi with a representation of Athena holding what might be spindle and distaff, cf. Perdrizet 1903, 263–5. An incised spindle and distaff can possibly be identified on an altar of Athena Ergane at Epidauros (*IG* IV.2.270).

[45] An epithet χρυσηλάκατος, possibly to be translated as 'of the golden distaff', is attested for Artemis and a number of other deities; cf. Bianchi 1953, 208–10.

[46] Cf. Strong and Garstang 1913. Lucian calls her 'Hera' and says she has something of the attributes of Athena, Aphrodite, Selene, Rhea, Artemis, Nemesis and the Fates.

[47] Akurgal 1949, pl. 42a (relief from Marash, here *Fig.* 11); Schachner and Schachner 1996 (relief from Marash, Antakya Museum 17915); Amiet 1966, 540, Figure 413 (relief from Susa, Paris, Louvre SB 2834).

[48] Pritchard 1969, 357; Bossert 1954–9, 349–59. The other two goddesses, however, hold mirrors, and one could suspect that the attributes merely designate the goddesses as female, without any further significance.

[49] One might also note that the earliest allegorical association of Athena with τέχνη is commonly attributed to an Ionian fifth-century philosopher, Metrodoros of Lampsakos: νοῦν μὲν τὸν Δία, τὴν δὲ Ἀθηνᾶν τέχνην (Diels and Kranz 1952, 50 no. 6).

[50] Cf. Forbes 1956, 12–13; Barnett 1975, 431.

[51] Cf. Özgan 1978; Boardman 1967, 23; Jung 1982, 117–22, 146–50. Note also that anthropomorphic Hittite cult statues were often seated; cf. Güterbock 1983b.

[52] Cf. e.g. Hippokrates' attribution of the east Greeks' lack of courage to the climate of the region and the contact with eastern peoples (*Aer.* 16); also Athenaios 12.534; Herodotos 1.143; Thucydides 6.77. On the subject, see especially Kurke 1992.

[53] Herodotos 1.142.3; cf. Graf 1985, 371–2. According to Strabo 13.1.41, an ancient seated cult statue of Athena existed also on Chios itself; cf. Simon 1986, 104.

[54] Boardman 1967, 5–31; Graf 1985, 44–7; Simon 1986, 110–16; Morton 1994.

[55] Boardman 1967, 23–4, 163–4 no. 785, pl. 60; Lemos 1991, 106 fig. 59; 270 no. 684, pl. 91.

[56] The cult statue may also have worn a griffin-crown, which has been reconstructed from finds of lead griffin protomes in the temple and may betray Anatolian influence; cf. Boardman 1967, 26–8, 203–5 no. 166, pls. 84–5.

[57] Athena's warlike character was, of course, well established throughout Greece from an early period onwards, and its possible eastern origin may date back to the Bronze Age.

[58] Lemos 1991, 292 no. 899, pl. 120.

[59] Lemos 1991, 280 no. 775, pl. 101; 282 no. 789, pl. 103.

[60] e.g. Blinkenberg 1931, 677 no. 2868, pl. 133; *Clara Rhodos* 4 (1931) 212–13 no. 13, fig. 226.

[61] Demargne 1984, 964–5 no. 63, pl. 711.

[62] Demargne 1984, 964 no. 60, pl. 710.

[63] Cf. most recently Muss 1994, 80, 82, fig. 104; Brinkmann 1994, 101–9.

5

A HISTORIAN'S HEADACHE
How to read 'Homeric society'?

Kurt A. Raaflaub

What is called 'Homeric society' is the social environment and background in and against which the epic heroes live, act, excel and suffer. Homer and Hesiod believed that this society existed in a somewhat distant past, before the contemporary Iron Age; from the eighth century, ancient tombs were venerated as those of heroes, and ancient sites and ruins attributed to them.[1] With the modern distinction between myth and history, the historicity of Homeric society has become an important problem. The debate on this problem is old and instructive. Every generation, it seems, has to come to terms with it. Currently, it is a 'hot' topic, as attested by the number of pertinent books published in the 1990s.[2] Many of the arguments are the same as those used fifty or one hundred years ago. But new insights have accrued as well, and it may just be that the collective weight of these insights, culled from many disciplines, has shifted the burden of proof to the side of those who continue to deny the substantial historicity of Homeric society or the 'Homeric world'.

In a recent publication, Paul Cartledge writes: 'The arguments for the existence of a genuinely historical single and uniform Homeric "society" or "period" or more vaguely "world" seem monumentally unpersuasive. My own view, which the mountain of recent investigation has merely hardened, is that Homer's fictive universe remains important precisely because it never existed outside the poet's or poets' fertile imagination(s) – just as Homeric diction was a *Kunstsprache* never actually spoken outside the context of an epic recital.' Sarah Morris has recently seconded this opinion: 'Homer's world is too variegated to be real or immediate, and we are jousting at windmills in trying to find it.'[3]

In responding to this challenge, I shall not try to prove the existence of a 'genuinely historical single and uniform' Homeric society, period or world. In staking this as the claim, Cartledge is both reaching impossibly high and throwing the baby out with the bathwater. The goal we should pursue is more modest and realistic: to make a plausible case (not to present proof) for the suggestion that within the epic narrative (not encompassing all that is mentioned in this narrative) there is much evidence (not complete and foolproof evidence) to show that the economic, social and political *background* to the heroic actions (not the events, heroes and actions themselves) is sufficiently (not completely) consistent to reflect elements of a historical society (that is, a society existing in time and space) or, perhaps more cautiously, to reflect a historical stage of social development in early Greece. In formulating my goal so cautiously, I simply limit myself to what seems to me possible, sensible and sufficient. For if we succeed in making a plausible case for the thesis that the social background description in the epics is sufficiently consistent to reflect elements of a historical society, we will be able to use the epics – despite their poetic nature and complicated history – as valuable literary evidence to illuminate a period for which we would otherwise have to rely almost entirely on archaeological sources. And we will be able to do so not just, as many have done before, by using a common-sense approach and assuming that Homer would naturally have modeled epic society after that of his own time,[4] but more confidently and rationally, on the basis of more specific criteria.[5]

By 'Homer' or 'the poet' I mean the poet(s) by whom the extant epics were composed. Whether or not they were the work of the same 'monumental' poet, they are sufficiently close to each other to be examined as one unit. They are usually dated to the second half of the eighth century, the *Iliad* perhaps a generation before the *Odyssey*, but serious arguments have been proposed for the first half of the seventh century.[6]

The question of 'Homeric society' should be distinguished from two related but different questions. One of these, *the* Homeric Question, concerns the origins of the extant epics. This question, once debated bitterly between Analysts and Unitarians, and focusing on the poet or poets and their making of the epics, has shifted considerably over the last few decades – so much so that today, as Gregory Nagy says, 'there is no agreement about what the Homeric Question might be'.[7] It now entails oral poetry, the performance of such poetry and its social function, the crystallization of oral epics into fixed poems that eventually were written down and recited by rhapsodes, and the various stories and traditions that may have influenced the elaboration of the extant epics;[8] it concerns anthropological research on the nature and

social function of oral traditions and oral history, and on the transformations they tend to undergo in the course of long-term transmission;[9] and it includes comparative research on heroic and oral epic,
and on the role of cultural memory and historical consciousness in
early societies.[10] All these approaches are directly relevant to our
investigation of Homeric society.

The other much-debated question is that of the historicity of the
Trojan War. It concerns an event rather than social conditions. The
discussion about whether or not concrete memories of such an event
are preserved in the epics is fascinating but, in my view, futile.[11] I shall
not discuss this question systematically, but some of the arguments
I shall advance for the historicity of Homeric society will prove
detrimental for that of the Trojan War.

I

A brief look at the development of scholarship on Homeric society is
illuminating. Every new discovery, every widening of the scope of
inquiry, in the end has helped solidify the same conclusion: the society
the epics describe is historical and belongs close to the period of the
poet himself. To begin with archaeology and the monuments, the
'Schliemann year' and the controversies it stirred up recently reminded us of the discoverer of Troy and Mycenae who used Homer as
his guide and was convinced he had found the world of Homer. So
were many of his successors.[12] In fact, as Moses Finley said later about
the time when he wrote his famous book, 'in the early 1950s, the
notion was generally accepted that the world of Odysseus was on the
whole the Mycenaean world... The small heretical minority, of whom
I was one, were in a difficult polemical position.' Wace and Stubbings'
Companion to Homer, published in 1962 but in the works for more than
twenty years, confirms this assessment. Even in 1972, Austin and
Vidal-Naquet still thought the adherents of the Mycenaean orthodoxy
were in the majority.[13] Of course, there had been dissenting voices:
Hasebroek, Schadewaldt, Strasburger in Germany, Calhoun in England, among others.[14] What brought about a crucial, though late, change
in opinion was another major discovery and one scholar's persistence.

In 1953, Ventris and Chadwick published their discovery of Greek
language on the Mycenaean Linear B tablets. These tablets revealed
a complex, centralized and highly hierarchical social-economic system
reminiscent more of contemporary Near-Eastern civilizations than of
anything known from later Greek history.[15] But words and names
were the same, at first sight suggesting continuity from the Bronze Age

to the archaic age. As Chadwick, who did not share this view, put it: 'All this can be made to add up to a strong case for the preservation of a large Mycenaean element in the epics; to this school of thought the Trojan War is a historical event, and Homer a guide book to Mycenaean Greece.'[16]

When Ventris' discovery was announced, Finley's *World of Odysseus* (1954) was already in press. Approaching the question from the perspective of social and economic history and anthropology, Finley clearly recognized the incompatibility of what the epics describe with the archaeological evidence from Mycenaean sites:

> From the very first publication announcing the decipherment, the literature of the Mycenaean tablets has been filled with references, parallels, analogies, arguments, and echoes from Homer. The procedure has tended to be haphazard and arbitrary in the extreme: an odd passage from the *Iliad*, the appearance of a particular word or name in both the tablets and the poems, and possible etymological relations are noted when they seem to prove a point or suggest a meaning... But there has been no systematic consideration of either the historical problems involved in juxtaposing the two sets of materials, or of the methodological principles which must be applied if the analysis is to have any validity. (Finley 1957, 133 = 1982, 213)

Hence Finley examined the evidence from the tablets and that from the epics side by side in an area where there is sufficient material to allow comparison, that of property and tenure. His conclusion: 'The Homeric world was altogether post-Mycenaean, and the so-called reminiscences and survivals are rare, isolated and garbled. Hence Homer is not only not a reliable guide to the Mycenaean tablets: he is no guide at all.'[17]

Finley's work represents a watershed in the discussion of Homeric society. The thesis for which he argued was threefold: (1) we should accept discontinuity between the Mycenaean and the archaic ages; (2) Homeric society is essentially consistent and coherent, and makes sense anthropologically; (3) this society is to be dated in the tenth or ninth centuries BC. I shall briefly discuss these three points.

First, Finley argued that the society described by Homer was separated from Mycenaean society by a deep gap; Greek Dark Age and archaic society was different in structure and developed in an entirely different direction. By contrast, Emily Vermeule states: 'There was no break between the Mycenaean and Homeric worlds, only change. The degree of change is arguable.'[18] When, we ask, is 'change' profound and comprehensive enough to represent a 'break'? In answer to this question it is important to assess not only the degree of continuity, but also the archaic Greeks' potential for reaching and understanding the world of the Bronze Age.[19] True, recent discoveries have shed welcome light on the 'Dark Ages'; the immense significance of this period in shaping the culture of later centuries is now increasingly recognized, and the concept of a 'Dark Age', with relatively sharp chronological boundaries, has itself been challenged seriously. In some outlying areas (Cyprus, Crete, to a lesser degree Athens or northern Boeotia/Phokis, among others) continuity was broad and substantial, and we now know that not all components of Mycenaean civilization were wiped out immediately. What is needed is not sweeping generalizations but assessments that differentiate carefully between regions and issues or objects, and new discoveries may prompt us in the future to revise such assessments further. But at this point it still seems clear that the destruction of the palaces, the nerve centers of Mycenaean economy and society, was a traumatic event with massive and irreversible consequences, and that in most areas by the Submycenaean period (*c.* 1125–1050) most traces of this civilization had disappeared. In dialects (pointing to the influx of new populations), settlement places and patterns, material culture, meaning and function of terminology (despite morphological affinity of many words), and much else, despite undeniable and substantial continuity on various levels, the changes were deep and pervasive.[20] The general impression of this period still is one of a massively reduced population living in small and scattered villages, in simple conditions and in relative isolation. 'If any period can truly be called a "Dark Age", it is this.'[21] The Protogeometric period (*c.* 1050–900) represents many new beginnings, in exceptional cases (especially Lefkandi) with indications of great wealth and international connections, and generally with features that soon resemble those of Homeric society. The eighth century witnessed especially rapid changes, a veritable 'structural revolution', in which 'everything was open to challenge: the world was turned upside down'.[22] Not surprisingly, therefore, Bronze Age survivals in the Homeric picture are rare and non-essential exceptions. Hence, even if, as is often argued, this debate should not be waged under the misleading headings of continuity and discontinuity, even if we consider the component of violent rupture relatively small and that of ongoing transformation relatively large, the Hellenic world after the Dark Ages was, in most essential respects, radically different from that of the Bronze Age four hundred years earlier.[23]

Second, the problem of consistency. On sociological and anthropological grounds, Finley argued for coherence in the epic description of

Homeric society. The essential point is that no one claims complete coherence and absence of any contradictions. In Finley's words,

> A model can be constructed, imperfect, incomplete, untidy, yet tying together the fundamentals of political and social structure with an appropriate value system in a way that stands up to comparative analysis, the only control available to us in the absence of external documentation... The critical point is...that the model is so coherent, and this also rules out the common statement that what we find in the poems is either a fiction...or a composite drawn from different eras. Given the profound differences between the Bronze Age and the eighth century BC, such a composite would be blatantly artificial, unable to withstand careful social analysis. (Finley 1977, 153; cf. 9, 48, 146)

Several scholars have since found in their research ample confirmation for a high degree of consistency in Homer's social picture. Among others, I mention Arthur Adkins' analyses of social values and political norms, Walter Donlan's examination of social and economic structures, Gabriel Herman's investigation of social relations, and recently Richard Seaford's discussion of reciprocity and ritual. Various studies of warfare and modes of fighting, the working and significance of political institutions, the conduct of interstate relations, and the customs of feasting have yielded further confirmation. Also recently, Christoph Ulf and Hans van Wees have broadly re-examined Homeric society and reached the same conclusion.[24]

Others, led by Geoffrey Kirk, Anthony Long and Anthony Snodgrass, have challenged Finley's claim and defended the view that Homeric society is essentially unhistorical because its description either reveals contradictions that seem insurmountable, or represents a fiction, or a hopeless amalgam of elements from various stages of social development ranging from the Mycenaean to the archaic ages, or all of the above combined. These objections must be taken seriously. Although not all have been accepted and some have since been refuted,[25] there clearly *are* contradictions, even important ones. But they are not insurmountable, and very similar ones are attested in other societies, both 'primitive' and medieval. Hence phenomena that are perceived as mutually exclusive in one society *can* coexist in another. The epics *do* contain anachronistic elements and a healthy dose of fiction and fantasy. But many of these elements are rather easily recognizable even to us – they must have been obvious to contemporary audiences. Moreover, and this is decisive, all these elements pale in significance when compared with the pervasive consistencies noticed by so many scholars throughout a broad range of economic, social, military and political structures.

174

The understanding of Homeric society that emerges from these discussions can be summarized as follows. First, persons, events and a few other elements *may* have formed an old, perhaps even historical, core of oral traditions reaching, perhaps, back into the Bronze Age. Certain conditions, such as forms of warfare or the scope of raiding expeditions, adventures, and international relations *may* have been remembered over many generations. Even if so, we shall see that long-term transmission and constant reinterpretation by generations of singers in ever-changing social conditions are likely to transform such core stories and memories so profoundly as to make it impossible to trace their beginnings or check their authenticity. Moreover, possible correspondences in this sphere between stories in the Homeric epics and Bronze Age archaeological discoveries (such as Mycenaean sherds in Troy VI) or visual representations (such as the miniature frescoes in a house on Minoan Thera), given their generic nature and the variety of possible explanations, so far seem incapable of establishing a specific link.[26]

Second, the picture includes some anachronisms, archaisms, and perhaps some genuine memories of the Mycenaean and Submycenaean periods and the Dark Ages. The list of such items is under constant revision; it includes, on one level, objects such as bronze weapons, war chariots and the famous boar's tusk helmet.[27] Explanations vary: chariots may have been remembered; they may be a heroic metaphor for horses; or they may have been in use in the eighth century in Asia Minor or even, at least for racing and hunting, in Greece.[28] The preponderance of bronze weapons may represent genuine memory or perhaps reflect a value scale connected with colors and metals – the shinier, the nobler; hence gold primarily characterized the gods' equipment, bronze the heroes'.[29] The boar's tusk helmet may have been an heirloom or found in Bronze Age tombs – an experience repeated by modern archaeologists – or still in use in some areas in the Submycenaean period.[30] The exclusion of 'modern' phenomena that must have been known to the poet probably represents another form of deliberate archaization: writing, attested only in the Bellerophon story (*Il.* 6.167–70), is a case in point; riding is another.[31] At any rate, archaisms had their proper place in such poetry, and the combined weight of these items is negligible.[32]

Third, exaggeration and fantasy form important elements in heroic poetry. For example, the shields of Hector and Ajax are described as man-sized, reaching from neck to feet, round, thick, with several layers of ox-hide and an outer layer of bronze. Van Wees observes rightly that there is no historical parallel for such a shield, and there cannot be one, since a man-sized shield can be neither round – this would make it uselessly wide – nor made of bronze because it would be too heavy to carry. The solution to the problem perhaps is not, as scholars usually assume, that Homer has amalgamated a small, round, hoplite shield and a large, oblong, Mycenaean tower shield, but that he is describing the fantastically big and heavy armor of fantastically big and strong heroes. Accordingly, in the poet's view, ideally the best fighters should carry the biggest shields, and Achilles has a spear 'so heavy, big and sturdy' that 'no other Achaean could brandish it'. Of course, as Archilochus tells us, in real life the best fighters were not necessarily the tallest and most beautiful men. We should think in the same way of the fabulous wealth and ostentation attributed to epic figures, the vastly exaggerated numbers (of the army at Troy or the slaves and herds of leading *basileis*) and the large and schematic time frames (ten years of war and ten of misfortunes on the return, hence twenty years on Ithaca without a 'king' or assembly, *Od.* 2.26–27).[33] Though too often taken seriously, such elements of fantasy and exaggeration usually can easily be identified. They combine with the elements of deliberate archaization, mentioned before, to create a 'heroic sphere' populated by figures who are larger than life, and thus to establish what James Redfield calls an 'epic distance' which consciously separates the world of song from the world of the audience.[34]

Fourth, the more we learn about it the clearer it becomes that knowledge of Near Eastern events, traditions, objects, and motifs has substantially influenced the epic narrative and picture. The exceptional importance attributed to the siege of cities or individual motifs such as the Trojan Horse may be part of such foreign influences – which, moreover, were at work both in the Bronze Age and in the Geometric and Orientalizing periods. Their impact and significance need to be assessed in the context of a much broader range of interactions between Anatolia, Mesopotamia, the Levant, and Egypt on the one side, and, on the other, the Aegean and Western Mediterranean.[35]

Fifth, what remains is the large bulk of the material used to depict the social background and environment of heroic events and deeds which, in contrast to the main events, persons, and individual objects, is not marked or emphasized. This background description is not entirely but sufficiently consistent to allow us to recognize a society that, as Finley has shown, makes sense from an anthropological perspective and can be fitted into a scheme of social evolution among early societies.

Sixth, of course, the epics represent poetic art of the highest order,

176

not a sociological or historical treatise. The poet does not tell us all he knows; he selects and emphasizes according to his own dramatic and interpretative purposes (Calhoun 1962, 431). This factor of 'poetic selection' is often underestimated: not all that the poet fails to empha- size is unimportant or non-existent in Homeric society. For example, the *Odyssey* is concerned with a hero's homecoming and his efforts to regain control in his *oikos*. Although the community is deeply affected by these events, the poet's primary attention rests on this *oikos*. Thus the community of Ithaka remains in the background. This does not mean, however, as many scholars have concluded, that this particular community was unimportant, undeveloped or even hardly existing; nor does it mean, more generally, that the *oikos* was the only social entity that counted for Homeric people.

The society thus described must have existed in time and space outside of the epics. In view of the traditions associated with Homer and the 'Homerids', the place most likely was Ionia – at least origi- nally.[36] Given the panhellenic aspiration, success, and validity of the epics, however, most local or even regional specificities must have receded early on and have been replaced by a panhellenic outlook and, accordingly, a deliberate focus on issues, values, patterns of life, and modes of behavior that were familiar, acceptable, and important to Greeks in many parts of Hellas. Homeric society thus is panhellenic in the sense that it allowed broad recognition and identification.[37] This, I should stress, only makes it less specific, not more fictitious or less historical.

How, then, should we date Homeric society? Finley believed that the epics ignore essential elements (including the *polis*) with which we know a late eighth-century poet should have been familiar, and that heroic poetry generally describes conditions that lie at least one cen- tury before the poet's own time. Hence he suggested the tenth and ninth centuries. Both presuppositions have been largely refuted. Sev- eral recent studies have argued, for example, that an early form of the *polis* is at the center of Homeric social structure.[38] For other reasons, too, recent publications tend to date Homeric society to the poet's own time, in the second half of the eighth or even the early seventh century.[39] Before we decide this question, we have to look at another area of research that has recently gained in importance.

II

Milman Parry's, Albert Lord's, and their successors' pathbreaking analyses of epic diction and composition and comparative studies of oral epic were absorbed into the mainstream of Homeric studies only late (in the 1970s). Although still in flux and debated, these studies have changed our understanding of the making of the epics and the relationship of the poet to his mythical material and to his own time and society.[40]

Oral poetry is a craft, learned from childhood by singers who grow up in a tradition that uses an elaborate system of formulae and set pieces as well as mnemonic devices to recreate in performance songs about memorable events and great individual exploits. Comparative analysis of a wide range of such poetry in many parts of the world has revealed a surprising number of shared characteristics.[41] Although the Homeric epics seem to be longer, more complex, more carefully composed and integrated, and artistically more accomplished than most comparable songs, these epics too are the product of such an oral poetic tradition. Their nature and background thus can be illuminated by comparison with other epic traditions.

Formulaic diction, with its well-known 'economy' of words and phrases and its preference for set pieces, is often taken to be conservative, inflexible and unadaptable, preserved from a distant past – perhaps, as West and others suggest, even the early Mycenaean period, 1000 years before Homer[42] – by repetitive use of generations of singers. In addition, as Joachim Latacz sees it, the artistic aim of such poetry was to improve upon a given tradition, not to deviate from it. Assumptions such as these have suggested to many that knowledge of events and social or political structures in the Mycenaean age (such as the Trojan War or the 'Catalogue of Ships'), enshrined in fixed poetic language, could be transmitted faithfully over centuries, even under changing social conditions, eventually to be shaped or integrated into Homer's great epic.[43]

This view faces several objections. One is that the crucial compositional role of formulae and set pieces does not at all stifle the singer's inventiveness and flexibility. Close examination of the formulaic system in Homer shows in fact that all the compositional units are dynamic and flexible and must have given the poet much freedom to expand, condense and vary any component of his story.[44] The other objection concerns the nature of oral tradition and poetry. With the exception of specific, almost ritualized contexts, oral tradition normally does not keep precise memories of persons and events beyond a limited timespan (often not surpassing three generations). The past is not remembered for its own sake but because it is meaningful to the present; this principle determines what is forgotten, what is remembered, and how it is remembered. Hence oral tradition is highly adaptable; it constantly adjusts to the changing experiences and needs of the society involved.[45] All this is no less true for oral poetry. Thriving in an atmosphere of intense interaction between singer and public, it is successful as long as it is meaningful and attractive to the audience and meets its needs.[46] Entertainment value is essential, but so is the potential for identification. Hence oral song prefers to focus on typical conflict situations and ethical dilemmas.[47] Under these circumstances, the description of the social background tends to adapt to changing conditions rather rapidly. In other words, the backbone of facts, the outline of the epic story, itself subject to change, was in each performance elaborated into a new full narrative with detailed description of background, scenes, actions and individual items. Taking advantage of the flexible composition technique of oral epic, each poet and each generation created a new picture, using as 'filling or background material' conditions familiar to the audience and corresponding to its changing needs and expectations.

The singer's interaction with the audience plays on several levels. For example, we learn in the *Odyssey* that people always want to hear the latest song (1.350–2). Odysseus praises Demodokos, the blind singer at the Phaeacian court:

> Surely the Muse...or else Apollo has taught you,
> for all too right following the tale you sing the Achaians'
> venture, all they did and had done to them, all the sufferings
> of these Achaians, as if you had been there yourself or heard it
> from one who was. (8.488–92, tr. R. Lattimore)

To sing as if one had been there: for the heroic events and exploits (the 'tale') the Muse guarantees truthfulness, but for the details of human experience ('the sufferings') and everyday life the audience assesses truth on the basis of its own knowledge. As Hermann Strasburger puts it, 'the more fabulous in the heroic sphere the better, but in the sphere of daily reality the listener demands verisimilitude'. Mathias Murko reports that audiences of South-Slavic singers measured truth in their songs precisely according to their experiences. Rather than performing poems about great events of the past, the singers preferred to compose songs on minor events in which they themselves and members of the audience had participated and which they were therefore able to describe truthfully. These songs were mostly concerned with duels – often provoked by quarrels about a woman or by offended pride – theft of women, ransoming of captured heroes, gifts to heroes, revenge for violence suffered, and raids provoked by malice, a desire for glory, greed, or simply by restlessness after a long period of peace.[48]

Assuming for a moment that a 'Trojan War' – say, as Emily Vermeule suggests, in the fifteenth century – soon became the subject of heroic song and that such song was performed regularly at the courts of the Mycenaean nobility, what might have happened to it after the destruction of the Mycenaean kingdoms? For a while it might have survived, now representing a nostalgic memory of great times that were quickly receding into a more and more remote past.[49] Soon, however, conditions became so different that such songs no longer had any relation to the world in which poets and their audiences were living. As John Bennet observes, for eighth-century Greeks the disjunction caused by the collapse of the Mycenaean palace societies and the subsequent period of instability was an 'unbridgeable gap'; in all essential respects, the Bronze Age simply was inaccessible to them. Hence singers entertaining the chieftains and their men in the apsidal houses found in some Protogeometric villages most likely sang about heroic exploits in local wars and raids rather than about great and complex wars in a distant past and in distant lands.[50] The earlier songs consequently would be forgotten or adapted to the new realities and thus transformed beyond recognition.

Some confirmation comes from the songs performed in the epics themselves. In the *Odyssey* the Trojan War and the sad *nostoi*, recent events, have become subjects of fame and song, meeting the audience's desire always to hear the newest story. In the *Iliad*, Phoenix tells a story about a war over the city of Kalydon, and Nestor about a series of cattle raids and a war between Pylians and Epeians in his youth.[51] The story which Phoenix characterizes as an 'action of old, not a new thing' (*Il.* 9.527) lies back only one generation; so does Nestor's tale. Both stories deal with heroics in raids for booty and wars between neighboring *poleis*, that is, wars of a type which corresponds precisely to the experience of eighth- or early seventh-century audiences. In fact, even essential components of the poet's conception of the Trojan War fit this pattern – a war between two cities at opposite ends of a large plain (Troy and the temporary *polis* of the Achaeans on the shore), a war fought in retaliation for a raiding expedition (Paris' abduction of Helen and many treasures from Sparta) and combined with (especially Achilles') raids for booty, and a war motivated largely by considerations of status, honor, revenge, and personal obligations.[52] And all this in a framework of social, economic and political structures, values, relations, and behavior patterns that were easily recognizable to the poet's audiences. The 'heroic grandeur' typical of such epic lay not in this framework but in the superhuman deeds of larger-than-life individuals, in the scope and dimension of their enterprises, and in the splendor of their possessions.

From whatever angle we approach the problem, therefore, the conclusion remains the same: apart from the 'heroic sphere', artificially created by the devices of 'epic distance', the society described in the epics must have been sufficiently coherent to be understandable and acceptable to the poet's audiences; it thus must essentially have corresponded to a social reality known to them from immediate experience or recent memory. The depiction of this society therefore cannot as a whole or in large parts have been the result of poetic invention or reflected a time that had long disappeared. The notion of a social and cultural 'amalgam' is only appropriate if it refers to the inclusion in the epic picture of reminiscences of earlier periods or of conscious archaisms. These are part of the picture only because at the time of the performance they were still generally remembered, fit the parameters of generally accepted poetic conventions, served specific poetic needs and, most importantly, did not impede recognition and identification on the part of the audience.

Yet in many respects, as Finley recognized, this is not the late eighth-century (or even later) society we know from other sources or can reconstruct from subsequent and well-attested developments. Even taking into account some lag-time for adjustments which must have been normal in traditional poetry, the poet clearly did not want epic society to appear blatantly contemporary. This phenomenon can be explained in various, perhaps not mutually exclusive, ways. On the one hand, there is much evidence for deliberate archaization on this level as well, especially through omission of recent phenomena. In other words, the social background of heroic epic needed to be 'modern' enough to be understandable but archaic enough to be believable. I have suggested, therefore, that perhaps the poet was consciously describing conditions that belonged to a recent past but were still accessible by the audiences' collective memory; if so, Homeric society as a whole should be considered near-contemporary rather than fully contemporary with the poet (Raaflaub 1993, 45).

On the other hand, this method of 'poetic distancing' – which differs from, but complements, that used to describe the heroic sphere in the sense of the strength, deeds and magnificence of a past generation of superhuman figures – may have been facilitated by the fact that, in contrast to earlier, more static periods, this was a time of profound and rapid change.[53] The old and new thus overlapped and coexisted in people's experience and memory, and this in itself may account for much of what in the epics appears to us inconsistent or contradictory. For such *Gleichzeitigkeit des Ungleichzeitigen* made it easy for the poet to ignore very recent developments and apply to the society he was describing an archaizing patina, or to combine traditional, old-fashioned, but dramatically attractive elements with more recent ones that were part of the audience's life. To us moderns, such poetic distortion is confusing, but the poet's listeners would have had no difficulty in understanding such mixture and juxtaposition: they knew well that things had been very different only a short time ago. To some extent, the result of such poetic distortion coincides with and is reinforced by the effect of 'ideological distortion' observed by Van Wees and Seaford, which causes the poet generally to focus on leaders and *oikos* rather than community and *polis*, and to present an idealizing picture of elite values and behavior.[54]

The following examples all reflect a society in transition.[55] The heroes count their wealth in herds; they are meat-eaters, and conspicuous consumption of meat is crucial for sacrifices, funerals and other feasts. At the same time, land is clearly important – as we know it was in the eighth century, when people ate mostly grain and only exceptionally meat. As Walter Donlan says, 'the Greeks of the epics were apparently stockbreeders who had adapted to farming'.[56] In the late eighth century, communal wars were often fought between *poleis* for the control of fertile land. The poet describes communal wars – which, as in history, coexist with private raids by warrior bands – but emphasizes the more heroic purpose of fighting about women, booty, honor and status. In war, the heroes monopolize the battlefield and the *laoi* seem little more than fodder for their killing sprees. Yet upon close inspection, the latter are constantly and equally involved in the fighting; mass fighting is the norm, the phalanx looms on the horizon.[57] In the community, institutions are informal and dominated by the elite. Yet a closer look reveals that the role of *demos* and assembly is significant. The individual seems almost autonomous, and foreign relations are conducted through elite guest-friendships. Yet public embassies and treaties between *poleis* are known and the *demos* is involved and capable of taking decisive action.[58] The list could be continued.

All these often seemingly contradictory elements are woven into a social picture that indeed represents an amalgam, but, I suggest, with few exceptions not an artificial or unhistorical one that arbitrarily combines components from wildly divergent periods and cultures.

Rather, this is a natural and organic amalgam, reflecting real historical development and perfectly understandable to the poet's listeners.

Some confirmation is provided by the observation that, like much else, the complex customs regulating the process of decision-making in the assembly and the equally complex rules and implications of gift-giving, though puzzling to the modern scholar, have their analogies in other cultures and can be decoded with the help of anthropology and sociology. What matters here is that the poet never explains these rules. He takes them for granted. His audience therefore must have been intimately familiar with all that was going on in these interactions. Spectacular examples are the conflict between Agamemnon and Achilles and the bizarre swap of armor between Glaucus and Diomedes, both convincingly interpreted recently by Donlan.[59] Such customs therefore cannot have been artificial poetic constructs or fossilized memories of things long gone. They are historical and belong to a culture that had existed in the recent past or still existed so that the poet's audience was able to understand them. The same, with few exceptions, is true for Homeric society as a whole.

III

Before we try to tie all this together, let me add a few observations that are perhaps less familiar to the ancient historian – and somewhat more tentative. All the considerations presented so far are based on the assumption that the poetic technique of heroic song, and the mythical traditions which Homer used to create the extant large and complex poems, had existed for generations if not centuries. To some extent, of course, this is true. But perhaps we should distinguish more consciously between form and content. Linguistic, pictorial and other evidence indicates that epic song as such originated way back in the Bronze Age.[60] By contrast, comparative research on *mythopoesis*, historical memory, and historical consciousness suggests that the stories themselves, just as their elaboration and social background, and the historical dimension in which they are couched, may be much younger than is usually believed. I shall present, with due caution and probably in vastly over-simplified terms, a few arguments that might support such a claim.[61]

The first point, mentioned before, is that collective memory is neither comprehensive nor automatic. It is not interested in the past, however great, *per se*. It concerns itself with the past only insofar as this past is relevant and meaningful to the present. The past, therefore, is never fixed: it can be re-shaped, re-organized, re-interpreted. Events that have entered the mythical sphere – often organized in three generations of kings and separated from the directly remembered past by a wide chronological hiatus (the 'floating gap') – are likely to bear little resemblance to their historical origins.[62]

Second, historical consciousness is not automatic either. By historical consciousness I mean an awareness of the existence of a long-term historical dimension pertinent to society and culture, as opposed to an awareness of a short-term past tied to memories of the individual and his immediate ancestors. Such historical consciousness emerges only under specific conditions at relatively advanced stages of social and communal development. It requires a strong sense of community and serves to further integrate the community. Its relevance, again, is tied to the meaning of the past for the present.[63]

Third, myths and oral traditions function as legitimizing, analytical and explanatory devices that are important to the present society. Historical and mythical 'traditions' can transmit historical memories; they can also be constructs that are retrojected into the past without having any grounding in the past. Especially in societies that have developed historical consciousness, such 'traditions' or myths can be provoked by remarkable historical objects, monuments or ruins; they can be etiological in nature, but etiology too serves the purposes of the present.

To a society, then, which has reached a sufficiently high level of culture and communal integration to develop historical consciousness, memories lost in previous generations that did not have such consciousness will be irretrievable. In other words, unless the memory of certain events or conditions of a distant past remains constantly and essentially important to all successive generations, it will be lost. If a society, having developed historical consciousness after an interval without such consciousness, boasts a rich array of myths dealing with events of a distant past, such myths are likely to reflect historicizing fiction rather than genuine historical memories. As said before, at the end of the Bronze Age the Greek world experienced deep and widespread ruptures; in the Dark Ages, conditions were hardly favorable to fostering historical consciousness. In this period, myths, traditions, and songs must soon have been concerned not with an increasingly remote past, however great and memorable it once was, but with the exigencies of survival and the challenges or excitement of competitive relations in a much smaller world.

Fourth, heroic epic – epic, that is, which explicitly refers to great deeds and events in a distant age of heroes – is often built around a core of historic persons and events. These, however, are grouped together, related to each other and interpreted in completely un-historical ways. What triggers heroic song is not interest in history *per se* but in human conflicts and drama – situations that are generally valid, though heroically exaggerated, and with which the audience can identify. The historical facts are incidental; the human deeds, deci-sions and concerns are primary. Hence we too should interpret the extant epics primarily as historical documents of the time in which they were created, informing us not least of the audiences' concerns.[64]

Fifth, it is usually assumed that the Greek cycle of myths originated in the Bronze Age. To the archaic Greek communities, however, the centuries after the end of the Bronze Age, not the Bronze Age itself, were the formative period. Similarly, the core of the Germanic heroic sagas seems to have been formed soon after the end of the tribes' migrations and settlement. The attachment of the Greek myths to the great Bronze Age ruins thus appears to be secondary. In addition, heroic sagas tend to incorporate migrating stories (*Wandersagen*), ma-terials connected with etiologies and rituals, and local myths: they are virtual 'magnets of myths'. Since all this is well visible in the Homeric epics, too, it is conceivable that the mythical material of which they are composed emerged in the timespan of only a few generations before Homer and was combined to form the outline of a grand war story centering on the site of Troy shortly before the great poet himself, who then elaborated and reshaped this story in a highly refined and dra-matic way that was aesthetically pleasing and ethically meaningful to widespread contemporary and later audiences.

Sixth, remarkably, some of the seemingly oldest objects in the *Iliad* occur in parts of the poem that have always been recognized as show-ing especially 'young' or 'modern' linguistic features. The famous boar's tusk helmet is described in Book 10 (the *Doloneia*) and, accord-ing to E. Visser's studies on the technique of epic verse-making, the Catalogue of Ships, often thought to be of Mycenaean origin, was versified in the eighth century.[65] Such examples betray a conscious historicizing or antiquarianizing intent. Possibly, therefore, many seemingly old elements in the cultural and social picture, adding to the amalgam which so disturbs many scholars, are the result of deliberate archaization and cultural amalgamation rather than genuine survivals of early traditions embedded in an old formulaic language.

Seventh, in the case of the German *Heldensage*, the heroic epics' focus on problems of general human interest helps explain their spreading over wide areas and assuming supra-local or supra-regional significance. Similar aspects, according to Gregory Nagy, are responsible for the panhellenic appeal of Greek heroic epic.[66] Such a panhellenic perspective in epic requires a corresponding perspective in the culture producing the epic. Both Greek epics betray a wide horizon and world view. The *Iliad* opposes a joint venture of a panhellenic army to the combined forces of the eastern non-Hellenic world, while the *Odyssey* elaborates a homecoming story in a broad Mediterranean context. The latter perspective seems characteristic of the age of exploration and colonization beginning in the eighth century. The conception underlying the *Iliad* clearly is tied to other panhellenic and supraregional phenomena emerging in the eighth and early seventh centuries, especially the great sanctuaries, the games, the early amphictyonies and religious homogenization.[67] Conceivably, therefore, the grand idea underlying the elaborated Trojan War myth is itself the product of the panhellenic worldview of elite society in Homer's time – artificially connected with an especially suitable site and retrojected into the heroic age.[68]

Eighth, several new phenomena document the emergence of historical consciousness in the eighth century, among them hero cults at sites of earlier burials, and sanctuaries connected with ancient sites and objects.[69] Both these phenomena had an important function in enhancing communal identity and cohesion. The creation of a heroic age, dramatized in the Homeric epics and conceptualized in Hesiod's *Theogony*, fits well into this context.

All these observations, if taken seriously, point in the same direction. We have no way of finding out what kind of traditions may have survived from earlier periods. There is no evidence to confirm the existence of genuine historical traditions about a Trojan War that may have taken place in the Bronze Age, and every reason to believe that such traditions as may have survived were radically transformed over time. Hence the events Homer describes and the combination of persons participating in these events, whatever their individual background, are historicizing fictions. In every respect, despite the long prehistory of epic song and the perhaps much shorter prehistory of myth and traditions, the epics are grounded in the time of their creation and reflect the outlook, ideology and culture of this period.

IV

To return to the question of Homeric society, the results we reached before seem to be confirmed by this latest series of considerations. The social background of the epic action is consciously archaized and heroicized, colored with an artificial patina, and to this effect endowed with anachronistic and artificial elements that to the modern student create the impression of a cultural amalgam. But this society is described from the perspective and with the knowledge of the poet's own time and intended to be recognizable and meaningful to the singer's audience. With few exceptions, it is the society existing in the poet's own time – or, as I suggested, perhaps shortly before then.

I end with two observations. First, the task of understanding how the evidence of Iron Age archaeology and that of the epics fit together is far from completed. On the one hand, Jan Paul Crielaard concludes 'that the new phenomena, which are manifest in the archaeological record of the eighth century and which together constitute the so-called Greek "Renaissance", are without exception attested in the epics'. He considers the depiction of the 'world of Homer' both internally consistent and largely compatible with the archaeological evidence for the poet's time. From this social and historical reality he separates the artistic devices of archaization and fantasy which the poet uses to create 'epic distance' and which result in an artificial and chronologically composite picture (Crielaard 1995, 273–5; cf. 201–9). Ian Morris, on the other hand, agrees with many archaeologists that 'the material world described by Homer cannot be paralleled by the excavated record from any single region of Greece at any single point within the Iron Age'. He therefore proposes that

> material culture and poetic culture were two ways in which people in eighth-century Greece constructed the social world within which they moved. Both were important areas in which people fashioned images of what they wanted their world to be, and challenged competing constructions which they did not like... I conclude that there is no way to use Iron Age archaeology to fix Homer in time or space; rather, Iron Age verbal and non-verbal representations must be read together, as sources for a fuller cultural history. (Morris 1997e, 539)

This view overemphasizes the elements that create 'epic distance' and underestimates the significance of the broad range of correspondences and consistencies emphasized above. Yet, in criticizing the 'amalgam theory' in its traditional form, insisting that the epics are artefacts created from the perspective of the poet's time and intended to be meaningful to the poet's audiences, and accepting that they reflect the panhellenic outlook of the period, Morris's position is closer to Crielaard's and my own than it may seem at first sight.[70]

Second, Martin West and Walter Burkert have long postulated that the composition of the epics should be dated to the first half of the seventh rather than the second half of the eighth century. Recently, West and others have added more arguments for the lower date.[71] Taken together, these arguments seem increasingly compelling. The later date has the advantage of reducing or eliminating some of the difficulties scholars have had with the earlier one, and it probably fits better into Nagy's evolutionary model for the text-fixing of the Homeric tradition.[72] Conversely, the later we date the composition of the epics, the wider the gap becomes in some respects between the world of the epics and the poet's contemporary world – or rather, the stronger and more pervasive becomes the element of 'epic distancing' in the poet's artistic picture. I mention but one example: in the seventh century many areas of Greece witnessed a broad range of institutional developments, including (s)election of officials and council members, fixed procedures for communal decision-making, and the enactment of written laws and 'constitutional' regulations. None of that is visible in the epics.[73] Here, as in many respects, the poet has skilfully used his technique of archaization through exclusion or omission. At the same time, he and most of his listeners must have lived at or remembered a time when such regulations did not yet exist, and they must have been aware that some Greek societies were faster in adopting them than others. It seems to me that under these circumstances the model proposed above for the Homeric world, of an 'organic amalgam' that was based partly on the experience of the *Gleichzeitigkeit des Ungleichzeitigen*, appears even more plausible.[74]

Acknowledgements

I thank Alan Boegehold, Sarah Morris, and Hans van Wees as well as the participants in the Cardiff conference, the Fellows of the Center for Hellenic Studies in 1995/96 (especially Carla Antonaccio and Kathryn Morgan) and the colleagues at Macquarie University in Sydney and the University of New England in Armidale (Australia) for valuable comments and suggestions. I owe special thanks to Paul Cartledge for showing me his excellent chapter on hoplites (1996c) and for engaging in a constructive dialogue, despite our disagreement on some important issues. This essay was revised during an extended stay at the University of New England in the summer of 1996, made possible by a Faculty Fellowship offered by the University; my heartfelt thanks go to the Dean of Arts and Sciences and the Classics Department. This is still work in progress; for earlier efforts to come to terms with various aspects of Homeric society, see Raaflaub 1991; 1993.

Notes

[1] Hes. *Op.* 157–68. Van Wees 1992, ch.1; Patzek 1992, ch.3; Kullmann 1995; see also Bennet 1997, 531–2, and n. 69 below.

[2] Ulf 1990, Patzek 1992, Van Wees 1992, Roisman and Roisman 1993, Andersen and Dickie 1995, Carter and Morris 1995, Crielaard (ed.) 1995. See also Thomas 1993a, Seaford 1994, Morris and Powell 1997.

[3] S. Morris, e-mail message of 26 June 1996; Cartledge 1996c, 687–8; see also Thomas 1993b.

[4] e.g. Hasebroek 1931, Strasburger 1953, Calhoun 1962.

[5] Few of my conclusions will be original; my purpose is mainly to summarize the broad range of arguments that militate against the views of Cartledge, S. Morris and others (below, n. 25). I find myself in substantial agreement with many scholars (including J. Bennet 1997, I. Morris 1997e, and J.P. Crielaard 1995), and have learned much from many more, esp. from B. Patzek, W. Donlan, and H. van Wees. On the importance of combining archaeological and literary evidence, see Morris, this volume.

[6] Eighth century: Lesky 1967, 687–93; Janko 1982, esp. 188–200, 228–31; Kirk 1985, 1–10; Latacz 1996, ch. 2, esp. 56–65. Seventh century: below, n. 71. See also Ballabriga 1990; Stanley 1993, 279–96.

[7] Nagy 1992, 17; cf. id. 1996. Lesky 1967, Heubeck 1974, Latacz 1996.

[8] e.g. Kullmann 1984; 1991, on 'neo-analysis'. Oral poetry: below, n. 41. Crystallization of the epics: Nagy 1979, 1–11; 1995; 1996; Foley 1990, 20–3.

[9] Henige 1974, 1982; Vansina 1985; cf. Goody and Watt 1968, Ungern-Sternberg and Reinau 1988.

[10] Epic: below, n. 41. Memory: Assmann and Hölscher 1988, Assmann 1992, Patzek 1992.

[11] e.g. Finley et al. 1964, Foxhall and Davies 1984, Mellink 1986, Patzek 1992.

[12] For discussion, see Wace and Stubbings 1962; McDonald and Thomas 1990; Sherratt 1990, 808; Buchholz 1991; I. Morris 1997a, 1997e. Schliemann: Calder and Traill 1986, Cobet and Patzek 1992, Gamer-Wallert 1992, Traill 1993.

[13] Finley 1977, 10; Wace and Stubbings 1962, e.g. vii, 328; Austin and Vidal-Naquet 1977, 37 (orig. French, 1972); cf. also Webster 1958. Critical views in Calhoun 1934, 193, 314; Vidal-Naquet 1963; Dickinson 1986.

[14] Hasebroek 1931, 7–9; Schadewaldt 1942; Strasburger 1953, esp. 97–8; 1954; Calhoun 1934; 1962; see also Hoffmann 1956.

[15] Finley 1957–8; 1970, pt. 1; Chadwick 1976; Deger-Jalkotzy 1987; Killen 1988. Decipherment: Ventris and Chadwick 1953, Chadwick 1958, Schachermeyr 1959.

[16] Thus, e.g., Webster 1958. Chadwick 1958 (also in Ventris and Chadwick 1956, 107–8).

[17] Finley 1957, 159 = 1982, 232; cf. id. 1977, 10. See now Bennet 1997.

[18] Vermeule 1964, 309; cf. S. Morris 1992b, xvii–xviii; Thomas 1993a, 69; Foxhall 1995, 249.

[19] See Bennet 1997, 531–2 (below, at n. 50); Kullmann 1995. We should consider here the ancients' general inability to perceive differences in social

conditions across two or three centuries, even without a traumatic rupture: late fourth-century interpretations of Solonian Athens (Hansen 1989, Rhodes 1993) or Roman perceptions of archaic Rome (Raaflaub 1986, 19–22) are obvious examples.

[20] Terminology: A. Morpurgo Davies and F. Gschnitzer, in Mühlestein and Risch 1979, 87–108, 109–34; Risch 1980; Patzek 1992, 56–8. Dialect changes: see the summary in Patzek 1992, 75–7, with bibliography. Generally: Desborough 1964, 1972, 1975; Snodgrass 1971; Deger-Jalkotzy 1983, and recently id. 1991a, 1991b; Ward and Joukowsky 1992; Patzek 1992, pt. 2; Thomas 1993a, 69–82; I. Morris 1997e. On the debate about the 'Dark Ages': S. Morris 1992b; Papadopoulos 1993, forthcoming, vs. I. Morris 1993c, 1997a, with bibliography. On continuity in some areas: Deger-Jalkotzy 1989, 143–7; 1991a; 1991b; 1991c. On Athens: Snodgrass 1982b; I. Morris 1991; Welwei 1992, 50–75. See also n. 49, below.

[21] I. Morris 1997e, 541; cf. 540: 'Population fell by perhaps 75% between 1250 and 1100'. See Snodgrass 1987, ch. 6; Donlan 1989a; Morris, this volume, at n. 22. How this can be reconciled with the more optimistic assessment of Muhly 1992, esp. 19–21, is a puzzle to me. The conclusions drawn by Latacz 1994, 357–8, from Deger-Jalkotzy's (1991a, 145–9; 1991c) remarkable finds in Elateia (Phokis) are far too sweeping: the 'essential basis of Greek culture was preserved undisturbed throughout the entire period'; it 'has been established that Mycenaean culture in Greece did not experience a thorough breakdown in 1200'. Elateia, though not unique, still seems exceptional rather than paradigmatic; so does Lefkandi in the subsequent centuries (n. 22, below). Much depends on what we consider 'essential'.

[22] Morris, this volume, 72. See summary in Patzek 1992, 104–20. Eighth century: Snodgrass 1980, 13–14, chs.1–2; Morris, this volume; Schadewaldt 1942, 126. Lefkandi: Popham et al. 1982, 1993; Blome 1984, 1991; Antonaccio 1995b; its exceptional nature: Morris 1997e, 543.

[23] Bronze Age survivals: Kirk 1960; 1975, 831–3; Sherratt 1990, 809–15; Deger-Jalkotzy 1991b; Hood 1995, 27–8. On the problem of objects as dating criteria: Finley 1977, 150–1; Crielaard 1995, 207–9. On the problem of 'continuity': e.g. Latacz 1996, 40–4.

[24] Ulf 1990; Van Wees 1992; Adkins, e.g. 1960, 1971, 1972, 1982; Donlan, e.g. 1980, ch. 1; 1981/82, 1985, 1989a, 1993; Herman 1987; Seaford 1994. Fighting: Latacz 1977; Pritchett 1985; Van Wees 1994, 1996; Raaflaub 1997a. Institutions: Havelock 1978; Gschnitzer 1983, 1991; Carlier 1984, ch. 2. Interstate relations: Wéry 1967/1979; Karavites 1992; Baltrusch 1994; Raaflaub, forthcoming. Feasting: Van Wees 1995. See also Starr 1961, 156–64; Austin and Vidal-Naquet 1977, 37–40; Heubeck 1974, 166–77; Dalby 1995.

[25] Long 1970; Snodgrass 1971, 388–94; 1974; cf. e.g. Lorimer 1950; Kirk 1962, ch. 9; 1975, esp. 821, 849; Lesky 1967, 717, 740–50; Coldstream 1977, 18; Sherratt 1990; Cartledge 1996c; from a different perspective: Whitley 1991a, 344; 1991b, 34–9. *Contra:* e.g. Adkins 1971; Qviller 1981, esp. 114; Morris 1986, esp. 102–20. See also, on the vagueness inherent in oral epic descriptions, Dalby 1995, 275 with n. 40.

[26] For a different view, see Davies 1984, 95–101; Vermeule 1986, 1987;

S. Morris 1989. Bennet 1997 remains cautious. For Hittite references to Ahhiyawa-Achaeans, see Güterbock 1983a, 1984, 1986; Mellink 1983; Easton 1984: these are fascinating but inconclusive; so are the undeniable relations between Mycenaeans and the west coast of Anatolia: e.g. Mee 1984, Bryce 1989. See also Schachermeyr 1986, Lehmann 1991. Latacz 1988, 160–1; 1994, 354, is surely wrong in seeing historical memories of Bronze Age conditions in the fact that the epics consider Asia Minor non-Greek territory: see Kullmann 1993, 136–8.

[27] Above, n. 23.

[28] Greenhalgh 1973; Anderson 1975; Latacz 1977, 215–23; Patzek 1992, 194–6; Hainsworth 1993, at *Il.* 11.150–3; Crouwel 1993; Van Wees 1994, 9–14; Kullmann 1995, 70.

[29] Gray 1954; Patzek 1992, 188–93.

[30] Yalouris 1960, 42–8; J. Borchhardt 1972, 18–37, 47–52; Patzek 1992, 193–4; Deger-Jalkotzy 1991c, 80. See, for Agamemnon's sceptre, *Il.* 2.101–8; Paus. 9.40.10–12.

[31] Writing: Crielaard 1995, 212–14 (with bibliography), but 273 for another explanation. Riding: Wiesner 1968, 110–35.

[32] See also Finley 1977, 149–51; Giovannini 1989; Bennet 1997, 532–3.

[33] Archilochus F114 West. *Il.* 6.117–18; 13.803–4 (Hector's shield); 7.222–3, 245–6; 11.485, 527 (Ajax' shield); 16.140–4 (Achilles' spear); 14.371–7; strength of heroes: e.g. 12.445–9; cf., on the shield, Van Wees 1992, ch. 1, esp. 17–21; H. Borchhardt 1977, esp. 44–52. Amalgamation: e.g. Sherratt 1990, 809–12, for none of whose three examples this is a necessary explanation; on iron, see Morris 1989. Numbers: Van Wees 1992, 269–71, considers them reasonable enough for the calculation of population figures.

[34] Redfield 1975, 35–9; cf. Vidal-Naquet 1986; I. Morris 1986, 89–91; Giovannini 1989; Kullmann 1995. Bennet 1997, 531–2, offers an interesting explanation.

[35] Siege: Crielaard 1995, 215–24; S. Morris 1995. The motif is popular in Mycenaean art as well (Vermeule 1964, 100–4) but contemporary models are perhaps more likely. Trojan horse: S. Morris 1995, 227–9 (with bibliography). Objects: e.g. the shield of Achilles, Fittschen 1973; Crielaard, *loc. cit.* Events: e.g. the sack of Egyptian Thebes by Assurbanipal in 663 BC (Burkert 1976) or the destruction of Babylon by Sennacherib in 689 BC (West 1995, 211–17). See generally, Dunbabin 1957, Austin 1970, Helck 1979, Braun 1982, Haider 1988, Burkert 1991a, 1992, S. Morris 1992a, Kopcke and Tokumaru 1992, Matthäus 1993, Burstein 1996.

[36] Vogt 1991; Latacz 1996, 24–30. For the poet's knowledge of Ionia: West 1988, 165; Heubeck 1986, 59–60. See also Emlyn-Jones 1980, ch. 4.

[37] Esp. Nagy 1979; 1990a, chs. 1–3; cf. Patzek 1992, 98–101, and the conclusion of Morris 1997e.

[38] Finley 1977, 47–8; cf. Donlan 1980, 2–3; 1981/82, 172–3; 1985, 298–305; Dickinson 1986. *Polis*: Finley, ibid. 34, 156; *contra:* e.g. Qviller 1981, esp. 113; Morris 1986; Raaflaub 1991, 239–47; 1993; Van Wees 1992, ch. 2; Crielaard 1995, 239–47.

[39] e.g. Morris 1986; Ulf 1990, ch. 6; Van Wees 1992, 261–5; 1994, 155;

Crielaard 1995. Dates of the epics' composition: nn. 6, above, and 71, below.

[40] The volume of Stolz and Shannon 1976 was instrumental. See Latacz 1979, 25–44, with bibliography, 573–618; Boedeker 1988; Foley 1988; Holoka 1991.

[41] M. Parry 1928/1971, Lord 1960, Bowra 1961, Finnegan 1977, Foley 1988, Hainsworth and Hatto 1989.

[42] Hoekstra 1981; West 1988, 156–9, with bibliography; cf. Bennet 1997.

[43] Foley 1990, 2–3, on the common prejudice (reservations about 'economy' in Shive 1987, Hoekstra 1995); Latacz 1984, 17, with bibliography; cf. Hoekstra 1981; Latacz 1988; 1994, 354 ('an essential characteristic of this traditional poetic genre' is 'its conservatism and its strong tendency to stick to tradition, at least in its most fundamental building blocks'). 'Catalogue of Ships': Hope Simpson and Lazenby 1970; *contra*: Giovannini 1969, Kullmann 1993, Anderson 1995; see also Minchin 1996; Visser 1997.

[44] A. Parry 1966; Patzer 1972; Nagler 1974; Russo 1978; several contributions in Latacz 1979; id. 1988; Visser 1987; 1988; Foley 1990, 2; cf. id. 1991, xii, chs. 1–2, 243–52. See De Jong 1995, esp. 132–4, on the place of such studies in literary analyses of the epics.

[45] See n. 9, above.

[46] Lord 1960, ch. 2; Finnegan 1977, esp. chs. 7–8; Wyatt 1989; Taplin 1992, 2–6; see also, generally, Martin 1989; Bakker and Kahane 1997.

[47] See below at n. 64.

[48] Strasburger 1953, 105 = 1982, 505; cf. Finley 1977, 145, 149; Redfield 1975, 35–9, 78–82; Murko 1919, 136–7, 140.

[49] Vermeule 1986; cf. S. Morris 1989. Most scholars date such a presumed war to the thirteenth, Hood 1995 to the late twelfth century, after the destruction of the Mycenaean palaces. On the uselessness of the dates proposed in antiquity, Burkert 1995. Deger-Jalkotzy 1989, 143–7; 1991b, and forthcoming, suggests that heroic song might have flourished during the Submycenaean period at the 'courts of nobles'; Sarkady 1975, 122; Latacz 1996, 35–56, postulate direct aristocratic continuity from the Mycenaean through the archaic period. This seems highly doubtful; 'the known genealogies of families in classical Greece reach back to a horizon in the mid-tenth century BC, but not earlier' (Davies 1984, 100; cf. Snodgrass 1971, 10–13; Raaflaub 1988c), and the nature and composition of Greek elites must have changed several times during this period (e.g. Raaflaub 1991, 230–8).

[50] Bennet 1997, 531–2; see also Kullmann 1995, 62, 64, who considers it 'nicht vorstellbar' that traditions about such a war could have survived in oral song through the Dark Ages; cf. id. 1993, 147: the thought that the epic tradition for 500 years kept substantial information about the Mycenaean period alive 'proves completely untenable'.

[51] *Nostoi*: *Od.* 1.325–6; cf. 8.75–82, 492–520; new story: 1.351–2. Phoenix: *Il.* 9.529–99. Nestor: 11.669–761.

[52] e.g. *Il.* 1.152–7; 18.509–40; see Nowag 1983, Van Wees 1992, Raaflaub 1997a, forthcoming.

[53] Above, n. 22.

[54] Van Wees 1992, 82–3, 88–9, 152–3, 156–7; Seaford 1994, 5–6;

cf. Raaflaub 1991, 251.

[55] Such transition, of course, extended over a long period of time, and some of the early elements (such as meat consumption at sacrifices, wars about booty and status, or the use of *xenia* as a political instrument) are visible even centuries later. The shift is important, nevertheless.

[56] Donlan 1981/82, 173; cf. 1989b, 139–43; Snodgrass 1980, 35–7; 1987, 193–209; Hennig 1980.

[57] See n. 24, above; for details, Raaflaub 1997a. Van Wees 1994 offers a different picture.

[58] See n. 24, above.

[59] Donlan 1989c, 1993. See also Flaig 1993, 1994, on decision making by consensus.

[60] See n. 42, above.

[61] For the following section, see generally the useful summaries and discussions by Patzek 1992, Hampl 1975, Kullmann 1995.

[62] Vansina 1985, Raaflaub 1988c, Ungern-Sternberg 1988. The great personalities of the German *Heldensage* are even condensed into two generations, although historically they are spread over two full centuries: Von See 1981, 10–11.

[63] See n. 10, above.

[64] Von See 1981, 11; Patzek 1992, 61–8. On audience interaction: above, n. 46; on the social class represented by the audiences: Latacz 1992, 204–7; 1996, 30–5 (elite); Dalby 1995 (distinctly non-elite).

[65] Visser 1997. Catalogue: see n. 43. *Doloneia*: Hainsworth 1993, 151–5.

[66] Von See 1981, 11–12; Nagy: above, n. 37.

[67] Sanctuaries: Rolley 1983; Morgan 1990, 1993. Amphictyonies: Tausend 1992. Religion: Vermeule 1974, Sourvinou-Inwood 1993, De Polignac 1995a, Crielaard 1995, 247–72. On parallel trends in material culture: I. Morris, this volume.

[68] Patzek 1992, pt. 3; Kullmann 1995.

[69] Cults: bibliography in Raaflaub 1991, 232 n. 94, and Patzek 1992, 162–77; Antonaccio 1994, 1995a; Crielaard 1995, 266–72. The famous burial of Lefkandi now seems to push the beginnings of hero cult back to the tenth century: n. 22, above; Morris 1997e, 541–4.

[70] See Morris' conclusion (1997e, 557–8).

[71] West 1966, 46–7; Burkert 1976; Taplin 1992, 33–5; Van Wees 1992, 54–8; 1994, 138–46; West 1995; Crielaard 1995; Dickie 1995, with J.K. Papadopoulos's review in *Bryn Mawr Classical Review* 7 (1996).

[72] Nagy 1995. Difficulties: e.g. West 1995; cf. Raaflaub 1993, 52–3, on city walls (cf. the bibliography cited there, and Crielaard 1995, 241 n. 150, 243–5), 92 n. 42 on houses (*dōmata*) of *basileis* (cf. Morris, this volume, 28–9; but see Dalby 1995, 272–5).

[73] So too, Van Wees 1992, 56–7. For institutional developments, see the bibliography cited in Raaflaub 1993, section 3.

[74] On various issues of the discussion on Homeric society, see also Pöhlmann 1992; Dickinson 1994; Olson 1995; Fitton 1996; Osborne 1996a.

6

HOMER'S ENEMIES
Lyric and epic in the seventh century

Andrew Dalby

'We are enemies of one another. It is torture for me when I see another singer who knows more than I.'

Anonymous poet quoted by M. Murko (1929, 21)

Research on archaic society builds on the varied evidence of the earliest recorded Greek literature in several genres. With the definitive establishment of literacy itself in Greece, choral lyric, personal lyric, satirical iambic verse, political and military elegiacs, and didactic hexameter all appear to blossom within the short period between about 700 and about 550 BC.

Divided from most of these by a sharply different world view, the *Iliad* and *Odyssey*, the two great epics traditionally attributed to Homer, have long been seen as originating in, and as reflecting, an earlier period of history. Apparently chronologically isolated from other literature, they were remarkably convincing in their depiction of a society which likewise was different in many of its traits from that which formed the background of the other genres. This 'Homeric society', which has been studied and explicated in great detail, was once widely thought to be a fairly accurate portrayal of the real world of the thirteenth century BC; a generation ago, Finley (1956) convinced the majority of scholars that it was a reflection of the ninth century; more recently, Morris (1986) has demonstrated that the epics cannot be expected consistently to depict any period earlier than that in which they were composed. Meanwhile the date of their composition, once placed between the tenth and the eighth centuries, has also been reconsidered: there is now a growing consensus that the *Iliad* and *Odyssey* that we know were composed about the middle of the seventh century[1] – the very time at which Greek iambic, elegiac and lyric poetry also begin to be known.

Thus archaeological and literary arguments come together: they

195

seem to reduce the chronological gap between the epics and the rest of archaic Greek literature to almost nothing. The social historian is faced with an unfamiliar question: can the world views characteristic of Greek epic and of the other genres possibly be views of the *same* world?

On the one hand, the student of the seventh and sixth centuries needs to reconsider what is known of Greek society and politics and thought of that period in the light of the epics, which – whatever their origins in oral tradition – were, it would seem, composed by a seventh-century poet or poets. On the other hand, the student of 'Homeric society' can no longer overlook the fact that the *Iliad* and *Odyssey* were in origin merely two poems among many, shaped by genre and by the occasion or occasions of performance, conditioned by poets' and audiences' expectations of genre and occasion: how did these influences colour the world seen in the epics? The question has to be approached in an awareness of what other genres and what other occasions there were, and thus in what other colours that same world was seen.

In re-exploring the relations among the poetic genres of Greece at the emergence of literacy it is helpful to make comparisons with other not wholly written literary cultures. But this means looking beyond epic. Although Parry's comparative study of modern Bosnian (Serbo-Croat) and archaic Greek epic was crucial in demonstrating that the *Iliad* and *Odyssey* stem from a tradition of oral composition, the Parry lineage has never achieved as much as might have been hoped for in the historical or literary criticism of either tradition, and this is partly because it discounts the wider literary context, oral and written, of the epics on which it focuses.[2]

The direct evidence for the exploration comes equally from the earliest surviving Greek literature in non-epic genres – and from the epics themselves. It is the latter source, somewhat neglected until now, that provides the framework of the present paper.[3]

Song and singer

In the world pictured by the makers of *Odyssey* and *Iliad*, singers (*aoidoi*) are several times depicted:[4] craftsmen, so it appears from the *Odyssey* episodes, who were recognised as possessors of a useful skill, and as such welcomed when they arrived, when one with nothing to offer might be ejected. They might also be well known in a single town, called to perform frequently at the same house. They sang to their own accompaniment on the *phorminx*, 'lyre'.[5]

Singers sang at wedding celebrations, which were also marked by instrumental music and dancing; they led laments at funerals; they sang in the market place (*Od.* 8.250–385); and they sang at dinner. At dinner they did not sit on the outside of the group, with the men, but on a stool placed 'in the middle' where the household was; those who served the diners are said to serve the singer also with food and drink.[6]

In spite of the poet's detachment, and in spite of the absence from end to end of the *Odyssey* of any overt address or personal appeal to the audience, one may certainly ask whether, in some of the episodes just cited, a special point is made of the honour that was properly done to a singer (Stanford 1958, vol. 1, 344). 'Who, when himself just arriving, calls in another stranger from elsewhere, unless one of those who are *demiourgoi*, a seer or a healer of sicknesses or a maker of spears, or again an inspired singer, who gives pleasure by singing? These are invited by mortals all over the boundless earth. No one would call in a beggar to be a drain on him' (*Od.* 17.382–7). Reading the protestations that the poet here gives to Eumaeus, it would even be possible to take it that a singer was not one of the *demiourgoi* but somehow on a higher plane,[7] if those proverbial lines did not bring one back to earth: 'Potter hates potter and joiner joiner; beggar is jealous of beggar, singer of singer' (Hesiod, *Works and Days* 25–6). The singer is indeed a *demiourgos*, an artisan.[8] In parallel, the Sumerian didactic piece *The Father and His Disobedient Son* (107–12) identifies singers as the only artisans whose skill is more demanding than that of scribes; and the 'seers' (poets) of the *Rigveda* frequently liken their own work to that of 'artisans and manual labourers (carpenters, weavers, chariot-makers)'.[9]

Now it is clear that song (*aoide*) was not the exclusive prerogative of an *aoidos*. Nausicaa leads her maids in song as they play ball; other women (Calypso and Circe, at any rate) sing at the loom.[10] The warrior Achilles is supposed to be the owner of a lyre, and when Nestor and Odysseus arrive to negotiate with him they find him singing to himself of the 'fame of men'.[11] This scene is a catalyst for our understanding of the ramifications of early Greek poetry as depicted in the epics.

Its realism has been doubted. 'A genuine amateur,' Hainsworth writes, 'like Akhilleus, or King Alfred among the Danes, is rare and the verisimilitude of such representations is called into question' (in Hatto 1980, 37). Yet one can find plenty of societies in which the making of poetry has been a very general skill: among the warrior Arabs,[12] the Vikings, the Japanese warriors, and the Tibetan students of early medieval times;[13] in modern East African cultures including the Fipa and the Muhima; among the Toda of south India.[14] Royal singers of lyric, and royal composers of lyric, are known from several cultures. What of the 'three dilettante poets', three amateur poets, of the *Welsh*

Triads, including the legendary Arthur (to whom surviving lyrics in Welsh are attributed) and the bloodthirsty Cadwallawn?[15] Whatever the literary status of those three, we may certainly adduce numerous high-born amateur improvisers of lyric from medieval European cultures: they range from King Richard 'Coeur de Lion' of England and the troubadour Dauphin, Count of Auvergne,[16] to King Harald Hardradi of Norway.[17] With all these potential parallels for Achilles, I believe Hainsworth's unspecified objection may be that Alfred [18] and Achilles, not being professional poets, could not have improvised an *epic*.

Another scholar, S. West, extrapolates from that same *Iliad* scene of Achilles singing to his lyre and asserts that all the singers in the *Iliad* are amateurs (they include Apollo and the Muses, and two singers depicted on the shield of Achilles).[19] Another again, Segal (1992, 5), highlights the fact that Patroclus is 'waiting for Achilles to leave off singing' and draws the moral that the singing of someone such as a warrior, unlike that of a 'bard', 'gives pleasure only to himself, not to others'.

All three, Hainsworth and West and Segal, are struggling to keep the singers of 'Homeric society' to a simple pattern: the ones that mattered were professional singers, and they were singers of epic. The pattern that we have discerned above is more complex, closer to what can be observed in real societies, and closer to what we know of archaic Greece in particular.

In the 'Homeric' world, then, song is of many kinds, and performed both by singers and by others. Singers have a varied repertoire of themes, though this is not to assume that all singers have the same repertoire, or the same range.[20] On four occasions the poet of the *Odyssey* gives us the narrative subject of the song of an *aoidos*. One, sung by Demodocus in the market place on Scherie to the accompaniment of dancing, tells of Hephaestus' trap for the adulterous Ares and Aphrodite.[21] As far as the plot of the *Odyssey* is concerned this naughty tale is an interlude.[22] The other three examples are all incidents in Odysseus' adventures at Troy, and their choice is necessary to the plot and design of the epic; thus it will be risky to argue just from them that the story of Troy was already overwhelmingly popular in the poet's own day; and risky to assume from them that the poets of *Iliad* and *Odyssey* performed epics at royal dinners (Dalby 1995). It is altogether too easy to add these three narratives to the story of Ares and Aphrodite, to summarise them in Penelope's words as 'the deeds of gods and men that singers make famous', and to make them define the repertoire of singers in 'Homeric society',[23] brushing aside the laments, wedding songs, choral songs and other occasions on which, in the world of the *Iliad* and *Odyssey*, singers went to work.

Aoide, 'song', was not coextensive with epic: there is no controversy there. But it goes beyond the evidence to assert that the singers (*aoidoi*) of the *Iliad* and *Odyssey* were solely or principally singers of hexameter epic. This is indeed controversial: some scholars even use *aoidos* as the technical term for a Homeric epic poet. The area of disagreement is wider than any question of the definition of terms, for it embraces the whole prehistory of Greek poetry.

On the one hand it has been argued that the non-epic metres of Greek poetry have relationships with Sanskrit hymns and lyrics of the *Rigveda* and with early Latin, Celtic, Germanic and other poetic traditions, and thus that a line of descent can be traced for these metres from the postulated culture that goes with the reconstructed proto-Indo-European language;[24] it would follow from this that the non-epic metres were cultivated throughout Greek prehistory. On the other hand, it has been said that the early Greek epic was in its own time the sole important art form of its community. Redfield writes: 'From the beginning, Greek high culture devoted itself, before anything else, to the art of [poetic] narrative' (1975, 31). There has been a widespread opinion that in archaic times a literary transition took place, from earlier epic to later shorter forms. To some, who like to look for a *protos heuron*, an 'inventor', as ancient literary historians did, this marks the beginning of personal poetry. Thus Campbell has described Homer and Hesiod uncomplicatedly as 'the predecessors of the lyric poets'; Fränkel wrote of 'the sudden swing from epic to lyric'.[25]

The ancient preoccupation with the *protos heuron* does indeed encourage the assumption that epic came first, and then, when epic tailed off, lyric was invented. There is now a newer twist to this set of views. 'In Greece,' as Rosalind Thomas expresses it, 'the transition from the leisurely style of epic to the briefer style of lyric has sometimes been taken to reflect a transition from orality to literacy,'[26] though it certainly did not in Old Norse literature, in which short lyric poetry and longer narrative coexisted;[27] nor in Arabian literature, in which shorter lyric was the best-known form before the literature began to be written, while oral epic is a feature of recent and modern times (Lyons 1995); nor in north Indian literature (in Sanskrit and related languages), which similarly begins with a collection of lyric, long orally preserved, and in which epic appears and reappears at later dates.[28] We should judge the ancient chronology of the genres harshly, knowing as we already do that many of the *protoi heurontes* are impostors. Arion did not invent dithyrambs (*pace* Herodotus 1.23, cf. Aristotle F677 Rose) for we know that Archilochus composed them far earlier (Archilochus F120 L-P); Phrynichus did not invent the tetrameter (*pace Suda* s.v. *Phrynikhos*); Stesichorus did not invent the hymn (*pace* Clement of Alexandria, *Stromateis* 1.16.78.5).

Early Greece would be highly unusual among oral cultures if it ever had no important art form but epic. And it would be a very strange coincidence indeed if the multiple poetic arts of Greece, relying as they did on oral delivery and very largely on oral transmission (Gentili 1988), and each tending to a distinct dialect colouring, only began to be practised at the moment of literacy. It is a relief, then, that ancient authors were happy to attribute to 'Homer' not only serious epic but also comic poems, hymns, epigrams and a wassail or *eiresione*; a relief, too, that some modern scholars, such as Page and Kirk, have explicitly envisaged a wider range than epic for pre-written Greek poetry.[29]

One area of confusion must be clarified. Not all oral poetry is formulaic. Early Greek epic is formulaic, as are many other long traditional narrative forms, especially verse ones. Other well known examples are the Bosnian epics and the closely related but much less widely known Albanian epics (e.g. Skendi 1954), the earlier French *chansons de geste*,[30] the Sanskrit *Mahabharata*. Formulas do assist the oral composition of large-scale verse narrative. But what of long traditional narratives that are not in verse, or not in a fixed metre: Sumerian, Akkadian and some modern Arabian epics, Icelandic sagas and Pali Buddhist dialogues? These may have features that suggest oral origin, oral transmission or oral performance, or all three, and yet not have the Parryan formulas that by definition fill defined spaces in metrical verse.[31] Meanwhile, in shorter lyric, whether Old Norse or Sanskrit or Chinese,[32] the poet's skill is to make every word count. Shorter poetry can perfectly well be performed orally, be transmitted orally, and be composed without the use of writing, and yet not be formulaic at all.[33] Thus the surviving shorter poetry of archaic Greece cannot be expected to display its oral antecedents in verbal formulas as epic does.

The genres of Homeric poetry

Let us return to the specific occasions and subjects given to song or poetry in the *Iliad* and *Odyssey*. The epic poets did not compose in a vacuum. We ought to be able to relate the performances that they themselves picture to what we otherwise know of archaic Greek literary culture,[34] and in the following section I will suggest how we may set about doing this.

The shield of Achilles, in *Iliad* 18, is a kind of sampler of the Greek poetry of 'Homer''s time. We find in it first the song for the vintage, the *linos kalos* sung by a boy to his own accompaniment on the *phorminx*, and taken up by the grape-pickers in song and in their stamping feet as they bring the baskets home (*Il.* 18.569–72). What sort of song was this *linos:* the same as, or different from, the *linos* performed in 'festivals and choruses' by 'all men who are *aoidoi* and *kitharistai*' (Hesiod F305, from the scholia on *Iliad* ad loc.)? More than one early poetic form may be adduced as appropriate for celebrating the vintage. One is dithyramb, a genre known to Archilochus, whose poems were composed at about the same date as the *Iliad* and *Odyssey* themselves: 'As I can lead the lovely song of King Dionysus, the dithyramb, when my mind is blown by the wine' (Archilochus F120 L-P). Aristotle discusses the gradual change towards 'imitation' and professionalism in this genre (*Problems* 918b13–29 (19.15)), 'imitation' here suggesting the use and re-use of written texts in place of earlier oral composition.

We are reminded of a second possibility by the story of the all-too-iambic verses that Archilochus devised for a festival chorus commemorating Dionysus and the fruit of the vine (*Monumentum Parianum*). There is no reason to reject the possibility that the poet of the *Iliad* had iambics in mind, or choliambics (if Hipponax was not after all the *protos heuron* of these). Choliambics, even more than iambics, and much more than any dithyrambs that I know, demand the accompaniment of stamping feet. We have a collection of guesses, rather than firm knowledge, as to the occasion for the performance of early iambi (West 1974, 22–39), but we know that the vulgarity, personal invective, sexual humour and innuendo, for which iambic verses served, belonged to the controlled release of inhibitions necessary in close-knit, almost claustrophobic communities such as archaic Greek cities and were typical of Dionysiac festival.[35] Is the performer imagined to be *any* child, or rather a young poet, a junior Homer or Archilochus – apprentice to a trade which in many societies is embarked on in youth[36] (like music in ours) and one of whose duties is very often to provide an accompaniment to agricultural work?[37]

Iambus differs from elegy, to our knowledge, in feeling. Solon is among the poets who used both. His iambics (Solon F24–27 Diehl) are lighter, more controversial, more personal; his elegiacs, expressions of moral philosophy and memoirs and histories told with a moral purpose – thoughts that others are expected to share.[38] This was exactly what was required of the *aoidos* whose services Agamemnon retained for

Clytemnestra's benefit (*Od.* 3.267–8). The scholia comment on this episode: 'In antiquity singers took the place of philosophers... So the singer left with Clytemnestra prevented her from adopting wicked ways by expounding the virtues of men and women.' Do we suppose, with the scholiasts, that the unfortunate *aoidos* was invented not just to keep an eye on Clytemnestra but to give her advice? I would argue that the scholiasts are right, for otherwise he need not be an *aoidos* at all. Naturally, as an *aoidos*, he would do his duty in verse. Not so much the discursive hexameter, more the elegiac couplet (assuming it was not still to be invented by Theocles of Naxos)[39] would be the appropriate metre for him to build a moral argument – and if necessary he might certainly do so on the spot. The use of elegiac couplets as dinner exchanges, and their improvisation by both men and women, is amply attested later – Homer's Clytemnestra may thus even be imagined *replying* in verse! Examples of a second metrical form suitable for the exchange of proverbs and moralities occur in the collection of anonymous *skolia* quoted by Athenaeus (695c–e).[40]

Let us return to Achilles' shield, and to the *molpe*, the singing dance of boys and girls depicted on it. There are several specific occasions for song on Achilles' shield, but this is song and dance for its own sake.[41] Now there is another occasion that seems rather similar to this one, an occasion that is described at length in the *Odyssey*. It takes place in the *agora* of the Phaeacians after the sports: Demodocus goes 'to the middle'; boys good at dancing stand around him, and they beat the 'holy *khoros*' with their feet. Demodocus plays on his lyre and begins his beautiful singing; this market-place song-and-dance is the story of Ares and Aphrodite (*Od.* 8.250–385). It would be wrong to overstress the similarity of the two occasions, in one of which we focus on the dancing boys and girls, in the other on the poet and his story, but in both the term *khoros* is used. Both belong to the realm of choral lyric, song accompanied by dance. We may conjecture that later performances of Stesichorus and Ibycus, and even Archilochus' poem on Deianeira (F286–288 L-P) may have been a little like the picture we get of Demodocus's performance in the market place. We may equally compare it with the longer Homeric Hymns, themselves mythical narratives, and should recall in the *Hymn to Apollo* (165–78) the poet's address to the girls who dance as he sings.

Achilles arouses the young Achaeans to sing a *paieon* as he prepares to drag Hector's body behind his chariot (*Il.* 22.391). This, surely, is to be imagined as a choral song in both senses – one sung in unison and in a processional dance. It was the praise poetry, the boasting song, of archaic Greece, and (at least in later opinion) a song which must be addressed to a god.[42] From the early fifth century we can read fragments of Pindar's *paianes*; earlier, such songs were known to Alcman. 'At feasts and at revels, among the diners of the men's house, it is right to lead off the *paian*' (Alcman F98 L-P). In the Homeric *Hymn to Apollo* (486–519) the god's destined worshippers are instructed, after sacrifice, prayer and feast, to return in procession to his temple singing the *iepaieon*. Led by the god himself, 'holding a lyre in his hands, playing sweetly, stepping high and fair', they do so 'like the *paieones* of Crete, and like those in whose breast the Muse, the goddess, has placed honey-voiced song'.

There are several wedding songs, *hymenaioi*, in the epics: one on the shield of Achilles (*Il.* 18.493), with women watching the procession from their verandas; a song at the wedding feast of the children of Menelaus (*Od.* 4.17–19) in which a godlike singer sings while playing, and two tumblers lead the song;[43] and then a false wedding song (*Od.* 23.133–6) arranged so that passers-by and neighbours will think a wedding is in progress while the suitors of Penelope are getting their just deserts. Wedding songs were another occasion for lyric poetry in archaic Greece. Those of Sappho come immediately to mind: the *epithalamia* (Sappho F103–117 L-P) that fit into the ribald jocularity of weddings, and also the two narratives of heroes' weddings, Peleus and Thetis, Hector and Andromache, probably appropriate for a more formal song to be performed during a wedding feast.

At the funeral of Hector (*Il.* 24.720–2) there came in 'singers, leaders of the lament, and they lamented in bitter song, and the women wailed after'. Then followed Andromache's dirge, and again 'the women wailed after'; then Hecabe's; then Helen's. On another occasion for mourning in the *Iliad* (18.316) no *aoidos* is introduced, but there is still Achilles himself to play the role played by Andromache, Hecabe and Helen at the funeral of Hector: that is, of singing the dirge for Patroclus in which others will join.[44] In the last book of the *Odyssey* the ghost of Agamemnon tells how the nymphs lamented Achilles and the Muses responded with a dirge for him, at which all the Argives wept (*Od.* 24.58–62). We know the kind of poetry that was made for these occasions a little later from the *threnoi*, laments, of Simonides and Pindar: we are told that the genre was discouraged by Solon, who is said to have forbidden 'lamenting to a text' (*threnein pepoiemena*; Plutarch, *Solon* 21.4).[45] The laments of Simonides, quite fragmentary, are made up of wholly pessimistic philosophical poetry concerning the condition of man, thoroughly appropriate to 'lead a lament'.[46] A clear picture of the rituals and their atmosphere is developed by Margaret Alexiou (1974, 4–14), though her emphasis is not on the verbal or poetic side. Much later, women's oral laments were said to use the 'political' verse.[47]

We may imagine as simpler and less formal than genres so far discussed the *molpe* in which Nausicaa leads her maids when, invisible to all except the hidden Odysseus and the epic audience, they throw off their veils and play on the shore. We know rather little of the lighter or more popular forms of poetry in archaic Greece, though we can place roughly in this category such texts as the swallow-song, traditional on Rhodes and traced there to the sage Cleobulus of Lindos, the slave-woman's milling song that appears to come from the reign of Pittacus in sixth century Lesbos, and the Athenian song of Harmodius, which displays the parallelism of verse and refrain typical of popular song in many cultures.[48] It is interesting that specifically in the popular forms (*skolia*, in the broad sense) a Hellenistic scholar hypothesised a development beginning with folk song in which all could join and ending with performance by professionals – and linked this development to the spread of literacy.[49]

Though it may be better not to ask what song the Sirens sang, let us at least consider what songs the Muses sang, while Apollo played the lyre, at dinner on Olympus (*Il.* 1.603–4). There is no need for segregation of the sexes on Olympus, for it is all one happy family; no difficulty, therefore, about women entertaining a party which includes men.[50] But we know altogether too little to allow easy generalisation on the place of women poets and singers in archaic Greece. The context of Nausicaa's song, above, was wholly feminine but for the watching eyes. What were the audiences of Sappho's songs? She sang to her women friends (Sappho F160 L-P); did others also listen to the songs in the 'halls of the servants of the Muse' where the *threnos* was out of place (Sappho F150 L-P)?

Lastly we return to the 'fame of men', and the song sung by Achilles, accompanying himself on the lyre (*Il.* 9.186–91). In one sense, it did not matter very much, to the poet or to his Achilles, what he was singing. Achilles was in a mood of calm meditation, and had nothing to do, so could be imagined 'pleasing himself' (186, 189), singing to himself. The scene is being set in some detail so something is said about his lyre; half a line remains, and so we hear that Achilles was singing about the 'fame of men'. In another sense, Achilles' subject does matter a great deal, for it is one half of the whole subject-field that lay open to oral Greek poetry, 'the fame of gods and men', as defined by Penelope (*Od.* 1.337–8). Hesiod (*Theogony* 100–1) uses the same definition, though not in the same formula. It can be compared with Stesichorus's more playful catalogue (F12 Diehl): 'Muse, discard wars and sing with me the matings of the gods, the feasts of men and the joys of the blessed.'

Many kinds of early Greek poetry could be said to be about the 'fame of men' – the praise poetry of such as Pindar, the stirring elegiacs of Tyrtaeus and Simonides, the iambics of Archilochus, the heroic legends of Stesichorus and of the epic poets. Achilles was making poetry of some kind, but Hainsworth was right to doubt that an 'amateur' would make or sing epic. Achilles is here a precursor of Alcaeus, singing – perhaps – the whole theme of the *Iliad* in eight lines, as Alcaeus himself would do (F44 L-P) or the story of Paris and Helen (cf. Alcaeus F283 L-P) or any other similiar theme that could be imagined as already belonging to a conceptual repertoire. Achilles is the analogue of one of the poets of Icelandic saga, Egil Skallagrimsson or Kormak Ogmundsson.[51] They did not tell long stories; they encapsulated a thought or a fateful turn of events in a well-turned short lyric.

The need for synthesis

'We know precious little', Nagy reminds us (1990a, 20), 'about the setting of ancient Greek oral poetry – beyond what we learn from the texts themselves.' It is all the more necessary to evaluate what the most discursive of these texts, the Homeric epics, can tell us of the earliest history of Greek literature. Much of the song depicted in the *Iliad* and *Odyssey* can be related to the lyric genres of archaic Greek poetry that are known to us. It does not need saying that some of the comparisons and links made in this paper are speculative. The relations between theme, genre and occasion were not simple or static in later Greece, and there is no reason why they should have been so in the seventh century or before. Yet the general picture is clear. It is not at all a bold step to suggest that, in the earliest years of known Greek lyric song, in its many different genres, in its many different and complex metres, and on its many different occasions, the poets of *Iliad* and *Odyssey* imagined some similar occasions and depicted the making of some similar songs. Epic depiction of its lyric rivals, and of the people who made and sang and listened to non-narrative poetry at the beginning of Greek literacy, can help the historian to place this poetry in its wider context, and thus to develop a picture of seventh-century literature and society which will take proper account of the epic poets' standpoint.

A corresponding search in early Greek lyric for depictions of narrative poetry and its poets will be less rewarding. If Solon, as is likely, means to criticise the epic poets with his famous phrase, '*aoidoi* tell many falsehoods' (Solon F21 Diehl),[52] few others in the seventh or sixth century say even as much as that about the tradition that gave birth to the two greatest works of European literature. It is true that from the narrative performances in the *Odyssey* and the hints in the *Theogony* and the *Works and Days* we can extract a convincing picture of the relationship between oral poets and their audiences. Narratives like those of Stesichorus and of 'Homer', traditional lore and wisdom like the 'Catalogue of Ships' and the works of Hesiod, really did emerge from negotiations like those between Odysseus or Phemius or Demodocus and their various audiences, and really were rewarded with such riches as an assured welcome, a warm cloak, a full begging bag and public acclaim at a market, fair or festival. Yet, in spite of all their apparent objectivity, we cannot expect from such masters of truth as the poets of the *Iliad* and the *Odyssey* an uncomplicated image of their own place in seventh-century Greek society. Patronage comes in many forms, but epic poetry has not often been observed to grow out of royal banquets. Philodemus and others have seen that 'Homer' is to be found in the lying vagrant Odysseus as well as in the laureate Demodocus;[53] the search for a social context and a performance context for archaic epic must range well beyond the internal evidence of the epics themselves.[54]

A balanced picture of archaic Greece will, somehow, reunite 'Homeric society' with its seventh-century context. The heroic values of the *Iliad* and *Odyssey*, the village satire of Archilochus, the collectivism of Solon and Tyrtaeus, the destructive politics of Alcaeus, were all approximately contemporary, and all were somehow relevant to contemporary audiences. From startlingly different perspectives, they are indeed visions of the same world.

Notes

[1] The precise dating is not essential to the present argument. West (1995) observes that current events in the Near East – the heyday of Egyptian Thebes, *c.* 715–663 BC (cf. Burkert 1976), and Sennacherib's destruction of Babylon in 689 – find echoes in the *Iliad* (9.381–4, 12.17–33). Similar echoes have assisted in the dating of several of the French *chansons de geste*.

[2] Mainstream historians of Serbo-Croatian literature have paid due attention to the literary contexts of early and modern oral poetry: see e.g. Subotic (1932) and more recently Koljevic (1981), who, though focusing on oral epic, attends from the outset to the 'range of collective singing in medieval Serbia'

(13) and to the interplay between oral and written composition (1–6). By contrast A.B. Lord, Parry's inheritor, 'arguing for the purity of the oral stream, denies any relationship at all' between oral epic and written literature (Matthias and Vuckovic 1987, 14, citing Lord 1960, 135).

³ Lanata 1963 is a useful collection of early Greek texts on poetics and performance – but it exemplifies the widespread neglect of the epic evidence for non-epic poetry. The extracts from the *Iliad* and *Odyssey* (pp. 4–19) cover only those four occasions which are generally supposed to represent the performance of epic: the story of Ares and Aphrodite and the three episodes from the Trojan War.

⁴ On the use of the terms *aeidein* and *aoidos* in early sources: West 1981, Detienne 1973.

⁵ *Od.* 1.153–4, etc.; *Od.* 8.43–4; *Od.* 3.267–8; *Od.* 17.382, quoted below. Later performers of the Homeric poems were highly mobile. Cf. Dalby (1995), 270 n. 6.

⁶ *Od.* 8.66; *Od.* 8.62–70 (cf. *Od.* 7.178–83); *Od.* 8.474–83. The singer Demodocus needs this help, being blind (*Od.* 8.64).

⁷ *Od.* 17.382–7. I agree with Stanford (1958, vol. 2, 292) in thinking that interpretation unlikely. On this passage and some anthropological parallels see Finley 1956, 58–9.

⁸ Literally one whose work has an 'association with or effect on the people' (Kirk 1962, 278–9: see his discussion of the implications of the word).

⁹ Gonda 1975, 73, for discussion. On the Sumerian text cited see Black 1992.

¹⁰ *Od.* 6.101, 5.61, 10.221. The term *aoidos* is not used of women: the lament for Hector was led by male *aoidoi*, to be taken up by women (see below). *Aoidos* has a feminine reference only in the case of Hesiod's nightingale, *Works and Days* 208.

¹¹ *Il.* 9.186–94. On the implications of *klea*, 'fame', see Nagy 1974, 244–52.

¹² The major sources are two compilations from the ninth and tenth centuries, one of them, the *Kitab al-Aghani* of Abu al-Faraj al-Isbahani, the fruit of extensive enquiries among exponents of oral poetry, the other, the thematic anthology *Hamasa* of Abu Tammam, collected from already-written sources. On the former work see Sawa 1989, esp. 20–32; for a summary of the evidence it provides on the contexts of performance, ib. 111–44; on improvisation and textual variation between performances, 142–4, 190–2. In general see Nicholson 1907, 30–140.

¹³ For Viking poets see e.g. *Kormáks Saga* (Collingwood and Stefánsson 1902) and the well-known *Egils Saga Skalla-Grimssonar*; for Japanese e.g. *Eiga Monogatari* (McCullough and McCullough 1980); for Tibetan e.g. *Bka' brgyud mgur mtsho* (Trungpa 1980), Heruka's life of Mar-pa (Trungpa 1982), and associated biographical literature.

¹⁴ 'In the past, every well-brought-up Muhima was expected to be able to compose and recite [praise-poetry concerning cattle raids], for not only was their recitation a pastime for the evening, but there were also certain occasions on which it was necessary for a Muhima to recite a praise-poem which he had composed... Inevitably some had the reputation of being particularly versatile

at the art' (Morris 1964, 12). On the Fipa, Willis 1978, esp. 21–6. On the Toda, Emeneau 1958.

[15] The term 'amateur' is suggested here by R. Bromwich in her commentary (1978, 22).

[16] For five of Dauphin's improvised poetic exchanges, one with King Richard, see Boutière and Schutz 1964, 284–98.

[17] The main source is 'King Harald's saga', a section of Snorri Sturluson's *Heimskringla*. See Turville-Petre 1966, 19–20; Whaley 1993.

[18] The story that Alfred spied on the Danish camp disguised as a *joculator* is not well-attested, and deserves questioning no doubt on grounds of historical likelihood. 'As one professing the art of a *joculator* [*jongleur*], he was admitted even to the intimacies of the dining-room: there was no secret that his eyes and ears did not uncover' (William of Malmesbury, *De Gestis Regum Anglorum* 2.4). The tale is not found in any earlier source. There is nothing in it, at any rate, that goes beyond Alfred's poetical abilities as attested in his own writings and in Asser's *Life* (if that source is genuinely contemporary). The story is not specific about the royal *joculator*'s repertoire and it need not be assumed that he was entertaining the Danes to an Anglo-Saxon *epic*.

[19] S. West in Heubeck et al. 1988–92, vol. 1, 96.

[20] Something of the real complexity of the interaction between genres and between kinds of performers is shown in the passages gathered by Athenaeus 620a–d. We know that similar complexity is to be found in other mainly oral cultures. The male and female *jongleurs* of medieval France were the composers of the epic *chansons de geste* (or of some of them) but were equally musicians, singers of short poems and songs often composed by others, and providers of all kinds of entertainment. Individuals had their varying skills, but all were *jongleurs* and there is no more specialised term that denotes the maker of a *chanson de geste*. Cf. Duggan 1986, 730–2; note especially his citations of Paris Bibl. Nat. Fonds Latin 16515, and of the thirteenth-century *Poème Moral*, both implying literary and non-literary skills combined in a single performer.

[21] Gentili (1985, 14–15) believes that dancing is supposed always to have accompanied the songs described in the epics, and connects this detail to the development of the hexameter. But, as will emerge below, we have no reason to be sure that the imagined Demodocus, Phemius and colleagues were singing in hexameter.

[22] Or a structural prefiguration of Odysseus' defeat of the Cyclops? Or an anti-aristocratic dig, because the 'grimy, hard-working little man' (or rather god) defeats the 'gorgeous hunk'? There are many readings of the epics. For these two, see Segal 1992, 8 n.7.

[23] *Od.* 1.337–8. See for example Hainsworth 1993, 38–9. Burkert (1987, 47) here ignores the gods: 'the subject of the singer's song in the largest sense is *kléa andrōn*, the glorious deeds of men. In practice this means the Trojan cycle.'

[24] Meillet 1923, Nagy 1974, West 1973a, West 1973b, West 1988.

[25] Campbell 1983, vii; Fränkel 1975, 133 ('der Umbruch vom Epos zur Lyrik' in the even more forceful expression of the German original, 1962 edn, 148).

[26] Thomas 1992, 37, citing Gentili 1985, in which see especially chapters 1, 3.

[27] The principal source on Old Norse poetics is the *Prose Edda* of Snorri Sturluson.

[28] On the *Rigveda* see e.g. Gonda 1975: 65–92 on the *rishis*, 'seers', and their poetry; 43–54 on the oral transmission of the collection. On the origins and transmission of the later epic *Mahabharata*, van Buitenen (1973–) vol. 1, xxiii–xxviii. On oral/written interplay in the composition of the Puranas, evidently later again, Rocher 1986, 49–80. The published corpus of modern Indian oral epic is now rapidly growing.

[29] Page (1965) proposed that a hypothesis of oral composition would help to explain the work of Archilochus. Kirk (1966) was to doubt this, yet had remarked in general on the probable variety of oral genres in Greek literature before the use of writing (1962, 56).

[30] Morris (1986, 95) takes the pre-Parryan view that the *Chanson de Roland* (the oldest and best-known example) was composed from written sources by a literate cleric, who, incidentally, would have courted damnation by dabbling in the literature of the *jongleurs*: Casagrande and Vecchio 1979. Against this view, there was certainly some tradition of oral poetry on the subject of Roland, for a song of Roland (whether part of such an epic as the rather later versions that we know, or a poem in some different form) was sung to the Normans before the Battle of Hastings. 'Then a song of Roland was begun, so that the man's warlike example would arouse the fighters. Calling on God for aid, they joined battle' (William of Malmesbury, *De Gestis Regum Anglorum* 3.1). In another early *chanson de geste* we hear that William of Orange took a skilled *jongleur* to war with him (*Chanson de Guillaume* 1257–74). In fact, following in Parry's footsteps, Rychner (1955; cf. Duggan 1973, 1981) demonstrated some time ago the oral formulaic nature of the earlier French *chansons de geste*, including Roland. Quite apart from their formulaic style, these epics provide unusually explicit testimony of oral composition (for references, Dalby 1995, n. 4).

[31] On the oral background of Icelandic sagas see e.g. Byock 1985; on Sumerian and Akkadian poetry, Alster 1992, esp. 27, and other papers in the same volume. The best survey of early Pali literature is Norman 1983.

[32] Old Norse lyric often seems formulaic in English translation, because to those unfamiliar with them, kennings are most conveniently paraphrased as noun plus epithet. In the original they do not match Parry's classic definition of the Homeric formula, 'a group of words which is regularly employed under the same metrical conditions to express a given essential idea' (Parry 1971, 272). On the essentially oral nature of the poems of the Chinese *Shih Ching*, see Granet 1932 and Wang 1974 (I have not been able to consult the latter).

[33] It is notorious that Lord (e.g. 1960) insisted on a concept of 'oral traditional poetry' that made it impossible to separate it from 'formulaic poetry' or from 'traditional epic', a highly misleading use of terms (cf. Kurt Raaflaub's definition of 'oral poetry' in the present volume) which few, outside the narrow field of Homeric studies, would now accept. For fuller discussion see e.g. Finnegan 1977; Finnegan 1988, 88–109; Russo 1992. In the present paper I mean different things by 'oral', by 'formulaic' and by 'epic'. It is necessary to keep an open mind as to the extent to which poetry may deserve one, or two, or all three of these epithets.

[34] A full survey of early Greek oral literature must include prose, cf. Kirk 1962, 107–9, and must draw e.g. on the arbitration or lawsuit on the Shield of Achilles, the political debates among Greeks at Troy and among citizens of Ithaca, the now much-discussed tales of Odysseus. Space does not allow this here. There is room for doubt, too, as to the dividing line between verse and prose. Kurt Raaflaub's paper in this volume is a reminder that Nestor's story of his cattle raid (*Il.* 11.656–761) might have been imagined in either form, as might the funeral laments that are discussed below.

[35] Iambic performances were seen by a later thinker as appropriate for adults only, among the things that go along with reclining at dinner, and with drinking after dinner (Aristotle, *Politics* 1336b20–2).

[36] Raaflaub, this volume.

[37] For the oral poets of modern Egypt there may be a wider repertoire than epic and 'there are less respected forms of income…even sitting at the edges of fields to entertain villagers as they harvest or plant in return for a meal and some small payment' (Reynolds 1995, 105).

[38] This is equally true of the elegiac couplets of Callinus, Tyrtaeus and others. Where elegiac verse was used for historical narrative, it was consciously political: typical subjects of sentences that unite singer and audience are 'we', 'our King', 'our city', 'our grandfathers' (Tyrtaeus F2 and 4 Diehl, Solon F3 Diehl, Mimnermus F12 Diehl), and such expressions were not felt to disprove any of the later, mutually contradictory stories of Tyrtaeus's personal origins. On the various genres and forms of the poetry that celebrated city foundation see now Dougherty 1994b.

[39] West 1974, 8–9 n. 12. It is also possible to imagine Clytemnestra's adviser using plain hexameters, morally neutral. Solon is supposed to have used hexameters for one perfectly appropriate purpose: for stating his laws (Solon F28 Diehl, cited by Plutarch, Solon 3 – if genuine). Aristotle speculates on the early 'singing' of laws, *Problems* 919b37–920a4 (19.28). Hesiod's use of hexameter in the *Works and Days* was similarly appropriate – a series of facts, rules and injunctions, already proverbial, largely unarguable in the context in which they were intended, and not intended for arguing but for stating. To this extent hexameter (though not epic) certainly does seem to have been the medium of the 'tribal encyclopaedia' for which Havelock used to argue (e.g. 1991). What is said in hexameter is said, uncomplicatedly, as a fact (Hesiod, *Works and Days* 10), whether or not it happens to be true (Hesiod, *Theogony* 27–8, quoted in n. 52 below)!

[40] Cf. West 1974, 17–18, on improvisation. In many cultures – even our own – rhythmical or metrical proverbs may be exchanged in the course of a search for the moral high ground. On the possible origins of elegiacs, ib. 1–21; Palmer 1980, 105–13. West observes (ib. 17 n. 26) that the invention of various elegiac riddles was ascribed to the (probably mythical) Cleobulina, daughter of a Sage.

[41] It is a matter of textual controversy whether this dance takes place with or without an *aoidos*, and thus whether tumblers 'lead the music' or follow the lead of the *aoidos* (*Il.* 18.604–6, Aristarchus quoted by Athenaeus 181c). The controversy has remained unsettled for over two thousand years, although

the logical requirement for a single *exarkhon*, person leading, argued by Athenaeus or his source against Aristarchus, can find support in Archilochus, who gives himself precisely this role, 'myself leading the Lesbian *paian*' (Archilochus F121 L-P, cf. F120 already quoted; West 1974, 24; Campbell 1983, 150–51; see also below, on laments).

[42] Or to a Hellenistic monarch; Athenaeus 606a–607b.

[43] That may be too many leaders: see Athenaeus 180c and n. 41 above.

[44] Holst-Warhaft 1992; West 1974, 33 n. 11.

[45] This does not in itself imply that *threnoi* were written down, only that they were learnt in advance; moreover, it is merely the rehearsing in advance that Solon outlawed, not the performances. Cf. Demosthenes 43.62; Alexiou 1974, 12–23.

[46] They are indeed so pessimistic that they worry Campbell, who theorises that the poet must have looked on the bright side in the sections no longer preserved, and that these laments were 'presumably intended to comfort the mourners' (1983, 235).

[47] Maximus Planudes comments on the adoption of this metre in written poetry about 1300 AD: 'One could say that [modern poets] filched such a practice from Ionian women. For this is the metre in which they mourn over the corpses of the dead at funerals' (*Dialogue on Grammar*, p. 100 Bachmann; translation by M. Jeffreys). For more on medieval Greek laments, see Jeffreys 1974; Beck 1971, 191–2.

[48] Swallow-song: Theognis, *Rhodian Festivals* quoted by Athenaeus 360c–d. Milling song: Plutarch, *Banquet of the Seven Sages* 157e. These and other anonymous and folk songs are collected as 'Carmina Popularia' in the lyric anthologies. The song of Harmodius: Athenaeus 695a–b and other sources; attributed to Callistratus (Hesychius s.v. *Harmodiou melos*).

[49] Artemon of Cassandreia, *On the Use of Books*, summarised by Athenaeus 694a–c.

[50] See the discussion of this scene by van Wees (1995, 162–3), with references given there.

[51] *Egils Saga Skalla-Grimssonar*; *Kormáks Saga*, both cited in n. 13 above.

[52] The context of this observation is lost, but its subtlety is not to be separated from the words that Hesiod gives to the Muses: 'we can tell many falsehoods as if real, and, when we wish, we can sing truths' (*Theogony* 27–8). Hesiod, an 'inspired *aoidos*' in the Homeric formula, here speaks of his own inspiration.

[53] Philodemus, *On Flattery*; cf. Nagy 1990, 44.

[54] See e.g. Nagy 1990b, Taplin 1992, and, for further discussion of the social context of epic, Dalby 1995.

7

WHAT WAS IN PANDORA'S BOX?

Daniel Ogden

The myth of Pandora, for which our primary accounts are the narratives of Hesiod in the *Theogony* (535–616) and the *Works and Days* (42–105), tells how, as the culmination of a series of deceptive exchanges between Zeus and Prometheus, Zeus foists upon Prometheus and his less forward-looking brother, Epimetheus, the first woman, Pandora. We know that she is the first (human) woman because Hesiod tells us that the entire race of women is descended from her (*Theog.* 590–1) (and she becomes the first woman more explicitly in later sources),[1] but it is an inconcinnity that Prometheus should himself have been born of a female creature, the nymph Clymene (*Theog.* 507–10), and that there should already be well-established and apparently unproblematic female deities in heaven, such as Athena, Aphrodite, Graces, Persuasion and Hours, to teach her her feminine crafts and wiles and to deck her out.[2] Pandora is, in a memorably jingling phrase, a 'beautiful evil' (*kalon kakon*) (*Theog.* 585), and she brings with her a jar of evils (not a 'box', as in the familiar modern reference: see below), which she proceeds to open, releasing disease, suffering and toil into the world of mortals (i.e. men), who had previously lived blessed lives (*Works and Days* 90–2). Hesiod only explicitly describes the opening of the jar as the work of 'a woman' (*gyne*) (*Works and Days* 94), but in context the phrase is most easily taken as referring to Pandora herself. Besides, what other woman exists at this point?[3]

The basic message of the myth is easily read: woman is the cause or source of all the world's ills. The similarities of the Pandora myth to that of Eve are manifest.[4] And the theme occurs elsewhere in Greek myth: for example, the cause of all the suffering in the Trojan war was also a beautiful woman, Helen.[5] But the Pandora story is among the richest in symbolism of all Greek myths, as a number of modern studies have shown to great effect, particularly those by Vernant and Faraone (see below).

213

The purpose of the paper

It is my purpose to add one more layer of analysis and context-ualisation to the myth. A number of the myth's features suggest that what its audience might have expected to have been in the jar, as the source, the cause and the embodiment of evils, was a *teras*-baby, Pandora's *teras*-baby.[6] A *teras* is properly an evil deformed offspring, human or animal, typically ugly and twisted, and often lame, that portends, causes, represents and embodies *loimos*, pestilence and steril-ity, and its close relative *limos*, famine, as was excellently expounded by Delcourt (1938). These babies must be cast out of the community if it is to be preserved; that is to say, they must be exposed, either by land or by sea, contained in a vessel, which might be a pot or a chest of some sort. The prime example of the *teras*-baby is Oedipus, the 'Swollen-foot' as his name describes him (Sophocles' famous explanation of his swollen feet with reference to the wiring of them at the time of his exposure is a rationalisation, see *Oed.Tyr.* 718, 1034). Oedipus was born in sterility (Euripides, *Phoen.* 13), and duly exposed by land, according to Sophocles, by sea according to others, variously in a pot (as Aristophanes says, *Frogs* 1190, etc.) or in a chest (as a scholiast to Euripides says, *Sch.Phoen.* 26–7). But he survived and eventually re-turned to Thebes, his community, and brought back with him the *loimos* of which he was the embodiment, and in turn caused the births of more *terata* (Sophocles, *Oed.Tyr.* 26–7). The city was only preserved when he was expelled a second time, this time as the adult equivalent of the *teras*, the scapegoat or *pharmakos*.[7]

Another *teras*, and one of greater relevance to the Pandora myth, was Erichthonius.[8] There are many variants in the myths relating to Erichthonius, but the core seems to be as follows: he was sired when Hephaestus attempted to rape Athena, but failed. His seed fell on the earth and produced from it Erichthonius, who, like his close counter-part Cecrops, was human in form down to the waist, but writhing snakes below it – a true monster (there are variants, admittedly, that make Erichthonius either fully human in form, or fully snake). The earth was the mother that bore him, but she was not the only mother he had.[9] This monstrous child was taken up by the virgin Athena, who was, in a peculiar and indirect way, also his mother, concealed in a vessel and given into the care of the three virgin daughters of Cecrops, themselves also, be it noted, apparently of an age and status to have been the child's mother. The vessel is described as a chest, *kibotos*, by Pausanias (1.18.2). However, in his *Ion* Euripides strongly associates the exposure-vessel of Ion with Erichthonius' vessel, and uses a wide range of words to describe it, words variously associated with boxes, baskets or pots; all these words may be compatible with the vessel having been an *antipex*, a lidded, hinged basket.[10] The concealment of Erichthonius is a symbolic exposure: this becomes particularly clear when we bear in mind the modern, surely correct conjecture, that the *kistai* which the Arrhephoroi used to carry into a subterranean cavern were supposed, at some level, to contain the baby Erichthonius,[11] and when we recall that deformed babies were disposed of at Sparta down a crevasse beside Taygetus, called *Apothetai* (Plutarch, *Lycurgus* 16). We may also compare Herodotus' famous account[12] of the concealment of baby Cypselus (whose name means 'footless')[13] in a ceramic beehive, a *kypsele*,[14] by his lame mother Labda, an act of which Plutarch actually employs the word *apotithemi* (*Moralia* 164a), one of the usual terms for the exposure of babies (and note again Sparta's *Apothetai*). Athena forbade the Cecropid girls to open the vessel she gave them, but open it two of them, Herse and Aglauros, did, out of curiosity: they were driven mad, and threw themselves off the acropolis to their deaths. Some variants say that a fully human-formed Erichthonius was guarded in the box by one or two snakes, and that it was fear of these that led the girls to throw themselves from the rock.[15] But other versions, such as Pausanias', simply say that they saw Erichthonius, went mad, and threw themselves from the rock (1.18.2). This could have been a madness induced by terror at the monstrous form of Erichthonius, but comparative material suggests rather that Erichthonius and the evil madness of which he was the embodiment were one and the same, and that it was the opening of the chest that released the madness on to the girls.[16] A similar thing happened to the Spartan heroes Astrabacus and Alopecus. They found the effigy of Artemis Orthia bound with withies. They released it, and were driven mad.[17] And when the pirates captured Dionysus, they bound him also with withies, but the god managed to free himself from them and turned the pirates mad, with the result that they all jumped off their ship into the sea.[18]

This provides us with a model for the analysis of the Pandora myth: in what ways might Pandora be seen as bringing with her from the gods, for the misery of men, an evil *teras* baby, her own, perhaps, in its exposure jar?

Vernant and Faraone

Consideration of some previous analyses of the myth will help us with the issue. Vernant has brilliantly shown how the myth is structured around a series of exchanges of deceptive objects, in which one thing is concealed within another, between Prometheus and Zeus.[19] Prometheus tricks Zeus into choosing the worse portion of the sacrifice by concealing within attractive white fat the worthless bones, whilst concealing the good meat in the disgusting belly (*gaster*);[20] Zeus, in punishment for the trick, withheld fire from mankind, but Prometheus stole it concealed in a fennel stalk;[21] in return for this theft, Zeus, with the help of the other gods, in particular Hephaestus, gave to mankind the first woman, who concealed evil within a beautiful exterior; the jar that she brought with her also concealed evils within it; in addition, Zeus concealed seed within the earth, so that man was doomed to agricultural toil (Hesiod, *Works and Days* 42–8).

There are high degrees of comparability between these objects of exchange. Pandora, within whom evil is concealed, is equated with the earth, within which the seed is concealed. Not only is Pandora made of clay, but her name, which means 'All-giving', is in fact known as an epithet of the earth itself, alongside '[A]nesidora', 'Sending-gifts-up', and Zeidoros, 'Corn-giving';[22] in some respects therefore Pandora is akin to a fertility goddess (more on this below). The use of agricultural metaphors for the sowing of seed in women became banal in Greek culture.[23] The shining white fat that concealed the worthless bones in the sacrificial portion corresponds with the shining white dress in which Pandora comes adorned.[24] And the *gaster* employed in the sacrificial trick also corresponds with Pandora herself, for it is the significant organ of a woman: the word denotes not only 'stomach' but 'womb', and the Hesiodic woman employs the organ in both its aspects to suck men dry, gluttonously eating them out of house and home, and draining the precious sperm out of them with her voracious sexual appetite.[25] In both ways the *gaster* must, like the earth, have seed buried within it, be it the seed of corn (as belly) or the seed of men (as womb).[26] Pandora is also made equivalent to fire, the thing in return for which she is given (*anti pyros*, 'in exchange for/equivalently to fire').[27] Hesiodic women accordingly 'roast their men without fire'.[28] Appropriately, Hesiod uses burning as a metaphor for voracious hunger.[29]

The equivalence between Pandora as a vessel containing evil and her jar of evils is manifest, but they are drawn more tightly together still if we bear in mind that both vessels are made of clay.[30] The equivalences of Pandora with clay-as-earth and with clay-as-pot are neatly demonstrated by vase images. On a volute krater of *c.* 450 BC in the Ashmolean are four beautiful figures, with their names inscribed above: Zeus, Hermes,[31] Epimetheus and Pandora. Pandora is welcomed by Epimetheus as she rises up out of the ground and raises her arms to him. She wears the crown that Hesiod describes, and above her hovers a cupid, ready to adorn her with a necklace. Epimetheus holds a mattock, with which he has no doubt helped Pandora emerge, plant-like, from the earth.[32] In rising out of the ground thus she broadly resembles Persephone as depicted in other images rising from her sojourn in the underworld (her *anodos*) to restore the earth's fruits,[33] or again Ge, as she rises to deliver Erichthonius.[34] A British Museum Campanian-style 'neck' amphora of the late fifth century BC from Basilicata similarly shows, on one side, a young man (Epimetheus? Prometheus?) leaning on a mattock and welcoming a young woman who is growing out of the ground and raising her arms in greeting (but not wearing a crown).[35] Comparison with the Ashmolean vase makes it clear that the woman is again Pandora. On the other side stands a bearded man, leaning on a stick, possibly stunted in growth or de-formed,[36] and possibly club-footed;[37] he gazes at a largish jar on a plinth, which culminates in a small woman's head (it thus appears that the woman and the jar are one, not that the woman is peeping out from inside the jar).[38] This pair is almost certainly Hephaestus and, again, Pandora, who is thus completely identified with the jar; it is even possible that the curves of the jar's sides are supposed to evoke the curves of a woman's hips.[39] The metaphoricity between Pandora and her jar perhaps travels in the other direction too in Hesiod's account: the jar is metaphorically portrayed as a belly, in that its rim, beneath which Hope lodges, is referred to as the jar's 'lips'.[40]

Faraone (1992, 100–2) has offered us another way of analysing the myth: it exemplifies the 'Ruse of the talismanic statue'. He shows that the tale of Pandora's construction by Hephaestus closely resembles other mythical narratives in which beautiful but evilly bewitched stat-ues are constructed and then palmed off on an enemy, onto whom they release their evil, to their destruction.[41] The pattern is best exem-plified by Medea's manufacture of a hollow statue of Artemis, into which she puts magic drugs, with which she is able to overthrow the Iolcians and the palace of Pelias (Hesiod, *Works and Days* 61, *Theogony* 571); it is found in the case of the Trojan horse, as Burkert had shown;[42] and we should again think of Astrabacus' and Alopecus' discovery of the statue of Artemis Orthia. The constructor of Pandora, Hephaestus, is familiar from Homer as the constructor of magical golden statues, or 'girl-robots'.[43] It is also significant that he is the protecting god of potters.[44] The similarity of Hesiod's Pandora to Medea's Artemis becomes particularly clear when we bear in mind that

Hesiod refers to Pandora as a 'likeness' (*ikelon*) of a woman,[45] and that Hyginus describes Pandora as an effigy (*effigies*) made by Vulcan/ Hephaestus, into which Minerva/Athena put a soul (*anima*).[46] Pandora-like figures are very much represented as (hitherto) inanimate mannequins being crowned by gods on two pots: a *c.* 470–460 British Museum white-ground Attic kylix portrays a rigid and static figure over whom '[A]nesidora' is inscribed being crowned by Athene and Hephaestus;[47] and a *c.* 460 Attic kalyx krater also in the British Museum portrays Athene alone crowning a similarly rigid and static female figure.[48] Another image seemingly unites Hephaestus' manufacture of Pandora in his workshop with Epimetheus' release of her from the ground with his mattock: a black-figure lekythos depicts the massive head and hands of a woman rising out of the ground and being hammered by two small but well-formed bearded figures.[49] Further context is provided by a lost satyr-play of Sophocles, which had the alternative titles of 'Pandora' and 'Hammerers' (*Sphyrokopoi*), and seems to have told of Hephaestus' manufacture of Pandora with the help of his workforce of hammering satyrs. It should be noted that hammers, or, perhaps better in this context, 'mallets', were used like mattocks to break up earth.[50] Dancing satyrs also appear on the kalyx krater to which we have just referred.[51]

However, despite his interest in the containment of evil in ancient Greece, Faraone strangely pays little attention to the significance of Pandora's jar, which he seems to regard as an abrupt addition and a redundant doublet of the woman herself, possibly influenced by Near Eastern ideas of the containment of evil (cf. Appendix).[52]

Pandora's jar

It is upon Pandora's vessel that I wish now to concentrate. Hesiod refers to it as a *pithos*, which was the largest Greek storage jar,[53] large enough to contain a man (Diogenes lived in one),[54] and familiar from Mycenean times.[55] He also tells us that its lid was 'great' (*mega*) (*Works and Days* 94).

But it is possible that the jar was not believed to have been as large relative to Prometheus and Pandora as a normal *pithos* is to a normal person, but that it was seen as something more portable.[56] It is strongly implied, though not explicitly stated, that Pandora brought the jar with her from Zeus and the other gods, for the *Works and Days* tells that the gods gave the evils to Pandora (82; cf. Reeder 1995, 277). These must surely have been in the jar. A scholiast to Hesiod thought the same, for he imaginatively suggested that the *pithos* was identical with the evil *pithos* of the two that Zeus kept from which to disburse good and evil to mankind.[57] (The alternative scholiastic suggestion that Prometheus got the jar 'from the Satyrs' presumably derives from the notion that Pandora was made in Hephaestus' workshop by his satyr workmen, the *sphyrokopoi*, and suggests another equivalence between Pandora herself and her jar: see Vernant 1989, 75.) That the jar should have been in Pandora's own charge suits well our analogy with the Cecropids. On the Campanian 'neck' amphora discussed above, the pot in the form of which Pandora is portrayed resembles in shape and size a large amphora rather than a *pithos* (see Sissa 1990, 155). Perhaps we should bear in mind that Prometheus was a Titan, and much bigger than modern mortals; presumably Pandora was made to scale.

If the jar was relatively small for a *pithos*, it might begin to look to us like a vessel suitable for exposure. We think of the reused amphoras from the Kerameikos in which babies are buried.[58] However, exposure pots need not always have been small. The *kypsele* in which Cypselus was hidden was probably also very large in comparison with the baby itself. The Suda and a scholiast to Aristophanes speak of *kypselai* that held six bushels.[59] These pots were built into the tops of furnaces, and surviving exempla and illustrations show them to have been very large jars indeed, much bigger than the size of a baby (see Ure 1922, 202–9).

The familiar reference is to Pandora's vessel as a 'box', but this is usually thought to be an error which originated with Erasmus in 1508,[60] who is alleged to have confused the *pithos* with the *pyxis* opened by Psyche in Apuleius' *Golden Ass* (6.19–20). A pity, for if the 'box' alternative could have been taken to be ancient, then this too would have supported our case. Jars and boxes alike function as exposure vessels, and indeed it is common for ancient sources to differ between themselves on the nature of the exposure vessels of specific *teras*-babies. As we have seen, variants of the Oedipus myth tell us he was exposed in both pot and chest; Euripides perhaps describes the exposure-vessel of Ion as both; and whereas Herodotus tells that Cypselus was exposed in a *kypsele*-pot (a ceramic beehive), Pausanias (5.15.5–9) understood the term (wrongly) to denote a *larnax*, and identified an ivory-appliqué chest that he saw at Olympia, and which he describes in great detail, as the concealment vessel of Cypselus.[61]

The contents of the jar

There is an apparent illogicality at the heart of the Pandora myth.[62] The jar, when firmly shut, contained evils and kept them out of the world of mortals, and when the jar was opened, they were consequently

219

released into that world. But, we are told, when Pandora opened the jar, the one thing that was not released, Hope (*Elpis*), which caught in the lid, was thereby retained in the world of mortals. We are clearly dealing with two models of action: one in which the closed jar keeps things out of the world of men, and one in which it keeps them within the possession of men. The former is the model employed by an important *Odyssey* parallel to Pandora's vessel, the leather bag that Aeolus gives Odysseus with all the pernicious winds sealed inside: when Odysseus' curious sailors, like the curious Cecropids, opened the bag, the winds rushed out and disaster ensued.[63] There is correspond-ing uncertainty as to to the status of Hope. Is it a bad thing (a poor exchange for lost *prometheia*, foresight, as Vernant 1989, 81–2 sees it), for it was after all within the jar of evils? Or is it, as one would perhaps more naturally expect, and as one would judge from its eventual separation from the evils, a good thing?[64] Vernant suggestively ob-serves that whether Hope is in itself ultimately good or bad, it only belongs in the company of evils.[65] Its ambivalence is perhaps best understood in terms of the ambivalence of talismanic objects, as inves-tigated by Faraone. Faraone (1991 and 1992, 36–53) has shown that there was an ambivalence in the case of buried and bound effigies of evil creatures: the act of containment was intended both to keep the evil represented out of society, but also also to retain the evil powers embodied in the effigy in one's own possession, so that they could protect one against rogue evil powers of a similar nature (on the principle of 'fighting fire with fire'). Perhaps then we are to imagine that Hope was after all an evil, but one that has been retained in man's possession to help him against other evils.

Just as evils emanating from Erichthonius flew out of the Cecropid chest when it was opened, sending the girls to their deaths, so too evils flew out of Pandora's jar, filling land and sea. They too might so well have emanated from a *teras* within it. The specific evils that flew out of Pandora's jar, as detailed by Hesiod, were precisely those things that we associate with *teras*-babies and their ensuing *loimos*: diseases (*nousoi*).[66] Comparable here is the Mediterranean plague of 166 AD, which was believed to have come from a sealed room or box in the temple of Apollo Comaeus (i.e., 'of the [sc. long] locks', the god in his plague-bringing/removing aspect) at Babylon, and which had been accidentally released by a Roman soldier.[67]

The use of containers for the restraint or control of powers or powerful objects or beings (beyond *terata*) can be well paralleled from Greek myth and culture. Often these containers were of metal (Faraone

1992, 6–7). At Messene a buried bronze *hydria* contained tin sheets on which mystery rites were inscribed (Pausanias 4.20.4 and 4.26.7–8); at Tegea a lock of the Gorgon given to the Tegeates by Heracles was kept sealed in a bronze pitcher;[68] and Homer tells that Ephialtes and Otus chained up Ares and kept him in a bronze cauldron.[69] On the basis of the ostensible parallel between this episode (and others) and that of Pandora, Walcot (1961, 250; 1966, 61) goes so far as to argue that Pandora's *pithos* was also bronze and prison-like. It would be a pity, however, to have to lose the associations of the *pithos* with clay.

The actual use of pottery vessels in this way is easily attested in the ancient world: Rome had such a sealed pottery jar, believed to contain possibly the Palladium or the images of the Samothracian gods.[70] From Roman Egypt comes the most elaborate of the *kolossoi* or 'voodoo dolls', the Louvre voodoo doll, a beautiful bound female figure run through many times with pins. This was found buried in a clay pot, accompanied by a Greek curse text on papyrus.[71] Columella (6.17.1–6: cf. Faraone 1992, 40) tells that cattle can be protected from the dangerous bite of the shrewmouse if a live shrew is encased in potters' clay and hung round the animal's neck as an amulet. It is less easy to find good Greek examples of the phenomenon employing pottery vessels. The *Geoponica* bids us bury a toad in a pot to avert noxious winds.[72] (The adorned pottery jars that the Athenians set up to Zeus Ktesios and filled with ambrosia do not appear to have been considered to contain a power within them, although they were used as defensive talismans.[73])

An importantly related phenomenon is that of so-called 'bottle imps', powerful beings kept imprisoned in containers, and thus, in some way, kept under control – much like Aladdin's genie.[74] The most obvious example from the ancient world is the Cumaean Sybil, kept hanging shrivelled up in a bottle, to whom Petronius tells us little boys used to address the question, 'Sibyl, what do you want?', eliciting the reply 'I want to die' (*Satyricon* 48). Ovid tells that she had asked of Apollo to live for as many years as there were grains of dust in a pile, but had forgotten also to ask for perpetual youth.[75] Petronius puts the Sibyl in an *ampulla*, a flattish flask; Pseudo-Justin in a bronze vessel of the same shape (*Cohortatio ad Graecos* 37); Pausanias puts her in a stone *hydria* or funerary urn (10.12.8); Ampelius in an iron cage (*Liber memorialis* 8.16).

Pandora and the Cecropids

We are not told directly why Pandora opened the jar. The vignette of the young woman opening the jar recalls strongly the Cecropids opening the chest of Erichthonius.[76] We are not told by Hesiod that Pandora's motive was curiosity, as was the case with the Cecropids (and of course the sailors of Odysseus), as opposed, for example, to simple malice[77] or pre-programming by Zeus,[78] but we can perhaps assume that this was the case.[79] The formal similarity of this scene with the Cecropid scene invites us to understand that the contents of Pandora's box and the Cecropids' chest were similar.

Pandora as the mother of a *teras*-baby

Pandora is a bride: not simply a beautiful young woman, but a woman whose purpose it is to bear children.[80] And in producing children, she inflicts on men the sexual system of reproduction, and the cycle of life that it entails. This inflicted life-cycle brings with it many woes, chief among which is the death of the individual, and a concomitant aware-ness of mortality (we may compare Eve's infliction of the loss of 'innocence').[81] Before the opening of the jar, Hesiod tells us in the *Works and Days* (91–2), men lived 'apart from evils and difficult toil and harsh diseases, which gave Deaths (*Keres*) to them'. (Hesiod quickly goes on to talk about men originally being un-aging and dying pain-lessly in their sleep, but this is within the context of a clearly marked alternative myth, that of the golden age.)[82] As Vernant notes (1989, 75 and 85), the rift between Zeus and Prometheus separates men from immortality; Hope is a compensation for mortality, for immortals do not need it; and the advent of Pandora and her sexual reproductive system is itself the equivalent of the opening of the jar (a further parallel between Pandora herself and the jar). In a sense, then, Pandora's reproductive capacity is evil, and Hesiod significantly fo-cuses on the bad children produced by women.[83] In a paradoxical way her reproductive capacity is represented as a kind of sterility, for it is made clear that the price of human reproduction is the wanton de-vouring by woman of the fruits of nature and of toil.[84] In these ways she is the fit mother of a *teras*-baby.

We have noted that Pandora is herself closely identified with the jar that she brings: both are made of clay, and both are containers for evil. There is only one way in which a woman can literally be considered to be a container: as a mother, she is the container of a baby, in her womb.[85] As we have seen, attention is particularly drawn to Pandora as a *gaster*. If Pandora is a container of evil, she is then easily seen as the container of a *teras*-baby, which is then appropriately hidden away in an exposure vessel akin to the mother from which it came. Indeed Hippocratic medical writing commonly visualised the womb as a pot.[86]

The jar's contents are associated with an (evil?) baby of Pandora's by those scholars who wish to make the retention of Hope in the jar an image for a baby carried in its mother's womb.[87] As an aspect of Earth too Pandora is the fit mother of a *teras*-baby: Earth produced not only the monstrous Erichthonius, but also, according to some versions of his myth, the monstrous Typhon, who similarly consisted of snakes below the waist.[88]

Prometheus had instructed Epimetheus not to accept any gift from Zeus, but 'to send back' or 'send away' (*apopempein*) anything he gave, lest some evil should befall mortals (Hesiod, *Works and Days* 87). The word is evocative of the term used by Plutarch to describe the despatch of Spartan babies to the *Apothetai* (Plutarch, *Lycurgus*, 16), and it is also a regular word for the dismissal of scapegoats and pollution in general: see Versnel (1993, 300). The association between the *teras*-baby and his adult correlate, the scapegoat, has been expounded by Delcourt and others, and is, as we have seen, particularly clear in the case of Oedipus.[89]

A further, indirect link between Pandora, pots and the *teras*-baby may be found in an obscure fragment of Hipponax, which is reconstructed and interpreted in various ways. The fragment speaks of a man 'slipping out and supplicating a seven-leafed cabbage', and goes on to say either that he sacrificed this cabbage to Pandora 'in a pot' (*enkythron*), or that Pandora sacrificed the cabbage in a pot, and that this was in the place of or before a scapegoat (*pro pharmakou*).[90] It seems, then, that Pandora was in some way associated with a pot which contained a substitute scapegoat, or with a pot in which a sacrifice was made in association with the expulsion of a scapegoat.

Conclusion

In conclusion, I do not wish to do anything as rash as to posit a lost 'alternative' or 'original' version of the Pandora myth in which she really did let a *teras* baby out of her jar. I merely wish to establish the parallel between the Pandora myth and Greek thinking about *terata*. The Pandora myth would have been contextualised by its consumers against their beliefs about, and their practices relating to, *teras*-babies, and this would have lent the myth a degree of immediacy and plausibility for them.

Appendix
The Pandora myth and Mesopotamian parallels
It is often now contended that one cannot mine the Pandora myth for

information about the way the Greeks perceived their world on the ground that it was borrowed wholesale from Mesopotamia, alongside several other myths. Such an objection is misconceived for a number of reasons. First, on the assumption that the Greeks did borrow 'the myth of Pandora' from Mesopotamia, we must still ask why they chose to borrow this myth, and such others as they borrowed alongside it, as opposed to all the other Mesopotamian myths that they did not borrow. Clearly the myths that were selected for borrowing were ones that spoke meaningfully to the Greeks in the first place. Secondly, if the Greeks did contrive to borrow into their own mythological system a myth that was alien to it at the point of borrowing, nonetheless once borrowed that myth ipso facto became part of the system that constituted Greek mythological consciousness as a whole. Thirdly, the identification of mythological 'borrowings' is in any case fraught with methodological difficulties, of which the chief, but by no means the only, one is the fact that we have no record of the Greek mythological system (Linear B affords very little help) prior to the supposed occasion of borrowing (ninth century BC?).[91] We cannot assert that the Greeks got their Pandora from Mesopotamia when we know nothing at all of Greek mythology prior to Homer and Hesiod: to do so would be repeat Herodotus' fallacy of deriving much of Greek culture from Egypt simply because the records of Egyptian culture preceded those of Greek. One would give much to know what Greek mythology prior to the supposed period of oriental 'borrowings' looked like.

Let us turn briefly to the specifics of the Pandora myth. While it is true that reasonably convincing 'parallels' (whatever we are to make of them once established) for the Promethean aspects of the Hesiodic tales can be found,[92] there is no simple and obvious Mesopotamian correlate for Pandora herself. In the most recent comparison of Greek and Mesopotamian myths Penglase has to piece together a model for Pandora from a number of disparate sources: her manufacture as a human from a clay figurine is derived from the manufacture of multiple male and female humans from clay figurines by Enki (= Hephaestus) and Ninmah (= Athena?);[93] her manufacture with hammers or mattocks (as in the satyric version of her myth) is derived from Enlil's (= Zeus') agricultural manufacture of the human race as a whole with a mattock;[94] her clothing-scene and her delivery to mankind by Hermes, conductor of souls, are derived from Ishtar/Inanna's ascent from the underworld with the help of the underworld figure Namtar;[95] the troubles she brings upon Epimetheus and mankind are derived from the demons that Ishtar/Inanna brings back with her from the underworld.[96] But Pandora's jar itself is derived not from a Mesopotamian source but from the Hittite conception of the underworld as a jar.[97] It emerges from this that while Mesopotamian and/or Hittite sources may provide parallels for individual motifs in the Pandora myth, none of them provides anything like the same collocation and system of motifs or details that we find in it. To all intents and purposes we may continue to consider the story of Pandora as preserved in the Hesiodic epics as a product of a Greek mythological mentality.[98]

Notes

[1] Apollodorus *Bibliotheca* 1.7.2 and Pausanias 1.24.7.

[2] Hesiod *Works and Days* 63–6 and 72–5 and *Theogony* 573–77 and 587. See Harrison 1900, 99; Rudhardt 1986, 237–42; Vernant 1989, 70; Faraone 1992, 101; Loraux 1993, 74 and 242–3; Penglase 1994, 197–8; Reeder 1995, 277 and Zeitlin 1995, 50.

[3] Faraone 1992, 101–2, who is anxious to portray Pandora as more magical statue than actual woman, implies that the opener of the jar was distinct from Pandora herself.

[4] For the Eve parallel see Séchan 1929 and West 1978, 155 n. 1.

[5] Cf. Loraux 1993, 80, with n. 45.

[6] The idea that Pandora's pot contained a *teras* is perhaps akin to the notion of Harrison (1900) that Pandora's pot was to be taken specifically as a grave-*pithos*, and that her opening of it ('Pithoigia') was therefore a release of ghosts. Cf. Walcot 1966, 61 and West 1978, 165.

[7] On Oedipus as *teras* and *pharmakos*, see Delcourt 1944; Lévi-Strauss 1963, 206–31; Guepin 1968, 89–91; Vernant 1981; Girard 1986, 26; and Ogden 1997, 29–30.

[8] For comparabilities between the myths of Pandora and Erichthonius, see Loraux (1993 passim), though her focus is on the comparability of their autochthonous origins, both alike under the guidance of Hephaestus and Athena, rather than on that of the opening of the vessels, since her main interest is in the *Theogony* narrative and the combination of Pandora and Erichthonius images in the Athena Parthenos statue. Particularly noteworthy is the vague similarity between the name of *Pandora* and that of *Pandrosos*, ('All-dew', a name therefore remarkably similar in meaning to that of the other Cecropid Herse), the Cecropid girl to whom specifically Erichthonius was entrusted in his box (Apollodorus *Bibliotheca* 3.14.6, Pausanias 1.2.6 etc.). Interestingly, some ancient lexicographical sources confuse the two, notably an MS of Harpocration s.v. *epiboion*, a citation of Philochorus FGH 328 F10, where Pandora is given by mistake for Pandrosos; cf. Deubner 1932, 26–7 and Loraux 1993, 115.

[9] Cf. Loraux 1993, 57–8.

[10] So Young 1941; cf. Bergson 1969 and Lissarrague 1995, 92.

[11] See Hamilton 1984.

[12] Herodotus 5.92; cf., generally, Vernant 1981.

[13] Aristotle *History of animals* 618a31; cf. Ogden 1997, 90.

[14] For the *kypsele* as a ceramic beehive see Ure 1922, 197–23, Roux 1963 and Ogden 1997, 89–90.

[15] One serpent: Apollodorus 3.14.6 and Euripides *Ion* 23. Two serpents: Hyginus *Astronomica* 2.13.

[16] On Erichthonius generally see Powell 1906, Parker 1987, Rosivach 1987, Brulé 1987, Loraux 1993, Shapiro 1995, Reeder 1995, 262–6 and Ogden 1997, 30–1.

[17] Pausanias 3.16.9–11; cf. Ogden 1997, 111–14.

[18] *Homeric hymn* 7 *(to Dionysus)* 13, 17 and 52.

[19] Vernant 1980, 168–85 (= Gordon 1981, 43–56, where see also Vernant at 57–79) and 1989, 62; cf. Zeitlin 1995, 50.

[20] Hesiod *Theogony* 535–60. At *Works and Days* 47–55 it appears that Zeus was plainly and simply tricked. However at *Theogony* 551–2 Hesiod actually tells that Zeus knew he was being tricked, but allowed himself to be so. This is presumably a pious development of the *Works and Days* notion, composed so as not to impugn the omniscience and omnipuissance of the god: see West 1966, 321. The hiding of the meat in the stomach has been seen as an aetiology for a haggis-like dish (cf. Homer *Odyssey* 18.44 and Herodotus 6.61): West 1966, 319 and Vernant 1989, 57–61.

[21] Hesiod *Theogony* 560–70. West (1966, 323) suggests that Zeus' specific purpose was to prevent Prometheus and mankind enjoying, by cooking, the nice meat he had tricked him out of.

[22] See Vernant 1980, 180–1 and 1989, 46–7. 'Pandora' is the epithet of a chthonic deity, or Earth herself: see the sources cited at West 1978, 164. For 'Anesidora' as an epithet of the earth, see Scholiast Aristophanes *Birds* 970 and Hesychius and *Etymologicum Magnum* s.v. *Anesidora*. On a white-ground *kylix* in the British Museum (inv. no. GR 1885.1–28.1 [D4] = *LIMC* Anesidora 1) of *c.* 470–460 Hephaestus and Athene are shown adjusting the crown of a statue-like woman (see below). Above her is inscribed not the name 'Pandora' but '[A]nesidora': see Harrison 1922, 281; Lendle 1957, Plate 2; Bérard 1974, 161–4; West 1978, 164; Loraux 1993, 78, 84; and Reeder 1995 278–81, with a detailed list of the pot's places of publication. For the earth described as *zeidoros*, see Hesiod, *Works and Days* 117. Hesiod himself explains the name 'Pandora' as 'Endowed by all' from the fact that all the gods gave something to help equip Pandora: *Works and Days* 80–2. But Faraone (1992, 101–2) persuasively argues that the name can be seen as part of Zeus' cruel deception: it is suggested that she will give everything, but in fact she will rather take away; cf. West 1978, 164.

[23] See, e.g., Dubois 1988, 65–85.

[24] Hesiod *Theogony* 574, cf. 583 (of the crown); Vernant 1980, 178.

[25] At Hesiod *Theogony* 599 woman, like a drone, reaps the toil of others into her stomach. The sexual ravenousness of women is explained at *Works and Days* 586–7. See Vernant 1980, 171, 178–9, and 1989, 60 and 66; and Zeitlin 1995, 53.

[26] Vernant 1989, 58 and 67, noting that the *gaster* also anticipates the culture of sacrifice in evoking the bowl of the tripod, the cooking pot which is placed on the fire, which was stomach-shaped and called a *gastre*.

[27] Hesiod *Works and Days* 57, *Theogony* 570, 585, 602.

[28] Hesiod *Works and Days* 702–5. See Vernant 1980, 179–80 and 1989, 62–8. The same phrase appears describing women in a more emphatic context in a fragment from Euripides' first *Hippolytus*, *TGF* 429N²; cf. Loraux 1993, 73.

[29] Hesiod *Works and Days* 363, *limos aithon*; at Hesiod F43a 5–10 Erysichthon is *Aithon*; cf. Vernant 1989, 66.

[30] Hesiod *Works and Days* 61, *Theogony* 571; for the general association between women and containers see Lissarrague 1995 and Reeder 1995, 277.

[31] The presence of the spirit-guiding (*psychopompos*) god both here and in the Hesiodic narrative (*Works and Days* 84) serves to underline Pandora's chthonic associations: Penglase 1994, 207–9.

[32] Volute *krater*, Ashmolean, Oxford, inv. no. G. 275 (V. 525) = *LIMC* Pandora 4. See Gardner 1901 with Plate 1; Harrison 1922, 281 with Figure 71; Bérard 1974, 161–4; West 1978, 164–5; Loraux 1993, viii, 89, 115 with Plate 2; Penglase 1994, 205 and 211; and Reeder 1995, 284–6 (this last with superb illustrations and a detailed list of prior publications).

[33] For depictions of the *anodos* of Persephone ('[Phe]rophatta') see Harrison 1922, 276–83, with Figures 67 and 68; and West 1978, 165.

[34] For Ge delivering Erichthonius, see, e.g., the British Museum hydria inv. no. GR 1837.6–9.54 (E 182), with Reeder 1995, 253–5; cf. also *LIMC* Erechtheus 11.

[35] British Museum inv. no. F147 = *LIMC* Elpis 13/Hephaestus 225/Pandora 5, illustrated also at Robert 1914, 36; Harrison 1922, 280; and Zeitlin 1995, 51.

[36] The figure certainly seems cramped in comparison with the youth, but this may simply have been due to the incompetence of the painter.

[37] As detected by Sissa 1990, 155, but this is not obvious to me.

[38] See Sissa 1990, 228 n. 40, rejecting the line taken by Simon 1963 and Zeitlin 1995, 51 that the tiny head belongs to Hope (*Elpis*), who remained inside the jar, which depends upon the assumption that woman and jar are separate. Penglase 1994, 211 similarly believes that the head comes from within the jar, but that it nonetheless represents Pandora, who emerges from a pot which represents the underworld.

[39] Thus Sissa 1990, 155. Zeitlin (1995, 51), however, identifies the bearded figure as Epimetheus, and reduces the figure I here identify as Epimetheus to an anonymous 'youth'.

[40] Hesiod *Works and Days* 97; cf. Vernant 1989, 77, and Zeitlin 1995, 53.

[41] Hesiod *Works and Days* 60–3, 70–1; *Theogony* 571–2, 578–87.

[42] Burkert 1979, 61–2 and 73–5; cf. Faraone 1992, 94, 99, 104.

[43] Homer *Il.* 18.417–20; cf. West 1966, 326, and 1978, 158 (arguing for the priority of Hesiod).

[44] See West 1966, 326 and Faraone 1992, 55–6.

[45] Hesiod *Theogony* 572 and *Works and Days* 71. Faraone (1992, 102) is wrong to say that Hesiod never refers to Pandora directly as a woman, for she is referred to as 'this woman (*gynaika*)' at *Works and Days* 80 and she is surely the

woman (*gyne*) that opens the lid of the jar at 94, as argued by West (1978, 168 and cf. 164); see also Loraux 1993, 77 with n. 31, and 241.

[46] Hyginus *Fabula* 147. Cf. Faraone 1992, 20 on the stages of manufacture of an animated statue, which involves first the casting of the metal and then the insertion of *pharmaka* to animate it.

[47] British Museum inv. no. GR 1885.1–28.1 (D4) = *LIMC* Anesidora 1; cf. Harrison 1922, 281 and 284; Penglase 1994, 202; and Reeder 1995, 278–81; see also above.

[48] British Museum inv. no. GR 1856.12–13.1 (E467) = *LIMC* Anesidora 2; Reeder 1995, 282–4, has full publication details.

[49] Paris, Bibliothèque Nationale cat. no. 298; see Harrison 1900, 106 Fig. 2, and 1922, 279 Fig. 69; and Kerenyi 1951, 219; cf. Penglase 1994, 205 and 207–9.

[50] Sophocles F482–6 Radt; see Harrison 1900, 106–7, and 1922, 282; Bérard 1974, 164; and West 1978, 165.

[51] Cf. Reeder 1995, 284.

[52] Faraone 1992, 110 n. 48 and 111 n. 55 for the derivation of the *pithos*-imagery from the East and 102 for the 'abruptly added' story of the *pithos*.

[53] Cf. Hesiod *Works and Days* 368 for the *pithos* in its role as a storage jar.

[54] Diogenes Laertius 6.23 and 43; 'the *pithos*-life' became proverbial of Cynicism (Zenobius 4.14).

[55] Hesiod *Works and Days* 94, 97, 98; cf. Harrison 1900, 99–100; West 1978, 168; and Faraone 1992, 101. Vernant (1989, 77–8 and 84) notes that as a storage jar, Pandora's vessel resembled both earth and woman in that it was something in which seed (grain) could be hidden for many months before being retrieved; and men must work hard to fill up what the woman so casually emptied. Sissa (1990, 155–6) and Zeitlin (1995, 52–5) note that as a storage jar the *pithos* has particular associations with female *oikonomia*. Harrison (1922, 285) rather connects Pandora's *pithos* with grave-*pithoi*, appropriately enough, perhaps, since Pandora releases deathly things from it.

[56] See Harrison 1900, 100, on the issue of portability.

[57] Scholiast Hesiod *Works and Days* 84, referring to Homer *Il.* 24.527–8; cf. Walcot 1961, 250, and Sissa 1990, 154.

[58] Knigge 1991, 37 with Fig. 34; cf. Penglase 1994, 210.

[59] Suda s.v. *kypsele* and Scholiast to Aristophanes *Peace* 631.

[60] Erasmus *Adagiorum Chiliades Tres* i.233; cf. Harrison 1900, 99; Panofsky 1956, 14–15; West 1978, 168; Faraone 1992, 110 n. 48; and Lissarrague 1995, 91.

[61] Cf. Jones 1894 and Roux 1963.

[62] Well articulated by West (1978, 169). See also Bonner 1937.

[63] Homer *Od.* 10.19–27 (cf. 5.383); Empedocles also used animal skins to control winds (Timaeus FGH 566 F30 apud Diogenes Laertius 8.60 and Clement of Alexandria *Stromateis* 6.3 p. 445 (Stählin)); cf. Faraone 1992, 86 nn. 1–2.

[64] The Aesopic tale told by Babrius *Fabula* 58 (Aesop no. 312 Perry) is simpler: Zeus gave man all *good things* gathered together in a *pithos* (the other Iliadic one?), which was opened by a man without self-control, so that they all flew up back to heaven, with Hope alone again sticking in the lid. Pandora's

jar contained good things also in the version of her tale told by Macedonius the Consul, *Palatine Anthology* 10.71. Cf. Theognis 1135–50, where the good gods, apart from Hope, quit the earth for Olympus. Some have argued therefore that Hesiod has conflated an original simple tale in which the jar contained good things with the notion that women bring bad things into the world; see West 1978, 170.

[65] Vernant 1989, 82–4. For further discussion of whether Hope is 'good' or 'bad', see Walcot 1961, Hoffman 1985, Noica 1984, Verdenius 1985, Penglase 1994, 211, and Zeitlin 1995, 55.

[66] Hesiod *Works and Days* 92 and 102. The contents of the jar are also described as: *kaka* (*Works and Days* 91, 101; *Theogony* 600, 602, 611), *ponos* (*Works and Days* 91), old age (*Theogony* 604; *Works and Days* 93, if genuine) and *kedea lygra* (*Works and Days* 95). See Vernant 1989, 78–80.

[67] *Historia Augusta*, *Verus* 8.1–2 and Ammianus Marcellinus 23.6.24; Faraone 1992, 63.

[68] Apollodorus *Bibliotheca* 2.7.3; cf. Pausanias 8.47.5 with Frazer 1898, ad loc. and Suda s.v. *plokion Gorgados*.

[69] Homer *Il.* 5.385–91; cf. Faraone 1991, 197 n. 111 and 1992, 74–5.

[70] Dionysius of Halicarnassus *Roman Antiquities* 1.69 and 2.66; further references at Faraone 1992, 15 n. 29.

[71] Faraone 1991, no. 27, with Fig.; Gager 1992, no. 28 with Figure 13; the curse text is reproduced at Daniel and Maltomini 1990–2 no. 47 and translated by Gager loc. cit.

[72] *Geoponica* 2.18.15; cf. Pliny *Natural History* 18.294; cf. Faraone 1992, 86 n. 2.

[73] Athenaeus 473b–c.

[74] On which see Bonner 1937.

[75] Ovid *Metamorphoses* 14.129–53; cf. Servius on Virgil *Aeneid* 6.321.

[76] Lissarrague 1995, 92 and Reeder 1995, 278–9.

[77] Malice is unlikely if we accept West's reading and analysis of *epembale* at *Works and Days* 98: Hesiod will thus have told us that Pandora slammed the lid back on the jar as soon as she realised what she had done. See West 1978, 171, also discussing Pandora's motivation.

[78] Sissa 1990, 155 characterizes Pandora opening the jar as 'like an automaton.'

[79] The facts that Pandora has a dog-like mind and deceitful nature (Hesiod *Works and Days* 67) and was 'sheer deception' (*Theogony* 589) perhaps suggest that curiosity was the motive.

[80] She is decked out as a bride at Hesiod *Theogony* 573–584; cf. Faraone 1992, 101–2; Reeder 1995, 278 and 286; and Zeitlin 1995, 51.

[81] Hesiod *Theogony* 602–11; cf., broadly, Vernant 1989, 64–6; Murnaghan 1993, 48 and 72–3 ; Reeder 1995, 277; and Zeitlin 1995, 50. We are reminded of Scott Fitzgerald's observation that only the mortal can be beautiful (*The beautiful and damned*).

[82] Hesiod *Works and Days* 112–15; note 106 for the distinctness and incompatibility of this myth.

[83] Hesiod *Theogony* 610, *atarteroio genethles*, 'baneful'; however West (1966 *ad loc.*) and Loraux (1993, 89) take *genethles* to mean here 'wife,' and to refer to Pandora herself; Zeitlin (1995, 52) reads the term as significantly ambivalent.

[84] She is a 'plague' (*pema*) to men that eat corn: Hesiod *Works and Days* 82, *Theogony* 592; cf. Vernant 1989, 69. At *Works and Days* 373–5 Hesiod warns men not to be bewitched by a woman's attractive bottom whilst she tries to get her hands on their granaries. And like drones, women reap the toils of others into their own bellies (*gastera*, *Theogony* 599). As we have seen, a bad wife 'roasts her man without fire, and brings him to raw old age' (*Works and Days* 702–5). Cf. West 1978, 155. See also Zeitlin 1995, 51 for Hesiod's 'suppression' of Pandora's 'fertility'.

[85] The association between Pandora's womb and her *pithos* is elaborately drawn by Zeitlin 1995, 53.

[86] e.g. Hippocrates *Ancient Medicine* 22 = i.628 Littré; see also Aristotle *Generation of animals* 737b28–34; cf. Hanson 1991, 210–11.

[87] Thus Hoffman 1985; Zeitlin 1995, 53; and Reeder 1995, 277–8.

[88] Apollodorus *Bibliotheca* 1.6.3; at *Homeric hymn* (3) *to Apollo* 343–55 he is, however, a son of Hera's parallel to the lame Hephaestus; cf. Ogden 1997, 35–7.

[89] See, e.g., Delcourt 1938, 50–66 and Ogden 1997, 9–23.

[90] Hipponax F104 lines 47–9 West apud Athenaeus 370b; cf. Harrison 1922, 283–4; Deubner 1932, 182; West 1974, 145–6; and Hughes 1992, 144–5. The reading of *enchyton*, 'cake', rather than *enkythron*, 'in a pot', together with the interpretation 'cabbage, to which Pandora sacrificed a cake...' now seems out of favour.

[91] Thus Penglase 1994, 241.

[92] In the *Epic of Atra-hasis*, for which see Lambert and Millard 1969 and Pritchard 1969, 104–6; cf. Walcot 1966, 56–7 and Penglase 1994, 216–29.

[93] *Enki and Ninmah*, for which see Kramer and Maier 1989; cf. Penglase 1994, 201.

[94] *Enlil and the Pickaxe*, for which see Jacobsen 1946, 134–7; cf. Walcot 1966, 55–6, and Penglase 1994, 203–5.

[95] *Ishtar's ascent to the netherworld* and *Inanna's descent to the netherworld*, at Pritchard 1969, 52–7 and 106–9; cf. Penglase 1994, 206–9 and 212–15.

[96] *Inanna's descent to the netherworld*; cf. Penglase 1994, 211.

[97] Wagenvoort 1956, 102–31; Walcot 1961 and 1966, 61; and Penglase 1994, 210–11.

[98] Even Penglase himself concedes a high level of creative re-shaping of the oriental prototype material by the Greeks (1994, 215–16, 228–9, 238–9 and 243).

8

THE NEW SIMONIDES AND
HEROIZATION AT PLATAIA

Deborah Boedeker

In a speech published a century after the event, Isokrates extravagantly suggests of the men who fought in the Persian War,

> I even believe that one of the gods, admiring their excellence (*arete*), brought about the war so that men of such natures would not remain unknown or end their lives without fame (*kleos*), but be deemed worthy of the same things that happened to the so-called demigods (*hemitheoi*) who are descended from gods. The bodies of those men the gods gave over to the constraints of nature, but the memory (*mneme*) of their *arete* they made undying (*athanatos*). (*Panegyrikos* 84)[1]

Not only the gods but the Greeks themselves kept alive the memory of those who fought in the Persian Wars. How were these same war-dead thought of and honored by their contemporaries, a century before Isokrates?

New evidence from the immediate aftermath of one of the great Persian War battles now helps us see more clearly how and when the transition from dead soldier to immortal hero took place. In 1992, Peter Parsons published a group of papyrus fragments which he identified as coming from Simonides' elegy on the battle of Plataia.[2] Almost simultaneously, the fragments were edited by M.L. West in the second edition of *Iambi et Elegi Graeci*, vol. 2; since then they have attracted a flurry of attention.[3] Their contents can be briefly summarized. A few broken lines, numbered Simonides fr. 10 by West, invoke (surely) Achilleus as 'famous son of the sea-maiden'. Fr. 11, the longest and most complete piece of the elegy, appears to be part of the proœmium. It begins by recounting Achilleus'(?) death and burial. The just destruction of Troy is then recapitulated, and the return home of the heroic Danaans. Simonides acknowledges the poet who made these men famous, bids Achilleus farewell, and summons his own Muse to help him preserve the memory of those who defended their land, remembering their *arete*; their *kleos* will be deathless. The Plataia narrative now begins, with the Spartans departing from their city, accompanied by the heroes Menelaos and the Dioskouroi as well as their general Pausanias. They march, it seems, through the lands of Corinthians, Megarians, and other neighbors, trusting in divine portents, toward a 'lovely plain', probably Eleusis, and Athens. Fr. 13 seems to describe a battle on a plain, presumably at Plataia, involving 'Medes and Persians' on one hand, 'sons of Doros and Herakles' on the other. West thinks that the badly damaged fr. 14 preserves part of a speech by the Spartans' seer Teisamenos, foretelling how the Greeks will win a memorable battle, with Zeus nodding in approval, and predicting that the enemy will even be driven out of Asia. Frr. 15 and 16 (which were quoted by Plutarch and partly preserved on a scrap of papyrus as well) cite the Corinthians' bravery in the center of the battle line. Little can be said about the rest of the poem, but fr. 17 preserves Demeter's name and may refer to the long duration of the battle.

Fragmentary as it is, this new text encourages a reconsideration of how the Persian War dead were thought of by their contemporaries. The Plataia elegy, I will argue, lends weight to the view that these fighters were honored with hero cult immediately after their death, and helps explain the process by which that happened.

My argument rests largely on the relationship between the two groups of Greek warriors mentioned in Simonides' poem, which posits the Danaans who fought at Troy as predecessors of the allied Greeks who fought at Plataia. The elegy appears to glide over the victory at Troy and focus more on the death and burial of one of the Danaans. In a passage from (probably) the prooemium of the poem, following M.L. West's plausible supplements, someone – probably Achilleus himself – is killed not by a Persian arrow at Plataia, but by Apollo's hand at Troy:

> str[uck you...and you fell, as when a larch]
>   or pine-tree in the [lonely mountain] glades
> is felled by woodcutters...
>   and much...
> [A great grief seized] the war-host; [much they honored you,]
>   [and with Patr]oclus' [ashes mingled yours.]
> [It was no ordinary mortal] laid you low,
>   ['twas by Apoll]o's hand [that you were struck.]
>   (fr. 11.1–8; translation M.L. West)[4]

In the following lines, the speaker summarizes the defeat of Troy, then states that 'undying fame' (*athanaton kleos*) was poured on the Danaans by the man who received the true story from the Muses (fr. 11.15–18) – surely a reference to Homeric epic. Now the poet bids farewell to Achilleus, son of Thetis, and calls on his own Muse to provide ordered beauty (*kosmos*) for this song (or a new key for his lyre),[5] so that '[fame] undying' ([*kleos*] *athanaton*)[6] will come to the brave men who went out from Sparta to save Greek freedom (fr. 11.19–28, as restored by West). Thus this very song is to provide a way for the Spartans and others[7] who fought at Plataia to achieve the kind of deathlessness that Homeric epic provided for the Greeks at Troy.

Another analogy between Greeks fighting Trojans and Greeks fighting Persians is made in what Felix Jacoby named the 'Eion poem' (*FGE* (Page) XL), fourteen verses inscribed on three herms in the Athenian agora, in praise of the Athenians who defeated the Persians at the Thracian city of Eion a few years after the battle of Plataia. Like the new Simonides, the Eion poem is composed in elegiacs; it too cites Homeric praise of earlier warriors, comparing the Athenians at Eion to their ancestors led by Menestheus at Troy, whom Homer called 'marshallers of battle'. The Eion poem, of course, must be dated after the city was captured in 476–475 BC, while the Plataia elegy, with its unapologetic mention of Pausanias and relatively panhellenic spirit, can best be ascribed to the period immediately after the battle in 479 BC.[8] Hence the new elegy provides the earliest extant verbal example of an analogy drawn between the Trojan and Persian Wars.[9]

The Plataia elegy differs from the Eion poem, however, in significant ways. It mentions Greeks from several cities instead of only one, and apparently it does not mention the contemporary combatants' relationship to the heroes who fought at Troy.[10] The role ascribed to the makers of the two elegies also differs radically. Homer's praise of heroic Athenians is deemed fitting also for their successors in the present generation; nothing is said of the poet who now praises the later group. In the Plataia elegy, however, the speaker is presented as key to the undying fame of those he praises, just as Homer, thanks to the Muses, was responsible for the immortal *kleos* of the heroes at Troy.[11] Similar self-consciousness is found also in Pindaric odes composed to celebrate winners in the panhellenic games. These lyric poems, roughly contemporary with the Plataia elegy, do not hesitate to mention the poet's essential role in perpetuating the athlete's achievement (e.g. *Ol.* 2.2, 89–95; *Ol.* 11.3–6).[12] The Eion poem's silence with regard to the poet corresponds to its mode of communication: the speaker's role is emphasized in praise poems that were meant for performance, such as the victory odes and the Plataia elegy, but not in those designated for inscription and reading.

The variation in how the poet's role is presented suggests another

233

difference between the two poems. The inscribed Eion poem com-
memorates Athenian valour, which is accepted as already established,
explicitly so that it may inspire future readers to equivalent efforts:

> seeing these (memorials), someone of those to come will be
> more willing
> to engage in strife for the common good.
>
> (*FGE* (Page) XL C.3–4)

The Plataia elegy, in contrast, is a dynamic speech act, intended to
perpetuate the memory of its subjects. Thus the speaker calls the Muse
to help him arrange his song 'so that someone in the f[uture] will recall
[the men]' who marched out of Sparta (fr. 11.21–5).

The speaker of the Plataia elegy, as we have seen, hopes to provide
the same kind of *athanaton kleos* to his contemporaries that the earlier
poet gave to the Danaans (assuming the restoration of *kleos*, 'fame', in
fr. 11.28 is correct). Such a close parallel between contemporary
hoplites and heroes of the Trojan War, however familiar to readers of
Herodotus,[13] would have been a bold stroke for a poet in 479. An
epinician ode, of course, may propose a Trojan-era hero as parallel to
a contemporary athletic victor, as Aias is parallel to Timodemos of
Acharnai in Pindar's *Nemean* 2.14–15 (although as Burnett points out
this is attested less frequently than modern readers might expect).[14]
Gregory Nagy describes this resemblance as ideological: the contemporary athlete's struggle to win in the Games is denoted in the same
terms (e.g. *ponos* 'labor', *aethlos* 'struggle') that apply in poetry to the
life-and-death efforts of heroes of old, at Troy and elsewhere.[15] But the
Plataia elegy postulates an even closer similarity, if indeed it aspires to
provide for contemporary Greek fighters the same kind of 'undying
fame' as that granted to their predecessors who fought at Troy.

This immortal fame is the *kleos* bestowed by poetry that will be re-
performed. But in the Plataia elegy it may mean something more as
well. The fame of both groups of Greek warriors is described not as
'unfading' (*aphthiton*) as in Homeric diction, but 'undying' (*athanaton*:
fr. 11.15 and 28);[16] I suggest that 'undying' here applies to the subjects
of *kleos* as well as to the *kleos* itself – that is, the Danaans have become
not only famous but deathless, and the speaker hopes that the Plataiamachoi too will share this fate. The reason for proposing this rests
largely on two passages in the prooemium, where the speaker apparently addresses Achilleus, referring to him as son of Thetis (an important distinction to which I shall return). A vocative is likely in the first
instance (fr. 10.5):

glorious [son] of the sea-dwelling [girl]
κούρης εἰ]αλίης ἀγλαόφη[με πᾶϊ

and virtually certain in the second (fr. 11.19–20):

[but] fare you well now, famous [son] of the goddess
[girl] of sea-dwelling Nereus, but I...
ἀλλὰ σὺ μὲ]ν νῦν χαῖρε, θεᾶς ἐρικυ[δέος υἱέ
κούρης εἰν]αλίου Νηρέος· αὐτὰρ ἐγώ[

Such invocations of men or women of the past are unusual in archaic epic and elegy. As Nagy points out, in Homeric epic praise consists of third-person narrative, whereas in epinician the victorious athlete can be praised in the second person[17] – but of course the athletic champion is (ideally) alive and present at the performance of the song in his honor.

Rarely, the narrator of epic apostrophizes a character. In the *Odyssey* this occurs only in a common formulaic line introducing a speech by Eumaios, and can be attributed to the metrical usefulness of the vocative form of his name: 'Responding you said to him/her, Eumaios the swineherd' (fifteen times in this form; twice more with variants in the first half of the line).[18] In *Iliad* 16, Patroklos is similarly addressed by the narrator: 'Groaning deeply you said to him, Patroklos the horseman' (*Il.* 16.20; cf. 16.744 and 843). More striking than these examples, and widely recognized for their pathetic quality, are the seven apostrophes to Patroklos in the space of 260 lines (the last five of them concentrated within a hundred lines) describing his final attack on the Trojans and the moment of his death.[19]

Direct address to a character at a critical moment is perhaps the most extraordinary trope of all those the epic performer uses to make present before his audience the story he is recreating. The pathos of the line 'Then and there, Patroklos, the end of your life appeared' (*Il.* 16.787) has been noted by critics for more than two millennia.[20] But even though Achilleus' death is also described in the Plataia elegy, the addresses to him are of a different nature. Fr. 10.5 is too fragmentary to encourage much conjecture about its context, but in fr. 11.19–20 the vocative is used not within a narrative, as is the case with Patroklos in the *Iliad* passages, but in the transition between one narrative and another. Achilleus at this point is not a character whose actions are being described or even lamented, as he is in Homeric epic; he is an addressee being honored by the poetic performance.

Obbink shows that the formula 'farewell...but I' (*chaire...autar ego*) accompanied by an invocation has parallels in passages where the speaker concludes his address to a god and turns toward another story – marking a transition from 'hymn' to 'epic' or from 'prooemium' to 'nomos' within a poetic performance.[21] In a Pindaric epinician, as Capra and Curti note, a similar formulation – 'farewell, but I...will proclaim' (Pindar, *Is.* 1.32–4: *chairete, ego de...garusomai*) – concludes the 'myth' section and introduces the praise of the current prize-winner.[22] In the Plataia elegy, correspondingly, *chaire...autar ego* marks the change in focus from the old Trojan War heroes to the recent battle of Greeks against Persians.[23]

In an illuminating general article on the new fragments, M.L. West asks why Achilleus receives so much attention in the prooemium, and suggests a casual answer: 'Possibly the poem happened to be composed at the time of some festival or ritual in Achilles' honor, and Simonides took his cue from that.'[24] Hugh Lloyd-Jones, however, maintains that Achilleus is not loosely connected but integral to the elegy's subject matter: he provides a model for the Greeks who fought at Plataia.[25] Important for my argument, however, is that the hero of Troy is not just *mentioned* in the Plataia elegy, but *invoked*.

In fr. 11.19–20, the address to Achilleus is followed immediately by the speaker's address to his 'many-named Muse'. Obbink shows that a double invocation is not unusual in 'early didactic, encomiastic, and paraenetic forms of rhapsodic composition. It is well attested in archaic hymnody, in which even addresses or admonitions to the poet's mortal audience may appear among a succession of invocations of divinities.' For example, Obbink continues, in the *Works and Days* Hesiod addresses Perses as well as the Muses, Pindar in *Pythian* 1 calls upon his patron Hieron as well as the Muse and other gods.[26] But the invocation of Achilleus in the Plataia elegy is also, in an important way, contrary to the practice Obbink describes. For although Achilleus is invoked as if he were a living, attentive presence, like the brother in the *Works and Days* or the laudandus in *Pythian* 1, in all probability his death is described in the same poem – and described to Achilleus himself, as it were, since the narrative is apparently framed in the second person (fr. 11.1–8, see above) and Achilleus himself is the addressee of this part of the poem.

Achilleus in the Plataia elegy thus has a double status: he dies, as befits an epic hero; but he is addressed as if alive, as befits a hero of cult. Invocation of a hero whose death has just been related recalls Christiane Sourvinou-Inwood's recent study of addresses to the dead on grave monuments. After a detailed study of the evidence, she concludes that before the fourth century *chaire/chairete* is restricted in epitaphs to the heroized dead, by analogy with salutation to gods and heroes.[27] Although clearly it is not intended for inscription on a grave stele, the narrator's *chaire* address to the 'dead' Achilleus in the Plataia elegy belongs to the same heroizing sphere.

Further, Achilleus is both times invoked not by name or patronymic, but as son of his sea-goddess mother. In Homeric tradition, significantly, Thetis helped preside at her son's burial and funeral games, which from the perspective of cult was also the locus of his immortalization.[28] Moreover, as Capra and Curti correctly assert, this genealogy emphasizes Achilleus' status as *hemitheos*, son of one divine parent, and indeed as representative *par excellence* of the entire 'race of demigods' (*genee hemitheon*, fr. 11.15) who received undying fame from Homer.[29] His emblematic role as representative of the Greeks at Troy strengthens the possibility that Achilleus serves as paradigm for the collective Greeks at Plataia[30] and not only for a single hero such as Pausanias or Leonidas, as proposed respectively by Lloyd-Jones and Pavese.[31]

Achilleus' dead-but-alive status resembles a passage in Tyrtaios (12.31–32 W), declaring that the (Spartan) war-dead will enjoy a special status after death:[32]

> Never will his noble fame (*kleos*) perish nor his name,
> but even though he is under the earth he becomes deathless (*athanatos*).

In a similar vein, Simonides' famous lyric on the dead of Thermopylai counts the ways in which the Three Hundred differ from ordinary dead, including: 'Their tomb is an altar; instead of laments is remembrance; sorrow for them is praise' (531.3 *PMG*). Although Spartans did not generally practise tomb cult for their war-dead, Pausanias the traveller reports centuries later that Spartans worshipped Alpheios and Maron, the two bravest heroes of Thermopylai (3.12.9).

The Plataia elegy too, as Eva Stehle has shown, can be seen as fulfilling the promise expressed in Tyrtaios' elegy.[33] Yet the concept that those who die in battle enjoy a special status is not restricted to Sparta; it was familiar, for example, in classical Athens as well.[34] If a cult of the Athenians who fell at Marathon indeed began soon after that battle, as is generally accepted, hero cult for Greeks who died fighting Persians would predate the battle of Plataia by more than ten years.[35] Further indication that Athenians believed in the immortality of their war-dead comes in a funeral speech given a few decades after the battle of Plataia: according to Plutarch's source, the late fifth-century biographer Stesimbrotos, Perikles asserted that those who fell in the Samian War became immortal (*athanatoi*) like the gods, who are not visible but are judged to be immortal 'because of the honors they receive and the benefits they confer' (ταῖς τιμαῖς ἃς ἔχουσι καὶ τοῖς ἀγαθοῖς ἃ παρέχουσιν).[36]

In the Plataia elegy, the invocation of Achilleus, together with the second-person narrative of his death, is strikingly different from the typical practice of Homeric epic vis-à-vis a narrative hero. Epic can grant its human characters unfading *kleos* but not that more active post-mortem existence associated with hero cult which seems to apply to the hero-addressee of the Plataia poem.[37] In Homeric epic, Achilleus serves precisely as the death-bound – rather than undying – hero *par excellence*; even in the *Odyssey*, where his shade makes several appearances, there is no reference to his enjoying a special kind of afterlife.[38] In the sphere of religious practice, by contrast, Achilleus was honored with hero cults in many places: from Sigeion near Troy to several sites around the Black Sea (most notably the 'White Island' Leuke at the mouth of the Danube) to a number of places in mainland Greece, including several in Sparta's homeland Lakonia.[39] Other Trojan War heroes – including Agamemnon, Aias, Diomedes, Menelaos, and Odysseus – also enjoyed multiple hero cults, but Achilleus clearly outdid them all in both the number and geographic range of cults attested. Direct evidence for these cults is considerably later than Simonides, and it is impossible to determine when and how they came into being; but even if they originated in the late archaic period as a result of the spread of the Homeric poems, it is still highly likely that by the fifth century Achilleus was for many Greeks a powerful figure to be sacrificed to and otherwise celebrated.[40]

In the prooemium of the Plataia elegy, Simonides alludes to both kinds of 'immortality' for the Greeks who fought at Troy: they are at once 'heroes' (fr. 11.14) – the term Homeric epic applies to its protagonists, the glorious warriors of old – and '*hemitheoi*' (fr. 11.18).[41] The latter, as Jenny Strauss Clay points out, is a rare and almost technical term in archaic poetry (e.g. *Iliad* 12.23, *Works and Days* 159–60, Kallinos 1.19 West, Alkaios 42.13 Voigt) that carries with it a retrospective view of epic heroes, where the poet is 'looking back at the legendary past from the vantage of the present'.[42] As narrative heroes, their reward is the undying fame of epic performance; as *hemitheoi*, they are almost impossible models for emulation by men of the present. Such heroes may also enjoy a robust afterlife, able to perceive (and respond to?) invocations from the world of the living – as implied by the second-person narrative and apostrophe to Achilleus (cf. also Isokrates, *Panegyrikos* 84, quoted at the beginning of this chapter).[43]

Is it possible that such a double heroic status applies to the Plataiamachoi as well? It is clear that the poet intends to make their *kleos* undying (fr. 11.28), but what about their immortality in cult? Too little remains of the Plataia elegy for us to determine whether the dead of that battle were invoked by the speaker as Achilleus was, but I consider it unlikely. Archaic and classical texts that deal with the heroization of the war-dead tend to be very circumspect;[44] apparently Simonides treats the ontological status of the Plataiamachoi with typical reticence. It seems unlikely that the poet would venture on his own authority to attribute to contemporaries the kind of immortality enjoyed by the famous heroes of cult. Individuals or groups in this period – and in connection with the Persian conflicts – could indeed be 'officially' designated as recipients of hero cult, but probably only when so authorized by a prestigious oracle or at least a remarkable sign.[45] Simonides can *suggest* that the Plataiamachoi have become heroes (probably offerings made to the fallen can suggest the same thing), but to declare this explicitly, on his own authority, would be going too far.

The parallels drawn in the elegy between the Plataiamachoi and Achilleus and his fellow Danaans, and the likelihood that Achilleus is presented as a hero of cult as well as *kleos*, encourage a brief re-examination of our evidence about honors paid to the Greeks who fell at Plataia. First of all, like most Greek war-dead of this period, they were buried in the place where they fell – although it was unusual for Greeks of so many cities to be buried at a single battlesite.[46] As at Marathon, where the Athenians and their Plataian allies had separate burial mounds,[47] so too at Plataia the dead were buried in separate tombs, city by city, according to Herodotus – distinct tombs for Athenians, Tegeans, Megarians, and Phliasians, with two tombs for Spartiates (differentiated according to age-grade) and another for their helots (Hdt. 9.85.1–2).[48] In an earlier passage Herodotus mentions only 159 Greek dead from the cities of Sparta, Athens, and Tegea (9.70.5),[49] but in later accounts the funeral celebrated after the battle was far more monumental. Plutarch reports that 1,360 Greeks fell (*Aristeides* 19.4) and the world-history writer Diodorus Siculus declares that there were more than 10,000 (11.33.1), no doubt making the number of casualties fit the importance of this battle in later Hellenic tradition. Yet whatever the actual numbers, even in Herodotus' account burial *in situ* at Plataia becomes an important issue for political self-image and propaganda: Aigina and other cities are said to have erected cenotaphs there some years after the battle, 'ashamed of their absence from the fight' (Hdt. 9.85.3).[50] I have suggested elsewhere that the funeral at Plataia may have been the occasion of the first performance of Simonides' elegy.[51]

Second, it is well attested that the Plataians brought annual offerings to the graves until 427, when their city was destroyed by the Spartans at Theban insistence during the Peloponnesian War. Thucydides attributes to the Plataians a speech in which they try unsuccessfully to convince the Spartans not to destroy their city, reminding them how every year they have brought gifts of garments, first fruits and other offerings to the tombs of 'your fathers who were killed by the Persians and are buried in our land' (Thuc. 3.58.4). It could be assumed from this speech that *only* Spartans received these gifts, but the point should not be pressed. Given their desperate circumstances, Thucydides' Plataians could be expected to downplay their special relationship to Athens, and may well be passing over in silence any rites connected with Sparta's current arch-enemy.

The annual offerings appear to have been re-instituted after Sparta allowed the Plataians to return to their city four decades after its destruction, if we can rely on Isocrates' *Plataikos*. This speech, supposedly delivered about 373 by Plataians asking Athens to restore their city after it was destroyed by Thebes, again mentions Plataian tomb cult on behalf of those who shared dangers in the fight for freedom (14.61).[52] Nearly five centuries later, Plutarch reports an elaborate ceremony celebrated by the Plataians in his own time, culminating in a bull sacrifice at the site of the funeral pyre and a libation by the archon of Plataia to those who died fighting for 'the freedom of the Greeks' (*Aristeides* 21).

What do such tomb offerings say about the status attributed to those who are honored by them? Recent studies of early hero cults make a strong case for thinking of a continuum of honors paid in various ways to the dead in the archaic and classical periods, rather than defining absolute categories such as 'ordinary dead', 'honored dead', and 'hero' (a term that our fifth-century sources avoid for the dead of the Persian Wars).[53] Regularly repeated festivals and offerings, nevertheless, signal that individuals or groups so honored were close to the 'heroic' end of this continuum – they were, in Snodgrass' deliberately loose formulation, 'somehow immortalized dead mortals'.[54] The Plataians' speech in Thucydides (cited above) further encourages this view of the Plataiamachoi, by referring to the Spartans buried there as if they were still alive, about to be abandoned in the territory of their old enemies the Thebans (3.58.5). As Simon Hornblower comments: 'The dead Spartans of the battle of Plataia are here virtually conjured back to life: what will they think about being left in hostile terrain among their murderers...?'[55]

In addition to their prestigious burial and annual tomb cult,

Plutarch writes that the Plataiamachoi were honored by an annual festival called the Eleutheria, held on a grander scale every four years when it included athletic contests; according to Plutarch, the panhellenic celebration was proposed by Aristeides soon after the battle.[56] Such an event would have precedents not only in the games held at the funerals of sixth-century aristocrats, but also in regularly-repeated festivals commemorating earlier battles, notably the Spartan Parparonia and Gymnopaidia.[57] Three bronze prize vessels, dating from roughly 480 to 440 and inscribed 'The Athenians [gave these] prizes for those [who died] in the war' (Ἀθεναῖοι· ἆθλα ἐπὶ τοῖς ἐν τῶι πολέμοι), possibly provide evidence for such a contest, jointly sponsored by Athens.[58] Eugene Vanderpool, the first to discuss the vessels as a group, believed they were prizes awarded at the official funeral games for war-dead celebrated in Athens, beginning shortly after the battle of Plataia (following the account of Diodorus Siculus 11.33.3).[59] Pierre Amandry, however, after analyzing all attested inscriptions on prize vessels, pointed out that in no other example does the name of the prize-givers appear in the nominative. The inscription 'the Athenians [gave these] prizes', in Amandry's view, indicates that the vessels were not awarded for games held in Athens itself; he proposed that they may have been awarded either for a fifth-century version of the Eleutheria at Plataia or for the Herakleia at Marathon, expanded to a panhellenic festival in honor of the Marathonomachoi.[60] In addition to the literary testimonia and this possible fifth-century evidence for the festival, several inscriptions from later centuries suggest that Athens and Sparta competed in a formal debate for leadership of the games each time they were held.[61]

In 1975, however, Roland Étienne and Marcel Piérart published an influential article arguing that – in contrast to the tomb cult attested in Thucydides – there is no clear evidence for the Eleutheria until the third century.[62] They conclude that the games were most likely founded when Alexander restored the city walls of Plataia in 338, influenced by a myth of panhellenism retrojected to the time of the Persian Wars and especially the battle of Plataia.[63] Many scholars continue to assume the existence of a fifth-century Eleutheria festival,[64] but most who have considered these arguments find them persuasive, though based only on silence and plausibility.[65]

The fragments of the Plataia elegy cannot prove that annual or quadrennial games were, or were not, held for the dead of Plataia in the fifth century. But with the striking parallel Simonides draws to Achilleus and the other *hemitheoi* of the Trojan War, the new text does imply that the Plataiamachoi acquired a special status from the very beginning. We already knew Thucydides' testimony of their tomb cult, and Herodotus' picture of a burial spot so prestigious that other *poleis* erected empty 'tombs' to gain a place in it. Now, the new Simonides offers another piece of evidence for how the (implicit) heroization of contemporaries *en masse* was facilitated or justified.

Precedents for treating the dead as heroes can be found in some well-known archaic elite funerals of individuals,[66] although I would emphasize that the rich burial of a prominent local individual, even if followed by regular offerings, is a practice very different from the solemn burial, away from home, of a group of soldiers fallen in battle. Sparta's veneration of its war-dead, as reflected in Tyrtaios' elegies or Simonides' Thermopylai lyric (discussed above), provides a certain precedent for the 'immortalization' of the Plataiamachoi, but ordinary Spartans killed in battle did not receive tomb cult.[67] Athens' cult of the Marathonomachoi, if indeed it began right after the battle, would be the closest parallel;[68] unfortunately we have no fifth-century literary or epigraphic evidence for the cult. The Plataia elegy uniquely shows how useful was another model in the delicate matter of elevating a group of contemporaries to a new status – the Trojan War heroes, celebrated in poetry and, some of them, 'immortalized' in cult. I do not mean that the Homeric epics, or the funerary practices described in them, pro- vided the primary motives or patterns for hero cults as they developed in earlier centuries.[69] On the contrary, as a number of recent studies have shown, the growth of Greek hero cults was a complex process intertwined with contemporary political and ideological developments – and archaic funerals, for their part, undoubtedly helped to shape epic descriptions of funerals at least as much as the reverse.[70] The new Simonides gives us a glimpse of how the heroes of Homeric poetry were used as predecessors of the Greeks who fell at Plataia, to help effect the transformation of dead contemporaries into heroes of cult as well as song. This is done in part, as we have seen, by adopting heroic poetry's perspective on its own immortalizing power: as the Danaans received undying *kleos* from Homer, so Simonides hopes to confer it upon the Plataiamachoi (fr. 11.15–17, 23–8). There is reason to be- lieve, however, that the elegiac poet is aiming even higher: he consid- ers Homer's heroes from a perspective broader than epic, a view signalled by the term *hemitheoi*.[71] In particular, by apostrophizing the son of Thetis, Simonides evokes Achilleus' undying nature as well as the mortality that so strongly characterizes him in the *Iliad*.

It would be natural to assume that the comparison between the heroes of Troy and Plataia rests upon the fact that both battles were panhellenic efforts against a barbarian, Asiatic force.[72] A contemporary audience might perhaps have made this connection, but the elegy's extant fragments do not emphasize the parallel in these terms, although they perhaps imply some sense of a Greek 'cause' at Plataia. For example, if West's suggested restoration of fr. 11.25–6 is correct, Simonides' Plataia narrative begins with the Spartans leaving their city to 'ward off the day of slavery from Sparta and Greece'.[73] A second possible 'panhellenic' reference appears in fr. 13.8–10, where the 'sons of Doros and Herakles'[74] are drawn up against 'Medes and Persians'. Even these readings, though, would convey a far more subdued sense of Hellenic identity than is found in the 'Greek vs. barbarian' dichotomy that developed a few decades later, particularly in Athenian tragedy.[75] In any case, I find in the elegy no evidence that the enemy was characterized as 'barbaric'.

What the elegy does focus on repeatedly are close relations with immortals, a feature shared by both groups of Greeks. Achilleus appears in connection with his divine mother Thetis and her father Nereus, probably with Apollo as his honorific killer as well; the destruction of Troy may be aided by Hera and Athena,[76] and involves the chariot of Justice (fr. 11.12). For the Plataiamachoi our meager fragments attest a remarkable number of gods and cult heroes.[77] Several local heroes of the Trojan War era (perhaps worshipped as gods in Sparta) – 'wide-ruling Menelaos' and the 'horse-taming sons of Zeus, the Tyndarid heroes' – apparently accompany the army departing from Sparta (fr. 11.30–1).[78] Simonides' brief account of the march to Plataia (fr. 11.36–41) is characterized by the names of local heroes as well: Pelops, Nisos (hero of Megara), Pandion (of Athens). Demeter would inevitably be linked with the 'lovely plain [of Eleusis]' (fr. 11.40), and her name is attested in fr. 17.1.[79] The Greeks at Plataia, like those at Troy, enjoy divine support for their cause: as West notes, Zeus must be 'nodding' approval in another fragment, and perhaps another god 'will drive' the enemy away (fr. 14.7).[80] Frr. 15–16 mention the Corinthians' hero Glaukos and their important deity Helios, evoked as witness of their bravery. Besides enjoying the company of immortal heroes and the approval of gods,[81] the Greeks seek divine help for the battle through divination ('trusting in [the gods' port]ents', fr. 11.39) and prophecy ('of the godlike [pro]phet,' fr. 11.42).[82]

Isokrates, as we have seen, calls those who fought in the Persian Wars even greater than the *hemitheoi* who fought at Troy, and proposes that the gods themselves were concerned to immortalize the valour and fame of both groups (*Panegyrikos* 84).[83] The orator's vocabulary is very close to Simonides' in fr. 11.15–28 (both speak of *arete*, *kleos*, undying memory or fame); despite the difference in time his 'theology' may be similar as well. In the new elegy, Achilleus and the other *hemitheoi* at Troy are presented as doubly immortal, thanks on the one hand to their poet and his Muses, on the other to their descent from, approval by, and close association with gods. Their counterparts at Plataia are also associated both with their poet and his Muse and (just as intensely, if a little differently from the Danaans) with divine patrons, gods and immortalized heroes – including several precisely from the Trojan era. The Plataia elegy thus deftly sets up an analogy between the two groups of Greeks that helps us understand how, in the early fifth century, ordinary contemporaries could be transformed to 'immortals' worthy of song and cult, even immediately after their death. Simonides' poem opens up the possibility that what happened to Achilleus, to Menelaos and the Dioskouroi, may be happening again.

Notes

[1] The passage is discussed also in Loraux 1986, 41.

[2] Parsons 1992, esp. 6.

[3] For bibliography cf. Boedeker and Sider (eds.) 1996, 283–93.

[4] The translation is from West 1993a, 168. Square brackets indicate where the preserved papyrus fragments have been supplemented by the editor.

[5] An attractive alternative reading is suggested by Capra and Curti (1995, 31–2), who argue for τόνδ[ε μελ]ίφρονα κ[όλλοπα χο]ρδῆς instead of West's τόνδ[ε μελ]ίφρονα κ[όσμον ἀο]ιδῆς (fr. 11.19): the poet asks the Muses not to grant *kosmos* to his song, but to regulate the key of his lyre, at this point of transition between epic and historical poetry.

[6] ἀθάνατον is attested, κλέος is restored by West (1992) in fr. 11.28.

[7] Spartans are predominant in the fragments we have, esp. fr. 11.25–34; Athenians may be mentioned in fr. 11.41, and Corinthians are subjects of praise in the verses of this poem cited by Plutarch, *De Malig. Hdt.* 872de. On 'panhellenism' in the Plataia elegy see Aloni 1994, Boedeker 1995, Pavese 1995.

[8] The Spartan regent was commander-in-chief of the Greek allies at Plataia; he came under suspicion and was recalled to Sparta probably by mid-477, according to the conservative calculation of Loomis 1990, and ended up starving to death rather than leaving his asylum in a Spartan temple, Thuc. 1.134. On the date of the Plataia elegy see also Aloni 1994, 16–18.

[9] Whitley 1994, 213 suggests however that already in 490 the cremation burial of the Marathonomachoi – in a mound, with stelai – was modeled after Homeric burials. See also Flashar 1996. For a somewhat later period, Francis and Vickers (1972, 110–11) discuss how Marathon in particular, and the Persian Wars as a whole, were being considered alongside legendary heroic

combats by the time the Stoa Poikile was built in the 460s.

[10] As Aeschines notes (3, *In Ctes.*, 183), the leaders of the Athenians at Eion are not mentioned in the epigrams. This silence contrasts with the naming of Pausanias in the Plataia elegy. But at the same time that it 'democratically' suppresses their names, the Eion poem does of course call to mind the Athenian leaders when it mentions the Homeric leader Menestheus.

[11] See Stehle 1996 for detailed discussion of the speaker's position in the Plataia elegy.

[12] For detailed discussion of the poet's role relative to the victor, see Nagy 1990a, 136–45.

[13] e.g. Hdt. 7.159 and 161.3: Spartan and Athenian speakers tell Gelon of Syracuse that their cities' roles in the Trojan War explain why they should supersede him as leaders of the Greek alliance. Hdt. 9.27.4 reports another (weak) argument based on Athenian prowess at Troy.

[14] Burnett (1985, 79–80) suggests that the epinician poets did not use Trojan War heroes very often because the Homeric epics had rationalized them too thoroughly: '...the fame of these warriors had become finite and natural; one admired them for their achievements and strength, but not as vessels in which a supernatural force had been conveyed to the surface of the earth... An awesome moment that strained rational belief was thus the deepest requirement for an epinician myth; a more superficial but equally essential one was that the fiction should show some structural or imagistic congruity with the occasion of victory.'

[15] Nagy 1990a, 151, cf. also 138. On *ponos* and *aethlos* see also Loraux 1982.

[16] Stehle (1996, 216–17) raises the possibility that *kleos athanaton* may be a conscious elegiac variant of the epic formula.

[17] This does not apply to all epic, however: see Nagy 1990a, 150 with bibliography.

[18] *Od.* 14.55, 165, 360, 442, 507; 16.60, 135, 464; 17.274, 311, 380, 512, 579; variants in *Od.* 15.325 and 22.194. Eumaios is the only character apostrophized in the *Odyssey*. See Heubeck and Hoekstra 1989, on 14.55.

[19] Apostrophes to Patroklos: 16.584, 693, 744, 754, 787, 812, 843; 744 and 843 introduce speeches. Menelaos is apostrophized seven times in the *Iliad*. On the pathetic quality of Iliadic apostrophes see Janko 1992, on 13.602–3, with Parry 1972 and Block 1982.

[20] See the scholia on this passage, as noted by Heubeck and Hoekstra (n. 18 above).

[21] Obbink 1996, 196, citing *Hom. Hymn Apollo* 545–6. Capra and Curti (1995, 30), however, point out that the invocation (they say nothing about *autar ego*) has a wider range of uses.

[22] Capra and Curti 1995, 30.

[23] See Obbink 1996, 203 (citing Parsons).

[24] West 1993b, 5; Obbink (1996, 199–200) leaves open the occasion of performance and the connection betweeen Achilleus and the Plataiamachoi. For further discussion of performance scenarios, see Aloni 1994 and Boedeker 1995.

[25] Lloyd-Jones 1994, 1; Capra and Curti (1995, 30) further discuss

Achilleus' role in the prooemium.

[26] Obbink 1996, 197–8.

[27] Sourvinou-Inwood 1995, 180–216, esp. 191–4 on the 'immortality' of fifth-century Athenian war-dead.

[28] *Odyssey* 24.73–92. See Pavese 1995, 9–10 for further testimonia on Thetis' role; Nagy 1979, 172, 175 on Achilleus' funeral/immortalization.

[29] Capra and Curti (1995, 30) also point out that in the *Iliad* only Achilleus receives the epithet ὠκύμορος 'swift-fated', which is applied to the ἡμιθέων γενέη in Sim. fr. 11.18.

[30] Capra and Curti (1995, 30) note that Simonides clearly emphasizes the collective nature of the expedition to Plataia.

[31] Lloyd-Jones (1994, 1) proposes the Spartan commander Pausanias as the logical parallel to Achilleus. Pavese (1995, 20–4) disagrees, especially since Pausanias did not die at Plataia, and suggests instead that the elegy included a comparison between Leonidas and Achilleus, two leaders killed in an ultimately victorious war. Thus Pavese hypothesizes that the poem began with a description of Thermopylai (although there is no evidence for this in our fragments) and ended with Plataia. On this hypothesis see further Burzacchini 1995, 24–5.

[32] Cf. Fuqua 1981, 221–5 and Stehle 1996, 217–20. Of course we should not exaggerate Spartan honors for warriors: as Parker (1989, 146) reminds us, '...it was the Athenians and not the Spartans who honored their war-dead with elaborate public rites'. Parker nevertheless concludes (148), 'Such heroisation for patriotic service is perhaps something distinctively Spartan, at least in its extent.'

[33] Stehle 1996, 218.

[34] The Tyrtaios elegy itself is quoted by Plato (*Laws* 629a–30b), showing that it was known in Athens by the early fourth century, admittedly long after the Persian Wars. Pritchett (1985, 94–260, esp. 174–5 on Plataia), discusses evidence for the burial of war-dead; see also Stupperich 1977, 62–70, on 'Gefallenenbestattung und Heroisierung'. Loraux (1986, 5) believes that Tyrtaios' elegies inspired fifth-century Athenian epitaphs, as well as some themes of funeral orations.

[35] Parker (1996, 137, n. 57) emphasizes that this cult is not attested until the second century. But see Vanderpool 1942, 334–6 on epigraphic evidence for an expansion of the Herakleia at Marathon, perhaps in honor of the fallen.

[36] Plut. *Per.* 8.9, citing Stesimbrotos (*FGH* 107 F 9). This passage is among those discussed by Loraux 1986, 39–41 and Parker 1996, 135–6 in their discussions of the 'immortality' of Athenian war-dead. Parker notes that the Stesimbrotos passage, 'if pressed, shows that the patriotic dead were believed still – note the present tense – to "confer benefits"...'

[37] See Nagy 1979, 184 and *passim* for discussion of the different kinds of immortality provided by epic and cult.

[38] See e.g. Nagy 1979 and Schein 1984 for elaborate analyses of the mortality of Achilleus.

[39] See Farnell 1921, 285–9 and references p. 409; on public laments for Achilleus, see also Seaford 1994, 139 n. 151. Hommel (1980) revives the

argument (*contra* Farnell) that Achilleus was essentially a god; Hooker (1988) provides a counterargument, whereas West (1993b, 5) writes that in cult Achilleus is sometimes venerated as a 'hero', sometimes a 'god'.

[40] For discussion of the origin of hero cults see below, notes 53–4.

[41] It does not affect my argument whether one restores fr. 11.14, with Parsons and West, to read 'he (Homer) *made* (ποίησ') the race of *hemitheoi* famous (ἐπώνυμον)' or with Capra and Curti (1995, 28–30), 'he *sang* (ἄεισ') the race named after (ἐπώνυμον) the *hemitheoi*'.

[42] Clay 1996, 244–5. See also West 1978, on *Works and Days* 160, and Nagy 1979, 159–61.

[43] On the significance of Simonides' *hemitheoi* see Capra and Curti 1995, Clay 1996, Rutherford 1996, 179–80.

[44] Loraux (1986, 38–41) discusses this question with regard to classical Athens, concluding that the Athenian war-dead were considered and treated as heroes in the annual public funeral ceremonies.

[45] As in the case of Onesilos of Cyprus during the Ionian revolt (Hdt. 5.114), or the Phokaian prisoners of war, stoned to death by their Etruscan captors (Hdt. 1.167).

[46] See Pritchett 1985, 94–106 with references and *passim*, on varying practices in this regard; the Athenian 'ancestral custom' of bringing the war-dead home for burial was fairly unusual, and probably began shortly after the Persian Wars.

[47] Mersch 1995 raises questions about the location of these tombs.

[48] Perhaps related to the funeral and tomb cult is a ceremony of which the Plataians remind the Spartans in a defensive speech in Thucydides, dated to 429: Pausanias presided at a bull-sacrifice to Zeus Eleutherios ('Zeus of Freedom') in the Plataian agora, and administered an oath guaranteeing that the allies would uphold forever the independence of Plataia (2.71).

[49] Nick Fisher plausibly suggests that the helot dead mentioned in Herodotus 9.85 are ignored in this low figure.

[50] Predictably, this passage is contested by Plutarch, *De Mal. Herod.* 872f–873a, who maintains that no one else ever charged fellow-Greeks with betraying the cause by being absent from the battle.

[51] Boedeker 1995.

[52] The identity of the συγκινδυνεύσαντες so honored is not specified, a fact which increases the likelihood that only Spartan graves were honored in this way: since the speech is designed to gain Athenian sympathy, one would expect the Plataians to single out any honors they paid to Athenian graves.

[53] e.g. Seaford 1994, 114–7; Parker 1996, 33–39. Antonaccio (1995a) analyzes the archaeological evidence for archaic hero cult.

[54] Snodgrass 1988, 20–1. Similar criteria for 'heroization' are set by Boehringer 1996, esp. 51.

[55] Hornblower 1991, on 3.58.5.

[56] Plutarch, *Aristeides* 21; the festival is mentioned also in Diodorus Siculus 11.29.1–2 (with a different story about its origin), Strabo 9.2.31, Pausanias 9.2.5. See Étienne and Piérart 1975, 63–7 for a succinct review of the evidence.

[57] See Roller 1981a, 1–7 for epigraphic and literary evidence of archaic

funerary games; also Parker 1989, 149–50.

[58] See Vanderpool 1969 and Amandry 1971, 612–25 on the three vessels. Vanderpool (2–3) dates the two *lebetes* to 'around or shortly after 480 BC' and 'a trifle later'; the hydria to 'the second half of the fifth century BC'; Amandry (612), dates the three vessels to roughly 480, 465, and 450; the editors of *IG* I[3] 523–5, to 480–470?, 460–450?, and 450–440?. Étienne and Piérart (1975, 55) note (in a different context) that ἐπί with the dative is regularly used of honors offered to heroes or to the dead, citing literary parallels. So too Nagy 1992, 121.

[59] Vanderpool 1969, 4–5; accepted e.g. by Roller 1981a, 7; Pritchett 1985, 107. Parker (1996, 132 n. 36) disagrees with Amandry's attribution of the bronze vessels 'to an (unattested) funerary context away from the city itself', without discussing Amandry's argument about the formulation of the inscription. Loraux (1986, 30) accepts Amandry's conclusions.

[60] Amandry (1971, 620–5), citing Vanderpool (1942) on the expanded Herakleia. Contra Stupperich (1977, 41 n. 5), directed mostly against a Marathonian provenance. The editors of *IG* I[3] 523–5 likewise disagree with Amandry's argument that the vases were not awarded in Athens, and support Vanderpool's attribution (1969) to the Athenian *agon epitaphios*.

[61] Robertson 1986.

[62] A fact which Amandry took into account as well; see 1971, 621: Plutarch must be describing a later revival of the festival.

[63] Étienne and Piérart 1975, 65–75. On this revival of Persian War ideology and its expression in 'false documents', see Habicht 1961.

[64] e.g. Haslam 1993, 135; Aloni 1994, 19; Pavese 1995, 22, 24.

[65] See especially Schachter 1994, 125–43, who lays out the ancient evidence with great clarity (although he does not discuss Amandry's view of the prize vessels), and substantially agrees with the chronology proposed by Étienne and Piérart; and Pritchett 1985, 119–20, with notes. As I argue above, Thucydides' Plataians (3.58.4), pleading with the Spartans for their survival, do not provide a strong argument from silence; a better case is provided by the silence of Isokrates' Plataians in *Plataikos* 14.61 (above, n. 52). I note that the expanded Herakleia festival at Marathon, which might provide a parallel to a fifth-century contest in honor of the fallen at Plataia, likewise leaves no trace in the literary record; cf. Vanderpool 1942.

[66] Most spectacularly, the late tenth-century 'hero of Lefkandi' (see Blome 1984 for comparison with Homeric burials), and the 'prince' buried near the West Gate at Eretria in the late eighth century, his tomb incorporated within the city wall about 680, and evidently honored with offerings for some two centuries thereafter; see Bérard 1982, recently discussed by Seaford (1994, 110) and Antonaccio (1995a, 227–36).

[67] See Pritchett 1985, 243–6.

[68] See above, at note 9. Shapiro (1991, 645) suggests that heroic honors offered to the fallen at Marathon may be a way to make up for the lack of an aristocratic individual burial. Significantly, Harrison (1972, 364) argues that in the painting of Marathon in the Stoa Poikile (dated to the later 460s), the achievement of the Athenian commander Kallimachos was presented as

'heroic, almost in the literal sense'.

69 Cf. Farnell 1921, esp. 284–342; this view has been developed more recently by Coldstream 1976 and Rupp 1988; against whose views see now the discussion of Iron Age 'heroic' graves by Antonaccio 1995a, 221–43.

70 See Whitley 1988, Boedeker 1993, Seaford 1994, esp. 180–6 with references, and Antonaccio (preceding note).

71 Cf. note 42 above.

72 As e.g. Castriota (1992) shows for later monuments. Conversely, Kierdorf (1966, 15) suggests that experiences of the Persian War (burning of temples) serve as a paradigm for the herald's report of the destruction of Troy in Aeschylus, *Agamemnon* 527 (cf. *Persai* 811).

73 e.g. Parsons (1992, 34) suggests restoring fr. 11.25 as οἳ Σπάρτ[ης ὥρμησσαν καρτερὸν ἄλκ]αρ or οἳ Σπάρτηι ----δούλιον ἦμαρ. In his edition of fr. 11.25–6 West (1992) proposes, *exempli gratia*, the restoration

ἀνδρῶ]ν, οἳ Σπάρτ[ηι τε καὶ Ἑλλάδι δούλιον ἦμ]αρ

ἔσχον] ἀμυνόμ[ενοι μή τιν᾽ ἰδεῖν φανερ]ῶ[ς

The phrase δούλιον ἦμ]αρ is of course Homeric; in the *Iliad*, however, it is used of the 'day of slavery' that *Trojans* will face if they lose the war (6.463); if Simonides used the same phrase here, he changed its application from the Asian to the Greek side. (The formula is also attested in *Od.* 14.340 and 17.323, but without referring to slavery as a result of large-scale war.)

74 This phrase, however, more likely indicates not all the Plataiamachoi but only Spartans and some other Peloponnesians; see Boedeker 1995, 224–5.

75 See Hall 1989.

76 If West's *exempli gratia* restoration of fr. 11.9–10 is correct '[Pallas Athena] being [near seized the famous cita]del, [together with Hera, ang]ry with the sons of [Pr]iam': cf. West 1993b, 6.

77 As mentioned by West (1993b, 7).

78 On the importance of Menelaos and the Dioskouroi at Sparta, see Parker 1989, 147–8, 152–3. Lloyd-Jones (1994, 3) cites an oracle that similarly pairs Spartan Menelaos and the Dioskouroi.

79 For Demeter in the Plataia tradition, see Boedeker 1996, 235–7.

80 So West 1993b, 8.

81 Divine descent (from Zeus, through Herakles) applies to the Spartan royal families as well, including Pausanias the commander at Plataia, a member of the Agiad clan: West's proposed restoration of fr. 11.32–3 is suggestive here: 'Pausanias...[son of divine Kleo]mb[r]otos'. Parsons (1992, 36) mentions 'Simonides' *FGE* (Page), XXXIX, an epigram where Pausanias is called 'son of Kleombrotos, of Herakles' ancient lineage'. See Parker 1989, 152–3, 169 n. 52 on the importance of Spartan kings' descent from Zeus.

82 See West 1993b, 7.

83 Divine favor is an aspect of heroization about which recent discussions have had rather little to say, and which probably does not apply to all instances. Cf. the sensible reconstruction by Parker (1996, 136–7) of the process in which Athenian war-dead were heroized.

9

EARLY GREEK COLONIZATION?
The nature of Greek settlement in the West

Robin Osborne

The big issue in the study of colonization has traditionally been the question of the causes of colonization. Some invoke overpopulation and land hunger, which are either seen as two sides of the same coin, or separated to stress that it is not absolute population size but the inability of the land to feed the people in climatic crises that is crucial,[1] others stress 'commercial' motives, while recently others, emphasising the nature of foundation stories, have effectively stressed political explanations (Dougherty 1993, 1994a). Much discussion of the causes of colonization has gone on without serious regard to the character of the early settlements. In this paper I want to reverse the direction of inference. I want to start by examining the character of early Greek colonies, and I want in the end to suggest that this has an implication for our views of how colonies came to be sent.

Back in 1964, John Graham noted that 'another distinction of clear relevance to the relations between colony and mother city is that between state and private enterprise... Oversimplifications, such as that all early colonies were private, or that colonial enterprises were generally official, should be avoided' (1964, 7). Graham went on to suggest that 'both state and private enterprises existed throughout the historical colonizing period', arguing that Herodotus clearly describes the foundation of Cyrene as a state act and Dorieus' abortive expedition as 'equally clearly a private enterprise' (1964, 8). Since Graham wrote, and partly perhaps because the issue of relations with the mother city has not been salient in scholars' enquiries, sensitivity to the 'state' versus 'private' distinction has been less often on display, and arguments about the causes of colonization seem frequently to make assumptions about the nature and character of the colony without explicitly addressing the question.

Part of what is at issue here is perhaps to do with terminology. Colony is a word which has strong 'statist' overtones. For all that we use the term figuratively to talk of plants and animals colonizing particular ecological niches, the model of a human colony remains tied up with states. Founding a colony is not an end in itself but a means to a further end, colonies are instruments of political and cultural control.[2]

Sensitivity to the differences between what the Greeks called an *apoikia* and what the Romans called a *colonia* goes back a long way. The Romans, true enough, dubbed Greek *apoikiai* colonies without, apparently, further thought. But not all Greeks were satisfied that *apoikia* was the appropriate word for a Roman colony. So St Luke in *Acts* 16.12 used not *apoikia* but *kolonia* of the Roman colony at Philippi, and although Luke's scruples were not universally shared, *kolonia* and *koloneia* are found used of such places in both epigraphic and literary texts.

Colony seems to have come into the English language through that passage of *Acts* in the translation of Wycliffe, although most immediately subsequent translators preferred some English periphrasis. Subsequently, colony not only became naturalised, and applied to English settlements abroad, but also used without scruple for Greek *apoikiai*. Most ancient historians used the term Greek colony as if Greek colony were a technical term where the epithet 'Greek' removed all unwanted overtones from the word 'colony', and voices of protest about this practice have been few.[3] But there are two important points to make. The first is that ancient historians cannot expect to communicate if they insist on communicating in private code: colony is a real live word with real live associations, and if we do not intend the associations we are better off not using the word. The second is that we should not be too ready to assume that Greek terms were technical – just as with *polis* itself, or *kōmē*, so with *apoikia* the evidence suggests that we are dealing with a word like 'game', to use the example familiar from philosophical discussions, not a word like 'mayor'.[4]

What, then, were early Greek settlements abroad like? Is the model clearly offered by classical Greek examples also appropriate to the settlements of the eighth and seventh centuries? I begin with those classical cases.

I

Fifth- and fourth-century settlements abroad *can* look quite like Roman colonies. Decisions to send settlers to a named location may be taken for military reasons, settlers may be specifically chosen because they will benefit from grants of land, and careful provision may be made for equal shares of land for all. Let me simply point to three familiar pieces of epigraphic evidence in support of this view. In the 320s the Athenians sent settlers to the Adriatic, and this decision is reflected in the records of the curators of the dockyards:

> In order that the resolution of the People concerning the Adriatic colony may be accomplished as quickly as possible, let it be voted by the People that the shipyard supervisors shall hand over to the trierarchs the ships and the equipment in accordance with the resolution of the People... In order that there may exist for the people for all time its own commercial outlet and supply of grain, and, when an anchorage of its own has been equipped there exists a guard against the Tyrrhenians, and Miltiades the founder of the settlement and the settlers may be able to use their own fleet, and those of the Hellenes and of the barbarians who sail the sea may also sail in to the anchorage of the Athenians with a view to keeping both their vessels and their other possessions safe, knowing that... [lacuna follows] (*IG* ii² 1629.174–83, 217–32)

Earlier in the fourth century, the Issaians sent settlers to Black Corcyra, also in the Adriatic, making the following provisions:

> With good fortune. When Praxidamos was *hiaramnamon*, in the month Makhaneus, agreement of the founders (or 'magistrates'?) of the Issaians and of Pullos (= Phyllos?) and of the son of Dazos. The founders (or 'magistrates'?) drew up the following specifications which the people agreed: the first who took the land were to take the selected land and having fortified the town were each to take one selected building plot of the fortified town along with the portion, and the same were to take of the land outside and the territory three *plethra* of land [suitable for vines (?)] as the first lot and parts of the rest. The lot and the parts are to be recorded as each obtains them by lot. One and a half *plethra* of the land are to remain with them and their descendants. Those who come later are to take one plot in the town and four and a half plethra of the land that has not been divided up. The magistrates are to swear never to redistribute land in town or country. If any magistrate proposes or citizen supports any measure contrary to the decree he is to lose his civic rights and his property is to be confiscated and anyone who kills him will not be subject to penalty [after a little more fragmentary text some 150 names are listed under the three Dorian tribal headings] (*SIG*³ 141)

Back in the fifth century, parts of the Athenian decree establishing an abortive colony in the northern Aegean are preserved:

> ...are to be provided for them by the apoikists to obtain good omens for the colony, however many they decide. *Geonomoi* shall be elected, ten in number, one from each tribe. These are to distribute the land. Demokleides shall establish the settlement at his discretion as best he can. The sacred precincts which have been reserved for the gods shall be left as they are, and others shall not be consecrated. A cow and panoply shall be brought

to the Great Panathenaia and a phallos to the Dionysia. If anyone wages a campaign against the territory of the settlers, aid shall be dispatched by the cities as swiftly as possible, as prescribed by the agreements [which, when ...]tos was Secretary, were contracted for the cities of the Thraceward region. They shall inscribe this on a stele and set it up on the Akropolis. Provision shall be made for the stele by the settlers at their own expense. If anyone proposes a decree contrary to the stele or if a public speaker advises or attempts to induce anyone to rescind or cancel any part of what has been voted, let him and his children lose their citizen rights and his property be confiscated and let the goddess receive the tithe, except if the settlers themselves... All those who are enrolled to go as settlers who are soldiers, after they have returned to Athens are to be in Brea within thirty days as settlers. They shall lead out the settlement within thirty days. Aiskhines shall accompany them and provide them with money.

Phantokles made the motion. Concerning the colony to Brea, let all the rest be as Demokleides moved. But Phantokles shall be introduced by Erekhtheis, the tribe in prytany, to the Council in its first session. Men from the *thetes* and the *zeugitai* are to go as settlers to Brea.

(*ML* 49, 4–42; Fornara 100)

In these three cases the initiative to send a settlement to a specific location is one backed by the citizen body of the 'home' community, although in two of the three cases there are signs that individuals have played a large part in championing the initiative – Demokleides at Brea and the rather shadowy Phyllos and son of Dazos at Black Corcyra. Military concern is very clear in the Athenian Adriatic settlement in the 320s but looks not far away in the Brea decree also. The role of the settlement in giving equal shares of land is clearest in the case of Black Corcyra but the amendment in the case of Brea suggests that some thought very much in those terms about that settlement too. While none of these is a veteran settlement in the sense that Roman colonies would often be, the Brea decree explicitly caters for the possibility that serving soldiers might be sent.

We can trace such foundations, where a city community decides that military and agrarian concerns can best be met by sending off settlers to a particular location, back into the sixth century, in the cases of such settlements as those of the Athenians at Salamis and Sigeion – at least if we accept the orthodox view that *IG* i³ 1 refers to settlers, not just to established residents, for there the settlers both have military obligations and are required not to lease out their land except on restricted conditions. These are both interesting cases: Salamis is obviously territory familiar to the Athenians, and Sigeion is a place deliberately snatched from the settlers there already, settlers with a Mytilenaean connection.

But this model of settlement equally clearly does not apply to other sixth-century episodes, such as Dorieus' abortive attempts to settle in North Africa and Sicily (Herodotos 5.42.2–47.2) or Miltiades' settlement in the Thracian Chersonnese (Herodotos 6.34–36), both of which are unofficial enterprises led by a charismatic individual whom the powers that be are glad to see the back of. It is therefore reasonable to ask whether the classical model of settlement abroad – state-led, at a pre-chosen site, for military and/or agrarian ends – can reasonably be retrojected to the earlier archaic period.

Stories told in the classical period of earlier foundations frequently shape themselves on the assumption that classical practice had a long history. An example of this is indeed the Theran version in Herodotos of the story of the foundation of Cyrene, the story to which Graham makes direct appeal in claiming that some early colonies have to be seen as state enterprises. In this story (Herodotos 4.150–3) it is the Theran King, Grinnos, who receives the Delphic direction to colonize; the expedition is carefully made up of children from all families and members of all the different geographical districts of Thera; and the Therans seek in advance expert advice from a Cretan purple-fisherman as to the best place to settle. That version is one which, in the fourth century, the people of Cyrene themselves found it convenient to adopt – as the inscription which claims to contain the famous oath of the original colonists makes clear (*ML* 5; Fornara 18) – but Herodotos in the fifth century had collected a very different Cyrenean version of the foundation of the city (4.154–6), a story which put all the emphasis on Battos and his individual initiative and stressed rejection by the Therans. While Cyrene from the end of the seventh to the middle of the fifth century needed a foundation story which justified its Battiad monarchy and put a distance between itself and Thera, in the fourth century Cyrenean democracy could welcome the equality of the colonists embedded in the Theran version. But we can surely no more take the Theran version, or the fact that it won through, as evidence that settlement at Cyrene was a Theran state-led enterprise than we can take the fifth-century Cyrene version as evidence that Battos' mother was called 'Sensible woman' (Phronime) daughter of 'True Ruler' (Etearkhos), was rescued by 'The man who does right' (Themison) or was married off to 'The man who woos much' (Polymnestor). Just as Menekles of Barke (*FGH* 270 F6; Fornara 17) seems to have found it useful to claim that Cyrene broke away from its mother city because of political dissension, since his own community apparently so broke away from Cyrene, so in the stories told to

255

Herodotos we have to recognise the political needs of the tellers as prime determinants.[5]

Most modern literature on early colonization, no doubt encouraged, as Graham was, by stories like the Theran story about Cyrene, assumes the classical model and limits itself to discussing why states sent out settlers. I will return to the question of foundation stories, but meanwhile if we begin not at the end but at the beginning and limit ourselves to the early evidence, both literary and archaeological, there would seem to be considerable grounds for questioning the retrojection of the classical model.

II

The Homeric poems are full of men who wander or settle abroad. Some have been pushed because of the hostility of powerful individuals or a community to their earlier behaviour, others have been pulled – kidnapped by Phoenicians or whatever, and still others again have jumped, by trading, pirating, or venturing as soldiers. Most move around alone, but Tlepolemos gathers others to join him: 'When Tlepolemos had grown up in the well-built palace he straightway killed his own father's uncle, Likymnios the already ageing son of Ares. And immediately he got ships together, collected a large folk and went off to sea in flight. For the other sons and grandsons of strong Herakles threatened him. But he came in flight to Rhodes, suffering ills, and he founded a settlement with three tribal groups and was loved by Zeus' (*Il.* 2.661–7).

Odysseus himself, in telling of his wanderings, sizes up the Cyclops' island for its suitability for settlement: 'For the Cyclopes have no ships with cheeks of vermillion, nor have they builders of ships among them, who could have made them strong-benched vessels, and these if made could have run them sailings to all the various cities of men, in the way that people cross the sea by means of ships and visit each other, and they could have made this island a strong settlement for them. For it is not a bad place at all; it could bear all crops in season, and there are meadow lands near the shores of the gray sea, well-watered and soft; there could be grapes grown there endlessly, and there is smooth land for ploughing; men could reap a full harvest always in season, since there is very rich soil. Also there is an easy harbour...' (*Od.* 9.125–36, trans. Lattimore).

The one case of a *community* establishing a settlement abroad in the *Odyssey* is the case of the Phaeacians who 'formerly lived in the spacious land, Hypereia, next to the Cyclopes, who were men too overbearing, and who kept harrying them, being greater in strength. From here godlike Nausithoös uprooted and led away and settled in Scheria, far away from men who eat bread, and drove a wall about the city, and built the houses and made the temples of the gods, and allotted the holdings' (*Od.* 6, 4–10). Here we have not a city sending out men to found another city but, under the leadership of a particular individual, a city moving and re-establishing itself.

Taken together, these episodes from *Iliad* and *Odyssey* reveal a world in which men routinely move about, because life is too hot in the place where they have been, to further gift-enhanced friendships with others (as Telemakhos visits Nestor and Menelaos), to achieve profit for themselves, whether by fair means or foul, or in search of security.[6] Only in a negative way, by making it impossible for individuals to stay, do communities control the movements of their members. Individuals regularly move on their own initiative, and as they move they keep an eye open for sites suitable for not just individual but also group settlement, aware of what is involved in settling a group on a new site. Nausithoos and the Phaeacians show that the Homeric world is one in which a community might decide to relocate itself, but relocation certainly does not wait on community decisions.

How seriously should we take this Homeric evidence? On the one hand the whole shape of both poems dictates that the individual is at the centre, for it is the decision-making and responsibility of the individual upon which attention is focused. On the other hand, episodes such as the interlude in Phaeacia did not require an individual-centred approach and could have been used to explore a different model of social organisation, but that opportunity is not taken. Moreover, the more or less contemporaneous world of Hesiod is similarly a world in which people do move around, whether Hesiod thinks that a good idea or not, where individuals can come in from distant places and still acquire a stake in land in the Greek mainland worth arguing over by their sons, as is presented as being the case for Hesiod's own father, and where individuals take their own decisions about exploring greener pastures across the seas. Local rulers may threaten with unjust judgements, but there seems no serious threat of being frogmarched off as a foreign settler on an expedition some petty prince has dreamt up.

How does this Homeric and Hesiodic picture accord with the archaeological evidence? There is some, perhaps general, acceptance that the picture accords quite well with the archaeological evidence from the earliest of western Greek settlements, Pithekoussai. Those who need a technical term pluck the term *emporion* for this settlement or acknowledge its difference by talking of it as 'pre-colonial', as does Ridgway (1992, 32): 'the hindsight of archaeology suggests that Pithekoussai was indeed some kind of pre-colonial establishment, succeeded at an early stage by the foundation, with full colonial honours, of Cumae'. (Later Ridgway (1992, 108) will go on to wonder whether 'an original trading settlement...could not simply have evolved into a colony'.)[7]

What is the 'archaeological hindsight' provided by Pithekoussai which Ridgway thinks marks it out as pre-colonial rather than having 'full colonial honours'? The answer seems to lie in the mixed nature of the archaeological record. The pottery at Pithekoussai does not come from any one mainland city. Euboean pottery is found, but there is more (Proto)Corinthian, and quite a range of east Greek pottery plus imports from Italy and from Carthage, the Levant, 'Phoenician' Rhodes, and the Iberian peninsula.[8] The presence of pots made in a particular Greek city does not mean that men from that city ever visited the site, but it does very strongly suggest that Pithekoussai was in contact with not just one or two cities of the Greek mainland but with a very large number of cities across the Greek world, and in contact with them in a different way from that in which Euboean communities, which display a rather less various material assemblage, were in contact with them. Would a community sent out to service one or two mainland Greek cities acquire such ramifying links?[9]

But there is more to Pithekoussai than the variety of its contacts. There is, above all, its size – both on the ground ('one kilometre from end to end by *c.* 750'; Ridgway 1994, 39) and in terms of population. Ridgway's estimate, on the basis of cemetery finds, is that the late eighth-century population of Pithekoussai was of the order of 5,000 to 10,000. Such a population in such a place requires us to believe in a very large number of Pithekoussai-focused ship movements occurring reliably year in year out and a very large amount of non-agricultural goods, whether raw materials or manufactured goods, being handled by Pithekoussai and its inhabitants. The rapidity with which Pithekoussai grows is inconceivable unless it grows out of a world where large numbers of individuals are already moving round in search of profit before their journeys become turned to any single location. Pithekoussai must build on the back of a large mobile population already sailing widely across the Mediterranean in the first half of the eighth century. That mobile population, moreover, has to be one that has half a mind to settle, in order for it to produce the spectacular growth of settlement at Pithekoussai. We should note the willingness of many of the displaced persons of the *Iliad* and *Odyssey* to stay for protracted spells: the Phoenicians of *Odyssey* 15.455 spend a year re-filling their ship, and Odysseus and his companions have a tendency to dally, Odysseus expressing a willingness to remain with the Phaeacians for a year if they gave him gifts. The long argument about Al Mina and whether it was a Greek settlement would perhaps be somewhat defused if the model was of this kind of opportunistic settlement, rather than of 'the establishment of a permanent trading post'.

What distinguishes Pithekoussai from Al Mina is the nature of the archaeological evidence (graves, largely, at Pithekoussai, store buildings at Al Mina) and the sheer quantity of evidence. Otherwise the picture of goods coming from a range of cities – albeit a slightly different range – is common to both. How far are those two sites different from sites like Cumae, to which Ridgway awards 'full colonial honours', or Megara Hyblaia, or other later eighth-century settlements in Italy and Sicily? In the case of Cumae, Coldstream (1977, 231) remarks that the material from the cemetery 'recalls the contemporary grave groups of Pithecusae. Here, too, Corinth is the chief source of imports; but there are also a few Euboean unguent vessels, many Pithecusan imitations of Corinthian *aryballoi*... and a few semi-oriental *aryballoi* of Rhodian origin.' Coldstream goes on to remark on Etrurian types among the fibulae and on the presence of scarabs. At Megara Hyblaia we have to depend largely on settlement rather than cemetery evidence,[10] but there eighth-century pottery includes much Corinthian Late Geometric, particularly Thapsos *skyphoi*, some Attic, some Euboean, some Argive (or 'Argive'), some Rhodian, and local imitations of both Corinthian and Euboean pottery. There may be a *different* 'mix' here from elsewhere, and it is true that Corinthian pottery is enormously dominant, but there is certainly a mix. And it is important to stress that such a mix is not to be found in Geometric graves at Athens, or Argos, or in settlement remains from eighth-century Eretria, etc. In material terms Megara Hyblaia is almost certainly – though we know all too little about the mainland city – *not* just like Megara.

There are two separate points which I want to stress. The first is that in terms of the nature of its pottery assemblage Megara Hyblaia shares with Pithekoussai the feature of attracting pottery from far-flung areas of the Greek world. To distinguish the one from the other on grounds of variety of contacts displayed in recovered material is simply not possible. Whatever variety of contacts is taken to imply in the case of Pithekoussai it should also imply in the case of Megara Hyblaia. The second point is that this variety of material contacts distinguishes Megara Hyblaia from mainland Megara. Megara Hyblaia was clearly tied in from the first to networks of which Megara was not a part. But if mainland Megara did not determine the nature of the contacts which the early settlement enjoyed, then in what sense can that settlement be described as a Megarian 'colony'?

Are there any archaeological grounds for believing that places like Cumae or Megara Hyblaia were different in character from Pithekoussai? Megara Hyblaia has long been the crucial early settlement abroad in any argument about character because of the evidence which it supplies of being a planned settlement from the beginning (Vallet 1973). Such planning has encouraged scholars to find acceptable assumptions about state-led enterprises, and has, indeed, led some (notably Snodgrass and Hansen, now joined by Malkin) to wonder whether it was not the experience of laying out a planned community abroad which encouraged the further planning of social and political arrangements at home, burgeoning in the birth of the *polis*.

The facts about Megara Hyblaia are straightforward: what is held to distinguish it are the existence of a grid plan, the reserving of streets and an *agora* from the beginning, the regularity with which houses are spaced, and the apparent advanced planning for walls between house-plots. Certainly an irregularly shaped piece of land in the middle of the settlement was never built on, and successive building activity around it respected its boundaries. In the middle of the seventh century this central area acquired monumental buildings, and extended itself slightly to the south into space previously occupied by houses (Vallet 1973, 40). That we have here a piece of land with a recognised communal role from the beginning cannot be disputed. But how significant is this? There is no doubt that the piece of reserved land came to act as a community focus in a big way, and little doubt that the name *agora* was relatively rapidly justified. But how important is it that the first settlers agreed that they needed a central communal space?

Similarly there is certainly a high degree of regularity in land division and house spacing: the eighth-century houses were aligned either with the streets or, more often, with the median line of the block in which each was located, and 1.5 foot spaces seem to have been allowed between houses. But the limits of this are revealed by the way in which there was not one single overall grid plan, but several separate grids. Five grids have been distinguished in the excavated area, and some have argued that this reflects the five villages of mainland Megara (Svenbro 1982). Such a connection puts unbearable stress on a coincidence of numbers, but that we have several groups planning things in their own way, and only co-ordinating their activities rather loosely, seems highly likely.

Scholars who put a great deal of emphasis on what they see as a high degree of communal decision-making involved in these elements of planning at Megara Hyblaia in the eighth century presuppose that such communal organisation was somehow new. But even Dark Age settlements such as Zagora on Andros have revealed a degree of planning and regularity which indicates that they were very far from being a free-for-all. Zagora is particularly important, for the settlement there shows no signs of having been dominated by any individual, family or group, and the regularity of the settlement there has to be seen as a result of communal agreement, not forced from outside. But if such a high degree of co-operative planning was possible at Zagora, why not similarly among the settlers at Megara Hyblaea? That there was a degree, indeed a high degree, of co-operation between settlers at any of these settlements abroad is demonstrable, for however friendly the native inhabitants were, the settlers had not arrived without co-operating with one another and could not expect to survive without sustaining such co-operation. Co-operative action of any sort – religious, 'commercial', or political – demands space, and the reserving of 'communal' space would seem to be evidence only for co-operation. From this as from many other points of view it is unfortunate that we know so little about the actual settlement areas at Pithekoussai.

The need for co-operative planning, whatever the character of the settlements, also means that arguments from the foundation or siting of religious sanctuaries indicate rather less about the character of the early settlements than their proponents sometimes suggest. Malkin manages to argue quite convincingly that sacred precincts at settlements abroad depended neither on the presence of native sites nor upon considerations of 'inherent sacredness' in the landscape, but his observations about (by no means universal) preferences for peripheral siting, which he sees as being promoted by eagerness to differentiate sacred and profane, to keep impurity away, and to facilitate town planning, in no case demand his conclusion – 'that it was the Greek founders of colonies themselves who decided and acted according to...functional and rational criteria for the organization of the territory of both city and countryside' (1987, 183). The more one accepts that the siting of sanctuaries is functional and rational the easier it is to believe that any group of co-operating settlers might have come to the same conclusion.

But if the siting of sanctuaries or the existence of a central *'agora'* at Megara Hyblaia does not *demand* state enterprise it certainly does not disprove it. I have already argued that archaeology does not give any good grounds for making a strong distinction between the situation at Pithekoussai and the situation at other settlements. But can the archaeology of the early western settlements offer any further means of distinguishing the character of the early settlements? Let me offer two archaeological observations: that the early settlements in the West are apparently very various; and that the highly planned 'colonial' city is repeatedly being found to be a result of second, rather than first, thoughts. I borrow my first observation from Di Vita (1990, 349) who notes that 'at Megara Hyblaea the houses in the area of the agora are too close together to have formed part of regular κλῆροι, and too far apart to speak of an urban setting... By contrast, the earliest houses at Syracuse are grouped together. The area to which they belong seems vast. Consequently, it seems most likely that the city was formed, like Corinth, by small clusters of dwellings grouped around water sources and occupying naturally privileged positions.' My second observation is best illustrated by the case of Selinous, where Martin suggests that a regular street system dates to the early sixth century – perhaps half a century after the foundation.[11] Similarly the regular plans at Himera, Naxos, Gela and Camarina are products of fifth-century revolutions, including expulsion of inhabitants, rather than simply the reinforcement of earlier plans (Di Vita 1990, 356–61).

Sicily has taken pride of place in scholarly treatments of Greek settlement in the West because of the richer literary sources on foundation, the outstanding monuments, the involvement of Sicily with mainland Greek affairs, and its altogether richer historical tradition. But none of these constitute a good reason for preferring later Sicilian evidence to earlier Italian evidence when we are trying to sort out the nature of early Greek settlement in the West. The Italian evidence looks distinctly different from the Sicilian, and unless we are to claim that Greek settlers went to Italy with different motives from those with which they went to Sicily we do need to be able to incorporate that Italian evidence into our picture.

I want to concentrate on just one area of Italy: the instep, and upon three sites: Siris/Policoro, Incoronata, and Metapontum. Incoronata is not a site about which we have any certain literary tradition; the traditions for Metapontum and Siris include both stories that are not the sort scholars attach much credence to (Strabo 6.1.4 has both founded as a result of the Trojan War; Siris by Trojans, Metapontum by Nestor) and stories generally assumed basically true because they relate to the seventh century – the tradition that Siris was founded by Colophonians fleeing Gyges (*c.* 680), and the tradition that Metapontum was a secondary Achaean foundation set up from Sybaris.

The earliest Greek pottery at Incoronata is a fragment of a Middle Geometric cup. Around 700 there are signs of the round huts of a native settlement being abandoned over part of the site – a road is built over them – and in part of the site replaced by small stone and mud-brick rectilinear buildings. Twenty-seven seventh-century tombs, mainly of adolescents, retain the foetal position and are regarded as securely native.[12] Earlier consensus that Greeks pushed out natives has now been replaced by the suggestion that, although the settlement and architectural changes, together with the dominance of the seventh-century pottery assemblage by Greek vessels, imply the presence of some Greeks, we should see Greeks as living side-by-side with natives. But somewhere in the third quarter of the seventh century all settlement seems to have been destroyed – the site has yielded no early Corinthian pottery.

At Policoro seventh-century burials show a mixture of burial rites – cremation, inhumation in supine position, inhumation in foetal position – which have been interpreted as Greek and native living side-by-side and sharing the same burial ground. Once more here there is a rich assemblage of Greek pottery, including a *dinos* as well as cups, Corinthian transport amphorae and Corinthian *aryballoi* (Greco 1992, 41). Nearby at Termitito and at S. Maria D'Anglona cemeteries show continuity from the eighth century. In the second half of the seventh century, perhaps, the hill at Policoro was surrounded by a 4 km long mud-brick wall, and, outside it, what Greco describes as a pastas house was built before 600, with a second building added a little later on the same orientation. There is some temptation to see this as the point of foundation of Siris – though that hardly squares with the chronology implied by the literary tradition of Kolophonians fleeing Gyges – but if so there are no archaeological signs of a compact foundation created in a single act.

At Metapontum the earliest Greek pottery, from the Andrisani plot, is Geometric, and from the early seventh century there is a quite extensive settlement with both Greek and native wares. This settlement was destroyed by fire. One site that has yielded Thapsos cups later received a wooden structure and after this was burnt, and probably shortly after 600, a cult structure (Sacellum C), but it is unclear whether the eighth-century use was cultic. Around 600 the site receives a permanent assembly-place equipped with wooden benches. These too were later destroyed by fire and in the middle of the sixth century the *Ekklesiasterion* was rebuilt in stone. In the nearby territory sanctuary sites with Greek votives of seventh-century date have been excavated (notably San Biagio), and these votives seem to be local production of strikingly high quality. Just what sort of story should be woven to account for these features it is currently hard to tell. Jo Carter has shown that one *could* fit them to the story told by literary sources (in which case the Andrisani huts become Nestor's settlement, their burning is the Samnite raid, and the wooden cult and political buildings are the foundation of the Akhaian colony) but it is far from clear that it is worth the effort (see below).

Famously, the territory of Metapontum was subject to regular division. Some five farm sites are known from survey from the first half of the sixth century, and Adamesteanu suggested that the land division dates back to that time; farm sites rise to some 116 in the early fifth century, but then drop to 46 in the early fourth century, and when farm site numbers leap from 46 for the first half of the century to 128 in the second half this may be because of some redivision (Carter 1990, 410, 426–8).

Metapontum survived into the classical period and acquired a colonial history. Incoronata perished at the end of the seventh century and did not. Should we account for their different fates in terms of different origins? Or have their different fates in fact given them different literary fates?

What I have tried to do in the second part of this paper is to undermine confidence that the archaeology distinguishes clearly between the nature of the settlements we have come to call 'colonies' and the nature of those settlements for which scholars cast about for an alternative term. I have argued, through examination of the pottery from Megara Hyblaia, that settlements abroad generally share the mixed archaeological record and the failure to mimic the material culture of a single Greek mainland city which is to be noted at Pithekoussai. I have also argued, through examination of the settlements of Basilicata, that a precise moment of 'Greek colonization' may be difficult or impossible to distinguish archaeologically in other than an arbitrary fashion, and that there is much in common between the archaeological record of places which did, and that of places which did not, get recorded as colonies. Becoming a Greek settlement, on this showing, may often have been a gradual process; becoming a colony more to do with the invention of a past than with a historical moment of invention.[13] The evidence for co-existence with a native population in this area further discourages big bang theories – for increasingly little sign is to be found that those there already felt any bang.

III

People *do* things with words. We don't need to invoke the example of Cato's *Origines* to see that stories about origins particularly lend themselves to being 'performative' utterances. For cities of the Greek mainland, prosperous communities abroad were communities worth keeping in touch with. Real kinship links could cement such claims, but with a little ingenuity even unconnected communities might be able to get themselves in on a city's past if there was some moment when this seemed mutually advantageous to both parties (one might think here of the Samian use of Kolaios to claim a tie with both Cyrene and Thera). Such claims to links need not be unwelcome: men who had chosen to move might nevertheless welcome any attention that kept them in contact with a wider world – they evidently relied on such contact for much of their imperishable material needs. For new settlements, stories about founders were one way of forging a community identity, one way of transposing current difficulties on to a past still more riven with hardship. Insistence that Delphi had picked the spot and inspired the founder were ways of encouraging those who found life hard to stick it out since Apollo, of course, must have known best (though if a move was required it could be noted that men might not interpret him quite correctly).

Let me briefly explore this line of reasoning for Siris and Metapontum. Siris has not one but a number of traditions which have come down to us. Strabo (6.264) records that 'Some say that both Siritis and Sybaris...were Rhodian foundations.' Strabo's main story (ibid.), however, is of Siris being a Trojan foundation superseded by the foundation of Herakleia from Taras:[14] 'Next there is the city of Herakleia a little in from the sea, and there are two navigable rivers, the Akiris and the Siris, on which was an homonymous Trojan town. Later when Herakleia had been founded there by the Tarantines this was the port of the Herakleots... As proof of the Trojan settlement they consider the *xoanon* of Trojan Athene which is set up there, which they say closed its eyes when the suppliants were dragged away on the taking of the city by the Ionians. For these came as settlers (οἰκήτορας), fleeing from Lydian rule, and they took by force the city which belonged to the Khones, and called it Polieion. They point to the fact that the statue now has closed eyes.'[15] Athenaios (12.523c) adds to this story the detail that these Ionians were from Kolophon: 'Those who settled Siris, which those from Troy first held, and later Kolophonians, according to Timaios and Aristotle, degenerated into luxury no less than the Sybarites.' But Justin (20.2.3–9) makes those who killed the suppliants at the altar Metapontines along with people of Croton and Sybaris: 'But right at the beginning Metapontines with people of Sybaris and Croton decided to expel other Greeks from Italy. When first they took the city of Siris, in the process of storming it they butchered fifty youths who had embraced the statue of Athene and the priest of the goddess dressed up in priestly regalia on the altar itself. Because of this they were troubled by plague and sedition.' The name Polieion is connected by Stephanus of Byzantium (s.v. Siris) and the *Etymologicum Magnum* (s.v. Polieion) with Athena Polias, in the former case Athena Polias at Troy, in the latter Athena Polias at Polieion; the name Siris is connected by the *Etymologicum Magnum* (s.v.) with Siris the daughter of Morges, King of Sicily.

Archaeologically there is no justification for the Trojan strand in the story, which serves to connect the fatal capture of Siris with the fatal capture of Troy. In Strabo the episode of fatal capture seems to be that by which the Ionians founded Polieion, in Justin it is that perpetrated by men from Metapontum, Sybaris and Kroton. In both cases mention of the Trojans draws attention to the violence involved in establishing the settlement, either to bring out the parallelism between Greek settlers expelling Anatolian residents in Italy and Lydians expelling Greek residents in Anatolia, or to import a weight of moral condemnation into an episode of warfare arising from local city rivalry. All the stories seem to be 'outsiders' ' stories about the settlement, not stories told by settlers about their own past. In such 'outsiders' ' stories it is pretty immaterial who the expelled residents are, and whom the violence is pinned upon will depend upon the vagaries of political alignments when the story is told. Whether the settlers are held to be any old Ionians, Kolophonians, or Rhodians, and how soft they are alleged to have become, is a matter of politics, not history. Scholarly concern to tie up the archaeology of Siris with plausible dates for Gyges making life uncomfortable for Kolophonians (not that the Siris traditions mention Gyges[16]) takes one strand of the tradition and, because it lacks obviously incredible details, believes it, while discarding other strands, some almost certainly equally old. We should hardly be surprised if archaeology does not oblige in yielding up the 'right' date.

Strabo is our main source for the foundation of Metapontum (6.264). He tells of its initial foundation by Nestor and its subsequent sack by Samnites; of Antiokhos' claim that it was founded by Akhaians summoned by the Akhaians of Sybaris, who wanted the city as a bulwark against Taras, and that it was at first called Metabus; of Ephoros' claim that its oikist was Daulius tyrant of Krisa; and of the story that it was founded by Leukippos who got use of the territory for a day and a night from the Tarantines and then refused to give it back.

Once more the earliest episode, the Pylian colonization, has no archaeological correlate. But the interest of the other stories in this case is their variety. Antiokhos' and Ephoros' claims are clearly claims already current in the classical period, but they give two totally different backgrounds to the colonists. We might rationalise the Antiokhan explanation as a *cui bono* approach to who might have been responsible for the foundation, but the greater difficulty of finding an explanation for Ephoros' attribution of the foundation to the tyrant of Krisa can hardly be taken to show that story to be true.

These two sites provide a good example, therefore, of the way in which modern scholarship, in classifying a colony as founded by a particular city of the Greek mainland, is often more or less arbitrarily selecting only one of a number of cities to which the ancient sources make reference. Such a selection is made on the presupposition that in fact only one city can have been responsible for a foundation (except for cases where there are not two stories, each about one founder, but one story about two founders, as for Gela (where it further helps that the story-teller is Thucydides (6.4.3)). That presupposition is part of a further scholarly consensus that also considers the founding city's consultation of the Delphic oracle as a basic feature of all acts of colonization (proven so, it is claimed, by the story about Dorieus being censured for not making such a consultation). But what the Dorieus story really shows is the power of the Delphic consultation motif in the political discourse about unsuccessful attempts of a rebellious individual separatist to establish himself and his supporters in foreign lands. It cannot be taken to show what such individuals regularly did, and the very fact that this story comes to circulate in Sparta suggests that whether or not a city takes up such a settlement may be determined rather by the success or failure of the settlement than by the circumstances in which the settlement was established. It is successful episodes of settlement which acquire Delphic justification.

IV

What I have been trying to do in this paper is to suggest that the model of 'colonization' is unsuitable as a model for Greek settlement in the

West in the eighth and seventh centuries. I have tried to argue that the features which mark the establishment of settlements abroad by cities in the classical period, features much like those of Roman *coloniae*, are not features which it is easy to parallel in eighth- and seventh-century colonies. I have argued instead that the 'private enterprise' which is widely and surely rightly assumed to have been responsible for the settlement at Pithekoussai, should be envisaged as responsible also for the vast majority of eighth- and seventh-century settlements, as shown by the way they attract pottery and metalwork from a wide, but usually peculiar, variety of Greek and Italian areas, by their very varied layouts and the fact that regular grids are demonstrably later in several cases, and by the marked discontinuities with which the settlement history at many of these sites is visited. The archaeological record may show no single moment of Greek settlement, and the literary tradition may reveal competing claims to the same foreign settlement. Charismatic individuals and venturesome or discontented groups from particular cities may well have been responsible for a good proportion of Greek settlements abroad, but the work done by their home communities to ensure that a good site was selected and that their welfare was in all events looked after is a product of the reclamation of advantageous contacts rather than the record of historical events.

We will never understand what is going on in Italy and Sicily in the eighth and seventh centuries until we properly understand the character of the settlements there. Without some idea of their character we have no choice but to treat literary tradition as historical record. If we treat those traditions as history we will go on calling the settlements 'colonies' and will go on mistaking both the causes and the nature of settlement in the West by invoking a colonization model. To do that is not only to fly in the face of the archaeology of settlements abroad, it is also to mistake the nature of the cities of the Greek mainland which are supposed to be sending out these colonies. Only when we accept that settlement in the West was a product of a world in which many were constantly moving across the seas, where there was a rich fund of knowledge about the shores of the Mediterranean, their peoples, and what those peoples' likes and dislikes were, and where individuals and small groups out for their own gain from time to time came to believe that more or less permanent settlement on foreign shores was both in their immediate best interests and was sustainable – only then will we get rid of the spectres of over-population, land shortage, and states with commercial policies. Talk of whether or not there was 'trade before the flag' is inappropriate, not because talk of trade is anachronistic, but because there was no flag. A proper understanding of archaic Greek history can only come when chapters on 'Colonization' are eradicated from books on early Greece.

Acknowledgements

Earlier versions of this paper were read to a Durham seminar organised by Lisa Nevett and David Levine, and at Oxford, as well as at Cardiff. I am grateful to participants on those occasions and to Franco De Angelis, Gillian Shepherd and Hans van Wees for comments on earlier drafts.

Notes

[1] So, recently, Cawkwell 1992.

[2] For a revealing study of the cultural control involved in colonization see Mitchell 1988.

[3] Most notable are Finley 1976, 173–4 ('The so-called Greek and Phoenician colonies of the eighth, seventh and sixth centuries BC...were more peaceful enterprises in some instances, less in others, but what is essential is that they were all, from the start, independent city-states, not colonies' and 'Commercial domination, monopoly, even export drives occur and recur in the literature [on early Greek and Phoenicians settlements]...simply because we have acquired the unfortunate habit of calling the settlements 'colonies'); Purcell 1990, esp. 55–6; Braund 1994, ch. 3, esp. 74, 78–9.

[4] See Casevitz 1985 and note also the recent discussion by Wilson 1997.

[5] I explore the case of Cyrene in more detail in Osborne 1996a, ch. 1.

[6] For further discussion of these aspects of the Homeric world see Van Wees 1992, 31–6, 105–6, 168–72, 207–48.

[7] The question of the precise status of Pithekoussai is much debated in *AION* n.s. 1 (1994): see Greco 1994, D'Agostino 1994, and Ampolo 1994, 34.

[8] Non-Greek imports on Pithekoussai are usefully catalogued in Docter and Niemeyer 1994.

[9] For a recent discussion of the variety of pottery found at Tocra and at Cyrene and its implications see Boardman 1994, 144–7.

[10] On the cemeteries see Cébeillac-Gervasoni 1975, 1976–7. The earliest material from the south cemetery dates to about 720 BC.

[11] *ASAA* 183–8; Di Vita 1990, 350–6.

[12] Greco 1992, 40; Carter 1993; 1994, 162–5.

[13] Although single sudden acts of foundation are not to be excluded, the assignment of a foundation date to a settlement seems to me likely in most cases to be a product of the alignment of archaic settlements to settlement foundation in the fifth century, rather than any genuine historical information.

[14] On the latter cf. also Diodorus Siculus 12.36.4.

[15] On all of this see Lykophron 978–92, with *schol. vet. ad* 984 and 989.

[16] Cf. Bérard 1957, 188–9: 'Ces conquérants lydiens ne peuvent être que ceux conduits par Gygès à l'assaut des villes grecques d'Ionie et d'Éolide vers la troisième décade du VIIe siècle, date à laquelle durent émigrer les Ioniens.'

10

TOWARDS THALASSOCRACY?
Archaic Greek naval developments

Philip de Souza

The purpose of this paper is to consider how we should interpret the evidence concerning naval developments in the archaic period. Ideally we might hope to be able to achieve some sort of 'marriage' of the (contemporary) archaeological evidence for archaic ships and harbour installations with the (largely non-contemporary) written evidence for navies and their use. From this combination of sources we might then be able to build up a picture of the development of naval power by the early Greeks.[1] The reality, however, is that such a harmonious union is impossible due to the irreconcilable differences between the various sources and the information which they provide.[2]

Consequently we must try to form a picture of naval developments among the archaic Greeks from texts of the classical period, or even later, which presents us with considerable problems of interpretation. In particular, those authors who describe the rise of sea powers in the years before the Persian Wars and the Athenian Empire need careful handling because, as will be seen, they are writing with a definite aim – to emphasize the greatness of the events which they are chronicling at length by briefly surveying the achievements of the past. Our best guides to the history of the archaic period are Herodotus and Thucydides, but their handling of naval developments is heavily coloured by the events and conditions of the fifth century. Thus, the principal limitation which we must overcome in trying to trace the naval history of the archaic Greeks is that it was written by and for the classical Greeks.

Ancient navies
It is important from the outset that we should have a clear idea of what constitutes a navy, in order to be able to identify and evaluate any naval developments in the archaic period. Too restrictive a definition of a navy would be unhelpful, however, because it would exclude

anything which might be the beginnings of naval resources, or might have some but not all of the characteristics of a navy. An important element in a developed navy is that its ships are not privately owned and operated, but that they are public vessels, whether purposely built as warships or not.[3] In the world of the classical Greeks the warships belonged to the *polis*, rather than to its individual citizens, as was apparently the case in the early archaic period. With public ownership comes public responsibility for maintenance and provision of adequate facilities. Strategic use of the naval resources of a *polis*, whether for military campaigns or for other purposes, such as colonization, or the suppression of piracy, is a further indication that an advanced stage of naval development has been achieved. Activities of this kind are likely to be long remembered and may even be documented in some fashion, enabling them to be incorporated into literary accounts, from which 'naval histories' can be constructed. Such naval developments are likely to take place in a competitive context. There is no need for one state to establish and improve its navy unless the naval capabilities of its potential opponents represent a significant threat, or unless the strategic ambitions of the *polis* require substantial naval forces for their realization.

Warships

The earliest ships used for warfare in the eastern Mediterranean were non-specialized vessels used for the transportation of goods and people as well as soldiers. References to fighting at sea can be found as early as the thirteenth century, in both pictorial form, such as the famous Medinet Habu reliefs of Rameses III, which depict his ships engaged in battle with those of the Sea Peoples, *c.* 1190 (Casson 1971, fig. 61), and in texts like the tablet of the Hittite king Shupilluliumash II recording a victory at sea against the ships of Alashiya (probably Cyprus) *c.* 1200.[4] Representations of archaic ships, found mainly on painted vases, seem to indicate that the development of the 'warship' was a phenomenon of the late eighth century BC in the eastern Mediterranean. The warship is characterized by its low, elongated hull, raised sides, oars rowed at one or more levels, a fighting platform for marines and the ram, extending out from the bows of the ship at the waterline.[5] Representations of this type of vessel are found on many painted ceramic vases of the late Geometric and early archaic periods. That they were also in regular use among non-Greeks is indicated by, amongst other items, a famous relief from the palace of Sennacherib which shows the flight of Lulli, king of Tyre and Sidon, *c.* 700, and includes several ships with two banks of oars, long, low hulls, fighting platforms and rams (Casson 1971, fig. 78; Wallinga 1993, fig. 19). There has been much debate among modern scholars about the exact nature of the ships depicted on these artefacts, but the consensus seems to be that vessels which could be called warships were widely used among the peoples of the eastern Mediterranean by *c.* 650, although vessels which were intended *only* for use as warships are not clearly attested until the mid-sixth century. At the same time ships which *cannot* be used for warfare, only for cargo transportation, because they lack multiple oars, the ram and the fighting platform, begin to appear.[6]

The ships which Homer describes in the *Iliad* and the *Odyssey* are apparently owned by individuals, rather than communities, although they are grouped together under various leaders. They do not engage in sea battles. Our fuller literary sources for the fifth century show that in the period between 'Homeric' and classical Greece a new fighting concept emerged in the Greek world – naval warfare between states.[7] We can define the nature of the development in terms of what was present before and after, but we are severely hampered in our attempts to describe the process by which it came about. The principal limitation to the available evidence is a lack of direct written testimony. The literary image of a fleet of ships under public ownership only emerges clearly in accounts of the battles of the Persian Wars, the earliest of which is Aischylos' description of the Battle of Salamis (*Persai* 302–471) and at several points in Herodotus' *Histories*.[8] The pattern of public rather than private warships is not rigid or complete, however, as there are still instances of privately owned ships, even triremes, in the fifth century.[9] It is also clear that what we might call the command structure of maritime expeditions changed dramatically over the course of time, with the collections of warrior bands under 'leaders of men' like Agamemnon and Odysseus giving way to squadrons and fleets following appointed or, eventually in the case of the fifth-century Athenians, elected generals and admirals. This shift in the leadership, and in the composition of maritime expeditions was accompanied, as Thucydides describes, by a change in the objectives from limited material ones to more expansive, political ones. Predatory warfare and piracy, aimed primarily at collecting booty and prestige, were superseded by campaigns aimed at securing control of territory and defeating potential rivals.[10] This process was a very gradual one, however, and there was never a complete divorce between predatory and political aims in Greek warfare.[11] Eventually the Greeks conceived of the idea that naval forces might be used to create a political supremacy which was based on 'sea power', and so the concept of *thalassocracy* was born. As we shall see, however, the resources which were required to create, maintain and deploy naval forces on a large scale and over an extended period of time were probably not possessed by the Greek *poleis* in the archaic period.

Naval facilities

Our best model for the requirements of an ancient Greek navy is that provided by classical Athens. The Athenians are credited by our sources with having deliberately developed a naval infrastructure in the early fifth century BC largely on the initiative of Themistokles, who persuaded them to employ the profits from a major silver strike in the Laurion region to build a large fleet. This fleet was enlarged so that by the summer of 480 the Athenians possessed 200 triremes. In addition to the ships, Themistokles proposed that the Athenians develop a fortified naval harbour at Peiraieus, a project apparently begun in 493 and continued after the defeat of Xerxes' invasion force in 480–479. Both the fleet and the facilities at Peiraieus which supported it were further expanded during the fifth century, partly with the tribute revenue provided by the Athenians' Delian League allies.[12] While it is unreasonable to expect archaic Greek *poleis* or other communities to have either a navy or naval installations on the scale of classical Athens, whose naval power was exceptional even in the eyes of her contemporaries, it is reasonable to expect that they would put in place a basic naval infrastructure, albeit over a long period of time. Clearly the financial capacity to build, equip, crew and maintain warships was not easily attained, as Thucydides is at pains to stress throughout his work. Although we are unable to calculate fully the cost of even the classical Athenian fleet, we can be sure that naval development could not have come cheaply, and it would not be possible for relatively small and impoverished *poleis* on their own.[13]

Limen kleistos

Several classical authors refer to harbours as *kleistos*, which is sometimes interpreted as enclosed or fortified, but seems to be best translated by the near-literal meaning of 'closeable'. The usual method of closing such a harbour was by means of a chain or boom, fixed to the ends of the moles at the harbour mouth, which would be reinforced and fitted with strong fixings for the barrier. Narrow entrances were easily closed off, and wider ones could be artificially narrowed by extending the moles or placing less permanent barriers across them.[14] The development or creation of a closeable harbour is *potentially* a strategic act, one which could be interpreted as an indication of basic naval development by an archaic *polis*. Identifying closeable harbours is, however, a very difficult matter, as in most cases it is only through the literary sources, such as Strabo, that we are informed that a particular harbour could be closed.[15] The silence of our sources on this matter is not necessarily indicative of the absence of arrangements to close a harbour. Where it is possible to identify the potential for closure of a harbour mouth, either through the narrowness of the entrance or the existence of suitable moles for fixing a boom or chain, then it is probably reasonable to assume that such arrangements were in place.[16] Dating the existence of a harbour and its security arrangements to the archaic period is, unfortunately, also often a matter of speculation. Few have been explored, and the literary sources which mention such arrangements do not tell us when they were first instituted. Archaic Greek *poleis* which *may* have had closeable harbours by the late sixth century include Korinth, Kyzikos, Miletos, Samos and Syracuse.[17]

Slipways and shipsheds

If they were allowed to remain exposed to sea water for long periods of time the hulls of ancient warships would become waterlogged, encrusted with barnacles, be subject to the attacks of marine borers, and eventually start to rot. This deterioration would affect their performance, slowing them down and making them more difficult to handle. Whereas merchant ships were usually heavily protected below the waterline, sometimes with lead sheathing, the weight added by such protection meant that it could not be used on warships, which were protected only by light coverings of pitch and paint. Instead it was necessary to remove warships from the water as often as possible, to allow the hulls to dry out and to careen, repair and re-paint them. If possible this was done on purpose-built slipways. The earliest slipways were probably semi-permanent wooden constructions of the kind referred to as *ouroi* by Homer (*Il.* 2.153). The Achaian ships are positioned upon these with the aid of props (*hermata*). As warships became larger, more sophisticated and more valuable elaborate ship-sheds were constructed, often made of stone and covered with a roof.[18] The usual Greek term for these installations is *holkoi*, and they were clearly an important part of the naval facilities of the Greek *poleis* in the classical period, as is shown by the pride the Athenians took in the Periklean shipsheds at the Peiraieus.[19]

The navy of the Persian Empire was, from the late sixth century to the time of Alexander, larger than that of any other state in the eastern Mediterranean. It is likely that there were Persian naval bases in Phoenicia, Kilikia, and in the Aegean at Abdera and Kyme (Wallinga 1987), but details of their facilities are lacking. It is also likely that several of the Levantine cities would have possessed substantial harbour installations by the end of the seventh century, but there is no evidence of slipways or shipsheds at any of the major sites, only securable inner harbours at Athlit, Tyre and Sidon.[20] Herodotus (2.159) refers to *holkoi* built on the coast of the Red Sea for the warships of the Egyptian pharaoh Necho (610–593). He also implies that similar ones existed on the Mediterranean seaboard.[21] No material evidence survives for any of these installations, and the situation in the Greek world is no better. We are given a stark indication of the severe limitations of the archaeological record for naval development in this period if we pause to consider the information available for one of the leading *poleis* of the archaic period – Miletos.

The Ionian city of Miletos was ideally situated for maritime communications with the rest of the Aegean and the regions beyond. With its direct access to the wealthy kingdom of Lydia and the populous Maeander valley it developed into one of the most important trading ports of the Aegean during the archaic period (Boardman 1980). Miletos had a privileged position among the Greek subjects of the Persian Empire. The city and its leaders played a major role in the Ionian revolt. There were four harbours at Miletos, although the oldest of them, the *Theaterhafen* (Theatre Harbour), does not adjoin the oldest *agora*, which is to the North. Instead it is the narrower inlet to the North, the so-called *Löwenbucht* (Bay of Lions), which is closest to the earliest *agora*. It would be reasonable to expect that such a prosperous maritime city would have invested in a naval infrastructure.[22] The *Löwenbucht* may have provided a securer, closeable harbour in the archaic period, which might well have had a naval function. There is no sign of shipsheds at Miletos before the classical period. Remains of some kind of storebuildings were excavated in the area of the *Löwenbucht* and the *Theaterhafen*. Archaic amphora sherds associated with these structures are a further indication that Miletos was a 'commercial' harbour or *emporion* in this period.[23] There is, however, no definite evidence of any naval installations in the archaeological record for archaic Miletos.

We are not much better served by the archaeological evidence for any other Greek *poleis* in the archaic period. Although there are many places where we might expect or hope to find some material remains which can be associated with naval developments, we are forced to rely very heavily on literary sources of the classical period. It is these that we must now examine closely.

Thalassocracy lists

Important, but problematical, written evidence for early Greek naval developments is provided by two lists of successive sea powers, one compiled by the Athenian historian, Thucydides, and contained within his *Archaiologia* (1.1–19), the other a composition of uncertain origin which is preserved in Armenian, Syriac, Greek and Latin texts derived from the *Chronika*, a two-part chronological work compiled by the fourth-century ecclesiastical historian Eusebius, bishop of Caesarea in Palestine (see Appendix). The Thucydidean list is the earliest attempt at a systematic account of early Greek naval developments, although there are some aspects of this account which correspond to statements made by the other great fifth-century historian, Herodotus of Halikarnassos. The latter author does not set out to provide a continuous or coherent account of a succession of naval powers. Consequently his work cannot be analysed independently of Thucydides, but must be seen as a kind of supplement, indicating further information and ideas about the early naval history of the Hellenes which may have been current among the Greek intellectual elite of the late fifth century.

Thucydides and Herodotus

Thucydides ascribes the first 'thalassocracy' to the Cretan king Minos, saying that he established the earliest navy and ruled over most of the Aegean, but giving no indication of a date, except that it clearly comes before the Trojan War (1.4). His use of the words *hōn akoēi ismen* ('of whom we know by hearsay') to qualify these statements is in keeping with his sceptical approach to early history and is similar to the attitude of Herodotus, who seems to consider Minos' thalassocracy as mythical, preferring to describe Polykrates the tyrant of Samos as the first to 'rule the sea' (*thalassokratein*), at least as far as mortals are concerned (3.122). Thucydides is more explicit than Herodotus about the status of his evidence for these ancient times, referring rather disparagingly to the exaggerations of Homer and the unreliability of old poets and the 'traditions' used by the *logographoi* (prose chroniclers) in general (1.10.3; 1.20–1). Scholars have tended to see the latter as including Herodotus, which is probably true in the sense that Thucydides believed that his own method of researching and writing about *recent* history was superior to any other writer's.[24] By positioning this claim to superiority *after* the *Archaiologia* he indicates that it does not apply to this part of his work. His intention is to make us see the main account of the Peloponnesian War as something better than the *Archaiologia*, which he realizes is open to criticism of a kind similar to that which he levels at Herodotus and other writers.

Minos is credited by Thucydides with having ruled over most of the Cyclades and established colonies on them, installing his sons as rulers or governors. Thucydides begins Minos' domination of the Aegean islands with the expulsion of the Karians, in contrast to Herodotus (1.171), who thinks that the Karians themselves were Cretan in origin and (therefore?) portrays them as partners of Minos, manning his ships and sharing in his successes. Thucydides suggests that Minos may have used his naval power to improve his revenues by suppressing piracy, which Thucydides felt was a common practice among the early Greeks, but once again he is deliberately cautious, adding the qualifying phrase *hōs eikos* (probably).[25] The process of increasing revenues and building up wealth is, in Thucydides' view, essential to the creation of a thalassocracy. Only a state or ruler with great resources could exercise political power over others through the deployment of military forces overseas. He also emphasizes the significance of a gradual intensification of maritime activity, for which the development of secure, prosperous coastal cities is an important indicator (1.7; 1.8.2; 1.13.5). We can be sure that he formed his opinions after an analysis of the successful development of the Athenian maritime empire in the fifth century. Herodotus seems, on the basis of what he says about Polykrates of Samos, to have had a similar view of what thalassocracy entailed.[26]

The next manifestation of sea power in Thucydides' account is the (undated) Trojan War.[27] He presents the expedition against Troy in terms of a deployment of the naval resources of Agamemnon's 'empire' (1.9). He assesses these resources by calculating the average size of the ships and their crews, as described in the *Iliad*, concluding that it was not a very large expedition compared to what the Greeks were able to mount in the fifth century (1.10.3–5), and that it did not achieve a great deal, mainly because the Greeks were forced to farm and raid in order to maintain themselves during the siege of Troy (1.11). We should note that Thucydides is very forthright about the limits of his evidence for the early history of Greek sea power. He considers Homer's evidence for the weakness and lack of unity among the early Greeks generally to be the best available (1.3.3), but he is doubtful about relying too closely upon the poet for details, because, as a poet, he is prone to exaggeration. So, although he is prepared to accept events described by Homer as historical, he does not consider the poet to be a reliable source (1.10.3). We must accept the limitations which Thucydides puts on his evidence up to this point. To his speculations about the early Greeks, modern scholars can add further information in the form of statements by later writers and archaeological evidence, but even this amalgam of sources is insufficient to enable us to draw firm conclusions in terms of the existence of navies or sea powers.[28]

Thucydides clearly relies upon different evidence for events which he places *after* the Trojan War and the coming of the Dorians (1.12), and which are part of his account of greater progress towards thalassocracy in the Greek world. From chapter 13 onwards he is describing developments which are, as far as we can tell, to be dated to the archaic period according to modern chronological divisions. He no longer has to rely upon the Homeric poems, but his cautionary words in chapters 20–1, about the limits of 'traditions' and the impossibility of checking the sources of the *logographoi* are still valid.[29]

Korinth is next on Thucydides' list of thalassocracies. He attributes the city's rise to its favourable position on trade routes and the wealth generated thereby. Like Minos, the Korinthians established a navy which they used to protect their maritime trade from pirates. Thucydides is still slightly hesitant about the reliability of his sources, using phrases like *legontai* ('they are said') and *phainetai* ('it appears') to qualify his more specific statements concerning Korinthian achievements. He does, however, claim that it was the Korinthians who first created something like a modern navy, that is, one similar to the navies of the fifth-century Greeks (1.13.2). There are various ways in which this statement might be interpreted, such as a reference to the use of decked ships, unlike the Homeric vessels of chapter 10, or to the use of the typical 'modern' warship of Thucydides' own day, the trireme.[30] In the context of Thucydides' earlier comments and the emphasis throughout his work on the deployment of its collective resources by a *polis* aiming to achieve thalassocracy, we could take him to mean that a modern navy involves state ownership of, or, at the very least, responsibility for, purpose-built warships and their facilities, making Korinth the archaic antecedent of the classical Athenian thalassocracy.

Should we, therefore, conclude that Korinth was the earliest *genuine* naval power among the archaic Greeks ? At first glance Thucydides seems to provide ample justification for such a conclusion. He says that the first triremes built in Greece were made at Korinth, that the

Korinthian Ameinokles built four ships for the Samians, and that the first known sea battle was fought between Korinth and Kerkyra. The reliability of these statements is distinguished from his other, more general, claims about Greek sea power by the assignment of specific dates to the last two: 704 for Ameinokles and 664 for the sea battle with Kerkyra (1.13.3).[31] Here we appear to have the basic requirements for a navy: state-owned Korinthian warships, the triremes, fighting a battle against a significant enemy, the prosperous Korinthian colony of Kerkyra. Herodotus' description of hostilities between the two in the reign of Periandros, tyrant of Korinth (3.39–53), even provides an historical context for the battle and a good reason for it to be remembered in the respective *poleis*.

Unfortunately there are some awkward problems with this interpretation. In the first place the mention of Ameinokles as a ship-builder does *not* seem to be directly connected to the mention of the earliest Greek triremes. Indeed, several scholars have argued that the invention of this highly complex, three-banked warship should be dated to the mid-sixth century. Whatever Ameinokles specialized in building, it seems unlikely to have been triremes.[32] Archaeology does not provide us with any further evidence, in spite of the wealth of excavation on the site of ancient Korinth. Some exploration has taken place at both the harbours which served the city of Korinth, Lechaion and Kenchreai, but no specifically naval installations have been found. Some scholars have argued that the famous *Diolkos*, a portage-way for transporting ships across the Isthmus of Korinth, was built for military purposes in the early sixth century, but there is no good evidence for this view, and it would make more sense to see the *Diolkos* as a commercial facility (Salmon 1984, 136–9).

Herodotus does not mention a sea battle between Korinth and Kerkyra, and the general context of Korinthian–Kerkyraian conflict which he provides, and which most scholars favour, the reign of Periandros, is about fifty years too late for Thucydides' date (Salmon 1984, chs. 15, 20). The usual response to this problem is a lowering of the dates to make the sea battle, assumed to be a victory for the Kerkyraians, coincide with Periandros' reign (*c*. 625–585) and leave Ameinokles somewhere in the middle of the seventh century. Justification for these dates is found in the view that Thucydides was not working from exact dates, but that he was simply counting back in 'generations' of forty years, which are too long for such a calculation.[33] Even if it is appropriate to adjust Thucydides' dates in this manner, we are still required to accept that Herodotus omitted to mention, or was unaware of, a naval defeat for the Korinthians under Periandros, and that Thucydides omitted to mention, or was unaware of, the connection between the Kypselids and this early Korinthian naval activity. There is often a tendency in the writing of ancient history for events to be 'attracted' to prominent individuals, especially in the fragmentary world of archaic Greece, but this tendency is one we should resist, even when it means that our main sources cannot be brought into agreement. Thucydides had a collection of facts about the Korinthians which he presented to justify his view that they were an emergent sea power, but this collection has to be kept separate from Herodotus' narrative on Periandros. The nature of the battle against Kerkyra and the activities of Ameinokles are, therefore, indeterminable and their dates at best uncertain. It may well be that the Kerkyraians and Korinthians came into conflict very soon after the foundation of Kerkyra in the early seventh century (Salmon 1984, 62–70).

The most we can say is that there were in the fifth century traditions of seventh-century Korinthian ship-building and of naval warfare which Thucydides thought were evidence for the early creation of something like a modern navy in Korinth.[34] A more positive attitude can, however, be taken to the next items in the Thucydidean narrative. He follows his remarks on Korinth with short accounts of three further naval powers – the Ionians under Persian rule, Polykrates of Samos, and Phokaia (1.13.6).

Persians and Ionians

It might seem paradoxical to us that the Ionians should attain naval power under Persian rule, until we take into account the context in which Thucydides makes this claim. Thucydides wrote the *Archaiologia* to demonstrate that the Peloponnesian War was the greatest conflict ever seen in the *Greek* world. He therefore describes archaic maritime developments in terms of the Greek *poleis*. The Ionians are credited with considerable naval strength by Herodotus (6.8), a total of 353 triremes which they attempt to use against Dareios I in 494. The important detail about this naval capacity which both Thucydides and Herodotus pass over is, as Wallinga has convincingly shown, that it belongs to the Persian king. On their own the Ionian *poleis* are not strong naval powers, but merely the providers of manpower for a Persian fleet which, as a remark in another section of Herodotus' account reveals (5.30), far outstrips the capacities of the Greeks under Persian rule.[35] There were, however, two notable exceptions to this rule of Ionian dependence on the Persians, which Thucydides specifies as

Samos, under the tyrant Polykrates, and Phokaia. We must take a closer look at these two sea powers.

Polykrates of Samos

Thucydides says very little about Polykrates. He calls him tyrant of Samos, ascribes his power to the use of a navy and mentions Rheneia, one of many islands which Polykrates conquered (1.13.6). It seems that, as with the Persian Wars (1.18.1–2), he felt it unnecessary to go to any length on a subject which his predecessor had covered in detail. Herodotus devotes several chapters of his third book to the Samian tyrant Polykrates. He describes Polykrates' rise to power and his establishment of a limited hegemony in the Aegean, in spite of Spartan attempts to help his Samian opponents overthrow him (3.39–49; 54–9). He justifies his lengthy Samian *logos* by referring to three famous *erga* of the Samians which he seems to associate with Polykrates' tyranny (3.60). It is clear, however, that Herodotus' main concern is with Polykrates as a potential opponent for, and ultimately a victim of, the Persians. Polykrates' fate also illustrates two major themes of Herodotus' history, namely that fortune never remains long in one place, and even the most powerful of mortals cannot avoid the destiny that fate has determined for them.[36] Thus Herodotus' decision to include a lengthy account of the Samian thalassocracy can be explained by its importance in his historiographic scheme, as much as by its political significance. The fact that Thucydides *also* considered Polykrates' naval power to have been of great significance gives us good reason to take his thalassocracy seriously.

The context in which Polykrates' naval power has to be placed is the rivalry between the newly created Persian Empire and the far more ancient Egyptian kingdom in the second half of the sixth century. Once again it is his concentration on Greek developments which makes Thucydides' evidence incomplete. Fortunately for us a combination of a re-reading of Herodotus and, finally, some reasonable archaeological evidence enables a much fuller picture to be drawn.[37] With the emergence of the Achaemenids as undisputed rulers of Western Asia in the mid-sixth century, the Saite Pharaohs were forced to look to the Greeks for allies. The ambitious, independent ruler of Samos was a logical choice, as he had already begun to build up his own defences aginst the threat from the East. Samian naval developments under Polykrates can be summarized as follows: he had a fleet of 100 pentekonters and (by 525) at least 40 triremes with the appropriate shipsheds; he conducted extensive maritime campaigns in the

Aegean, defeating both the Lesbians and the Milesians at sea, and capturing many cities and islands. He was probably also responsible for the harbour mole at Samos which was about 400 m long and extended out into over 30 m of water. Its main purpose was to furnish a sheltered harbour large enough to accommodate the Samian warfleet. We can speculate that there may well have been a closeable harbour of some sort, but our earliest evidence for this is a fourth-century text.[38] A set of defensive walls, fragments of which have been dated to the sixth century, is also reasonably attributed to the Polykratean period (Shipley 1987, 75–8). The famous tunnel through the mountain west of Samos, providing a secure water supply for the *polis* (Rihll and Tucker 1995) is probably also part of this defensive programme.

According to Herodotus, Polykrates contributed to Kambyses' Egyptian expedition in 525 his 40 triremes, crewed by Samians of whose loyalty Polykrates was uncertain.[39] After their defection Polykrates is said by Herodotus (3.45) to have imprisoned their women and children in his ship-sheds (*neosoikoi*) and threatened to burn them. It therefore seems clear that the Samian tyrant possessed both triremes and the shipsheds to house them by 525. Wallinga has even suggested that a special type of ship, the *samaina*, which Hellenistic and Roman writers claim was built by Polykrates, may have been a type of *pentekonter* intended to function as a troop-transport, needed to ferry Polykrates' large land forces around, and to help support his ally Amasis (Wallinga 1993, 93–9). Thus the Samian navy which Thucydides thought worthy of special attention is a rapid creation of the late sixth century, given extra impetus and resources by Amasis' urgent need to counter the threat posed by the Persian Empire. There is good reason to accept that the Samians under Polykrates developed the makings of a strong navy, based around a core of purpose-built, 'public' warships.

Phokaia

Thucydides' treatment of the Phokaians is similar to that of Polykrates. He says only that they defeated the Carthaginians while they were founding Massalia (1.13.6). Further information about the Phokaians as seafarers is to be found in Herodotus. He claims that they were the earliest of the Greeks to make long sea voyages, exploring the western Mediterranean in pentekonters, rather than in round sailing vessels (1.163). He elaborates upon their success in trade and the assistance they received from the king of Tartessos as they prepared to resist the advance of the Persians. His account of their adventures after the flight from Ionia to Corsica includes a brief description of their sea battle against the combined Carthaginian and Etruscan fleet at Alalia (1.164–7). According to Herodotus there were 60 ships on each side and the Phokaians lost 40 of their vessels and had the rams of the remaining 20 badly damaged. This battle can be dated *c.* 540, a few years after the Persians conquered Ionia, whereas the date for the founding of Massalia is *c.* 600.[40] While it would be tempting to try to match the two accounts by dating the foundation of Massalia to the 540s, or even to amend the text of Thucydides to say 'Alalia', there is no further evidence to justify this. Thucydides' Phokaian victory against the Carthaginians must be a separate, otherwise unknown, event. It seems reasonably likely that the Phokaians would have been able to obtain the resources to build warships as a result of their prosperous trading activities, although neither Herodotus nor Thucydides implies that they had a purpose-built navy.[41] By Thucydides' reckoning the Phokaians would qualify as a sea power because they had wealth, a favourable trading position, which gave them the incentive to develop their naval capabilities, and they had some kind of reputation as a result of their clashes with the Carthaginians and Etruscans. There are obvious similarities here with his appraisal of the Korinthians. For our purposes the most significant point which emerges from the literary evidence is that the Phokaians may well have *needed* to develop a navy, in order to carry on their struggle against the rival powers of Etruria and Carthage. That this rivalry was in some fashion still current in the early fifth century is indicated by the exploits of Dionysios of Phokaia in Sicily after the Battle of Lade (Herodotus 6.17).

Wallinga has recently proposed a connection between the Phokaians and the invention of the trireme. He believes that the most likely context in which the triple-banked warship was first created is the conflict between the Phokaians and their Carthaginian and Etruscan neighbours. Wallinga argues that it was the need to obtain an advantage in terms of ramming speed which prompted the Carthaginian shipwrights to add a third level of oars to their galleys, this being their response to the superior tactical skills of the Phokaians.[42] He cites a tradition preserved by the second-century AD Christian writer Clement of Alexandria, who says that the Sidonians were the first to build a *trikrotos naus* (three-banked warship), arguing that the word 'Sidonians' is to be understood as a generic term for Phoenicians.[43] This hypothesis implies that the Phokaians were a substantial naval power in the middle of the sixth century, but it rests upon a highly speculative interpretation of the evidence. It obtains a little further support from a statement in Thucydides' *Archaiologia* (1.14.2) to the effect that it was the Sicilian tyrants and the Kerkyraians who were the first to make use of large numbers of triremes, just prior to the death of Dareios I (522–486). This does not mean that the Carthaginians could not have used triremes earlier than these two powers, since Thucydides is concerned with Greek sea powers. Thucydides here indicates a western Mediterranean location for the early development of the highly specialized, trireme-based navy, but we lack any precise evidence on this matter. The process by which the trireme concept was transferred from one maritime community to another is similarly obscure.

Athens and Aigina
The weakness of the Greek *poleis* is, in Thucydides' view, further illustrated by the fact that, until just prior to Xerxes' invasion, even the navies of Athens and Aigina, which Herodotus (5.81–7; 6.87–94) describes as engaging in a substantial maritime conflict in the early 480s, were mainly composed of pentekonters, similar to the ships of the Trojan War (1.14.3). Herodotus may have felt that Aigina counted as some kind of thalassocracy, but only on a very local scale, and it is clear that Athens cannot be considered a strong naval power before the Themistoklean trireme-building programme of 483.[44] It may well be that the earliest Athenian navy, in terms of publicly owned ships, was the small core of twenty vessels purchased from the Korinthians,[45] whose late sixth-century naval resources are thus implied to be greater, although we have no figures for them earlier than the 40 triremes they contributed to the Greek fleet at Artemision in 480 (Herodotus 8.1). Herodotus' statement that Athens and Aigina had about 70 ships[46] each may explain why Thucydides felt it necessary to justify the exclusion of these *poleis* from his thalassocracy list. We must accept his claim that, unlike the Korinthians and Samians, they still did not have large fleets of purpose-built warships at this point.[47]

The navies of the early fifth century
The gradual nature of the development of substantial fleets of publicly owned warships among the Greek *poleis* can be traced through several instances mentioned by Herodotus. In about 524 the Elder Miltiades sailed off to set up a new regime in the Thracian Chersonese, taking many Athenians with him (6.38). It is difficult to see this as a state-controlled or state-sponsored enterprise, and it is likely that the ships used were multi-purpose pentekonters belonging to the individuals

285

and families involved (Haas 1985, 40). When the Younger Miltiades was sent to the Chersonese *c.* 516 by Hippias and Hipparchos, he travelled in a trireme. The nature of the mission suggests it was a public initiative, for which a new state-owned trireme might have been allocated, but there is a problem of interpretation for *poleis* governed by individuals (tyrants, kings, etc), as opposed to those governed by elected or appointed groups, be they oligarchic or democratic. In the case of the former, a distinction between public and private is difficult to maintain. Similarly, the trireme used by the exile Philippos of Kroton, son of the ruler Boutakides, to participate in Dorieus' colonising expedition in 510 (Herodotus 5.47), is described as 'private' by Herodotus – but were there any Krotonian 'public' vessels at this time? When Miltiades set out to return to Athens in 493 he had five triremes at his disposal (Herodotus 5.41). Were these (expensive) ships his own private flotilla, or did they represent the newly created naval resources of his semi-autonomous principality in the Chersonese, now likely to be brought under Persian control? The number of vessels is small, and it seems that Miltiades was trying to salvage the best resources he could before he was overwhelmed by Dareios' superior forces.

Another suggestive report in Herodotus concerns Thasos. This wealthy island *polis* was attacked by Histiaios of Miletos in 494, with a flotilla of eight triremes from Lesbos. After his withdrawal the Thasians decided to use their mining revenues to strengthen their walls and build some warships. Mardonios subsequently ordered them to transfer the ships to his naval base at Abdera (Herodotus 6.5, 28, 46).[48] For the Thasians it seems that building triremes was an appropriate step for a strong, prosperous *polis* to take, in conjunction with strengthening its land defences. The aspirations for political autonomy which the creation of a navy implies are confirmed by the Persian king's desire to retain control of all warships in his dominions, especially those belonging to potential rebels like Thasos.

There seems to be a pattern here of the wealthier Greek *poleis* taking relatively small steps in the creation of naval resources, gradually building or acquiring fleets of purpose-built warships. Their actions were influenced by both their local rivalries and, at least for the eastern Greeks, the presence of the far larger navy of the Persian king. Inspired, perhaps, by the Korinthians, and spurred on by the inconclusive results of their conflict with Aigina, the Athenians used profits from their newly available mineral resources in 483 to build the largest fleet of *polis*-owned warships yet seen. The extent of the transformation of naval power in the Greek world since the mid-sixth century is clearly illustrated by the situation in 480, when Kleinias' 'private' trireme at the Battle of Artemision was a highly exceptional vessel among the publicly-owned ships of the Athenians.[49]

Conclusion

The impression which we have formed from this consideration of the evidence for early Greek naval developments is that there were no Greek navies before the sixth century, and that the 'thalassocracies' of the earlier archaic period are largely the creations of later historical writers who are interpreting events of doubtful historicity, based upon dubious sources, and somewhat exaggerating their scale and significance, in order to make the history of the archaic period fit a particular intellectual scheme. While it would be desirable to test their accounts against the archaeological record this is not possible, except in a few isolated and inconclusive cases.

Nevertheless, it seems clear that the latter part of the sixth century witnessed the creation of small naval forces by several Greek *poleis* with ambitions to protect their independence from external threats and to project their political influence overseas. In many cases these archaic naval developments can be seen as a response to the power of non-Greek states – Carthage and Persia. From the situation in the middle of the sixth century, when there is no Greek *polis* which can be *definitely* described as having a navy, there was a rapid development of naval power in the Greek world, to the position described by Herodotus in 480, when there are large fleets owned by some *poleis* and it is only very small ones like Melos, Siphnos and Seriphos which do not have substantial naval forces, consisting in whole or in part of triremes (8.48). As with many other important themes in the history of the ancient Greeks, it is in the second half of the sixth century, when many Greek *poleis* are politically and economically stronger than they have ever been, and eager to establish their superiority over others, that the move towards thalassocracy begins.

Appendix
Eusebius thalassocracy list

An alternative thalassocracy list, clearly not dependent on the material in Thucydides or Herodotus, is provided by the Eusebian tradition mentioned above.[50] It seems to have been drawn up from the early books of Diodorus' *Library of History*, compiled in the first century BC, although parts of it may ultimately derive from two separate sources – the first-century BC *Register* of Kastor of Rhodes, and a Hadrianic work called *The Nine Muses*, written in imitation of Herodotus by one Kephalion.[51] This list consists of a succession of naval powers whose predominance begins with the demise of a predecessor and ends either as a result of their own defeat or through the rise of a stronger sea power. The Eusebian list, with its dates revised to their most credible form by Forrest,[52] can be summarized as follows: Phrygians 750–720; Cypriots 720–710; Phoenicians 710–668; Egyptians 668–625; Milesians 625–600; Karians (?Korinthians[53]) 600–585; Lesbians 585–575; Phokaians 575–540; Samians 540–516; Spartans 516–510; Naxians 510–500; Eretrians 500–490; Aiginetans 490–480. It should be noted that the early entries on this list are non-Greeks, and that the first Greek *polis* to make an appearance, Miletos, is one which does not appear in its own right in Thucydides' list, nor does it receive much attention from Herodotus. Although the Eusebian list does coincide with Herodotus and Thucydides in some respects, it does not provide further information of a kind which can be used either to check or to supplement their accounts. Nor are there any other extant accounts of early Greek history which match this list, even partially. Forrest's revision is heavily dependent upon fragments of later Greek historians and other writers.[54] Does the Eusebian list represent a credible alternative tradition to that found in Thucydides and Herodotus? Forrest speculates about a fifth-century original which lies behind both the Eusebian and Thucydidean lists, but although the idea of a succession of thalassocracies was, as we have seen, current at that time, the discrepancies between the two versions are considerable and, as Forrest (1969, 98) admits, the list is at times incredible. The Eusebian list has a similar purpose to Thucydides' *Archaiologia*, namely to give an account of naval developments up to the time of the Athenian Empire, but although it was probably created from a wide range of ancient historical literature it is more of an intellectual fantasy than a serious piece of historiography. It does not merit consideration on the same level as Thucydides and Herodotus.

Acknowledgements

I would like to thank the audience who listened to the first version of this paper in September 1995 for their comments, especially Paul Cartledge, John Davies, Kurt Raaflaub, Hans van Wees and Sitta von Reden. I am also very grateful to the library staff at the Institute of Classical Studies, Royal Holloway, University of London and St Mary's University College for their assistance. Debra Birch and Hans van Wees gave invaluable help during the completion of the written version.

Notes

[1] For an example of such a marriage of archaeological and literary evidence see Reddé 1986, on the Roman navy of the imperial period.

[2] There is a growing tendency in modern scholarship towards rejection of even the idea of such a union of written and material evidence. Archaeologists have become (justifiably) frustrated with the impossibility of 'marrying'their findings to the literary evidence, especially the Homeric poems. See, for example, the comments in the preface to Foxhall and Davies 1984 and also Morris 1986.

[3] Public ownership need not extend to *all* vessels involved in naval enterprises and may, of course, be temporary. For more recent examples of the gradual transition to 'state' navies, see Scammell 1981.

[4] Nougayrol et al. 1968, 87–9; Sandars 1985, 142.

[5] See Casson 1971, ch. 4. The development of the ram in the Eastern Mediterranean is difficult to trace. Morrison and Williams (1968, 7) consider it to be already present on some representations of ships dated to the Mycenaean period, but Casson favours 'the obscure period after 1000 BC' for its development. In any case, the ram is not the only attribute of a warship in ancient times. Naval warfare in the ancient world almost always involved missile exchanges and hand-to-hand fighting among marines, even in the fifth and fourth centuries, the heyday of the most sophisticated of ramming vessels, the trireme.

[6] See Casson 1971, Morrison and Williams 1968, Wallinga 1993, for illustrations and discussion. I have deliberately taken a conservative approach to the consensus on the development of purpose-built warships. The importance of the fighting platform is stressed by Thucydides, who describes ships without such a platform as 'pirate ships' (1.10.4).

[7] I take the Homeric poems to be generally representative of conditions in the late eighth and early seventh centuries.

[8] e.g. Hdt. 5.83 (Aigina); 6.89 (Corinth and Athens); 7.158 (Syracuse under Gelon); 7.185; 8.43–8 (the Greek *poleis* opposing Xerxes). See below on the emergence of 'public' navies in individual *poleis*. Contrast Sappho's poetic fleet (F16 West), the status of which is not specified.

[9] e.g. the private trireme of Kleinias, the son of Alkibiades, who was the most distinguished of the Greeks at the Battle of Artemision (Hdt. 8.17).

[10] See de Souza 1995, and, on the Homeric warrior band, Van Wees 1992.

[11] The Parian campaign of the Younger Miltiades in 489 is a good example of the overlap between private and public, predatory and political (Hdt. 6.132–36). On the 'commercial' politics of imperialism, see Von Reden 1995.

[12] The main sources are Hdt. 7.144; Plut. *Them.* 4; Thuc. 1.93. On the development of naval installations at Peiraieus see Garland 1987, 14–28, 96–8, 203.

[13] See further the remarks in Gabrielsen 1994, 1–39.

[14] Blackman 1982, 194. See Lehmann-Hartleben 1923, 65–74, for full references. Thuc. 7.38 describes a stockade-type barrier erected in front of their beached or anchored ships by the Athenians at Syracuse in 413 as a *limen*

kleistos, illustrating the flexible application of the term.

[15] e.g. Strabo 14.1.37, describing the harbour of Smyrna as a *limen kleistos*.

[16] Occasionally the existence of arrangements for a boom or chain is revealed by archaeological investigations, as in the case of Halieis in the Argolid: Jameson 1973.

[17] See Lehmann-Hartleben 1923, 65–74. The evidence is very sketchy in all cases.

[18] The best known examples of such shipsheds are those of the Peiraieus, on which see Blackman 1968.

[19] Diodorus Siculus 22.76; Isokrates 7.66 says that the shipsheds cost 1,000 talents to build.

[20] Arenson 1990, 59–64, Blackman 1982, 92–3, and Harden 1962. For the existence of a substantial quay at Tyre as early as the eighth century, see Bunnens 1983, 7–11.

[21] The latter installations may be the same as the *holkoi* of the Ionian and Karian 'bronze men' who helped Psammetichos (664–610) gain the throne, although Herodotus' description of them as 'men sailing out to obtain booty' (2.154) suggests that they would not have used warships of the kind Herodotus envisaged, namely triremes.

[22] Such an infrastructure need not have been on the same scale as that found in classical Athens. This is indicated by Herodotus in his account of Aristagoras of Miletos' reply to the Naxian exiles in 500, where he implies that the naval capacities of Miletos are insufficient to undertake a campaign against Naxos, and that both are greatly inferior to the Persian navy (Hdt. 5.30).

[23] Kleiner 1968, ch. 5; Lehmann-Hartleben 1923, ch. 3.

[24] 1.22. This claim to methodological superiority rests largely on the fact that he was able to *check* his sources of information, which were mainly eyewitness reports or accounts based upon the reports of eyewitnesses. In trying to discover what took place more than a few generations back in time, however, there could be no such cross-checking because the original witnesses, and those who first heard their accounts, were dead.

[25] Thucydides' uncertainty about the evidence for Greek history in the distant past is indicated very early in the *Archaiologia* with the phrase *dokei de moi*: 'I think' or 'it seems to me' (1.3.2).

[26] See below, pp. 282–3. On the later history of the idea of sea power in Greek political thought see Momigliano 1944.

[27] Thucydides' reluctance to give a specific date for the Trojan War may be related to his sceptical attitude to the evidence. It is likely that he envisaged a relatively 'high' date, perhaps *c.* 1250; see Hornblower 1991, 39.

[28] The limits of modern speculation on the Minoan thalassocracy are explored in Starr 1955, Buck 1962, Hägg and Marinatos 1984.

[29] He still refers to 'old poets' (1.13.5) as evidence for the origin of Korinthian power. It should be noted that Thucydides does not make systematic use of what we would call 'archaeological' evidence, although his comments about the relative size and political power of cities in Homeric times and in his own day (1.10.1–3) are based upon the study of material remains.

[30] For discussion of these possibilities see Hornblower 1991, 42–3; Meijer 1988.

[31] Thucydides says that Ameinokles went to Samos about 300 years before the end of the Peloponnesian War (404), and that the sea battle between Korinth and Kerkyra took place about forty years later.

[32] Most recently Wallinga 1993, esp. 23. The earliest mention of a trireme in Greek literature is in a fragmentary poem by Hipponax (F28 West), whose work is dated *c*. 540–520. No visual depiction of a trireme survives which can be dated earlier than the fourth century.

[33] e.g. Forrest 1969, 106; Hornblower 1991, 44–5.

[34] It is worth considering here what level of conflict might actually be thought to constitute a sea battle in the archaic period. While Thucydides clearly judged such events by the standards of his own times, and therefore was happy to conclude that all earlier Greek naval activities had been on a lesser scale than those of the Persian and Peloponnesian Wars, we cannot be certain that the historical traditions which informed him about Korinth and Kerkyra would have been as exacting. Representations of maritime conflict on archaic Greek vase paintings are rare, and never show more than two vessels at a time; would a gathering of two or more be enough for a 'battle'?

[35] Wallinga 1987; 1993, ch. 5. Aristagoras of Miletos is made by Herodotus to say (in 500) that the king has many ships under his control along the coast of Asia Minor, and he asks for 100 ships from the satrap Artaphrenes for the expedition against Naxos, but is given 200 (5.31). These ships are clearly part of the Ionian fleet which Herodotus enumerates at Lade.

[36] Hdt. 1.5; the story of Polykrates' ring (3.40–3), used by Herodotus to explain the end of Amasis' alliance with Polykrates, is also an excellent illustration of the inevitability of a man's fate.

[37] What follows is mainly based upon Shipley 1987, Wallinga 1993, and parts of Lloyd 1988.

[38] Pseudo-Skylax 98; see also Lehmann–Hartleben 1923, 58, 70.

[39] I am strongly persuaded by Wallinga's suggestion that Polykrates' triremes were actually supplied to him by Amasis, and that their alliance continued up until the Egyptians' defeat at the hands of Kambyses: Wallinga 1987; 1993, ch. 4. It is conceivable that these 'Samians' were in fact from other Ionian cities or islands which were subject to Polykrates, hence the doubts about their loyalty.

[40] This date is based on a fragment of the historian Timaios, *FGH* 566 F71.

[41] On Phokaian trade in the Western Mediterranean see Cunliffe 1988, ch. 1.

[42] The man who attempted to train the Ionians in naval tactics in the late 490s was Dionysios of *Phokaia* (Hdt. 6.11–12).

[43] Clement of Alexandria, *Stromateis* 1.16.76; Wallinga 1993, 111–14. Wallinga also believes that the trireme was adopted by the Persians, the Egyptians and, eventually, the Greeks as much for its greater transport capacity as for its speed. All ancient naval campaigns were essentially amphibious operations.

[44] The fighting which is associated with Athenian settlements on Salamis and at Sigeion in the first half of the sixth century need not have involved a public fleet, since the forces could easily have been transported in

pentekonters, or similar vessels belonging to families or individuals, rather than to the *polis* itself. See Haas 1985, 42–43.

[45] Herodotus 6.89; he uses the word *naus* for these ships, which could mean anything from triakonters to triremes. The balance of probability is that they were triremes. The decision of the Korinthians to sell the twenty ships to Athens for five drachmas each because they had a law preventing them being given away is intriguing (Hdt. 6.89). Was the law one which related to all public property? Or was it specific to warships? One possible interpretation is that it was intended to prevent the decommissioning of public vessels without provision for their replacement. In any case it seems that the law implies a public naval policy of some kind at Korinth, which would fit with Thucydides' views on Korinthian primacy in naval organization. For further speculation see Wallinga 1993, 23–31.

[46] Again it must be inferred that these were mostly not triremes; see Haas 1985, 44–6.

[47] Wallinga believes that Athens, and other Greek *poleis*, possessed a naval finance infrastructure based around the *naukrariai* ([Aristotle], *Ath.Pol.* 8.3), which he envisages as similar to the medieval English Cinque Ports: Wallinga 1993, 17–18. The relevance of this institution to naval matters is a matter of some dispute. There is, in my opinion, no good evidence to support the association of the *naukrariai* with warships in the archaic period. See further Gabrielsen 1994, 19–24; contra Figueira 1986, 270–6.

[48] Herodotus does not specifically call them triremes but it seems most likely that they were.

[49] Hdt. 8.17. On the lack of clear evidence for private triremes after 480, see Gabrielsen 1994, 202, 266. The institution of the trierarchy must date either to 483, or, as Gabrielsen argues, to the acquisition of a smaller public fleet based around the Korinthian ships in 488/7: Gabrielsen 1994, 31–9, with Figueira 1986 for the date.

[50] The only version of the thalassocracy list in Eusebius' *Chronika* which survives appears to be an Armenian text of the first part, the *Chronographia*, giving the latter part of the sequence from Samos to Aigina and adding Alexander. Other versions deriving from the second part, the *Canons*, can be found in several later chronographic works which are based upon Eusebius. For full references to the texts and (German) translations see Miller 1971.

[51] The different versions and their possible origins are discussed at length in Miller 1971, 52–85.

[52] This summary is based on the table in Forrest 1969, 105. I have omitted the first four entries (Lydians, Pelasgians, Thracians and Rhodians) whose putative dates, as recorded by the Eusebian tradition, are all before the ninth century BC and whose claims to thalassocracy are not taken seriously by Forrest.

[53] Forrest 1969, 98–9, suggests that the Korinthians are better candidates than the Karians at this point, largely because of the correspondence in the original dates (730–669) with Thucydides (1.14.3–4) and the nearness in time to the Kypselid era of his own revised version. Such an emendation does not have any support in the manuscript traditions.

[54] e.g. Forrest's re-dating of the Milesian thalassocracy from its original mid-eighth-century position to the late seventh century is established on the strength of Strabo's version of the foundation of Naukratis by Milesians, following their naval victory over the Egyptians at the time of Psammetichos (Str. 17.1.18). This story is incompatible with Herodotus' account, which ascribes the foundation of Naukratis to Amasis, in the mid-sixth century (Hdt. 2.178). The earliest Greek finds suggest a mid-seventh-century date for the city's foundation: Boardman 1980.

11

CARGOES OF THE HEART'S DESIRE
The character of trade in the archaic Mediterranean world

Lin Foxhall

This paper is the first step in an attempt to reinterpret 'trade' in early Greece. It is formulated as a theoretical sketch utilising only limited examples of supporting data: much more information could be assembled to back the arguments outlined here. I wish to try out a new way of looking at the phenomenon of expanding, cross-cultural, pan-Mediterranean contact and exchange which characterizes the late ninth through early fifth centuries BC, especially the later part of this time span for which evidence is more abundant. It would be wrong to imply that the character of contact and exchange was uniform over the period and of course it continues beyond this latter date (though probably its character changes), and perhaps starts earlier. Like many others I have alighted on this period as critical for shaping the character of 'the Mediterranean world' for many generations to come.

Many different theoretical approaches have been brought to bear on trade, exchange, and cross-cultural contact. Substantivist perspectives (Polanyi 1968), emphasising how 'the economy' is not separable from other aspects of life in the ancient world (in sharp contrast to the modern West), underpin much of the foundation provided by the work of Finley (1985) and Sahlins (1972). Such views have informed the work of succeeding generations in various ways (see, e.g., Garnsey et al. 1983). In the past few years much emphasis has been placed on world systems theories,[1] in conjunction with Greek-barbarian relations (Wells 1980, Champion and Megaw 1985, Pare 1997) and post-colonial perspectives (Webster and Cooper 1996; Miller, Rowlands, and Tilley 1989). Most recently Osborne has taken up a revisionist position, claiming that it is not unrealistic to view the archaic Greek world as 'a world of interdependent markets' (Osborne 1996b, 31). In contrast I shall begin from the burgeoning literature on theories of consumption and material cultural studies.[2] This is not to say that this

body of theory provides 'the' answer which will 'explain' the phenomenon. Obviously the social, economic and political processes of first
millennium BC Mediterranean cultural interchange are complex and
any kind of over-arching, universalising explanation (e.g. the simplistic way in which world systems models or the notion of 'reciprocity'
have sometimes been applied) must ultimately be unsatisfactory.
Rather I hope to add another new tool for understanding how that
world worked, in conjunction with others which have proved useful.
Moreover, this material offers an interesting case study for critiquing
the ways in which consumption has often been studied, and the assumptions made about the social and economic settings in which it
operates.

The study of consumption has been developed from the perspective
of several different disciplines, notably sociology/social theory, economics, geography, psychology, anthropology, and history. This is not
the place for a history of the subject,[3] but since the later 1980s interest
in the field has largely been inspired by post-modernist thinking (e.g.
Harvey 1989). Consumption, especially 'mass consumption', is often
viewed as symptomatic of modernity (i.e. the interplay between the
ephemeral and rapidly changing aspects of society and deeper, more
permanent social structures and values), and a product of the industrial revolution, or at least as part of a trajectory of modernity beginning in early modern Europe and culminating in the Industrial Revolution (Gibb 1996, Brewer and Porter 1993, also Glennie 1995). Frequently it is tied to a developing notion of 'fashion'. These approaches,
though interesting, seem to me too narrow, limiting the potential
which exploring consumption might offer for a wider range of societies, and limiting the impact which notions of consumption might have
on them. Even those scholars who have realised that this body of
theory might have implications for societies of the distant past have
hesitated to apply it to periods earlier than the Industrial Revolution
(e.g. Fine and Leopold 1993). Miller (1987), with a background in
archaeology and anthropology, has been sensitive to the idea that
consumption need not be a mode of behaviour limited to emerging
industrial societies. However, he has tied his notion of consumption
and the significance of materiality largely to the 'artefact', defined in
his terms not only as concrete, but also as substantially permanent and
as 'manufactured' – a reified 'thing' rather than a 'commodity' or any
other aspect of the material world which might be consumed.[4] I hope
to demonstrate that the praxis of consumption as an element of social
and economic interaction which both constitutes and transforms culture

need not be limited to 'modern' societies and economies, nor restricted to 'artefacts' in any narrow sense.

Consumption and the study of antiquity

In the context and cultural settings of ancient societies, consumption and its significance were undoubtedly different than in more recent settings. However, the advantage of using the notion of consumption as a starting point is that it then may be possible to avoid using some of the categories and terminology of modern, 'classical', economics to describe and explain ancient economic institutions. It is very difficult, even for those of us who accept that ancient economies were radically different from the ways modern ones are usually described, to find positive terms of analysis: too frequently we accept the use of terms like 'market', 'price', 'credit', 'demand' although we may deem them inappropriate, or look for their absence, in the ancient world.

Fine and Leopold (1993, 10) have observed that 'economic history has tended to be a supply side subject'. That goes equally for the economic history of antiquity which has focused largely on production and the point of origin of commodities – Osborne's recent paper (1996b) is typical in this regard. The snag here is that starting with production, however 'obvious' a focus it may be for dealing with the archaeological record in particular, almost automatically casts the rest of the debate in the terminology of supply and demand intersecting to form a 'price' in a 'market'. It is implicit in the terminology itself that such a 'market' takes its shape on the demand side as the result of informed choice of a kind that almost certainly did not exist (because it was not feasible) in most ancient economies (and in plenty of more recent ones). Moreover, it has long been plain that many social and cultural forces distorted the 'pure' operation of supply and demand in ancient economies (as they do in modern ones): 'price' was not often merely a balance of the two, and it may not be appropriate to assume that the precise measure of that balance was always an important objective in non-monetary economies.

With consumption, however, the starting point is not demand, but desire, on which the textual evidence is especially explicit. Desire and the goods which foster it are intimately and dynamically related, each changing in response to the other as part of the dynamics of culture. Nonetheless, desire is limited to goods (services, rituals, or whatever) which have come within a person's reach: you cannot desire what you have not experienced directly, or indirectly by seeing it in the hands of another or hearing others speak (or indeed sing) of it.

It would be easy at this point to slip into explanations of desire for things which reduce it to 'status', 'conspicuous display', and so forth. While it would be wrong to dismiss the significance of such motivations, the desire for things is more complex.[5] Frequently things become so embedded in the workings of social life that without them social life would not work 'properly'. The pins which fastened a *peplos* were as essential to constituting 'appropriateness' (or its absence) in the social lives of Greek women as the grey suit and tie are for modern professional men. Desirable things from far away may become so entwined with the specialness of special occasions that they become part of their constitution and without them the event is not deemed to be 'right'. The significance of dates and sultanas in traditional English Christmas foods, or of perfume or highly-esteemed imported wine in the context of a symposium both offer examples of this phenomenon.

Consumption therefore implants the element of self- or group-definition into the notion of demand. Material things and their consumption (e.g. dress, food preferences, etc.) are important elements of personal and communal identities in many times and places. During the first half of the first millennium BC such identities, along with the social and political orders they constituted, were being questioned and redefined in many different ways across the Mediterranean world. The discourse of eliteness, notably the question of who might claim to have a share in the eliteness of political activity, is particularly problematised in the textual sources (for example the concern in Greek poetry from Theognis to Pindar about the role of wealth in claims to elite status, cf. Kurke 1991). Simultaneously, the dynamics of material wealth (especially imported objects) and the uses to which it is put are manifest in the archaeological record.

The character of trade
The study of archaic Mediterranean trade is ultimately founded on a huge number of painstaking regional and local studies. Out of these a range of empirical and theoretical overviews has been gradually built up, and various overarching theoretical models have been proposed. Given the wide range of very different societies in regular contact with each other during the period and the complexity of their relationships, any generalisations are likely to be reductionist, simplistic and misleading. Though I have tried to take this diversity into account, a work of this small scale exploring the interface between the local and the 'global' (in this case, the Mediterranean littoral and its hinterlands) is bound to over-simplify.

The best evidence of Greek, Cypriot and Phoenician/N. Syrian trading activity is archaeological. We have abundant material remains of both Greek and Phoenician overseas settlements, and the extent to which imported items penetrated the hinterlands where these settlements arose has been a major focus of scholarly interest. Similarly there is much evidence of the import of foreign items into Greek and Phoenician 'homelands'. One of the problems, of course, is that the largest preserved component of this activity consists of pottery, and this has led to fierce debates on the overall quantity and significance of pottery, notably finewares, in relation to other trade items. This is not an argument in which I wish to become embroiled, though for the record I suspect that Gill and Vickers are largely right that fineware pottery was virtually never the major component of trade and that generally it accompanied other goods which were qualitatively and quantitatively considered to be more important.[6]

Many guesses have been made, some better than others, about what the main commodities of trade were. The contents of shipwrecks have often been adduced to indicate their diversity; nonetheless the full range of items of trade and any realistic hope of large-scale quantification of trade is beyond our reach. The main suggestions are well known and many are fairly well accepted: non-precious metals and ores, timber, oil and perfumed oil, wine, textiles, hides and slaves. The evidence of shipwrecks (Bass 1967, 163; 1986) and transport containers (Grace 1961, Johnston and Jones 1978, Whitbread 1995) have regularly turned up other foodstuffs as well: olives, honey, pistachios, almonds, fish sauce and pickled fish have all been attested. The degree to which grain was imported by Greek cities (especially Athens) in the archaic period has also been hotly debated over the years (Garnsey 1988, 105–12; Arafat and Morgan 1994, 128–9; Tsetskhladze 1994, 124). And many of the small 'manufactured' goods classed as trade items are also regularly categorised as 'luxuries' – notably precious metals and outstanding exotica (e.g. ostrich eggs, ivory, tridacna shell), but sometimes less obviously 'luxurious' items as well, such as Greek fineware pottery.

Most studies of trade across the archaic Mediterranean world emerge from the perspective of production: this is hardly surprising since so many of the material remains of trade are or represent 'manufactured' goods, or at least processed products. This has sometimes led to a focus on 'luxury' items as the backbone of trade. I think this is a dangerous term – surely what makes a 'luxury' must depend on who is consuming it and where it originated in relation to the consumer (see Berry 1994, 32, 40–1). So, for example, fineware Greek pottery or olive oil might have been a 'luxury' in the Heuneberg, though they probably were not for a wealthy Etruscan (but I wonder how they would have been viewed by a less rich Etruscan).

Frequently, too, trade is postulated as established on the basis of 'gift-giving' relationships in a rather simplistic way. There is certainly convincing evidence for such relationships lying behind Greek and Phoenician mercantile activity in parts of the Black Sea, Iberia and W. Europe, and even in not-so-far-flung locations such as Italy and Sicily relationships between traders and colonisers on the one hand and local community leaders on the other may well have been sealed and maintained via regular gift exchange.[7] However the now-standard use of the concept of 'reciprocity' (that is long-term relationships established on the basis of the exchange of gifts, in which their exact monetary value is irrelevant, and at any particular moment in the relationship there is no exact equivalence in the value of gifts exchanged), seems to me quite inadequate as an over-arching explanation for the full volume of Greek and Phoenician trade. Not only does it unjustly primitivise all of the societies with which we are dealing, but as an explanatory model it also fails to deal with either the complexity or the volume of the phenomenon. For settlements such as those of the Phoenicians on Cyprus or the Greeks in Egypt political and economic relationships between locals and foreigners can hardly be reduced to a crude notion of 'reciprocity'.

Guesses about the impetus for trade have been even less well founded. Generally it has simply been assumed by most writers that 'need' in some kind of absolute sense is the fundamental reason for trade, especially for metals, other bulk commodities and foodstuffs, even where scholars are specifically arguing that there is no evidence for imports because there is no demonstrable shortage or need.[8] This basic assumption is one I wish to question in the arguments which follow.

Consuming trade
The bulk of the commodities for which we in fact have the most substantial evidence as traded items are foodstuffs. Given the pottery-based nature of the evidence there is somewhat more certainty about the movement of food, even if we do not always know what kind or how much, than of metals, though the latter might have formed a more 'important' component of trade overall. That this is so even in the seventh and sixth century is striking and demands explanation. Let us start then with the question of why people wanted the things

they were importing and consuming from overseas, then move on to consider, first, the evidence for imports into and around Greece, and second, exports into the eastern Mediterranean.

As soon as we look closely, 'need', 'shortage' and similar explanations fall apart. There are too many instances of the well-established import of goods of which there is no obvious long-term need, lack or shortage. For example, why would the inhabitants of the northern Levant wish to import Corinthian and other aryballoi (presumably full of perfumed oil, Ploug 1973, 18–22) when at roughly the same time or only a little earlier there is good evidence for the import of Cypriot and North Syrian perfume containers to Rhodes and Kos, followed by the manufacture of local imitations of these imported wares (Coldstream 1982, 268–9), in addition to the considerable evidence for the Phoenician export of perfume (Aubet 1993, 246; Culican 1970; 1975)? Why would Cypriots living near the sea have needed to import pickled fish from the Nile in Egypt (Griksson 1995, 200)? Why did North Syrian and Phoenician towns import Greek oil or wine,[9] when the olive and vine are indigenous local crops and there is evidence also for the large-scale Phoenician export of such products (Aubet 1993, 244–5, 290)? More peculiarly, why were wine cups and serving vessels (Ploug 1973, 18–22, 27–38; Waldbaum 1994, 59–61) imported into the Levant when there were well-established indigenous Levantine customs attached to consumption of wine (Isaiah 5; 28; Jeremiah 48.11–12)? For that matter why did Greek cities apparently trade commodities like wine and oil with each other on a regular basis (Grace 1961; Whitbread 1995)? One can document an uncomfortable number of examples of what appears to be trade in coals to Newcastle all over the Mediterranean world, which cannot be explained simply by short-term food crises. Even the widely-held belief that the olive and the vine were not widely cultivated in Italy before the sixth century BC depends primarily on the assumption that Italian peoples would not have bothered to import wine and oil in Greek transport amphorae if they had had their own supplies (Vallet 1962). In fact, the archaeobotanical evidence does not uphold the assertion that these crops only came into cultivation so late (Barker 1988).

The trade in grain in the archaic period provides a particularly interesting case. Garnsey (1988) has persuasively argued that even Athens, the grain-importing city par excellence from the fifth and fouth centuries, had no absolute need, in subsistence terms, to import grain in the seventh or sixth century, and this view has been fairly widely accepted (Gill 1994, 102; Arafat and Morgan 1994, 129;

Tsetskhladze 1994, 124); certainly I accept it. However, there is still some suggestion that trade in grain existed earlier which had little to do with subsistence needs. The 'Solonian' legislation restricting agricultural exports to olive oil (whether it is really Solonian or not does not matter), need not mean that there was a permanent surplus of oil,[10] but it does suggest that other foodstuffs, not necessarily just grain though perhaps including it, might regularly have been the objects of trade. In this regard it is interesting, and possibly significant, that virtually the only instances in which the contents of SOS amphorae (which are the earliest Greek transport amphorae manufactured and exported in quantity and have been frequently assumed to be oil containers, Vallet 1962; Johnston and Jones 1978, 134, 140) are hinted at, indicate that they regularly contained wine: Dionysos on the François vase is holding one (Johnston and Jones 1978, 133 and n. 48; Minto 1960, pl. 11). Obviously, they are capable of carrying many products other than oil.

More to the point, it is difficult, given the later involvement and significance of Thrace, the Hellespont and Black Sea regions, as well as Egypt, in grain trade, to explain this entirely as a later development. Herodotos (7.147) mentions grain ships at the Hellespont in the early fifth century BC – are we to assume they are the first? Nor can the import of grain be laid entirely at the door of Athens and our heavily Athenocentric sources. Other Greek cities are documented as attempting to regulate grain exports and imports or being involved in grain trade comparatively early.[11] More significantly, the eighth/seventh century writer of Isaiah (23.2–3) speaks of the merchants of Sidon:

> whose goods travel over the sea, the grain of the Nile, the harvest of the river, formed your revenues, traded between nations.

And at Isaiah 55.1–2 grain is classed with other purchased 'semi-luxury' foods in an invocation of 'the good life':

> though you have no money, come, buy grain and eat;
> come, buy wine and milk,
> not for money, not for a price.
> Why spend your money for what is not food,
> your earnings on what fails to satisfy?
> Listen to me and you will fare well,
> you will enjoy the fat of the land.

Certainly for Athens, the critical feature of imported grain is that it is wheat, not barley which is imported. From Egypt it is likely that exported grain consisted of durum (macaroni) type wheats – considered highly desirable for bread. We are used to thinking of cereals as staples, but 'high-quality' wheat, imported to a barley-growing region, is a delicacy on a par with good quality wine, perfumed oil, or pickled fish.

Ancient peoples in the Mediterranean and the Near East were demonstrably connoisseurs of specialness in foodstuffs from overseas. Foreign produce, from particular places, was deemed to have regionally-specific, desirable qualities not attributed to the local and home-grown. Elites could of course afford to develop their tastes to a fine art, and there is much documentation of all periods, starting with archaic poetry, which suggests that they did. Archilochos, according to Athenaios (1.30), compares the wine of Naxos with nectar; the passage then goes on to quote the famous fragment (Archilochos 2 West), referring to Ismaric wine:[12]

> There's kneaded barley bread for me in my spear, there's Ismaric wine in my spear, and I drink leaning on my spear.

Even Hesiod drinks wine from Byblos at his summer holiday barbecue (*Works and Days* 589), though Boeotia is full of vines. Similarly, the sixth/seventh century Sicilian poet Stesichoros (fr. 187 Page) mentions 'Kydonian apples' (= quinces).[13] 'Garlands of Naukratis' appear in the fragments of Anakreon (fr. 434 Page), along with 'sea-purple dye' (fr. 447) and 'Lydian style' (i.e. luxurious, fr. 481), while the game of *kottabos* is described as Sicilian (fr. 415). 'Sympotic' and celebratory lyric poetry is full of references to perfume, spices, fine foods and wines and rich clothing.[14] Sappho (frs. 2.4 L-P and 44.30 L-P) first mentions frankincense (*libanos*), myrrh and cassia (cinnamon):

> hither to me from Crete, on this holy ship, where your lovely grove of apples is, and altars are burning with frankincense (2.1–4).

Far-away places which offer desirable goods are also often vaunted in Greek poetry. One fragment of Stesichoros (fr. 272 Page) mentions a 'trading station' (ἐμπορικὸς οἶκος). Pindar's poetry from the first half of the fifth century BC regularly invokes images of exotic locations (e.g. *Nemean* 4, see also Kurke 1991, 21–5). Entwined with the complex metaphorical use of these images, those of traded commodities and delicacies appear regularly. In *Nemean* 6.32–3 a family is described as bearing 'a freight of fame' (ναυστολέοντες ἐπικώμια)[15] while in *Nemean* 8.21 stories (λόγοι) are described as a 'delicacy' (ὄψον), and in *Pythian* 2.67–8 songs sail swiftly like Phoenician cargo (κατὰ Ψοίνισσαν ἐμπολάν).

On the other hand, it is around this time, probably in the later seventh or early sixth century that the Madonna lily[16] is first exported to Egypt, probably by Greeks, where it was cultivated in the Delta (with some difficulty) as a perfume ingredient. Six Late Period Egyptian paintings document the processes of tending and processing the plants (Leahy 1988).[17]

In the Song of Solomon[18] the lovers shower the beloved with and compare her/him to foreign produce and distant places in terms which closely echo Sappho:

> your dress has the scent of Lebanon; your two cheeks are an orchard of pomegranates, an orchard full of choice fruits; spikenard and saffron, aromatic cane and cinnamon, with every frankincense tree, myrrh and aloes, with all the most exquisite spices.
>
> (Song of Solomon 4.11–14, tr. Revised English Bible)

> his cheeks are like beds of spices, terraces full of perfumes, ...his aspect is like Lebanon, noble as cedars (5.13, 15).

> How beautiful are your sandalled feet, O prince's daughter!
> The curves of your thighs are like ornaments devised by a skilled craftsman.
> Your navel is a rounded goblet that will never lack spiced wine.
> Your belly is a heap of wheat encircled by lilies...
> Your neck is like a tower of ivory (7.1–4).

Attaching special qualities to particular wines is readily comprehensible in the modern world. However in antiquity, regionally specific desirable qualities are also regularly attributed to many other foodstuffs. Oil is the most obvious, but figs, fruit, nuts, cheeses, table olives, fish sauces, other condiments and spices and, yes, wheat, are also treated in a similar way.

Similarly with clothing: it has long been established that foreign textiles, in conjunction with items of clothing and new styles of dress, are entering Greece in this period. Their adoption is well documented in sculpture and vase painting, as well as in literature: Alkman's girls know about Lydian headgear (Alkman 1.67–8 Page). Textiles were exported by Greek cities as well. In the sixth-century compilation of Ezekiel 27,[19] purple, blue and red 'canvas' and saddle-cloths are said to come from Cyprus (Alishah = Alashiya) and the Greek islands/Ionia (Javan), along with bronze utensils, slaves, iron, cassia(!) and ivory and ebony from Rhodes(!) (the latter presumably originated in Egypt).

Most interestingly, the available evidence suggests that ornate, and perhaps in many cases imported, textiles became essential parts of ritual activity in this period. In Sparta we have not only the testimony of Alkman (cited above) that young girls wore specially rich and elaborate clothing for ritual performances, but also the evidence of the finds from Artemis Orthia and other Spartan sanctuaries. Model textiles were dedicated as votives in the sanctuary (Foxhall and Stears 1998), perhaps as a replacement for or supplement to the dedications of 'real' textiles.[20] Moreover, enormous care was taken to depict the patterns on the model textiles and the dresses of the female figurines. Given their small size (most are under 5 cm high) the effort made to show these patterns (especially in comparison with, e.g., facial features which are sketchy) seems disproportionate. It suggests that the patterns were considered important, and that the very ornateness of textiles and dresses was integral to the rituals performed and the significance of votive donations.

Food is close to the heart, and something about which we might expect people to be quite conservative. Similarly dress is frequently at the heart of constructed identities. Why foreign food and clothing, then, so often appear especially desirable is an interesting question. The most obvious answer was that their consumption enhanced the status of the consumer, but this is probably too simple in its raw form. Why was the quality of foreignness apparently as important as the quality of rarity (especially since some of these products were not all that rare)? Some of these foods indeed have multiple uses: perfumed oil was consumed internally as well as externally (used as food and as perfume and body treatment). Indeed, many of the items imported on a fairly large scale seem to be used in intimate contact with the body: including textiles, some craft items (jewellery, small bronzes, some ivory items, cosmetics) as well as the perfumes and foodstuffs already mentioned.

Nor were most of these products unattainable luxuries for all but a few. The significant thing is that such products would have been accessible to a considerable portion of the socioeconomic spectrum in many parts of the Mediterranean world, even though poorer people undoubtedly consumed less 'Biblian' wine or Samian oil than rich people. These are not products used solely by the rich to demarcate their eliteness, which were out of reach for everyone else. Rather, with 'good quality' imported wine, olive oil, wheat, fish sauce or whatever, the less-well-off consumed such products occasionally (frequently, one might guess, on special occasions, with entertainment being a factor), while for the rich such commodities might have been what was expected every day. Religious celebrations and rituals, themselves a major constituting factor in group and community identities in Greece in this period (Murray 1983; Schmitt-Pantel 1990, 1992; cf. Bowie 1986), might have played a major part as settings for the consumption and distribution of these commodities. Hence demand for them must have been elastic – should greater quantities be imported, people probably just consumed more – 'gluts on the market' in any modern sense would probably not generally have occurred with such products. From the merchant's point of view, such commodities would have been the most secure kind of cargo. These goods would always have been in demand (though fashions and tastes might have changed over time), and there was a large potential pool of consumers for such products (perhaps in comparison with the potential consumers of gold, precious stones, tridacna shells or ostrich eggs!). In a period when overall wealth was increasing in many parts of the Mediterranean world, this trend was probably enhanced.

If anything, the consumption of such commodities would seem to me to be something akin to the modern concept of 'fashion', that is the consumption of products through which the individual links him- or herself to larger, global sets of values and ideologies. Such consumption habits allow those less well off to situate themselves relative to their social and economic superiors: though they cannot be the same, they can aspire by partaking of the same set of values via the same commodities. Moreover, the elite can maintain their eliteness by the scale and the manner in which they consume such products. In other words, they constitute an agreed set of symbols which different groups within a society construct and use with different meanings, not necessarily even aware of some or all of the meanings attributed by others. Elites can feel themselves distinct, while the poorer can feel that they can step one rung up the ladder, at least for a moment.[21] The dynamics of consumption patterns in the first half of the first millennium BC might best be understood as the economic expression of shifting social and political boundaries, simultaneously constituted by and manifesting the complex processes of these transformations, and facilitating trajectories which seem to occur in a number of different, but interconnected, societies over the course of this period.

Rethinking consumption

In summary, within the Mediterranean world at this time, especially (though not exclusively) during the seventh and sixth centuries BC, a number of commodities, apparently important in bulk trade, share some interesting features:

    1) They were both imported and exported simultaneously.

    2) They consisted in large part of agricultural products, usually processed, which were not expensive and unattainable 'luxuries', though they may have been 'delicacies' – I have called them 'semi-

luxuries' because I can't think of a better term.[22] Textiles can be included in this category. Small, though I think not large, items of metal and other small-scale craft products (even fineware pottery in some cases) were probably treated in a similar manner.

3) Most of these commodities were literally consumed, while others, like textiles, had comparatively short life spans. Though concrete, they were not in any sense permanent artefacts. Moreover, many were intimately associated with the adornment and nourishment of the body: food, perfumed oil, small metal items, jewellery, cosmetics, and textiles all served these roles.

4) Hence they were commodities which wealthy people consumed in large quantities regularly though they were still within reach of less wealthy folk who consumed them in smaller quantities occasionally. Consumption of such commodities for all social groups may frequently have taken place in the settings of entertainment and ritual. Indeed, as suggested by the poems of Alkman in juxtaposition with the care taken to depict the elaborate decoration and patterns on the representations of textiles from Artemis Orthia, it is likely that in many instances the very act of consuming such imported 'semi-luxury' goods had become incorporated into ritual (whether social or religious) as part of the 'right way' to perform it.

5) Demand for them was elastic – if more were available, more would be consumed precisely because of the multiple significances attached to the consumption of these products and the circumstances in which they were most often consumed.

In terms of post-industrial theories of consumption, these observations on the world of the archaic Mediterranean are important. Many of the traits attributed to modern notions of fashion and post-industrial consumption clearly can be found within the social and political relations of a world which is not only pre-capitalist but indeed pre-market in any modern sense, and pre-monetary. It is, however, a world in which social and political relations were intricately balanced, complex and undergoing a series of major transformations comparable in scale, though qualitatively very different from, the economic, political and social transformations of early modern Europe. This is also a time in which the diverse societies of the Mediterranean world were becoming increasingly integrated into 'global systems' of sorts. Cultural diversity remained paramount, but there was increasing awareness of similarities and differences with others, at the levels of both self and community. The praxis of consumption may well both have constructed and displayed the links of self to community within

307

ranked social systems, as well as offering a means by which the local and the global could accommodate each other.

This is not to say that a body of theory developed to explain modernity can be overlaid directly on to antiquity. Rather, 'modernity' in a general sense and its modes of constitution via materiality may not simply be a feature of a post-capitalist world, and cannot thus be isolated and cut off from the rest of the past. It seems to me arrogant in the extreme to view ourselves as utterly unique within historical time and space because of our modes of materiality.

Acknowledgements
I am very grateful to Nick Fisher and Robin Osborne for their suggestions on earlier drafts of this paper.

Notes

[1] e.g. Rowlands et al. 1987, Sherratt and Sherratt 1993, Arafat and Morgan 1994, cf. Gibb 1996, 8–9, for a brief but incisive critique of the limits of world systems theory.

[2] Bocock 1993, Fine and Leopold 1993, Miller 1987, Miller (ed.) 1995, Brewer and Porter 1993, Harvey 1989, Berry 1994, etc.

[3] For which see Miller 1987, Miller (ed.) 1995, Fine and Leopold 1993.

[4] e.g. Miller 1987, 107: 'its [the artefact's] physical presence exemplifies the concept of praxis, in that this materiality is always an element in cultural transformation', see also Miller 1987, 129–30.

[5] For a good discussion of these distinctions see Berry 1994, 30–2; for an archaeological example of setting 'status display' in the broader context of consumer behaviour, see Gibb 1996, 2 and *passim*.

[6] For the full range of publications see the references in Gill 1994, Vickers and Gill 1994, though the problem has been most recently tackled in an interesting way by Osborne 1996b.

[7] For examples see Ridgway 1992; Shefton 1994, 68; Wells 1980, 1984; Coldstream 1993, 1994; Pare 1997.

[8] e.g. Boardman 1980; Tsetskhladze 1994, 123–4; Ridgway 1992, 1994, 40; the idea of 'need' is questioned, if not tackled head-on, by Arafat and Morgan 1994, 116, 127–30.

[9] If that is what Aegean transport amphorae might indicate at sites like Al Mina, Ras el Bassit and Tell Defenneh; see Johnston and Jones 1978.

[10] I am sure this is wrong; see Foxhall 1998.

[11] e.g. Teos *ML* 30, perhaps dating to the first half of the fifth century BC; the grain ships Xerxes saw are said by Herodotos (7.147) to be heading for Aegina and the Peloponnese.

[12] Ismaros is on the Thracian coast. Whether this is a type of wine or an import is irrelevant to the argument: in either case there is the implication of

'specialness', perhaps enhanced by the fact that it is already referred to by Homer (*Od.* 9.196 ff., cf. *Il.* 9.71 f.).

[13] Kydonia is in Crete, also Alkman fr. 99 Page and Ibykos fr. 286.1–2 Page.

[14] Alcaeus fr. 50 L-P; Sappho frs. 29, 30, 94 L-P; Xenophanes fr. 1 D-K; Solon frs. 38–40 West; Theognis 879–84, 891–4. Cf. the significance of spices as an imported 'consumer good' in the otherwise subsistence-based economy of colonial North America, Gibb 1996, 16.

[15] Cf. *Nemean* 6.57–61; Kurke 1991, 58–9.

[16] *Lilium candidum*, a plant native to Greece; Huxley and Taylor 1984, 146.

[17] The lily-processing scenes are datable to the mid-twenty-sixth dynasty, i.e. the first half of the sixth century, and the earliest Egyptian depiction of a Madonna lily is a single one in a tomb dating to Psammetichos I who reigned 664–610 BC.

[18] An anthology of erotic poems ranging in date from the beginning of the post-exilic period (539 BC+) down to the Hellenistic period – the exact date and origin of the text are irrelevant for this argument.

[19] Some of the poetic bits of the text may be seventh century BC.

[20] Compare also the epigram attributed to Anakreon (108D Diehl = FGE vii; *Anth.Pal.* 6.136) celebrating the dedication of a robe made by two women.

[21] The same could probably be said of the meanings attributed by different cultures.

[22] Berry 1994, 40–1, would categorize them as luxuries under his taxonomic scheme, though I am uneasy that he fails to distinguish fully between the attainable and the unattainable in his focus on desire.

12

LITERACY AND LAW-MAKING
The case of archaic Crete

James Whitley

In George Orwell's *Animal Farm* the animals, having successfully re-belled against their human owners, agree upon a set of laws, laws that are to enshrine the principles of their new state, their new *politeia*. As Orwell puts it:

> They [the pigs] explained that by their studies of the past three months the pigs had succeeded in reducing the principles of Animalism to Seven Commandments. These commandments would now be inscribed on the wall; they would form an unalterable law by which all the animals on Animal Farm must live for ever after.[1]

Orwell goes on to describe how two pigs, Snowball and Squealer (who is later to emerge as the orator, remembrancer and scribe of this community) write down this unalterable law.

> The Commandments were written on the tarred wall in great white letters that could be read thirty yards away. They ran thus:
>
> THE SEVEN COMMANDMENTS
> 1. Whatever goes upon two legs is an enemy.
> 2. Whatever goes upon four legs, or has wings, is a friend.
> 3. No animal shall wear clothes.
> 4. No animal shall sleep in a bed.
> 5. No animal shall drink alcohol.
> 6. No animal shall kill any other animal.
> 7. All animals are equal.[2]

In the initial stages of this 'animal revolution' the writing down of laws is accompanied by a determined effort on the part of some animals to remember them, and by an educational campaign intended to make all animals literate. As the novel progresses, however, and as it becomes clearer that the pigs have in fact established an oligarchy not dissimilar to the old regime, such attempts and such educational programmes are abandoned. Eventually, only the pigs, Muriel the goat, and the old donkey, Benjamin, remain literate, and, after Muriel dies, it is only Benjamin who is capable of recognising that things have changed.

> 'My sight is failing' she [the horse Clover] said finally. 'Even when I was young I could not have read what was written there. But it appears to me that the wall looks different. Are the Seven Commandments the same as they used to be, Benjamin?' For once Benjamin consented to break his rule, and he read out to her what was written on the wall. There was nothing there except a single Commandment. It ran:
>
> ALL ANIMALS ARE EQUAL
> BUT SOME ANIMALS ARE MORE EQUAL THAN OTHERS.[3]

Animal Farm is, of course, a fable about Soviet Communism and the betrayal of a socialist ideal. But it does share with classical scholarship a number of assumptions concerning the relationship between literacy, the rule of law, social progress and social justice. Widespread literacy is a good thing, a necessary condition for liberty and democracy. Written law too is good. If a law is written and publicly displayed, the public will notice if its terms are being adhered to. The public will be alerted to disparities between what was written and what is being done. The public will be enabled to criticize, amend and improve. That written law serves the interest of democracy is a view shared by many ancient and modern commentators. Zaleukos, Charondas, Lycurgus, Pittakos, Drakon, Solon and other legendary and historical law-givers are still thought to deserve honourable mention in most recent histories of archaic Greece. Snodgrass is not untypical in his view of the benefits of alphabetic literacy and the development of written law.

> What is much clearer is that the alphabet, once adopted, proved an enormous asset to the progress of Greek society. By making the art of reading and writing widely available, it enabled organizations to communicate beyond the close circle of those actually operating them, and individuals beyond their immediate acquaintances. Governments could write down procedures and law codes, cult associations could record forms of rituals and names of officials, sanctuaries could list their property and record information of wider interest... At the same time, merchants could record payments, craftsmen sign their products, property owners publish their claims against potential usurpers, poets set down their compositions. But permanency did not necessarily mean immutability: on the contrary, once a thing is set down in writing, it becomes inherently more open to analysis and criticism than when it is secreted in the memories of a specialist group. In this way, alphabetic writing, despite the fact that in our view it was adopted with no such intention, must have made a considerable contribution to the speed of development in the institutions of archaic Greece.[4]

Snodgrass later cites the early legal inscriptions from Dreros as evidence that these processes were at work in Crete in the seventh century.[5] Such benefits may not have been apparent, however, if literacy were restricted to a small group. Certainly in *Animal Farm*, the lawgivers themselves, the pigs, do not merely breach the principles of animal socialism. They break their own laws. They befriend humans; they betray other animals; they learn to wear clothes, sleep in beds and to drink alcohol; they kill other animals. It must be admitted, however, that in this respect they differ profoundly from legendary Greek lawgivers, who, as Andrew Szegedy-Maszak has pointed out, were famously literal-minded in the application of laws they themselves had given, often putting the law before their own interests.[6] Mainland and colonial lawgivers were more scrupulous than Orwell's pigs. Whether the same is true of the legendary lawgivers of archaic Crete is a matter I will return to later.

In any case it would be silly to pursue the analogy of *Animal Farm* much further. The purpose of an analogy is, after all, to clarify a problem, by bringing out both the similarities and the differences between two cases, and not to force facts into a mould they will not fit. It is my intention to explore the relationship between alphabetic literacy and the practice of producing written laws, and to cast doubt on the liberal, progressive metanarrative that still informs many histories of archaic Greece.[7] If such a narrative still works for some regions of Greece during the archaic period, it conspicuously ignores the situation in Crete, where epigraphic evidence for the widespread production of written law and for its gradual codification sits uneasily with other evidence indicating an otherwise very restricted use of alphabetic literacy. For law making, and in particular the appearance of publicly accessible written law, can only play the role assigned to it in such a narrative, the role of midwife to democracy, if the population at large is widely literate already. Widespread literacy must precede written law if law is to serve democratic interests. In recent years, a number of scholars have cast a sceptical eye over the evidence for widespread literacy in archaic Greece.[8] Some have gone further, and questioned the presumed relationship between written law and the development of Greek democracy.[9] These scholars have made good use of the Cretan evidence, but have nonetheless tended to treat Crete as one region of Greece which has abundant epigraphic evidence for written law. The same social processes were, it seems, at work in Crete as they were elsewhere in archaic Greece.[10] This is another example of that widespread prejudice held by many ancient historians, the belief that differences in the pattern of archaeological finds from different regions of Greece result from nothing more than the hazards of discovery and survival. It is my contention that such differences do tell us something real about the diverse natures of the polities, societies and cultures that existed in Greece in the archaic period. I am not claiming here that the relationship between patterns in the archaeological (including the epigraphic) record and the social order of the various communities of archaic Greece is direct and straightforward. No one who has eavesdropped on the debate between processualists and post-processualists in archaeology could possibly hold such a belief. I am merely asserting that the 'epigraphic habits' of the various communities of archaic Greece are facts we ought to take seriously.[11] From an archaeological perspective it is clear that such epigraphic habits varied enormously from region to region. An example from outside Crete may clarify this point. For the purposes of comparison it may be worth looking at one Greek *polis* where democracy did develop and where alphabetic literacy was widespread in archaic times, namely Athens. Here I believe the epigraphic evidence can be used to answer a number of key questions, namely: What kind of literacy existed in archaic Athens? Which groups of people used writing, and for what purposes? In brief, what, in archaic Athens, was writing for?

Inscriptions of archaic date from Athens and Attica survive in a whole variety of forms. It is clear that writing, from very early times, was put

TABLE 1: Attic Inscriptions

Date range	Inscribed dedications	Graffiti	Dipinti	Inscribed tombstones	Laws etc
700–650	2	49	2	0	0
650–600	8	64	6	2	0
600–550	35	63	45	12	0
550–500	101	32	531	66	4
500–480	249	32	174	2	4

to a wide range of uses. The earliest Athenian inscription, a graffito on the so-called Dipylon *oinochoe*, is a hexameter verse that accords very well with Barry Powell's 'sympotic' or 'poetic' theory of the adoption of the alphabet.[12] From the seventh century onwards there is no lack of graffiti from Attica, such as one saying 'the boy is hateful' (*misetos ho pais*) from the Athenian Agora.[13] Owners' names too are not uncommon.[14] There are also a number of abecedaria, practice alphabets of seventh-century date from both the Athenian Agora and Mt Hymettus.[15] Clearly, from very early times, a number of people in Attica found it a worthwhile exercise to practise the new-found skills of writing. From 620 BC onwards, painted inscriptions, dipinti, are increasingly to be found incorporated into the visual images on vases.[16] These dipinti are first used to clarify, or perhaps amplify, narrative scenes. By the early sixth century this practice had developed considerably. Sophilos has a tendency to name everything and everyone on his *dinoi*, a habit if anything accentuated by Kleitias and Ergotimos on the François vase.[17] Here, apart from pygmies and cranes, everything is named; each one of the heroes and hounds who took part in the Calydonian boar hunt, each participant in Patroclos' funeral games, and every deity attending the marriage of Peleus and Thetis. This naming goes much further than simply clarifying a narrative scene; in some cases, an inscription takes the place of an image. Some deities are named attending the marriage ceremony who are not depicted. In others, inanimate objects, whose identity cannot really be in doubt, are named; absolutely unambiguous images of springs (*krenai*) and seats (*thakoi*) are accompanied by a totally unnecessary inscription. What purpose is served by such redundancy? However we may want to answer this question, it is clear that in the François vase the skills of literacy and the development of complex visual narrative, narratives whose origins must stem from a tradition of oral poetry or story telling, are closely intertwined.[18] Visual, oral and literate culture were not clearly demarcated in archaic Athens – indeed the writing that accompanies complex visual narratives and the the oral performance of the same stories from 'written works' must be seen as two sides of the same coin.[19] This interdependence of the written word and visual representation is not confined to images on vases. It also applies to many Attic funerary monuments where inscriptions accompany images. Svenbro's subtle reading of the statue of Phrasikleia has shown us that the inscription is there to be read aloud, and, once read, sets up a chain of associations between the written (now spoken) word and the iconography of Phrasikleia's statue.[20] The purpose of such inscriptions is not easily conveyed by the English word 'commemorate' (though that is what they do), unless we also remember that 'commemorate' can also 'bringing the man/woman to mind', and all that that implies.

There are many indications that literacy was widespread amongst craftsmen in archaic Attica. We know the names of at least 51 vase painters or potters who lived in the sixth century from the signatures on 496 pots.[21] Sculptors too, such as Phaidimos, were in the habit of signing their works.[22] More significant is the general frequency of personal names on inscriptions in archaic Attica. Of the 80 or so inscribed bases from tombstones that date to before 500 BC, we know the names of 58 persons commemorated and 15 family members who helped to erect the monument. Of these works 13 are signed by sculptors.[23] A similar pattern is evident on the 395 marble dedications from the Athenian Acropolis which date to before 480 BC.[24] Most of these have the dedicator's name, and many the name of the sculptor who executed them.

There are four points to emphasize here. First, alphabetic literacy, albeit in a rather elementary form (Harris's 'phonebook literacy'), was widespread in archaic Attica. It is impossible otherwise to account for the variety and quantity of inscriptions found during this period. Secondly Athenian literacy was almost obsessively concerned with naming and with commemorating the actions and achievements of named individuals – fame appears to be the inspiration for hundreds of dedications and tens of funerary monuments. Thirdly Attic literacy was inextricably bound up with the oral, narrative and visual culture of the time, as can be seen vividly both on the François vase and in the statue of Phrasikleia. This observation suggests that the presumed contrast or conflict between 'literate' and 'oral' culture has been over-drawn, and that such terminology is in itself misleading. Lastly, there is little epigraphic evidence to suggest that literacy was put to wide-spread public use in the archaic period.

This last point raises a number of issues, for there is plenty of contemporary and later literary evidence to support the traditional view that both Drakon and Solon were responsible for the promulga-tion of written law in the period 640 and 560 BC. The archaisms in the 're-publication' of Drakon's law on homicide, and the testimony of Solon's poems cannot easily be explained away. Whatever the precise physical form of the *axones* and *kyrbeis*, the existence of some written law, accessible to all those who could read, cannot seriously be doubted. One or two qualifications should be entered here. Whilst Drakon and Solon were certainly responsible for much written legislation, a set of legal, written decrees does not in itself constitute a law code. Much of what we would regard as 'law' remained unwritten. Moreover it seems that, in its earliest form, written law did not take monumental form.[25] Nonetheless the virtual absence of any surviving legal inscription before 520 BC in Athens and Attica is distinctly odd.[26] This is not a trivial fact, nor merely a matter of the 'accident of survival'. Athenians went to considerable trouble to commemorate themselves in public places. They inscribed their names both on expensive funerary monuments and on highly visible marble dedications on the Athenian Acropolis, but, in the archaic period at least, did not care to monumentalize their laws. Law may have been made public in archaic Athens, but there seems to have been no desire to make of law a *monumentum aere perennius*.

How does this compare with the situation in archaic Crete? The most striking feature of the Cretan evidence is the rarity of all other forms of inscription of archaic date apart from legal fragments. There are no abecedaria, no signs of private individuals feeling a need to

---

TABLE 2: Cretan Inscriptions

Date range	Inscribed dedications		Graffiti	Dipinti	Inscribed tombstones	Laws etc (separate single texts)
	(a)	(b)				
700–650	0	0	5	0	0	0
650–600	2	13	2	0	1	3
600–550	0	0	0	0	0	7
550–500	2	0	4	0	1	16
500–480	2	0	2	0	3	12

Note: For the inscribed dedications, (a) represents those which are standard dedicatory inscriptions (or presumed to be such) and (b) inscribed armour, which may not be classed as dedications properly speaking.

---

practise the skills of writing. Graffiti are rare: there are early examples from Prinias, Knossos and quite a number from the 'port of trade' of Kommos.[27] The latter are written in Boeotian script. There is a later group from the very eastern extremity of Crete near Itanos.[28] Two vessels datable to the late eighth to seventh century, one from Knossos and one from Phaistos, appear to be inscriptions of their owners' names.[29] Inscribed tombstones are also uncommon. Apart from one seventh-century stele from Prinias, all tombstones are late and have a marked coastal distribution. The majority (three out of five) come from Kydonia in Western Crete.[30] These Kydonian tombstones date from a time when we know from Herodotus Kydonia was being fought over between Samians and Aeginetans, and perhaps it is not surprising that they are written in Aeginetan script.[31] More curious still is the complete absence of dipinti, and the extreme rarity of dedicatory inscriptions. Two daedalic figurines from sanctuaries, one from Gortys, the other from Praisos, are inscribed on their reverse sides, but it is not clear what the function of these inscriptions is.[32] There are some inscribed bronzes from Kato Symi which are probably dedications.[33] There is an inscribed base, and an earlier collection of inscribed bronze armour from Afrati.[34] These last however are not dedications strictly speaking, but records of personal victories over opponents in battle. There are only two real dedicatory inscriptions, that is, inscriptions which follow the dedicatory formula of the name of the dedicator, the verb *'anetheke'* and the name of the deity in the dative case. One is the inscribed base from Afrati (see above). The other is a bronze cauldron dedicated by one Thalios (or Tharios) to Apollo and found at Panormos near Heraklion. It too is written in Aeginetan script.[35] Nor are personal names at all common. If we exclude Aeginetan gravestones and dedications, we know the names of no more than 31 Cretans for the whole archaic period up until the time of the Gortys law code, less than 10% of the number of names from archaic Attica (see Appendix 2). Signs of informal, personal literacy are rare in Crete. It would be difficult to argue that literacy was widespread. As TABLE 2 and Maps 2 to 5 (pp. 323–4) show, if someone did want to make such a case, it would be easier to argue for widespread literacy in the seventh rather than the sixth century. Here at least archaeological evidence is confirmed by other sources, since what little literary evidence we do possess suggests that literacy was not a highly regarded accomplishment in Crete even in the fourth century BC.[36]

For me, however, the most striking difference between Attica and Crete in this period is the total absence in Cretan art of any inscription which has any role in narrative – whether the narrative be in stone, bronze or on the surface of a vase. This is not merely to say that there is no evidence for literate craftsmen. It is rather to emphasize the apparent disconnection between literacy, oral performance and visual art that appears to have prevailed in Crete. Crete was, to be sure, hardly famed for its poetry in this period – there are no known poems at all apart from the Song of Hybrias.[37] But it is still an odd fact that, while Cretan art had long made use of images, it is difficult to argue that any of these images either form a part of a story, or synoptically represent the whole of a story. The best candidates for narrative art in archaic Crete are some of the bronze shields from the Idaean cave, in particular the Hunt Shield, which date to the eighth century, a time when the alphabet was only just being adopted in Greece. By the end of the seventh century most Cretan figurative art is, as Hoffmann rightly observed, heraldic.[38] It is full of single figures or antithetical opposed groups of humans or animals. There are some more complex scenes, such as the one on the Rethymnon *mitra*, but it is not clear whether this is an excerpt from a story or a scene, generic in character, from a particular ritual. [39] Here again the scant literary evidence we possess seems to confirm an interpretation based on the firmer ground of material evidence. There is a remarkable passage in Plato's *Laws* where the Cretan Kleinias expresses his admiration for Homer, for him a relatively unknown 'foreign poet' for whom generally Cretans had little use.[40] Homer's stories, with their emphasis on narrative and personalities rather than ritual or 'founder myths', seem to have had little currency in archaic and classical Crete. They were simply not useful to Cretans. My point here is not simply that this relative ignorance of Homer on the part of Cretans partly explains why 'mythological' interpretations of Cretan iconography have proven so difficult and unconvincing. It is that, whereas in Athens and other regions of Greece oral and visual narratives were frequently linked by the practice of writing, no such relationship existed in Crete. Crete was not, as it were, a 'narrative culture' in the sense that Athens was.

What do survive in large numbers from archaic Crete are fragments of laws, or at least inscriptions of legal character in stone or (more rarely) in bronze. There would be little point in counting each and every one of these fragments, since some pieces are no more than one or two letters, but it is important to emphasize that they are widely distributed in both time and space. Inscriptions from Crete are difficult to date as we cannot associate changing letter forms with a series of datable artefacts, as we can for Attica, but it appears that the earliest, from Dreros, dates to around 650 BC; some date to the sixth century, and there is a large cluster 'circa 500 BC'. For my purposes, the Gortys Law Code, usually dated to circa 450 BC, is the last in this series. Legal fragments are to be found in most of the major archaic cities – Eleutherna, Axos, Phaistos, Gortys, Prinias (Rhizenia), Knossos, Eltynia, Lyttos, Dreros and Praisos (see Appendix 1). These 'laws' seem for the most part to be very specific regulations which seem to have been written down in response to a specific problem. The early inscription from Dreros, for example, decrees that no-one can serve as a *kosmos* more than once every ten years.[41] Such decrees rarely leave room for much ambiguity, and sometimes go into considerable detail. The recently published inscription from Lyttos regulating pasturage rights tells us what appear to be the limits of common land for pasture, defined by particular roads.[42] Where their context can be reconstructed, these laws seem to have been displayed in public places, often in temples or sanctuaries. The majority of sixth century legal fragments from Gortys come from the temple of Apollo Pythios; most of the fragments from Dreros come from the temple there; and the Eteocretan fragments from Praisos (which are probably laws) were found to have been 'cast down' from the open-air sanctuary on the Third Acropolis.[43] Moreover there is at Gortys good evidence for the progressive codification of these various decrees during the sixth and early fifth century, a codification that was eventually to lead to the Great Code itself, which must have been set up in its very own, semi-circular public building.[44] Moreover, like early laws from elsewhere in Greece, archaic Cretan laws are overwhelmingly concerned with *procedure*. In the inscription from Dreros as in many others, due process is defined and punishments for its infringement laid down.[45] In these respects, Cretan laws conform to the expectations of those who would see the production of written law and its codification as a progressive measure, gradually placing law in the public domain.

There remain a number of paradoxes or difficulties with such an interpretation. Firstly, if law was put in the public domain, it clearly did not help to bring about democracy in Crete. Cretan cities remained obstinately oligarchic throughout the archaic and classical periods, as all our literary sources (particularly Aristotle) attest. Secondly, our literary sources indicate that Cretan *kosmoi* took very little notice of written law; they made judgements not *kata grammata* but *autognomonas*.[46] Thirdly, other evidence seems to indicate that the skills of literacy were not widespread in the archaic period (see above). There is no evidence to suggest that there was a literate, critical public out there, capable of noticing contradictions and able to press for improvements to the law. Indeed there is, if anything, more evidence for widespread literacy in the earlier part of the period, the seventh century, than there is in the sixth. Lastly there is the evidence of the Spensithios decree (*Fig.* 1), which is worth discussing in some detail.

Fig. 1. The Spensithios decree. London, British Museum, BM 1969.4-2.1, side A.

The Spensithios decree is a bronze *mitra* (an archaeological term for an abdominal guard) inscribed on both sides in boustrophedon script, and dated by Jeffery and Morpurgo-Davies to *c.* 500 BC.[47] It sets out the terms, in the manner of a contract rather than a law, of the man Spensithios who is to become the 'remembrancer and scribe' (*mnamon* and *poinikastas*) of this community, which is probably to be identified with the modern Afrati.[48] His office is to be hereditary, and he is to be awarded privileges and duties which put him and his family on a par with those families from whom the *kosmoi* were taken. His payment is written down, and his dues to the 'men's club' (*andreion*) outlined. The decree gives Spensithios a monopoly of public writing, all writing concerning public and divine affairs. Before this discovery, public scribes were thought to be a rarity in Greece, and, if known about, were not persons of high status. But Spensithios' role is clearly an important one. He is a part of the oligarchy – as was Squealer in Animal Farm.

In Crete, there appears to have been limited literacy amongst crafts-men and most sections of the population. The main use of writing was for legal and public purposes. The Spensithios decree is further evidence that Crete was a region where 'scribal literacy' prevailed; that is, where literacy is virtually confined to a small, specialist group, for whom the practice of writing is a specialist (and sometimes) hereditary skill. Scribal literacy is usually thought to have been characteristic of Near Eastern society, and there are other features which align Cretan writing practices more with the north Semitic area (Syria and northern Mesopotamia) than with the rest of Greece. The first is, of course, the very existence of a public scribe; second the noun *poinikastas* and the verb *poinikazen* suggest that the idea of 'letters' were still strongly associated in the minds of Cretans even by the late archaic period with Phoenicians and the Near East; and thirdly, the practice of invoking the gods or (as on the Dreros decree) a god at the beginning of every decree is something we find in a certain class of Near Eastern public inscriptions.[49] My point here is not that Crete was more directly or profoundly 'influenced' by the Near East than other regions of Greece. It is rather that the social practices of Near Eastern and Cretan alphabetic literacy remained very similar, and that writing operated within a similar social and cultural context. There is good reason to suppose that alphabetic literacy had different points of origin in archaic Greece.[50] It was certainly put to very different social uses in different regions.

If limited, scribal literacy prevailed in Crete in the archaic period (and perhaps later), then what is the function of legal inscriptions, publicly displayed? And why are the terms of such decrees so specific? One matter I will concede: the Dreros decree and other inscriptions are clearly there partly to regulate aristocratic competition, to write down in stone laws to which others can appeal if any one person becomes excessively powerful. But, I would argue, this regulatory effect would only have operated within the small group that ran Cretan city states. The ruling families (like the pigs) could probably read. But what was the effect of such decrees as far as the general run of the population was concerned? If the Gortys law code was not written down, and displayed in its own special building, so that Gortynians could know their own law, what was it for? Why devote so much care to the careful, written execution and public display of written law? I would argue that this law code in particular should be seen first and foremost as a monument, and not a text. It was there to represent the majesty of the law to a population that was largely illiterate. It was designed to present the particular regulations and practices of a small city state as eternal and immutable – permanent and beyond criticism, like some platonic form existing above and beyond the day-to-day concerns of the average Gortynian. Not being able to read its specific terms, an unfree or only partially free Gortynian (such as an *apetairos*) would not be able to notice the disparity between the punishment that would be meted out to him, were he to commit adultery or rape, and what punishment a free man would receive.[51] He would not be able to criticize the fact that offences to him would, under the law, receive only a small recompense. He would not be able to notice that the spirit of the code would be well represented by the adage that some men are equal, but some are much more equal than others.

Map 1. Cities and sanctuaries of archaic Crete.

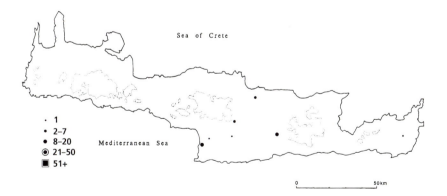

Map 2. Early Cretan inscriptions: non-legal 750–600 BC.

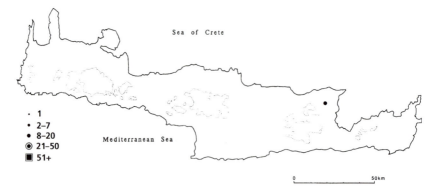

Map 3. Early Cretan inscriptions: legal 750–600 BC.

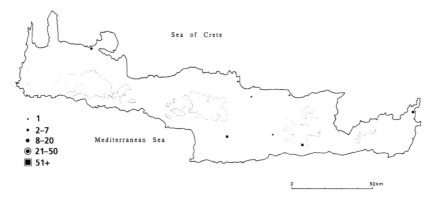

Map 4. Cretan inscriptions: non–legal 600–450 BC.

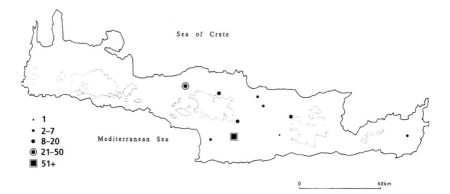

Map 5. Cretan inscriptions: legal 600–450 BC.

324

Appendix 1
Legal inscriptions in archaic Crete

I have not summarized all the legal inscriptions in the footnotes, as this would encumber the text too much. What follows is a city-by-city account of all the legal inscriptions from archaic Crete and all inscriptions associated with city sites (references for inscriptions from sanctuaries and other locations are given in the endnotes). This should give the reader some idea of the evidence on which my tabulations have been made. The cities are listed according to geographical location, easternmost first and westernmost last (see Map 1). Some references are given in abbreviated, 'non-Harvard' form.

Itanos: There are no known public, legal inscriptions from here. Some late sixth century graffiti (*I.Cret.* III.vii.2, 3 and 4) inscribed on stone were however found nearby.

Praisos: There are two 'Eteocretan' public inscriptions from this site (*I.Cret.* III.vi.1 and 4). These are datable to just before 500 BC. The context of these inscriptions (close to the Altar Hill) makes it probable that they are fragments of laws, or some other kind of public inscription. The inscribed daedalic figurine (*I.Cret.* III.viii.1) also came from this sanctuary site, see Halbherr 1901, 386.

Dreros: There are numerous individual legal inscriptions from this site, all found close to the Geometric temple of Apollo. The most famous is the *kosmos* decree, Demargne and Van Effenterre (1937b) (=Jeffery 1990, 315 no. 1a). Then there is an alleged Greek/Eteocretan bilingual (Van Effenterre 1946a = Jeffery 1990, 315 no. 1b) and a number of other legal inscriptions (Van Effenterre 1946b = Jeffery 1990, 315 nos. 1c–1h). All date to around 650 BC.

Chersonisos: This was probably an archaic Cretan city, but no legal inscriptions have been found here. The only inscription is a late archaic tombstone, Masson 1979, 64–5 and fig. 5.

Lyttos (or *Lyktos*): There are a number of legal texts dating to between 550 and 525 BC (*I.Cret.* I.xviii.1–7). The most recently published legal text from here dates to around 500 BC (Van Effenterre and Van Effenterre 1985).

Afrati: The ancient name of this site is not known. It has usually been identified with 'Arkades', but, as Viviers (1994, 230–4 and 238–43) has recently argued, it is more likely to be 'Dattalla'. The only legal inscription which probably (but not certainly) comes from this site is the Spensithios decree (Jeffery and Morpurgo-Davies 1970), which dates to circa 500 BC. Other inscriptions include the inscribed armour (Hoffmann 1972), datable to circa 600 BC and one other dedicatory inscription (*I.Cret.* I.v.4), datable to around 500 BC.

Eltynia: This small city near Knossos is known to us largely from its two archaic legal inscriptions (*I.Cret.* I.x.1 and 2), the former dating to *c.* 600 BC, the latter to around 500 BC.

Knossos: Despite the size and importance of this site in the archaic period, archaic legal inscriptions are few and far between. Knossos has probably suffered more severely than other sites in Crete from robbing of stones for re-use in later buildings. Knossos was too useful a quarry, too close to Heraklion and so to the Venetians' demand for large defensive walls. There are in fact only three very fragmentary legal inscriptions: *I.Cret.* I.viii.2; Jeffery 1949, 35–6; and one published in *Ergon tis en Athenais Arkhaiologikis Etaireias* 1972 (1972, 129–30). All date to the very end of the archaic period. There are however a number of early informal inscriptions from this site; see Cold-stream et al. 1981, 157 no. 117; Jeffery 1990, 468 no. B; Sackett 1992, 141–2 (no. X.32).

Prinias (ancient *Rhizenia*): There are a number of early legal inscriptions from this site (*I.Cret.* I.xxviii.2–15) which date to the earlier part of the sixth century BC. There is also one early graffito (*I.Cret.* I.xxviii.1) and one seventh century inscribed tombstone, Lebessi 1976, 21–2 no. A1.

Gortys: There are more inscriptions from here than from any other site in Crete. Here the epigraphic evidence does suggest that something akin to a progressive codification of law was taking place. The earliest legal fragments, datable to the first half of the sixth century, are mostly associated with the walls of the temple of Apollo Pythios (*I.Cret.* IV.1–40). There are a number of late sixth legal inscriptions (*I.Cret.* IV.62–3) and a whole host dating to the early fifth century (*I.Cret.* IV.41–9, 51, 52–61 and 65–70; see also now *SEG* XXIII. 585). The Great Code (*I.Cret.* IV.72; Willetts 1967) forms the end of this series as far as I am concerned.

There are few signs of informal literacy in archaic Gortys: one inscribed daedalic figurine, Rizza and Santa Maria Scrinari 1968, 187–8 no. 257; a *kalos* inscription on stone (*I.Cret.* IV.50); a 'treaty' which appears to grant privileges to a certain Dionysios (*I.Cret.* IV.64); and a simple graffito of a name (*I.Cret.* IV.71). Inscriptions of this type, which would form the majority in archaic Athens, are in Gortys few and far between. The overwhelming number of inscriptions here are legal.

Phaistos: Until fairly recently no (Greek) inscriptions were known from this site. Two legal inscriptions have come to light in the past few decades, both dating to circa 500 BC, see Manganaro 1965, 296–7 no. A1; and Cantarella and Di Vita 1978. An early eighth century graffito has also been found here; see Levi 1969.

Axos: This is Herodotos' *Oaxos* (Hdt. IV.154). All the inscriptions recovered from this site seem to have been legal in character (*I.Cret.* II.v.1–14; Jeffery 1949, 24–36) and date to between 600 and 450 BC.

Eleutherna: Many inscriptions have been recovered from this large and impor-tant Cretan city, some as a result of recent investigations by the University of Crete at Rethymnon (*I.Cret.* II.xii.1–19; Van Effenterre et al. 1991, 17–23 and 73–4 nos. E1, E2 and E8–13; Kalpaxis and Petropoulou 1989, 130 no. II; I.A.

Papastolou, *Praktikas tis en Athenais Arkhaiologikis Etaireias* 1975 (1975, 516–17). They date to between 600 and 450 BC.

Kydonia: Although this must have been a large and important city, no archaic legal fragments have been discovered here. The only inscriptions of archaic date are found on three tombstones (*I.Cret.* II.x.7, 10 and 13). These all date to the very end of the sixth century, the period of Aeginetan and Samian interference (Hdt. III.44.1 and III.59). It is perhaps no coincidence that the inscriptions are written in Aeginetan script; see Jeffery 1990, 314–16 nos. 29a–c.

Appendix 2
Personal names known from Cretan archaic inscriptions
There seem to be very few personal names known from archaic Crete. I have listed below all known to me as having been found on inscriptions datable to between 750 and 450 BC. These are arranged into a number of categories.

1. Inscriptions marking personal property, with personal names given (5 examples): from Phaistos, Levi 1969; from Knossos, Jeffery 1990, 468 no. B; and from Kommos, Csapo 1991, 1993. All these inscriptions are early, and date to between 750 and 600 BC.

2. Names found on tombstones (5 examples): from Chersonisos, Masson 1979, 64–5; from Prinias, Lebessi 1976, 21–2 no. A1; and from Kydonia (*I.Cret.* II.x.7, 10 and 13).

3. Names found on dedications (3 examples): from Apollonia/Panormos, Alexiou 1984; from Kato Symi, Viannou, Lebessi 1975, 191; from Afrati (*I.Cret.* I.v.4). I exclude here the inscriptions on the bases of the daedalic figurines from Praisos and Gortys, which may not be names. The dedications from the cave of Lera near Khania (Guest-Papamanoli and Lambraki 1976) all date to after 450 BC.

4. Names found inscribed on armour (13 inscriptions giving us 9 names): from Afrati, Hoffmann 1972. These inscriptions are often misleadingly called dedications. They are probably nothing of the sort. The inscriptions are boasts, not dedications, and the context may not be a sanctuary so much as an *andreion* (see Viviers 1994).

5. Names found on 'graffiti', including such things as *kalos* names (6 examples): from near Itanos (*I.Cret.* III.vii.2, 3 and 4); from Prinias (*I.Cret.* I.xxviii.1); and from Gortys (*I.Cret.* IV.50 and 71).

6. Names mentioned in legal texts (3 examples): from Gortys (*I.Cret.* IV.64); and Willetts 1967, 43 col. V. lines 5–6; and probably from Afrati (the Spensithios inscription), Jeffery and Morpurgo-Davies 1970.

It could be argued that the names of alleged Cretan mercenaries found inscribed on the walls of the temple at Abydos should be added to this list (see

Perdrizet and Lefebvre 1919, p. 45 no. 405 and p. 79 no. 445; and Masson 1976, 305–9 nos. 1 and 2). But of these graffiti, only no. 405 is certainly that of a Kydonian mercenary (though it is likely, as Masson argues, that 'Hyperballon' is a common Cretan name). None of these inscriptions is in Cretan script. Their date is uncertain. If they are to be associated with the revolt of the Egyptian Amyrtaios, mentioned by Thucydides (Thuc. I.110) they may be as early as 460 BC (see Perdrizet and Lefebvre 1919, p. ix; Jeffery 1990, 314). But it is equally probable that they are later in date, and are to be associated with a later Amyrtaios. If we exclude these mercenary graffiti, our list gives us a total of 31 separate names of individuals from 35 inscriptions. By any calculation this is far fewer than those from archaic Athens.

Acknowledgements

This is a revised version of talks given at the Institute of Classical Studies in London, the conference in Cardiff and at the Seminar für Altgeschichte in Freiburg. A longer version of this paper, entitled 'Cretan Laws and Cretan Literacy' (with many more footnotes) appears in the *AJA* 101(1997), 635–61. I would like to thank all those who offered comments on all those occasions when the paper was read, particularly Alan Johnston. I have also benefited considerably from Nick Fisher's, John Bennet's and Anthony Snodgrass's comments on earlier drafts of this paper, though they are not to be held accountable for any of my views. The points raised by the anonymous referees of the *American Journal of Archaeology* have also saved me from many errors. Finally I would like to thank Ian Dennis, who drew the maps.

Notes

[1] Orwell 1971, 20–1.

[2] Orwell 1971, ibid.

[3] Orwell 1971, 99.

[4] Snodgrass 1980, 83–4.

[5] Snodgrass 1980, 120. For this inscription see also Jeffery 1990, 215 no. 1a, first published by Demargne and Van Effenterre 1937b.

[6] Szegedy-Maszak 1978.

[7] See again Snodgrass 1980, 83–4; Murray 1980, 96. Both Murray and Snodgrass seem to have been persuaded by the arguments of Goody and Watt 1963, Murray explicitly so when he claims that 'Archaic Greece was a literate society in the modern sense'.

[8] See for example Harris 1989, 45–64; R. Thomas 1992; and Stoddart and Whitley 1988.

[9] For example, Thomas 1994b, 1995a; Hedrick 1994 and Hölkeskamp 1992b, 1994. Gagarin too (1986, 121–6) doubts that written law and democratic interests are necessarily connected in any obvious way.

[10] In this respect both R. Thomas and Hölkeskamp are in general agreement with a number of other scholars, in particular Gagarin (1986), all of

whom tend to treat Crete primarily as a region which is simply richer in epigraphic evidence for written laws than other parts of Greece.

[11] One of the criticisms voiced at the conference in Cardiff was that I was taking the 'absence of evidence (sc. for widespread literacy in Crete) as evidence for absence'. If this were the case it would indeed be an example of naive positivism, and I do not think that I am guilty of that. All I am asserting is that archaeological (and epigraphical) absences, or gaps in the record, are facts which the historian or archaeologist is obliged to explain, and no historical interpretation that neglects to explain such phenomena can be taken at all seriously. The 'hazards of survival' have too often been taken as a rather lame excuse not to think hard about archaeological evidence.

[12] B.P. Powell 1988, 1991; see also Jeffery 1990, 76 no. 1.

[13] Lang 1976, 12 no. C1. For other examples of early Athenian graffiti, see Jeffery 1990, 76 nos. 2–4; Immerwahr 1990, 8 and 11; Lang 1976 nos. C1–C5; Langdon 1976.

[14] For owners' names, see Lang 1976, 30–1 nos. F1–F20.

[15] Lang 1976 no. A1; Langdon 1976, 3–31 nos. 20–6.

[16] Immerwahr 1990, 9–10 and 20–1.

[17] For Sophilos' inscriptions and narrative, see Bakır 1981, 5–7 and 64–72; Beazley 1956, 37–42; Brownlee 1995. For Kleitias, Ergotimos and the François vase, see Beazley 1956, 76–7; Immerwahr 1990, 24–5; Furtwängler and Reichold 1904, 1–14, 55–62 and plates 1–3 and 11–13.

[18] For the relationship between narrative, image and inscriptions on the François vase, see Immerwahr's shrewd comments 1990, 24, to the effect that 'Their purpose (sc. the purpose of the inscriptions) is not so much to clarify the scenes as to accompany them in an independent narrative.'

[19] For discussions of these issues, see C.G. Thomas 1989, Hurwit 1990 and Brownlee 1995.

[20] Svenbro 1993, 8–25.

[21] Figures from Beazley 1932, 1956, 1963, 1971. This is, if anything, an underestimate of the numbers of inscriptions on vases, though not of the number of literate painters and potters.

[22] Jeffery 1962, 151–3 and 137; Richter 1961, 157.

[23] Figures from Jeffery 1962; Willemsen 1963; *IG* I^3 nos. 1194–1236, 1240–9, 1251–3, 1255–69, 1271–3 and 1274–8 (pp. 789–824) and elsewhere. Full information is given in the longer version of this paper. Meyer (1993) probably underestimates the number of archaic Attic tomb inscriptions.

[24] Raubitschek 1949; *IG* I^3 pp. 489–607, also discussed in Stoddart and Whitley 1988.

[25] For the evidence for Drakon's and Solon's laws, see Stroud 1968; 1979, and Gagarin 1986, 86–9. I have followed Stroud (rather than Immerwahr 1985) in believing that the laws were first inscribed on wooden *axones* housed in their own special building; that is, they were first published in non-monumental form. It was only later, sometime before 461 BC, that these laws were inscribed on bronze *kyrbeis* which were suitable for display in the open air. So the monumentalization of Athenian laws dates to sometime before 461 BC, and probably no earlier than 510 BC. The re-publication of Drakon's law on homicide

survives (*IG* I³ 104). In one of his poems Solon says explicitly that he 'wrote down' (ἔγραψα) his laws (Sol. F 36.18–20 West). It should be noted however that there is an important difference between individual written laws and a complete law code, for which see most recently R. Thomas 1995a, 71.

[26] The earliest surviving legal texts are *IG* I³ 1–5 and 230–2, which date to between 520 and 480 BC. They are 'legal' only in the broadest sense of the term. I exclude from consideration the misleadingly termed '*dromos* decrees', *IG* I³ 507 and 508, which date to between 565 and 558 BC. The context and the language of these inscriptions make it clear that these must be thought of primarily as *dedications*.

[27] For graffiti from Knossos, see Coldstream *et al.* 1981, 157 no. 117 fig. 5; and Sackett 1992, 141–2 no. X.32. For graffiti from Prinias, see *I.Cret*. I.xxviii.1. For the Kommos inscriptions, see Csapo 1991, 1993.

[28] For the Itanos graffiti, see *I.Cret.* III.vii.2, 3 and 4. For 'graffiti' of early fifth century date from Gortys, see *I.Cret.* IV.50 and 71.

[29] For Knossos, see Jeffery 1990, 468 no. B; for Phaistos, see Levi 1969 = Jeffery 1990, 468 no. 8a.

[30] For Prinias, see Lebessi 1976, 21–2 no. A1; for the inscription from Chernosisos, see Masson 1979, 64–5. The Kydonian inscriptions are *I.Cret*. II.x.7, 10 and 13.

[31] The letter forms of the Kydonian inscriptions are discussed in Jeffery 1990, 314, 316 nos. 29a–c. Herodotos describes events concerning Kydonia in Hdt. III.44.1 and III.59.

[32] For the Gortynian figurine, see Rizza and Santa Maria Scrinari 1968, 187–8 no. 257. For the figurine from Praisos (wrongly attributed to Sitia in *I.Cret.* III.viii.1), see Halbherr 1901, 386 and plate X.

[33] Lebessi 1975, 191 and plate 193 *gamma*.

[34] For the Afrati armour, see Hoffmann 1972, esp. 15–16. The other dedication from here is *I.Cret.* I.v.4.

[35] The stone base from Afrati is *I.Cret.* I.v.4. The Thalios inscription is published by Alexiou 1984. For the letter forms see Jeffery 1990, 468–9 (no. H). The dedicatory inscriptions from the cave of Lera near Khania published by Guest-Papamanoli and Lambraki 1976 do not date to before 450 BC.

[36] Aristotle F 611.15. ll. 9–11 Rose.

[37] PMG 909 (Page), quoted by Athenaeus 695f–6b; cf. Bowra 1961, 398–403.

[38] For the Hunt Shield, see Kunze 1931, 8–12, also discussed in Blome 1982, 15–23 and Boardman 1961, 138–9. For Hoffmann's view on later archaic Cretan art, see Hoffmann 1972, 34–40. It must be admitted, however, that Hoffmann's view is not widely shared by more traditional scholars such as Blome (1982, 105–8) or Boardman (1961, 129–59), who still tend to see Cretan material culture through the prism of 'Greek Art', with all that this term implies.

[39] For the Rethymnon *mitra*, see Poulsen 1906, Boardman 1961, 142–4 and Hoffmann 1972, 25–6 and 31–2.

[40] Plato *Laws* 680.c.2–680.c.5. It is worth quoting the Greek: ἔοικέν γε ὁ ποιητὴς ὑμῖν οὗτος γεγονέναι χαρίεις. καὶ γὰρ δὴ καὶ ἄλλα αὐτοῦ διεληλύθαμεν μάλ᾽ ἀστεῖα, οὐ μὴν πολλά γε· οὐ γὰρ σφόδρα χρώμεθα οἱ Κρῆτες τοῖς ξενικοῖς

ποιήμασιν. My (colloquial) translation is: [Kleinias] 'That poet of yours [Homer] seems charming. And we have gone through other works of his (very fine they were too), but not many, I'm afraid. We Cretans don't have much use for foreign poems'. The Spartan Megillus goes on to say that Spartans have quite a lot of use for this particular 'foreign poet'.

[41] For this inscription see Demargne and Van Effenterre 1937b, also discussed in Jeffery 1990, 315 no. 1a. For the most recent discussion, see Hölkeskamp 1992b, 93–6 and 101–2.

[42] Van Effenterre H. and Van Effenterre M. 1985.

[43] *I.Cret.* IV.1,3,8–14, 16, 18, 19 and 21–6 were found in the temple of Apollo Pythios at Gortys (see *I.Cret* IV, pp. 42–87). For the context of the laws from Dreros, see Demargne and Van Effenterre 1937a, 1937b; and Marinatos 1936. For the context of the 'Eteocretan' laws from Praisos (*I.Cret.* III.vi .1 and 4) see Halbherr 1894, 1901 and Bosanquet 1902, 254–7.

[44] For this see *I.Cret.* IV.72 (pp. 123–71) and Willetts 1967, 3.

[45] Demargne and Van Effenterre 1937b. See discussion in Gagarin 1986.

[46] Aristotle *Politics* 1272a 33–9.

[47] Jeffery and Morpurgo-Davies 1970 = Jeffery 1990, 468 no. 14b. For the most recent discussion of this inscription, see R. Thomas 1995a, 66–71.

[48] For the most recent discussion of the context of the Spensithios *mitra*, and its association with the Afrati armour (on which Hoffmann 1972, Raubitschek 1972), see Viviers 1994, 243–9. I agree with Viviers that modern Afrati should not be identified with ancient 'Arkades', but with the 'Dattalla' or rather the 'Dataleis' of the Spensithios inscription.

[49] Though words like '*poinikazen*' and '*poinikastas*' are not entirely exclusive to Crete (we find '*phoinikographein*' on an inscription from Teos, where 'write as a scribe' may be understood, see Hermann 1981, 8–9 and 12), the word is more common there than elsewhere, being also found (partly restored) at Eleutherna (*I.Cret.* II.xii.11). The use of the word '*theos*' or '*theoi*' as an inscription heading has been thoroughly discussed by Pounder 1984.

[50] This statement requires some justification. It seems that both Crete and Euboea (and Euboean colonies) have equal claims to be the regions where the Greek alphabet was first discovered. The Euboean case has recently been eloquently argued by Powell 1991 and the Cretan by Duhoux 1981. Problems only arise if we assume that the Greek alphabet must have had a single origin, an Ur-alphabet. It is equally likely (and equally consistent with the evidence for divergent scripts as summarised by Jeffery 1990) that it had several origins, and that what we can observe in the archaeological/epigraphic record is a process of convergence.

[51] For the rights (or otherwise) of the *apetairos*, see Willetts 1967, 40 col. II lines 4–45, and discussion on pages 10, 12–23 and 58–60.

13

GREEKS BEARING ARMS
The state, the leisure class, and
the display of weapons in archaic Greece

Hans van Wees

The Second Amendment of the U.S. constitution lays down that 'the right of the people to keep and bear arms shall not be infringed'. Anyone inclined to question the meaning or wisdom of this provision is called to order by the National Rifle Association: it prints T-shirts with the slogan *What part of 'Infringed' do you not understand?* Such enthusiasm for owning and carrying weapons is regarded with puzzlement elsewhere. In Britain, attitudes are so different that the government has been able to pass quite severe gun laws without meeting much resistance, and even the police force has repeatedly voted against arming itself. On the other hand, Americans carrying guns discreetly in holsters and handbags are a picture of restraint beside, say, Cretan shepherds, with their habit of noisily showing off their firepower at weddings and baptisms. In the lives of these shepherds, in turn, weapons play only a small role compared with their constant display in parts of the Philippines, where 'ammunition belt or sling, bladed weapon, rifle, amulets, and sometimes a pistol' are part of the normal dress code for men, or in parts of Papua New Guinea, where 'without an axe tucked in his belt...a man feels naked'.[1]

Ancient Greece moved from one end of this spectrum to the other in a matter of two or three centuries. Thucydides and Aristotle tell us that carrying a weapon as a matter of daily routine, or 'bearing iron' (*sidērophorein*/σιδηροφορεῖν), was once common in the Greek world. It is generally assumed that this was so until about 700 BC, at least.[2] Yet by 400 BC at the latest, the usage of weapons in Athens in many ways ranged somewhere between that of the U.S. and that of Britain. Many citizens had at home a full set of arms and armour, and most or all men owned at least some weapons, but these were used only in war. Common as brawling and assault were, they rarely led to so much as a knife being drawn. Men fought with bare hands, wielded potsherds – the broken bottles of antiquity – or beat each other with sticks. 'Bearing iron' had come to be seen as a quaint old custom, now found only in backward parts of Greece, and among barbarians.[3]

Thucydides thought that the habit had been dropped when the Greeks 'changed to a life of greater luxury and slacker habits' (I.6.3), and scholars have largely left it at that. Hardly any effort has been made to determine precisely how and when this happened.

Yet the problem is of more than antiquarian interest. Attitudes towards weapons reflect levels of state-formation: the more highly valued is personal autonomy, and the less developed or accepted are forms of central control, the more widespread ownership and display of weapons is likely to be. In Papua New Guinea, before colonization, there was no form of central government at all. In the Philippines, certain regions largely evade government control. In Crete, central control is rather more effective, yet in some places it is still felt that special occasions call for a display of firepower to demonstrate family strength within the community and village defiance of governmental authority. Even in the U.S., advocates of an unrestricted right to keep and bear arms appeal to a need for personal autonomy. It is claimed that arming all citizens is the only way to deter criminal and other offensive behaviour ('the armed society is the polite society'), and, above all, that citizens require weapons to protect themselves from oppression by the federal government, thought by some to have 'an obvious plan to destroy the fabric of America'.[4] British citizens feel the least need to defend themselves against their fellows or their government. There may or may not be good grounds for their feeling this way; it is their greater *belief* in the effectiveness and legitimacy of the state that matters.

In short, the usage of weapons indicates how close a community has come to creating a central monopoly on the legitimate use of violence, and this is generally regarded as a key element in what distinguishes the 'state' proper from other kinds of political organization.

As an index of state-formation, the pattern of ownership and display of weapons in ancient Greece is potentially of great significance for the study of the development of the Greek *polis*. In what follows, therefore, we shall investigate how the social and cultural roles of arms and armour changed from the eighth to the fifth century BC, and how these changes reflected and affected the development of the state in early Greece. The evidence, including a body of iconographic evidence which to date has been almost entirely ignored, suggests that Thucydides' thinking about the role of increasing 'luxury' was on the right lines, and can tell us with some precision in what ways, when, and why the presence of weapons in civic life came to be reduced. As we shall see, the process was gradual, closely related to the transformation of the ruling elite into more and more of a leisure class, and probably not completed until the very end of the archaic age.

Sword, spear, and staff: heroes, tyrants, and lawgivers

As soon as they get out of bed, the heroes of the *Iliad* and *Odyssey* put on their swords, even before they put on their sandals. They follow this routine in time of peace as in time of war, whether they are about to leave the house or to stay in all day. Swords are worn in formal assemblies, by men meeting friends in the town square, by spectators at games, and by youths at a dance. At feasts, host and guests retain their swords even as they sit down to dinner. During the day, a man and his sword are evidently inseparable.[5]

Spears, too, are commonly carried outdoors, not only by travellers, but also by men merely going about town. Telemakhos never appears in public without a spear. Arriving back home in Ithaca, he picks up his spear from the deck of the ship. The slave whose cottage he first visits relieves him of it temporarily, but he picks it up again when he sets off for town. Back at his mother's house, he leaves it outside, leaning against a pillar. Moments later, he takes it up yet again when he goes out to the town square, just as he does on two other occasions.[6] Like him, the warriors of the *Iliad* carry spears at meetings early in the morning and late at night, when they are not otherwise armed or armoured, but are wearing tunics and cloaks, or lion and leopard skins in the heroic manner.[7]

Not everyone goes around in arms, however. Although slaves in charge of farms and herds do have spears and swords 'as a defence against dogs and men', they do not carry these weapons when they come to town.[8] Since the heroes wear swords even in the safety of their own homes, while their slaves, despite disposing of weapons, refrain from carrying these even in less safe public places, we must conclude that bearing arms is a custom not dictated purely by practical necessity, but also by symbolic considerations. At the very least, it sets apart free man from slave.

Further distinctions are hinted at: the old, infirm, and destitute carry walking-sticks instead of spears. A simple wooden staff is part and parcel of a beggar's outfit, and the poet goes out of his way to stress the pitiful impression it helps create. Forgetting that Odysseus in his disguise of elderly vagrant already has a staff, Homer makes him pretend to worry about the difficulty of the long walk ahead, and ask for 'a stick, already cut' with which to support himself. The hero is then led towards town, 'looking like a miserable beggar and an old man, leaning on his staff' (*Od.* 17.195–203). The only other men said to walk with a stick are crippled Hephaistos and aged Priam.[9] In Homeric society, men of Priam's advanced age are regarded as unable to defend themselves, cripples are seen as a legitimate butt of ridicule, and beggars are forced to put up with all sorts of humiliation for the sake of food.[10] There may thus be symbolic significance in the contrast between walking-stick and spear: the staff may indicate those too old, weak, or poor, to fight, while the spear is a badge of status for those deemed capable of standing up for themselves. In practice, of course, a wooden staff can be quite an effective weapon, even if by contrast with the spear it is a symbol of impotence.[11]

At the other end of the social scale, an ornate version of the walking-stick, the hereditary sceptre, serves as an emblem of aristocratic status. A sceptre is handed down within each of the families which rule a Homeric community, and is held by the heads of the families, the 'sceptre-bearing princes', in the exercise of their privileges in assembly and court.[12] On the other hand, the display of weapons, which in some societies is an aristocratic prerogative, does not appear to be thus restricted in the Homeric world. Here, hosts may present visitors, even those who are quite poor, with gifts of spears and swords, along with sets of clothes and sandals, and it is not a statement of fact, but an insult, to tell a humble traveller that his hosts may give him food, but never a sword.[13] Clearly, the poet treats weapons as a regular item of male apparel; the right to carry a sword and spear in public is not the preserve of an elite, but extends to all independent and physically fit men who know how to use them.[14]

We cannot simply assume that the epic picture in this, or any other respect, mirrors the realities of life in early Greece, but in what follows we shall find evidence to suggest that there was indeed a time when men carried weapons in the Homeric manner. By the late fifth century, the picture had changed dramatically. In 411 BC, for instance, the very year in which the Athenians instituted a short-lived regime under which political rights were restricted to those who owned a panoply, a comedy could mock those who entered the public meeting place in arms: 'among the cooking pots and vegetables they stalk about the *agora* with their weapons, like men possessed' (Aristophanes, *Lysistrata* 555–64).

In the most recent, indeed almost the only, study of how and when the change came about, Sepp-Gustav Gröschel argued on the basis of literary evidence that the old habit of 'bearing iron' was ended by state intervention in the sixth century (1989, 80). His case, however, is weak. It rests chiefly on deeply unreliable stories about tyrants confiscating the weapons of their subjects. In the fourth century, when some rulers could rely on large mercenary armies, they might be in a position to seize the citizens' arms, but in the sixth century this would have been extremely difficult, as well as entirely self-defeating since by disarming his subjects the ruler would deprive himself of his citizen-army. The late fourth-century *Constitution of the Athenians* is the earliest source to attribute such an initiative to an archaic tyrant, Peisistratos, and its version is clearly at odds with previous accounts of the reign of that tyrant and his sons.[15] We should therefore reject this evidence. Even if we were to accept it, it would not imply that the custom of 'bearing iron' was necessarily abandoned. Citizens of classical Greek states continued to possess their own military equipment: if they had ever lost it, it was regained when the tyrants fell, and 'bearing iron' became a possibility once more.

Worthy of serious consideration, on the other hand, is the evidence for early laws restricting the usage of weapons. Zaleukos of Locri in southern Italy is credited with a law decreeing that 'no one is to carry weapons in the Council House' (μηδένα φορεῖν ὅπλα ἐν βουλευτηρίῳ). Kharondas of Catana, whose laws were also used in the other Chalcidian cities in Sicily and southern Italy (including Naxos, Leontini, Zankle, Rhegion, and Kyme), allegedly legislated that 'no-one is to attend an assembly in possession of a weapon' (μηδένα μεθ' ὅπλου ἐκκλησιάζειν). The lawcode of Syracuse, drawn up by a committee led by Diokles in 412 BC and adopted widely in Sicily, contained a law to the effect that 'if anyone entered the *agora* with a weapon, he would be punishable by death'. In each case, we are told about the law for the sake of an anecdote: the lawgiver in person inadvertently breaks the rule and kills himself so as to uphold it.[16] The stories are clearly apocryphal, but it seems likely that the laws to which they were attached were indeed common in the Greek cities of Sicily and southern Italy. What is not immediately obvious, however, is whether these laws were designed as special provisions against plotters and troublemakers or as general measures to ban from certain public spheres the weapons which were still routinely carried by the citizens. Moreover, as so often with laws, they are impossible to date.[17]

A final anecdote deals with the Spartan lawgiver Lycurgus, who, it is claimed, was once caught up in a brawl in the assembly, and had his eye accidentally gouged out with a staff. As a result, the carrying of staffs in assembly, normal in other Greek states, was prohibited in Sparta.[18] The story about the lawgiver is supposed to explain his alleged dedication of a cult to Athena 'of the Eye' (*Optilletis*), and is obviously fictional, but surely reflects a historical situation: the notoriously competitive Spartans must at some stage have gone so far as to ban, whether by law or by custom, all kinds of weapons, even sticks, from their public meetings in order to prevent eruptions of violence.

So much for the literary sources. They offer tantalizing glimpses of early Greek custom, and of what may have been done subsequently to limit the use of weapons in civic life, but they do not allow us to determine when or why the habit of 'bearing iron' disappeared. We must turn to the archaeological and iconographic evidence.

The decline of the 'warrior' grave

We may begin at the end, with the funerals at which the dead showed off their weapons one last time. Quite a few Dark Age graves contain arms: on or alongside inhumed bodies, spears, swords, and daggers may be laid out as if the dead were carrying them; cremation burials, too, may be accompanied by weapons, including swords, sometimes bent so as to fit round the urn, and detached spearheads, placed in or beside it.

By no means all men were buried with arms or armour. In Athens, of 57 Dark Age graves with demonstrably adult male remains, only 15, i.e. about a quarter, contained weapons. This is roughly in line with the total numbers of graves found. Of about 650 burials 36 contained weapons; on the assumption that not much more than a quarter of all graves would have held adult males, at most 1 in 5 men would have taken weapons to the grave. One suspects that burial with arms was the prerogative of the wealthy, and this is confirmed by the fact that such burials tend to be rich in other grave goods as well, in clear contrast to the relative poverty of male burials without arms (TABLE 1).[19] The situation is not dissimilar in eighth-century Argos: the proportion of male graves with weapons may be higher (1: 2), but their richness in additional valuables contrasts even more sharply with the other male burials, which contain hardly any grave goods at all.[20] When we occasionally encounter burial groups in which *most* of the dead are accompanied by arms, therefore, we may safely conclude that these represent cemeteries used exclusively by members of the elite.[21]

The fact that it was first and foremost the wealthy who were buried with weapons does not mean either that only the rich *owned* swords and spears, or that weapons represented wealth pure and simple. As for ownership, being able to afford weapons for practical use in life is one thing, being able to afford them for symbolic use in death quite another. Many who possessed arms may well have felt that it would be beyond their families' means, or indeed above their station, to dispose of these in such a dramatic act of conspicuous consumption. As for the symbolism of burial with weapons, as opposed to other iron, bronze, or precious metal objects, we need to look more closely at what was deposited in graves.

Scholars usually refer to burials with arms as 'warrior graves', implying that the dead were inhumed or cremated in full combat gear.[22] Yet it is not obvious that this was so, since finds of armour, as opposed to weapons, are extremely rare. Well over two hundred weapons, but not a single helmet, cuirass, or shield, turned up in cemeteries at Knossos spanning the Dark Age and the seventh century. Of thirty-six Dark Age 'warrior' burials from Athens, only three very early ones contained armour: none of these had any weapons, but each had a shield, of which the central metal boss survives.[23] Easily the highest proportion of pieces of armour in any set of central Greek graves is found in Argos, where eleven 'warrior' burials between them produced three helmets and two cuirasses, as well as nineteen weapons.[24]

The scarcity of armour may be partly accounted for by assuming that, until the very end of the Dark Age, much of it was made of perishable materials, and that when bronze armour began to be used it was either too precious to be buried at all, or first to be looted when graves were disturbed. Such considerations, however, cannot explain the rarity of shield-bosses, or the complete absence of other metal

---

TABLE 1: Weapons and other grave goods in male burials, Athens, 900–700 BC

Source of information: Strömberg 1993; including all Geometric male burials from categories 'A' and 'B', as well as cat. nos. 400 and 440b.

Male burials with weapons:		22	Male burials without weapons:		31
Burials with additional metal grave goods:			*Burials with additional metal grave goods:*		
Iron knives:	4	18%	Iron knives:	2	6%
Bronze/iron pins:	6	27%	Bronze/iron pins:	0	0%
Bronze vessels:	8	36%	Bronze vessels:	3	10%
Gold/silver bands:	7	32%	Gold/silver bands:	1	3%

attachments for wooden shields or leather helmets and corslets. Nor can they explain why an undisturbed, rich 'warrior' grave from Eretria, dating to the same period as the Argive burials with armour, contained a cremation in a *bronze* cauldron, with *four* swords and *six* spears, but still no shield or body armour.[25]

We should therefore take seriously a suggestion made long ago by Wolfgang Helbig – but apparently completely ignored since – that Dark Age graves with weapons normally held, not 'warriors', in the sense of men equipped as they would have been for battle, but men 'in peace-time costume, yet with spears and swords' (1909, 49–51). Helbig plausibly inferred that the burial of weapons reflects a custom of carrying them in daily life. It is noteworthy that the sword, constantly worn by Homeric heroes, is indeed much the most common weapon in Geometric Athenian graves.[26] However, we should not imagine too direct a relation between what was buried and what was used: some men were buried with more arms than they could ever have worn, and it is very likely that others were buried without the weapons which they had habitually carried. A cautious conclusion might be that offensive weapons, used in all kinds of conflict, rather than defensive armour, used only in war, followed a man into the grave because they were seen as more fitting symbols of what he had been, or should have been: not specifically a warrior, but generally a man capable of using force.[27]

The ultimate disappearance of weapons from graves is of great potential significance. It need not – and, as we shall see, does not – mark the moment at which weapons stopped being carried in daily life, but it might indicate when they became a less vital prop of male identity. The problem, however, is that in large parts of Greece their disappearance tends to coincide with a general abandonment of the habit of depositing metal objects and other valuables in graves; it therefore tells us something about changes in the disposition of wealth rather than about changes in attitude towards the ownership and display of weapons.[28] Nevertheless, the statistics of grave goods are suggestive.

Argos is representative of many parts of central Greece insofar as weapons here disappear from graves at the same time as all other metal grave goods; this happens around 690 BC, as it did, for example, in Eretria. Weapons enter the archaeological record relatively late: in the Early Geometric period, when metal grave goods appear in considerable numbers, weapons do not feature at all. Throughout the eighth century, however, weapons form a sizeable proportion of grave goods. When in the Late Geometric period the number of burials per year suddenly more than doubles and the quantity of metal grave goods follows suit, arms and armour lag behind only slightly, and probably not significantly (TABLE 2).

Knossos is representative of many parts of Greece outside the central regions insofar as both weapons and other metal grave goods continue to be found throughout much of the archaic period. The two main excavated sites, a group of tombs at Fortetsa and the Knossos North Cemetery, differ notably in their development, but have in common that the number of weapons buried per year first increases by a factor of about 1.5 from the ninth to the eighth century, but then, in the seventh century, falls to half its previous level, despite the fact that the number of burials at the time rises in one cemetery and remains steady in the other (TABLE 3). This is particularly interesting because other metal grave goods appear to suffer less of a decline.[29] If 'warrior' burial became less widespread in seventh-century Crete, it is tempting to suggest that there may have been a more general waning of the symbolic significance of weapons, which the total absence of metal grave goods does not allow us to see elsewhere.

The evidence from Athens, finally, tells the most interesting story. Here, the deposition of weapons reaches a peak in the ninth century, then falls quite fast in the eighth century to *stop completely* by about 735 BC. This is all the more striking because, throughout, the number of other valuables deposited per year continues to rise slowly, and, in the last third of the century, the number of burials per year grows

---

TABLE 2: Graves and grave goods in Argos

Absolute figures, with one minor modification, as given in Whitley 1991b, 190 (table 13), which offers a breakdown of 'other valuables' into gold/silver, bronze, and ivory.

Period	Burials	per year	Weapons	per burial	per year	Other valuables	per burial	per year
PG								
1050–900	50	0.33	2	0.04	0.01	26	0.52	0.17
EG								
900–825	28	0.37	0	0	0	45	1.61	0.60
MG								
825–750	22	0.29	9	0.41	0.12	29	1.32	0.39
LG								
750–690	46	0.77	15	0.33	0.25	59	1.28	0.98

TABLE 3: Graves and grave goods in Knossos

Sources of information: Fortetsa, burials: Morris, this volume, TABLE 1; Fortetsa, weapons: Brock 1957 (excluding weapons not datable to within one of the periods defined below); Knossos North Cemetery: Coldstream and Catling 1996 (again excluding weapons not datable to within one of the periods defined below; number of burials based on numbers of *pithoi* dated to each of these periods).

	Fortetsa Tombs		North Cemetery		Total	
Period	*Burials* (per year)	*Weapons* (per burial /per year)	*Burials* (per year)	*Weapons* (per burial /per year)	*Burials* (per year)	*Weapons* (per burial /per year)
LPG–PGB						
870–810	54 (0.9)	8 (0.15/0.13)	17 (0.3)	18 (1.06/0.3)	71 (1.2)	26 (0.37/0.43)
EG–LG						
810–710	67 (0.7)	20 (0.3/0.2)	158 (1.6)	47 (0.3/0.47)	225 (2.3)	67 (0.3/0.67)
EO–LO						
710–630	102 (1.3)	8 (0.08/0.1)	123 (1.5)	18 (0.15/0.23)	225 (2.8)	26 (0.12/0.33)

TABLE 4: Graves and grave goods in Athens

Absolute figures as given in Whitley 1991b, 183 (table 11), which offers a breakdown of 'other valuables' into gold/silver, bronze, and ivory.

Period	*Burials*	per year	*Weapons*	per burial	per year	*Other valuables*	per burial	per year
PG								
1050–900	194	1.29	16	0.08	0.11	48	0.25	0.32
EG–MGI								
900–800	77	0.77	22	0.29	0.22	76	0.99	0.76
MGII–LGI								
800–735	68	1.00	8	0.12	0.12	52	0.76	0.80
LGII								
735–700	141	4.03	0	0	0	35	0.25	1.00

exponentially (TABLE 4). Interestingly, a couple of Athenian vases from before 735 BC show a dead man fitted out with weapons or armour, while later vases tend to show arms or armour merely placed on, or seemingly suspended above, the bier (*Fig.* 1). Perhaps weapons might be displayed during the funerary ritual even when they were no longer buried.[30] Furthermore, funerary vases depicting scenes of battle are much rarer after 735 than they had been.[31] This is surely no coincidence, but part of a trend: at funerals, symbols of physical prowess lost ground in Athens a generation or more before that happened anywhere else.

It comes as something of a surprise to find that weapons play virtually no part in the heroic funerals of the *Iliad*. Akhilleus, it is said, did once arrange for the cremation of one of his victims, Eëtion, 'with his arms', as an expression of 'awe' (*Il.* 6.417–18) which we may infer was due to the man's advanced age. Yet the two prime candidates for warrior burial, Patroklos and Hektor, casualties of war, and outstanding, much-loved warriors both, are burnt and buried without weapons or armour, dressed only in a tunic or robe, and covered with a shroud. It is not cremation in arms, but in rich clothes, which is explicitly cited as a source of fame. Nor do the offerings placed on Patroklos' funeral pyre include weapons, though they range from amphoras of honey and oil to sacrificed livestock, horses, dogs, and prisoners of war.[32] It would seem that Homer reflects a state of affairs which in most of Greece did not exist until the seventh century; the *Iliad* reflects a degree of dissociation of men from their weapons which in the late eighth century obtained only in Athens.[33]

Fig. 1. Shield, pair of spears, and helmet (only partially preserved) placed on bier.
Fragment of neck of Late Geometric II amphora, Workshop of Athens 984 (Kerameikos 5643; after Rombos 1988, pl. 9).

343

Swords, cloaks, and the leisure class, *c.* 760–600 BC

When weapons disappear from graves, they are still being portrayed in art as items of everyday male attire. Swords worn by civilians[34] feature prominently in Athenian and Boeotian vase-painting of the Late Geometric period (*c.* 760–700 BC) and the early seventh century. Men may carry swords, for example, as they gather to mourn the dead (*Fig.* 2).[35] Although Geometric male figures are conventionally referred to as 'naked', unless they wear a helmet or hold a shield, the appearance of nudity is merely the result of the high stylization of the human figure.[36] It is a fair assumption that male mourners, unless they are shown wearing armour, are envisaged as dressed in a tunic and cloak, as worn by their more naturalistic counterparts in archaic and classical art, and indeed by Greeks throughout antiquity. The majority of sword-bearing mourners in civilian dress is Athenian and belongs to the eighth century, but a Boeotian Subgeometric hydria (680–670 BC), too, shows men with large swords slung from their shoulders, standing round the bier, tearing out their hair.[37]

In other Geometric settings we also find civilians carrying swords, such as the men in a departure scene who wave goodbye to travellers boarding a ship (*Fig.* 3). It is no coincidence that those who leave are kitted out with sword and spear, while those who stay behind wear only a sword, surely as part of their normal dress. An Attic picture of a mixed company dancing features several men, including musicians, who are armed with swords, just like Homer's youths at a dance (*Fig.* 4). A Boeotian painting of a boxing match has the unarmed contenders flanked by their horses and by two groups of men wearing swords (*Fig.* 5). In each case, the peaceful nature of the event means that participants and onlookers must be civilians, not equipped for war.

Fig. 2. Sword-bearing mourners.
(a) Attic Late Geometric I (after Athens NM 806)
(b) Attic Late Geometric II (after Oxford 1916.55)
(c) Boeotian Subgeometric (after Louvre A575)

Fig. 3. Departure scene.
Right to left: travellers embarking, equipped with sword and spears;
four men waving goodbye, equipped with swords; two women,
lamenting. Late Geometric II oinochoe (Hobart 31; after Ahlberg 1971a,
pl. 65b).

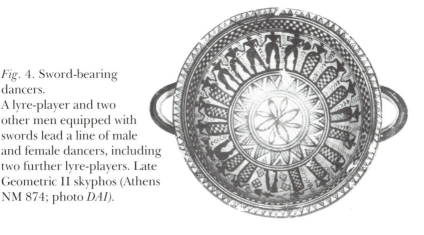

Fig. 4. Sword-bearing
dancers.
A lyre-player and two
other men equipped with
swords lead a line of male
and female dancers, including
two further lyre-players. Late
Geometric II skyphos (Athens
NM 874; photo *DAI*).

Fig. 5. Sword-bearers and horses flanking boxers.
Two views of Boeotian Geometric krater, from Thebes, *c.* 700 BC (Athens
NM 12896; photo courtesy of *Ministry of Culture of the Hellenic Republic*).

345

A particularly common motif on Athenian, Boeotian, and especially Argive Geometric vases is that of a man leading one or two horses. Since horses are associated with elite status, it is likely that such scenes represent, so to speak, portraits of aristocrats. On Argive pottery, these aristocrats are always posing 'naked', without any weapons, whereas on Athenian vases more than half are wearing a helmet or are dressed in full armour. Some Athenian and Boeotian figures, however, pose with swords only, which presumably means that they carry these weapons as part of their civilian costume (*Fig.* 6).[38]

Finally, a Late Geometric II amphora (735–700 BC) depicts a line of seven men who wear no armour, but nevertheless carry swords, and hold spears as well.[39] This is paralleled by a picture of a striding man equipped with both sword and spear on an Early Protoattic amphora in New York (700–675 BC; *Fig.* 7), which is remarkable because it is among the first to show explicitly that these weapons are indeed carried in combination with civilian dress, consisting of a long tunic (*khitōn*/χιτών) and a large cloak (*khlaina*/χλαῖνα). The visibility of the

Fig. 6. Men with swords, between horses.
(a) Late Geometric I kantharos (after Athens EPK 630.)
(b) Boeotian Geometric oinochoe, *c.* 750–735 BC (after Athens NM 236).

Fig. 7. Well-dressed man with sword and spear. Man wearing long tunic and large, tasselled cloak, apparently pinned across chest.
Neck panel of Early Protoattic amphora, *c.* 690–680 BC (New York 21.88.18; photo courtesy of the *Metropolitan Museum of Art*).

'naked' legs under the long tunic is further confirmation that the earlier, more stylized figures are in fact also imagined as fully dressed.

The cloak of the man on the New York amphora is almost identical to those worn by men in a procession on a few Early Protoattic fragments: it is apparently worn over both shoulders and fastened at the front, presumably by means of a pin or fibula.[40] The style of dress matches that of Homer's heroes, who carry their swords underneath cloaks pinned with fibulae, too.[41] In view of later developments, it is worth noting that the habit of carrying swords should indeed encourage the wearing of fastened cloaks, rather than cloaks thrown loosely over the shoulders. A cloak not firmly fixed in place would tend to be dislodged by the bulk and the movement of the sword underneath, and it would have to be thrown off, rather than simply thrown back, for the sword to be drawn.

Artistic representations from the second half of the eighth and the early seventh century BC thus depict men dressed and equipped in the Homeric manner. For the next quarter of a century there is no evidence, until around 650 BC a sudden change of fashion is detectable in Attic and Corinthian art. The sword disappears as an item of civilian dress, and a new type of cloak is introduced: a draped garment conventionally known as the *himation* (ἱμάτιον). Neither development appears to have attracted scholarly comment, but both phenomena are quite distinct and, I believe, of historical importance.

Thousands of men dressed in tunics and long cloaks or in long cloaks alone – *Mantelmänner*, as German scholars have got used to calling them – appear in archaic and classical vase-painting. As we shall see, a large proportion of these figures hold a spear. Yet barely a single one carries a sword.[42] The change from earlier representations is radical. From the middle of the seventh century onwards, swords are carried only by warriors in battle scenes, or by figures stripped for action, usually heroes such as Heracles and Theseus and their attendants. Such figures wear either a short tunic or nothing but a baldric; if they have a cloak at all, it is a short wrap around the shoulders, known as a *khlamys* (χλαμύς; *Fig.* 8), which may or may not be fixed with a pin or brooch. The persistence of the sword with these styles of dress may have obscured for scholars the extent of the change in fashion, but it is nevertheless unmistakable. Before 650 BC, men in full civilian dress regularly carry swords; thereafter, they do not.

The introduction of a new type of cloak at the same time is rather less securely attested, since so few earlier vases illustrate male dress, but it is clear that the first representations of the *himation* appear from

Fig. 8. The *khlamys*.
Drawings: as worn by youths in the works of the Heidelberg painter
(after Brijder 1991, fig. 84mn). Photos: as worn (with short tunic) in
reconstruction by Margarete Bieber (1928, pl. 56).

the middle of the century onwards. The *himation*, unlike the Homeric
khlaina or the *khlamys*, is never fastened, but wrapped around the
wearer. It may be simply draped symmetrically over both shoulders,
but more commonly it is draped around the whole body in a variety of
intricate ways. Typically, one end of the cloth hangs down in long folds
over the left arm, while the other end goes along the back, under the
right arm, and then across the front, to be thrown over the left
shoulder, from which it hangs down in loose folds (*Fig.* 9).[43] This style
and variations on it are universal in the classical period, when it is
described in literary sources and drawn in realistic detail in vase-
paintings. Even in the more stylized and at times fragmentary paintings of the archaic age it is easily recognizable by the folds under the

Fig. 9. The *himation*.
Drawings : as worn (with long tunic) by men in the works of the Heidelberg painter (after Brijder 1991, fig. 84be). Photos: as worn (with short
tunic) in reconstruction by Margarete Bieber (1928, pls. 57, 3; 58, 1–3).

left arm and behind the left shoulder, as well as by the hem running
diagonally upwards across the front.

In Attic iconography the *himation* worn in this way first appears on
two stands attributed to the Polyphemus Painter, dated to 650 and
640 BC, respectively. Both show a line of heroes or mortal men in
procession, all clad in the same way, as are figures on a couple of
fragments dated to the same period (*Figs.* 10, 19).[44] In Corinthian

349

vase-painting, the *himation* is first worn thus by a man leading a bull, on a fragment attributed to the Sacrifice Painter and dated to 650–30 BC (*Fig.* 11).[45] A group of gods wrapped in *himatia* is found engraved on the spectacular Crowe corslet, dated variously, but not earlier than 650 or later than 600 BC (*Fig.* 12).[46] Along with the short *khlamys*, the long *himation* accounts for the vast majority of cloaks pictured in all subsequent Greek art. The absence of this garment, worn in wrap-around

Fig. 10. Procession of spear-bearers.
A line of men in *himatia* and long tunics, holding spears; central figure labelled 'Menelas'. Middle Protoattic stand, Polyphemos Painter, *c.* 650 BC (Formerly Berlin A42; photo courtesy of *Antikensammlung, Staatliche Museen zu Berlin – Preussischer Kulturbesitz*).

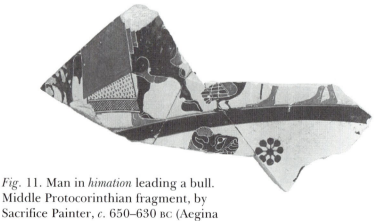

Fig. 11. Man in *himation* leading a bull.
Middle Protocorinthian fragment, by
Sacrifice Painter, *c.* 650–630 BC (Aegina
K340; photo *DAI*).

Fig. 12. Three gods in *himatia.*
Zeus and two other gods, wearing wrap-around *himatia,* face Apollo, who
wears his cloak bunched around the shoulders. Detail of engraving on
'Crowe' corslet, from Olympia, *c.* 650–600 BC (Athens NM; after Schefold
1966, fig. 5).

fashion, from earlier representations, and its sudden proliferation in
the iconography of two regions at the same time, strongly suggest that
it had not been in use before the middle of the seventh century, but
was then quickly and widely adopted.

It is no surprise that swords are never worn with the new model
cloak. As suggested, it would be difficult to carry a sword under any
kind of unfastened cloak, but it would have been particularly hard to
do so under a *himation* when it covered the left side of the body – the
sword-side – twice over. Moreover, the draped arrangement of the
himation was easily undone: many vase-paintings depict seated or reclining figures whose cloaks have fallen down and are lying in disarray
around their waists. Walking in such a precariously balanced garment
would have been tricky; walking in it while wearing a sword would
have been next to impossible. Classical sources show that a small
dagger might be concealed in one's cloak, 'under the arm',[47] but
himation and sword clearly did not mix.

There is no doubt that the countless gods, heroes, and mortals in art
who go without swords and are wrapped in *himatia,* reflect the style of
dress current for men in archaic and classical Greece. We cannot be
entirely certain that the earlier figures equipped with swords, long
tunics, and long, pinned cloaks equally reflected an actual, older,
fashion but it seems highly probable that they did. It is theoretically
possible that the sword in epic and art was a fictional attribute intended to mark its bearers as heroes rather than mortals, but, if so, it is
hard to see why it would have been abandoned by later artists

portraying the same gods and heroes. The most plausible explanation for the change in artistic representation is therefore that it mirrors a historical change of fashion.

Why did the Greeks abandon the sword and adopt an intricate style of wearing the *himation*? Recent discussions of the classical evidence have pointed out that 'wearing the cloak, with no fixed point at either shoulder or waist, must have required skill and unremitting attention'. Apart from its general tendency to slip and fall down, matters were complicated by etiquette, which required that the cloak should be draped neither too tightly nor too loosely, neither hitched up too high nor trailed too low. 'So careful had the arrangement to be, and achieved without belt or pins, that for all its theoretical simplicity it was very impractical.'[48] When a man donned a *himation*, he virtually immobilized his left arm and seriously inhibited all other movement. 'The only thing he was capable of doing now was watching, listening, talking, and taking decisions'; in short, what the draped cloak did was to 'enforce and proclaim leisure'.[49] This would have been no less true in the seventh century, of course, and this must be precisely why the *himation* was adopted in the first place, and why the most complex, wrap-around style of wearing it becomes the most widespread – because it is *a means of displaying conspicuous leisure*.[50]

The middle of the seventh century BC thus marks a turning point in the history of bearing arms: the sword rapidly and widely loses its place as an item of male civilian dress, at least among the elite, as those who can afford to do so begin to present themselves more as men of leisure and less as men of strength.

The spear in archaic art and society

Spears are almost as commonly carried as swords by civilians in Geometric art, although they do not appear before its last phase (LGII, 735–700 BC). Only one vase pictures a pair of spears held by a mourner beside a bier, but this vase and four others do have scenes in which men, each holding two spears but otherwise unarmed, perform what is evidently a funeral dance (*Fig.* 13).[51] As for the motif of the aristocrat posing with his horses, one late eighth-century Athenian and one early seventh-century Boeotian painting have a subject apparently in civilian dress and equipped with a spear rather than sword (*Fig.* 14). And, apart from the two instances, already cited, of men striding out, or lined up, with a spear in hand as well as a sword at their side (*Fig.* 7), there are three vases on which the men standing in line have spears only.[52]

The introduction of the draped cloak did not cause spears to go the

Fig. 13. Funeral dancers holding pairs of spears.
After a Late Geometric II amphora by the Philadelphia Painter (Texas MFA Houston).

Fig. 14. Men with spears and horses.
(a) After an early seventh-century Boeotian Geometric krater in the Ludwig Collection.
(b) After a Late Geometric II amphora by the Philadelphia Painter (Gothenberg Röhska Museum).

way of swords and vanish as an item of civilian costume in art. In the earliest surviving Athenian picture of men wrapped in the *himation*, all are holding spears (*Fig.* 10), and the motif remains common until about 500 BC,[53] reaching a peak of popularity in Attic vase-painting around the middle of the sixth century, in the work of artists such as the Heidelberg Painter (565–540) and the Amasis Painter (560–515).

The most numerous category of spear-bearers are the so-called 'onlookers' (*Fig.* 15). These are figures of men, women, and youths flanking a central scene without being part of it. Long dismissed as incongruous space-fillers, such figures have recently been the object of several studies, which agree that onlookers are meant to constitute an audience for the event depicted in the central image – often a heroic or athletic feat – and thereby to highlight its importance. These audiences are identified by their dress and personal adornment as contemporary

Fig. 15. Onlookers.
Man and youth in *himatia*,
holding spears, in the style of
the Heidelberg Painter (after
Brijder 1991, fig. 84a, l).

upper-class Athenians.[54] By no means all cloaked men and youths among them carry spears, but many do, and in the works of the painters just mentioned onlookers with spears are very common indeed.[55]

Flanking figures may hold spears regardless of whether they form the audience for a scene of arming, departure, or battle, a mythical event, a sporting contest, a dance, a *symposion*, or even a scene of courtship. It has been pointed out that 'their equipment therefore indicates, not the situation they are in, but their *status*. They are members of the upper class, and in line with the ideology of merit they are shown, not as men of wealth, but as warriors' (Kaeser 1990, 153). I would modify this. The symbolic significance of the spear is beyond question, but if the onlookers were meant to represent warriors pure and simple, this would have been much more effectively conveyed by portraying them as hoplites in full armour. Dressing them instead in the *himation*, the garment of the leisure class, and adorning them with long tunics and impressive hair-styles, the painters surely intended to show them as *both* warriors *and* men of wealth.

The same may be said of the well-dressed men and youths holding spears who are not just marginal decoration, but form the central subject of paintings, as they regularly do – in the work of the Heidelberg Painter above all. At one remove from the purely symbolic onlookers, we find, as a theme in its own right, 'a pair of motionless men facing each other in mirror-symmetry', dressed in *himatia* and holding spears 'stiffly'.[56] At a further remove, spear-bearers play an active part in narrative images. They may be found mingling with hoplites who are arming or taking their leave, a kind of scene in which boundaries between onlookers and participants are often blurred in any case.[57] Most intriguing are the spear-bearers pictured in meetings with one another or with women (*Figs.* 16, 17). These scenes may involve the juxtaposition of stock types, but the gestures of greeting and the direction of the glances make it quite clear that they are not random compositions. They represent social encounters, and seem such everyday images, without any heroic dimension, that the presence of spears is quite remarkable.[58]

On the other hand, spears are never carried by mourners in archaic vase-painting, which is not surprising, since even in Geometric art there is but a single surviving instance of this. We know that the spear could play a symbolic role at funerals of murder victims: if a male relative sought revenge, he was supposed to announce his intentions by carrying a spear in the funeral cortège and planting it on the grave.[59] The ritual function of the weapon highlights its significance as a token of masculine force and family autonomy, but also confirms that it was not normally carried by mourners. More surprisingly, in Athenian art spears do not feature in wedding processions either, although Corinthian vases do show bride and groom being escorted by relatives

Fig. 16. Spear-bearers socializing.
Men in *himatia,* holding spears; after a Siana Cup by the Heidelberg Painter, *c.* 550–540 BC (Taranto IG 4408).

Fig. 17. Meeting of men, youths and women.
Men dressed in *himatia,* holding spears. Details from a Siana Cup by the Heidelberg Painter, *c.* 560–550 BC (Heidelberg S61; photo courtesy of H.A.G. Brijder).

carrying spears (*Fig.* 18), which is what one might have expected, given the cross-cultural popularity of weddings as occasions for the display of weapons.[60]

In general, archaic painters felt no need to equip all, or even the majority, of their male figures with weapons; large numbers of cloaked men in archaic art lean on staffs instead, or stand empty-handed. A few scraps of literary evidence suggest that in reality spears were by no means universally carried either. We are told that, around 600 BC, the aristocrats of Mytilene had a habit of prowling the streets armed with clubs (*korynai*/κορύναι) and beating up commoners, and again that, in 561 BC, Peisistratos was granted a bodyguard of fifty men armed with clubs to protect him from his enemies.[61] The choice of weapon would have been most peculiar if, at the time, it had been the norm for men to go equipped with spears.

Evidently, spears were not as ubiquitous in archaic Greece as guns are in the Philippines, or axes in New Guinea, but nevertheless their presence in art is far from negligible. May we infer that, to the end of the archaic age, men could at least occasionally be seen in the town square or the streets armed with a spear as they attended to their daily business? To my knowledge, the question has never been asked, but I suspect that it has largely been taken for granted that the answer must be no; that spears in the hands of civilians must be purely an artistic convention, designed to 'heroize' a picture, or more generally to hint at the warriorhood and masculinity of their bearers.

Fig. 18. Wedding procession.
Featuring men and and a youth with spears. Middle Corinthian krater, Cavalcade Painter, *c.* 570 BC (Vatican 126; photo courtesy of *Archivio fotografico, Musei Vaticani*).

If, however, one accepts the argument that in the late eighth and early seventh centuries civilians did carry swords in life as in art, it would be perverse to argue that the same is not true of spears; men probably did routinely carry spears until the middle of the seventh century. Whether the custom continued after that is another matter. It certainly could have. Unlike the sword, the spear need not have been banished from social life by the introduction of the draped cloak, for, as hundreds of vases testify, one could perfectly well carry a spear while wearing a *himation*. In fact, a *himation* would only stay in place so long as its wearer kept his lower left arm raised, and this pose would be more easily maintained with a spear or staff to support the left hand. On the other hand, it is conceivable that spears were abandoned at the same time as swords, or fairly soon thereafter, yet were retained in art as a convenient symbol.

A more comprehensive investigation of the iconography than I have been able to undertake might throw further light on the matter, but for the moment the only consideration that seems to me to carry much weight is that, if our spear-bearers were unrealistic hybrids of civilians and warriors, they would look odd mingling with realistic hoplites, and odder still in 'meetings', as a group of abstractions socializing amongst themselves. This may not be decisive, but tends to favour the view that painters were familiar with a habit of 'bearing iron' which did not altogether fall into disuse until the end of the sixth century. From *c*. 650 to 500 BC, the role of spears may have been roughly analogous to that of guns in the mountain villages of modern Crete: most of the time, men do not actually carry them, but these weapons are a source of pride, and may therefore be taken out and displayed in public if the occasion seems to demand it. A cloaked man with a spear in Greek art, then, is no more (and no less) a symbolic figure than a Cretan shepherd posing with a machine gun or pistol to have his picture taken.[62]

The ultimate disappearance of such images is of interest regardless of their precise relation to reality. They are last seen in any numbers around 500 BC, on *lekythoi* by the painter of the so-called 'arming group' within the 'Phanyllis class': 'figures with spears held in front of them, just standing there, with impassive dull faces'.[63] After this, they only rarely appear even in explicitly heroic scenes. A decline appears to set in a few decades earlier. Trends in their popularity are hard to quantify, since their frequency clearly varied with the preferences of individual artists – they are rare in the works of, for instance, Exekias and the Swing Painter, created at roughly the same time as the works of the Amasis painter and the Affecter, in which they are common.

Still, it is probably no coincidence that, despite their popularity with the Amasis Painter in the early and middle phases of his career (560–530), they barely feature in his last phase (530–515). Similarly, nine out of ten of the Affecter's subjects carry spears between 550 and 530, but between 530 and 520 nine out of ten are empty-handed.[64] We may cautiously conclude that the spear as an item of civilian apparel, or as a conventional marker of manhood, lost ground from about 530 BC onwards, to disappear entirely a generation later.

Another major shift in perception of masculinity and social status must have been taking place in the late sixth century if, outside military contexts, men no longer felt it appropriate to present them-selves in public, or to be represented in art, with any kind of weapon. After the abandonment of the sword, the combination of *himation* and spear had struck a symbolic balance, advertising leisure and strength in equal measure. With the abandonment of the spear, the balance swings away from physical force as an integral part of male self-presentation. It is as if a man now has two distinct identities: one in his role as a soldier, represented in art by the figure of the armed and armoured hoplite, a picture of strength and courage; another in his role as a civilian, represented in art by the figure of the cloaked, unarmed male. A man's civilian costume – a term which only now becomes truly appropriate, although I have been using it throughout for want of a better word – barely hints at prowess and proclaims him above all a gentleman of leisure.

Staffs, poses, and parasols: further displays of leisure

The trends sketched so far are mirrored in the changing usage of the staff, and the introduction of the parasol. In *The Theory of the Leisure Class*, Thorstein Veblen noted that 'the walking-stick serves the pur-pose of an advertisement that the bearer's hands are employed other-wise than in useful effort, and it therefore has utility as an evidence of leisure. But it is also a weapon.' Hence, he explained, it is in 'modern life' carried by 'men of the leisure class proper, sporting men, and the lower-class delinquents', but not by 'the common run of men engaged in industry', nor by women 'except in case of infirmity, where it has a use of a different kind' (1899, 176). The dual role of the staff as a simple weapon and a symbol of leisure no doubt explains its ubiquity in classical Athenian vase-painting. Even scenes of sexual intercourse may feature a gratuitous staff, leaning against the wall as a reminder of its owner's status and masculinity.[65]

Yet it had not always been like this. In Homer, as we have seen, staffs, other than ornamental sceptres signifying hereditary privilege, are carried only 'in case of infirmity', and staffs find no place at all in vase-painting until 640 BC, when they make a first appearance in the hands of bearded men wearing *himatia* (*Fig.* 19).[66] Surely this is no coincidence. In a world where sword and spear are carried routinely and the attire of men is designed to symbolize prowess, the staff is second best, and stigmatizes the old and the weak. When the sword is abandoned and the display of leisure becomes more prominent, on the other hand, the staff can take on the significance attributed to it by Veblen: it becomes an emblem of leisure, and a weapon acceptable as an alternative to the spear.

The next change comes in the late sixth century, when the staff's potential use as a weapon is dramatically played down in favour of its role as an 'advertisement that the bearer's hands are employed otherwise than in useful effort'. Until the mid-sixth century, artists always show staffs carried like spears, held upright, at right angles to the ground. In 550 BC, however, an entirely new pose makes its first appearance. Instead of standing upright, the cloaked man leans heavily forward on his staff, which is placed at a sharp angle to provide a counterbalance (*Fig.* 20). For about a generation, this rather ungainly-looking posture remains unusual and tends to be awkwardly drawn, but from about 520 BC, it is commonly found and becomes increasingly elegant. Instead of keeping both feet on the ground and bending the knees, only the right leg is now used for support, while the left leg is

Fig. 19. Procession of staff-bearers in *himatia*.
Middle Protoattic stand, Polyphemos Painter, *c.* 640 BC (Berlin A41; photo courtesy of *Antikensammlung, Staatliche Museen zu Berlin – Preussischer Kulturbesitz*).

Fig. 20. Early representation of 'leaning' pose.
Men watching wrestlers; Siana cup, Manner of Heidelberg Painter,
c. 550–540 BC (Paris F67; photo courtesy of H.A.G. Brijder).

stretched backwards, the left foot barely touching the ground or indeed dangling in the air. Sometimes, the staff rests against the chest or under the left arm, and the whole body is balanced against it without the use of hands (*Fig.* 21). 'The man in *himation* leaning on his stick' has been dubbed 'the late archaic type of "onlooker" ' (Haspels 1936, 151), and remains much in vogue during the first half of the fifth century, peaking in popularity between 470 and 450. He all but disappears after 430 BC.[67]

The extraordinary new pose fits a pattern. 'The potential for bodily movement is reduced to a minimum by this posture. Only the lower left arm, the right arm, the head, and – at considerable risk to one's stance – the left leg can still be moved... The use of bodily strength is confined to keeping one's balance and keeping one's head up' (Hollein 1988, 22). For a century or so, the *himation* had immobilized a man's left arm, prevented him from using a sword, and signified that he could afford to restrict his movements. Now, the precarious balancing act involved in the new pose amplifies that message. It immobilizes a man's entire body, prevents him from using his stick in an aggressive manner, and signifies that he is not about to go anywhere or do anything. Appropriately, it is first adopted in art by men engaged in the most leisurely of pursuits: watching other men engage in sports. That, and the fact that it begins to grow popular in art just when the popularity of the spear begins to decline, leaves little doubt that the leaning posture is designed to display leisure at the expense of any display of strength.[68]

The introduction of the parasol as an item of male apparel caps the trend. The period of the greatest popularity of the leisurely pose, from 520 to 450 BC, coincides with the appearance of men dressed in such

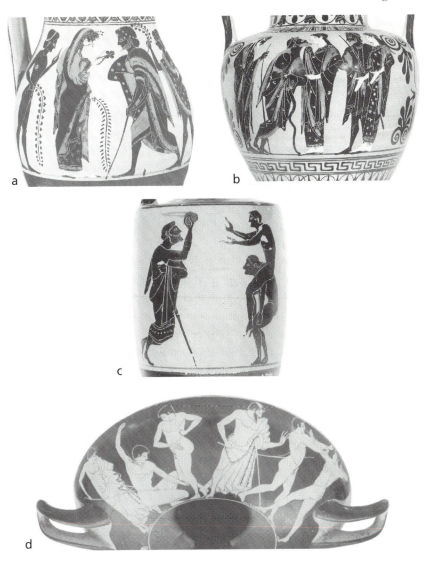

Fig. 21. Later representations of 'leaning' pose.
(a) Man courting a woman; Black-Figure olpe, Amasis Painter, *c.* 520 BC
(New York 59.11.7; photo courtesy of the *Metropolitan Museum of Art*).
(b) Man courting a woman; Black-Figure neck-amphora, Medea Group,
c. 520 BC (New York 56. 171.21; photo courtesy of the *Metropolitan Museum of Art*).
(c) Man tossing a ball to players; Black-Figure lekythos, Edinburgh Painter,
c. 500 BC (Oxford 1890.27; photo courtesy of *Ashmolean Museum*).
(d) Men umpiring boxing matches; Red-Figure kylix, Triptolemos Painter,
c. 490 BC (Toledo 61.26; photo courtesy of *Toledo Museum of Art*).

Fig. 22. Parasol-bearer.
Man in *himation,* long tunic, and
head dress, holding staff and
parasol. Red-Figure cup, Brygos
Painter, *c.* 480 BC (Louvre G285;
photo *La Licorne*/courtesy of
Musée du Louvre).

a seemingly feminine manner that they were long taken for transves-
tites. As recent studies have shown, however, their costume is not in
fact that of women. The long, flowing garments, soft boots, turbans,
and ear-rings are, rather, exceptionally luxurious items of male attire,
with more than a nod towards exotic, Oriental costumes. This style of
dress must be what Thucydides had in mind when he spoke of the
'luxury' of male attire in Athens and Ionia 'not long ago', and it offers
yet more evidence that conspicuous consumption and leisure were
reaching increasingly high levels.[69] The latest addition to the ensemble,
and the first to go out of fashion again, is the parasol, which appears
on a vase dated to 505 and disappears around 470 BC. Like the staff,
'the parasol identified its user as one who was not compelled to engage
in manual labour'; all the more so when the bearer was carrying a staff
in his other hand (*Fig.* 22).[70] Unlike the staff, however, it could not
double as a weapon. The parasols we see are small, dainty, and vulnerable; their decorative character is obvious from a poetic fragment
which refers to a newly wealthy man who 'travels in carriages, wearing
golden ear-rings, and carries a little ivory parasol – just as women
do'.[71]

That last comment speaks volumes. At the very end of the sixth
century, the adoption of the parasol by some members of the elite –
who had already abandoned a symbolic association with the spear and
made new symbolic use of the staff – was the final step. Devoting their
appearance as civilians wholly to the display of wealth and leisure, they
accepted that they would look 'like women', and gave up any show of
masculine strength.

The place of weapons in the home

The history of the display of weapons in public is complemented by the history of their storage at home. The earliest evidence reveals arms and armour on show in the most public part of the house, hung up on the walls of the dining room. In Homer, the richest men and the greatest warriors decorate their halls with dozens of weapons and pieces of armour, some captured in war. Odysseus' hall contains seventeen shields and helmets, and some twenty spears placed in a special rack (*dourodokēs*/δουροδόκης, *Od.* 1.128). Other valuables such as tripods may be on show in the same room, but weapons in such quantities would have dominated the scene.[72] Outside the world of epic fantasy, the picture is no different. Around 600 BC, Alkaios exhorted his companions at a *symposion* to keep up the fight against their political rivals, taking inspiration from the weapons and armour surrounding them.

> The great house glitters with bronze, and the whole room is decorated for War, with gleaming helmets...and gleaming bronze greaves, hanging from hidden pegs...and new linen corslets and hollow shields slung below them; next to them, swords from Chalkis; next, many belts and tunics. These we cannot forget...[73]

An impressive archaeological variation on this theme has recently been recognized in the five helmets, eight corslets, and sixteen belly-guards of 650–600 BC, from Afrati, Crete. Several pieces are inscribed with phrases such as 'Neon captured this', 'The Phrygian captured this', or 'Syenitos, son of Euklotas, this one'. Since these formulae are quite different from what one would find on objects placed in sanctuaries as dedications, it has been convincingly argued that the armour was hung up instead in a secular building, most probably the town's public dining hall, the *andreion* (ἀνδρεῖον).[74]

In the early sixth century, Corinthian vase-paintings repeatedly show shields, swords, bows and quivers, and more rarely helmets and cuirasses, suspended behind reclining drinkers and diners; one vase even has spears leaning against the wall (*Fig.* 23). Other vases feature cups, ribbons, and lyres in their place, and after *c.* 570 BC arms and armour are entirely supplanted by these paraphernalia of partying. When Athenian artists begin to paint *symposia* around 580 BC, they hardly ever include weapons except in heroic scenes.[75] This has led some to argue that the disappearance of weapons from convivial scenes in art corresponded to their disappearance from contemporary dining rooms. Thereafter, arms and armour would have been placed out of sight, in 'deep storage', along with the household implements. Plausible as this seems, it is not quite what happened.[76]

Classical literary evidence for the practice is very thin, but two passages in Herodotos indicate that this author, at any rate, took the custom of hanging weapons on dining room walls for granted; no other author says anything to the contrary.[77] Iconographic evidence is relatively abundant, and, although it is not without its problems, provides a clinching argument. As already said, weapons on walls do continue to feature in images from myth, such as Akhilleus or Heracles reclining, and also appear in non-heroic *symposion* scenes on two Athenian black-figure cups and two red-figure vases.[78] They are shown again on several archaic and classical reliefs from different parts of the Greek world, and, finally, on dozens of classical Athenian reliefs dedicated to heroes.[79] One might argue that all such late representations must be deliberately 'archaizing' or 'heroizing', but that would be to disregard a remarkable feature of some of the hero-reliefs. In these reliefs, above a reclining male figure, we often find armour and weapons indicating his heroic status, but in some cases only the bottom half of the armour is visible within the frame, although there would have been plenty of room to represent the whole of the symbolically significant armour on the large stretch of blank wall behind the hero.[80] The peculiar composition only makes sense if there is still a habit of hanging military equipment high above the couches in a dining room, faithfully rendered by the sculptor.

Neither in the sixth century nor later, then, did arms and armour go into the closet or chest. They remained on view, but vase-painters

Fig. 23. Symposium.
Featuring a cuirass and two helmets behind the diners. Middle Corinthian krater, Athana Painter, *c.* 600–570 BC (Louvre E629; photo *La Licorne*, courtesy of *Musée du Louvre*).

chose not to include them in their pictures any longer. Reasons for this are suggested by two trends spotted by Gröschel (1989, 83–4). Firstly, whereas the early poetic and artistic evidence refers to numerous sets of armour decorating a rich man's hall, and being used to equip his supporters in time of conflict, it was later apparently the norm for anyone to possess just a single panoply, for personal use. A fourth-century military manual recommends keeping an eye on 'those who have more than one': they must 'register their weapons' (Aineias Tacticus X.7). Secondly, the early evidence makes much of the 'gleam' of bronze armour illuminating the room, but a late sixth-century relief from Paros shows a shield hanging on the wall in a cloth cover (*sagma/ σάγμα*) and in the classical period shields and other pieces of military equipment were regularly kept under wraps.[81] This would no doubt sensibly protect the equipment from, say, being damaged by smoke, a problem raised in the *Odyssey* (16.288–90; 19.7–9, 17–20), but would detract much from its role as an object of display. So not only were fewer arms and less armour available in the household, but they began to be regarded as utilitarian items rather than showpieces deserving pride of place. Presumably this is why vase-painters, in choosing what features of the dining room to represent, came to ignore the weapons on the wall.

Two structural changes in archaic Greek society underlie this development. The first is of great importance, but will here be mentioned only in passing. When hierarchical relations prevailed and military service was a matter of private arrangements between aristocrats and their followers – as in Homer's epics – the possession of multiple sets of armour enabled a man to equip a band of friends and followers. The display of arms and armour thus symbolized his ability to mobilize force, as well as his personal masculinity and wealth. When, by contrast, egalitarian relations came to the fore, and military service became an obligation owed to the state – as was clearly the case in Athens, and perhaps elsewhere, by the end of the archaic age – aristocrats could no longer make practical use of spare panoplies, and these lost their meaning as symbols of power.[82]

The second major change is the rise of the *symposion*, an eating and drinking session which offered much scope for conspicuous consumption and even more for conspicuous leisure. Some features of sympotic culture are attested from the late eighth century onwards, when verse inscriptions on drinking vessels indicate that reciting or improvising poetry, dancing, and erotic pursuit are associated with conviviality.[83] The most significant development takes place in the mid-seventh century, when fragments of poetry allude to the custom of reclining on couches. The practice may have been adopted rather later in mainland Greece, where our literary and iconographic sources do not refer to it until the very end of the century.[84] Lying down to dinner is as dramatic an expression of leisure as one could convey by means of posture, much more so than sitting down on a chair or stool. Further activities associated with the *symposion*, such as drinking games and especially the habit of taking to the streets in a drunken procession (*kōmos*/κῶμος), also effectively advertise that one has time and energy to spare. At the same time, wealth is displayed in the decoration of the dining room. By the late fifth century, guests could be expected to admire its ornamental bronzes, its tapestries with figured decoration, and its ornate ceiling, wall-paintings, and mosaic floor – all regarded as excessively luxurious by more austere contemporaries.[85]

Such signs of wealth, however, are not yet conspicuous in archaic vase-painting. Instead, as noted, much space is devoted to representations of cups and musical instruments in the hands of the symposiasts or on the walls behind them. Nothing suggests that either the cups or the instruments are particularly valuable, and their significance is surely that they draw attention to the time spent at leisure, singing and drinking, rather than to the wealth expended in the process. It would seem, then, that the importance of the conspicuous display of leisure first, and wealth second, continued to grow after the introduction of reclining, until, about 570 BC, they came to dominate the culture of the *symposion* to the point of forcing the display of arms and armour, as symbols of warlike prowess, into a distant third place. It was not long before the poet Anakreon, speaking for those most dedicated to the life of luxury, pronounced it uncouth at a *symposion* even to *talk* about war and violence.[86]

Conclusion

In the middle of the eighth century, arms and armour were everywhere to be seen: panoplies covered the walls of dining rooms; swords and spears were carried in the streets; weapons, shields and other armour were deposited in graves. All of these customs show that physical prowess was seen as an essential quality of men. The decline of 'warrior' burials in Athens from about 735 BC was the first move away from this state of affairs, accompanied by growing expenditure on the visible parts of tombs, now covered by ever larger burial mounds and provided with offering trenches. A generation or so later, other central Greek states also abandoned the burial of weapons and turned increasingly to dedicating armour and other valuables in sanc-tuaries. Like Athenian funerary monuments, such highly visible dedi-cations were a form of conspicuous consumption which remained in the public eye, and thus had a broader and more lasting impact than the burial of riches.

Next, in a dramatic set of changes between 650 and 600 BC, the sword was abandoned, as the display of leisure grew exponentially with the introduction of the draped *himation* and the habit of reclining at dinner, as well as the transformation of the staff from a support for the infirm into a substitute weapon and symbol of status.

By 570 BC, arms and armour, although still visibly displayed at home, were no longer the showpieces they had been. Finally, in Ath-ens between 530 and 500 BC, the spear lost its place as an item of civilian costume to become strictly an item of military, hunting, and travelling gear. Again this trend was accompanied by the introduction of new forms of conspicuous leisure. First, the habit of leaning on one's stick, balancing precariously, constituted an almost histrionic display of leisure which no longer made any reference to physical prowess; then, the habit of carrying parasols as part of the most luxurious costume yet seen, blurred even the boundaries between the sexes.

How do these developments relate to the process of state-formation? One plausible scenario is that the Greek state, as it developed, imposed restrictions on private violence and on the usage of weapons, and thereby forced its citizens to find alternative channels for status rivalry. Competitive displays of wealth thus replaced competitive displays of prowess. This sort of thing has certainly been known to happen: when colonial authorities in, say, North America or Melanesia put a stop to violent local conflict, the natives often resorted to 'a war of wealth' in which they sought to defeat their rivals in gift-giving or potlatching. The evidence for legislation on weapons in the Greek cities in the West would fit this picture, and could be seen as revealing a gradual widen-ing of state-imposed bans on weapons: they were excluded first from meetings of the Council (Zaleukos), then from meetings of the popular assembly (Kharondas), and finally from the *agora* (Diokles), which would be tantamount to removing them from social life altogether. More generally, it may not be a coincidence that both the abandonment of the sword and the earliest surviving written laws date to the mid-seventh century. One could argue, then, that it was the state which created the leisure class.

There are, however, a couple of problems with this theory. For one thing, it cannot easily explain why warrior burials declined or why weapons lost their glamour as objects of display at home. More importantly, it leaves one wondering why we hear of no legislation, or any kind of central initiative, against 'bearing iron' in Athens, although we are rather well informed about Athenian law and history. That this is not merely an accident of survival is suggested by the contrast between the relatively *late* development of state institutions in Athens, and Thucydides' claim that the Athenians were *quicker* than the rest of the Greeks to restrain the usage of weapons – a claim which receives some support from the early discontinuation of warrior burial in Athens and from the absence of weapons from archaic Athenian, but not Corinthian, pictures of wedding processions. It therefore seems likely that in Athens, at any rate, the gradual demise of 'bearing iron' and rise of the leisure class *preceded* the crucial stages of the rise of the state.

An alternative explanation for the shrinking role of weapons in Athenian society and elsewhere may lie in another key development of the archaic period, often remarked upon by scholars: the relative decline of birth in favour of wealth as a prime criterion of status. This process has left traces in many an archaic poem lamenting the neglect of good 'stock', the growing importance of wealth, or the pernicious effects of greed, and above all in the reforms of Solon, which took political power out of the hands of the hereditary aristocracy to redistribute it amongst the citizens according to property class. As it grew in importance, the possession of wealth needed to be more emphatically demonstrated. New forms of conspicuous consumption and conspicuous leisure (including, alongside the *symposion*, gymnastic and pederastic competition) duly developed, and superseded old symbols of status – not only the hereditary sceptre, but also, step by step, the weaponry that had symbolized masculine prowess. If this is true, we may conclude that, in at least some parts of the Greek world, it was not the state which created the leisure class, but the leisure class which pushed weapons behind the scenes of social life, undercut the ideology of personal autonomy, and thereby made it possible for the state to develop.

These developments must have been a source of much tension and conflict, both among the upper classes and between the elite and the rest of the population. Since hereditary aristocrats resented the newly rich and the new importance of wealth *per se*, one would expect them to have reasserted their traditional claims to both high birth and masculine prowess. There may be evidence for this in early sixth-century poetic denunciations of, and legislation against, 'luxury' and *hybris*. Deploring and legally restricting the display of wealth is likely to have been a response on which a threatened aristocracy of birth and the excluded majority of the population could agree. Indulging in gratuitously aggressive behaviour against inferiors, on the other hand – as did the Eupatridai in Athens, to judge from the poems and laws of Solon, and the Penthilidai in Mytilene, beating up citizens at random[87] – may have been the way in which nobles chose to assert their physical prowess in the face of a changing social hierarchy and new values. Such acts of *hybris* were bound to unite the non-noble rich and the poor against them. The resulting three-way struggle dominated the history of archaic Greece.

It was not until the classical period that egalitarian ideals associated with democracy gave rise to a compromise. In the course of the fifth century, the growth of 'luxury' was partially reversed in Athens. Parasols, elaborate dress, and matching hairstyles, presumably always confined to a small group of very rich men, had gone out of fashion by about 450 BC. Leaning leisurely on one's stick, a pose much more widely attested, became less common at the same time, and virtually disappeared from art within the next two decades. Not only were levels of display by the elite toned down to what Thucydides called 'moderation in dress as it is practised now' (I.6.4), but at the same time a greater part of the citizen body was enabled to share in the life of leisure, through the provision of opportunities for the common man to take part in sympotic and athletic activities. It became a common notion that ideally *no* citizen should have to work for a living.[88]

Forms of conspicuous consumption and leisure, then, became less extreme, but were more widely shared and remained vital in classical Athenian social life. 'Bearing iron', with its emphasis on physical force as the key to high status, never made a come-back.

Acknowledgements

This paper has benefited from the generous advice and criticism of Paul Cartledge, Nick Fisher, Alan Johnston, Lloyd Llewellyn-Jones, and James Whitley. An embryonic version of it was delivered at the Cardiff conference, and provoked helpful comment from the participants, especially David Harvey, Daniel Ogden, Kurt Raaflaub, and P.J. Shaw. Herman Brijder, Lucilla Burn, Herbert Cahn, Alan Johnston, and Alexandra Villing kindly assisted in obtaining illustrations and permissions.

Notes

[1] US: *The Guardian* newspaper, 22 May, 1995; Crete: Herzfeld 1985, 68–70; Philippines: Kiefer 1972, 77; New Guinea: Meggitt 1977, 57.

[2] Thucydides I.5.3–6.3; Aristotle, *Politics* 1268b25–40. No-one has questioned

the accuracy of these claims; they are positively accepted by e.g. Helbig 1909, 49–51; Snodgrass 1980, 100; Gröschel 1989, 80–5.

³ Fisher, forthcoming a; Herman 1996, 28–9; 1994, 101–5; also 1993, 1995.

⁴ So Sheriff Richard Mack, the NRA's Law Enforcement Officer of the Year 1995. References as in n. 1.

⁵ Swords put on when getting dressed (1) for assembly: *Il.* 2.42–7; *Od.* 2.2–14; implicitly also *Il.* 1.190, 210, 219–20; (2) for informal meeting in agora: *Od.* 20.124–7; (3) for dealing with guest at home: *Od.* 4.307–11. Swords worn (1) at games: *Od.* 8.403–6, 416; (2) at dance: *Il.* 18.597–8; (3) at feasts: well into the feasting, Telemakhos takes off his sword to dig up the floor of his dining hall (21.119); he puts it back on again when fighting breaks out (21.431), while his guests draw the swords they had apparently been wearing all along (*Od.* 22.74, 79, 90, 98, 326–8). See n. 7 for an exception. On the Homeric evidence, see also Gröschel 1989, 75–9.

⁶ *Od.* 15.551–2; 16.40; 17.4, 29, 61–2; also 2.10; 20.127. Relieving a travel-ler of his spear is as much part of hospitality as an offer of food and drink: *Od.* 1.121–9; 15.282.

⁷ Spears brought into morning assembly: *Il.* 19.47–9; cf. 14.38. Five heroes get dressed for a late night meeting: three wear 'civilian' dress (see n. 34, below), but pick up a spear (*Il.* 10.21–4, 131–5, 177–8); a fourth puts on a helmet, and picks up a spear (28–31); the fifth picks up a shield only (149). Unlike elsewhere in the epics, swords are not mentioned, and were clearly not put on (10.255–6, 260–1); their absence might be used to support the com-mon view that Book Ten was a later addition, since, as will be argued below, the sword was abandoned earlier than the spear.

⁸ The swineherd Eumaios takes along a sword and spear when he guards the animals at night (*Od.* 14.528–31), and it is implied that the slave Dolios and his sons, who live on an outlying farm, dispose of weapons, too (*Od.* 24.496–8). Clearly, however, neither Eumaios nor the other shepherds are armed when they come to town: there is no reference to weapons when they quarrel on the way in (*Od.* 17.197–255), and later that day they are only able to join the fight between Odysseus and his enemies after weapons have been fetched for them from Odysseus' stores (*Od.* 22.101–4).

⁹ Beggars: *Od.* 13.437; 14.31; 18.103. Hephaistos: *Il.* 18.416–17; Priam: *Il.* 24.247. Wounded warriors, limping to meetings, support themselves with spears rather than staffs: *Il.* 14.38; 19.47–9.

¹⁰ Helpless old men: *Od.* 11.494–503; *Il.* 24.488–9; ridiculed cripples: *Il.* 1.571–600; 2.212–70. The humiliation of beggars is a theme throughout *Odyssey* 17 and 18.

¹¹ Priam chases away the Trojans with his stick (*Il.* 24.247) and Odysseus, as beggar, considers using his staff to hit an aggressive goatherd (*Od.* 17.236). Even a formal sceptre (see below) may be used to hit unruly commoners (*Il.* 2.198–9, 265–8).

¹² For this view of the role of princely sceptres, see Van Wees 1992, 276–80. Priests and prophets, too, carry special staffs symbolic of their status, and when Poseidon strikes the Aiantes with his *skēpanion* (*Il.* 13.59), this staff is presumably part of his disguise as the prophet Kalkhas, rather than a divine attribute.

[13] Gifts: *Od.* 16.78–81; 21.338–42; insult: *Od.* 17.222.

[14] Contra Gröschel 1989, 79.

[15] [Aristotle], *Athenaiōn Politeia* 15, 4–5 claims that the tyrant tricked the Athenians out of their weapons in 536 BC or shortly thereafter. Neither Herodotos I.64 nor Thucydides VI.54 hints at any such radical measure, and Thuc. VI.58 explicitly says that in 514 BC the citizens still held *armed* processions; *Ath.Pol.*, sticking by its story, is therefore forced to disagree and claim that processions at the time were unarmed (18.4). Similar stories are found in Polyainos I.21.2 (Peisistratos); I.23.2 (Polykrates); V.1.2 (Phalaris). The story about Aristodemos of Kyme is slightly more plausible than other such tales: after coming to power in 504 BC, he ordered people not to keep their weapons at home, but place them in temples so that they would be able to retrieve them in time of war, but would have no access to them for use in 'civil war and political assassinations' (Dionysios of Halikarnassos VII.8.2–3). Whether the tale is true is another matter.

[16] The little-known law of Zaleukos (Eustathios, *Comm. ad Hom. Iliad.* I.131.7–132 (*ad* I.190)) is noted by Hansen 1994, 41 n. 64. The other laws are more familiar: Kharondas: Diod.Sic. XII.19.2; Val.Max. VI.5, ext. 4 (using *contio* for *ekklesia*); Diocles: Diod.Sic. XIII.33, 2–3. Fisher, forthcoming a, suggests that Aristotle's discussion of bearing arms (n. 2, above), too, may imply legislation against the practice. See Osborne 1997, 78–9, for the view that such laws were designed specifically to ban the carrying of weapons 'at a time of civil strife'. Zaleukos' other legislation: Link 1992; Van Compernolle 1981. Greek lawgivers in general: Szegedy-Maszak 1978; Hölkeskamp 1992a, 1992b.

[17] The traditional floruit of Zaleukos is 663 BC, and Kharondas is variously placed in the seventh or sixth century. There is no guarantee that the laws of Zaleukos and Kharondas were not in fact added to 'their' legislation at a much later date. Conversely, Diocles' code, although reliably dated to 412 BC, was clearly a revision of existing laws, and the law associated with him may well be much older.

[18] Plutarch, *Lykourgos* 11 (discussed in detail by Piccirilli 1978, 917–36; 1980, 251–3, but without reference to the change of custom). Staffs in assembly at Athens: Aristophanes, *Wasps* 31–3; *Ekklesiazousai* 74–5, 150, 275–7; in jury courts: [Aristotle], *Ath. Pol.* 65, 1.

[19] The above and TABLE 1 are based on the catalogue in Strömberg 1993; cf. her comments, ibid., 81–3, and Whitley 1991b, 183 (table 11).

[20] This is based on a comparison of Courbin's chart of 'sexed' graves (1974, 5; based on osteological examination) with his catalogue of burials. It must be acknowledged that the numbers are small, but Late Geometric 'warrior graves' 6/2, 45, and 176/2, contain many additional valuable metal objects (although 179 does not), while of the other LG male graves, 172, 173/1, and 189 contain no goods at all; only 175 contains some pots, and a pair of large bronze pins. For the whole of the Dark Age, Courbin lists 15 known male burials; among these only 5 have weapons.

[21] So Morris 1987, 151 (Table 11): 16 out of 21 intact adult male burials in the Kerameikos cemetery between 1050 and 800 BC contained weapons, which is surely 'the result of exclusion in burial practices, rather than the

consequence of a very egalitarian society'. Something similar might be said for the group of burials by the West Gate, Eretria, *c.* 700 BC, where 5 out of 6 intact adult cremations contained weapons: Bérard 1970, 13–32.

[22] Explicitly Snodgrass 1967, 48 (burial with arms 'gives a homogeneous picture of the equipment of a single warrior'). In what follows, I am indebted to James Whitley for comment and for letting me see a forthcoming paper on gender in Greek burial customs.

[23] Strömberg 1993, cat. nos. 72, 83, 85 (Kerameikos PG24, 40, 43). Snodgrass 1964, 40 (A26), 47, and pl. 21, lists one further Athenian shield-boss, dated to the eighth century.

[24] Courbin 1974, 133–4 (helmet and cuirass in 'Panoply Tomb', T.45); Hägg 1983, 30 (helmets and cuirass in 'Stavropoulos' and 'Theodoropoulos' plot). The rarity of armour has recently been noted by Jarva 1995, 12–13; Kunze 1991, 71.

[25] Bérard 1970, 13–17 (Tomb 6).

[26] Of 22 Geometric 'warrior graves', just over three-quarters (17) include a sword; exactly half (11) include nothing but a sword. By contrast, only about 40% (9) include one or two spears, and only 14 % (3) contain nothing but a spear. Count based on Strömberg 1993.

[27] Härke 1990, 36, points out that the inclusion of weapons in Anglo-Saxon burials may be symbolic rather than a reflection of actual use, since '8% of those buried with weapons were below the age of about fourteen' and there is one striking case of a spina bifida sufferer buried with a spear and sword which he would have been incapable of using. Furthermore, as in Greece, there are instances of men buried with shields only (6.7%; p. 33), which clearly cannot correspond to any form of actual military equipment. Anglo-Saxon graves much more commonly than Greek ones contained shields (shield-bosses were found in 45.2% of a sample of 702 burials; p. 26), but, as in Greece, body armour is extremely rare ('helmets and mailcorslets have been found in only a handful of very rich burials'; pp. 25–6).

[28] Snodgrass 1977; 1980, 52–4, 99–100, places the disappearance of warrior burials *c.* 700 BC in the context of this trend, but still echoes Helbig in saying that Greek aristocrats 'certainly appear to have dropped the practice, at about this time or shortly after, of going about their ordinary daily business armed' (1980, 100). For a survey of weapons and other grave goods in the archaic period: Morris, this volume.

[29] See Whitley 1991b, 189 (table 12) and Morris, this volume (table 1).

[30] Unless they feature on grave goods and markers to compensate for the absence of the real thing. Vases from LGI (760–735 BC): Ahlberg 1971a, nos./pls. 19 (sword and dagger across the waist); 22c (helmet). Vases from LGII (735–700 BC): Ahlberg 1971a, nos./pls. 41c (sword, shield, spears on bier; corpse wears helmet); 46b (sword, spears 'above' bier); 49 (2 or 3 swords 'above' bier); Rombos 1988, pl. 9 (here *Fig.* 1) (shield, helmet, spears on bier).

[31] Ahlberg 1971b: vases with battle scenes: LGI: 18; LGII: 2. The dates of two further vases are contested, and of another six uncertain. For the role of 'heroic' images, including some of battle, in Protoattic vasepainting, see Whitley 1994b; Houby-Nielsen 1992.

[32] Patroclus: linen *heanos* and white *pharos*, *Il.* 18.352–3; Hector: *khiton* and

pharos, *Il.* 24.580–8. Before Hector's body is recovered, his wife has already promised that she will burn his 'fine and graceful garments' even if she cannot dress his corpse in them, 'to bring you fame among Trojan men and women' (*Il.* 22.510–14); cf. the importance of the shroud woven for Laertes (e.g. *Od.* 2.97–9). Offerings on pyre: *Il.* 23.166–76.

[33] For the likelihood of an early seventh century date, see Raaflaub, this volume; recently also Osborne 1996a, 157–60; Crielaard 1995; Dickie 1995; West 1995; Van Wees 1994, 138–46.

[34] In what follows, 'civilian' is used to denote a man not *currently* fulfilling a military role; in our period, 'civilians' and 'soldiers' are not distinct social groups. The phrase 'civilian dress/costume' does not refer to 'ordinary' or 'drab' clothing, but to all forms of non-military costume; 'full' or 'formal' civilian dress excludes the scantier clothing worn by hunters, travellers, and others engaged in strenuous physical activity.

[35] Geometric mourners with swords: Ahlberg 1971a, nos./pls. 8, 19, 20, 32. The presence of swords alone does not mean that these figures are fully armed warriors, as is evident from the contrast with other figures standing round the bier, who wear helmets as well (Ahlberg 1971a, nos./pls. 22, 32, 47, 48), and the contrast with the very common figures in funeral processions who carry shields and spears in addition.

[36] Note that female figures are often seemingly nude, too, especially in the first phase of Late Geometric, but it becomes clear in paintings of the later phase that they are imagined as wearing long dresses – just as one would have expected (see briefly Van Wees, forthcoming).

[37] Louvre A575 (e.g. Ahlberg 1971a, no./pl. 52; dated by Coldstream 1968, 211).

[38] Men posing with swords and horses: Attic: Rombos 1988, no. 89, pl. 61a (Athens EPK 630; here *Fig.* 6a), and no. 442 (Oxford 1929.24); Boeotian: Ruckert 1976, pl.4,1 (Oi9; Athens NM 236; here *Fig.* 6b) and pl. 13,2 (BA 39; Thebes Museum). See below for similar figures with spears. For full lists of Athenian, Boeotian and Argive armoured and 'naked' figures, and for their interpretation as aristocratic portraits, Rombos 1988, 272–83.

[39] Amphora formerly in the Hirschmann Collection: Rombos 1988, no. 163, pl. 24a.

[40] Cloaked men in procession on fragments of an Early Protoattic amphora from Phaleron: Cook 1935, pls. 48, 49ab. On these fragments, the attachment of the cloak at the front is not as clear as on the New York amphora, and they might therefore instead represent a *himation* (see below) simply draped across the shoulders. As for the New York amphora, Geddes 1987, 308 n. 14, is surely wrong to identify it as an early 'attempt' to draw a *himation*, and Marinatos 1967, 40, right to identify it with the pinned Homeric *khlaina* (though he goes too far in seeing in it a representation of *Il.* 10.131–5). Amphora and Phaleron fragments are dated by Cook 1935, 184–5, to 'not too early in Early Protoattic'.

[41] Cloaks pinned with ornate fibulae: *Il.* 10.133–4; 19.225–31. That swords are worn underneath the cloaks is clear from sequences of dressing (see n. 5, above) and undressing: men take off their cloaks without removing their swords: *Od.* 20.248–9 (cf. 22.74, 79, etc.); 21.118–9.

[42] I cannot claim to have seen every single relevant vase, but a quite extensive search has revealed only *one* civilian cloaked figure equipped with a sword: Odysseus in the famous scene of a Greek embassy dealing with a delegation of Trojan women, led by Theano, on a Late Corinthian krater (570–550; Vatican, Astarita 565; Amyx 1988, 264, pl. 116a). For the total number of *Mantelmänner*: Hollein 1988 discusses just over a thousand from Red-Figure pottery alone; there are probably at least as many on Black-Figure vases.

[43] See Losfeld 1991, 136–70, on classical evidence for the *himation*. The styles of dress – pinned versus draped – are clearly distinct, but a sharp terminological distinction between *khlaina* and *himation* is not found in our sources; it has been adopted by scholars for ease of reference.

[44] 'Menelas' stand (Berlin A42), dated and attributed by Morris 1984, 41, 43; 'Flowery ornaments' stand (Berlin A41), Morris 1984, 41, 46. Fragments: Morris 1984, pl. 4,555 (from Aegina); Cook 1935, pl. 51b (from Eleusis).

[45] Fragment Aegina 340 (Kraiker); Amyx 1988, 35 (Sacrifice Painter, no. 7).

[46] Hoffmann 1972, 50–3 (and pl. 25), discusses the various dates and places of origin suggested; he himself opts for 630–10, and for a 'Peloponnesian origin', while not ruling out the possibility that it may be Attic.

[47] The hidden weapon of plotters is never the sword, but always the dagger (*enkheiridion*/ἐγχειρίδιον), as used by Harmodios and Aristogeiton (Thucydides VI.57.1; 58.2), the aristocratic faction in Corcyra (III.70.6), the Four Hundred (VIII.69.4), and the assistants of the Thirty (Xenophon, *Hellenika* II.3.23 ('under the arm') and 55). Lysias refers to the dagger as the typical murder weapon (IV.6).

[48] Quotations from Geddes 1987, 312–13, discussing also the evidence for *himation*-etiquette, as does Hollein 1988, 278. Geddes' fine discussion is unfortunately marred by the assumption that the *himation* is adopted as a regular form of dress only *c.* 500 BC, to 'replace' the long tunic (*khitōn*; 1987, 312). In fact, the long tunic is replaced by a short tunic, or by nothing at all, while the *himation* continues to be worn as it had been for a century and a half, except perhaps that it becomes plainer and more uniform.

[49] Geddes 1987, 323–4. Note also that it reinforced the impression of self-control which men sought to cultivate at the same time (Van Wees, forthcoming).

[50] Bieber noted the appearance of the wrapped *himation* in archaic art without dating it, or discussing its significance (1934, 27), but commented that the simpler style of wearing it 'symmetrically' across the shoulders, initially quite common, had become rare by the late archaic period and is never found in classical art (30, 32). This suggests that the display of leisure in dress became increasingly widespread.

[51] Mourner with spear: Ahlberg 1971a, 96; no. 38/pl. 38a (amphora in private collection in Athens). Funeral dancers with spears: Rombos 1988, no. 147/pl. 22, and no. 172, pl. 9; Ahlberg 1971a, nos./pls. 38, 39, 43 (there are also dancers without spears: Ahlberg 1971a, nos./pls. 35, 41, 42).

[52] All three from the LGII Workshop of Athens 894: Rombos 1988, no. 183 = Villard 1957, figs. 1 and 4; *CVA* Louvre 16, pls. 40–1 (Louvre CA 3468, featuring on each side a procession of 12 men, who are clearly civilians, in contrast to the helmeted men with square shields or corslets elsewhere on the

vase); Rombos 1988, no. 184 (Swiss market) and no. 208 (Marathon K134), with 9 men each.

[53] As in the discussion of the sword, we are concerned only with images of fully dressed men and youths: nude and semi-nude figures of hunters, travellers, or men otherwise stripped for action continue to be shown with spears as well as swords in classical art, too.

[54] Brijder 1991, 337; Kaeser 1990, 151–6; Scheibler 1988, 547–57; Carpenter 1986, 37–40; Korti-Konti 1979 (with catalogue). Von Bothmer 1985, 70, treats onlookers as merely 'supernumeraries' required to fill space on certain types of vases.

[55] The bulk of these painters' works are illustrated in: Von Bothmer 1985 (Amasis Painter) and Brijder 1991 (Heidelberg Painter, who embraces most of the range, including spear-bearing onlookers at a symposion, no. 366/pl. 120de (Taranto 110339), and at a dance, no. 367/pl. 121d (Louvre CA576)). A few examples from the work of other Attic painters: Bakır 1981, A15/pls. 18, 23 (Athens NM 12587 by Sophilos, *c.* 600–590); Böhr 1982, nos. 4, 7, 65, 123, 133, 135, 138–9 (Swing painter, 540–520); Brijder 1983, pls. 10b, 13c, 161c; Callipolitis-Feytmans 1974, pls. 29.48, 36.7, 39.25, 40.42, 41.33, 61.1. See also Mommsen 1975 for the many cloaked men with spears in the work of the Affecter (below n. 64), some of whom flank scenes of homosexual courtship (e.g. no. 3/pl. 17; no. 68/pl. 74). Boeotian: Kilinski 1990, pl. 18,3 (*c.* 550). Corinthian: Amyx 1988, pls. 80b (*c.* 590–570) and 119,2a (*c.* 570–550).

[56] Brijder 1991, 365; no. 419/pl. 134d; no .423/pl. 137c; no. 425/pl. 138d; Von Bothmer 1985, no. 51 (all 550–540); see also e.g. the unattributed paintings on *CVA* Munich 7, pls. 328,3–4; 329,2–3 (Munich 1448, 1449; *c.* 570 and 560).

[57] Brijder 1991, no. 407/pl. 133ab; no. 426/pl. 139df; Von Bothmer 1985, nos. 1, 7, 25 and figs. 20, 51, 56; Mommsen 1975, nos. 69/pl. 74 (Affecter) and pl. 131 (Elbows-Out Painter).

[58] Meeting of men: Brijder 1991, no. 385/pl. 129b; also pl. 159a, c (by C-Painter, *c.* 570). Men and youths: ibid., no. 367/pl. 121e. Men and women: ibid., no. 362/pl. 118ef, 119; no. 446/pl. 144a.

[59] [Demosthenes] 47.69 and Pollux VIII.65, for carrying the spear; Hellanikos FGH 323a F1 and Istros FGH 334 F14 (*ap.* Harpokration, s.v. ἐπενεγκεῖν δόρυ), for planting it on the grave; see Seaford 1994, 90.

[60] Athenian wedding processions are discussed and illustrated in Oakley and Sinos 1993 (note p. 27 for the threat of violence at weddings). One Attic scene which has been plausibly interpreted as the bride being brought before her father-in-law does have cloaked spear-bearers on both sides (Brijder 1991, 394; no. 369/pls. 122–3; Cambridge 30.4). 'Armed' wedding processions in Middle Corinthian art (*c.* 590–570): Amyx 1988, pl. 79b (New York 27.116); Guarducci 1928, pl. 20, 4–5 (Vatican 126).

[61] Penthilidai of Mytilene: Arist. *Pol.* 1311b26–8. Peisistratos: Hdt. I.59; Arist. *Ath.Pol.* 14, 1–3; Plut. *Solon* 30 (50 men); Diod.Sic. XIII.95.6; for an interesting discussion of their significance: McGlew 1993, 74–8. 'Club-bearers' are also attested for Sikyon, but our sources believe that the term referred to the local serf population: Stephanos of Byzantium, s.v. Χίος; Pollux III.83; cf. VII.68.

[62] Herzfeld 1985, esp. 89, 181–2, and, for posing with guns, pl. 1.

[63] Haspels 1936, 64; Appendix VIII.B–E; for a recent illustrated catalogue: Giudice 1983.

[64] For the Amasis Painter, see Von Bothmer 1985: the only cloaked spear-bearer in late work appears in no. 25 (Boston 01.8027, showing Achilleus arming). As for the Affecter, on the basis of Mommsen 1975, I calculate that on the 65 earliest vases (Groups I–IV and all but the last 3 from Group V) there are 272 relevant figures, of whom 119 (44%) carry spears, and another 125 (46%) carry what I take to be a stylized version of the spear (which does not have a spear-head, but consists only of a shaft as long as a spear, and is certainly too long to be a regular staff, which is never more than chest-high); only 27 figures (10%) are empty-handed; a single one carries a short staff. On the 42 later vases (the remainder of Group V, and Groups VI–VIII), there are 116 relevant figures, of whom 7 (6%) carry spears of some description, and 107 (92%) are empty-handed; two carry a short staff.

[65] See Dover 1978, R502, 520, 543, 545, 573; also R454 (staff beside washing youth), R1027 (beside dressing youth); R59, 196ab (youths embracing boys without letting go of their staffs).

[66] On the Protoattic 'Flowery Ornaments' stand (see n. 44 above). It is a measure of the general lack of scholarly concern with our subject that Sarah Morris in her detailed study failed to note that the cloaked men are carrying staffs rather than spears, and misleadingly referred to them as 'warriors' (1984, 46–7, 122).

[67] Earliest instances of the new pose: Paris F67 (Brijder 1991, no. 472/ pl. 148d; here *Fig.* 20); Oxford 1966.768 (*ABV* 113,80; Boardman 1974, fig. 70); Munich 1468 (*CVA* Munich 7, pl. 344,1–2); all dated to 550–540 BC, and all involving men watching wrestlers or boxers. Same pose, *c.* 520: Brussels A130 and Munich 1411 (Böhr 1982, pls. 123, 183); New York 59.11.7 (Von Bothmer 1985, no. 30; here *Fig.* 21a; this last one is so awkwardly drawn that Von Bothmer (1960, 75) suggested that the staff might represent a crutch, and its bearer the lame god Hephaistos. The earliest more elegant version of the pose appears to be New York 56.171.21 (Von Bothmer 1985, fig. 88; here *Fig.* 21b), dated to 520–510. Other Black-Figure examples are listed by Haspels 1936, 151, and hundreds of Red-Figure examples are catalogued and analysed by Hollein 1988.

[68] So Hollein 1988, 23: 'according to the vase-paintings, from 520 BC the ostentatious display of skole [sic: *skholē*/σχολή, 'leisure'] becomes ever more important'; he refers to our leaning figures as the 'skole-type'. Despite recent challenges (Jenkins 1985; B. Nagy 1992), it still seems most likely that the ten men in various 'leaning' poses on the East Frieze of the Parthenon represent the Athenian tribal heroes (Kron 1984); if so, this is dramatic confirmation of the extent to which leisure has displaced prowess by the mid-fifth century: 'their warrior status has been tamed' (Spivey 1995, 48–9).

[69] Thucydides I.6.3, referring to the wearing of 'linen tunics' and hair 'done up in a bun'. The reference must be to *long* tunics (cf. Asios F13 Kinkel) such as are frequently depicted in archaic art, and are last seen, in their most elaborate form, on these vases depicting exotically dressed men (nicknamed 'the boon companions'; discussed by Kurtz and Boardman 1986; Price 1990;

Frontisi-Ducroux and Lissarrague 1990). Hair worn in a bun at the back of the head is a common late archaic and early classical hairstyle; Thucydides and others also mention the use of 'golden grasshoppers' as part of the head-dress; the reference is still not satisfactorily explained: see Gomme 1959; Hornblower 1991, *ad* I.6.3. In his commentary on the *Iliad* (*ad* 13.685), Eustathios notes: 'It is said that they had a habit of wearing tunics reaching to the feet, and grasshoppers, until the generalship of Perikles.' This presumably means *c.* 450 BC, which fits the vases and Thucydides' claim that it was 'not long ago'.

[70] Miller 1992, 105; her article offers a full discussion of the evidence.

[71] Anakreon F388, 11–12 Page. See Miller 1992; Slater 1978 for discussions of this passage.

[72] For the number of weapons in Odysseus' hall, and for the decoration of such halls generally, see Van Wees 1995, 148–54 (esp. n. 4). For captured arms and armour, see esp. *Il.* 13.260–5.

[73] Alkaios F140 West, Campbell (203, 357 L-P). See Colesanti 1995 for the view that the fragment does indeed refer to a normal sympotic setting; my translation incorporates some of his suggestions.

[74] Armour and inscriptions: Hoffmann 1972, esp. 15–16. Deposition in the *andreion*, identified with a building measuring 11 x 6 m: Viviers 1994, 244–9; cf. Lebessi 1969, 415–18 (I owe the references to James Whitley; see his chapter in this volume for the inscription on a related piece of armour, the Spensithios *mitra*).

[75] The evidence is catalogued and discussed in Fehr 1971, esp. 29, 55, 61, and nos. 7, 10, 11, 12, 15, 31; Dentzer 1982, 85, 96–9.

[76] Gröschel 1989, 82–4; briefly also Bremmer 1990, 144.

[77] Herodotos I.34 is the best evidence; Colesanti 1995, 386, points out another instance at III.78. Both passages refer to non-Greeks, and could therefore be explained away as referring to a barbarian custom; however, it is so obliquely mentioned by Herodotos that it must have been very familiar to his audience. A reference in Aristophanes' *Akharnians* to hanging a shield over the embers (279; adduced by Jackson 1991, 233) is a joke, and should not be taken to mean that armour was normally hung up above the hearth. Gröschel 1989, 83, relies heavily on Xenophon, *Oikonomikos* IX.6 ff., which discusses household storage, but in fact leaves it quite unclear how and where weapons were stored: all it does is to list weapons as a distinct category of household implements which must be given an 'appropriate' place in the house – the dining room is included in the list of rooms available for storage.

[78] Black-figure: Fehr 1971, nos. 75, 76 (see Brijder 1991, no. 366/pl. 120de; no. 421/pl. 135e; dates 560–550 and 550–540 BC; both show a single sword). Red-figure: Fehr, nos. 430, 463.

[79] Catalogued and illustrated in Dentzer 1982; see also Fehr 1971, nos. 465–8.

[80] Dentzer 1982, R439/pl. 107/fig. 661 (flaps of corslet); R458/pl. 110/ fig. 679 (lower part of corslet, and what appears to be a 'shield-apron' of a shield outside the frame). Contrast the other token of heroic status, the horses' heads which appear in little square frames and are clearly only sym-bolically present.

[81] Fehr 1971, no. 467; Dentzer 1982, R286/pl. 88/fig. 536 (*c.* 510 BC). For

the literary evidence, Gröschel 1989, 83–4. Diod.Sic. XX.11.2 shows that shields could be kept in their covers even on campaign.

[82] Gröschel 1989, 83–5; see also Raaflaub 1997a, 53–7, for changes in military organization. Gröschel 1989, 85, has argued that, as arms and armour became more widely available, they were no longer prestige items and the rich no longer bothered to show them off.

[83] Murray 1994, 49–51, on 'Nestor's Cup' (Pithekoussai, *c.* 725–720 BC); dancing is referred to in a verse on an LGII *oinokhoe* from Athens: Jeffery 1990, 68, and pl. 1,1; Alan Johnston has alerted me, however, to the recent (and not to my mind altogether convincing) suggestion by Chadwick (1996, 218–21) that (a) the text is a funerary inscription, rather than a sympotic poem, and (b) 'dancing' may be a euphemism for sexual intercourse. In Homer, 'sympotic' elements are few – perhaps deliberately kept to a minimum – but the performance of poetry by host and guests (as opposed to hired entertainers) is famously illustrated by Achilleus (*Il.* 9.186–91), and the suitors dance while a bard sings (*Od.* 1.421–2). See Dalby, this volume.

[84] Earliest Greek allusions to reclining: see Murray 1994, 52–3, on Kallinos F1 West and Arkhilokhos F2 West (both *c.* 650 BC). First mainland reference: Alkman F19 Page (*c.* 600); earliest symposion scene on (Corinthian) vase: 'Eurytion' krater (Louvre E635), *c.* 610; see Dentzer 1982, 123–5; Fehr 1971. Murray's suggestion (1994, 51) that the reference in the inscription on Nestor's Cup (n. 83 above) to being seized by 'the desire of Aphrodite' 'implies the arrival of the reclining couch' as early as the late eighth century, on the grounds that 'the seated banquet with food is much less well adapted to the pleasures of love than the reclining *symposion*' surely cannot carry much weight. The appearance of scenes of conviviality in art must indicate that eating and drinking in company had acquired a new significance, and the move towards conspicuous leisure inherent in the introduction of reclining seems the most likely occasion.

[85] Aristophanes, *Wasps* 1214–15, *Frogs* 937–8, and FF436, 611; Attic Stelai (Pritchett 1956, 244–54); Lysias IX.27; Xenophon, *Memorabilia* III.8.10; Plato, *Republic* 529b; Menander, *Dyskolos* 914–30; Theophrastos, *Characters* 21.15; Plutarch, *Alkibiades* 16.

[86] Anakreon, Eleg. F2 Page: 'I do not like him who speaks of conflicts and tearful war as he drinks his wine beside a full krater, but him who is mindful of the pleasant atmosphere of the feast as he mixes the splendid gifts of the Muses and Aphrodite.' Contrast the linking of war and symposia by Arkhilokhos FF1, 2 West, and the martial exhortations of Tyrtaios and Kallinos (Bowie 1990). The rejection of stories of war by Stesikhoros (F210 West) is a possible parallel to Anakreon which would date to *c.* 600–560, but the context is not clear. The superficially similar rejection by Xenophanes (FB1 West) refers primarily to tales of war and conflict among the gods.

[87] For these archaic expressions of aristocratic *hybris*, see especially Fisher 1992, 36–85, 201–46.

[88] See Donlan 1980 for changes in social hierarchy; Morris 1996a, and this volume, for the conflict of elite and 'middling' ideologies; Fisher, forthcoming(b), on the spread of sympotic and gymnastic culture in classical Athens.

14

WRITING THE HISTORY OF
ARCHAIC GREEK POLITICAL THOUGHT

Paul Cartledge

Poetry makes nothing happen (W.H.Auden)

Problematics

We live, according to the director of the suitably hellenizing 'Demos'
thinktank, in an 'Antipolitical Age'; or at any rate in an age in which
the most we can aspire realistically to practise is some form of
'subpolitics'.[1] One respected political commentator, now the editor of a
national newspaper, has emotively but not inaptly characterised 'Britannia' as 'a hemmed-in nation, whose ancient sources of authority
have been polluted, whose political culture has been eroded and
whose centralising state reforms have thrown up new questions of
democratic control'.[2] It has therefore occurred to me and others in this
country, as to colleagues in France, Australia and the United States in
comparable circumstances, to ask whether we can or should look or
turn back to the ancient Greeks for inspiration or guidance to help us
on the road to political, and more especially democratic, reconstruction or at least renewal.[3] Since it is agreed that there can be no
question of treating the ancient Greek *polis* (city, city-state, citizen-
state, city-republic) or even the Athenian democratic *polis*, as a simple
model or paradigm to imitate, the emphasis tends to be displaced on to
the Greeks' conceptions of the political and their more or less self-
conscious reflection upon the politics of their and other societies.
Hence, in significant part, but nevertheless only in part, has arisen my
current book project, *Political Thought in Ancient Greece: Elite and Mass from
Homer to Plutarch*.[4] The present essay consists of methodological pre-
liminaries to the portions of this forthcoming book which are essentially concerned with what is conventionally called the archaic period.

There are apparently two broadly distinguishable modes or styles of
writing political theory, or the history of political thought: the reflective
and the prescriptive. By temperament and inclination, I strongly incline

towards the latter, though what exactly it is that on the basis of my study of the ancient Greeks I shall wish to prescribe to my modern readers has – perhaps fortunately – not yet become sufficiently clear. The dual problematic of my book is, however, clear enough. On the one hand, it will seek to re-open the question of the relationship between political theory (or plain thought) and practice, *theōria* and *praxis*: which of the two came first and/or took causal precedence, or did so more often, in the Greek world from the time of Homer (understood as the era or moments of the monumental composition of the two epics between about 750 and 650 BCE) to that of Plutarch (first-second century CE)? On the other hand, it will take as its *leitmotif* the relations, in both theory or ideology and concrete actuality, between the Elite and the Mass (the few and the many, the rich/well-born/morally superior and the common citizenry, and other formulations and specifications): why and how did Greek political thought or theory typically operate in terms of such a binary and polarised representation of the relevant political actors?

The latter theme not only follows on directly from my previous book, *The Greeks* (Cartledge 1993/1997), but will also, I hope, help me to reduce the otherwise almost limitless scope of the new book to manageable proportions, as well as giving it a coherent axis of argument. But that is not my topic, or my main topic, here. It is on the relationship of theory with (or as opposed to) practice that I aim here to engage in a dialogue with my readers. This is not of course a new problematic in our field. Whole books have been devoted to it, and many heavyweight articles.[5] Nor *a fortiori* is it new in the field of the history of western political thought more generally, or in histories of particularly dramatic or pivotal political events or processes that are considered to have borne an especially heavy freight of ideas or ideology. One might, for example, begin by noting a programmatic remark of Bertrand Russell: 'Philosophers are both effects and causes...causes (if they are fortunate) of beliefs which mould the politics and institutions of later ages.'[6] That could perhaps be dismissed outright as mere self-referential and self-serving idealism, in more than one sense. But harder to dismiss out of hand is Leon Trotsky's more temperate and modest comparison of intellectuals to the topmost branches of a tree, which are the first to shake when a tempestuous wind blows but not sufficiently powerful or detached to uproot the tree by themselves. Trotsky, after all, might be thought to have known what he was talking about. And when one conjures further with the names of (to indicate a wide range of intellectual-political projects, styles and performances)

Voltaire and Rousseau, James Madison, the Thomases Paine and Jefferson, Marx and Engels, Adolf Hitler, Vaclav Havel – then perhaps it becomes at least initially promising to start thinking in similar terms about, say, Solon and Cleisthenes, and the Greek or Athenian democratic 'revolution' of the sixth century BCE.[7] Anyhow, even if the problematic is not new, I shall hope to give it a fresh spin or two.

Let us begin with a seeming paradox: on the one hand, there is easily detectable in much Greek thinking, not only political, an all-pervasive conservatism. Greeks often found themselves or perceived themselves as being in the grip of the past, with the linguistic consequence that political ideas and practices which we might want to label positively as 'revolution', such as the invention of democracy, they would habitually and automatically anathematise as 'new' or 'newer things', opposing them unfavourably to that which was traditional (*patrion*), in accordance with ancestral custom and practice, even – or especially – when the supposed tradition was perceptibly or demonstrably an invented one.[8] On the other hand, the Greeks did actually achieve revolutions or at any rate profound and lasting transformations in both their political practice and their political consciousness, something structurally far deeper and more permanent than is conveyed by the terms *metabolē* or *metastasis* (transformation) employed by the author of the 'Constitution of the Athenians' attributed to Aristotle.[9] Again, the case of democracy comes to our mind, especially as the Greeks' direct, participatory democracy was – within its self-imposed limits – far more radical and unsettling, almost literally the world turned upside down, than anything we have had to operate or cope with since the re-invention and taming of democracy in the last couple of centuries.[10]

To meet that seeming paradox, with special reference to democracy's 'emergence' (or however otherwise the process should be labelled) at Athens, three explanatory hypotheses might be proposed, each capable of variant expression or emphasis. First, an evolutionary, or teleological, approach might suggest that the seeds of the *nuova scienza* of fifth- and fourth-century political theory (as of physical science, historiography, and so forth) were sown already perhaps as far back as Homer, in terms of the extant literary sources,[11] or not too long thereafter,[12] and indeed were implicit in the very idea and structure of the new and distinctively Greek (as I take it to be), early historical state-form called *polis*.[13]

A second hypothesis might hold that there was nothing or little predictable and inevitable about the political revolution of theory and practice, at the centre of which was democracy, and that therefore some special, individual factor needs to be invoked. It has been said bitterly of official communism that ideas do have consequences, and that those who hold them are not their only victims; perhaps, inverting that, one might want to say cheerfully that Cleisthenes was not the sole beneficiary of his, highly consequential, political ideas. In other words, without going to the lengths of invoking mere accident or serendipity, one might go as far as to credit particularly gifted, forceful or transcendent individuals, such as Cleisthenes may have been, with the historic and heroic role of successfully applying political thought, if not theory, to political (re)construction.[14]

A third hypothesis, a sort of Aristotelian *via media*, might try to combine elements of the preceding two. Although the democratic experiment or revolution was not inevitable, it might be suggested, it was crucially facilitated by conditions peculiar to Greek political life, or to archaic Greek political life, or to archaic Athenian political life. These conditions might include the possibility that Greek political thought and thinkers were unusually influential on events and processes – thanks to either the nature of Greek political society in general or that of the Athenian *polis* in particular in the precise circumstances of the archaic period. The operation in combination of both these causal variables is, roughly speaking, the hypothesis I shall outline and endorse below.

At all events, the case seems to demand as open an approach as possible, at least to start with. Openness is enjoined further by a brief consideration of the available sources in the abstract. The substantive part of the paper will retain a strong source-critical slant, in keeping with the present book's overall problematic.

Sources

The first main problem is one of selection or rather selectivity. There is plenty of contemporary visual art available, generally well classified and understood typographically. This may include not just visual allusions *via* myth to political propaganda – for example, the myths of Heracles as deployed (allegedly) in sixth-century Athenian ideological and factional struggle – but art as political theory or at least political thought.[15] Yet it is hard to get a purchase on the 'language' of visual art at other than a rather general and so to speak broadbrush level. The semantics of archaic visual art will never be as well understood as the lexicon of Homer, Alcaeus or Solon, as that has been explicated, for example, with respect to the changing significance of the meaning of '*dēmos*' from Homer onwards.[16] Perhaps the most we can achieve in this regard is some grasp of the expressive symbolism of an age or a political milieu.

Next, there is a handful of contemporary and authentic documentary inscriptions of a precisely political character – laws, sacred and less sacred, passed by cities in old Greece, and foundation-decrees of and for new cities in the colonial world, which somehow imply political thinking at various levels of explicitness and sophistication.[17] Connected with these are the later and heavily mythicised traditions regarding the early archaic lawgivers, of which only those to do with Solon of Athens can be tested at all rigorously against other more obviously reliable types of evidence.[18] In a class by itself, but straddling some aspects of all the above, is the so-called Spartan Great Rhetra, an oracle or a law, or both, not only attributed to the at least semi-legendary lawgiver Lycurgus but also somehow involving two putatively genuine Spartan co-kings, and apparently prescribing as well as describing some crucial aspect or aspects of Spartan decision-making procedure in the sixth century or earlier.[19]

Apart from these, the extant sources for the political thought of archaic Greece are scattered and exclusively poetic: Homer, Hesiod, Tyrtaeus, Alcaeus, Solon, Theognis, and Xenophanes, chief among them. The question of how most appropriately to wring significance from these mainly fragmentary remains of early Greek poetry involves the problem, first, of how to distinguish characteristically archaic ways of thinking or talking from individual and conventional idioms of style.[20] Then, there is the uncertainty as to how far the extant sources are representative even of the genres that they exemplify. At least, there seems to be consensus that attention to genre and context and especially to their interrelation is of the essence to a proper understanding of their political thought and role.[21] Thirdly, even if they are in some degree representative, how politically influential were they, theoretically or pragmatically? Whereas for Shelley poets were the unacknowledged legislators of the world, an archaic Greek poet such as Solon was literally the acknowledged legislator of his admittedly small, *polis*-shaped world. The trick would seem therefore to be to see how, on the one hand, the development of the *polis* marked epic and early lyric poetry, and, on the other, how representations of the *polis* in these early composers and performers, beginning (perhaps) with Homer, contributed in turn to the (or an) evolving conceptualisation of political community. At any rate, we are 'in a better position to reconstruct the ideological or symbolic systems at work than the "realities" of events'[22] – small comfort though that may be.

Methods

Studying any political thought or theory requires deep thinking; but, given our particular evidential problems, the study of archaic Greek political thought makes Aeschylus' analogy of the diver's plunge into the depths (*Supp.* 407–8, 1057) seem especially apt. So here goes, head first. My approach to the history of political thought or theory is, understandably, somehow indebted to that of the rightly influential 'Cambridge School', in that it is contextual, and discourse-oriented, opposed to the notion of transcultural and ahistorical universals and in favour of the view that political thought is and should be written with a view to the interest of a historically conditioned community.[23] It will not, therefore, be at all (Leo) Straussian, since I do not believe that we can understand an ancient thinker as he or she understands himself or herself, although it may sometimes be legitimate to read between and behind as well as on a thinker's lines. I shall indulge also in a certain amount of *Begriffsgeschichte*, especially the history of 'Grundbegriffe' such as Freedom, and the rather less basic Revolution.[24] But above all my approach is historiographical in one quite particular sense: that is, I do hope to be able to make some measurable progress in resolving what Arnaldo Momigliano (1952/1994, 27) once identified as a key element in the then general crisis of Greek history, namely the divorce of the history of political ideas from the study of Greek political and social history.

There probably remains a crisis of some sort in Greek history, but this aspect of it seems to be at last becoming rather less evident or threatening.[25] No doubt there still are some benighted ancient philosophers who treat politics as mere background; and some ancient historians who treat political theory as just so much gloss (or dross). But I shall be endeavouring to put them both in the same ballpark and on as level a playing field as can be. Not that it will be simple: as one of the pioneers of the 'Cambridge School' has put it, 'I do not think that political philosophy possesses a unified and narratable history, or that the efforts of those who disagree with me to prove otherwise are likely to provide legitimate paradigms for the coming *paideia*' [26] – by which he meant courses or books on political thought and theory such as the book I am writing. I press on regardless.

The political and politics in archaic Greece

So much for problematics, sources and methods. Now for terrain, subject-matter, field of operation: politics and the political. Greek political theory (and perhaps thought) presupposes politics in a strong

384

sense: communal and collective decision-making, in public, effected after substantive discussion among more or less equals, on issues of principle as well as purely technical, operational matters.[27] Such politics were intrinsic to the institution of the *polis*, not merely the outcome of a sort of etymological wordplay. Of course, scholars have advanced different, often conflicting interpretations of the nature and meaning of the *polis*, influenced by 'national' and other contemporary considerations, and quite rightly there has of late been a multiculturally inspired movement of recuperation that would diminish the uniqueness of Greek politics in favour of allowing at any rate Phoenicia and Phoenician-founded Carthage a place in the political sun.[28] Yet, despite the excessive denial of Gawantka at one pole and the excessive affirmation of Burckhardt at the other, it should at least be agreed or conceded that there was a distinctive Greek *polis* for us to study today, and that, as an ideal type, the Greek city was a 'city of reason'.[29] More precisely, this *polis* was, ideologically as well as practically, a 'citizen-state', in which the *politeia* meant not only (or merely) constitution, but the community's very life and soul, the beating heart of a truly soulful corporation.[30] It was of the essence of the identity of the citizens in such a polity that they be conceived interchangeably as those who rule and are ruled in turn, 'as if', to quote the greatest analyst of the *polis*, 'becoming other persons' (Aristotle, *Politics* 1261b2–3).

Such citizen politics was, in its turn, premised on 'the political', a phrase of dubious origin (in the thought of the nazi Carl Schmitt) but considerable theoretical and heuristic utility.[31] It signifies abstractly the carving out of a civic space within the *polis*, and the social and communal allocation of primacy to politics therein. Concretely, it stands for the civic space located *en mesōi* or *es meson*, 'in' or 'towards the centre' of collective life.[32] If the Homeric poems were composed *c.* 700, this was a space invented perhaps round about 750 BCE.[33] That suggestion is at least compatible with the physical layout of eighth-century Cretan Dreros, with its dedicated *agora*, and perhaps also with some examples of de Polignac's controversial thesis identifying the rise of the *polis* with the symbiosis of 'urban' and 'extra-urban' religious sanctuaries in the latter part of the eighth century.[34] After *c.* 700 civic-political space increased, symbolically, so greatly indeed as to engulf society in its maw. Thus the *polis* was, on Aristotle's definitive as well as definitional construction, both state and society. Yet, even as he wrote, in the real world it was beginning, thanks not least to his former pupil Alexander, to be reduced once again – at different speeds in different areas of the hugely enlarged Greek world – to the narrow proportions envisaged in the Plutarchan essay *Praecepta rei gerendae*, which constitutes my terminal reference-point.[35]

The political thus defined embraces, fundamentally, devotion to the gods, an absolute moral valuation of freedom, and the gendering of the military function, on top of what we automatically associate with the political sphere: with the result that, as Kurt Raaflaub – forthcoming(a) – has nicely put it, Greek political thought 'from the beginning was interested not only in matters that *we* consider specifically political, but in a wide range of social, religious, moral, economic, and military aspects as well'. Here I am concerned just with the earliest tranche of this complex movement of thought and action, that which either falls within or is coterminous with the so-called 'archaic' period of Greek history.

The archaic period: the theoretical moment

That 'either...or' is not a mere rhetorical flourish. All periodisation is conventional, a matter primarily of convenience, as is its labelling.[36] And 'archaic' as a label would seem to have long passed its sell-by date. Originating within art-historical discourse, 'archaic' meant formative, as applied to an epoch putatively not only preceding but heralding a mature 'classical' era. Hence, unfortunately, it is irredeemably teleological and misleading. Sparta's 'archaic' period, for example, chronologically speaking, was also its 'classical' epoch in terms (if such organic terms be permitted) of its political and social maturity.[37] There is the same problem, or rather danger, of reading backwards, with anachronistic hindsight, the whole of Greek culture and civilisation, including its specifically political component. The danger is perhaps especially acute with regard to the development or emergence or invention of democracy. There are those scholars who regard the very *polis* concept as intrinsically democratic or at least proto-democratic, inasmuch as it is egalitarian.[38] That characteristic tends to be presented today as an unalloyed good, since we are of course all democrats now. But actually democracy could equally, or better, be seen as the gigantic anomaly of ancient Greek politics in the long run; and anyhow even during its peak, during the second quarter of the fourth century, ancient democracy did not mean what we understand by it today, even in its least class-antagonistic and most pluralistic versions.[39]

The conventional lower dividing-line between the archaic and the classical, the Persian Wars, has also caused difficulty. As Anthony Snodgrass brilliantly observed, the Persian Wars of 490–480 did not make the difference that the traditional terminology and chronography implied they did in key areas of Greek culture: the crucial break-throughs, both intellectual and political, had already been made by about 500.[40] One of these breakthroughs was of course democracy or proto-democracy itself, and the question I should like to pose, within the terms of my book's problematic as outlined above, is whether, and if so to what extent and in what way, the development of some relevant political theory, as distinct from and as opposed to mere thinking or thought, was necessary to that breakthrough. If a distinguished German historian of both ancient Greek and modern British political thought is right, 'the development towards democracy would not have been possible without intellectual anticipations, even if the goal in its entirety could not be present to the eyes'.[41] But did those 'anticipations' amount to the construction of (a) theory?

It would, I think, be generally agreed that the distinction and opposition of the *vita activa* and the *vita contemplativa* were phenomena of the fifth century BCE at the earliest, being neither conceptually nor practically possible before Socrates (born *c.* 470) – or even Plato's 'Socrates' (almost a century later). Hence, the cut-off point for the emergence or invention of political theory would be pre-Socratic in this sense. But how far back can we legitimately push it? Debates about government and the state, as Moses Finley rightly pointed out, 'abound in ancient [Greek] cultural expressions, in epic, tragedy and historiography as well as in ethics or political theory in the narrower sense', in other words from the very beginnings of extant Greek literature in (*ex hypothesi*) *c.* 750–700.[42] What concerns me here, though, is the narrower and sharper distinction drawn by Alasdair MacIntyre, according to whom political theories properly so called 'are, by and large, articulate, systematic, and explicit versions of the unarticulated, more or less systematic and implicit interpretations, through which plain men and women understand this experience of the actions of others in a way that enables them to respond to it in their own actions'.[43]

The *terminus ante quem* for the emergence of Greek political theory in this strong sense would seem to me to be Herodotus' Persian Debate (3.80–2).[44] The Debate in its preserved literary form is a three-cornered fight, not a *dissoi logoi* ('twofold arguments'), although each individual *logos* takes the form of a Protagorean antilogy, predominantly against one of the other two *logoi*, not against both equally.[45] Whenever one dates the supposed original of Herodotus' version, if indeed there was a really existent textual or oral original, its extant form does seem to presuppose the emergence of democracy as the 'third position', rule by all, between rule by one and rule by some in either theory or practice. So the *terminus post quem* would have to be *c.* 500 or not much before, which is entirely compatible with the shared usage of *isonomia* in both the literary Debate and Cleisthenic actuality (see below). In any case, we may surely not push it back as much before 500 as Herodotus asks his readers to accept by placing the debate in 522 BCE. This was too long before the medism of Athens's ex-tyrant Hippias raised the Persian Question in Greek intellectual minds in the form of the polar opposition of oriental despotism and Greek liberty, and even longer before the Ionian Revolt gave that ideological polarity a decisively concrete form.[46]

But there is more to it even than the emergence of democracy. A further precondition for the invention of political theory in Greece is the mental and symbolic transformation so well described and ana-lysed by Jean-Pierre Vernant and others.[47] This complex transforma-tion of consciousness comprised the search for a new secularising rationality, the allegorical interpretation of myth, the birth of historical reflection, in short, the crisis of the traditional forms of communica-tion and of the values that accompanied them. All contributed in their different ways to delineate a series of profound changes in the theory and practice of politics (in the broadest sense) in late archaic Greece: from myth to *logos*, from gift-exchange to instituted political exchange, from divine to human understanding, from concrete to abstract rea-soning, from unwritten to written law – in sum: from a city of gods to the city of reason. The strong temptation therefore arises to adopt an idealist, Kuhnian view of this intellectual transformation.[48] By 500, it might be claimed, the old paradigms for understanding the world of gods and the – ever more distinct – world of men no longer held good; 'normal' science, as it were, would no longer work, so that there occurred, and had to occur, an intellectual revolution which did not only precede but also precipitated, and maybe in a deeper sense caused, a political revolution.

Alternatively, one might hold with a more materialist and context-ualist explanation of the changes. The list of conditions or factors forming a framework in which independent political thought was not suppressed but enabled, encouraged and eventually necessitated, even outside the politically dominant circles, would include at least the following: the absence of a rigidly hierarchical, religiously sanctioned communal structure; the evolution of small, topographically confined *poleis* – not centralised territorial states; the existence of the *poleis* for centuries outside the orbit of great imperial powers, so that they were able to develop their own civic ideologies, absorbing without being dominated by outside influences; and (already noted) the strong egalitarian foundations of the *poleis*. Against such a background – of necessary but not sufficient conditions – one might postulate the occurrence of an objective crisis, differently shaped in different cities of course, engendered either by contact with other non-Greek cultures, or with other Greek *poleis* or polities such as Sparta (which had their own very different solutions to often broadly comparable problems), or by endogenous political or social breakdown. Such a crisis might have been a sufficient condition for not only the questioning in theory but also the demolition in practice of the reigning doxic order.[49]

Of course, whichever view, or combination of them, one prefers, the transition or transformation was not necessarily everywhere an identically neat and tidy, let alone quick and complete, process. To bring us back to Athens and democracy, I want to conclude this section by concentrating on the relationship of myth and *logos* with special reference to the new and specially, perhaps indeed uniquely, democratic genre of tragedy. 'Whereas the performance of choral lyric tends to reinforce the traditions and the values of the aristocratic families, the relatively new art of the dramatic spectacle is the distinctive form of the democratic *polis*.'[50] No one I think would quarrel with Segal's idea that Greek tragedy as we know it was a new and specifically Athenian democratic space for competitive performance and civic viewing. But what was it like in the time of its supposed inventor Thespis – did it already under the dictator Peisistratos in the 530s, before it was, or could have been thought likely to be, institutionalised within a democratic political frame of civic religious ritual (whenever precisely that was), bear within it the seeds of its specially democratic flowering?[51]

Lack of space forbids yet another in-depth exploration of this well-worked terrain, but a brilliant suggestion as to how and why tragedy, democracy and Dionysos might all have become bound up in a single coherent package *en mesōi*, at the heart of Athenian democratic civic space, seems well worth noting in passing.[52] At the centre of the early City Dionysia, Sourvinou-Inwood has suggested, was the myth (or myths) of human resistance to Dionysos as god of cosmic and civic disorder; the lesson of the myth(s), she continues, was the paradox that cosmic-civic order can be maintained only 'by surrendering control and embracing disorder in the service of Dionysos', that is, by behaving irrationally, or at least in accordance with a deeper than human rationality. If that is right, there could have been no straightforward 'myth to *logos*' progression in this case anyhow, for tragedy

389

was simultaneously both myth and *logos*, and democratic Athens was thus essentially a city of both Reason and Unreason.

The particular relevance and resonance of that hypothesis for my purposes come from tragedy's role as a prime site – perhaps indeed the original site – of democratic political theory.[53] It therefore matters to me very much when the City Dionysia became thus organised as a politicised play-festival, and especially whether that was before, thanks to, or after Cleisthenes.[54] Sadly, I doubt that we shall ever be able to decide that issue for sure. Instead, therefore, I conclude by re-opening the case of Cleisthenes himself, and his possible model or *prodromos*, Solon.

A democratic revolution?

Democracy, ancient Greek-style, is the key theme of my 'Key Theme'. It could hardly be more acutely topical. In Burma today, for instance, ordinary people are, literally, dying for democracy, or what is counted as democracy nowadays – they want the opposite, anyhow, of what the Greeks would have called the *dunasteia* or non-responsible collective tyranny of the Burmese military junta. In the longer established of the modern democracies, however, the very fact of democracy is somewhat old hat or *vieux jeu*. Perhaps indeed it is only at its instauration that democracy really tastes 'sweet'.[55] But when exactly should we date its instauration? The Athenians at different times and in different contexts held to two different views. According to conservative fourth-century Athenians (and most fourth-century Athenians were conservative), democracy was their 'ancestral constitution' (Finley 1971), and its founder was Solon. According to Herodotus (6.131), and the Athenian source or sources he followed, the founder of 'the democracy and the tribes for the Athenians' was Cleisthenes.

We may of course choose to regard both views as merely typical instances of the Greeks' personalisation of historical process, and their invincible devotion to *prōtos heuretēs* mythology. But the two alleged founders have an interest and importance above and beyond mere ideology. John Milton, it has been well said, was more profoundly involved in public affairs than any other major English poet. But even he was not as profoundly, directly and centrally involved as Solon. Retrospective appropriation has done its worst, and the original motives and intentions, and indeed the precise verbal details of his laws are for the most part unrecoverable. But we do at least have some of his *ipsissima verba*, including some self-justificatory verses that take us to the heart of his preferred understanding of the socio-economic and political crisis he was called upon to resolve as both arbitrator and lawgiver.[56]

Solon seems to have thought it his proper task to strike the appropriate balance of political power and privilege between two contending socio-economic groups or classes:

> I gave the common people (*dēmos*) as much privilege as they needed
>   neither taking honor from them nor reaching out for more.
> But as for those who had power and were admired for their wealth,
>   I arranged for them to have nothing unseemly.

In another poem he resumes his fundamentally dichotomous representation of the citizenry for whom he was writing laws, using the characteristic archaic (but not solely archaic) mixture of moral and social terminology:

> I wrote laws (*thesmoi*) equally for poor and rich (literally 'for bad and good').[57]

What little reliable evidence we have suggests that the political essence of his reforms consisted in a twofold movement: on the one hand, depriving aristocrats of their monopoly of political power and throwing the major offices of government open to the wealthiest rather than only the best-born; on the other, giving a voice – including the formal registering of their vote – on some major issues to ordinary, poor citizens.[58] The latter marked indeed a major advance in status and privilege for the majority of Athenians, but it did not amount to anything like majority rule. It would be strictly anachronistic therefore to describe Solon as in any sense a democrat – though that is precisely what later Athenians did. At most, certain of his measures might be allowed to acquire retrospectively a proto-democratic connotation.

The fate of Cleisthenes' reputation as a political innovator has been almost the opposite of Solon's. In antiquity he sank virtually without trace, while moderns either have denied him any more than a figurehead role in the reform bill associated with his name, or have debited him with a proto-Machiavellian ambition, or sought to transfer the credit for introducing true, or full, democracy from him to Ephialtes and his junior coadjutant Pericles in the late 460s.[59] Against the latter move, at least, a strong protest must be entered. It is common ground, among ancients and moderns alike, that the deme (local village, ward or parish) was crucial to the Cleisthenic reforms, even if the interpretation of its rationale and more especially its motivation has been hotly disputed, and that the deme remained throughout its history the 'basis of the Athenian democracy'.[60] The significance of that for our problematic, the mutual relationship of political theory and practice, is twofold. First, the deme formed part of a political system, one that was both complex and theoretically informed.[61] Second, the new system was remarkably successful from almost the word go, triumphantly satisfying one of Aristotle's thoroughly pragmatic criteria for a constitutional order's success, namely that the relevant groups and interested individuals should want it to work.[62] It is illegitimate, no doubt, to argue from observed consequences directly back to inferred intentions, but those two facts in combination would seem at least to imply the existence of some sort of organising intelligence or guiding spirit.

Nevertheless, the question still remains how precisely we are to assess the role of ideas (whether one man's or a committee's) in its foundational history. For reasons of space I shall concentrate on one of the latest and most original attempts at understanding the Cleisthenic reforms or revolution, which indeed allots a crucial role to ideas but locates them in an unexpected quarter.[63] It was, on Ober's picture, not so much the case that Cleisthenes, as the motor force of political revolution, won over the Athenian *dēmos* to him, as that he was won over to and by the *dēmos*, the mass of citizens whose thought and aims he proved peculiarly skilled at interpreting.[64]

Let me begin by putting Ober's construction of the Cleisthenic episode in a wider, historiographical context. There is, on the one hand, the Athenian local tradition, at least partly invented, of non-violent reformers running from Drakon *via* Solon and Cleisthenes to Ephialtes and the post-403 Restoration constitutionalists. On the other hand, there is the persistent and unsuppressible evidence that the reformers were opposed by, or that their reforms were preceded or accompanied by, violence – the murders of Kylon and his co-conspirators, of Hipparchos, and of Ephialtes, and the reign of the so-called Thirty Tyrants. Ober's thesis seems decisively to privilege the constitutional over the violent tradition, although he does allow for a violent mass riot by leaderless Athenians to eject Isagoras and his alleged Spartan sponsor Cleomenes.

The second marked feature of Ober's interpretation is his understanding of the late-sixth-century *dēmos*, apparently for him a broad term, representing the Athenian 'masses' in some sense, which was somehow exceptionally politicised. Hence, so far from Cleisthenes aristocratically 'adding the *dēmos*' to his *hetaireia* (political faction), as Herodotus (5.66) has it, the *dēmos* on Ober's view in effect added Cleisthenes to theirs. They were all now 'comrades' (*hetairoi*), relating to each other on a basis of *isonomia*, being 'equal sharers in regard to the *nomoi'*, the new reformed laws of Cleisthenes, in opposition both to old-style tyranny and to new-style oligarchy, especially when either of those was supported by the foreign power of Sparta.

Numerous problems and questions arise. Who exactly was this *dēmos*? How had it become so politicised, and in the direction specifically of *isonomia*? And why should Cleisthenes (and/or his immediate circle) be seen merely as a relatively passive tool? I take up just two, linguistic aspects: the contemporary language of *isonomia* and the retrospective language of Herodotus. The latter Ober's thesis requires him to play down, but actually, as long as it is appreciated that Herodotus's source – not (primarily) Herodotus himself – is a tainted witness, it need constitute no impediment to the notion of an intellectually as well as pragmatically active (or proactive) Cleisthenes. For the source was of course aristocratic and so literally, by the mid-fifth century (Herodotus' time), anti-'democratic'.[65] Above all, the formulation is replete with the embarrassment of aristocrats that one of their own should have become in effect a class traitor and handed over power to a *dēmos* that, however precisely it was composed, was certainly non-aristocratic. From their biased standpoint Cleisthenes was – merely – adding the *dēmos* to his *hetaireia*, and, moreover, for his own personal advantage (that is the force of the middle form, *prosetairizetai*) rather than out of any considerations of altruistic statesmanship. In less biased – or rather oppositely biased – hindsight, however, Cleisthenes can and perhaps should be seen rather to have broken the mould of old-style *hetaireia*-based aristocratic faction-politics altogether, much as Caius Gracchus was to end old-style aristocratic patronage politics at Rome.[66] In that case, Ober's suggestion that the *dēmos* had become (somewhat) politicised and were surprisingly keen on the new plans could well have acted as an important stimulus to Cleisthenes' mould-breaking.

What, then, might Cleisthenic *isonomia* have meant? As later worked out under the developed democracy, it stood for an exact equality of distribution of *timē* for citizens under the laws or the Law, and an exact equality of status for citizens *qua* citizens; for instance, every citizen was to count for one and none for more than one both in eligibility for most offices (hence the practice of sortition), and in voting in the Assembly (hence the contractual acceptance of majority votes as binding on minority).[67] But in 500 *isonomia* was still, arguably, a slogan rather than a theory, available to all opponents of unconstitutional tyranny and not only to democratic or proto-democratic ones. Cleisthenes (or his spin doctors) should not therefore be automatically taken for political theorists of democracy *avant la lettre*. Although in Herodotus' Persian Debate (our earliest extant example of Greek constitutional political theory) *isonomia* does service for 'democracy' in the mouth of the notionally pro-democracy speaker, it does so for tactical and rhetorical as well as discursive and philosophical reasons. Political theory proper, I would still want to contend, was invented somewhere after Cleisthenes' reforms, precisely because it was dependent on the prior invention of democracy as a working practice and (perhaps) also as a label.[68]

Here, finally, is another possible paradox. On the one hand, political theory itself is a use of the intellectual space provided by and only by democracy. On the other hand, there was always relatively little democratic theory proper, at least theory as explicitly and systematically articulated as that of its various anti-democratic rivals. Why so? It might be argued – as it has been for modern political theory – that theory was itself an anti-democratic practice. The very Persian Debate, for example, is couched in the form of a progression from the democratic *via* the aristocratic to the monarchic.[69] Then again, secondly, the development of such articulated and sophisticated theory would seem to have depended crucially on the use of writing – which was or might be constructed as oligarchic, if not tyrannical.[70] Thirdly, it has been argued quite plausibly that 'the daily evidence of a system actually in use minimised the need for theoretical justification', especially as an everyday, mundane form of democratic philosophy is evident in the mass forums of the Assembly and theatre by or from about 500 and the lawcourts after about 460.[71]

Envoi

The career of the praise-poet Simonides spans precisely the transition period I have identified between the implicitly theory-laden reforms of Cleisthenes and the explicit theorizing of Herodotus' Otanes, the period that has also been labelled the 'tragic moment'.[72] According to a *bon mot* of Simonides, *polis andra didaskei*, by which he surely meant that practical experience of politics in the strong Greek sense teaches a *politēs* what it is to be a political man. Formal Greek political theory, as that was developed under the Sophists and their successors or opponents, was dedicated to the proposition that Simonides' dictum was but a partial truth. To *praxis* must, later, be added *theōria*.

Consider, finally, the proem to Aristotle's *Nicomachean Ethics* (1095a2–5): 'a young man is not a fit person to attend lectures on political theory, because he is not versed in the practical business of life from which politics draws its premisses and subject-matter'. So much for the teaching of political thought and its history at university today... Yet we are not all that far here from the 'reconstruction' of modern American democracy that has recently been advocated with special reference to a re-reading or even re-appropriation of ancient Greek democratic theory and practice.[73] My forthcoming *Political Thought in Ancient Greece* doubtless cannot legitimately aspire to fostering any such reconstruction of the way in which Britannia is ruled, but I should like to think that, even if it achieves nothing else, it can at least introduce a touch more political correctness into the lexicon, or at any rate into the *Oxford English Dictionary*. If you look up there the epithet 'Thersitical', you will not, curiously enough, find it defined as 'visionary', 'progressive' or 'egalitarian', but as 'abusive and foul-mouthed'. The aristocratic Homer, by way of Socrates and the – until very recently – dominant 'anti-democratic tradition in western thought' triumphs still, theoretically or ideologically speaking.[74]

Acknowledgements

In the writing of this paper I have incurred many debts – too many to name individually, but above all to the following three friends: Nick Fisher and Hans van Wees for inviting me to the Cardiff conference and ensuring its success; and Kurt Raaflaub, with whose conclusions I find myself in disagreement more than I should ideally like, but whose learning, skill in argument and generosity of scholarly spirit are never less than disarming. In accordance with the paper's proleptic and protreptic character – this is strictly a *Denkschrift* – I have severely restricted references to both the ancient sources and the disproportionately immense modern literature; others may be found in Cartledge 1996b.

Notes

[1] 'Antipolitical age': Mulgan 1994; 'subpolitics': Beck 1995.

[2] Marr 1995. Regardless of one's political affiliation, it is still hard to disagree with the manifesto declaration by the leader of the (then – July 1996) British Opposition that 'Our system of government is centralised, inefficient and bureaucratic. Our politics produce meaningless confrontation rather than serious debate. Our citizens lack basic rights to challenge unfair government decisions. Parliament symbolises much that is out of date in the British political system.'

[3] France: Lévêque and Vidal-Naquet 1996; Loraux 1996, 190–216. America: Euben *et al.* 1994. Australia: special issue of the journal *Thesis Eleven* 40 (1995), 'In the Mirror of the Classical'.

[4] This monograph, to be published in the C.U.P. series 'Key Themes in

Ancient History' (C.U.P.), is in several ways a sequel to my earlier attempt to understand and re-present the Greeks' self-construction, in that case mainly through the medium of their written historiography, Cartledge 1993; cf. Cartledge 1995.

[5] Humphreys 1978, 209–41; Wood and Wood 1978; Vatai 1984; Hahn 1989; Erskine 1990 – with the review of Green 1994; Schubert 1993.

[6] Russell 1995.

[7] On the allegedly decisive intellectual role of James Madison in the American Revolution, see Banning 1995. Another American Revolutionary, John Adams, suggestively claimed that the Revolution had been made in people's minds before it was enacted on the ground.

[8] On the concept of 'invented' tradition, see Ranger and Hobsbawm 1983. The Athenian tyrannicides myth is a good case in point: Loraux 1996, 102–27 (at 112 she raises the question whether Cleisthenes himself might have been involved in the initial mythopoiesis).

[9] Finley 1986 denied the validity of 'revolution' in application to the ancient world, but on pedantic grounds. On the concept, see Meier 1984. On the *metabolai/metastaseis* concept of the *Ath. Pol.* see Keaney 1992.

[10] The differences are well brought out by Finley 1983, 1985a; Dunn 1996, 178–95 ('Democracy: the politics of making, defending and exemplifying community: Europe 1992'); and Loraux 1996, 190–216.

[11] Advocates of a political (in a strong sense) Homeric world include Raaflaub 1988a, 1988b, 1989, 1991, 1993; Scully 1990; Carlier 1991; and van Wees 1992. Morris 1986, Seaford 1994 and Yamagata 1994 go in the opposite direction, rightly to my way of thinking. Further reading is cited in Eder 1994, 247–8, 'Analytische Bibliographie', §L15.

[12] Snell 1953 and Gagarin 1986 are among those advocating an evolutionary approach; but against the latter see Hölkeskamp 1990; and in general Fränkel 1975 and Konstan 1997, ch. 2, offer salutary cautions.

[13] Morris 1996a; on the comparison of Greek and non-Greek early political development, see n. 28.

[14] Lévêque and Vidal-Naquet 1996 have made perhaps the most powerful case for Cleisthenes the intellectual activist; cf. Murray 1993, 274–80. Possibly, too, one might want to include him among the 'transcendent' intellectuals of Humphreys (1978, 209–41), except that 'intellectuals' is perhaps itself a questionable label for anyone before the fifth-century Sophists and Socrates; cf. Stanton 1973, Miralles 1996.

[15] Art as propaganda: references are conveniently collected in Sparkes 1994, 76 n. 36; add Neils 1994; art as political theory or at least political thought: Sparkes 1994, 61 n. 1. See further the varying approaches to the interpretation of ancient visual art in broadly political terms in Bérard *et al.* 1989 and Goldhill and Osborne 1994. A recent (non-aesthetic) attempt at a political construction of archaic Greek artefactual evidence, de Polignac 1995b, relies tellingly on literary sources.

[16] Donlan 1970; cf. Lévêque in Lévêque and Vidal-Naquet 1996, 128–33.

[17] See a series of published articles by Hölkeskamp 1990, 1992a, 1992b, 1993, 1994; and his monograph (forthcoming); also Koerner 1985, Eder 1986,

and Gehrke 1993.

[18] On early lawgiver traditions/myths, see Szegedy-Maszak 1978. On Solon, see below, n. 56.

[19] The literature on the Rhetra is unmanageably huge: see recently (e.g.) Ruzé 1991; and cf. n. 37.

[20] Most of the obviously 'political thought' fragments are collected and translated in Gagarin and Woodruff 1995; see also, for translation and commentary of the more obviously 'philosophical' fragments, Kirk, Raven and Schofield 1983. On the problems of reading them: Fränkel 1975, Calame 1995.

[21] Genre counts: Griffiths 1995, Thomas 1995b. Capizzi 1990 protests against what he sees as Aristotle's anachronistic misreading of the Presocratics; cf. Osborne 1987.

[22] Kurke 1994, 69 n. 6.

[23] Pocock 1962, Skinner 1969, Pocock 1987, Tuck 1991, Pocock *et al.* 1994, Dunn 1996, 11–38 ('The history of political theory'); cf. MacIntyre 1983, 19 ('the serious political theorist must also *be* to greater or lesser degree a historian'); Rorty *et al.* 1984; Pagden 1987; Ball, Farr and Hanson 1989; Tully 1988, 1994, 1996; Ober 1994, 155; Ball 1995.

[24] In homage to Koselleck *et al.* 1972–, Brunner *et al.* 1984, Meier 1990, and Raaflaub 1985; cf. Richter 1986. For freedom, see n. 55; revolution, n. 9.

[25] The forthcoming *Cambridge History of Greek and Roman Political Thought* (Schofield and Rowe, forthcoming), for example, brings together historians, philosophers – and even literary critics.

[26] Pocock 1980, 140, in a collection of essays on the problem of political theory in relation to political education.

[27] 'Politics': Finley 1981, 1983; Farrar 1988; Vidal-Naquet in Lévêque and Vidal-Naquet 1996, 103.

[28] On contemporary non-Western polities and politics in relation to early Greece, see Carlier 1991, Gehrke and Wirbelauer 1994, Raaflaub and Müller-Luckner 1993.

[29] Sakellariou 1989, Murray 1990, 1991.

[30] 'Citizen-state': Runciman 1990, taken up by Hansen 1993; cf. Manville 1990. *Politeia*: Bordes 1982.

[31] The 'political' (das Politische, le [as opposed to la] politique): Meier 1990 (the English title mistranslates Meier's *Die Entstehung des Politischen bei den Griechen*); Lévêque and Vidal-Naquet 1996, 104.

[32] *en mesōi/es meson*: Vernant 1965, Detienne 1965, Raaflaub 1994, 116 n. 25.

[33] Despite n. 11, I am willing to concede that the Homeric poems do contain references or passages (e.g. the description of the Shield of Achilles in *Iliad* 18) which arguably presuppose the existence of some features of the *polis* properly so called. That is not the same as saying that the 'world' of Homer is a world of the *polis*.

[34] de Polignac's 1984 French original, *La naissance de la cité grecque. Cultes, espace, et société VIIIe–VIIe siècles av. J.-C.* has been issued in an English translation (de Polignac 1995a) updated to try to take account of criticisms; note also his contribution to Alcock and Osborne 1994, 'Mediation, competition, and

sovereignty: the evolution of rural sanctuaries in Geometric Greece', which the author describes as 'a summation and completion of the changes' made for de Polignac 1995a. Dreros *agora*: de Polignac 1995a, 22.

[35] Hellenistic 'politics': see Cartledge 1997, 8–11.

[36] Periodization: Golden and Toohey 1997.

[37] For Sparta's 'archaic' period as also her 'classical' era, see Cartledge 1980.

[38] e.g. Morris 1996a.

[39] See n. 10.

[40] Snodgrass 1980.

[41] Nippel 1994, 18.

[42] Finley 1975, 115.

[43] MacIntyre 1983, 23.

[44] On the Persian Debate, see most recently Thompson 1996, 52–78; cf. Brock 1991, 165–6.

[45] Protagoras: see Gagarin and Woodruff 1995, 173–89, at 187, nos. 23–4.

[46] It would be interesting to know why Herodotus (6.43) was quite so insistent that the Persian Debate really had taken place as and where he said. Oriental despotism *v.* Greek liberty: below, n. 55.

[47] Vernant 1983, Meier 1986, Brillante 1991, 103, Lloyd 1979, Raaflaub (forthcoming(a)).

[48] Kuhn 1997; cf. Hoyningen-Huene 1993.

[49] *Doxa* is Bourdieu's (1977) Greek-borrowed term for 'the objective consensus on the sense of the world'.

[50] Segal 1995, 211.

[51] For tragedy viewed as political thought, see Euben (ed.) 1986, Meier 1993, Williams 1993, Griffith 1995.

[52] Sourvinou-Inwood 1994.

[53] Euben 1986; cf. Euben (ed.) 1986.

[54] Connor 1989 makes a powerful case for the institution of the Great/City Dionysia as a Cleisthenic play-festival of liberation.

[55] This is the adjective used of freedom by Herodotus' Spartan interlocutors (7.133), when setting Greek freedom in polar opposition to the slavery of Persian oriental despotism: Cartledge 1993, 143–5; cf. generally Raaflaub 1985.

[56] Vlastos 1945, Andrewes 1982, Oliva 1988, Anhalt 1993, McGlew 1993, ch. 3. On Solon's posthumous reception, or invention, see Hansen 1989, and Kyrtatas 1992.

[57] Woodruff and Gagarin 1995, 26, no. 2, ll. 1–4; 27, no. 4, ll.18–19.

[58] Larsen 1949.

[59] Cleisthenes as a proto-Machiavelli: Lewis 1963, Lavelle 1993, 101–6. *Contra*: Hamilton 1993. Ephialtes/Pericles as true founders of democracy: Raaflaub 1995. Balanced views of the Cleisthenic reforms may be found in Stein-Hölkeskamp 1989, 189 ff.; Manville 1990, 187 ff.; Ostwald 1988.

[60] Hopper 1957, Whitehead 1986.

[61] Lévêque and Vidal-Naquet (1996) have made out probably the best case for the systematic character of the reforms; cf. n. 14.

[62] Arist. *Pol.* Book 5, *passim*.

[63] Ober 1993. Rather unexpectedly, this has been forcefully, if not entirely persuasively, countered by David Ames Curtis, the American translator of Lévêque and Vidal-Naquet (1996), xiii–xvii.

[64] As Ober (pers. comm.) once put it to me, self-caricaturally, his picture is of a 'Cleisthenes-the-miserable-tool-of-the-politicized-masses'; take the picture seriously, and the coincidence with his striking thesis about the fourth-century democracy, that the elite politicians were obliged to operate within parameters of ideology and discourse set by the controlling *dēmos* (see Ober 1989), is presumably not merely fortuitous. Nor may be the resemblance of Ober's Cleisthenes to the Lincoln who in 1864 declared: 'I claim not to have controlled events, but confess plainly that events have controlled me.'

[65] *Dēmokratia* as the title of a system of self-government was of course available to Herodotus (6.131), though he did not always choose to use it (see below and n. 68). According to one quite appealing modern view, however, the word was actually coined as a slur (meaning roughly 'dictatorship of the proletariat') by its elite opponents, playing on the ambiguity and ambivalence of both *dēmos* and *kratos*.

[66] Brunt (1966) is still, for me, the best short account of Rome's Late Republican 'constitution', despite revisionist claims that it was actually much more 'democratic' than the view Brunt then represented would hold.

[67] Cartledge 1996a; cf. Loraux 1991, Carlier 1991.

[68] *Isonomia:* Cartledge 1996b. Nagategawa 1988 wishes to push *isēgoria* (Hdt. 5.78) right back to Cleisthenes, as a specifically democratic practice. Persian Debate: see n. 44.

[69] Possible exceptions are extremely few; besides Protagoras of Abdera (Farrar 1988), there are perhaps just Democritus of Abdera (Vlastos 1945–6; Cole 1967; Salem 1996, 344–50) and (maybe) Hippodamus of Miletus.

[70] Loraux 1988a; Steiner (1994, 127–241) argues a controversially strong thesis linking writing essentially with tyranny. For the publication of written laws and decrees as a matter of publicity as much as of writing *per se*, see Thomas 1992, 1994b; cf. Detienne 1988.

[71] Quotation from Brock 1991, 169. Mass arenas: Ober 1989.

[72] Vernant in Vernant and Vidal-Naquet 1988, 23–8.

[73] Euben *et al.* 1994. See also n. 3.

[74] Roberts 1994; cf. Ober 1994.

BIBLIOGRAPHY

Adkins, A.W.H.
1960   *Merit and Responsibility: A Study in Greek Values*, Oxford.
1971   'Homeric values and Homeric society', *JHS* 91, 1–14.
1972   *Moral Values and Political Behaviour in Ancient Greece*, London.
1982   'Values, goals, and emotions in the *Iliad*', *CPh* 77, 292–326.
Ahlberg, G.
1971a   *Prothesis and Ekphora in Greek Geometric Art*, Stockholm.
1971b   *Fighting on Land and Sea in Greek Geometric Art*, Stockholm.
Akurgal, E.
1949   *Späthethitische Bildkunst*, Ankara.
1983   *Alt-Smyrna I. Wöhnschichten und Athenatempel*, Ankara.
1987   *Griechische und Römische Kunst in der Türkei*, Munich.
Alcock, S.
1993   *Graecia Capta*, Cambridge.
1994   'Breaking up the Hellenistic world: survey and society', in Morris (ed.) *Classical Greece*, 171–90.
Alcock, S., Cherry, J.F. and Davis, J.L.
1994   'Intensive survey, agricultural practice and the classical landscape of Greece', in Morris (ed.) *Classical Greece*, 137–70.
Alcock, S.E. and Osborne, R.G. (eds.)
1994   *Placing the Gods: Sanctuaries and sacred space in ancient Greece*, Oxford.
Aleshire, S.
1989   *The Athenian Asklepieion*, Amsterdam.
Alexiou, M.
1974   *The Ritual Lament in Greek Tradition*, Cambridge.
Alexiou, S.
1984   'Une nouvelle inscription de Panormos-Apollonia en Crète', in Nicolet (ed.) *Aux origines de l'Hellénisme*, 323–7.
Aloni, A.
1994   'L'elegia di Simonide dedicata alla battaglie di Platea (Sim. frr. 10–18 W²) e l'occasione della sua performance', *ZPE* 102, 9–22.
Alster, B.
1992   'Interaction of oral and written poetry in early Mesopotamian literature', in Vogelsang and Vanstiphout (eds.) *Mesopotamian Epic Literature*, 23–69.
Amandry, P.
1971   'Collection Paul Canellopoulos (I)', *BCH* 95, 585–626.
Amiet, P.
1959   *Elam*, Auvers-sur-Oise.
Ampolo, C.
1994   'Tra *empòria* ed *emporìa*: note sul commercio greco in età arcaica e classica', in D'Agostino and Ridgeway (eds.) *Apoikia*, 9–36.
Amyx, D.A.
1988   *Corinthian Vase-painting of the Archaic Period*, Berkeley.
Andersen, L.H.
1977   *Relief pithoi from the archaic period of Greek art*, Diss. Ann Arbor.
Andersen, O. and Dickie, M. (eds.)
1995   *Homer's World: Fiction, Tradition, Reality*, Athens.

Bibliography

Anderson, J.K.
1975 'Greek chariot-borne and mounted infantry', *AJA* 79, 175–87.
1995 'The geometric catalogue of ships', in Carter and Morris (eds.) *The Ages of Homer*, 181–91.

Andreiomenou, A.
1980 *To kerameikon ergasterion tis Akraiphias*, unpublished Ph.D. thesis, Athens University.
1985 'La nécropole classique de Tanagra', in *La Béotie Antique*, Paris, 109–30.

Andrewes, A.
1956 *The Greek Tyrants*, London.
1982 'The growth of the Athenian state'; 'The tyranny of Pisistratus', *CAH²* III.3, Cambridge, 360–416.

Andronikos, M.
1969 *Vergina I: To Nekrotapheion ton Tymvon*, Athens.

Anhalt, E.K.
1993 *Solon the Singer: Politics and poetics*, Lanham, Md.

Antonaccio, C.
1994 'Contesting the past: hero cult, tomb cult, and epic in early Greece', *AJA* 98, 389–410.
1995a *An Archaeology of Ancestors: Tomb cult and hero cult in early Greece*, Lanham, Md.
1995b 'Lefkandi and Homer', in Andersen and Dickie (eds.) *Homer's World*, Athens, 5–27.

Arafat, K. and Morgan, C.
1994 'Athens, Etruria and the Heuneberg: mutual misconceptions in the study of Greek–Barbarian relations', in Morris (ed.) *Classical Greece*, 108–43.

Arenson, S.
1990 *The Encircled Sea. The Mediterranean maritime civilization*, London.

Arthur, M.
1973 'Early Greece: the origins of the western attiutude toward women', *Arethusa* 6, 7–58.
1982 'Cultural strategies in Hesiod's *Theogony*', *Arethusa* 15, 63–82.
1983 'The dream of a world without women: poetics and the circles of order in the *Theogony* prooemium', *Arethusa* 16, 97–116.

Assmann, J.
1992 *Das kulturelle Gedächtnis. Schrift, Erinnerung und politische Identität in frühen Hochkulturen*, Munich.

Assmann, J. and Hölscher T. (eds.)
1988 *Kultur und Gedächtnis*, Frankfurt am Main.

Aston, A.E. and Philpin, T. (eds.)
1985 *The Brenner Debate*, Cambridge.

Auberson, P.
1968 *Eretria I: Le Temple d'Apollon Daphnéphoros*, Berne.

Aubet, M.E.
1993 *The Phoenicians and the West*, Cambridge.

Auslander, L.
1995 *Taste and Power*, Berkeley.

Austin, M.M.
1970 *Greece and Egypt in the Archaic Age*, *PCPhS* Suppl. 2, Cambridge.

Austin, M.M. and Vidal-Naquet, P.
1977 *Economic and Social History of Ancient Greece: An Introduction*, Berkeley.

Badian, E.
1982 'Greeks and Macedonians', in B. Barr-Sharrar and E.N. Borza (eds.) *Macedonia and Greece in late classical and early Hellenistic times*, Washington, 33–51.

Bakır, G.
1981 *Sophilos: Ein Beitrag zur seinem Stil*, Mainz.

402

Bakır, T.
1974   *Der Kolonnettenkrater in Korinth und Attika zwischen 625 und 550 v.Chr.*
Bakker, E. and Kahane, A. (eds.)
1997   *Written Voices, Spoken Signs: Tradition, performance, and the epic text*, Cambridge, Mass.
Ball, T.
1995   *Transforming Political Discourse. Political theory and critical conceptual history*, Cambridge.
Ball, T., Farr, J. and Hanson, R.L. (eds.)
1989   *Political Innovation and Conceptual Change*, Cambridge.
Ballabriga, A.
1990   'La question homérique: pour une réouverture du débat', *REG* 103, 16–29.
Baltrusch, E.
1994   *Symmachie und Spondai: Untersuchungen zum griechischen Völkerrecht der archaischen und klassischen Zeit, 8.–5. Jh. v. Chr.*, Berlin.
Bammer, A.
1984   *Das Heiligtum des Artemis von Ephesos*, Graz.
Bammer, A. and Muss, U.
1996   *Das Artemision von Ephesos* (*Antike Welt* Sonderheft), Mainz.
Banning, L.
1995   *The Sacred Fire of Liberty. James Madison and the founding of the Federal Republic*, Ithaca.
Barber, E.W.
1994   *Women's Work: The First 20,000 Years*, New York and London.
Barker, G.
1988   'Archaeology in the Etruscan countryside', *Antiquity* 62, 772–85.
Barnett, R.D.
1975   'Phrygian Religion', in *CAH*[3] II.2, Cambridge, 435–8.
Bass, G.
1967   *Cape Gelidonya: A Bronze Age Shipwreck*, Philadelphia.
1986   'A Bronze Age shipwreck at Ulu Burun (Ka)', *AJA* 90, 269–96.
Bats, M. and Ruby, P. (eds.).
Forthcoming   *Les princes de la protohistoire*, Naples.
Baudrillard, J.
1968   *Le système des objets*, Paris.
1981   *Toward a Critique of the Political Economy of the Sign*, trs. C. Levin, St. Louis.
Beazley, J.D.
1932   'Little Master cups', *JHS* 52, 167–204.
1956   *Attic Black-Figure Vase Painters*, Oxford.
1963   *Attic Red-Figure Vase Painters*, 2nd edn, Oxford.
1971   *Paralipomena*, Oxford.
Beck, H.-G.
1971   *Geschichte der byzantinischen Volksliteratur*, Munich.
Beck, U.
1995   *Ecological Politics in an Age of Risk*, Oxford.
Bellinger, A.R.
1961   *Troy. The Coins* (Troy Suppl. Monograph 2), Princeton.
Bencivenga Trillmich, C.
1990   'Elea: problems of the relationship between city and territory, and of urban organization in the archaic period', in Descoeudres (ed.) *Greek colonists*, 365–71.
Bennet, J.
1997   'Homer and the Bronze Age', in Morris and Powell (eds.) *A New Companion to Homer*, 511–33.
Béquignon, Y.
1937   *Recherches archéologiques à Phères de Thessalie*, Paris.

Bibliography

Bérard, C.
  1970   *Eretria: Fouilles et recherches III: L'héroon a la porte de l'ouest*, Bern.
  1974   *Anodoi: essai sur l'imagerie des passages chthoniens*, Neuchâtel.
  1982   'Récupérer la mort du prince: héroïsation et formation de la cité', in Gnoli and Vernant (eds.) *La mort*, 89–105.
Bérard, C. et al.
  1989   *A City of Images*, Princeton (French original 1984).
Bérard, J.
  1957   *La colonisation grecque de l'Italie méridionale et de Sicile dans l'antiquité: histoire et légende*, 2nd edn, Paris.
Bergson, L.
  1960   'Zur Bedeutung von *Antipex* bei Euripides', *Eranos* 58, 12–19.
Bergquist, B.
  1973   *Herakles on Thasos*, Uppsala.
Berry, C.J.
  1994   *The Idea of Luxury*, Cambridge.
Beyer, I.
  1976   *Die Tempel von Dreros und Prinias A und die Chronologie der kretischen Kunst des 8. und 7. Jhs.*, Freiburg.
Bianchi, U.
  1953   *Dios Aisa. Destini, uomini e divinità nell'epos, nelle teogonie e nel culto dei Greci*, Rome.
Bieber, M.
  1928   *Griechische Kleidung*, Berlin.
  1934   *Entwicklungsgeschichte der griechischen Tracht*, Berlin.
Bile, M.
  1988   *Le dialecte crétois ancien* (Études crétoises 27), Paris.
Bintliff, J. (ed.)
  1991   *The Annales School and Archaeology*, Leicester.
Bintliff, J. and Snodgrass, A.M.
  1985   'The Cambridge/Bradford Boeotia expedition', *Journal of Field Archaeology* 12, 123–61.
Bitrakova-Grozdanova, V.
  1993   'La nécropole antique de Delogozda et sa chronologie', in *Ancient Macedonia V*, Thessaloniki, 167–73.
Bittel, K. (ed.)
  1975   *Bogazköy-Hattusa IX. Das Hethitische Felsheiligtum Yazilikaya*, Berlin.
Black, J.
  1992   'Some structural features of Sumerian narrative poetry', in Vogelzang and Vanstiphout (eds.) *Mesopotamian Epic Literature*, 71–101.
Blackman, D.J.
  1982   'Ancient harbours in the Mediterranean', *International Journal of Nautical Archaeology* 11, 79–104, 185–211.
  1968   'The ship-sheds', in Morrison and Williams (eds.) *Greek Oared Ships*, 181–6.
Blackman, D.J. (ed.)
  1973   *Marine Archaeology: Colston Papers 23*, London.
Blakeway, A.
  1935   Review of Ollier 1933, *CR* 49, 184–5.
Blanton, R.E.
  1994   *Houses and Households*, New York.
Bleicken, J. and Bringmann, K. (eds.)
  1993   *Colloquium aus Anlass des 80. Geburtstages von A. Heuss*, Kallmünz.
Blinkenberg, C.
  1931   *Lindos. Fouilles de l'acropole 1902–1914 I. Les petits objets*, Berlin.
Block, E.
  1982   'The narrator speaks: apostrophe in Homer and Vergil', *TAPA* 112, 7–22.

Blome, P.
1982   *Die figürliche Bildwelt Kretas in der geometrischen und früharchaischen Periode*, Mainz.
1984   'Lefkandi und Homer', *Würzburger Jahrbücher für die Altertumswissenschaft*, n.s. 10, 9–22.
1991   'Die dunklen Jahrhunderte – aufgehellt', in Latacz (ed.) *Zweihundert Jahre Homer-Forschung*, 45–60.
Boardman, J.
1961   *The Cretan Collection at Oxford: The Dictaean Cave and Iron Age Crete*, Oxford.
1963   'Artemis Orthia and chronology', *BSA* 58, 1–7.
1967   *Excavations in Chios 1952–1955. Greek Emporio* (*BSA* Suppl. 6), London.
1974   *Athenian Black Figure Vases. A Handbook*, London.
1980   *The Greeks Overseas*, 2nd edn, London.
1990   'Al Mina and history', *Oxford Journal of Archaeology* 9, 169–90.
1994   'Settlement for trade and land in North Africa', in Tsetskhladze and De Angelis (eds.) *The Archaeology of Greek Colonisation*, 137–49.
Boardman, J. and Hammond, N.G.L. (eds.)
1982   *The Cambridge Ancient History, Vol. III, part 3. The Expansion of the Greek World, Eighth to Sixth Centuries bc* , 2nd edn, Cambridge.
Boardman, J. and Hayes, J.
1966   *Excavations at Tocra 1963–65, I. The Archaic Deposits* (*BSA* Suppl. Vol. 4), London.
1973   *Excavations at Tocra 1963–65, II. The Archaic Deposits II and Later Deposits* (*BSA* Suppl. Vol. 10), London.
Bocock, R.
1993   *Consumption*, London.
Boedeker, D.
1988   'Amerikanische Oral-Tradition-Forschung. Eine Einführung', in Ungern-Sternberg and Reinau (eds.)*Vergangenheit in mündlicher Überlieferung*, 34–53.
1993   'Hero cult and politics: the bones of Orestes', in Kurke and Dougherty (eds.) *Cultural Poetics in Archaic Greece*, 164–77.
1995   'Simonides on Plataea: narrative elegy, mythodic history', *ZPE* 107, 217–29.
1996   'Heroic historiography: Simonides and Herodotus on Plataea', in Boedeker and Sider (eds.) *The New Simonides*, 223–42.
Boedeker, D. and Sider, D. (eds.)
1996   *The New Simonides, Arethusa* 29.2.
Boehlau, J.
1898   *Aus ionischen und italischen Nekropolen*, Leipzig.
Boehmer, R.M. and Hauptmann, H. (eds.)
1983   *Beiträge zur Altertumskunde Kleinasiens. Festschrift für Kurt Bittel*, Mainz.
Boehringer, D.
1996   'Heroisierung historischer Persönlichkeiten', in Flashar, Gehrke and Heinrich (eds.) *Retrospektive*, 37–61.
Boffo, L.
1985   *I re ellenistici e i centri religiosi dell'Asia Minore*, Florence.
Böhr, E.
1982   *Der Schaukelmaler* (*Kerameus*, vol. 4), Mainz.
Bölte, F.
1929   'Zu lakonischen Festen', *Rh. Mus.* 78, 124–43.
Bonnechere, B.
1994   *Le sacrifice humain en Grèce ancienne*, Athens and Liège.
Bonner, C.
1937   'The Sibyl and bottle imps', in Lake (ed.) *Quantulacumque*, London, 1–8.
Borchhardt, H.
1977   'Frühe griechische Schildformen', in H.-G. Buchholz and J. Wiesner (eds.), *Archaeologia Homerica E: Kriegswegen, Teil 1, Göttingen*, 1–56.

Bibliography

Borchhardt, J.
1972   *Homerische Helme: Helmfunde der Ägäis in ihren Beziehungen zu orientalischen und europäischen Helmen in der Bronze- und frühen Eisenzeit*, Mainz.

Bordes, J.
1982   *Politeia dans la pensée grecque des origines jusqu'à Aristote*, Paris.

Boring, T.A.
1979   *Literacy in Ancient Sparta* (*Mnemosyne*, Suppl. 54), Leiden.

Borza, E.N.
1990   *In the Shadow of Olympus*, Princeton.

Bosanquet, R.C.
1901   'Excavations at Praesos, I', *BSA* 8, 231–70.

Bossert, H.T.
1954   'Die Schicksalsgötter der Hethiter', *Die Welt des Orients* 2, 349–59.

Bothmer, D. von
1960   'New vases by the Amasis Painter', *Antike Kunst* 3, 71–80.
1985   *The Amasis Painter and his World*, New York and London.

Bourdieu, P.
1977   *Outline of a Theory of Practice*, Cambridge (French original 1972).
1984   *Distinction*, Cambridge, Mass.

Bourke, S. and Descoeudres, J.-P. (eds.)
1995   *Trade, Contact and the Movement of Peoples in the Eastern Mediterranean. Studies in honour of J. Basil Hennessy* (*Mediterranean Archaeology*, Suppl. 3), Sydney.

Boutière, J. and Schutz, A.-H.
1964   *Biographies des troubadours,* new edn, Paris.

Bouzek, J.
1973   *Graeco-Macedonian Bronzes (Analysis and Chronology)*, Prague.

Bouzek, J. and Ondrejová, I.
1988   'Sindos–Trebenishte–Duvanli', *Mediterranean Archaeology* 1, 84–94.

Bowie, E.
1986   'Early Greek elegy, symposium and public festival', *JHS* 106, 13–35.
1990   '*Miles ludens*? The problem of martial exhortation in early Greek elegy', in Murray (ed.) *Sympotica*, 221–9.

Bowman, A.K and Woolf, G. (eds.)
1994   *Literacy and Power in the Ancient World*, Cambridge.

Bowra, C.M.
1961a   *Greek Lyric Poetry: From Alcman to Simonides*, Oxford.
1961b   *Heroic Poetry*, London.

Braudel, F.
1972   *The Mediterranean and the Mediterranean World in the Age of Philip I*, London.

Braun, T.F.R.G.
1982   'The Greeks in the Near East'; 'The Greeks in Egypt', *CAH²* III.3, Cambridge, 1–56.

Braund, D.
1994   *Georgia in Antiquity*, Oxford.

Bremmer, J.N.
1990   'Adolescents, *symposion*, and pederasty', in Murray (ed.) *Sympotica*, 135–48.

Brewer, J. and Porter, R. (eds.)
1993   *Consumption and the World of Goods*, London and New York.

Brijder, H.A.G.
1983   *Siana Cups and Komast Cups I*, Amsterdam.
1991   *Siana Cups II: The Heidelberg Painter*, Amsterdam.

Brillante, C.
1990   'Myth and history: history and the historical interpretation of myth', in Edmunds (ed.) *Approaches to Greek Myth*, 91–140.

Brinkmann, V.
1994   *Die Friese des Siphnierschatzhauses*, Ennepetal.

Brock, J.K.
1957   *Fortetsa: Early Greek Tombs Near Knossos*, Cambridge.
Brock, R.
1991   'The emergence of democratic ideology', *Historia* 40, 161–9.
Bromwich, R. (ed.)
1978   *Trioedd Ynys Prydein: the Welsh Triads*, Cardiff.
Brownlee, A.B.
1995   'Story lines: observations on Sophilan narrative', in Carter and Morris (eds.) *The Ages of Homer*, 363–72.
Brückner, A.
1902   'Geschichte von Troja und Ilion', in W. Dörpfeld et al., *Troja und Ilion*, Athens, 549–93.
Brulé, P.
1987   *La fille d' Athènes*, Paris.
Brunner, O., Conze, W. and Koselleck, R. (eds.)
1984   *Geschichtliche Grundbegriffe*, Stuttgart.
Brunt, P.A.
1966   'The Roman mob', *P&P* 35, 3–22.
Bryce, T.R.
1989   'The nature of Mycenaean involvement in Western Anatolia', *Historia* 38, 1–21.
Buchholz, H.-G.
1991   'Die archäologische Forschung im Zusammenhang mit Homer: Gesamtüberblick', in Latacz (ed.) *Zweihundert Jahre Homer-Forschung*, 11–44.
Buck, R.J.
1962   'The Minoan thalassocracy re-examined', *Historia* 11, 129–37.
Buckler, W.H. and Calder, W.M.
1923   *Anatolian Studies presented to Sir W.M. Ramsay*, Manchester.
Buitenen, J.A.B. van (trsl.)
1973   *The Mahabharata*, Chicago.
Buitron-Oliver, D. (ed.)
1991   *New Perspectives in Early Greek Art*, Hanover and London.
Bunnens, G.
1983   'Tyr et la mer', in Gubel et al. (eds.) *Studia Phoenicia I–II*, 7–21.
Burford, A.
1993   *Land and Labor in the Greek World*, Baltimore.
Burke, P. (ed.)
1991   *New Perspectives on Historical Writing*, Oxford.
Burkert, W.
1976   'Das hunderttorige Theben', *Wiener Studien* 89, 5–21.
1979   *Structure and History in Greek Mythology and Ritual*, California.
1987   'The making of Homer in the 6th century BC: rhapsodes versus Stesichorus', *Papers on the Amasis Painter and His World*, Malibu, 43–62.
1991a   'Homerstudien und Orient', in Latacz (ed.) *Zweihundert Jahre Homer-Forschung*, 155–81.
1991b   'Homer's anthropomorphism: narrative and ritual', in Buitron-Oliver (ed.) *New Perspectives in Early Greek Art*, 81–91.
1992   *The Orientalizing Revolution. Near Eastern influence on Greek culture in the early archaic age*, Cambridge, Mass.
1995   'Lydia between East and West or how to date the Trojan War: a study in Herodotus', in Carter and Morris (eds.) *The Ages of Homer*, 139–48.
Burnett, A. P.
1985   *The Art of Bacchylides*, Cambridge, Mass.
Burstein, S.
1996   'Greek contact with Egypt and the Levant: ca. 1600–500 BC: an overview', *The Ancient World* 27, 20–8.

Bibliography

Burzacchini, G.
    1995   'Note al nuovo Simonide', *Eikasmos* 6, 21–38.
Buschor, E. and Massow, W. von
    1927   'Vom Amyklaion', *AM* 52, 1–85.
Byock, J.L.
    1984   'Saga form, oral prehistory and the Icelandic social context', *New Literary History* 16 (/5), 153–73.
Calame, C.
    1995   *The Craft of Poetic Speech in Ancient Greece*, Ithaca (French original 1986).
Calder, W.M.III and Traill, D.A. (eds.)
    1986   *Myth, Scandal, and History: The Heinrich Schliemann controversy and a first edition of the Mycenaean diary*, Detroit.
Calhoun, G.M.
    1934   'Classes and Masses in Homer', *CPh* 29, 192–208, 301–16.
    1962   'Polity and Society', in Wace and Stubbings (eds.) *A Companion to Homer* , New York, 431–52.
Callaghan, P.
    1992   'Archaic to Hellenistic pottery', in Sackett et al. *Knossos*, 89–136.
Calligas, P.G.
    1992   'From the Amyklaion', in Sanders (ed.) *Philolakōn*, London, 31–48.
Callipolitis-Feijtmans, D.
    1974   *Les plats attiques à figures noires*, Paris.
Cambitoglou, A.
    1981   *Archaeological Museum of Andros*, Athens.
Cambitoglou, A., Coulton, J.J., Birmingham, J. and Green, J.R.
    1971   *Zagora I*, Athens.
    1988   *Zagora II*, Sydney.
Campbell, D.A.
    1983   *The Golden Lyre: The themes of the Greek lyric poets*, London.
Canciani, F.
    1970   *Bronzi orientali e orientalizzanti a Creta nell' VIII e VII sec. a. C.*, Rome.
Cantarella, E. and Di Vita, A.
    1982   'Iscrizione arcaica giuridica dà Festos', *Annuario della Scuola Archeologica di Atene e delle Missioni Italiane in Oriente* 56 (1978), 429–35.
Capizzi, A.
    1990   *The Cosmic Republic: Notes for a non-peripatetic history of the birth of philosophy in Greece*, Amsterdam.
Capizzi, A., Capra, A. and Curti, M.
    1995   'Semidei Simonidei. Note sull'elegia di Simonide per la battaglia di Platea', *ZPE* 107, 27–32.
Carapanos, C.
    1878   *Dodone et ses ruines*, Paris.
Carlier, P.
    1984   *La royauté en Grèce avant Alexandre*, Strasbourg.
    1991   'La procédure de décision politique du monde mycénien à l'époque archaïque', in Musti et al. (eds.) *La transizione dal Miceneo all'Alto Arcaismo*, 85–95.
Carpenter, T.H.
    1986   *Dionysian Imagery in Archaic Greek Art. Its development in black-figure vase painting*, Oxford.
Carsten, J. and Hugh-Jones, S. (eds.)
    1995   *About the House: Lévi-Strauss and Beyond*, Cambridge.
Carter, J.B.
    1988   'Isotopic analysis of seventh century *perirrhanteria*', in Herz and Waelkens (eds.) *Classical Marble*, 419–31.

Carter, J.B. and Morris, S.P. (eds.)
1995   *The Ages of Homer: A tribute to Emily Townsend Vermeule*, Austin, Tex.

Carter, J.C.
1990   'Metapontum – land, wealth, and population', in Descoeudres (ed.) *Greek Colonists*, 405–41.
1993   'Taking possession of the land: early Greek colonisation in southern Italy', in Scott and Scott (eds.) *Eius Virtutis Studiosi*, 342–67.
1994   'Sanctuaries in the chora of Metaponto', in Alcock and Osborne (eds.) *Placing the Gods*, 161–98.

Cartledge, P.A.
1978   'Literacy in the Spartan oligarchy', *JHS* 98, 25–37.
1979   *Sparta and Lakonia: A Regional History 1300–362 BC*, London.
1980   'The peculiar position of Sparta in the development of the Greek city-state', *PRIA* 80C, 91–108.
1981   'The politics of Spartan pederasty', *PCPhS* 30, 17– 36.
1982   'Sparta and Samos: a special relationship?', *CQ* 32, 243–65.
1985   Review of Rolley 1982, *JHS* 105, 238–40.
1987   *Agesilaos and the Crisis of Sparta*, London.
1988   Review of Herfort-Koch 1986, *CR* 38, 342–5.
1993   *The Greeks. A Portrait of Self and Others*, Oxford. (Revised edition 1997.)
1995   ' "We are all Greeks"? Ancient (especially Herodotean) and modern contestations of Hellenism', *BICS* 40, 75–82.
1996a   'Comparatively equal', in Ober and Hedrick (eds.) *Demokratia*, 175–85.
1996b   'La Politica', in Settis (ed.) *I Greci*, 39–72.
1996c   'La nascita degli opliti e l'organizzazione militare', in Settis (ed.) *I Greci*, 681–714.
1996d   Review of Ducat 1994, *CR* 46, 379–80.
1997   'Introduction' to P. Cartledge, P. Garnsey and E. Gruen (eds.) *Hellenistic Constructs*, Berkeley.

Casagrande, C. and Vecchio, S.
1979   'Clercs et jongleurs dans la société médiévale', *Annales· économies, sociétés, civilisations* 34, 913–28.

Casevitz, M.
1985   *Le vocabulaire de la colonisation en grec ancien*, Paris.

Casson, L.
1971   *Ships and Seamanship in the Ancient World*, Princeton.

Castriota, D.
1992   *Myth, Ethos, and Actuality. Official Art in Fifth-Century BC Athens*, Madison.

Catling, R.W.V.
1996   'The archaic and classical pottery', in Cavanagh et al. *The Laconia Survey* II, 33–89.

Cavanagh, W.G. and Laxton, R.
1984   'Lead figurines from the Menelaion and seriation', *BSA* 79, 23–36.

Cavanagh, W.G., Crouwel, J., Catling, R.V.W. and Shipley, G.
1996   *The Laconia Survey* II. *Archaeological Data*, *BSA* Suppl. Vol. 27, London.

Cavanagh, W.G. and Walker, S. (eds.)
1998   *Sparta in Lakonia. Proceedings of a conference at the British Museum, December 1995*, London.

Cawkwell, G.
1992   'Early colonisation', *CQ* 42, 289–303.

Cébeillac-Gervasoni, M.
1975   'Les nécropoles de Megara Hyblaea', *Kokalos* 19, 3–36.
1976/7 'Une étude systematique sur les nécropoles de Megara Hyblaia: l'exemple d'une partie de la nécropole méridionale', *Kokalos* 22/3, 587–97.

Chadwick, J.
1958   *The Decipherment of Linear B*, Cambridge.

Bibliography

1976 *The Mycenaean World*, Cambridge.
1996 *Lexicographica Graeca*, Oxford.
Champion, T.C. (ed.)
1989 *Centre and Periphery: Comparative studies in archaeology*, London.
Champion, T.C. and Megaw, J.V.S. (eds.)
1985 *Settlement and Society: Aspects of Western European prehistory in the first millennium BC*, Leicester.
Champion, T., Gamle, C., Shennan, S. and Whittle, A.
1984 *Prehistoric Europe*, New York.
Charbonneaux, J.
1958 *Les Bronzes Grecs*, Paris.
Chartier, R.
1988 *Cultural History: Between practices and representations*, Ithaca.
Cherry, J., Davis, J. and Mantzourani, E. (eds.)
1991 *Landscape Archaeology as Long-Term History: Northern Keos in the Cycladic Islands*, Los Angeles.
Christou, Chr.
1964a 'Archaic graves in Sparta and a Laconian funeral figured relief amphora', *Archaiologikon Deltion* 19 A', 123–63 and 283–5. (In Greek; English summary.)
1964b 'The new amphora from Sparta: the other amphorae with reliefs of Laconian manufacture', *Archaiologikon Deltion* 19 A', 164–265 and 285–8. (In Greek; English summary.)
Clay, J.S.
1996 'The New Simonides and Homer's *Hemitheoi*', in Boedeker and Sider (eds.) *The New Simonides*, 243–5.
Cobet, J. and Patzek, B. (eds.)
1992 *Archäologie und historische Erinnerung: Nach 100 Jahren Heinrich Schliemann*, Essen.
Cohen, A.
1995 'Alexander and Achilles – Macedonians and Mycenaeans', in Carter and Morris (eds.) *The Ages of Homer*, 483–505.
Cohen, D.
1991 *Law, Sexuality, and Society: The enforcement of morals in classical Athens*, Cambridge.
1995 *Law, Violence, and Community in Classical Athens*, Cambridge.
Coldstream, J.N.
1968 *Greek Geometric Pottery*, London.
1973 *Knossos: The Sanctuary of Demeter*, London.
1976 'Hero-cults in the age of Homer', *JHS* 96, 8–17.
1977 *Geometric Greece*, London.
1982 'Greeks and Phoenicians in the Aegean', *Madrider Beiträge* 8, 261–75.
1984 'A protogeometric nature goddess from Knossos', *BICS* 31, 93–104.
1992 'Early Hellenic pottery', in Sackett (et al.), *Knossos*, 67–87.
1993 'Mixed marriages at the frontiers of the Greek world', *Oxford Journal of Archaeology* 12, 89–107.
1994 'Prospectors and pioneers: Pithekoussai, Kyme and Central Italy', in Tsetskhladze and De Angelis (eds.) *The Archaeology of Greek Colonisation*, 47–59.
1995 'The rich lady of the Areiopagos and her contemporaries', *Hesperia* 64, 391–403.
Coldstream, J.N., Callaghan, P.J. and Musgrave, J.H.
1981 'Knossos: an early Greek tomb on the Lower Gypsadhes Hill', *BSA* 76, 141–65.
Coldstream, J.N. and Catling, H.W. (eds.)
1996 *Knossos North Cemetery: Early Greek Tombs* (*BSA* Suppl. 28).
Cole, A.T.
1967 *Democritus and the Sources of Greek Anthropology*, Cleveland.

410

Colesanti, G.
1995   'La disposizione delle arme in Alc. 140 V', *Rivista di Filologia* 123, 385–408.
Collingwood, W.G. and Stefánsson, J. (trsl.)
1902   *The life and death of Cormac the skald*, Ulverston.
Conkey, M.W. and Gero, J.M.
1991   'Tensions, pluralities, and engendering archaeology', in J.M. Gero and M.W. Conkey (eds.) *Engendering Archaeology*, Oxford, 3–30.
Connor, W.R.
1989   'City Dionysia and Athenian democracy', *C&M* 40, 7–32.
Cook, J.M.
1935   'Protoattic pottery', *BSA* 35, 165–219.
1962   *The Greeks in Ionia and the East*, London.
1975   'Greek settlement in the Eastern Aegean and Asia Minor', *CAH*[3] II.2, Cambridge, 773–804.
Cook, R.M.
1959   'Die Bedeutung der bemalten Keramik für den griechischen Handel', *JdI* 74, 114–23.
1962   'Spartan history and archaeology', *CQ* 12, 156–8.
1969   'A note on the absolute chronologies of the eighth and seventh centuries BC', *BSA* 64, 13–15.
1981   *Clazomenian Sarcophagi*, Mainz.
Coulson, W.D.E.
1986   *The Dark Age Pottery of Messenia* (Studies in Mediterranean Archaeology), Göteborg.
Coulson, W.D.E. et al. (eds.)
1994   *The Archaeology of Athens and Attica under the Democracy*, Oxford.
Courbin, P.
1974   *Tombes géométriques d'Argos I*, Paris.
Crane, G.
1993   'Politics of consumption and generosity in the carpet scene of the Agamemnon', *CPh* 88, 117–36.
Crielaard, J.P.
1995   'Homer, history and archaeology. Some remarks on the date of the Homeric world', in Crielaard (ed.) *Homeric Questions*, Amsterdam, 201–88.
Crielaard, J.P. (ed.)
1995   *Homeric Questions*, Amsterdam.
Croissant, F.
1988   'Tradition et innovation dans les ateliers Corinthiens archaïques: matériaux pour l'histoire d'un style', *BCH* 112, 91–166.
Crouwel, J.H.
1992   *Chariots and Other Wheeled Vehicles in Iron Age Greece*, Amsterdam.
Crowther, N.B.
1990   'A Spartan Olympic boxing champion', *AntClass* 59, 198–202.
Csapo, E.
1991   'An international community of traders in late 8th–7th century BC: Kommos in southern Crete', *ZPE* 88, 211–16.
1993   'A postscript to "An international community of traders"', *ZPE* 96, 235–6.
Culican, W.
1970   'Phoenician oil bottles and tripod bowls', *Berytus* 19, 5–16.
1975   'Sidonian bottles', *Levant* 7, 145–50.
Cunliffe, B.
1988   *Greeks, Romans and Barbarians*, London.
D'Agostino, B.
1994   'Pitecusa – una *apoikìa* di tipo particolare', in D'Agostino and Ridgeway (eds.) *Apoikia*, 19–27.

D'Agostino, B. and Ridgway, D. (eds.)
1994 *Apoikia: Scritti in onore di Giorgio Buchner* (*AION*, n.s. 1), Naples.
D'Onofrio, A.M.
1982 'Korai e kouroi funerari attici', *AION* 4, 135–70.
1988 'Aspetti e problemi del monumento funerario Attico arcaico', *AION* 10, 82–96.
1995 'Santuari "rurali" e dinamiche insediative in Attica tra il Protogeometrico e l'Orientalizzante (1050–600 a.C.)', *AION* n.s. 2, 57–88.
Dakaris, S.I.
1971 *Dodona. Archaiologikos Odigos*, Athens.
Dalby, A.
1995 'The *Iliad*, the *Odyssey* and their audiences', *CQ* 45, 269–79.
Danforth, L.
1995 *The Macedonian Conflict*, Princeton.
Daniel, R.W. and Maltomini, F. (eds.)
1990/2 *Supplementum Magicum* (Papyrologica Coloniensia vols. xvi.1 and xvi.2), Cologne.
David, E.
1989 'Dress in Spartan society', *Ancient World* 19, 3–13.
Davies, J.K.
1971 *Athenian Propertied Families 600–300 BC*, Oxford.
1984 'The reliability of the oral tradition', in Foxhall and Davies (eds.) *The Trojan War*, Bristol, 87–110.
Davis, J.
1992 *Exchange*, Buckingham.
Dawkins, R.M. (ed.)
1929 *The Sanctuary of Artemis Orthia* (Society for the Promotion of Hellenic Studies, Suppl. Paper 5), London.
De Angelis, F.
1994 'The foundation of Selinous: overpopulation or opportunities?', in Tsetskhladze and De Angelis (eds.) *The Archaeology of Greek Colonisation*, 87–110.
De Jong, I.J.F.
1995 'Homer as literature: some current areas of research', in Crielaard (ed.) *Homeric Questions*, 127–46.
De Ste. Croix, G.E.M.
1972 *The Origins of the Peloponnesian War*, London.
De Vries, K.
1975 'Greeks and Phrygians in the Early Iron Age', in De Vries (ed.), *From Athens to Gordion*, 33–49.
De Vries, K. (ed.)
1975 *From Athens to Gordion: The Papers of a Symposium for Rodney S. Young*, Pennsylvania.
Deetz, J.
1977 *In Small Things Forgotten*, New York.
Deger-Jalkotzy, S.
1987 ' "Near Eastern economies" versus "Feudal society": zum mykenischen Palaststaat', in Killen et al. (eds.) *Studies in Mycenaean and Classical Greek*, 137–50.
1989 'Frühgriechische Herrschaftsformen in mykenischer Zeit', *Jahrbuch der Universität Salzburg 1985–87*, 133–51.
1991a 'Die Erforschung des Zusammenbruchs der sogenannten mykenischen Kultur und der sogenannten dunklen Jahrhunderte', in Latacz (ed.) *Zweihundert Jahre Homer-Forschung*, 127–54.
1991b 'Diskontinuität und Kontinuität: Aspekte politischer und sozialer Organisation in mykenischer Zeit und in der Welt der homerischen Epen', in Musti et al. (eds.) *La transizione dal Micenae all'Alto Arcaismo*, 53–66.
1991c 'Elateia (Phokis) und die frühe Geschichte der Griechen: Ein österreichisch-

griechisches Grabungsprojekt', *Anzeiger der phil.-hist. Klasse der Österreich-ischen Akademie der Wissenschaften* 127 (1990), 77–86.

Forthcoming 'Zwischen Mykene und Homer. Der Beginn eines heroischen Zeitalters', Salzburg.

Deger-Jalkotzy, S. (ed.)
1983 *Griechenland, die Ägäis und die Levante während der 'Dark Ages' vom 12. bis zum 9. Jh. v. Chr* (Sitzungsber. Österreichische Akademie der Wissenschaften 418), Vienna.

Delcourt, M.
1938 *Stérilités mystérieuses et naissances maléfiques dans l'antiquité classique*, Liège and Paris.
1944 *Oedipe ou la légende du conquérant*, Paris and Liège.

Demargne, P.
1984 'Athena', *LIMC II*, 955–1044.

Demargne, P. and Effenterre, H. van
1937a 'Recherches à Dreros I', *BCH* 61, 5–32.
1937b 'Recherches à Dreros II', *BCH* 61, 333–48.

Dentzer, J.-M.
1982 *Le motif du banquet couché dans le Proche-Orient et le monde grec du VIIe au IVe siècle avant J.-C.*, Paris/Rome.

Desborough, V.R.d'A.
1964 *The Last Mycenaeans and Their Successors*, Oxford.
1972 *The Greek Dark Ages*, London.
1975 'The end of the Mycenaean civilization and the Dark Age', in *CAH²* III.1, Cambridge, 658–77.

Descoeudres, J.P. (ed.)
1990 *Greek Colonists and Native Populations*, Oxford.

Detienne, M.
1965 'En Grèce archaïque: géométrie, politique et société', *Annales (ESC)* 20, 425–41.
1973 *Les maîtres de vérité dans la Grèce archaïque*, 2nd edn, Paris.
1988 'L'espace de la publicité, ses opérateurs intellectuels dans la cité', in Detienne (ed.) *Les savoirs de l'écriture en Grèce ancienne*, 29–81.

Detienne, M. (ed.)
1988 *Les savoirs de l'écriture en Grèce ancienne*, Lille.

Deubner, L.
1932 *Attische Feste*, Berlin.

Di Vita, A.
1955 'Atena Ergane in una terracotta della Sicilia ed il culto della dea in Atene', *Annuario della Scuola archeologica di Atene e delle Missioni italiane in Oriente* n.s. 14–16 (1952–4), 141–54.
1990 'Town planning in the Greek colonies of Sicily from the time of their foundation to the Punic wars', in Descoeudres (ed.) *Greek Colonists*, 343–63.

Di Vita, A., La Rose, V. and Rizzo, M.A. (eds.)
1984 *Creta antica. Cento anno di archeologia italiana (1884–1984)*, Rome.

Dickey, K.
1992 *Corinthian burial customs ca. 1100–550 BC*, unpublished Ph.D. thesis, Bryn Mawr College.

Dickie, M.
1995 'The geography of Homer's world', in Andersen and Dickie (eds.) *Homer's World*, 29–56.

Dickins, G.
1908 'The art of Sparta', *The Burlington Magazine* 14, 66–84.
1912 'The growth of Spartan policy', *JHS* 32, 1–42.

Dickinson, O.T.P.K.
1986 'Homer, the poet of the Dark Age', *G&R* 33, 20–37.

413

1994   *The Aegean Bronze Age*, Cambridge.

Diehl, E.

1964a   *Die Hydria: Formgeschichte und Verwendung im Kult des Altertums*, Mainz am Rhein.

1964b   'Fragmente aus Samos', *AA*, 493–612.

Diels, H. and Kranz, W.

1952   *Die Fragmente der Vorsokratiker II*, 6th edn, Berlin.

Docter, R.F. and Niemeyer, H.G.

1994   'Pithekoussai: the Carthaginian connection. On the archaeological evidence of Euboeo-Phoenician partnership in the 8th and 7th centuries', in D'Agostino and Ridgeway (eds.) *Apoikia*, 101–15.

Donlan, W.

1970   'Changes and shifts in the meaning of *demos* in the literature of the archaic period', *PdP* 135, 391–5.

1980   *The Aristocratic Ideal in Ancient Greece*, Lawrence, Kans.

1981/2   'Reciprocities in Homer', *Classical World* 75, 137–75.

1985   'The social groups of Dark Age Greece', *CPh* 80, 293–308.

1989a   'The pre-state community in Greece', *Symbolae Osloenses* 64 , 5–29.

1989b   'Homeric *temenos* and the land economy of the Dark Age', *Museum Helveticum* 46, 129–45.

1989c   'The unequal exchange between Glaucus and Diomedes in light of the Homeric gift-economy', *Phoenix* 43, 1–15.

1993   'Duelling with gifts in the *Iliad*: as the audience saw it', in Roisman and Roisman (eds.) *Essays on Homeric Epic*, 155–72.

Dörpfeld, W. et al.

1902   *Troja und Ilion*, Athens.

Dougherty, C.

1993   'It's murder to found a colony', in Dougherty and Kurke (eds.), *Cultural Poetics*, 178–98.

1994a   *The Poetics of Colonization: From city to text in archaic Greece*, Oxford.

1994b   'Archaic Greek foundation poetry: questions of genre and occasion', *JHS* 114, 35–46.

Dougherty, C. and Kurke, L. (eds.)

1993   *Cultural Poetics in Archaic Greece. Cult, performance, politics*, New York.

Douglas, M. and Isherwood, B.

1979   *The World of Goods: Towards an anthropology of consumption*, New York and London.

Dover, K.J.

1978   *Greek Homosexuality*, London.

Dragendorff, H.

1903   *Thera II*, Berlin.

Drerup, H.

1969   *Griechische Baukunst in geometrischer Zeit (Archaeologia Homerica,* Bd. O), Göttingen.

Droop, J.P.

1929   'Pottery'; 'Bronzes', in Dawkins (ed.) *The Sanctuary of Artemis Orthia*, 52–116, 196–202.

DuBois, P.

1988   *Sowing the Body*, Chicago.

Ducat, J.

1994   *Les penèstes de Thessalie*, Paris.

Duggan, J.J.

1973   *The Song of Roland: formulaic style and poetic craft*, Berkeley.

1980/1   'Le mode de composition des chansons de geste', *Olifant* 8, 286–316.

1986   'Social functions of the medieval epic in the Romance literatures', *Oral Tradition* 1, 728–66.

Duhoux, Y.
1981   'Les Etéocrétois et l'origine de l'alphabet grec', *L'Antiquité Classique* 50, 287–94.
Dunbabin, T.J.
1957   *The Greeks and their Eastern Neighbours: Studies in the relations between Greece and the countries of the Near East in the eighth and seventh centuries BC*, London.
Dunn, J.
1996   *The History of Political Theory and Other Essays*, Cambridge.
Easton, D.F.
1984   'Hittite History and the Trojan War', in Foxhall and Davies (eds.) *The Trojan War*, 23–44.
Eder, B.
1994   *Staat, Herrschaft, Gesellschaft in frühgriechischer Zeit. Eine Bibliographie 1978–1991/2*, Vienna.
Eder, W.
1986   'The political significance of the codification of law in archaic societies', in Raaflaub (ed.) *Social Struggles in Archaic Rome*, 262–300.
Edmunds, L. (ed.)
1990   *Approaches to Greek Myth*, Baltimore.
Ehrenberg, V.
1925   *Neugründer des Staates*, Munich.
1929   'Sparta (Geschichte)', *RE* III, A2, 1373–1453.
Eisenstadt, S.N. (ed.)
1986   *The Origins and Diversity of Axial Age Cultures*, NewYork.
Emeneau, M.B.
1958   'Oral poets of South India: the Todas', *Journal of American Folklore* 71, 312–24.
Emlyn-Jones, C.J.
1980   *The Ionians and Hellenism: A study of the cultural achievement of the early Greek inhabitants of Asia Minor*, London.
Engelmann, H. and Merkelbach, R. (eds.)
1973   *Die Inschriften von Erythrai und Klazomenai II (Inschriften griechischer Städte aus Kleinasien* 2), Bonn.
Erskine, A.W.
1990   *The Hellenistic Stoa: Political thought and action*, London and Ithaca.
Étienne, R. and Piérart, M.
1975   'Un décret du koinon des Hellènes à Platées en l'honneur de Glaucon, fils d'Étéoclès, d'Athènes', *BCH* 99, 51–75.
Euben, J.P.
1986   'The battle of Salamis and the origins of political theory', *Political Theory* 14, 359–90.
Euben, J.P. (ed.)
1986   *Greek Tragedy and Political Theory*, Berkeley and London.
Euben, J.P., Wallach, J.R. and Ober, J. (eds.)
1994   *Athenian Political Thought and the Reconstruction of American Democracy*, Princeton.
Fagerström, K.
1988   *Greek Iron Age Architecture. Developments through changing times (Studies in Mediterranean Archaeology* 81), Göteborg.
Faraone, C.
1991   'Blinding and burying the forces of evil: the defensive use of "voodoo" dolls in ancient Greece', *CA* 10, 165–205.
1992   *Talismans and Trojan Horses: Guardian statues in ancient Greek myth and ritual*, Oxford.
Farnell, L.R.
1921   *Greek Hero Cults and Ideas of Immortality*, Oxford.
Farrar, C.
1988   *The Origins of Democratic Thinking. The invention of politics in Athens*, Cambridge.

Bibliography

Fehr, B.
    1971   *Orientalische und griechische Gelage*, Bonn.

Felsch, R.
    1983   'Zur Chronologie und zum Stil geometrischer Bronzen aus Kalapodi', in Hägg
            (ed.)*The Greek Renaissance*, 123–9.

Felsch, R. et al.
    1996   *Kalapodi: Ergebnisse der Ausgrabungen*, Vol. I, Mainz am Rhein.

Fernández Castro, M.C.
    1995   *Iberia in Prehistory*, Oxford.

Fetscher, I. and Münkler, H. (eds.)
    1988   *Pipers Handbuch der politischen Ideen* I: *Frühe Hochkulturen und die europäische
            Antike*, Munich.

Figueira, T.J.
    1986   'Xanthippos, father of Perikles, and the *prytaneis* of the *naukraroi*', *Historia*
            35, 257–79.

Filow, B.
    1927   *Die archaische Nekropole von Trebenischte*, Berlin.
    1934   *Die Grabhügelnekropole bei Duvanlij in Südbulgarien*, Sofia.

Fine, B. and Leopold, E.
    1993   *The World of Consumption*, London.

Finley, M.I.
    1956   *The World of Odysseus*, London.
    1957   'Homer and Mycenae: property and tenure', *Historia* 6, 133–59; repr. in id.
            1982, 213–32.
    1957/8 'Mycenaean Palace archives and economic history', *Economic History Review* ser.
            2, 10, 128–41; reprinted. in id. 1982, 199–212.
    1970   *Early Greece. The Bronze and Archaic Ages*, London.
    1975   *The Use and Abuse of History*, London.
    1976   'Colonies – an attempt at a typology', *Transactions of the Royal Historical
            Society* 26, 167–88.
    1977   *The World of Odysseus*, 2nd edn, London.
    1981   'Politics', in Finley (ed.) *The Legacy of Greece*, 22–36.
    1982   *Economy and Society in Ancient Greece*, New York.
    1983   *Politics in the Ancient World*, Cambridge.
    1985a   *Democracy Ancient and Modern*, 2nd edn, London.
    1985b   *The Ancient Economy*, 2nd edn, London.
    1986   'Revolution in antiquity', in Porter and Teich (eds.) *Revolution in History*,
            47–60.

Finley, M.I. (ed.)
    1973   *Problèmes de la terre en Grèce ancienne*, Paris.
    1981   *The Legacy of Greece. A new appraisal*, Oxford.

Finley, M.I., Caskey, J.L., Kirk, G.S. and Page, D.L.
    1964   'The Trojan War', *JHS* 84, 1–20.

Finnegan, R.
    1977   *Oral Poetry: Its nature, significance and social context*, Cambridge.
    1988   *Literacy and Orality*, Oxford.

Fisher, N.
    1989   'Drink, *hybris,* and the promotion of harmony in Sparta', in Powell (ed.)
            Classical Sparta, 26–50.
    1992   *Hybris. A study in the values of honour and shame in ancient Greece*, Warminster.
    Forthcoming(a) 'Violence, masculinity, and the law in classical Athens', in
            L. Foxhall and J. Salmon (eds.) *When Men Were Men*, London.
    Forthcoming(b) 'Gymnasia and the democratic values of leisure', in P. Cartledge,
            P. Millett and S. von Reden (eds.) *Kosmos*, Cambridge.

Fitton, J.L.
    1996   *The Discovery of the Greek Bronze Age*, Cambridge, Mass.

Fittschen, K.
1973   *Der Schild des Achilleus* (*Archaeologia Homerica*, Bd. N1), Göttingen.
Fitzhardinge, L.F.
1980   *The Spartans*, London.
Flaig, E.
1993   'Die spartanische Abstimmung nach der Lautstärke', *Historia* 42, 139–60.
1994   'Das Konsensprinzip im homerischen Olymp', *Hermes* 122, 13–31.
Flashar, M.
1996   'Die Sieger von Marathon — Zwischen Mythisierung und Vorbildlichkeit', in
        Flashar, Gehrke and Heinrich (eds.) *Retrospektive*, 63–85.
Flashar M., Gehrke, H.-J. and Heinrich, E. (eds.)
1996   *Retrospektive. Konzepte von Vergangenheit in der griechisch-römischen Antike*,
        Munich.
Fleischer, R.
1973   *Artemis von Ephesos und verwandte Kultstatuen aus Anatolien und Syrien* (*Etudes
        préliminaires aux religions orientales dans l'empire romain* 35), Leiden.
Foley, A.
1988   *The Argolid 800–600 bc. An Archaeological Survey* (Studies in Mediterranean
        Archaeology 80), Göteborg.
Foley, J.M.
1988   *The Theory of Oral Composition: History and methodology*, Bloomington, Ind.
1990   *Traditional Oral Epic: The Odyssey, Beowulf, and the Serbo-Croatian Return Song*,
        Berkeley.
1991   *Immanent Art: From structure to meaning in traditional oral epic*, Bloomington, Ind.
Forbes, R.J.
1956   *Studies in Ancient Technology IV*, Leiden.
Forrest, W.G.
1969   'Two chronographic notes', *CQ* 19, 95–106.
Forssman, B.
1991   'Schichten der homerischen Sprache', in Latacz (ed.) *Zweihundert Jahre
        Homer-Forschung*, 259–88.
Förtsch R.
1994   *Kunstverwandung und Kunstlegitimation im archaischen und frühklassischen
        Sparta*, Habilitationsschrift, Köln.
1995   'Zeugen der Vergangenheit', in Wörrle and Zanker (eds.) *Stadtbild und
        Bürgerbild im Hellenismus*, 172–88.
1998   'The many ways of dying in Spartan art', in W.G. Cavanagh and S. Walker
        (eds.) *Sparta in Lakonia*, London.
Foucault, M.
1985   *The Uses of Pleasure*, New York.
Foxhall, L.
1995   'Bronze to iron: agricultural systems and political structures in Late Bronze
        Age and Early Iron Age Greece', *BSA* 90, 239–50.
1998   *Olive Cultivation in Classical Greece: Seeking the ancient economy*, London.
Foxhall, L. and Davies, J.K. (eds.)
1984   *The Trojan War: Its Historicity and Context*, Bristol.
Foxhall, L. and Stears, K.
1998   'Redressing the Balance: Dedications of Clothing to Artemis and the Order
        of Life Stages', in McDonald and Hurcombe (eds.) *Gender and Material
        Culture*.
Francis, E.D. and Vickers, M.J.
1981   'Leagros kalos', *PCPhS* 27, 97–136.
1983   'Signa priscae artis: Eretria and Siphnos', *JHS* 103, 49–67.
1985a   'Greek Geometric pottery at Hama and its implications for Near Eastern
        chronology', *Levant* 17, 131–8.
1985b   'The Oenoe painting in the Stoa Poikile and Herodotus' account of

Marathon', *BSA* 80, 99–113.

1988   'The Agora revisited: Athenian chronology *c.* 500–458 BC', *BSA* 83, 143–67.

Fränkel, H.
1962   *Dichtung und Philosophie des frühen Griechentums*, 2nd edn, Munich.
1975   *Early Greek Poetry and Philosophy*, Oxford.

Frazer, J.G.
1898   *Pausanias* (Loeb Classical Library), Cambridge, Mass.

Frisch, P.
1975   *Die Inschriften von Ilion* (*Inschriften griechischer Städte aus Kleinasien* 3), Bonn.

Frontisi-Ducroux, F. and Lissarrague, F.
1990   'From ambiguity to ambivalence: a Dionysiac excursion through the "Anakreontic" vases', in Halperin et al. (eds.) *Before Sexuality*, 211–56.

Fuqua, C.
1981   'Tyrtaeus and the cult of heroes', *GRBS* 22, 215–26.

Furet, F.
1983   'Beyond the Annales', *Journal of Modern History* 55, 389–410.

Furtwängler, A. and Reichold, K.
1904   *Griechische Vasenmalerei: Auswahl hervorragender Vasenbilder*, Munich.

Fusaro, D.
1982   'Note di architettura domestica greca nel periodo tardo-geometrico e arcaico', *Dialoghi di Archeologia* 4, 5–30.

Gabrielsen, V.
1994   *Financing the Athenian Fleet. Public taxation and social relations*, Baltimore.

Gagarin, M.
1986   *Early Greek Law*, Berkeley, Los Angeles and London.

Gagarin, M. and Woodruff, P. (eds.)
1995   *Early Greek Political Thought from Homer to the Sophists*, Cambridge.

Gager, J.G.
1992   *Curse Tablets and Binding Spells from the Ancient World*, New York.

Gamer-Wallert, I. (ed.)
1992   *Troia: Brücke zwischen Orient und Okzident*, Tübingen.

Garland, R.
1987   *The Piraeus*, London.

Garnsey, P.
1988   *Famine and Food Supply in the Graeco-Roman World*, Cambridge.

Garnsey, P., Hopkins, K. and Whittaker, C.R. (eds.)
1983   *Trade in the Ancient Economy*, Cambridge.

Gauer, W.
1996   'Überlegungen zum Mythos vom Krieg um Troia und zur Heimat Homers', *Gymnasium* 103, 507–34.

Geddes, A.G.
1987   'Rags and riches: the costume of Athenian men in the fifth century', *CQ* 37, 307–31.

Geertz, C.
1973   *The Interpretation of Cultures*, New York.

Gehrig, U.
1971   'Der krater lakonikos', *Archäologischer Anzeiger*, 602–12.

Gehrke, H.-J.
1993   'Gesetz und Konflikt. Überlegungen zur frühen Polis', in Bleicken and Bringmann (eds.) *Colloquium*, 49–67.

Gehrke, H.-J. and Wirbelauer, E. (eds.)
1994   *Rechtskodifizierung und soziale Normen im interkulturellen Vergleich*, Tübingen.

Gellner, E.
1985   *Relativism in the Social Sciences*, Cambridge.

Gentili, B.
1985   *Poesia e pubblico nella Grecia antica da Omero al V secolo*, Bari.

Georges, P.
1994   *Barbarian Asia and the Greek Experience*, Baltimore and London.
Gergova, D.
1993   'Common elements in the ritual behaviour of Thracians and Macedonians',
         in *Ancient Macedonia* V, 471–8.
Gesell, G.
1985   *Town, Palace, and House Cult in Minoan Crete* (Studies in Mediterranean
         Archaeology 67), Göteborg.
Gibb, J.G.
1996   *The Archaeology of Wealth: Consumer Behaviour in English America*, New York
         and London.
Gill, D.
1994   'Positivism, pots and long distance trade', in Morris (ed.) *Classical Greece*,
         99–107.
Giovannini, A.
1969   *Etude historique sur les origines du Catalogue des Vaisseaux*, Berne.
1989   'Homer und seine Welt', in *Vom frühen Griechentum bis zur römischen
         Kaiserzeit. Gedenk- und Jubiläumsvorträge am Heidelberger Seminar für Alte
         Geschichte.* HABES 6, Stuttgart, 25–39.
Girard, R.
1977   *Violence and the Sacred*, Baltimore. (French original 1972.)
1986   *The Scapegoat*, Baltimore. (French original 1982.)
Giudice, F.
1983   *I pittori della classe di Phanyllis, Vol. I*, Catania.
Gjødesen, M.
1963   'Greek bronzes: a review article', *AJA* 67, 333–51.
Glennie, P.
1995   'Consumption within historical studies', in Miller (ed.) *Acknowledging Con-
         sumption*, 164–203.
Gnoli, G. and Vernant, J.-P. (eds.)
1982   *La mort, les morts dans les sociétés anciennes*, Cambridge.
Goethert, F.W. and Schleif, H.
1962   *Der Athenatempel von Ilion* (Denkmäler antiker Architektur 10), Berlin.
Golden, M. and Toohey, P. (eds.)
1997   *Inventing Ancient Culture. Historicism, periodization and the ancient world*,
         London.
Goldhill, S. and Osborne, R. (eds.)
1994   *Art and Text in Ancient Greek Culture*, Cambridge.
Gomme, A.W.
1959   *A Historical Commentary on Thucydides, Vol. I*, Oxford.
Gonda, J.
1975   *Vedic literature: Samhitas and Brahmanas*, Wiesbaden.
Goody, J. (ed.)
1968   *Literacy in Traditional Societies*, Cambridge.
Goody, J. and Watt, I.
1963   'The consequences of literacy', *CSSH* 5, 304–45.
1968   'The consequences of literacy', in Goody (ed.) *Literacy in Traditional Societies*,
         27–68.
Gordon, R.L. (ed.)
1981   *Myth, Religion and Society*, Cambridge.
Grace, V.
1961   *Amphoras and the Ancient Wine Trade*, Princeton.
Graf, F.
1985   *Nordionische Kulte: religionsgeschichtliche und epigraphische Untersuchungen zu
         den Kulten von Chios, Erythrai, Klazomenai und Phokaia*, Rome.

Graham, A.J.
1964   *Colony and Mother City in Ancient Greece*, Manchester.
1982   'The colonial expansion of Greece', *CAH²* III.3, Cambridge, 83–162.
Grandjean, Y.
1988   *Recherches sur l'habitat thasien à l'époque grecque (Études thasiennes* 12), Paris.
Granet, M.
1919   *Fêtes et chansons anciennes de la Chine*, Paris.
Gray, D.H.F.
1954   'Metal-working in Homer', *JHS* 74, 1–15.
Grayson, A.K.
1991   'Assyria: Tiglath-Pileser III to Sargon II, (744–705 BC)', *CAH²* III.2, Cambridge, 71–102.
Greco, E.
1992   *Archeologia della Magna Grecia*, Rome.
1994   'Pithekoussai: *empòrion* o *apoikìa*', in D'Agostino and Ridgeway, (eds.) *Apoikia*, 11–18.
Green, P.
1994   'Philosophers, kings, and democracy, or, how political was the Stoa?', *Ancient Philosophy* 14, 147–56. (Review of Erskine 1990.)
Greenhalgh, P.A.L.
1973   *Early Greek Warfare: Horsemen and chariots in the Homeric and archaic ages*, Cambridge.
Gregor, T.
1977   *Mehinaku*, Chicago.
Griffith, J.G.
1988   *Festinat Senex, or An Old Man In A Hurry*, Oxford.
Griffith, M.
1995   'Brilliant dynasts: power and politics in the *Oresteia*', *Classical Antiquity* 14, 62–129.
Griffiths, A.
1995   'Non-aristocratic elements in archaic poetry', in Powell (ed.)*The Greek World*, 85–103.
Griksson, K.O.
1995   'Egyptian amphorae from late Cypriot contexts in Cyprus', in Bourke and Descoeudres (eds.) *Trade…in the Eastern Mediterranean*, 199–205.
Gröschel, S.-G.
1989   *Waffenbesitz und Waffeneinsatz bei den Griechen*, Europäische Hochschulschriften, Reihe 38, Bd. 23, Frankfurt.
Gschnitzer, F.
1983   'Der Rat in der Volksversammlung', in P. Händel and W. Meid, (eds.) *Festschrift Robert Muth*, Innsbruck, 151–63.
1991   'Zur homerischen Staats- und Gesellschaftsordnung', in Latacz, (ed.) *Zweihundert Jahre Homer-Forschung*, 182–204.
Guarducci, M.
1928   'Due o più donne sotto un solo manto in una serie di vasi greci arcaici', *AM* 53, 52–65.
Gubel, E., Lipinski, E. and Servais-Soyez, B. (eds.)
1983   *Studia Phoenicia I–II*; *Orientalia Louvaniensia Analecta* 15, Leuven.
Guepin, J.
1968   *The Tragic Paradox*, Amsterdam.
Guest-Papamanoli, A. and Lambraki, A.
1980   'Les grottes de Léra et de l'Arkoudia en Crète occidentale aux époques préhistoriques et historiques', *Archaiologikon Deltion A: Meletai* 31 (1976), 178–243.
Güterbock, H.G.
1983a   'The Hittites and the Aegean World: 1. The Ahhiyawa problem reconsidered',

AJA 87, 133–8.

1983b   'Hethitische Götterbilder und Kultobjekte', in Boehmer and Hauptmann (eds.) *Beiträge zur Altertumskunde Kleinasiens*, 203–17.

1984   'Hittites and Akhaeans: a new look', *Proceedings of the American Philosophical Society* 128, 114–22.

1986   'Troy in Hittite Texts? Wilusa, Ahhiyawa, and Hittite History', in Mellink (ed.) *Troy and the Trojan War*, 33–44.

Haas, C.J.

1985   'Athenian naval power before Themistokles', *Historia* 34, 29–46.

Habicht, C.

1961   'Falsche Urkunden zur Geschichte Athens im Zeitalter der Perserkriege', *Hermes* 89, 1–35.

Hägg, R.

1974   *Die Gräber der Argolis I*, Uppsala.

Hägg, R. (ed.)

1983   *The Greek Renaissance of the Eighth Century BC: Tradition and innovation*, Stockholm.

Hägg, R. and Marinatos, N. (eds.)

1984   *The Minoan Thalassocracy: Myth and reality*, Stockholm.

Hägg, R., Marinatos, N. and Nordquist, G. (eds.)

1988   *Early Greek Cult Practice*, Stockholm.

Hahn, J.

1989   *Der Philosoph und die Gesellschaft. Selbstverständnis, öffentliches Auftreten und populäre Erwartungen in der höhen Kaiserzeit*, Stuttgart.

Haider, P.W.

1988   *Griechenland-Nordafrika: Ihre Beziehungen zwischen 1500 und 600 v.Chr.*, Darmstadt.

Hainsworth, J.B.

1993   *The* Iliad*: A Commentary*, Vol. 3: Bks 9–12, Cambridge.

Hainsworth, J.B. and Hatto, A.T. (eds.)

1989   *Traditions of Heroic and Epic Poetry*, London.

Halbherr, F.

1894   'American expedition to Crete under Professor Halbherr', *AJA* 9, 538–44.

1901   'Report on the researches at Praesos', *AJA* 5, 317–92.

Hall, E.

1989   *Inventing the Barbarian. Greek self-definition through tragedy*, Oxford.

Hall, E.R.

1914   'Excavations in eastern Crete, Vrokastro', *University of Pennsylvania, the Museum Anthropological Publications* 3.3, 79–185.

Halperin, D., Winkler, J.J. and Zeitlin, F.I. (eds.)

1990   *Before Sexuality*, Princeton.

Halstead, P.

1987   'Traditional and ancient rural economy in Mediterranean Europe: plus ça change?', *JHS* 107, 77–87.

Hamilton, C.D.

1993   'Cleisthenes and the *demos*', in W.J. Cherf (ed.) *Alpha to Omega. Studies in honor of George John Szemler on his sixty-fifth birthday*, Chicago, 69–93.

Hamilton, R.

1984   'Sources for the Athenian *amphidromia*', *GRBS* 25, 243–51.

Hammond, N.G.L.

1967   *Epirus*, Oxford.

1972   *A History of Macedonia I*, Oxford.

1982   'Illyria, Epirus and Macedonia', in *CAH*² III.3, Cambridge, 261–85.

Hampl, F.

1975   'Die "Ilias" ist kein Geschichtsbuch', in id. *Geschichte als kritische Wissenschaft*, vol. 2, Darmstadt, 51–99.

Hanfmann, G.M.A.
  1983   *Sardis from Prehistoric to Roman Times*, Cambridge, Mass., and London.
Hänsel, B.
  1989   *Kastanas: Die Baubefunde*, Berlin.
Hansen, M.H.
  1989   'Solonian democracy in fourth-century Athens', *C&M* 40, 71–99.
Hansen, M.H. (ed.)
  1993   *The Ancient Greek City-State*, Copenhagen.
Hansen, M.H. and Fischer-Hansen, T.
  1994   'Monumental political architecture in archaic and classical Greek *poleis*.
          Evidence and historical significance', in D. Whitehead (ed.) *From Political
          Architecture to Stephanus Byzantius*, Stuttgart, 23–90.
Hansen, M.H. and Raaflaub, K.A. (eds.)
  1995   *Studies in the Ancient Greek Polis* (*Historia Einzelschriften* 95), Stuttgart.
Hanson, A.E.
  1991   'Continuity and change: three case studies in Hippocratic gynaecological
          therapy and theory', in S.B. Pomeroy (ed.) *Women's History and Ancient
          History*, Chapel Hill, 48–72.
Hanson, V.D.
  1995   *The Other Greeks*, New York.
Harden, D.
  1962   *The Phoenicians*, London.
Härke, H.
  1990   ' "Warrior Graves"? The background of the Anglo-Saxon burial rite', *P&P*
          126, 22–43.
Harris, D.
  1995   *The Treasures of the Parthenon and Erechtheion*, Oxford.
Harris, W.V.
  1989   *Ancient Literacy*, Cambridge, Mass.
Harrison, E.B.
  1972   'The south frieze of the Nike Temple and the Marathon painting in the
          Painted Stoa', *AJA* 76, 353–78.
Harrison, J.E.
  1900   'Pandora's box', *JHS* 20, 99–114.
  1922   *Prolegomena to the study of Greek religion*, 3rd edn, Cambridge.
Harvey, D.
  1989   *The Condition of Postmodernity*, Oxford.
Harvey, D.
  1994   'Lacomica: Aristophanes and the Spartans', in Powell and Hodkinson (eds.)
          The Shadow of Sparta, 35–58
Hasebroek, J.
  1931   *Griechische Wirtschafts- und Gesellschaftsgeschichte bis zur Perserzeit*, Tübingen.
Haslam, M.W.
  1993   Review of West 1992, *Bryn Mawr Classical Review* 4, 131–5.
Haspels, C.H.E.
  1936   *Attic Black-figured Lekythoi*, Paris.
Hatto, A.T. (ed.)
  1980   *Traditions of Heroic and Epic Poetry*, Vol. 1, London.
Havelock, E.A.
  1978   *The Greek Concept of Justice from its Shadow in Homer to its Substance in Plato*,
          Cambridge.
  1991   'The oral-literate equation', in D.R. Olson and N. Torrance (eds.) *Literacy
          and Orality*, Cambridge, 11–27.
Hawkes, C.
  1954   'Archaeological theory and method: some suggestions from the Old World',
          American Anthropologist 56, 155–68.

Hedrick, C.W. Jnr.
1994   'Writing, reading, and democracy', in Osborne and Hornblower (eds.) *Ritual, Finance, Politics*, 157–74.

Helbig, W.
1909   'Ein homerischer Rundschild mit einem Bügel', *Jahreshefte des öster-reichischen archäologischen Institutes in Wien* 12, 1–70.

Helck, W.
1979   *Die Beziehungen Ägyptens und Vorderasiens zur Ägäis bis ins 7. Jahrhundert v. Chr.*, Darmstadt.

Helly, B.
1978   *Gonnoi I*, Paris.

Henige, D.P.
1974   *The Chronology of Oral Tradition*, Oxford.
1982   *Oral Historiography*, London.

Hennig, D.
1980   'Grundbesitz bei Homer und Hesiod', *Chiron* 10, 35–52.

Herdejürgen, H.
1969   'Bronzestatuetten der Athena. Bemerkungen zur Herkunft des archaischen Promachostypus', *Antike Kunst* 12, 102–10.

Herfort-Koch, M.
1986   *Archaische Bronzeplastik Lakoniens*, Münster.

Herman, G.
1987   *Ritualised Friendship and the Greek City*, Cambridge.
1993   'Tribal and civic codes of behaviour in Lysias I', *CQ* 43, 406–19.
1994   'How violent was Athenian society?', in Osborne and Hornblower (eds.) *Ritual, Finance, Politics*, 99–117.
1995   'Honour, revenge, and the state in fourth-century Athens', in W. Eder (ed.) *Die Athenische Demokratie im 4. Jahrhundert v. Chr.*, Stuttgart, 43–60.
1996   'Ancient Athens and the values of Mediterranean society', *Mediterranean History Review* 11, 5–36.

Hermann, P.
1981   'Teos und Abdera in 5. Jahrhundert v. Chr. Ein neues Fragment der Teiorum Dirae', *Chiron* 11, 1–30.

Herrmann, H.V.
1964   'Werkstätten geometrischer Bronzeplastik', *JdI* 79, 17–71.
1983   'Altitalisches und Etruskisches in Olympia (neue Funde und Forschungen)', *ASAA* 61, 271–94.

Hertel, D.
1991   'Schliemanns These vom Fortleben Troias in den "Dark Ages" im Lichte neuer Forschungsergebnisse', *Studia Troica* 1, 131–44.

Herz, N. and Waelkens, M. (eds.)
1988   *Classical Marble: Geochemistry, technology, trade*, NATO ASI Series E: Applied Sciences, Vol. 153, Dordrecht, Boston and London.

Herzfeld, M.
1985   *The Poetics of Manhood. Contest and identity in a Cretan mountain village*, Princeton.

Heubeck, A.
1974   *Die Homerische Frage*, Darmstadt.
1984   'Homer und Mykene', *Gymnasium* 91, 1–14.
1986   'Geschichte bei Homer', in id. *Kleine Schriften zur griechischen Sprache und Literatur*, Erlangen, 39–62.

Heubeck, A., West, S. et al.
1988/92 *A Commentary on Homer's Odyssey*, Oxford.

Heubeck, A. and Hoekstra, A.
1989   *A Commentary on Homer's Odyssey* Vol. II: Books 9–16, Oxford.

423

Hodder, I.
1987   'The contextual analysis of symbolic meanings', in id. (ed.), *The Archaeology of Contextual Meanings*, Cambridge, 1–10.
1991   *Reading the Past*, 2nd edn, Cambridge.
1992   *Theory and Method in Archaeology*, London.
Hodder, I. (ed.)
1978   *The Spatial Organisation of Culture*, Cambridge.
Hodkinson, S.
1983   'Social order and the conflict of values in classical Sparta', *Chiron* 13, 239–81.
1986   'Land tenure and inheritance in classical Sparta', *CQ* 36, 378–406.
1988   'Animal husbandry in the Greek polis', in C.R. Whittaker (ed.) *Pastoral Economies in Classical Antiquity* (*PCPhS* Suppl. Vol. 14), Cambridge, 35–74.
1989   'Inheritance, marriage and demography; perspectives upon the success and decline of classical Sparta', in Powell (ed.) *Classical Sparta*, 79–121.
1994   'Blind Ploutos?: contemporary images of the role of wealth in classical Sparta', in Powell and Hodkinson (eds.) *The Shadow of Sparta*, 183–222.
1997   'The development of Spartan society and institutions in the archaic period', in Mitchell and Rhodes (eds.), *Development of the Polis*, 83–102.
1998   'Patterns of bronze dedications at Spartan sanctuaries, *c*. 650–350 BC: towards a quantified database of material and religious investment', in W.G. Cavanagh and S. Walker (eds.) *Sparta in Lakonia*, London.
Hoekstra, A.
1981   *Epic Verse Before Homer*, Amsterdam.
1995   'Phrase clusters in the Homeric poems', in J.A. López Férez (ed.) *De Homero a Libanio*, Madrid, 1–8.
Hoepfner, W. and Schwandner, E.-L.
1986   *Haus und Stadt im klassischen Griechenland*, Munich.
Hoffman, G.
1986   'Pandora, la jarre et l'espoir', *Études rurales* (1985), 98–9, 119–32; reprinted at *Quaderni di storia* 24, 55–89.
Hoffmann, H.
1972   *Early Cretan Armorers*, Mainz.
Hoffmann, W.
1956   'Die Polis bei Homer', in *Festschrift für Bruno Snell*, Munich, 153–65.
Hogarth, D.G.
1908   *The Archaic Artemision*, London.
Hölkeskamp, K.-J.
1990   Review of Gagarin 1986, *Gnomon* 62, 116–28.
1992a   'Arbitrators, lawgivers and the "codification of law" in archaic Greece. Problems and perspectives', *METIS* 7, 49–81.
1992b   'Written law in archaic Greece', *PCPhS* 38, 87–117.
1993   'Demonax und die Neuordnung der Bürgerschaft von Kyrene', *Hermes* 121, 404–21.
1994   'Tempel, Agora und Alphabet. Die Entstehungsbedingungen von Gesetzgebung in der archaischen Polis', in Gehrke and Wirbelauer (eds.) *Rechtskodifizierung und soziale Normen*, 135–64.
Forthcoming   *Schiedsrichter, Gesetzgeber und Gesetzgebung im archaischen Griechenland*.
Holladay, A.J.
1977   'Spartan austerity', *CQ* 27, 111–26.
Hollein, H.G.
1988   *Bürgerbild und Bildwelt der attischen Demokratie auf den rotfigurigen Vasen des 6.– 4. Jahrhunderts v. Chr.* (Europäische Hochschulscriften, Reihe 38, Bd. 17), Frankfurt.
Holoka, J.P.
1991   'Homer, oral poetry theory, and comparative literature: major trends and

controversies in twentieth-century criticism', in Latacz (ed.) *Zweihundert Jahre Homer-Forschung*, 456–81.

Holst-Warhaft, G.
1992   *Dangerous Voices: Women's laments and Greek literature*, London.

Hommel, H.
1980   *Der Gott Achilleus*, Heidelberg.

Hood, S.
1995   'The Bronze Age context of Homer', in Carter and Morris (eds.) *The Ages of Homer*, 25–32.

Hood, S. and Smyth, D.
1981   *An Archaeological Survey of Knossos* (*BSA* Suppl. Vol. 12), London.

Hooker, J.T.
1980   *The Ancient Spartans*, London.
1988   'The cults of Achilles', *Rheinisches Museum für Philologie* 131, 1–7.

Hope Simpson, R. and Lazenby, J.F.
1970   *The Catalogue of the Ships in Homer's* Iliad, Oxford.

Hopper, R.J.
1957   *The Basis of the Athenian Democracy*, Sheffield.

Hornblower, S.
1991   *A Commentary on Thucydides. Vol. I: Books I–III*, Oxford.

Houby-Nielsen, S.
1992   'Interaction between chieftain and citizens? Seventh-century burial customs in Athens', *Acta Hyperborea* 4, 343–74.
1995   ' "Burial language" in archaic and classical Kerameikos', *Proceedings of the Danish Institute at Athens* 1, 129–91.
1996   'The archaeology of ideology in the Kerameikos: new interpretations of the *Opferrinnen*', in R. Hägg (ed.) *The Role of Religion in the Early Greek Polis*, Stockholm, 41–54.

Hoyningen-Huene, P.
1993   *Reconstructing Scientific Revolutions*: *Thomas S. Kuhn's Philosophy of Science*, Chicago (German original 1989).

Hughes, D.D.
1991   *Human Sacrifice in Ancient Greece*, London.

Humphreys, S.C.
1978   *Anthropology and the Greeks*, London, Henley and Boston.
1980   'Family tombs and tomb-cult in ancient Athens: tradition or traditionalism?', *JHS* 100, 96–126.

Hunt, L.
1984   'French history in the last twenty years: the rise and fall of the *Annales* paradigm', *Journal of Contemporary History* 21, 209–24.
1989   'Introduction: history, culture, and text', in L. Hunt (ed.) *The New Cultural History*, Berkeley, 1–22.

Hurwit, J.M.
1990   'The words in the image: orality, literacy and early Greek art', *Word and Image* 6, 180–97.

Huxley, A. and Taylor, W.
1984   *Flowers of Greece and the Aegean*, London.

Huxley, G.L.
1962   *Early Sparta*, London.

Immerwahr, H.M.
1985   'The date of the construction of Solon's *Axones*', *Bulletin of the American Society of Papyrologists* 22, 123–35.
1990   *Attic Script: A Survey*, Oxford.

Isler-Kerényi, C.
1984   'Boreade oder Eros?', *AA*, 383–6.

Bibliography

Isaac, B.
    1986   *The Greek Settlements in Thrace until the Macedonian Conquest*, Leiden.
Isager, J. (ed.)
    1994   *Hekatomnid Caria and the Ionian Renaissance* (Halicarnassian Studies I), Odense.
Isager, S. and Skydsgaard, J.E.
    1992   *Ancient Greek Agriculture*, London.
Jackson, A.H.
    1991   'Hoplites and the gods: the dedication of captured arms and armour', in V.D. Hanson (ed.) *Hoplites. The classical Greek battle experience*, London and New York, 228–49.
Jacobsen, T.
    1946   'Sumerian mythology: a review article', *JNES* 5, 128–52.
James, P., Thorpe, I.J., Kokkinos, N., Morkot, R. and Frankish, J.
    1991   *Centuries of Darkness*, London.
Jameson, M.H.
    1973   'Halieis at Porto Cheli', in Blackman (ed.) *Marine Archaeology*, 219–31.
Jameson, M.H., Runnels, C. and Andel, T. van
    1994   *A Greek Countryside: The Southern Argolid from prehistory to the present day*, Stanford, Calif.
    1998   'Religion in the Athenian democracy', in I. Morris and K. Raaflaub (eds.) *Democracy 2500? Questions and challenges*, Dubuque, Iowa.
Janko, R.
    1982   *Homer, Hesiod, and the Hymns: Diachronic development in epic diction*, Cambridge.
    1992   *The* Iliad*: A Commentary*, Vol. 4: Bks 13–16, Cambridge.
Jarva, E.
    1995   *Archaiologia on Archaic Body Armour*, Rovaniemi.
Jeffery, L.H.
    1949   'Comments on some archaic Greek inscriptions', *JHS* 69, 25–38.
    1962   'The inscribed gravestones of archaic Attica', *BSA* 57, 114–53.
    1976   *Archaic Greece*, London.
    1990   *The Local Scripts of Archaic Greece*, 2nd edn, with additions by A. Johnston, Oxford.
Jeffery, L.H. and Morpugo-Davies, A.
    1970   '*Poinikastas* and *Poinikazen*: BM 1969.4–2.1, a new archaic inscription from Crete', *Kadmos* 9, 118–54.
Jeffreys, M.J.
    1974   'The nature and origins of the political verse', *Dumbarton Oaks Papers* 28, 141–95.
Jenkins, I.
    1985   'The composition of the so-called eponymous heroes in the east frieze of the Parthenon', *AJA* 89, 121–7.
Joffroy, R.
    1954   'La tombe de Vix', *Monuments et Mémoires de la Fondation Piot* 48, 1–68.
    1962   *Le Trésor de Vix*, Paris.
Johannowsky, W.
    1974   'Un corredo tombale con vasi di bronzo laconici da Capua', *Rendiconti dell'Accademia di Archaeologia, Lettere e Belle Arti di Napoli* 49, 3–20.
Johnston, A.W. and Jones, R.E.
    1978   'The SOS Amphora', *BSA* 73, 103–41.
Johnstone, S.
    1994   'Virtuous toil, vicious work: Xenophon on aristocratic style', *CPh* 89, 219–40.
    Forthcoming   'Cracking the code of silence: Athenian legal oratory and the history of slaves and women', in S. Joshel and S. Murnaghan (eds.) *Differential Equations: Women and slaves in Greco-Roman culture*, London.

Jones, S.
    1894   'The chest of Kypselos', *JHS* 14, 30–80.

Jost, M.
    1985   *Sanctuaires et cultes d'Arcadie* (Études péloponnésiens), Paris.

Jucker, H.
    1965/6   'Bronzehydria und Bronzehenkel in Pesaro', *Studia Oliveriana* 13/14, 1–128.

Jung, H.
    1982   *Thronende und sitzende Götter. Zum griechischen Götterbild und Menschenideal in geometrischer und früharchaischer Zeit*, Bonn.

Kaeser, B.
    1990   'Zuschauerfiguren', in K. Vierneisel and B. Kaeser (eds.) *Kunst der Schale, Kultur des Trinkens. Antikensammlungen München*, Munich, 151–6.

Kalpaxis, T. and Petropoulou, A.B.
    1988/9   'Tmemata duo Epigraphon apo tin Eleftherna', *Kretika Khronika* 26–7, 127–33.

Kanta, A.
    1991   'Cult, continuity and the evidence of pottery at the sanctuary of Syme Viannou, Crete', in Musti et al. (eds.) *La transizione dal Miceneo all'Alto Arcaismo*, 479–505.

Karagiorga, Th.
    1965   'Un miroir laconien au musée de Sparte', *Archaiologikon Deltion* 20 A', 96–109 and 191. (In Greek; French summary.)

Karavites, P.
    1992   *Promise-Giving and Treaty-Making: Homer and the Near East*, Leiden.

Keaney, J.J.
    1992   *The Composition of Aristotle's Athenaion Politeia: observation and explanation*, Oxford.

Keene Congdon, L.O.
    1981   *Caryatid Mirrors of Ancient Greece*, Mainz am Rhein.

Kent, S.
    1990   'A cross-cultural study of segmentation, architecture, and the use of space', in S. Kent (ed.) *Domestic Architecture and the Use of Space*, Cambridge, 127–52.

Kerenyi, C.
    1951   *The Gods of the Greeks*, New York.

Keuls, E.
    1985   *The Reign of the Phallus*, Berkeley.

Kiefer, T.M.
    1972   *The Tausug. Violence and law in a Philippine moslem society*, New York.

Kierdorf, W.
    1966   *Erlebnis und Darstellung der Perserkriege. Hypomnemata* 16, Göttingen.

Kilian, K.
    1975   *Fibeln in Thessalien von der mykenischen bis zur archaischen Zeit* (Prähistorische Bronzefunden 14.2), Mainz.
    1983   'Weihungen aus Eisen und Eisenverarbeitung im Heiligtum zu Philia', in Hägg (ed.) *The Greek Renaissance*, 131–46.

Kilian-Dirlmeier, I.
    1985   'Fremde Weihungen im griechischen Heiligtümern von 8. bis zum Beginn des 7. Jhs', *Jahrbuch des römisch-germanisch Zentralmuseums Mainz* 32, 215–54.

Kilinski II, K.
    1990   *Boeotian Black-Figure Vase-painting of the archaic period*, Mainz.

Killen, J.T.
    1988   'The Linear B Tablets and the Mycenaean Economy', in A. Morpurgo Davies and Y. Duhoux (eds.) *Linear B: A 1984 Survey*, Louvain-La-Neuve, 241–305.

Killen, J.T., Melena, J.L. and Olivier, J.-P. (eds.)
    1987   *Studies in Mycenaean and Classical Greek Presented to John Chadwick, Minos* 20–22, Salamanca.

Kinch, F.
1914   *Fouilles de Vroulia*, Berlin.
Kinzl, K.H. (ed.).
1995   *Demokratia. Der Weg zur Demokratie bei den Griechen*, Darmstadt.
Kirk, G.S.
1960   'Objective dating criteria in Homer', *MusHelv* 17, 189–205.
1962   *The Songs of Homer*, Cambridge.
1966   'Formular language and oral quality', in G.S. Kirk and A. Parry (eds.)
        Homeric studies (Yale Classical Studies 20), 155–74.
1975   'The Homeric poems as history', in *CAH*³ II.2, Cambridge, 820–50.
1985   *The* Iliad: *A Commentary*, Vol. 1: Bks 1–4, Cambridge.
Kirk, G.S., Raven, J.E. and Schofield, M.S.
1983   *The Presocratic Philosophers*, 2nd edn, Cambridge.
Kitchen, K.A.
1986   *The Third Intermediate Period in Egypt (ca. 1100–650 bc.)* , 2nd edn, Warminster.
Kleiner, G.
1968   *Die Ruinen von Milet*, Berlin.
Knapp, A.B. (ed.)
1992   *Archaeology, Annales, and Ethnohistory*, Cambridge.
Knigge, U.
1976   *Kerameikos IX. Die Südhügel*, Berlin.
1991   *The Athenian Kerameikos*, Athens. (German original 1988.)
Koerner, R.
1985   'Tiryns als Beispiel einer frühen dorischen Polis', *Klio* 67, 452–7.
Koljevic, S.
1981   *The Epic in the Making*, Oxford.
Konova, L.
1995   'The necropolis from Trebeniste – studies and problems', *Thracia* 11, 195–202.
Konstan, D.
1997   *Friendship in the Classical World*, Cambridge.
Kopcke, G. and Tokumaru, I. (eds.)
1992   *Greece between East and West: 10th to 8th Centuries bc.* , Mainz.
Korti-Konti, S.
1979   ' "I theates" stis parastaseis athlon kai agonon stin arkhaia elliniki tekhni',
        Epistimoniki Epeteris Philosophikis Skholis Thessalonikis 18, 167–204.
Koselleck, R., Brunner, O. and Conze, W. (eds.).
1972   *Geschichtliche Grundbegriffe: Historisches Lexicon zur Sprache in Deutschland*,
        Stuttgart.
Koukouli-Chrysanthaki, Ch.
1984   *I Proistoriki Thasos I*, Athens.
1993   'I proimi epochi tou sidirou stin anatoliki Makedonia', in *Ancient Macedonia*
        V, 679–711.
Kramer, S.N. and Maier, J.
1989   *Myths of Enki, the Crafty God*, Oxford.
Krause, C.
1977   'Grundformen des griechische Pastashauses', *Archäologischer Anzeiger*, 164–77.
Kron, U.
1984   'Die Phylenheroen am Parthenonfries', in E. Berger (ed.) *Parthenon-Kongress
        Basel I*, Mainz, 235–44.
Kübler, K.
1950   *Alt-attische Malerei*, Tübingen.
1976   *Kerameikos VII.1*, Berlin.
Kuhn, T.S.
1970   *The Structure of Scientific Revolutions*, 2nd edn, Chicago.
Kullmann, W.
1984   'Oral Poetry: theory and neoanalysis in Homeric research', *GRBS* 25, 307–23.

1991   'Ergebnisse der motivgeschichtlichen Forschung zu Homer (Neoanalyse)', in Latacz (ed.) *Zweihundert Jahre Homer-Forschung*, 425–55.

1993   'Festgehaltene Kenntnisse im Schiffskatalog und im Troerkatalog der *Ilias*', in id. and J. Althoff, (eds.) *Vermittlung und Tradierung von Wissen in der griechischen Kultur*, Tübingen, 129–47.

1995   'Homers Zeit und das Bild des Dichters von den Menschen der mykenischen Kultur', in Andersen and Dickie (eds.) *Homer's World*, 57–75.

Kunze, E.
1931   *Kretische Bronzereliefs*, Stuttgart.
1991   *Beinschienen* (Olympische Forschungen XXI), Berlin/New York.

Kurke, L.
1991   *The Traffic in Praise: Pindar and the poetics of social economy*, Ithaca/London.
1992   'The politics of *habrosune* in Archaic Greece', *ClAnt* 22, 91–120.
1994   'Crisis and decorum in sixth-century Lesbos: reading Alkaios otherwise', *QUCC* 47, 67–92.

Kurke, L. and Dougherty, C. (eds.)
1993   *Cultural Poetics in Archaic Greece*, Cambridge.

Kurtz, D. and Boardman, J.
1986   'Booners', *Greek vases in the J. Paul Getty Museum III*, Malibu, 47–70.

Kyrieleis, H.
1979   'Babylonische Bronzen im Heraion von Samos', *JdI* 94, 32–48.
1992   'Neue Ausgrabungen in Olympia', in W. Coulson and H. Kyrieleis (eds.) *Proceedings of an International Symposium on the Olympic Games*, Athens, 19–24.
1993   'The Heraion at Samos', in Marinatos and Hägg (eds.) *Greek Sanctuaries*, 125–53.

Kyrtatas, D.
1992   'I metarrythmiseis tou Solōna, o Aristotelēs kai i synkhroni politiki theōria', *Mnemon* 14, 205–22.

Lacroix, L.
1949   *Les reproductions de statues sur les monnaies grecques*, Liège.

Lamb, W.W.
1926/7 'Bronzes from the Acropolis, 1924–27'; 'Notes on some bronzes from the Orthia site', *BSA* 28, 82–106.
1969   *Ancient Greek and Roman Bronzes* (Chicago 1929; reprint with additions).

Lambert, W.G. and Millard, A.R.
1969   *Atra-hasis: the Babylonian story of the flood*, Oxford.

Lambrinoudakis, V.G.
1988   'Veneration of ancestors on Geometric Naxos', in Hägg et al. (eds.) *Early Greek Cult Practice*, 141–48.

Lanata, G.
1963   *Poetica preplatonica*, Firenze.

Lane, E.A.
1933/4 'Laconian vase painting', *BSA* 34, 99–189.

Lang, M.
1976   *The Athenian Agora XXI: Graffiti and Dipinti*, Princeton.

Langdon, M.K.
1976   *A Sanctuary of Zeus on Mount Hymettus*, Princeton.

Langlotz, E.
1975   *Studien zur Nordostgriechischen Kunst*, Mainz.

Larsen, J.A.O.
1949   'The origin and significance of the counting of votes', *CPh* 44, 164–81.
1968   *Greek Federal States*, Oxford.

Laslett, P. and Runciman, W.G. (eds.)
1962   *Politics, Philosophy and Society*, 2nd ser., Oxford.

Latacz, J.
1977   *Kampfparänese, Kampfdarstellung und Kampfwirklichkeit in der Ilias, bei Kallinos*

          und Tyrtaios, Munich.

1979   'Tradition und Neuerung in der Homerforschung. Zur Geschichte der Oral poetry-Theorie', in Latacz (ed.) *Homer*, 25–44.

1984   'Das Menschenbild Homers', *Gymnasium* 91, 15–39.

1988   'Zu Umfang und Art der Vergangenheitsbewahrung in der mündlichen Überlieferungsphase des griechischen Heldenepos', in Ungern-Sternberg and Reinau (eds.) *Vergangenheit in mündlicher Überlieferung*, 153–83.

1992   'Homers Ilias und die Folgen: Wie der Mythos Troias entstand', in Gamer-Wallert (ed.) *Troia*, 201–18.

1994   'Between Troy and Homer: the so-called Dark Ages in Greece', in *Storia, poesia e pensiero nel mondo antico: Studi in onore di Marcello Gigante*, Naples, 347–63.

1996   *Homer: His art and his world*, Ann Arbor.

Latacz, J. (ed.)

1979   *Homer: Tradition und Neuerung* (Wege der Forschung 463), Darmstadt.

1991   *Zweihundert Jahre Homer-Forschung: Rückblick und Ausblick* (Colloquium Rauricum 2), Stuttgart and Leipzig.

Lateiner, D.

1995   *Sardonic Smile. Non-verbal communication in Homer*, Ann Arbor.

Lauter, H.

1985a   *Die Kultplatz auf dem Turkovuni*, Berlin.

1985b   *Lathuresa. Beiträge zur Architektur und Siedlungsgeschichte in spätgeometrischer Zeit*, Mainz.

Lauter-Bufe, H.

1974   'Fragment eines lakonischen Reliefpithos', *Antike Kunst* 17, 89–91.

Lavelle, B.M.

1993   *The Sorrow and the Pity. A prolegomenon to a history of Athens under the Peisistratids, c. 560–510 BC* (Historia Einzelschriften 80), Stuttgart.

Lawrence, D. and Low, S.M.

1990   'The built environment and spatial form', *Annual Review of Anthropology* 19, 453–505.

Leach, E.R.

1976   *Culture and Communication*, Cambridge.

Leaf, W.

1923   *Strabo on the Troad*, Cambridge.

Leahy, L.M.

1988   *Private Tomb Reliefs of the Late Period from Lower Egypt,* Diss., Oxford.

Lebessi, A.

1975   'Hierou Ermou kai Aphroditis eis Symen Viannou', *Praktika tis en Athenais Arkhaiologikis Etaireias* 1973, 188–99.

1976   *I Stiles tou Prinia*, Athens.

1978   'Monumento funerario dell VII sec.a.C. a Creta', in *Antichità Cretesi*, Catania, 120–31.

1985   *To Iero tou Ermi kai tis Aphroditis sti Symi Viannou* I.1, Athens.

Lebessi, I.

1969   Excavation report, *Archaiologikon deltion 24 B: Chronika*, 415–18.

Lehmann, G.A.

1991   'Die "politisch-historischen" Beziehungen der Ägäis-Welt des 15.– 13. Jh.s v. Chr. zu Ägypten und Vorderasien: einige Hinweise', in Latacz (ed.) *Zweihundert Jahre Homer-Forschung*, 105–26.

Lehmann-Hartleben, K.

1923   *Die Antiken Hafenanlagen des Mittelmeeres* (Klio Beiheft 14), Berlin.

Lemos, A.A.

1991   *Archaic Pottery of Chios*, Oxford.

Lendle, O.

1957   *Die 'Pandorasage' bei Hesiod*, Würzburg.

Leon, C.
    1968   'Statuette eines Kouros aus Messenien', *MDAI (AM)* 83, 175–85.
Lesky, A.
    1967   'Homeros', *RE* Suppl. vol. 11, 687–846.
Lévêque, P. and Vidal-Naquet, P.
    1964   *Clisthène l'Athénien*, Paris.
    1996   *Cleisthenes the Athenian. An essay on the representation of space and time in Greek political thought*, Atlantic Highlands, N.J.
Levi, D.
    1969   'Un pithos iscritto dà Festos', *Kretika Khronika* 21, 153–6.
Lévi-Strauss, C.
    1963   *Structural anthropology*, New York. (French original 1958.)
Lewis, D.M.
    1963   'Cleisthenes and Attica', *Historia* 12, 22–40.
Lieber, H.-J. (ed.)
    1994   *Politische Theorien von der Antike bis zur Gegenwart*, Bonn.
Link, S.
    1992   'Die Gesetzgebung des Zaleukos im epizephyrischen Lokroi', *Klio* 74, 11–24.
Lissarrague, F.
    1995   'Women, boxes, containers: some signs and metaphors', in Reeder (ed.) *Pandora*, 91–101.
Lloyd, G.E.R.
    1979   *Magic, Reason and Experience. Studies in the origins and development of Greek science*, Cambridge.
Lloyd-Jones, H.
    1994   'Notes on the new Simonides', *ZPE* 101, 1–3.
Long, A.A.
    1970   'Morals and values in Homer', *JHS* 90, 121–39.
Loomis, W.T.
    1990   'Pausanias, Byzantion and the formation of the Delian League. A chronological note', *Historia* 39, 487–92.
Loraux, N.
    1982   'Ponos. Sur quelques difficultés de la peine comme nom du travail', *Annali del seminario di studi del mondo classico, Napoli: Archeologia e storia antica* 4, 171–92.
    1985   'Enquête sur la construction d'un meurtre en histoire', in Loraux 1996, *Né de la terre*, 102–27.
    1986   *The Invention of Athens: The funeral oration in the classical city*, Cambridge, Mass.
    1988a   'Solon et la voix de l'écrit', in Detienne (ed.) *Les savoirs de l'écriture...*, 95–129.
    1988b   'La démocratie à l'épreuve de l'étranger', in Loraux 1996, *Né de la terre*, 190–216.
    1991   'Reflections of the Greek city on unity and division', in Molho, Raaflaub and Emlen (eds.) *City States...*, 33–51.
    1993   *The Children of Athena*, Princeton (French original 1984).
Loraux, N. (ed.)
    1996   *Né de la terre. Mythe et politique à Athènes*, Paris.
Lord, A.
    1953   'Homer's originality: oral dictated texts', *TAPA* 94, 124–34.
    1960   *The Singer of Tales*, Cambridge, Mass.
Lorimer, H.L.
    1950   *Homer and the Monuments*, London.
Losfeld, G.
    1991   *Essai sur le costume grec*, Paris.

431

Bibliography

Lubar, S. and Kingery, W.D. (eds.)
1994   *History From Things*, Washington.
Lyons, M.
1995   *The Arabian Epic*, Cambridge.
MacDowell, D.M.
1986   *Spartan Law*, Edinburgh.
MacIntyre, A.
1983   'The indispensability of political theory', in Miller and Siedentop (eds.) *The Nature of Political Theory*, 17–33.
Malkin, I.
1994a   'Inside and outside: colonisation and the formation of the mother city', in D'Agostino and Ridgway (eds.), *Apoikia*, 1–9.
1994b   *Myth and Territory in the Spartan Mediterranean*, Cambridge.
Manganaro, G.
1965   'Nuove iscrizioni della Creta centrale ed orientale', *Rendiconti della Accademia Nazionale dei Lincei: Classe di Scienze morali, storiche e filologiche* 20, 295–307.
Manville, P.B.
1990   *The Origins of Citizenship in Ancient Athens*, Princeton.
Margreiter, I.
1988   *Frühe lakonische Keramik der geometrischen bis archaischen Zeit (10. bis 6.Jahrhundert v. Chr.)*, Bayern.
Marinatos, N. and Hägg, R. (eds.)
1993   *Greek Sanctuaries: New Approaches*, London.
Marinatos, S.
1936   'Le Temple géométrique de Dreros', *BCH* 60, 214–85.
1967   *Kleidung. Archaeologia Homerica Bd. A*, Göttingen.
Marr, A.
1995   *Ruling Britannia*, London.
Martin, R.P.
1989   *The Language of Heroes: Speech and Performance in the* Iliad, Princeton.
Masson, O.
1976   'Nouveax graffites grecs d'Abydos et de Bouhen', *Chronique d'Egypte* 51, 305–13.
1979   'Cretica', *BCH* 103, 57–82.
Matthäus, H.
1993   'Zur Rezeption orientalischer Kunst-, Kultur- und Lebensformen in Griechenland', in Raaflaub and Müller-Luckner (eds.) *Anfänge politischen Denkens in der Antike*, 165–86.
Matthias, J. and Vuckovic, V. (trsl.)
1987   *The battle of Kosovo*, Leek.
Mazarakis-Ainian, A.
1985   'Contribution à l'étude de l'architecture religieuse grecque des âges obscurs', *L'Antiquité Classique* 54, 5–48.
1988   'Early Greek temples: their origin and function', in Hägg et al. (eds.) *Early Greek Cult Practice*, 105–19.
1994   'Lathouriza: mia agrotiki katastasi ton proimon istorikon khronon sti Vari Attikis', in P.N. Doukellis and L.G. Mendoni (eds.) *Structures rurales et sociétés antiques* (Annales littéraires de l'Université de Besançon 508), Paris, 65–80.
1995   'New evidence for the study of the Late Geometric–Archaic settlement at Lathouriza in Attica' in C. Morris (ed.) *Klados: Essays in honour of J.N. Coldstream* (*BICS* Suppl. Vol. 63), London, 143–55.
McCullough, W.H. and H.C. (trsl.)
1980   *A Tale of Flowering Fortunes*, Stanford.
McDonald, M. and Hurcombe, L. (eds.)
1997   *Gender and Material Culture*, London.

McDonald, W.A., Coulson, W.D.E. and Rosser. J.J.
   1983   *Excavations at Nichoria in Southwest Greece* III, Minneapolis.
McDonald, W.A. and Thomas, C.G.
   1993   *Progress into the Past: The discovery of Homeric Greece*, 2nd edn, Bloomington, Ind.
McGlew, J.F.
   1993   *Tyranny and Political Culture in Ancient Greece*, Ithaca.
McPhee, I.
   1986   'Laconian red-figure from the British excavations at Sparta', *BSA* 81, 153–65.
Mee, C.B.
   1984   'The Mycenaeans and Troy', in Foxhall and Davies (eds.) *The Trojan War*, 45–56.
Meggitt, M.J.
   1977   *Blood Is Their Argument. Warfare among the Mae Enga tribesmen of the New Guinea Highlands*, Palo Alto.
Meier, C.
   1984   ' "Revolution" in der Antike', in Brunner et al. (eds.) *Geschichtliche Grundbegriffe*, 656–70.
   1986   'The emergence of an autonomous intelligence among the Greeks', in Eisenstadt (ed.) *The Origins and Diversity of Axial Age Cultures*, 65–91. (German version in Meier 1989, 70–100.)
   1989   *Die Welt der Geschichte und die Provinz des Historikers*, Berlin.
   1993   *The Political Art of Greek Tragedy*, Oxford. (German original 1988.)
Meijer, F.
   1988   'Thucydides 1.13.2–4 and the changes in Greek ship-building', *Historia* 37, 461–3.
Meillet, A.
   1923   *Les origines indo-européennes des mètres grecs*, Paris.
Mellink, M.J.
   1983   'The Hittites and the Aegean World: 2. Archaeological comments on the Ahhiyawa-Achaians in Western Anatolia', *AJA* 87, 138–41.
Mellink, M.J. (ed.)
   1986   *Troy and the Trojan War: A symposium held at Bryn Mawr College, Oct. 1984*, Bryn Mawr.
Merkelbach, R.
   1976   *Die Inschriften von Assos* (Inschriften griechischer Städte aus Kleinasien 4), Bonn.
Mersch, A.
   1995   'Archäologischer Kommentar zu den "Gräbern der Athener und Plataier" in der Marathonia', *Klio* 77, 55–64.
Meyer, E.
   1993   'Epitaphs and citizenship in classical Athens', *JHS* 113, 99–121.
Michell, H.
   1952   *Sparta*, 1st edn, Cambridge.
   1964   *Sparta*, 2nd edn, Cambridge.
Miller, D.
   1987   *Material Culture and Mass Consumption*, Oxford.
Miller D. (ed.)
   1995   *Acknowledging Consumption: A review of new studies*, London.
Miller, D., Rowlands, M. and Tilley, C. (eds.)
   1989   *Domination and Resistance*, London.
Miller, D. and Siedentop, L. (eds.)
   1983   *The Nature of Political Theory*, Oxford.
Miller, M.
   1971   *The Thalassocracies. Studies in Chronology II*, New York.
Miller, M.C.
   1992   'The parasol: an oriental status symbol', *JHS* 112, 91–105.

1997 *Athens and Persia in the Fifth Century bc. A Study in Cultural Receptivity* , Cambridge.

Miller, S.G.
1994 'Architectural terracottas from Ilion', in Winter (ed.) *Proceedings ...Greek Architectural Terracottas*, 269–73.

Minchin, E.
1996 'The performance of lists and catalogues in the Homeric epics', in Worthington (ed.) *Voice into Text*, 3–20.

Minto, A.
1960 *Il vaso François*, Firenze.

Miralles, C.
1996 'Poeta, saggio, sofista, filosofo: l'intellettuale nella Grecia antica', in Settis (ed.) *I Greci*, 849–82.

Mitchell, L. and Rhodes, P.J. (eds.)
1997 *The Development of the Polis in Archaic Greece*, London.

Mitchell, T.
1988 *Colonising Egypt*, Cambridge.

Molho, A., Raaflaub, K.A. and Emlen, J. (eds.)
1991 *City States in Classical Antiquity and Medieval Italy*, Stuttgart.

Momigliano, A.D.
1944 'Sea-power in Greek thought', *CR* 58, 1–7.
1952 'George Grote', in Momigliano, *Studies*, 15–31.
1994 *Studies on Modern Scholarship*, Berkeley and London.

Mommsen, H.
1975 *Der Affekter*, Mainz.

Moretti, L.
1957 'Olympionikai, i vincitori negli antichi agoni olympici', *Atti della Accademia Nazionale dei Lincei, Memorie*, Ser. 8, vol. 8, fasc. 2, Rome, 53–198.

Morgan, C.
1990 *Athletes and Oracles: The transformation of Olympia and Delphi in the eighth century bc*, Cambridge.
1991 'Ethnicity and early Greek states: historical and material perspectives', *PCPhS* 37, 131–63.
1993 'The origins of Pan-Hellenism', in Marinatos and Hägg (eds.) *Greek Sanctuaries*, 18–44.

Morris, H.F.
1964 *Heroic Recitations of the Bahima of Ankole*, Oxford.

Morris, I.
1986 'The use and abuse of Homer', *Classical Antiquity* 5, 81–138.
1987 *Burial and Ancient Society. The Rise of the Greek City-State*, Cambridge.
1988 'Tomb cult and the "Greek renaissance": the past in the present in the eighth century bc', *Antiquity* 62, 750–61.
1989 'Circulation, deposition and the formation of the Greek Iron Age', *Man* 23, 502–19.
1990 'The Gortyn code and Greek kinship', *GRBS* 31, 233–54.
1991 'The early polis as city and state', in Rich and Wallace-Hadrill (eds.) *City and Country*, 24–57.
1992 *Death-Ritual and Social Structure in Classical Antiquity*, Cambridge.
1993a 'Poetics of power: on the interpretation of Archaic Greek ritual', in Dougherty and Kurke (eds.) *Cultural Poetics*, 15–46.
1993b 'Geometric Greece', *Colloquenda Mediterranea* 3.A.2, 29–38.
1993c 'Response to Papadopoulos (I): The Kerameikos stratigraphy and the character of the Greek Dark Age', *Journal of Mediterranean Archaeology* 6, 207–21.
1994a 'Archaeologies of Greece', in Morris (ed.) *Classical Greece*, 8–47.
1994b 'The Athenian economy twenty years after *The Ancient Economy*', *CPh* 89, 351–66.

1995	'Burning the dead in Archaic Athens: gods, men, and animals', in A. Verbanck-Piérard and D. Viviers (eds.) *Culture et cité en Athènes archaïque*, Brussels.
1996a	'The strong principle of equality and the archaic origins of Greek democracy', in Ober and Hedrick (eds.) *Demokratia*, 19–48.
1996b	'The absolute chronology of the Greek colonies in Sicily', *Acta Archaeologia* 67.
1997a	'Periodization and the heroes: inventing a Dark Age', in Golden and Toohey (eds.) *Inventing Ancient Culture*, 96–131.
1997b	'The art of citizenship', in S. Langdon (ed.) *New Light on a Dark Age*, Columbia, 9–43.
1997c	'*Burial and Ancient Society* after ten years', in R. Étienne, M.-T. Le Dinahet and J.-F. Salles (eds.) *Théories de la nécropole antique*, Lyon.
1997d	'Beyond democracy and empire: Athenian art in context', in D. Boedeker and K. Raaflaub (eds.) *Democracy, Empire, and the Arts in Fifth-Century Athens*, Cambridge, Mass.
1997e	'Homer and the Iron Age', in Morris and Powell, *A New Companion to Homer*, 535–59.
Forthcoming	*Darkness and Heroes: Manhood, equality, and democracy in Iron Age Greece*, Oxford.

Morris, I. (ed.)

1994	*Classical Greece. Ancient histories and modern archaeologies*, Cambridge.

Morris, I. and Powell, B. (eds.)

1997	*A New Companion to Homer*, Leiden and New York.

Morris, S.P.

1984	*The Black and White Style*, New Haven.
1989	'A tale of two cities: the miniature frescoes from Thera and the origins of Greek poetry', *AJA* 93, 511–35.
1992a	*Daidalos and the Origins of Greek Art*, Princeton.
1992b	'Introduction', in Kopcke and Tokumaru (eds.) *Greece between East and West*, xiii–xviii.
1995	'The sacrifice of Astyanax: Near Eastern contributions to the siege of Troy', in Carter and Morris (eds.) *The Ages of Homer*, 221–45.

Morrison, J. and Williams, R.T.

1968	*Greek Oared Ships 900–322 BC*, Cambridge.

Morton, J.

1994	'Sanctuary use at Emporio on Chios, 800–600 BC', *Archaeo* 2, 67–83.

Mosshammer, A.A.

1979	*The Chronicle of Eusebius and Greek Chronographic Tradition*, Lewisburg, Pa.

Mühlestein, H. and Risch, E. (eds.)

1979	*Colloquium Mycenaeum. Actes du 6e colloque internationale sur les textes mycéniens et égéens*, Neuchâtel 1.

Muhly, J.D.

1992	'The crisis years in the Mediterranean world: transition or cultural disintegration?', in Ward and Joukowsky (eds.) *The Crisis Years*, 10–26.

Mulgan, G.

1994	*Politics in an Antipolitical Age*, Oxford.

Müller-Wiener, W.

1986	'Bemerkungen zur Topographie des archaischen Milet', in W. Müller-Wiener (ed.) *Milet 1899–1980* (Istanbuler Mitteilungen Beiheft 31), Tübingen, 95–104.

Munn, M. and Zimmerman Munn, M.L.

1989	'Studies on the Attic-Boeotian frontier: the Stanford Skourta Plain Project, 1985', in J.M. Fossey (ed.) *Boeotia Antiqua I*, Amsterdam, 73–127.

Murko, M.

1929	*La poésie populaire épique en Yougoslavie au debut du XXe siècle*, Paris.
1979	'Neues über südslavische Volksepik' (1919), in Latacz (ed.) *Homer*, 118–52.

Bibliography

Murnaghan, S.
1993   'Maternity and mortality in Homeric poetry', in C.N. Seremetakis (ed.)
        *Ritual, power and the body: historical perspectives on the representation of Greek
        women*, New York. (Reprinted from *Classical Antiquity* 11.2, 1992, 242–64.)
Murray, O.
1980   *Early Greece*, Glasgow.
1983   'The symposium as social organisation', in Hägg (ed.) *The Greek Renaissance*,
        Stockholm, 195–9.
1990   'Cities of reason', in Murray and Price (eds.) *The Greek City*, 1–27.
1991   'History and reason in the ancient city', *PBSR* 59, 1–13.
1993   *Early Greece*, 2nd edn, London.
1994   'Nestor's cup and the origins of the Greek symposion', in D'Agostino and
        Ridgeway (eds.) *Apoikia*, 47–54.
Murray, O. (ed.)
1990   *Sympotica. A Symposium on the Symposion*, Oxford.
Murray, O. and Price, S. (eds.)
1990   *The Greek City. From Homer to Alexander*, Oxford.
Muss, U.
1994   *Die Bauplastik des archaischen Artemisions von Ephesos*, Vienna.
Musti, D. et al. (eds.)
1991   *La transizione dal Miceneo all'Alto Arcaismo: Dal palazzo all città*, Rome.
Nafissi, M.
1989   'Distribution and trade', in Stibbe (ed.) *Lakonian Mixing Bowls*, 68–88.
1991   *La Nascita del Kosmos: Studi sulla Storia e la Società di Sparta*, Napoli.
Nagler, M.N.
1974   *Spontaneity and Tradition: A study in the oral art of Homer*, Berkeley.
Nagy, B.
1992   'Athenian officials in the Parthenon frieze', *AJA* 96, 55–69.
Nagy, G.
1974   *Comparative Studies in Greek and Indic metre*, Cambridge, Mass.
1979   *The Best of the Achaeans: Concepts of the hero in archaic Greek poetry*, Baltimore.
1990a   *Pindar's Homer: The lyric possession of an epic past*, Baltimore.
1990b   *Greek Mythology and Poetics*, Ithaca.
1992   'Homeric questions', *TAPA* 122, 17–60.
1995   'An evolutionary model for the making of Homeric poetry: comparative
        perspectives', in Carter and Morris (eds.) *The Ages of Homer*, 163–79.
1996   *Homeric Questions*, Austin, Tex.
Nakategawa, Y.
1988   '*Isegoria* in Herodotus', *Historia* 37, 257–75.
Neils, J.
1994   'The Panathenaia and Kleisthenic ideology', in Coulson et al. (eds.) *The
        Archaeology of Athens and Attica*, 152–60.
Neils, J. (ed.)
1992   *Goddess and Polis. The panathenaic festival in ancient Athens*, Princeton.
Nevett, L.
1994   'Separation or seclusion? Towards an archaeological approach to investig-
        ating women in the Greek household in the fifth to third centuries BC', in
        Parker Pearson and Richards (eds.) *Architecture and Order*, 98–112.
1995   'Gender relations in the classical Greek household: the archaeological
        evidence', *BSA* 90, 363–81.
Nicholson, R.A.
1907   *A Literary History of the Arabs*, London.
Nicolet, C. (ed.)
1984   *Aux origines de l'Hellénisme: la Crète et la Grèce: Hommage à Henri van Effenterre*,
        Paris.

Nilsson, M.P.
   1936   *The Age of the Early Greek Tyrants*, Belfast.
Nippel, W.
   1994   'Politische Theorien der griechisch-römischen Antike', in Lieber (ed.) *Politische Theorien*, 17–46.
Noethlichs, K.L.
   1987   'Bestechung, Bestechlichkeit und die Rolle des Geldes in der spartanischen Aussen- und Innenpolitik vom 7. bis 2. Jh. v. Chr.', *Historia* 36, 129–70.
Noica, S.
   1984   'La boite de Pandore et l'ambiguité d'Elpis', *Platon* 36, 100–24.
Norman, K.R.
   1983   *Pali Literature*, Wiesbaden.
Nougayrol, J. (ed.)
   1968   *Ugaritica*, Vol. V, Paris.
Nowag, W.
   1983   *Raub und Beute in der archaischen Zeit der Griechen*, Frankfurt am Main.
Oakley, J.H. and Sinos, R.
   1993   *The Wedding in Ancient Athens*, Madison.
Obbink, D.
   1996   'The hymnic structure of the new Simonides', in Boedeker and Sider (eds.) *The New Simonides*, 193–203.
Ober, J.
   1989   *Mass and Elite in Democratic Athens. Rhetoric, ideology and the power of the people*, Princeton.
   1993   'The Athenian revolution of 508/7 BC: violence, authority, and the origins of democracy', in Dougherty and Kurke (eds.) *Cultural Poetics*, 215–32. (Reprinted in Ober 1996 *The Athenian Revolution*.)
   1994   'How to criticize democracy in late fifth- and fourth-century Athens', in Euben et al. (eds.) *Athenian Political Thought*, 149–71. (Reprinted in Ober 1996 *The Athenian Revolution*.)
   1996   *The Athenian Revolution. Essays on ancient Greek democracy and political theory*, Princeton.
Ober, J. and Hedrick, C.W. (eds.)
   1996   *Demokratia. A conversation on democracies, ancient and modern*, Princeton.
Ogden, D.
   1997   *The Crooked Kings of Ancient Greece*, London.
Oliva, P.
   1988   *Solon – Legende und Wirklichkeit*, Konstanz.
Olson, S.D.
   1995   *Blood and Iron: Stories and storytelling in Homer's* Odyssey, Leiden.
Orwell, G.
   1971   *Animal Farm*, 3rd edn, London.
Osborne, C.
   1987   *Rethinking Early Greek Philosophy*, London.
Osborne, R.
   1988   'Death revisited, death revised: the death of the artist in archaic and classical Greece', *Art History* 11, 1–16.
   1989   'A crisis in archaeological history? The seventh century BC in Attica', *BSA* 84, 297–322.
   1996a   *Greece in the Making 1200–479 BC*, London.
   1996b   'Pots, trade and the archaic Greek economy', *Antiquity* 70, 31–44.
   1997   'Law and laws: how do we join up the dots?', in Mitchell and Rhodes (eds.) *The Development of the Polis*, 74–82.
Osborne, R. and Hornblower, S. (eds.)
   1994   *Ritual, Finance, Politics: Athenian democratic accounts presented to David Lewis*, Oxford.

Bibliography

Ostwald, M.
    1988   'The reform of the Athenian state by Cleisthenes', *CAH²* IV, Cambridge,
           303–46.
    1969   *Nomos and the Beginnings of the Athenian Democracy*, Oxford.
Özgan, R.
    1978   *Untersuchungen zur archaischen Plastik Ioniens*, Bonn.
Pagden, A. (ed.).
    1987   *The Languages of Political Theory in Early-Modern Europe*, Cambridge.
Page, D.L.
    1965   'Archilochus and the oral tradition', *Entretiens Hardt* 10, 119–179.
Palavestra, A.
    1994   'Prehistoric trade and a cultural model for princely tombs in the central
           Balkans', in K. Kristiansen and J. Jensen (eds.) *Europe in the First Millennium
           BC* (Sheffield Archaeological Monographs 6), Sheffield, 45–56.
Palmer, H.
    1964   'The Classical and Roman periods', in C.W. Blegen, H. Palmer and R.S.
           Young (eds.) *Corinth XIII: The North Cemetery*, Princeton, 65–327.
Palmer, L.R.
    1980   *The Greek Language*, London.
Panofsky, D. and E.
    1956   *Pandora's Box. The changing aspects of a mythical symbol*, New York.
Papadopoulos, J.K.
    1993   'To kill a cemetery: the Athenian Kerameikos and the Early Iron Age in the
           Aegean', *Journal of Mediterranean Archaeology* 6, 175–206.
    1996   'Euboians in Macedonia? A second look', *Oxford Journal of Archaeology* 15,
           151–81.
    Forthcoming   ' "Dark Age" Greece', *Oxford Companion for Archaeology*, Oxford.
Pare, C.
    1997   'La dimension européenne du commerce grec à la fin de la periode
           archaïque et pendant le début de la periode classique', in P. Brun and
           B. Chaume (eds.) *Vix et les éphemeres principautés celtiques*, Paris.
Parker Pearson, M. and Richards, C. (eds.)
    1994   *Architecture and Order*, London.
Parker, R.
    1987   'Myths of early Athens', in J.N. Bremmer (ed.) *Interpretations of Greek
           mythology*, London, 187–214.
    1989   'Spartan religion', in Powell (ed.) *Classical Sparta*, 142–72.
    1996   *Athenian Religion: A History*, Oxford.
Parry, A.
    1966   'Have we Homer's Iliad?', *YCS* 20, 177–216 (reprinted in Latacz (ed.) 1979
           Homer, 428–66),
    1972   'Language and characterization in Homer', *HSCP* 76, 1–22.
Parry, A. (ed.)
    1971   *The Making of Homeric Verse. The collected papers of Milman Parry*, Oxford.
Parry, M.
    1928   *The Traditional Epithet in Homer* (Reprinted in A. Parry 1971, *The Making of
           Homeric Verse*, 1–190).
Parsons, P.J.
    1992   '3965. Simonides, Elegies', *The Oxyrhynchus Papyri* 58, 4–50.
Patzek, B.
    1992   *Homer und Mykene. Mündliche Dichtung und Geschichtsschreibung*, Munich.
Patzer, H.
    1972   *Dichterische Kunst und poetisches Handwerk im homerischen Epos*, Wiesbaden.
Pavese, C.O.
    1995   'Elegia di Simonide agli Spartiati per Platea', *ZPE* 107, 1–26.

Payne, H.
1931   *Necrocorinthia*, Oxford.
Pelagatti, P.
1989   'Ceramica laconica in Sicilia e a Lipari', *Bollettino d'Arte* 54, 1–62.
Pelagatti, P. and Stibbe, C.M.
1988   'Una forma poco conosciuta di vaso laconico: il cratere a campana', *Bollettino d'Arte* 52, 13–26.
1992   *Lakonika: Ricerche e nuovi materiali di ceramica laconica* i–ii, *Bollettino d'Arte*, Suppl. vol. 64 (1990), Rome.
Pendlebury, J.
1939   *The Archaeology of Crete*, London.
Penglase, C.
1994   *Greek Myths and Mesopotamia: Parallels and influence in the Homeric Hymns and Hesiod*, London.
Perdrizet, P.
1903   'De quelques monuments figurés du culte d'Athéna Ergane', *Mélanges Perrot*, Paris, 259–67.
1908   *Fouilles de Delphes V*, Paris.
Perdrizet, P. and Lefebvre, G.
1919   *Les graffites grecs du Memnonion d'Abydos*, Paris.
Perlman, P.
1992   'One hundred-citied Crete and the "Cretan politeia" ', *CPh* 87, 193–205.
Piccirilli, L.
1978   'Due ricerche spartane', *ASNP* 8, 917–47.
1980   *Plutarco. Le vite di Licurgo e di Numa*, a cura di M. Manfredini and L. Piccirilli, Milan.
Pipili, M.
1987   *Laconian Iconography of the Sixth Century BC*, Oxford.
Plommer, H.
1960   'The archaic acropolis', *JHS* 80, 127–59.
Ploug, G.
1973   *Sukas II. The Aegean, Corinthian and Eastern Greek Pottery and Terracottas*, Copenhagen.
Pocock, J.G.A.
1962   'The history of political thought – a methodological enquiry', in Laslett and Runciman (eds.) *Politics, Philosophy and Society*, 183–202.
1980   'Political ideas as historical events', in Richter (ed.) *Political Theory*, 139–58.
1987   'The concept of a language and the *métier d'historien*: some considerations of practice', in Pagden (ed.) *The Languages of Political Theory*, 19–38.
Pocock, J.G.A., Schochet, G.J. and Schwoerer, L.G.
1994   *The Varieties of British Political Thought, 1500–1800*, Cambridge.
Pöhlmann, E.
1992   'Homer, Mykene und Troia: Probleme und Aspekte', *Studia Troica* 2, 187–99.
Polanyi, K.
1968   *Primitive, Archaic and Modern Economies: Essays of Karl Polanyi* (ed. G. Dalton), New York.
Polignac, F. de
1992   'Influence extérieure ou évolution interne?', in Kopcke and Tokumaru (eds.) *Greece between East and West*, 114–27.
1995a   *Cults, Territory, and the Origins of the Greek City-State*, Chicago.
1995b   'Repenser la "cité"? Rituels et société en Grèce archaïque', in Hansen and Raaflaub (eds.) *Studies in the ancient Greek polis*, 7–19.
Politis, L.
1936   'Halki idria ex Eretrias', *Archaiologikē Ephemeris*, 147–74.
Pompili, F.
1986   'Le officine', in id. (ed.) *Studi sulla ceramica laconica* (Archaeologia Perusina 3), Roma, 65–74.

Popham, M., Kalligas, P.G. and Sackett, L.H. (eds.).
  1980/93   *Lefkandi I and II*, London.
Popham, M., Toloupa, E. and Sackett, L.H.
  1982   'The Hero of Lefkandi', *Antiquity* 56, 169–74.
Popovic, L.
  1956   *Katalog Nalaza iz Nekropole kod Trebenishte*, Belgrade. (In Serbo-Croat and French.)
Poralla, P.
  1913   *Prosopographie der Lakedaimonier bis auf die Zeit Alexanders der Grossen*, Breslau. (Revised English edition Chicago 1985.)
Porter, R. and Teich, M. (eds.)
  1986   *Revolution in History*, Cambridge.
Poulsen, F.
  1906   'Ein kretische Mitra', *AM* 31, 373–91.
Pounder, R.
  1984   'The Origin of *theoi* as inscription heading', in Rigsby and Boegehold (eds.) *Studies*, 243–50.
Powell, A.
  1980   'Athens' difficulty, Sparta's opportunity: causation and the Peloponnesian War', *AC* 49, 87–114.
  1988   *Athens and Sparta*, London.
  1994   'Plato and Sparta: modes of rule and of non-rational persuasion in the *Laws*', in Powell and Hodkinson (eds.), *The Shadow of Sparta*, 273–321.
Powell, A. (ed.)
  1989   *Classical Sparta. Techniques behind her success*, London.
  1995   *The Greek World*, London and New York.
Powell, A. and Hodkinson, S. (eds.)
  1994   *The Shadow of Sparta*, London and New York.
Powell, B.
  1906   *Athenian Mythology: Erichthonius and the three daughters of Cecrops*, Ithaca. (Reprinted 1976.)
Powell, B.P.
  1988   'The Dipylon oinochoe inscription and the spread of literacy in 8th-century Athens', *Kadmos* 27, 65–86.
  1991   *Homer and the Origin of the Greek Alphabet*, Cambridge.
Price, S.D.
  1990   'Anacreontic vases reconsidered', *GRBS* 31, 133–75.
Pritchard, J.B.
  1969   *Ancient Near Eastern Texts Relating to the Old Testament*, 3rd edn, Princeton.
Pritchett, W.K.
  1956   'The Attic stelai', *Hesperia* 25, 178–317.
  1985   *The Greek State at War, Part IV*, Berkeley and Los Angeles.
Purcell, N.
  1990   'Mobility and the polis', in Murray and Price (eds.) *The Greek City*, 29–58.
Qviller, B.
  1981   'The dynamics of the Homeric society', *SO* 56, 109–55.
Raaflaub, K.A.
  1985   *Die Entdeckung der Freiheit. Zur historischen Semantik und Gesellschaftsgeschichte eines politischen Grundbegriffes der Griechen*, Munich.
  1988a   'Die Anfänge des politischen Denkens bei den Griechen', in Fetscher and Münkler (eds.) *Pipers Handbuch*, 189–271.
  1988b   'The beginnings of political thought among the Greeks', *Boston Area Colloquium in Ancient Philosophy* 4, 1–25.
  1988c   'Athenische Geschichte und mündliche Überlieferung', in Ungern-Sternberg and Reinau (eds.) *Vergangenheit*, 197–225.
  1989   'Die Anfänge des politischen Denkens bei den Griechen', *HZ* 248, 1–32.

440

1991   'Homer und die Geschichte des 8.Jhs. v. Chr.', in Latacz (ed.) *Zweihundert Jahre Homer-Forschung*, 205–56.

1993   'Homer to Solon: the rise of the polis. The written evidence', in Hansen (ed.) *The Ancient Greek City-State*, 41–105.

1995   'Einleitung und Bilanz: Kleisthenes, Ephialtes und die Begründung der Demokratie', in Kinzl (ed.) *Demokratia*, 1–54, 451–2.

1997a   'Citizens, soldiers, and the evolution of the early Greek polis', in Mitchell and Rhodes (eds.) *The Development of the Polis*, 49–59.

1997b   'Homeric Society', in Morris and Powell (eds.) *A New Companion to Homer*, 624–48.

Forthcoming(a)   'Poets, lawgivers, and the beginnings of political thought in archaic Greece', in Schofield and Rowe (eds.) *Cambridge History of Ancient Political Thought*.

Forthcoming(b)   'Politics and interstate relations in the world of early Greek *poleis*: Homer and beyond', *Antichthon* 31.

Raaflaub, K.A. (ed.)

1986   *Social Struggles in Archaic Rome: New perspectives on the conflict of the orders*, Berkeley.

Raaflaub, K.A. and Müller-Luckner, E. (eds.)

1993   *Anfänge politischen Denkens in der Antike: Die nahöstlichen Kulturen und die Griechen*, Munich.

Raeck, W.

1984   'Zur Erzählweise archaischer und klassischer Mythenbilder', *JdI* 99, 1–25.

Ranger, T.O. and Hobsbawm, E.J. (eds.)

1983   *The Invention of Tradition*, Cambridge.

Rathje, W.

1992   *Rubbish! The Archaeology of Garbage*, New York.

Raubitschek, A.E.

1949   *Dedications on the Athenian Acropolis: A catalogue of the inscriptions of the sixth and fifth centuries BC*, Cambridge, Mass.

1972   'A mitra inscribed with a law', in Hoffmann, *Early Cretan Armorers*, 47–9.

Reddé, M.

1986   *Mare Nostrum*, Rome.

Redfield, J.

1975   *Nature and Culture in the* Iliad*: The Tragedy of Hector,* Chicago.

Reeder, E.D. (ed.)

1995   *Pandora: Women in classical Greece*, Baltimore.

Renard, L.

1967   'Notes d'architecture proto-géométrique et géométrique en Crète', *L'Antiquité Classique* 36, 566–95.

Renfrew, C. and Wagstaff, M. (eds.)

1982   *An Island Polity*, Cambridge.

Rhodes, P.J.

1993   '"Alles eitel Gold"? The Sixth and Fifth Centuries in Fourth-Century Athens', in M. Piérart (ed.) *Aristote et Athènes*, Fribourg and Paris, 53–64.

Rich, J. and Wallace-Hadrill, A. (eds.)

1991   *City and Country in the Ancient World,* London.

Richter, G.M.A.

1961   *Archaic Gravestones of Attica*, London.

Richter, M.

1986   'Conceptual history (*Begriffsgeschichte*) and political theory', *Political Theory* 14, 604–37.

Richter, M. (ed.)

1980   *Political Theory and Political Education*, Princeton.

Ridgway, B.S.

1992   'Images of Athena on the Akropolis', in Neils (ed.) *Goddess and Polis*, 119–142.

Ridgway, D.
  1992   *The First Western Greeks*, Cambridge.
  1994   'Phoenicians and Greeks in the west: a view from Pithekoussai', in
          Tsetskhladze and De Angelis (eds.) *The Archaeology of Greek Colonisation*, 35–46.
Rigsby, K.J. and Boegehold, A. (eds.)
  1984   *Studies Presented to Sterling Dow on his Eightieth Birthday*, Durham, N.C.
Rihll, T.E. and Tucker, J.V.
  1995   'Greek engineering: the case of Eupalinos' tunnel', in Powell (ed.), *The
          Greek World*, 403–31.
Riis, P.J.
  1970   *Sukas I. The North-East Sanctuary and the First Settling of Greeks in Syria and
          Palestine*, Copenhagen.
Risch, E.
  1980   'Die griechischen Dialekte im zweiten vorchristlichen Jahrtausend', *Studi
          Micenei ed Egeo-Anatolici* 20, 91–112.
Rizza, G.
  1973   'Tombes de cheveaux', in *The Relations Between Cyprus and Crete, ca. 2000–
          500 BC*, Nicosia, 294–301.
  1991   'Priniàs. La città arcaica sulla Patela', in Musti et al. (eds.) *La transizione dal
          Miceneo all'Alto Arcaismo*, 331–47.
Rizza, G. and Santa Maria Scrinari, V.
  1968   *Il Santuario sull' Acropoli di Gortina*, Rome.
Robert, C.
  1914   'Pandora', *Hermes* 49, 17–38.
Robertson, N.
  1986   'A point of precedence at Plataia. The dispute between Athens and Sparta
          over leading the procession', *Hesperia* 55, 88–102.
Robinson, D.M. and Graham, J.W.
  1938   *Excavations at Olynthus VIII: The Hellenic House*, Baltimore.
Rocher, L.
  1986   *The Puranas*, Wiesbaden.
Rodenwaldt, G.
  1939/40 *Korkyra, Archaische Bauten und Bildwerke*, Berlin.
Roisman, H.M. and Roisman, J. (eds.)
  1993   *Essays on Homeric Epic*, Colby Quarterly 29.3.
Roller, L.E.
  1981a   'Funeral games for historical persons', *Stadion* 7, 1–18.
  1981b   'Funeral games in Greek art', *AJA* 85, 107–19.
Rolley, C.
  1958   'L'origine du krater de Vix: remarques sur l'hypothèse laconienne', *BCH*
          82, 168–71.
  1977   'Le problème de l'art laconien', *Ktema* 2, 125–40.
  1982   *Les Vases de Bronze de l'Archaïsme récent en Grande-Grèce*, Naples.
  1983   'Les grands sanctuaires panhelléniques', in Hägg (ed.) *The Greek Renaissance*,
          109–14.
  1986a   'Les bronzes grecs: recherches récentes', *Revue Archéologique*, 377–91.
  1986b   *Les Bronzes Grecs*, Fribourg.
  1989   'Les bronzes grecs et romains: recherches récentes', *Revue Archéologique*,
          342–56.
Romano, I.B.
  1980   *Early Greek Cult Images*, Ann Arbor.
Rombos, T.
  1988   *The Iconography of Attic Late Geometric II Pottery*, Jonsered.
Rorty, R., Schneewind, J.B. and Skinner, Q.R.D. (eds.)
  1984   *Philosophy in History: Essays in the historiography of philosophy*, Cambridge.

Rose, C.B.
  1992   'The 1991 Post-Bronze Age Excavations at Troia', *Studia Troica* 2, 43–60.
  1993   'The 1992 Post-Bronze Age Excavations at Troia', *Studia Troica* 3, 97–116.
  1995   'The 1994 Post-Bronze Age Excavations at Troia', *Studia Troica* 5, 81–105.
Rosivach, V.J.
  1987   'Autochthony and the Athenians', *CQ* 37, 294–306.
Roux, G.
  1963   'Kypselé: ou avait-on caché le petit Kypselos?', *REA* 65, 279–89.
Rowlands, M., Larsen, M. and Kristiansen, K. (eds.)
  1987   *Centre and Periphery in the Ancient World*, Cambridge.
Ruckert, A.
  1976   *Frühe Keramik Boötiens*, Antike Kunst, Beiheft 10.
Rudhardt, J.
  1986   'Pandora: Hésiode et les femmes', *MH* 43, 231–46.
Rumpf, A.
  1957   'Krater lakonikos', in Schauenburg (ed.) *Charites*, 127–35.
Runciman, W.G.
  1990   'Doomed to extinction: the *polis* as an evolutionary dead-end', in Murray
          and Price (eds.) *The Greek City*, 347–67.
Rupp, D.
  1988   'The "Royal" tombs at Salamis (Cyprus): ideological messages of power and
          authority', *Journal of Mediterranean Archaeology* 1, 111–39.
Russell, B.
  1995   *A History of Western Philosophy* (new edn), Basingstoke.
Russo, J.
  1978   'How, and what, does Homer communicate? The medium and message of
          Homeric verse', in E.A. Havelock and J.P. Hershbell (eds.) *Communication
          Arts in the Ancient World*, New York, 39–52
Russo, J.A.
  1992   'Oral theory: its development in Homeric studies and applicability to other
          literatures', in Vogelzang and Vanstiphout (eds.) *Mesopotamiam Epic
          Literature*, 7–21.
Rutherford, I.
  1996   'The new Simonides: towards a commentary', in Boedeker and Sider (eds.)
          The New Simonides, 167–92.
Rutkowski, B.
  1986   *The Cult Places of the Aegean*, New Haven.
Ruzé, F.
  1991   'Le Conseil et l'Assemblée dans la grande *rhètra* de Sparte', *REG* 104, 15–30.
Rychner, J.
  1955   *La chanson de geste*, Geneva.
Sackett, L.H. et al.
  1992   *Knossos: From Greek city to Roman colony: The unexplored Mansion II*, London.
Sahlins, M.
  1972   *Stone Age Economics*, New York and London.
Sakellariou, M.B.
  1989   *The Polis-State: Definition and Origin*, Athens.
Salem, J.
  1996   *Démocrite. Grains de poussière dans un rayon de soleil*, Paris.
Sallares, R.
  1991   *The Ecology of Ancient Greece*, London.
Salmon, J.B.
  1984   *Wealthy Corinth*, Oxford.
Sancisi-Weerdenburg, H.
  1987   *Achaemenid History I: Sources, structures, synthesis*, Leiden.

Sandars, N.K.
1985   *The Sea Peoples*, 2nd edn, London.
Sanders, J.M. (ed.)
1992   *Philolakōn: Lakonian studies in honour of Hector Catling*, London.
Sarkady, J.
1975   'Outlines of the development of Greek society in the period between the
        12th and 8th centuries BC', *Acta Antiqua Academiae Scientiarum Hungaricae* 23,
        107–25.
Sawa, G.D.
1989   *Music Performance Practice in the Early 'Abbasid Era 132–320 AH / 750–932 ad* ,
        Toronto.
Scammell, G.V.
1981   *The World Encompassed. The first European maritime empires c. 800–1650*,
        London.
Scarlatidou, E.
1986   'The archaic cemetery of Abdera', *Thracia Pontica* 3.
Schachermeyr, F.
1959   'Die Entzifferung der mykenischen Schrift', *Saeculum* 10, 48–72.
1986   *Mykene und das Hethiterreich*, Vienna.
Schachner, S. and Schachner, E.
1996   'Eine späthethitische Grabstele aus Maras im Museum von Antakya', *Anatolica*
        22, 203–26.
Schachter, A.
1994   *Cults of Boiotia*, Vol. 3, London.
Schadewaldt, W.
1942   'Homer und sein Jahrhundert', in *Das neue Bild der Antike,* Vol. 1, Leipzig,
        51–90. (Reprinted in id. *Von Homers Welt und Werk*, 4th edn, Stuttgart, 87–129.)
Schalles, H.J.
1985   *Untersuchungen zur Kulturpolitik der pergamenischen Herrscher im dritten
        Jahrhundert vor Christus*, Tübingen.
Schauenburg, K. (ed.)
1957   *Charites. Studien zur Altertumswissenschaft*, Bonn.
Schaus, G.
1978   *Archaic Greek Pottery from the Demeter Sanctuary, Cyrene, 1969–76: Minor
        Fabrics*, Diss. University of Pennsylvania.
Scheibler, I.
1988   'Die Kouroi des Amasis-Malers', in J. Christiansen and T. Melander (eds.)
        Proceedings of the Third Symposium on Ancient Greek and Related Pottery,
        Copenhagen, 547–57.
Schein, S.L.
1984   *The Mortal Hero. An Introduction to Homer's* Iliad, Berkeley and Los Angeles.
Schilardi, D.U.
1983   'The decline of the Geometric settlement at Koukounaries of Paros', in
        Hägg (ed.) *The Greek Renaissance*, 173–83.
1988   'The temple of Athena at Koukounaries', in Hägg et al. (eds.) *Early Greek
        Cult Practice*, 41–8.
Schmidt-Dounas, B.
1991   'Zur Datierung der Metopen des Athena-Tempels von Ilion', *Istanbuler
        Mitteilungen* 41, 363–415.
Schmitt-Pantel, P.
1990   'Sacrificial meal and symposium: two models of civic institutions in the
        archaic city', in Murray (ed.) *Sympotica*, 14–33.
1992   *La cité au banquet: histoire des repas publics dans les cités grecques*, Paris.
Schofield, M. and Rowe, C.J. (eds.)
Forthcoming   *The Cambridge History of Ancient Political Thought*, Cambridge.

Schubert, C.
1993   *Die Macht des Volkes und die Ohnmacht des Denkens. Studien zum Verhältnis von Mentalität und Wissenschaft im 5. Jahrhundert* (Historia Einzelschriften 77), Stuttgart.

Schuller, W., Hoepfner, W. and Schwandner, E.-L. (eds.)
1989   *Demokratie und Architektur*, Munich.

Scott, R.T. and Scott, A.R. (eds.)
1993   *Eius Virtutis Studiosi: classical and postclassical studies in Memory of Frank Edward Brown*, Washington.

Scrinari, V.S.M. and Rizza, G.
1968   *Il sanctuario sull'acropoli di Gortina*, Rome.

Scully, S.
1990   *Homer and the Sacred City*, Ithaca.

Seaford, R.
1994   *Reciprocity and Ritual. Homer and tragedy in the developing city-state*, Oxford.

Séchan, L.
1929   'Pandora, L'Eve grecque', *Bulletin de l'association Guillaume Budé* (April), 3–36.

See, K. von
1981   *Germanische Heldensage: Stoffe, Probleme, Methoden*, 2nd edn, Wiesbaden.

Seeberg, A.
1966   'Astrabica (Herodotus VI.68–9)', *SO* 41, 48–74.
1971   *Corinthian Komos Vases* (*BICS* Suppl. 27), London.

Segal, C.
1992   'Bard and audience in Homer', in R. Lamberton et al. (eds.) *Homer's Ancient Readers*, Princeton, 3–29.
1995   'Spectator and listener', in Vernant (ed.) *The Greeks*, 184–217.

Serdaroglu, Ü.
1990   'Zur Geschichte der Stadt Assos und ihrer Ausgrabungen', in Serdaroglu, Stupperich and Schwertheim (eds.) *Ausgrabungen in Assos*, 1–5.

Serdaroglu, Ü., Stupperich, R. and Schwertheim, E. (eds.)
1990   *Ausgrabungen in Assos* (Asia Minor Studien 2), Bonn.

Settis, S. (ed.)
1996   *I Greci: Storia-Cultura-Arte-Società* I. *Noi e I Greci*, Turin.

Shanks, M.
1995   'Art and an archaeology of embodiment', *Cambridge Archaeological Journal* 5, 307–30.
1996   *Classical Archaeology of Greece. Experiences of the discipline*, London.

Shapiro, H.A.
1991   'The iconography of mourning in Athenian art', *AJA* 95, 629–56.

Shear, T.L. Jr.
1993   'The Persian destruction of Athens: evidence from Agora deposits', *Hesperia* 62, 383–482.
1994   '*Isonomous t'Athenas epoiesaten*: the Agora and the democracy', in W.D.E. Coulson, O. Palagia, T.L. Shear Jr., H.A. Shapiro, and F.J. Frost (eds.) *The Archaeology of Athens and Attica under the Democracy* (Oxbow Monograph 37), Oxford, 225–48.

Shefton, B.B.
1994   'Massalia and colonization in the north-western Mediterranean', in Tsetskhladze and De Angelis (eds.) *The Archaeology of Greek Colonisation*, 61–86.

Shepherd, G.
1995   'The pride of most colonials: burial and religion in the Sicilian colonies', *Acta Hyperborea* 6, 51–82.

Sherratt, A.
1995   '*Fata Morgana*: illusion and reality in "Greek-Barbarian" relations', *Cambridge Journal of Archaeology*, 1–15.

445

Bibliography

Sherratt, E.S.
 1990 ' "Reading the Texts": archaeology and the Homeric Question', *Antiquity* 64, 807–24.

Sherratt, E.S. and Sherratt, A.
 1993 'The growth of the Mediterranean economy in the early first millennium BC', *World Archaeology* 24.3, 361–78.

Shipley, G.
 1987 *A History of Samos 800–188 BC*, Oxford.
 1992 '*Perioikos*: the discovery of classical Lakonia', in Sanders (ed.) *Philolakōn*, 211–26.

Shive, D.
 1987 *Naming Achilles*, New York.

Simon, C.G.
 1986 *The Archaic Votive Offerings and Cults of Ionia*, Ann Arbor.

Simon, E.
 1963 'Pandora', *EAA* V, 930–3.
 1985 *Die Götter der Griechen*, Darmstadt.

Sissa, G.
 1990 *Greek Virginity*, Cambridge, Mass., and London. (French orginal 1987.).

Skendi, S.
 1954 *Albanian and South Slavic Oral Epic Poetry*, Philadelphia.

Skinner, Q.R.D.
 1969 'Meaning and understanding in the history of ideas', in Tully (ed.), 1988, *Meaning and Context*, 26–67.

Slater, W.J.
 1978 'Artemon and Anacreon', *Phoenix* 32, 185–94.

Snell, B.
 1953 *The Discovery of the Mind: The Greek origins of European thought*, Oxford. (German original 1948.)

Snodgrass, A.M.
 1964 *Early Greek Armour and Weapons*, Edinburgh.
 1971 *The Dark Age of Greece: An archaeological survey of the 11th to the 8th centuries BC*, Edinburgh.
 1974 'An historical Homeric society?', *JHS* 94, 114–25.
 1977 *Archaeology and the Rise of the Greek State*, Cambridge.
 1980 *Archaic Greece: The age of experiment*, Berkeley and Los Angeles.
 1982a 'Les origines du culte des héros dans la Grèce antique', in Gnoli and Vernant (eds.) *La mort...dans les sociétés anciennes*, 107–19.
 1982b 'Central Greece and Thessaly', in *CAH*² III.3, Cambridge, 657–95.
 1983 'Two demographic notes', in Hägg (ed.) *The Greek Renaissance*, 169–71.
 1986 'Interaction by design: the Greek city-states', in C. Renfrew and J.F. Cherry (eds.) *Peer Polity Interaction and the Development of Socio-Cultural Complexity*, Cambridge, 47–58.
 1987 *An Archaeology of Greece. The present state and future scope of a discipline*, Berkeley.
 1988 'The archaeology of the hero', *AION* 10, 19–26.
 1989/90 'The economics of dedication at Greek sanctuaries', *Scienze dell'Antichità* 3–4, 287–94.
 1993 'The rise of the polis: the archaeological evidence', in Hansen (ed.) *The Ancient Greek City-State*, 30–40.
 1994a 'Response: the archaeological aspect', in Morris (ed.) *Classical Greece*, 197–200.
 1994b 'The Euboeans in Macedonia: a new precedent for westward expansion', in D'Agostino and Ridgway (eds.) *Apoikia*, 87–93.
 1996 'The iron objects', in Coldstream and Catling (eds.) *Knossos North Cemetery*.

Sourvinou-Inwood, C.
 1993 'Early sanctuaries, the eighth century and ritual space: fragments of

a discourse', in Marinatos and Hägg (eds.) *Greek Sanctuaries*, 1–17.

1994   'Something to do with Athens: tragedy and ritual', in Osborne and Hornblower (eds.) *Ritual, Finance, Politics*, 269–90.

1995   *'Reading' Greek Death. To the end of the classical period*, Oxford.

Souza, P. de

1995   'Greek piracy', in Powell (ed.) *The Greek World*, 179–98.

Sparkes, B.A.

1994   *Greek Art* (Greece and Rome New Surveys in the Classics), Oxford.

Spencer, N.

1995   'Early Lesbos between East and West: A "grey area" of Aegean archaeology', *BSA* 91, 269–306.

Spivey, N.

1994   'Psephological heroes', in Osborne and Hornblower (eds.) *Ritual, Finance, Politics*, 39–51.

Stampolidis, N.

1990   'Eleutherna on Crete: an interim report on the Geometric-Archaic cemetery', *BSA* 85, 375–403.

1993   *Eleftherna III.1. Geometrika-Archaika Chronia kai Odigos stin Ekthesi*, Rethymno.

1995   'Homer and the cremation burials of Eleutherna', in Crielaard (ed.) *Homeric Questions*, 289–308.

Stanford, W.B. (ed.)

1958   *The Odyssey of Homer*, 2nd edn, London.

Stanley, K.

1993   *The Shield of Homer: Narrative Structure in the* Iliad, Princeton.

Stanton, G.R.

1973   'Sophists and philosophers: problems of classification', *AJP* 94, 350–64.

Starr, C.G.

1955   'The myth of the Minoan thalassocracy', *Historia* 3, 282–91.

1961   *The Origins of Greek Civilization, 1100–650 bc* , New York.

1977   *The Economic and Social Growth of Early Greece, 800–500 BC*, New York.

1986   *Community and Individual*, New York.

Stehle, E.

1996   'Help me to sing, Muse, of Plataea', in Boedeker and Sider (eds.) *The New Simonides*, 205–22.

Stein-Hölkeskamp, E.

1989   *Adelskultur und Polisgesellschaft. Studien zum griechischen Adel in archaischer und klassischer Zeit* , Stuttgart.

Steiner, D.T.

1994   *The Tyrant's Writ. Myths and images of writing in ancient Greece*, Princeton.

Steinhauer, G.

1972   'Arheotites ke mnimia Lakonias', *Archaiologikon Deltion* 27, B'1, *Chronika*, 242–51 *Museum of Sparta*, Athens.

Stibbe, C.M.

1972   *Lakonische Vasenmaler des 6 Jahrhunderts v. Chr.*, Amsterdam.

1974   'Il Cavaliere Laconico', *PDI* (Rome) 1, 19–37.

1976   'Neue Fragmente lakonischer Schalen aus Cerveteri', *Med. Ned. Inst. Rom.* 38, 7–16.

1978   'Lakonische Kantharoi', *Mededelingen van het Nederlandsch Historisch Instituut te Rome* 40, n.s. 5, 23–42.

1984a   'Lo stamnos laconico', *Bollettino d'Arte* 27, 1–12.

1984b   'Reisende lakonische Töpfer', in *Ancient Greek and Related Pottery*, Amsterdam, 135–8.

1985   'Chilon of Sparta', *Mededelingen van het Nederlandsch Historisch Instituut te Rome* 46, n.s. 11, 7–24.

1989   *Laconian Mixing Bowls*, Amsterdam.

1994   *Laconian Drinking Vessels and Other Open Shapes*, Amsterdam.

447

Bibliography

Stoddart, S. and Whitley, J.
 1988   'The social context of literacy in archaic Greece and Etruria', *Antiquity* 62, 761–72.
Stolz, B.A. and Shannon, R.S. (eds.)
 1976   *Oral Literature and the Formula*, Ann Arbor.
Strasburger, H.
 1953   'Der soziologische Aspekt der homerischen Epen', *Gymnasium* 60, 97–114; reprinted in Strasburger *Studien*, 491–518.
 1954   'Der Einzelne und die Gemeinschaft im Denken der Griechen', *Historische Zeitschrift* 177, 227–48; reprinted in Strasburger *Studien*, 423–48.
 1982   *Studien zur Alten Geschichte*, Vol. I, Hildesheim.
Strøm, I.
 1992   'Evidence from the sanctuaries', in Kopcke and Tokumaru (eds.) *Greece between East and West*, 46–60.
Strömberg, A.
 1993   *Male or Female? A methodological study of grave-gifts as sex-indicators in Iron Age Athens*, Jonsered.
Strong, H.A. and Garstang, J.
 1913   *The Syrian Goddess*, London.
Stroud, R.S.
 1968   *Drakon's Law on Homicide*, Berkeley and Los Angeles.
 1979   *The Axones and Kyrbeis of Solon and Drakon*, Berkeley and Los Angeles.
Stubbs, H.
 1950   'Spartan austerity: a possible explanation', *CQ* 44, 32–7.
Stucchi, S.
 1956   'Una recente terracotta Siciliana di Atena Ergane ed una proposta intorno all'Atena detto di Endoios', *MDAI (RM)* 63 122–8.
Stupperich, R.
 1977   *Staatsbegräbnis und Privatgrabmal im klassischen Athen*, Diss., Münster.
Subotic, D.
 1932   *Yugoslav Popular Ballads: Their origin and development*, Cambridge.
Suhr, E.G.
 1969   *The Spinning Aphrodite. The evolution of the goddess from earliest pre-hellenic symbol through late classical times*, New York.
Svenbro, J.
 1982   'A Mégara Hyblaea, le corps géomètre', *Annales (ESC)* 37, 953–64.
 1993   *Phrasikleia: An anthropology of reading in ancient Greece*, Ithaca, N.Y.
Symeonoglou, S.
 1985   *The Topography of Thebes*, Princeton.
Szegedy-Maszak, A.
 1978   'Legends of the Greek lawgivers', *GRBS* 19, 199–209.
Taplin, O.
 1992   *Homeric Soundings. The shaping of the* Iliad, Oxford.
Tausend, K.
 1992   *Amphiktyonie und Symmachie: Formen zwischenstaatlicher Beziehungen im archaischen Griechenland* (Historia Einzelschriften 73), Stuttgart.
Thomas, C.G.
 1989   'Greek Geometric art and orality', *Art History* 12, 257–67.
 1993a   *Myth Becomes History: Pre-Classical Greece*, Claremont.
 1993b   'The Homeric epics: strata or a spectrum?', in Roisman and Roisman (eds.) *Essays on Homeric Epic*, 273–82.
Thomas, R.
 1982   'Die "schwebende Athena" in Basel. Bemerkungen zur Darstellung der Athenageburt im 5. Jahrhundert v. Chr.', *JdI* 97, 47–63.
Thomas, R.
 1989   *Oral Tradition and Written Record in Classical Athens*, Cambridge.

1992   *Literacy and Orality in Ancient Greece*, Cambridge.

1994a   'Law and the lawgiver in the Athenian democracy', in Osborne and Hornblower (eds.) *Ritual, Finance, Politics*, 119–33.

1994b   'Literacy and the city-state in archaic and classical Greece', in Bowman and Woolf (eds.) *Literacy and Power*, 33–50.

1995a   'Written in stone? Liberty, equality, orality and the codification of law', *BICS* 40, 59–74.

1995b   'The place of the poet in archaic society', in Powell (ed.) *The Greek World*, 104–29.

Thompson, N.

1996   *Herodotus and the Origins of the Political Community. Arion's Leap*, New Haven.

Tilley, C.

1990   'Claude Lévi-Strauss: structuralism and beyond', in C. Tilley (ed.) *Reading Material Culture*, Oxford, 3–81.

Tilley, C. (ed.)

1993   *Interpretative Archaeology*, New York.

Tod, M.N. and Wace, A.J.B.

1906   *A Catalogue of the Sparta Museum*, Oxford.

Traill, D.A.

1993   *Excavating Schliemann* (Illinois Classical Studies, Suppl. 4), Atlanta.

Trémouille, M.C.

1994   'L'iconographie de la déesse Hebat à la lumière des textes', *Studi Micenei ed Egeo-Anatolico* 34, 87–105.

Triandaphyllos, A.

1990a   'Ochyromatikoi perivoloi stin endochora tis Aigaiakis Thrakis', in *Mnimi D. Lazaridi*, Thessaloniki, 683–99.

1990b   'I Thraki tou Aigaiou prin apo to Elliniko apoikismo', *Thrakiki Epetirida* 7, 297–322.

Trungpa, C. et al. (trsl.)

1980   *The Rain of Wisdom: The Vajra songs of the Kagyü Gurus*, Boulder.

1982   *Tsang Nyön Heruka: The life of Marpa the Translator*, Boulder.

Tsetskhladze, G.R.

1994   'Greek penetration of the Black Sea', in Tsetskhladze and De Angelis (eds.) *The Archaeology of Greek Colonisation*, 111–35.

Tsetskhladze, G.R. and De Angelis, F. (eds)

1994   *The Archaeology of Greek Colonisation* (Oxford Committee for Archaeology, Monograph 40), Oxford.

Tuck, R.

1991   'History of political thought', in Burke (ed.) *New Perspectives*, 193–205.

Tully, J.

1995   *Strange Multiplicity. Constitutionalism in an age of diversity*, Cambridge.

Tully, J. (ed.)

1988   *Meaning and Context. Quentin Skinner and his critics*, Princeton.

Turville-Petre, G.

1966   *Haraldr the Hard-ruler and His Poets*, London.

Ulf, C.

1990   *Die homerische Gesellschaft. Materialien zur analytischen Beschreibung und historischen Lokalisierung* (Vestigia 43), Munich.

Ungern-Sternberg, J. von,

1988   'Überlegungen zur frühen römischen Überlieferung im Lichte der Oral-Tradition-Forschung', in Ungern-Sternberg and Reinau (eds.) *Vergangenheit in mündlicher Überlieferung*, 237–65.

Ungern-Sternberg, J. von and Reinau, H. (eds.).

1988   *Vergangenheit in mündlicher Überlieferung* (Colloquium Rauricum 1), Stuttgart.

Ure, P.N.

1922   *The Origin of Tyranny*, Cambridge.

449

Vallet, G.
  1962   'L'introduction de l'olivier en Italie centrale d'après les donnés de la céramique', in *Hommages à Albert Grenier* III, 1445–63.
  1973   'Espace privé et espace public dans une cité coloniale d'Occident (Mégara Hyblaea)', in Finley (ed.) *Problèmes de la terre*, 83–94.
Vallet, G. and Villard, F.
  1955   'Un atelier de bronziers: sur l'école du cratère de Vix', *BCH* 79, 50–74.
  1976   *Mégara Hyblaea I: Le quartier de l'agora archaïque*, Paris.
Van Compernolle, R.
  1981   'La législation aristocratique de Locres Epizéphyrienne, dite législation de Zaleukos', *Antiquité Classique* 50, 759–69.
Van Effenterre, H.
  1946a   'Une bilingue etéocrétoise?', *Revue de Philologie* 20, 131–8.
  1946b   'Inscriptions archaïques crétoises', *BCH* 70, 588–606.
Van Effenterre, H. and M.
  1985   'Nouvelles lois archaïques de Lyttos', *BCH* 109, 157–88.
Van Effenterre, H. and M., Kalpaxis, T., Petropoulou, A.B. and Stavrianopolou, E.
  1991   *Eleutherna: Tomeas II:1 Epigraphes apo to Pyrgi kai to Nisi*, Rethymnon.
Vanderpool, E.
  1942   'An inscribed stele from Marathon', *Hesperia* 11, 329–37.
  1969   'Three prize vases', *Archaiologikon Deltion* 24, 1–5.
Vansina, J.
  1985   *Oral Tradition As History*, Madison.
Vatai, F.L.
  1984   *Intellectuals in Politics in the Greek World*, London and New York.
Vatin, C.
  1969   *Médéon de Phocide*, Paris.
Veblen, T.
  1899   *The Theory of the Leisure Class. An economic study of institutions* (cited from Unwin Books edition 1970, London).
Ventris, M. and Chadwick, J.
  1953   'Evidence for Greek dialect in the Mycenaean archives', *JHS* 73, 84–103.
  1956   *Documents in Mycenaean Greek*, Cambridge.
Verdenius, W.J.
  1971   'A "hopeless" line in Hesiod: *Works and Days* 96', *Mnemosyne* 24, 225–31.
  1985   *A Commentary on Hesiod: Works and Days, vv. 1–382*, Leiden.
Vermeule, E.T.
  1964   *Greece in the Bronze Age*, Chicago.
  1974   *Götterkult. Archaeologia Homerica*, Bd. 3. V, Göttingen.
  1986   ' "Priam's castle blazing". A thousand years of Trojan memories', in Mellink (ed.) *Troy and the Trojan War*, 77–92.
  1987   'Baby Aigisthos and the Bronze Age', *PCPhS* 213, 122–52.
Vernant, J.-P.
  1957   'The formation of positivist thought in archaic Greece', in id. *Myth and Thought Among the Greeks*, London 1983, 343–74.
  1965   'Espace et organisation politique en Grèce ancienne', *Annales ESC* 20, 576–95.
  1980   *Myth and Society in Ancient Greece*, London. (French original 1974.)
  1981   'Ambiguity and reversal. On the enigmatic structure of the *Oedipus Rex*', in J.-P. Vernant and P. Vidal-Naquet (eds.) *Myth and Tragedy in Ancient Greece*, Brighton, 87–119.
  1989   'At man's table: Hesiod's foundation myth of sacrifice', in M. Detienne and J.-P. Vernant (eds.) *The Cuisine of Sacrifice Among The Greeks*, Chicago, 21–86. (French original 1979.)
Vernant, J.-P. (ed.).
  1995   *The Greeks*, Chicago.

Versnel, H.S.
  1993   *Transition and Reversal in Myth and Ritual. Inconsistencies in Greek and Roman religion* II, Leiden.
Vickers, M. and Gill, D.
  1994   *Artful Crafts: Ancient Greek Silverware and Pottery*, Oxford.
Vidal-Naquet, P.
  1963   'Homère et le monde mycénien. A propos d'un livre récent et d'une polémique ancienne', *Annales ESC* 18, 703–19.
  1986   'Land and sacrifice in the *Odyssey*: A study of religious and mythical meanings', in id. *The Black Hunter: Forms of thought and forms of society in the Greek world*, Baltimore, 15–38.
Villard, F.
  1954   *Corpus Vasorum Antiquorum Louvre 11*, Paris.
  1957   'Une amphore géométrique attique au musée du Louvre', *Mon.Piot* 49, 17–40.
Visser, E.
  1987   *Homerische Versifikationstechnik. Versuch einer Rekonstruktion*, Frankfurt am Main.
  1988   'Formulae or single words? Towards a new theory on Homeric verse-making', *Würzburger Jahrbücher* 14, 21–37.
  1997   *Homers Katalog der Schiffe*, Stuttgart.
Viviers, D.
  1992   *Recherches sur les ateliers des sculpteurs et la cité d'Athènes à l'époque archaique. Endoios, Philergos, Aristokles*, Gembloux.
  1994   'La cité de Dattalla et l'expansion territoriale de Lyktos en Crète centrale', *BCH* 118, 229–59.
Vlastos, G.
  1945/6 'Ethics and physics in Democritus', *Philosophical Review* 54, 578–92; 55, 53–64.
  1946   'Solonian justice', *CPh* 41, 65–83.
Vogelzang, M.E. and Vanstiphout, H.L.J. (eds.).
  1992   *Mesopotamian Epic Literature: Oral or Aural?*, Lewiston.
Vogt, E.
  1991   'Homer – ein grosser Schatten? Die Forschungen zur Person Homers', in Latacz (ed.) *Zweihundert Jahre Homer-Forschung*, 365–77.
Vokotopoulou, I.
  1986   *Vitsa*, Athens.
  1990   *Oi Taphikoi Tymvoi tis Aineias*, Thessaloniki.
Vokotopoulou, I., Despini, A., Michailidou, V. and Tiverios, M.
  1985   *Sindos. Katalogos tis Ekthisis*, Thessaloniki.
Von Gerkan, A.
  1925   *Milet I.8. Kalabaktepe, Athenatempel und Umgebung*, Berlin.
Von Reden, S.
  1995   *Exchange in Ancient Greece*, London.
Voyatzis, M.
  1990   *The Early Sanctuary of Athena Alea at Tegea* (Studies in Mediterranean Archaeology Pocket Book 97), Göteborg.
Wace, A.J.B.
  1929   'The lead figurines', in Dawkins (ed.) *The Sanctuary of Artemis Orthia*, 249–84.
  1937   'A Spartan hero relief', *Archaiologikē Ephemeris* 100, 217–20.
Wace, A.J.B. et al.
  1908/9 'Excavations at Sparta, 1909. The Menelaion', *BSA* 15, 108–57.
Wace, A.J.B. and Stubbings, F.H. (eds.)
  1962   *A Companion to Homer*, New York.
Wade-Gery, H.T.
  1925   'The growth of the Dorian states', *CAH* III, Cambridge, 527–70.
  1949   'A note on the origin of the Spartan Gymnopaidiai', *CQ* 42, 79–81.

Bibliography

Wagenvoort, H.
1956   *Studies in Roman Literature, Culture and Religion*, Leiden.
Wagstaff, J. and Renfrew, C. (eds.).
1982   *An Island Polity*, Cambridge.
Walcot, P.
1961   'Pandora's jar, *Erga* 83–105', *Hermes* 89, 249–51.
1966   *Hesiod and the Near East*, Cardiff.
Waldbaum, J.C.
1994   'Early Greek contacts with the Southern Levant, *ca.* 1000–600 BC: the Eastern perspective', *Bulletin of the American Schools of Oriental Research* 293 (Feb.), 53–66.
Walker, S.
1983   'Women and housing in Classical Greece', in A. Cameron and A. Kuhrt (eds.) *Images of Women in Antiquity*, London, 81–91.
Wallinga, H.T.
1987   'The ancient Persian navy and its predecessors', in Sancisi-Weerdenburg (ed.) *Achaemenid History I*, 47–76.
1993   *Ships and Sea Power before the Great Persian War. The ancestry of the ancient trireme*, Amsterdam.
Wang, C.H.
1974   *The Bell and the Drum: Shih Ching as formulaic poetry in an oral tradition*, Berkeley.
Ward, W.A. and Joukowsky, M.S. (eds.)
1992   *The Crisis Years. The 12th Century BC: From beyond the Danube to the Tigris*, Dubuque.
Webster, J. and Cooper, N. (eds)
1996   *Roman Imperialism: Post-Colonial Perspectives*, Leicester.
Webster, T.B.L.
1958   *From Mycenae to Homer*, London.
Wees, H. van
1992   *Status Warriors: War, violence and society in Homer and history*, Amsterdam.
1994   'The Homeric way of war: the *Iliad* and the hoplite phalanx', *G&R* 41, 1–18, 131–55.
1995   'Princes at dinner: social event and social structure in Homer', in Crielaard (ed.) *Homeric Questions*, 147–82.
1996   'Heroes, knights and nutters: warrior mentality in Homer', in A.B. Lloyd (ed.) *Battle in Antiquity*, London, 1–86.
Forthcoming   'A brief history of tears. Gender differentiation in archaic Greece', in L. Foxhall and J. Salmon (eds.) *When Men Were Men*, London.
Weicker, G.
1902   *Der Seelenvogel in der alten Literatur und Kunst*, Leipzig.
Wells, B.
1983   *Asine II.4.2–3. The Protogeometric Period*, Stockholm.
Wells, P.S.
1980   *Culture Contact and Culture Change: Early Iron Age Central Europe and the Mediterranean world*, Cambridge.
1984   *Farms, Villages and Cities: Commerce and urban origins in Late Prehistoric Europe*, Ithaca.
Welter, G.
1938   *Aigina*, Berlin.
Welwei, K.-W.
1992   *Athen: vom neolithischen Siedlungsplatz zur archaischen Grosspolis*, Darmstadt.
Wéry, L.-M.
1967   'Le fonctionnement de la diplomatie à l'époque homérique', *Revue internationale des droits de l'antiquité*, 3d ser. 14, 169–205 (German translation in E. Olshausen (ed.) *Antike Diplomatie*, Darmstadt 1979, 13–53).

West, M.L.
  1966   *Hesiod: Theogony*, edited with prolegomena and commentary, Oxford.
  1973a   'Greek poetry 2000–700 BC', *CQ* 23, 179–92.
  1973b   'Indo-European metre', *Glotta* 51, 161–88.
  1974   *Studies in Greek Elegy and Iambus*, Berlin and New York.
  1978   *Hesiod: Works and Days*, edited with commentary, Oxford.
  1981   'The singing of Homer and the modes of early Greek music', *JHS* 101, 113–29.
  1988   'The rise of the Greek epic', *JHS* 108, 151–72.
  1992   *Iambi et Elegi Graeci*, Vol. 2², Oxford.
  1993a   *Greek Lyric Poetry*, translated with introduction and notes, Oxford.
  1993b   'Simonides Redivivus', *ZPE* 98, 1–14.
  1995   'The date of the Iliad', *Museum Helveticum* 52, 203–19.
Whaley, D.
  1993   'Skalds and situational verses in Heimskringla', in A. Wolf (ed.) *Snorri Sturluson: Kolloquium anläßlich der 750. Wiederkehr seines Todestages*, Tübingen, 245–66.
Whitbread, I.
  1995   *Greek Transport Amphorae: A petrological and archaeological study*, Athens.
Whitehead, D.
  1986   *The Demes of Attica*, Princeton.
Whitley, J.
  1988   'Early states and hero cults: a re-appraisal', *JHS* 108, 173–82.
  1991a   'Regional diversity in Dark Age Greece', *BSA* 86, 341–65.
  1991b   *Style and Society in Dark Age Greece*, Cambridge.
  1994a   'The monuments that stood before Marathon: tomb cult and hero cult in archaic Attica', *AJA* 98, 213–30.
  1994b   'Protoattic pottery: a contextual approach', in Morris (ed.) *Classical Greece*, 51–70.
  1995   'Tomb cult and hero cult: the uses of the past in Archaic Greece', in N. Spencer (ed.) *Time, Tradition and Society in Greek Archaeology*, London, 43–63.
  1997   'Beazley as theorist', *Antiquity* 71, 40–7.
  Forthcoming   'Gender and hierarchy in early Athens: the strange case of the disappearance of the rich female grave', *Metis*.
Wickert-Micknat, G.
  1982   *Die Frau. Archaeologia Homerica*, Bd. R, Göttingen.
Wiesner, J.
  1968   *Fahren und Reiten. Archaeologia Homerica*, Bd. F, Göttingen.
Wilkes, J.
  1992   *The Illyrians*, Oxford.
Willemsen, F.
  1963   'Archaische Grabmalbasen aus der Athener Stadtmauer', *AM* 78, 104–53.
Willetts, R.F.
  1967   *The Law Code of Gortyn*, Berlin.
Williams, B.A.O.
  1993   *Shame and Necessity*, Berkeley and Oxford.
Williams, D.
  1991/3 'The "pot-hoard" pot from the Archaic Artemision at Ephesus', *BICS* 38, 98–103.
Willis, R.
  1978   *There Was A Certain Man. Spoken art of the Fipa*, Oxford.
Wilson, J.-P.
  1997   'The nature of Greek overseas settlements in the archaic period: *emporion* or *apoikia?*', in Mitchell and Rhodes (eds.) *The Development of the Polis*, 199–207.
Winter, N.A. (ed.)
  1994   *Proceedings of the International Conference on Greek Architectural Terracottas of the*

       Classical and Hellenistic Periods, December 12–15 1991 (Hesperia Supplement 27), Princeton.

Wiseman, J.
1978   *The Land of the Ancient Corinthians* (Studies in Mediterranean Archaeology 50), Göteborg.

Wood, N. and E.M.
1978   *Class Ideology and Ancient Political Theory*, Oxford.

Wörrle, M. and Zanker, P. (eds.)
1995   *Stadtbild und Bürgerbild im Hellenismus*, Munich.

Worthington, I. (ed.)
1996   *Voice into Text. Orality and literacy in ancient Greece*, Leiden.

Wyatt., W.F. Jr.
1989   'The intermezzo of Odyssey 11 and the poets Homer and Odysseus', *Studi micenei ed egeo-anatolici* 27, 235–53.

Yalouris, N.
1960   'Mykenische Bronzeschutzwaffen', *AM* 75, 42–67.

Yamagata, N.
1994   *Homeric Morality*, Leiden.

Young, R.S.
1941   '*Antipex*: a note on the *Ion* of Euripides', *Hesperia* 10, 138–42.

Zapheiropoulou, Ph.
1994   'Une nécropole à Paros', in J. de la Genière (ed.) *Nécropoles et sociétés antiques*, Naples, 127–52.

Zeitlin, F.I.
1995   'The economics of Hesiod's Pandora', in Reeder (ed.) *Pandora*, 49–56.
1996   *Playing the Other*, Chicago.

Ziehen, L.
1949   'Palladion', *RE* 18.3, 171–89.

Zimmermann, J.-L.
1989   *Les chevaux de bronze dans l'art géometrique grec*, Mayence.

INDEX

The index does not cover introductory matter or footnotes; some subjects which feature prominently throughout the book (e.g. archaeology, material evidence, literary evidence, archaic age, Iron age, polis, politics, society, culture, ideology) are not given entries. Greek names which appear in different spellings in the text here have only one entry, in which they usually appear in their Latinized form.